RACE AND STATE IN CAPITALIST DEVELOPMENT

RACE AND STATE IN CAPITALIST DEVELOPMENT

COMPARATIVE PERSPECTIVES

STANLEY B. GREENBERG

NEW HAVEN AND LONDON, YALE UNIVERSITY PRESS

Published under the auspices of the Southern
African Research Program, Yale University.
Copyright © 1980 by Yale University.

Designed by Sally Harris
and set in Times Roman type.
Printed in the United States of America by
Vail-Ballou Press, Binghamton, N.Y.

Library of Congress Cataloging in Publication Data
Greenberg, Stanley B   1945–
Race and state in capitalist development.
Bibliography: p.
Includes index.
1. Race relations—Economic aspects. 2. Race
relations—Economic aspects—South Africa. 3. Race
relations—Economic aspects—Alabama. I. Title.
HT1531.G73   301.45'1'042   79–22324
ISBN 0–300–02444–4
ISBN 0–300–02527–0 pbk.

10   9   8   7   6   5   4   3   2

To
Rosa

CONTENTS

CONCLUSION

PREFACE

This book begins with a problem: the persistence of racial conflict and domination. Despite the development of nation-states and capitalist economies, seemingly archaic identities intrude on our lives. We do not easily escape Birmingham and Watts, nor are we very far removed from events in southern Africa, the Middle East, or, oddly enough, Great Britain and Western Europe. Whatever our image or model of contemporary society, we cannot after all ignore W. E. B. Du Bois's prognosis at the outset of this century: "The problem of the Twentieth Century is the problem of the color-line."

The problem began to intrude on my thinking in the concluding days of an earlier project, *Politics and Poverty: Modernization and Response in Five Poor Neighborhoods.* I asked then why a shared modernizing experience—rural marginality, migration, urbanization, and proletarianization—brought such diversity in the politics and political attitudes of the poor? With C. Wright Mills's "sociological imagination" in mind, I looked for patterns among seemingly scattered and random events. Where were the connections between the immediate "troubles" that poor people lived with daily and the larger "issues"? *Politics and Poverty,* I think, uncovered some patterns. By interviewing a large sample of poor Americans and studying community history and migration, I was able to outline some of the common experiences of poor neighborhoods. I was also able to talk about differing attitudes and their political consequences. But the approach raised some fundamental questions: Why had so radical a social transformation left so much intact, including the pattern of racial domination? Why had class issues not dislodged concerns and conflicts originating in the pre-capitalist countryside? And why had class coalitions not shattered earlier the anomalous alignment of poor blacks, southern "Bourbons," and industrialists?

These paradoxes and questions set my present course. The problem of persistent racial conflict and domination is at the center of this research.

The setting, however, has changed. From inner-city poor neighborhoods in the United States, I turned to a number of societies where race lines or, more broadly, ethnic lines are socially pervasive and formalized and where capitalist development threatens to redraw them. South Africa and Alabama are my primary research settings. I have also included two related cases—Northern Ireland and Israel—to help establish the generality of the problem and process.

The vantage point too has changed. This book is researched and written from the "top down," focusing primarily on businessmen, workers, and farmers in the dominant racial group. It examines in particular the role these class actors play in elaborating, accommodating, or undermining racial barriers in the market and society and studies the class actors' role in forging a state racial apparatus. This perspective, however, deflects attention from peasants and workers of the subordinate racial group. They are an integral part of the story and, indeed, the point of it. But they are not the entire story and, in certain periods, perhaps not the principal forces shaping social relations and making for political change and conflict.

The shift in vantage point also reflects my response to what was becoming an untenable research position: the days when outside white researchers could observe and roam freely through the East Side of Detroit and North Central Philadelphia had passed, and those days had yet to come in Soweto and the Bogside.

The need for a "sociological imagination" has not changed. But imagination, if it is to focus and find patterns, must be guided by some notion of society or historical process. This work draws, in the first place, on Marxian political economy. In its historicism and materialism, I sought the connections between development and growth, on the one hand, and social and political relations, such as racial domination, on the other. In the second place, I turned to a range of middle-level theories, or mediations, to help explain the role of class actors in particular settings. Here the work displays an eclecticism that others, better tutored in their paradigms, will find troubling.

This book is divided into three major sections on farmers, businessmen and workers. Each section includes an introductory chapter, one that examines the role of particular class actors during capitalist development and that considers as a logical and theoretical question the probable impact of these actors in a multiracial context. Can we expect, for example, that businessmen or industrial workers will attempt to eliminate racial barriers in the labor market? Or will businessmen or farmers call on the state to elaborate controls over a racially subordinate laboring population? The introductory chapter creates a number of expectations (or hypotheses) that are tested in the specific cases that fill out each section. By examining these expectations in a number of multiracial settings, using broadly comparable data, I establish some propositions about class actors in racial orders and begin perhaps to respond to my initial query: What is the impact of capitalist development on patterns of racial domination?

Though there is a shared logic within each section, there is also a lack of symmetry that betrays the learning process I underwent during this research. I had presumed from the beginning that the final product would devote a comparable amount of attention to two major settings, South Africa and Alabama, and somewhat less attention to the related settings, Northern Ireland and Israel. But as the text shows, I allowed my interest in racial conflict in South Africa to develop and affect both the allocation of my research energies and the structure of the book, which devotes nearly twice as much space to South Africa as Alabama. In the end, I concluded that this imbalance was less important than the added richness of the South African materials.

The project at the outset neglected the rural economy, focusing instead on two groups within the emerging industrial framework: businessmen and workers. I prepared interview guidelines for each (appendix C) and began gathering material on the two primary research settings and, in each case, a related setting (businessmen in Northern Ireland and workers in Israel) where the expectations might face a broader test. But the project was too narrowly focused: it neglected the rural economy—farm owners and farm laborers—which helped shape the racial state apparatus and the framework of race domination.

In the end, the book could not avoid asking how developing societies free themselves from race domination. This book is not a political tract or handbook, but there are lessons here for those who despise racism and those who live with its burdens from day to day. Both groups in the end must understand the consequences of growth and the opportunities and obstacles that it creates.

I have managed in five years of research to accumulate a remarkable number of debts. It is sobering to consider how many people thought this project worth their time and commitment.

Two fellowships, above all else, made this project possible. Near the end of the work, 1976–77, the John Simon Guggenheim Foundation provided support for a critical year of writing and for field research in Northern Ireland, Israel, and South Africa. At the beginning, 1973–74, the Junior Faculty Fellowship at Yale University made it possible for me to conduct the initial year of field research in South Africa. A whole series of smaller but nonetheless important grants carried this project along from beginning to end. The Institution for Social and Policy Studies at Yale provided start-up funds, allowing a research assistant and some "primitive accumulation" in information, books, periodicals, and newspapers. It later released an enormous amount of secretarial time for typing the South Africa and Alabama interview transcripts. At two points, the Stimson Fund of the Concilium for International and Area Studies, Yale University, covered travel costs: allowing my family to join me in South Africa in 1973 and later allowing me to travel to Israel, South Africa, and Northern Ireland. The

American Philosophical Society also came to my aid at two junctures: in 1973, it provided air fare to South Africa, and in 1975, it supported my travel and research in Alabama. The Behavioral Sciences Publication Fund provided support for the final typing of this manuscript.

I cannot acknowledge all the people who interrupted their routines and chose in one way or other to assist the fieldwork. Nonetheless, I am grateful for their anonymous efforts. A few individuals and organizations, however, went far out of their way to ease my adjustment and provide access to documents and people: in South Africa, Jeffrey Lever (University of South Africa and, later, Wesleyan and Stellenbosch Universities), Alfred Stadler (University of the Witwatersrand), C. J. P. Cilliers (director, South African Agricultural Union), Myrna and David Margolis, Robert Kraft (assistant general secretary, Trade Union Congress of South Africa), Dennis Etheridge (director, Gold Mining Division, Anglo-American Corporation); in Alabama, Higdon Roberts (director, Research and Labor Education, University of Alabama), Barney Weeks (president, Alabama Federation of Labor), John H. Dorrill, Jr. (assistant to the president, Alabama Farm Bureau Federation); in Israel, Jusuf Khamis and Reubin Katzav (associate and director, Arab Department of the Histadrut), Jacob M. Landau (Hebrew University); in Northern Ireland, G. L. Auret (secretary, Northern Ireland Chamber of Commerce and Industry). A number of libraries freely gave of their time and resources: Gubbins Library (University of the Witwatersrand), Johannesburg City Library, Parliamentary Library (Cape Town), Trade Union Council of South Africa Library (Johannesburg), Chamber of Mines Library (Johannesburg), Rhodes House at Oxford University, the Royal Commonwealth Society (London), British Museum, Birmingham City Library (Alabama), Mobile Public Library, Alabama Department of Archives and History (Montgomery), National and University Library (Hebrew University), Library of the Histadrut (Tel Aviv), Queens University Library (Belfast).

John M. D. Crossey, African curator at the Sterling Memorial Library, Yale University, took care of virtually all my research needs, including some that must have seemed whimsical. During the last five years at Yale, I have also been aided by a number of remarkably talented Yale undergraduate and graduate students—Randy Perry, Mark Foley, Kennieth Pittman, Robert Shell, Robert Baum, and William Worger.

Marilyn Satterthwaite, Patricia Campbell, Sandy Ruggiero, Pamela Baldwin, Ruth Coddington, and Rita Santoroski typed the various drafts of the manuscript with skill and patience. Joyce Romanow proved a tireless, and unpaid, proofreader.

At two critical points in the writing, George and Betty Hill and Harold and Ruth Romanow graciously provided me with well-stocked and secluded quarters in New Hampshire and Long Island, respectively.

Students in my undergraduate and graduate courses at Yale—"Marxian Political Economy and the Social Sciences," "Politics of Divided Societies," and "Race and Ethnic Conflict in Southern Africa"—patiently listened to my partially formulated ideas and read and criticized drafts of the manuscript.

Individual chapters were presented at the Workshop on the Social and Economic History of Southern Africa (Oxford University, 1974), the Yale-New England Southern African Workshop (1976), Symposium on Urbanization and Agriculture (Duke University, 1976), meetings of the American Political Science Association (1976), and of the African Studies Association (1976 and 1977), and the Workshop on the Rural Community and Political Change (State University of New York, Buffalo, 1977).

A large number of friends and colleagues read and commented on chapters or sections of the book. I want to thank Heribert Adam, Benjamin Beit-Hallahmi, Belinda Bozzoli, Aharon Cohen, Robert Dahl, Leonard Doob, André DuToit, Hermann Giliomee, Edward Greenberg, Keith Hart, Thomas Karis, John Kendrick, Jacob Landau, Joseph LaPalombara, Martin Legassick, Jeffrey Lever, John Mollenkopf, David Montejano, Kogila Moodley, Sam Nolutshungu, Hasu Patel, Kenneth Pittman, Richard Ralston, Lawrence Schlemmer, James Scott, Harold Stanley, Newell Stultz, Victoria Suddard, Leonard Thompson, Stanley Trapido, C. Vann Woodward, Charles Van Onselen, H. Bradford Westerfield, David Yudelman, and Maurice Zeitlin.

At Yale Press, Marian Neal Ash maneuvered the manuscript between supportive, critical, and even dilatory readers. Bowden Anderson brought some grace and logic to my stumbling prose.

The Southern African Research Program at Yale and Wesleyan Universities (supported by grants from the National Endowment for the Humanities and the Ford Foundation) is a unique community of scholars and friends that has devoted enormous energies to encouraging my work, somehow combining tough criticisms with personal support. Leonard Thompson, Jeffrey Butler and William Foltz, in particular, introduced me to Africa and struggled with this book as if it were their own.

To Rosa DeLauro, my wife, who, thank God, is not an academic, who did not help write or research this book, who lives her own life but provided more support than I can relate here, this book is dedicated.

Stanley B. Greenberg

New Haven, Connecticut

INTRODUCTION

POLICE ALERT IN SOWETO

Strong police patrols watched the streets of Soweto yesterday as a big standby operation came into force, aimed at preventing a recurrence of last month's bloody township riots.

A new wave of security arrests could follow the proclamation... of the new Internal Security Act which makes provision for "preventive detentions for up to a year."

The West Rand Administration Board has ruled that all Whites are to be barred from Soweto "because it is impossible to guarantee their safety at this stage."

The move, [the Commissioner of Police] said, followed rumours ...that there would be "trouble" next Tuesday, scheduled reopening date for Soweto schools....

The security police round-up of key members of Black consciousness movements...is continuing.

The Star
International Edition
July 17, 1976

DOGS, WATER USED TO HALT NEGRO MARCH

BIRMINGHAM (AP) -- Police dogs and fire hoses routed crowds of Negroes Friday as hundreds of school-age youngsters attempted to stage anti-segregation marches. . . . .

About 60 Negroes were jailed in the first series of attempted marches. Two hours later, 50 other marchers were turned back by water hoses.

After two diversionary marches in the block around the church, about 50 teen-agers started marching toward the downtown area....

Police blocked off the entire section surrounding the church....

With firemen brandishing their hoses, a policeman with a loud-speaker warned the marchers, "Disperse or you'll get wet."

Then the water hit them. Cowering, first with hands over their heads, then on their knees or clinging together with their arms around each other, they tried to hold their ground....

The hoses were turned on the crowd of several hundred Negro spectators. They began yelling [in] protest....

Commenting on the use of water hoses and police dogs Friday, [Gov. George C.] Wallace added: "Birmingham has a very fine police commissioner (Eugene "Bull" Connor) and I am satisfied that the Birmingham Police Department has taken the necessary action as far as force is concerned to maintain law and order."

Montgomery Advertiser
May 4, 1963

BELFAST TO LONDONDERRY MARCH
BRINGS ULTRA ATTACKS

January 1, 1969 -- The [civil
rights] march to Derry began to
be harassed shortly after it
left Belfast....The climax...
occurred at Burntollet Bridge
outside Londonderry. There the
marchers were ambushed by an
organized crowd of Protestant
Ultras armed with stones and
cudgels. No one was killed, but
many marchers were injured as
they ran...for protection. RUC
policemen and members of the
Ulster B Special Constabulary
talked congenially with the
Ultras as they waited in ambush.
...In the weekend that followed,
Royal Ulster Constabulary men
entered the Catholic Bogside
area of Derry, batoning men, wom-
en and children on the streets
and inside their houses. In the
antiseptic words of a Commission
of Inquiry: "A number of policemen were guilty of misconduct
which involved assault and bat-
tery, malicious damage to property...giving reasonable cause
for apprehension of personal in-
jury among other innocent inhabitants, and the use of provocative sectarian and political
slogans. (E.g., 'Come out you
Fenian bastards and we'll give
you one for the Pope.')"
        Richard Rose
        Governing Without Consensus
        1971

FIVE ISRAELI ARABS DEAD,
MANY PEOPLE HURT, IN RIOTS

NAZARETH, Israel, March 30 --
A general strike by Israel's
Arab citizens erupted today into
violent clashes with security
forces in more than a dozen villages...that left at least five
Arabs dead and about 70 people
wounded.
    Israeli policemen and security
forces opened fire repeatedly to
break up demonstrations by Arabs
who were protesting a Government
plan to appropriate Arab land as
part of a regional housing and
development program in predominantly Arab Galilee.
    The rioters set up scores of
roadblocks and fought policemen
and soldiers with stones and
flaming kerosene bombs. A
spokesman said that 38 of the
wounded were from the security
forces.
    ...[The] dimension of the
day's disturbances clearly
startled Israeli officials....
    The Police Minister, Shlomo
Hillel,...expressed hope that
the riots would "prove to be a
single, isolated incident in
the history of coexistence between Israelis and their Arab
fellow citizens."
    Here in Nazareth, a group of
green-uniformed border guards
appeared to panic when stones
were hurled at them from roofs
on the eastern quarter of the
town. Shouting and waving their
nightsticks they charged through
the streets beating any Arab
they could find.
        New York Times
        March 31, 1976

CHAPTER 1

The Problem: Growth and Racial Domination

The dogs and firehoses in Birmingham, the internal security laws in Soweto, the nightsticks in Nazareth, and the stones and cudgels at Burntollet Bridge near Londonderry dramatize the brutal in modern political life. They, along with the protestors and marchers, capture the headlines—and our consciousness, leaving vivid memories of dead in the streets, bombed-out churches, and communities divided by barricades and police.

If these events were isolated incidents in a pervading serenity, we could dismiss them as anomalies. But there is more than drama and violence here. The "children" of Soweto, the Bogside, Birmingham, and Lower Nazareth have exposed what modern social thought has effectively obscured: the continuing reality of racial and ethnic domination.[1] That message would not be particularly startling if our universe were confined to Ogaden, where Somali nationalism has yet to fix its territorial boundaries, or Burundi, where a Hutu majority and governing Tutsi minority have yet to achieve social harmony. Few observers expect these fragile societies, economically

---

1. A racial group should be seen in this work as a social grouping distinguished from others by physical criteria. See Pierre L. van den Berghe, *Race and Racism: A Comparative Perspective,* p. 9. Racial differentiation may also be considered a form of ethnic differentiation, where groups are distinguished more broadly by cultural criteria. Here, differing values and belief are closely correlated with, or stem from, socially perceived physical differences. See Cynthia H. Enloe, *Ethnic Conflict and Political Development,* pp. 24–25.

Our principal concern in this book is racial domination. But because race is so closely associated conceptually with other forms of ethnicity, the analysis may be more generally applicable. The consideration later of secondary research settings is an explicit recognition of the more general aspects of this work.

The term domination—and the later terms *dominant* and *subordinate section*—should not be viewed as an authority relation as conceived by Ralf Dahrendorf, where "superordinate elements" exercise "legitimate" control over others (*Class and Class Conflict in Industrial Society,* pp. 166–67.) Domination for our purposes represents the relative standing of social groups apparent in a range of possible contexts, including the economy and polity. In the case of racial domination, one social group distinguished by physical criteria may monopolize landholdings and may have a preferred access to the state when compared to another social group also distinguished by physical criteria. The group in the preferred position will be considered the "dominant section," and the group in the less-favored position will be considered the "subordinate section." See chapter 2 for the definition of racial domination in the context of racial orders.

undeveloped and politically unstable, to escape the fires of "cultural pluralism." But racial and ethnic discord exists within the "modernizing" and "modern" societies as well: Arabs and Jews in Israel; Catholics and Protestants in Northern Ireland; blacks and whites in South Africa and the American South; Chicanos and Anglos in the American Southwest; Flemmings and Walloons in Belgium; Maronite Christians and Muslims in Lebanon; foreign workers and burghers in Switzerland; English-speakers and French-speakers in Canada; and Welsh, Scots, and English in Great Britain.

The durability of such divisions casts doubt on powerful assumptions in modern social theory. Indeed, if such parochial and ascriptive loyalties continue to organize social and political life today, despite the growth of rationalism, nations, industry, and capitalism, then it may be, as Nathan Glazer and Daniel Moynihan suggest, that "a very great deal of radical and even liberal doctrine of the past century and a half is wrong,"[2] or at least overstated. Orthodox Marxist-Leninism, Parsonian sociology, and modernization theory offer widely divergent pictures of the contradictions in industrialization, but they all agree that modernization itself, variously defined, is a transcendent process: a "single secular, national political authority" and "overarching loyalties" replace "a large number of traditional, religious, familial, and ethnic political authorities" and attachments;[3] "all fixed, fast-frozen relations, with their train of ancient and venerable prejudices and opinions, are swept away. . ."[4] There is apparently little room in this expansive process for the narrower concerns of race or ethnicity.

And yet the events of Birmingham, Soweto, Derry, and Nazareth are hardly trivial or isolated. They highlight the bitter racial and ethnic divisions in societies that have managed high levels of urbanization, mass communication, economic growth, wage labor, trade-union organization, bureaucratization, political mobilization, indeed, all the essentials of developing capitalist societies.[5] They leave us, therefore, with a difficult and

---

2. Nathan Glazer and Daniel P. Moynihan, *Ethnicity*, p. 5.
3. David E. Apter, *The Politics of Modernization*, p. 294; Samuel P. Huntington, *Political Order in Changing Societies*, p. 34; and Clifford Geertz, "The Integrative Revolution." These arguments are described in substantially more detail in the next section.
4. Karl Marx and Frederick Engels, "The Manifesto of the Communist League," pp. 46–47. Their arguments, like those of the modernization theorists above, will be elaborated in the next section.
5. The discussion in this section considers both the concept of modernization and capitalist development, though the emphasis of the book is on the latter. I assume that capitalist development necessarily takes in processes associated with modernization, particularly urbanization, rational accounting, mass communication, and bureaucratization though I do not assume the converse. These processes are not confined to capitalist settings.

unanswered question: What is the impact of capitalist development on patterns of racial and ethnic domination?[6] The answer requires an appreciation of the dynamics of growth and the tenacity of ethnic and racial differentiation.

MODERNIZATION AND CAPITALIST DEVELOPMENT: BEYOND DIVERSITY

The presumptions about growth and its impact are not confined to the obscure reaches of social theory. The presumptions pervade not only the advanced capitalist societies, where there is evidence of both assimilation and persistent ethnic conflict, but also strife-ridden, racially divided societies, where they stand against the enormous weight of counterevidence. Indeed, that is the tragedy of the growth school: spokesmen within both the dominant and the subordinate racial or ethnic sections look to growth as a salve for racial or ethnic antagonisms. The optimism of those at the top of these societies is understandable enough. In Northern Ireland, Protestant businessmen who watch the reenactment of the Reformation daily and live with the memory of three centuries of recurrent violence speak almost facilely of the rewards of economic growth: "Extra slices of a bigger cake" will bring increasing harmony in "community relations."[7] In South Africa, white businessmen who live with equally bitter divisions and violence maintain that racial barriers are incompatible with rapid economic growth; given free rein, businessmen would generate wealth and a new relationship between black and white.[8] But what is surprising is that even in the lower reaches of these divided societies, there are important groups where hope—and faith in growth—spring eternal. Prominent black leaders in the American South, like Booker T. Washington, identified the struggle of poor blacks not with the political initiatives of a Frederick Douglass, the rebellions of a Toussaint L'Ouverture in Haiti or a Nat Turner and those who followed in their tradition, or even with an emergent, potentially interracial labor movement. Progress for black southerners lay with the "Atlanta Compromise," an identification of black interests with industrial education, thrift, and industry, with a "triumphant commercialism."[9]

---

6. Implicit in the structure of the question is a presumption that racial domination may precede the development of capitalist relations within a particular society. This argument is set out more explicitly in chapter 2.

7. Northern Ireland Community Relations Commission, *First Annual Report*, 1971, p. 16.

8. *Optima* 24, no. 1, p. 4. See the extended discussion of this issue in chapters 7 and 8.

9. W. E. Burghardt DuBois, *The Souls of Black Folk*, pp. 42–54; see also Stanley B. Greenberg, *Politics and Poverty*, pp. 182–83.

During a full century of industrial development and increasing racial antagonisms in South Africa, successive leaders, like J. T. Jabavu and John L. Dube and now Manas and Gatsha Buthelezi,[10] have allied themselves with liberal capitalists and, while not advocating an "Atlanta Compromise," have urged programs of self-help and economic expansion.

These sentiments place Jabavu and Washington in prominent company— with Marx and Lenin on the one hand and with Weber, Huntington, Deutsch, and Apter on the other. They all believe that modernization and capitalist development take us beyond diversity to new forms of community and new forms of social conflict.

That is not to say that the Marxist and modernization literatures have mindlessly dismissed tradition, social distinctions, and precapitalist economic forms, ignoring their strength or their potential role in emerging social conflicts. The short term in these literatures is uncertain, disorderly, and frequently violent. Samuel Huntington, for example, emphasizes the immediate costs in the surge toward modern social formations. Income inequalities may be exacerbated; new forms of consciousness, like class, may be accompanied by renewed interest in traditional forms, like tribe, region, clan, religion, or caste. The consequences may prove tumultuous:

> Ethnic or religious groups which had lived peacefully side by side in traditional society become aroused to violent conflict as a result of the interaction, the tensions, the inequalities generated by social and economic modernization. Modernization thus increases conflict among traditional groups, between traditional groups and modern ones, and among modern groups.[11]

These contradictions are more likely to arise, Karl Deutsch argues, where culturally or linguistically distinct groups remain unassimilated but, for a variety of reasons related to modernization, become mobilized. Gaelic-speaking Highlanders in Scotland, for example, drawn to the cities, evicted from their farms, emerged during the height of English industrialization (1760–1860) as a distinct and mobilized urban population. But the Gaelic-speaking community in Glasgow soon gave way to larger forces: "In the absence of any large continuous reinforcements from the Highlands, however, the 'bottom of the barrel' was soon reached, and assimilation

10. The characterization of Manas Buthelezi is based on his involvement with the Urban Foundation, an organization funded by large South African firms and concerned with black living conditions in the urban areas.

11. Huntington, *Political Order,* pp. 37–39. For an excellent discussion of the resurgence of ethnic consciousness, particularly during anti–colonial struggles or modernization, see Donald L. Horowitz, "Cultural Movements and Ethnic Change"; and Geertz, "The Integrative Revolution."

made English the sole language of the industrial areas well before the end of the nineteenth century."[12]

Marx and Lenin were sensitive to the "national question" and the historical role of national, linguistic, and racial differences. Ireland, for Marx, was not simply the source of surplus labor for English industry or the "bulwark of the English landed aristocracy"; Irish laborers also provided the critical social diversity in the English working class that militated against its political cohesion. "All English industrial and commercial centres now possess a working class *split* into two *hostile* camps: English proletarians and Irish proletarians," Marx wrote. "This antagonism is artificially sustained and intensified by the press, the pulpit, the comic papers, in short, by all the means at the disposal of the ruling classes." Only with the severing of the Irish connection, Marx wrote Engels in 1869, would the English working class be free of such divisions and capable of forging a revolutionary social movement.[13]

If the English working class and socialists had their "Irish question," then the "Great Russian" proletariat and socialists had their Poland; indeed, they had their Bundists, Ukrainian nationalist-socialists, and, after the Revolution, their Georgians and other Caucasian nationalists as well. The 1903 program of the Russian Marxists already included a commitment to the "right of nations to self-determination." Before World War I, Lenin insisted that the proletarian parties accommodate, as Switzerland had, a babble of languages. He rejected any "artificial Russification of non-Russian nationalities";[14] indeed, he insisted on the applicability of Marx's "Irish solution" to the Ukraine and Poland.[15] The collapse of czarism and Austria-Hungary raised the "national question" to a new prominence, dominating debate within and among the Eastern European socialist parties. Even after 1917, when attempting to forge a union of socialist republics, Lenin refused to play down the issue: "The fundamental interest of proletarian class struggle, requires that we never adopt a formal attitude to the national question, but always take into account the specific attitude

---

12.   Karl W. Deutsch, *Nationalism and Social Communication,* pp. 128–29, 137. The emphasis on the continued importance of tradition and premodern social groupings is apparent throughout the modernization literature and is considered in the text only by example. Additional discussion might include David Apter's portrayal of traditional Japanese culture and its impact on modern institutions and C. E. Black's emphasis on the viability of traditional institutions (Apter, *The Politics of Modernization,* pp. 330–35; C. E. Black, *The Dynamics of Modernization,* pp. 47–49).

13.   Correspondence, Marx to Engels, London, 10 December 1869 and Marx to Meyer and Vogt, London, 9 April 1870, in David Fernbach, ed., *Karl Marx: The First International and After,* pp. 166–71.

14.   V. I. Lenin, "Critical Remarks on the National Question," pp. 12–13.

15.   V. I. Lenin, "The Right of Nations to Self-Determination," pp. 85–92.

of the proletarian of the oppressed (or small) nation towards the oppressor (or great) nation."[16]

The discussion of the short term and "national question," however, does not convey the full thrust and tone of these literatures. Lenin, for example, believed that the "national question"—the dispute over language, cultural autonomy, and national self-determination—would seem compelling only during certain periods. In the early stages of capitalism, with the "collapse of feudalism and absolutism" and the "formation of the bourgeois-democratic society and state," Lenin wrote, the mass of the population is drawn into the "struggle for political liberty in general, and for the rights of the nation in particular."[17] Hence, the national issue emerges in "backward" areas: in Ireland and the Ukraine; for Jews, in "semi-barbarous" Galicia and Russia rather than for those in "civilized" Paris and New York;[18] and for American blacks in the South rather than the North.[19] But the emerging dominance of the bourgeois order, the triumph of commodity production, buries such issues. Supporting Kautsky, Lenin wrote that "the national state is the rule and the 'norm' of capitalism; the multi-national state represents backwardness, or is an exception." Eventually, the "international unity of capital, of economic life in general" moves the nation beyond these limits:

> What is left is capitalism's world-historical tendency to break down national barriers, obliterate national distinctions, and to assimilate nations—a tendency which manifests itself more and more powerfully with every passing decade, and is one of the greatest driving forces transforming capitalism into socialism.[20]

Marx himself showed more impatience with than interest in the tenacity of the "Irish question." The issue was a distraction that kept the proletariat and bourgeoisie in England and the landed aristocracy in Ireland from their

16. V. I. Lenin, "The Question of Nationalities or 'Autonomisation,' " p. 169; also see the discussion of this issue in Robert C. Tucker, *Stalin as Revolutionary*, pp. 254–67.

17. Lenin, "The Right of Nations," p. 51.

18. Lenin, "Critical Remarks," pp. 19–24.

19. Ibid., p. 30.

20. Lenin, "Right of Nations," pp. 20–21, 50. Oliver C. Cox's posthumous work, *Race Relations, Elements and Social Dynamics*, follows on this argument. The book concludes:

Since the early sixteenth century, under the powerful and irreversible pressures of capitalist culture, the whole world entered a process of unification and assimilation. The emergent cultural standard of this assimilation has been first that of Great Britain and then the United States. There seems to be every indication that the trend will continue. In the interest of efficiency and growth, national barriers will lose significance. Demographic and ecological imperatives would increasingly force the total population to deal with the resources of the planet as a whole (p. 302).

historic roles. Their destinies were inevitably bound up not with the "Irish question" but with a revolutionary process that "explodes, rips-up" such precapitalist traditions. "Ties of personal dependence—of blood, education, caste, or estate—fall away before the progressive pre-eminence of "free wage labor." Individuals "collide with one another," not as lord and vassal, black and white, but as "things" or "commodities": the individual "carries his social power, as well as his bond with society, in his pocket."[21]

Though Max Weber did not define capitalism in terms of these transformations, he nonetheless considered them powerful "presuppositions" of capitalist society. Without "freedom of the market," mechanization, the "commercialization of economic life," private property, and "free wage labor,"[22] capitalist enterprise would be difficult to sustain. Indeed, "free wage labor" emerges as a critical factor:

> Persons must be present who are not only legally in the position, but are also economically compelled, to sell their labor on the market without restriction. It is in contradiction to the essence of capitalism, and the development of capitalism is impossible, if such a propertyless stratum is absent, a class compelled to sell its labor services to live; and it is likewise impossible if only unfree labor is at hand.[23]

Though it is possible to imagine a society where racial or ethnic domination and "rational capitalistic calculation" coexist, Weber's emphasis was upon eliminating impediments to individual mobility.[24]

At the simplest level, the modernization literature makes the bold assumption that problems of "assimilation," "integration," and "primordial diversity" are somehow peculiar to the premodern world. The modern societies maintain national unity by "allegiance to a civil state"; the premodern world grapples with "calls to blood and land." Somewhere in the movement from the latter to the former, blood dissolves into an "overarching and somewhat alien civil order."[25] At a more complex and

---

21.   For a good discussion of the force of capitalist development and its impact on traditional relationships, see Karl Marx, *Grundrisse,* pp. 157–64, 252–53. Cynthia Enloe offers an excellent discussion of the national question in Marxism, particularly the association with "backwardness" and the treatment of the issue in revolutionary China (*Ethnic Conflict,* pp. 40–53).

22.   Weber also includes "calculable adjudication and administration," not emphasized in the discussion of Marx above (*General Economic History,* pp. 276–77).

23.   Ibid., p. 277.

24.   For a more extended discussion of Weber's notions of "free wage labor" and rationality, see Anthony Giddens, *The Class Structure of the Advanced Societies,* pp. 45–50; Maurice Dobb, *Studies in the Development of Capitalism,* pp. 4–11; and K.R. Hughes, "Challenges from the Past: Reflections on Liberalism and Radicalism in the Writing of Southern African History," pp. 59–60.

25.   Geertz, "The Integrative Revolution," pp. 109–10. Also, see the discussion of modern and traditional in Samuel P. Huntington, "The Change to Change," p. 286.

dynamic level, the modernization literature emphasizes a radical transcendence, a "pulverization"[26] of the old and substitution of new relations and unknown possibilities. "Familiar communities are twisted out of shape. . . cherished institutions are swept away and beliefs come to be regarded as outmoded," Apter writes. "The future appears as a sea of adventures, not all of them pleasant." This transcendence is carried along by a revolutionary, systemic, and integrating process.[27] Individuals are loosed from "local, regional, and other intermediate structures" and joined with a "larger and more diffuse urban and industrial network."[28] They reflect a new pattern of life ("increased occupational, vertical and geographical mobility"), an enormous expansion of knowledge ("increased literacy, mass communication, and education"), and new patterns of status ("cumulative inequalities" give way to "dispersed inequalities").[29]

The implications for race and ethnicity are staggering. Social communication and economic intercourse are increasingly organized around the center rather than the periphery; the claims of nationality supersede and, in time, sweep away those of race, religion, and ethnicity.[30] The traditional bases for inequality associated with the periphery and these lesser claims, therefore, lose legitimacy and social standing. "One might say," Apter writes, "that as secular beliefs associated with the modernization process are universalized there is a corresponding peeling off of different layers of belief associated with inequality." Roles and boundaries go the way of beliefs. Modernization breaks down the "ritualized role relationships between members of different castes," whether religious, as in India, or "racial-cultural, as between Europeans, Asians and Africans in East Africa."[31] Such distinctions and boundaries survive only as remnants in societies that give increasing prominence to "germaneness," that define marginality in functional rather than racial-cultural terms.[32]

ALTERNATIVES TO GROWTH AND TRANSCENDENCE

In light of the events in Belfast and Londonderry, Soweto, Birmingham, and Nazareth—indeed, the conflict and disorder in a wide variety of multiracial and multinational contexts—it is difficult to remain comfortable with the

---

26. The term is suggested by Crawford Young, *The Politics of Cultural Pluralism*, p. 10.
27. See Huntington, "The Change to Change," pp. 288–90.
28. Black, *The Dynamics of Modernization*, pp. 68, 81–82.
29. Huntington, *Political Order*, pp. 32–33.
30. Deutsch, *Nationalism and Social Communication*, pp. 101–03.
31. Apter, *Politics of Modernization*, pp. 73–74, 124.
32. See David E. Apter, *Choice and the Politics of Allocation*, pp. 57–60, 78–79.

conventional models. That the growth and transcendence argument reflects a remarkable integration of diverse thought lends weight to the presumptions and seriousness to the issue but does not lessen our discomfiture. The problems are rudimentary and compelling: the facts, the tenor of events, do not fit the theory. The counsels of a "world-historical tendency," of modernization as "a special kind of hope,"[33] lend meaning to a quest but do not bring fact and theory into closer alignment. With perhaps more Pangloss than Sisyphus put behind us, we are wise to consider the alternatives.[34]

Persistence

The most obvious alternative to a theory that posits the death of racial and ethnic distinctions is one that insists upon their persistence. No well-developed body of theory, however, gives a central place to the idea of persistence and, at the same time, offers the consistency, power, and sense of historical movement apparent in orthodox Marxism and the development literature. But enduring ethnic and racial identities do figure in the sociological literature. We may turn to two loose bodies of theory that separate identity and development and emphasize the tenacity, perhaps pre-eminence of the former. The first body of theory stresses the strong emotional attachments associated with race and ethnicity; the second focuses on the social and historical settings that give formality and permanence to these distinctions.

Primordialism and the Beginnings

Race and ethnicity, this first literature maintains, are not simply attributes, identities, or memberships in a larger array of individual associations. Being black or Irish is not like being a trade-union member, a carpenter, or a Democrat. Race and ethnicity elicit strong emotional attachments and a sense of "sameness"; but more than that, they are "primordial," grounded in what Clifford Geertz calls the "givens"[35] or what Edward Shils calls a "common biological origin that is thought to establish ties of affinity."[36] The "givens" contrast with all that is ephemeral in

---

33. See Lenin, "Critical Remarks," pp. 20–23; and Apter, *The Politics of Modernization,* pp. 1–2.
34. Apter likens modernization to Sisyphus's repeated attempts to roll his rock up the hill. Camus, and Apter, emphasize the hope brought to the task, despite its apparent futility (Apter, *The Politics of Modernization,* pp. 1–2).
35. Geertz, "The Integrative Revolution," p. 109.
36. Edward Shils, "Color, the Universal Intellectual Community, and the Afro-Asian Intellectual," p. 4.

modern and traditional societies; indeed, they transcend and infuse them. Ties of language, color, religion, or culture, unlike other identities, are established at the beginning—with the family. Harold Isaacs writes, "These legacies come to the child bearing the immense weight of the whole past as his family has received it. They shape the only reality in his existence and are made part of him before he has barely any consciousness at all."[37] This "beginning" gives race and ethnicity a special tenacity and emotional force. Before an individual becomes a member of a society or nation, modernizing or otherwise, he or she already has a sense of common origins, of cultural or physical sameness,[38] or of simple affinity—of "our kind."[39]

The emphasis in this literature on the "beginnings" is well-placed, countering to some extent the earlier focus on the developing capitalist mode of production or the growth of functionality. Nonetheless, the emphasis is an inadequate response to our primary question.

In the first place, racial and ethnic identities are not uniformly primordial and, if primordial, not always emotion-laden and determinative. Group identities emerge in social and historical contexts, sometimes with deep primordial roots but at other times with only an artificial or circuitous connection to the "beginnings." The "basic units of contemporary cultural conflict, themselves fluid and shifting," Crawford Young writes, "are often entirely novel entities, in other instances substantially altered and transformed, in most cases redefined versions of cultural groups."[40] There may be a distant connection to the common origins, to a tortuous one-thousand mile trek or a potato famine that left millions dead and millions more in the diaspora; there may be a genuine "sameness" that comes from a shared language and rural experience. But identities emerge and disappear as groups fuse or split off, as new authorities or political boundaries are imposed, or as groups find themselves in new and strange surroundings. The Kikuyu, for example, whose coherence is now so important to understanding Kenyatta and nationalism in Kenya, had no certain identity before the imposition of British rule and the alienation of land to the settlers; distinctive groups like the Sikhs in India, Ibo in Nigeria, and Malays in Malaysia were barely conscious of their "sameness" one hundred years

37. Harold R. Isaacs, "Basic Group Identity: The Idols of the Tribe," p. 32.
38. Harold Isaacs maintains that physical sameness is a particularly powerful basis for identification: "Because the body is the most primordial of all features of basic group identity, extraordinarily powerful taboos and sanctions have been attached in many groups to exogamous unions or marriages that threaten their physical sameness, their 'racial purity' " (ibid., p. 40). Groups may adopt special practices to accentuate or create "physical sameness," like circumcision or disfiguring of the nose or ear.
39. See William J. Foltz, "Ethnicity, Status, and Conflict," pp. 105–06.
40. Young, *The Politics of Cultural Pluralism*, p. 34.

ago.[41] Even race, seemingly universal and "primordial," central to the entrenched group conflicts in southern Africa and the United States, only became a basis for broad group identity and ideology in the mid-nineteenth century. The literary skill and power of a DuBois and Senghor should not deflect us from the ephemeral in what is often considered a primordial identity.

Even if we grant the strength and emotional content in racial and ethnic identities, it does not follow necessarily that industrialization and capitalist development proceed without disturbing or trampling on them. The empirical evidence is contradictory and fragmentary. In some cases, ethnic and racial groups may acquire a new salience by serving fundamental identity needs threatened by political change and commercialization;[42] prevailing patterns of racial and ethnic cleavage may simply be reproduced in industrial enterprises and modern institutions;[43] and in other cases, ethnic and racial distinctions may survive intact while the relations between these groups are fundamentally altered.[44] The assertion of viability and persistence by itself, then, is essentially unresponsive to the question at hand.

Finally, too much of the discussion of race and ethnicity, and particularly the discussion of "primordialism," examines group identity outside considerations of power and domination. While group identities sometimes emerge in a free-formed setting, without any prior relationship between groups, very often this is not the case. Patterns of dominance between identifiable ethnic and racial groups exist prior to modernization and may survive, be invigorated, or be transformed by the process. The emotional bonds may have something to do with the persistence of these groups, but so too, I expect, do the continuing and perhaps added advantages in the relationship between them. The "beginnings" provide an identity and meaning, but they are also a claim on the state, nation, and economy, and a claim against other groups. That the Kikuyu in independent Kenya gained preferred access to productive land in the "White Highlands" and disproportionate representation in governmental, party, and university posts, while denying these positions to Asians, Luos, and other groups, was probably not incidental to their group identity.[45] Similar material and

41. Donald L. Horowitz, "Ethnic Identity," pp. 117–18, 135–40; Horowitz, "Cultural Movements and Ethnic Change"; and Young, *The Politics of Cultural Pluralism,* pp. 35–37.
42. Enloe, *Ethnic Conflict,* p. 268; Horowitz, "Cultural Movements and Ethnic Change."
43. Herbert Blumer, "Industrialization and Race Relations."
44. Van den Berghe, *Race and Racism,* pp. 31–32. Van den Berghe argues that industrialization destroys the "paternalistic" brand of race relations apparent in the "Old South," for example, and creates a no less onerous "competitive" type.
45. Young, *The Politics of Cultural Pluralism,* pp. 125–35; Colin Leys, *Underdevelopment in Kenya,* pp. 195–206.

political advantages are important to group identity for white southerners, Ulstermen, Israeli Jews, and—the Great Trek and Blood River notwithstanding—Afrikaners.

Primordialism—the emphasis on identities formed early in life—is a basic analytic concept that, at least in a theoretical sense, can be considered separately from questions of social transformation. The impact of modernization on primordialism is an empirical issue, not a theoretical necessity. Relations of dominance and modernization, however, are analytically and historically inseparable. Changes in the form of political control, the capacity of the state, patterns of ownership, and status might leave race or ethnic domination untrammeled only if that domination were independent of the economy, society, and state. Indeed, it is their intimacy that underlies our primary question.

Pluralism and Plural Societies

The second alternative emphasizing persistence draws on the literature and experience of plural societies. Its starting point is not the nation-state, conventionally conceived, with its overarching community and institutions, shared values, and loyalties. It begins with divided societies where the members share almost nothing except a common territory, a marketplace, and the state. What holds these societies together is coercion. A culturally distinct group, probably a minority, gains control within a territory, institutionalizes its distinctiveness,[46] and uses the state apparatus to maintain its ascendancy. The guiding principles in such societies are cultural diversity, inequality, and political domination.[47]

The classic consideration of plural societies is J. S. Furnivall's study of Burma and Netherlands India and the imperatives of tropical economy. There Furnivall found what he describes as a "medley of peoples— European, Chinese, Indian and native." The term "medley" is carefully chosen:

> It is in the strictest sense a medley, for they mix but do not combine. Each group holds by its own religion, its own culture and language, its own ideas and ways. As individuals they meet, but only in the marketplace, in buying and selling. There is a plural society, with different

---

46.   M. G. Smith describes this process as the "systematic disassociation between members of institutionally distinct collectivities" ("Institutional and Political Conditions of Pluralism," p. 27).

47.   Leo Kuper, "Plural Societies: Perspectives and Problems," pp. 14–17.

sections of the community living side by side, but separately, within the same political unit.[48]

For M. G. Smith, and later Leo Kuper, that medley represents not just a peculiarity of tropical economies but a central organizing idea for other societies in North America, the West Indies,[49] Africa, and elsewhere. Pluralism finds "its purest expression and most profound effects," Smith writes, in colonial settings: a European minority establishes unquestioned political dominance, while insuring the economic and social disadvantage of indigenous groups. But pluralism is not confined to any particular region, historical epoch, or economic arrangement. The notion of plural society is "equally consistent with industrial or preindustrial levels of economic and technological organization," Smith writes, and therefore independent of them.[50] Societies governed by a culturally distinct minority and riddled by inequality and conflict are theoretically possible in both the traditional and modern worlds.

The pluralism literature insists on persistence by countering principal assumptions in the modernization and nation-building literature, particularly the notion that modern societies are economically and politically integrated: racial and ethnic divisions are neither modern nor traditional.[51]

The pluralists also insist on persistence by turning the Marxists, and even Furnivall, on their heads. The binding force and principal organizing idea in plural societies, Smith writes, is political domination by a cultural minority: "Economic inequalities . . . were based upon antecedent conditions of political and jural domination and presupposed them."[52] Kuper's discussion of pluralism reflects that theme: "The state precedes and constitutes society; it is the state that is primary and imposes some measure of ordered relations on otherwise hostile or dissociated groups."[53] The state, in short, is not superstructure, dependent on changing material relations; the state is the

48. J. S. Furnivall, *Colonial Policy and Practice,* p. 304.
49. See M. G. Smith, "The Plural Framework of Jamaican Society," in Paul Baxter and Basil Sansom, eds., *Race and Social Difference.*
50. Smith, "Institutional and Political Conditions," p. 29; also see the discussion in R. A. Schermerhorn, *Comparative Ethnic Relations: A Framework for Theory and Research,* pp. 148–56.
51. In emphasizing these cleavages, Smith, Kuper, and others in the pluralist school place themselves on the side of what are sometimes called "power–conflict" theories of society. See Kuper, "Plural Societies," pp. 7–18; also see Schermerhorn, *Comparative Ethnic Relations,* p. 43; and Michael Banton, *Race Relations,* pp. 288–92.
52. Smith, "Institutional and Political Conditions," p. 59.
53. Kuper, "Plural Societies," pp. 17–18.

independent variable whose machinations structure class and ethnic relations. Our primary question, in this view, is misstated from the outset; there is no reason to believe that changes in the economy reverberate back to a system of racial domination and transform it. Kuper maintains, for example, that industrialization may create "tensions" in "settler societies," but only political transformations open the way for "revolutionary" change: "the central political system is the basis of settler domination."[54]

But where do political changes come from? How does a cultural minority lose control of the bureaucracy, the military, and the politicians? Why does a cultural minority whose position has been built on "differential incorporation" begin "incorporating" other groups? The literature on plural societies provides almost no clues to understanding political change. The closest it comes is in Smith's discussion of "important requisites" for "structural stability." Two of these—minimizing external intervention and maintaining the demographic ratios—are easy enough to appreciate in idiosyncratic, historical, or empirical terms. But three of the remaining requisites are almost inseparable from other processes in the society and economy: there must be "substantial continuity of the economic and ecological conditions in which the structure was first stabilized"; "inequalities and differences" must be generalized to all spheres ("religious, familial, educational, occupational, economic and other"); and the "cohesion, esprit de corps, and superior organization and resources to which the rulers owe their initial dominance should be maintained or enhanced."[55] To some extent, the dominant political actors can control economic change and channel the resources and antagonisms that come with it. But evolution of the economy and society sometimes have unknown and, more often, uncontrolled effects on unity within the dominant group, on the resources of various communities and actors, and on the generality of group differences.

The pluralism literature properly emphasizes the role of the state in divided societies, and we will return to that question later; but in divorcing the state from the economy and society, it creates a model that negates rather than responds to our primary question.

Uneven Development: Beyond Persistence

The literature on "dependency" and "underdevelopment" does not include a well-developed analysis of racial and ethnic domination; it does provide a

---

54. Leo Kuper, "Political Change in White Settler Societies: The Possibilities of Peaceful Democratization," pp. 186–88.
55. Smith, "Institutional and Political Conditions," p. 54.

basis, however, for going beyond theories of growth and persistence. The basis comes in the literature's polemic and presumption: capitalist development creates inequalities, unevenness, and underdevelopment. "Backward" areas or groups are not anomalies; they are integral to the process. "Economic development and underdevelopment," Gunder Frank writes, "are the opposite faces of the same coin." They are "the product of a single, but dialectically contradictory, economic structure and process of capitalism."[56] That process, though it includes an integration of disparate elements, generates a "core" and "periphery" within the same overall framework. Core-periphery relations characterize internal developments within the late-developing countries; they are also central to what Immanuel Wallerstein describes as a "world division of labor": coerced labor in the plantations and mines of the periphery, sharecropping in the semiperiphery of Europe and parts of the Americas, and wage labor in the core economies of Europe and, later, the United States.[57] But above all, they suggest a pattern of generated and functional uneven development.[58]

A variety of social and historical paradoxes associated with race begin to make sense in light of this pattern. Why, Eugene Genovese asks, did "the most advanced capitalist countries, notably England and Holland, [spawn] an archaic mode of production," like slavery? Creating a slave-owning class that was essentially antibourgeois and a slave class that was unfree would seem to run counter to historical process. Yet there is sense in that "unevenness." The Girondist bourgeoisie in 1790 had little difficulty harmonizing its own ascendancy in France and the planters' ascendancy in San Domingo. The merchants' prosperity and status were intimately tied up with the survival of slavery and the slave trade.[59] Similarly, when capitalism penetrated into the distant interior of Mesoamerica, it decimated and transformed the Indian societies but did not bring free wage labor of a capitalist variety. It brought instead forms of forced labor and dependent serfdom that, like slavery, now seem archaic or precapitalist.[60]

56. André Gunder Frank, *Capitalism and Underdevelopment in Latin America,* p. 9.
57. Immanuel Wallerstein, *The Modern World System,* pp. 87–127, 349–50.
58. The emphasis of this discussion is on the presumption of unevenness, not on the important debate over capitalism and feudalism in the third world and "underdevelopment" and "dependent capitalist development." For a consideration of those issues, see my discussion in chapter 3 and further discussion in Wallerstein, *The Modern World System,* pp. 126–27; Frank, *Capitalism and Underdevelopment,* pp. 5–6; Ernesto Laclau, "Feudalism and Capitalism in Latin America"; and Fernando Henrique Cardoso, "Imperialism and Dependency in Latin America," pp. 11–16.
59. Eugene D. Genovese, *The World the Slaveholders Made,* pp. 22, 44–46.
60. See Frank, *Capitalism and Underdevelopment,* pp. 126–35; Rodolfo Stavenhagen, *Social Classes in Agrarian Societies,* pp. 170–74.

Uneven development is also apparent in the marked social inequalities that persist and grow within developing societies. Gunder Frank associates those inequalities with the dependent relationship between the metropolitan centers and their satellites and peripheries: São Paulo and the provincial centers; the provincial centers, like Recife or Belo Horizonte, and their "local satellites" and peripheries.[61]

But the principal arguments about inequality in the dependency literature focus on the "distorted" class structure within developing nations or periphery. Class formation and development here look altogether different from these historic processes in the core economies of Western Europe and the United States. With the growth of state enterprise and multinational investment, wage workers emerge as a small but strategic section in the population, what Giovanni Arrighi and John Saul call the "labor aristocracy of tropical Africa."[62] They represent not a demoralized and exploited mass, the dynamite that will make a revolution, but a drain on the society's resources and a prop for existing patterns of uneven development. Likewise, the bourgeoisie does not forge some new order built around free wage labor and industrialization. Some elements within the bourgeoisie emerge as a kind of "comprador" group, closely allied with foreign business and its dominance within the third-world economies.[63] The bourgeoisie as a whole appears too weak to shatter the hold of entrenched landowning groups. It "yielded one strategic position after another," Paul Baran writes, and "sought nothing but accommodation to the prevailing order." What resulted was a little hideous: "an economic and political amalgam combining the worst features of both worlds—feudalism and capitalism—and blocking effectively all possibilities of economic growth."[64]

These patterns of core-periphery relations and uneven development do not by themselves enable us to construct a theory of race or ethnic relations. They give rise, however, to two tentative but important propositions: first, growth may create or exacerbate divisions and inequalities; and second, "archaic" social relations, like race and ethnicity, are potentially compatible with and perhaps functional to capitalist development.

Only the literature on "internal colonialism"[65] considers these propositions together with the problems of racial and ethnic domination. Like the

---

61. Frank, *Capitalism and Underdevelopment*, pp. 146–47.
62. Giovanni Arrighi and John S. Saul, *Essays on the Political Economy of Africa*, pp. 13–21.
63. Paul A. Baran, *The Political Economy of Growth*, p. 195; also see Leys, *Underdevelopment in Kenya*, pp. 26–27.
64. Paul A. Baran, *The Longer View: Essays Toward a Critique of Political Economy*, pp. 252–56.
65. The outlines of such a discussion are discernible in Lenin's analysis of the "national question." But his emphasis on "lagged" development—the belief that "backward" areas would ultimately catch up and escape "national" concerns—runs counter to the emphasis here on a prolonged and functional "unevenness."

work on uneven development, the literature emphasizes the vivid economic disparities between the core and periphery, though within societies: the core organized along capitalist and the periphery along precapitalist lines; members of the former command the dominant positions in the economy and polity, while members of the latter exercise little control over credit, commerce, the vagaries of the market, or the movement of labor.[66] But the disparity between the core and periphery, no matter how marked, is less important than the relationship between them. The development and growth of the core is dependent upon the stagnation and marginality of the periphery. So that, for example, the modernization of England is built upon the political subjugation and material exploitation of the Celtic fringe— Scotland, Wales, and Ireland. Similarly, the Witwatersrand in South Africa has its Zululand, Transkei, and Northern Transvaal; coastal Peru, its Sierra; and Great Russia, its Ukraine.

What is striking for my purposes is the association of internal colonialism with racial or cultural domination. For Robert Blauner, that association is more a historic than theoretical proposition: "world wide patterns of white European hegemony" were imposed within national borders, creating in the process oppressed, "racial colonies." People of color "became ethnic minorities en bloc, collectively, through conquest, slavery, annexation, or a racial labor policy." In the American experience, they remained for long periods outside of mainstream culture and society: their labor was unfree; their communal ties and culture were shattered; their lives were bound to preindustrial peripheral regions.[67] Michael Hechter frees the discussion of internal colonialism from questions of "European hegemony" and historically specific explanations. The unevenness of development creates "advanced" and "less advanced" groups. "The superordinate group, now ensconced as the core," Hechter writes, "seeks to stabilize and monopolize its advantages" by institutionalizing the differences between groups and allocating roles and benefits in ways that perpetuate the difference. The contrast between core and periphery, consequently, emerges as a "cultural division of labor," a superimposition of cultural differences upon economic inequalities.[68]

In Harold Wolpe's analysis, that superimposition is based not on inequality or advantage but on a specific relationship between the capitalist core and noncapitalist periphery. In some societies, the capitalist mode of production becomes dominant and pervasive, penetrating city, countryside,

66.. Harold Wolpe, "The Theory of Internal Colonisation—The South African Case," p. 9; Michael Hechter, *Internal Colonialism*, p. 33.
67. Robert Blauner, *Racial Oppression in America*, p. 72; see the extended discussion on pp. 51–75.
68. Hechter, *Internal Colonialism*, pp. 9, 39–43.

and diverse regions, shattering precapitalist labor patterns and social relations. Internal colonialism is not at issue there; nor are racial divisions likely to retain their importance in the face of developing commodity relations. But in other societies, the capitalist mode of production becomes dominant within a territory without dissolving the noncapitalist relations that prevail in certain regions or in the countryside. National capitalist development proceeds here very much like international capital on a larger scale—by intense exploitation and prolonged pauperization of precapitalist societies. That process creates, Wolpe says, "internal colonialism." It is also a process that gives free play to race and ethnicity. Capitalist development that builds on the conservation of noncapitalist modes of production, as in South Africa,

> necessarily requires the development of ideologies and political poli-
> cies which revolve around the segregation, and preservation and
> control of African "tribal" societies. The ideological focus, it must be
> stressed, is always necessarily on the "racial" or "tribal" or "national"
> elements, precisely because of the "tribal" nature of what is being
> preserved and controlled.[69]

The discussion of internal colonialism, however, does not take us very far beyond the propositions raised in the discussion of uneven development. It highlights the origins of racial or ethnic stratification, and we will take up that issue later in this chapter, but understanding the "roots"—the origins of Mexican-Americans as a peripheral and subordinate group in the Southwest or the Irish in the British Isles—is not synonymous with understanding development. The historical processes that brought blacks and whites together, with great advantages for one and disabilities for the other, may tell us nothing about their subsequent interaction. It is as easy to imagine that capitalist development and modernization would betray these roots as that it would reproduce them. "Tribal societies" may dissolve under the pressures of development; wage labor may diffuse through the periphery; and subordinate groups may migrate to the cities and themselves diffuse through the core. Or none of this may happen.

The discussion of uneven development, nonetheless, leaves us with an alternative presumption about growth and a sense of the origins of our problem. It does not resolve the primary question: What impact does capitalist development have on patterns of racial and ethnic domination? But it is a beginning.

---

69. Wolpe, "The Theory of Internal Colonialism," p. 13. Harold Wolpe's analysis in this article builds on his earlier discussion of capitalist and precapitalist modes of production in South Africa ("Capitalism and Cheap Labour-Power in South Africa: from Segregation to Apartheid").

CLASS FORMATION AND THE RACIAL ORDER

This analysis takes as a starting point the presumptions in uneven development theory—that is, the importance of capitalist development in understanding the persistence and elaboration of racial and ethnic domination.
But I begin by disaggregating the problem posed in that literature and
earlier discussions of the issue and by focusing on the narrower question of
racial domination.[70] I do not dwell on the relationship of "core" and
"periphery" or the conflict between an emergent rationalism and "archaic"
or "primordial" social identities: those formulations did not get us very far
beyond presumptions and perhaps a restatement of the problem. Instead,
my analysis focuses on class formation in racial orders as a concrete process,
incorporating both sides of the question—development and racial differentiation. Specifically, it focuses on class actors who accompany and make for
development and who cope with, ignore, or exploit the racial barriers and
presumptions that surround them.

The book considers three sets of individuals and roles in the dominant
section: commercial farmers, businessmen, and industrial workers.[71] These
class actors emerge in the process of increasing commercialization, capital
accumulation, and proletarianization and at the same time shape both
capitalist development and the racial barriers.[72] Their organizations—
agricultural cooperatives, business associations, and trade unions—
articulate the interests of these actors, make demands on the state, and

70. While the analysis will concentrate on racial domination and racial orders, it will later
take up related settings where ethnic differentiation is pervasive and where our propositions
face a broader test.

71. The terms *dominant section* and *subordinate section* refer here and elsewhere in the book
to privileged and unprivileged groups in a system of racial or ethnic domination. In South
Africa or the American South, the terms refer to whites and Africans, respectively; in Israel, to
Jews and Arabs; and in Northern Ireland, to Protestants and Catholics. The emphasis on the
dominant section is outlined in the Preface and Appendix A, "Sources and Methods." It
reflects, to some extent, a self-conscious research bias but also a view of historical process: the
motor forces in capitalist development and racial orders, particularly in the early stages, are
found in the dominant section. With control over capital, skilled labor, land, and the state,
dominant class actors play a critical part in shaping society and development.

But because of this emphasis, we may only take account of the "political disorder" created
by the subordinate section, not explain it. In the end, that disorder will play an increasingly
important part in the politics of the dominant section and will itself help shape development
and the racial order.

72. The class actors may or may not constitute classes in themselves. But I have tried at this
point to avoid joining the debate over "fractions" of classes; establishing whether some
workers constitute a "petty bourgeois" element or whether they and subordinate workers
constitute a proletariat; and determining at what point commercial farmers stop extracting
feudal rents and emerge as an agrarian bourgeoisie. For the moment, class actors should be
considered individuals with particular roles in the productive framework who form a part of an
emerging class or constitute a class-in-themselves.

inevitably grapple with problems of growth and race. At the individual level, my analysis examines how these class actors, while acting to secure their own interests, affect the framework of race domination. At the societal level, I ask how coalitions, power relations, and conflict among them influence the developing racial pattern.

By focusing upon these class actors, I disaccentuate, without abandoning, capitalist development as a "movement of historical totalization," as Jean-Paul Sartre describes it, as a conceptualization of whole societies embodying rules of conflict and historical development. I focus instead on the "moments," the events, facts, and the "living men," without which "there is no history."[73] My choice of particular "moments," however, is largely determined by the conceptualization of historical process, and my account of them should influence our understanding of it.

But the choice permits, as a research strategy, an emphasis on individual actors,[74] in particular, on actors who live simultaneously in a class and racial milieu: the European factory worker in a racially divided working class or the white landowner and commercial farmer in a setting where whites monopolize productive land. It is within these "moments" that my primary question is posed most vividly.

It is at this level that positivist social science has contributed most to an understanding of individual action and social relationships.[75] Marxist social science can no more dismiss its findings and methods than disregard the "moments." That, I believe, is what Sartre and Henri Lefebvre had in mind

73. Jean-Paul Sartre, *Search for a Method*, pp. 26, 82, 127–33. The emphasis on particular historical situations rather than formal theory is apparent in Eugene Genovese's work and is faced directly in his preface to the *World the Slaveholders Made* (p. viii). Nicos Poulantzas, though wedded to formal theory, also emphasizes specific historical settings or "social formations" where particularity, not abstractions, are pre-eminent: "The classes of a social formation cannot be 'deduced,' in their concrete struggle, from an abstract analysis of the modes and forms of production which are present in it, for this is not how they are found in the social formation" (*Classes in Contemporary Capitalism*, p. 23). Anthony Giddens also distinguishes between Marx's "pure" and "concrete" models, the latter emphasizing the "specific characteristics of classes in particular societies" (*The Class Structure of the Advanced Societies*, p. 27).

74. I presume here that individual members of society by their actions—their labor and "praxis"—make society and history, rather than adapting to an environment whose reproduction and development have other roots. See the discussion of these questions in Anthony Giddens, *New Rules of Sociological Method: A Positive Critique of Interpretative Sociologies*, pp. 98–104, 110–13.

75. At the same time, Marxism itself provides only limited tools for understanding behavior and identities at the individual level. Instead of developing such "mediations" or employing the "mediations" in bourgeois social science, Marxist social science sometimes situates phenomena within a totality of social contradictions and class struggle or examines consequences while inferring the process. The oppositional nature of things and historical process in this view prevent our grabbing hold of the "moments" or, if we grab the "moments," our understanding the movements. Like the physicist trying to establish the position of rapidly moving electrons,

when they urged Marxist inquiry to incorporate "certain Western disciplines," just as Paul Baran, no lackey of bourgeois economics, urged socialist societies to exploit conventional micro-level economics in certain areas of planning and administration.[76] In this analysis we will depend heavily on these "mediations" from contemporary social science, trying not to lose sight of the fact that "moments" exist alongside other "moments," that "moments" are part of a movement, and that their reconstruction makes for history and society.[77]

In this book, we will consider the three sets of class actors in turn, in each case attempting to understand its position and mode of conduct in nonracial settings and to project its likely role under conditions of developing capitalist relations in a racial order. How should each deal with a racially divided working class, the restricted mobility of labor and capital, the partial proletarianization of the subordinate peasantry, racial segregation and discrimination, and the recurrent or developing racial conflicts and political disorder? Here our analysis will depend on diverse historical experiences and a wide range of concepts, from theories of class formation and the neoclassical labor market to theories of organization and the firm. The preliminary answers to these questions form the expectations or hypotheses that will be tested in a number of multiracial and related settings. Only after those tests will we attempt to generalize beyond class actors in specific settings and attempt a "reconstruction" of historical process. Only then will we attempt to move from these "moments" to our primary question: What impact does capitalist development have on patterns of racial and ethnic domination?

Marxist social scientists may have to look at the "tracings," rather than the actual moments, and speculate about the movements.

The costs of abandoning people and the moments, except as a short-term expedient, however, are much too high. People are not incidental to historical process and grand theory. (See footnotes 73 and 74 and the discussion of "praxis" in Henri Lefebvre, *The Sociology of Marx*, pp. 25–58.) There are situations—where the line of sight is blocked, for example—where we should rely on inference. Some political relationships, whether dialectical, historical, or at a given time, are self-consciously surreptitious. No historian or social scientist, indeed no journalist and few other political actors, will be allowed access to the relationship. Bribery, lobbying, perhaps political influence have their privileges. But a bad observation point should not be promoted to a principle of inquiry. See the excellent discussion of these issues in Joel Samoff, "Class, Class Conflict, and the State: Notes on the Political Economy of Africa"; also see Bertell Ollman, "Prolegomenon to a Debate on Marx's 'Method,' " pp. 503–04.

76. Sartre, *Search for a Method*, pp. 82–83; Lefebvre, *The Sociology of Marx*, pp. 36–37, 188; Paul Baran, *The Longer View*, p. 85.

77. In the end, we embark on what Heinz Eulau calls "construction" and Sartre, the "progressive method"; we attempt to move from moments to history, to answer our primary questions. In Heinz Eulau's terminology, the class actors are essentially our "subject units"— the "unit whose behavior is observed"—and the society our "object units"—the "unit whose behavior is to be explained" (*Micro-Macro Political Analysis*, pp. 8–9; 12; see also Sartre, *Search for a Method*, pp. 146–47).

PREVIEW OF A CONCLUSION

It will be apparent that in some societies rigid racial divisions are present during early capitalist development and that perhaps a century of emerging capitalist relations does not eliminate them.[78] But we should not rush to the conclusion that development does not affect racial domination or that the two evolve independently. Capitalist development in our research settings both preserves and remakes the racial order, extending and reinforcing racial barriers, but also creating new contradictions that paradoxically threaten to dismantle them.

In its early stages, capitalist development brings an elaboration of racial disabilities and a growth of the state racial apparatus, in effect, a period of intensification. Each of the dominant class actors—commercial farmers, businessmen, and trade unionists—demands increasing control over the subordinate population and an expanded state role in the labor market. Commercial farmers, more than any other set of actors, set the tone for this intensification. They respond to growing commercial opportunities by plundering the subordinate peasantry—undermining subsistence prod-uction, intensifying labor services, and limiting the scope of the labor market. During an extended transition to capitalist agriculture, commercial farmers demand the elaboration of the labor-repressive and racial framework. Businessmen, particularly in primary, extractive industries like mining, depend on the racial order and the racial state to dislodge subordinate labor from the subsistence economy, to help organize a labor force, but also to help insure labor's continuing cheapness, immobility, and political impotence. Dominant workers, particularly those in unskilled positions, insist on state vigilance in the labor market, setting out areas of protected employment and limiting the proletarianization and mobility of subordinate laborers.

These dominant class actors are frequently at odds over the forms of racial domination. There is significant difference between the farmer's effort to bottleup subordinate labor in the rural areas and limit the labor market and the businessman's attempt to organize a labor force for the mines or factories; and between the trade unionist's attempt to create areas of protected employment and the employer's interest in substituting "cheap," subordinate labor. Nonetheless, each in his own way lends legitimacy to the racial order and race domination. Each calls on the state to take control of the subordinate worker, to draw racial lines somewhere in the society and

78.   This preview of a conclusion presents the book's findings in very bold terms. It does little justice, therefore, to the nuances in each setting or the differences between them—which are considerable. It barely gives a full account of business, trade-union, or farmer behavior.

economy. And no matter how acrimonious their conflicts over racial policies, each insists that political power remain in dominant hands.

The period of intensification, when class formation and conflict lead to heightened racial differentiation, is not fully coincident with developing capitalist relations in these settings, however. It gives way to a period best characterized as a continuing crisis of hegemony.

By what will seem like a tortuous process, each of the class actors comes to depend less on the racial order and state racial apparatus. Increasing mechanization, intensive land uses and wage labor transform a rural economy that had relied on various forms of unfree labor and a large laboring population in the countryside. Commercial farmers may not easily forego the traditional racial divisions, but with a diminishing and more mobile labor force, they no longer require or demand an elaborated state role in the labor market. Businessmen in the developing manufacturing and commercial sectors conventionally accommodate prevailing racial practices and the needs of other dominant groups. Still, they are more interested in labor stability and domestic markets than in labor repression. For them, the state racial apparatus and the disabilities on subordinate labor look increasingly anachronistic. Some dominant workers never successfully enlisted state protection in the labor market, even during the period of intensification, but others who did no longer seem in a position to demand the traditional state role. The movement of subordinate workers into some industries, the upward mobility of dominant workers, the splintering of the labor movement, the difficulties in maintaining racial boundaries in the labor market, the increasing importance of business and farm groups, all contribute to the diminished political role of dominant labor.

Capitalist development peels away the class character of the racial order but does not immediately or necessarily undermine it. The well-developed racial state, very much a product of capitalist development and the period of intensification, does not wither away with its feckless business, farm, and perhaps trade-union supporters. The ideologies that justified segregation in urban life and unfree labor in the rural economy do not immediately lose favor and currency. The bureaucrats, military, and police who administered the lives and movements of the subordinate population under the repressive framework, the public servants who worked under various forms of subsidy and preferential employment, as well as the public officials who articulated and rose with the dominant population's monopoly on access to the state do not easily relinquish the old ideas, hierarchy, and barriers.

But in the absence of clearly articulated class interests in the dominant section, the racial order and the racial state tend toward an amorphous racism, "mere dominance" in the face of the dominant class actors' diminishing interest in the racial framework and the subordinate population's increasing resistance to it.

Indeed, increasing political disorder in this period, unlike the less widespread disorder during the period of intensification, sets off a political crisis that threatens the survival of the racial order. Businessmen in the developed manufacturing and commercial sectors in particular, content at other times to accommodate prevailing ideas and practices, may now support sweeping changes in the labor framework, franchise, and ruling ideology. They may demand the dismantling of a state racial apparatus that fails to serve their labor requirements in any case and that embodies the coercion and illegitimacy at the heart of the society. They find increasingly attractive state structures that lack a racial character and ruling ideas that can gain adherents among the subordinate population.

Whether the racial order persists and in what form depends on the strength of the business challenge to the traditional racial hegemony, but also on the resources and coherence of the racial state, and increasingly on the strength of the subordinate challenge, on the violence in Soweto, Birmingham, Nazareth, and Derry.

It will be apparent from this reconstruction of development in these settings that class actors carry forward and elaborate the traditional racial patterns. Rather than transcending diversity, these class actors breathe new life into racial categories, associating race with privilege in the labor market, bringing the elaboration of a state machinery to control and limit the proletarianization of the subordinate population. Growth also brings changing labor needs, disunity, and political disorder that threaten to undo the racial order, but only after turning "primordial" identities into social barriers and only after racial domination has emerged as a modern social and political construction.

CHAPTER 2

The Racial Orders

LAND AND LABOR

There are many societies where color has moved from a neutral "spectroscopic fact," inherently no different from height or weight, to a social attribute of groups. Race, often encrusted in genetic or deterministic theory, becomes a "role sign" and barrier to opportunity, thus fostering marginal populations. In many other societies, cultural or linguistic issues set groups apart. Feelings of common ancestry, "real or putative," a "shared historical past," and clusters of "fundamental beliefs and values" rarely diffuse throughout a territory without fostering or encountering groups that live with different ancestries, histories, and beliefs. Trading minorities (including the Jews, Indians, and Chinese of their respective diasporas), political refugees (including Hungarians, Poles, and Russian Jews), and immigrants (including Italians and Eastern European Jews) populate the developed and undeveloped worlds alike.[1] England has its Commonwealth "coloured" populations; France, its Algerians; Vietnam, its ethnic Chinese; Holland, its Moluccans; Germany, its Yugoslavs, Turks, and Portuguese; Canada, its French-speakers; Spain, its Basques; and the United States, its Appalachia and not-so-well-stirred "melting pot."

But our focus is not simply on diversity and marginality. While racial distinctions may set off some groups, they need not pervade the whole society. The divisions may not be so universal that other forms of stratification, including class, are obscured or take on a "profound racial dimension."[2]

My primary research settings are racial orders, societies where racial differences are formalized and socially pervasive. Other identities and forms

1. Edward Shils, "Color and the Afro-Asian Intellectual," pp. 1–2; John Rex, *Race Relations in Sociological Theory*, pp. 28, 116–18; Michael Banton, *Race Relations*, pp. 57–59; R.A. Schermerhorn, *Comparative Ethnic Relations*, p. 12; Nathan Glazer and Daniel P. Moynihan, eds., *Ethnicity*, p. 4; Cynthia H. Enloe, *Ethnic Conflict and Political Development*, p. 15.

2. Banton, *Race Relations*, pp. 65–66; Eugene Genovese, *The World the Slaveholders Made*, pp. 103, 113.

of differentiation, no matter how important to the development and characterization of the society, must contend with a powerful social schism: to one side, a dominant section with disproportionate control over economic resources, a presumptive privilege in social relations, and a virtual monopoly on access to the state; to the other side, a subordinate section with constrained economic resources and with little standing in social or political relations.[3]

The racial orders are conventionally rooted in the historic interplay between race and the domination of peasant societies. Here, race emerged not simply as an attribute of social groups but as an integral part of a larger process and division: the expansion of a world market economy, largely European in origin, and its intrusion on peasant economies in Africa, Asia, and the Americas of varied cultures and hues. Intrusive European actors and the developing colonial-administrative machinery broke down the "social order" and disintegrated "native organic society," Furnivall writes, in effect, barring the peasant producer's access to land and threatening to incorporate him as an unfree laborer.[4] In this historic context, race lines were identified with land alienation, unfree labor, and state power—all the ingredients of a racial order.

But a racial order did not follow automatically on such tumult. In some cases, European settlement in colonial settings was followed by the rapid displacement or destruction of the indigenous populations, as in parts of North America, Australia, and New Zealand, the Caribbean Islands, and lowland areas of Latin America. Where indigenous populations gave up their land, and perhaps their lives, to European settlers, but failed to give up their labor as well, there was little need of racial distinctions or a state racial apparatus.[5] In other cases, the alienation of land and the threat to peasant society were partial or sporadic, as in Chad or Niger. In yet others—India, parts of Southeast Asia, and West Africa, for example—serious intrusions into the peasant economy but only sparse European settlement allowed land and labor questions to develop without taking on a pronounced racial character.[6]

---

3. While this characterization suggests a two-section model, there is no reason why a racial order cannot encompass a range of racial sections. For conceptual simplicity in a very complex historical process, this analysis will focus on the single divide, ignoring multiple divisions and "middle groups." The empirical research in the primary settings also will neglect, for the most part, middle groups, like the Sephardi communities in Israel and the Coloured and Indian communities in South Africa.

4. See J. S. Furnivall, *Colonial Policy and Practice*, p. 293; James C. Scott, *The Moral Economy of the Peasantry*, pp. 7–9; and Paul Baran, *The Political Economy of Growth*, p. 143.

5. See Marvin Harris, *Patterns of Race in the Americas*, pp. 1–24.

6. See discussion in Guy Hunter, ed., *Industrialization and Race Relations*, pp. 256–59.

In two settings, however, land and labor questions proved inescapable and racial distinctions shaped the society: the slave plantation economies of the New World and the European settler societies that exploited rather than eliminated their indigenous populations. Not all societies in these settings evolved into racial orders, but all racial orders began here.

Slave Plantation Economies

Race and unfree labor came together in plantation slavery. It began in the modern West on a small scale, with the African slave community on Cyprus, the slave trade in the Black Sea and Mediterranean, and the expanding slave markets in Castille and Portugal. Before it ended in the mid-nineteenth century, all the major European sea powers had become involved in the Atlantic slave trade, and African slaves had been employed in Canada, all the American colonies, the Caribbean Islands, and Latin America as far South as Rio de la Plata. African slaves had worked in the mines and ports and had helped clear the land; they had been a significant presence in Newport and New York and nearly dominant in Mexico City and Lima.[7] But slavery had not become the predominant labor form throughout the New World. Only in the plantation areas did slaveowners manage to create a slave economy.

No other "inter-group sequence," Schermerhorn writes, had "more pronounced racist consequences."[8] European settlers usually found indigenous labor unsuited to organized and commercial agriculture; the Amerindians were too sparsely settled and too mobile or succumbed too readily to European diseases.[9] Plantation agriculture was built instead on African slavery: Europeans controlled land and life in the New World and forcibly extracted labor from peasant societies in Africa. The European planters, continually short of labor, fearing that their servile laborers would flee or, worse, fall into insurrection, constructed an elaborate framework of labor control and racial domination.[10] The principal plantation slave economies were found in the southern United States, northeast Brazil, and the West Indies.

7. David Brion Davis, *The Problem of Slavery in Western Culture*, pp. 9–10, 44–45, 129–35.
8. Schermerhorn, *Comparative Ethnic Relations*, p. 101.
9. George L. Beckford, *Persistent Poverty: Underdevelopment in Plantation Economies of the Third World*, pp. 88–89; Carl N. Degler, *Neither Black Nor White: Slavery and Race Relations in Brazil and the United States*, pp. 212–13; and Harris, *Patterns of Race*, pp. 11–12.
10. Eric R. Wolf, "Specific Aspects of Plantation Systems in the New World: Community Sub-Cultures and Social Classes," pp. 136–37; Ida C. Greaves, "Plantations in World Economy," p. 15; Jay R. Mandle, "The Plantation Economy: An Essay in Definition."

Racial domination and unfree labor did not always survive emancipation. In some cases, like Haiti, slave rebellions brought a rapid end to the racial order; in others, like Cuba, many former slaves found land and recreated a rudimentary peasant agriculture; in others, like Brazil, Guyana and Trinidad, mixed racial groups or new waves of indentured laborers altered the original racial divisions.[11]

Nonetheless, discrimination and race lines persisted throughout the plantation world. Beckford maintains that none of the postslave plantation societies in the New World fully escaped the "caste lines."[12] Even in Brazil, where Gilberto Freyre proclaimed a "racial democracy," the latifundias remained largely in white hands, and until the twentieth century, laws against vagabondage and social contact dogged the former slaves.[13] In a few plantation societies—Jamaica, Guyana, and the southern United States, for example—rigid race lines and unfree labor persisted well into the modern period.[14] The South in particular, with its highly developed slave economy, clear and rigid racial-caste lines, and white monopoly of state power, provided the essentials for a racial order.[15]

Settler Societies

The European settlers that intruded on and exploited indigenous societies provide a second setting conducive to persistent racial domination. Had the settlers sought land alone, had their armies pushed back the "frontier," making room for an essentially European and racially homogeneous society, race lines might never have emerged as a principal divide. But the settlers in some colonial contexts were also intent on drawing labor out of the peasant economy. They turned increasingly to the state: land expropriation, reserves, population removals, taxes, forced labor, pass laws, and corvée services.

Settler societies emerged in much of Central and Latin America. Spanish conquest sometimes brought the destruction of Indian communities, as in Hispaniola and on the Peru coast; elsewhere, however, Spanish and Portuguese conquest brought new forms of tribute and new patterns of

11.   Degler believes that the mulattoes are the key, the "escape hatch," that differentiates race relations in Brazil and the United States (*Neither Black Nor White*, pp. 223–27).
12.   Beckford, *Persistent Poverty*, pp. 68–69.
13.   Degler, *Neither Black Nor White*, pp. 220–24.
14.   M. G. Smith, "The Plural Framework of Jamaican Society"; Jay R. Mandle, *The Plantation Economy: Population and Economic Change in Guyana, 1838–1960*.
15.   Davis, *The Problem of Slavery*, p. 60. Genovese argues that the American South came closer than any other slave society in the New World to turning slavery into a distinct mode of production (*In Red and Black*, p. 340).

agriculture and labor exploitation. In Peru, Spanish and mestizo penetration of the Sierra led to the rapid alienation of arable and common lands and the emergence of a land and labor form commonplace in Spanish America, the hacienda. Amerindians, sometimes living in the free villages, sometimes on the hacienda itself, faced a host of labor obligations. The framework depended on hacienda, indeed on Spanish and mestizo, control of national and local political institutions.[16] In Mexico and parts of Guatemala, similar patterns of conquest and Spanish penetration brought similar consequences for the Amerindian communities. The "voracity of the hacienda for land and labor,"[17] Eric Wolf writes, intruded on the pueblo and Indian communal lands, creating a servile and dependent labor force. "While each local hacienda had its own apparatus of coercion, its own policy and whipping post, the entire structure of coercion depended ultimately on the apparatus of coercion maintained by the government."[18]

The growth of a large white and mestizo population by the outset of the nineteenth century (almost two of every three persons across Latin America)[19] insured that other cleavages would accompany or dominate Latino-Amerindian differences. In the settler societies of Africa, however, race was not so easily obscured.

Had Europeans not lost political control in central and east Africa and in the former Portuguese colonies, settler regimes and racial orders might still order relations between blacks and whites there as they still do to the south, particularly in South Africa. In Angola, like Mozambique, exiled Portuguese criminals and, later, settlers under rural development schemes demanded widespread land alienation and forced labor. Portuguese rule, particularly in the twentieth century, established a firm barrier between settlers and the indigenous African population—with political rights and land concessions for the former and land expropriations, reserves, "native work books," and "native labor codes" for the latter.[20] In Kenya, the British colonial administration alienated to European settlers fertile Kikuyu and Masai land in the highlands. But land was not enough. From the time of early settlement before World War I until the time of Mau Mau, European settlers complained of acute labor shortages. In the intervening years, the British constructed the familiar framework of a racial order: land

---

16. Jeffrey Paige, *Agrarian Revolution,* pp. 161–67; Julio Cotler, "The Mechanics of Internal Domination and Social Change in Peru," pp. 413–15, 420–22.

17. Eric R. Wolf, "Aspects of Group Relations in a Complex Society: Mexico," p. 56.

18. Eric Wolf, *Peasant Wars of the Twentieth Century,* p. 22; also see the discussion in Rodolfo Stavenhagen, "Classes, Colonialism and Acculturation," pp. 266–76.

19. Richard M. Morse, "The Heritage of Latin America," p. 138.

20. See Paige, *Agrarian Revolution,* pp. 233–54; and Gerald J. Bender, *Angola Under the Portuguese,* pp. 57–131.

alienation was accompanied by hut and poll taxes, pass laws, masters and servants ordinances, and crowded tribal reserves; Europeans controlled the marketing boards, the civil service and police, and diverted African tax revenues to the railroads, roads, and extension services for white farmers.[21] Today, white political domination, land alienation, and labor compulsion in South Africa provide a contemporary example of a settler society and racial order.

THE PRIMARY RESEARCH SETTINGS

My primary research settings include two societies—South Africa and Alabama—where conflicts over racial domination in our time have captured the headlines and dramatized the problem. In both instances, the expansion of the market economy and European settlement raised questions about land and labor that were answered in race terms. In the period before capitalist relations dominated these societies, race lines were pervasive and formalized, affecting questions of social and economic privilege and access to the state. In both settings, the process of class formation and articulation were affected by a preexisting, "profound racial dimension." Who gained access to capital and industrial enterprises, who won control over markets and labor supplies, and who cornered the skilled job positions were all decided within this racial context. But in South Africa, developing capitalist relations over an entire century did not eliminate and may have enlarged the racial dimension. In Alabama, race lines survived three-quarters of a century of development and only failed in the wake of political disorder and external intervention.[22]

South Africa

The essential outlines of the racial order in South Africa were drawn during European colonial expansion that predates capitalist development within South Africa itself.[23] The Dutch East India Company established a re-

21. Colin Leys, *Underdevelopment in Kenya*, pp. 28–36; Richard D. Wolff, *The Economics of Colonialism*, pp. 96–127; Crawford Young, *The Politics of Cultural Pluralism*, pp. 125–38.
22. This book will not attempt to explain the increasing black resistance and violence but will focus on their effect on class actors in the dominant section and their impact on the state coercive and racial structure.
23. For background reading on this overview, see C. W. de Kiewiet, *A History of South Africa: Social and Economic;* Richard Elphick, *Kraal and Castle: Khoikhoi and the Founding of White South Africa;* Monica Wilson and Leonard M. Thompson, eds., *The Oxford History of South Africa;* R. E. and H. J. Simons, *Class and Colour in South Africa, 1850–1950;* Sheila T. van der Horst, *Native Labour in South Africa;* Heribert Adam, *Modernizing Racial Domination.*

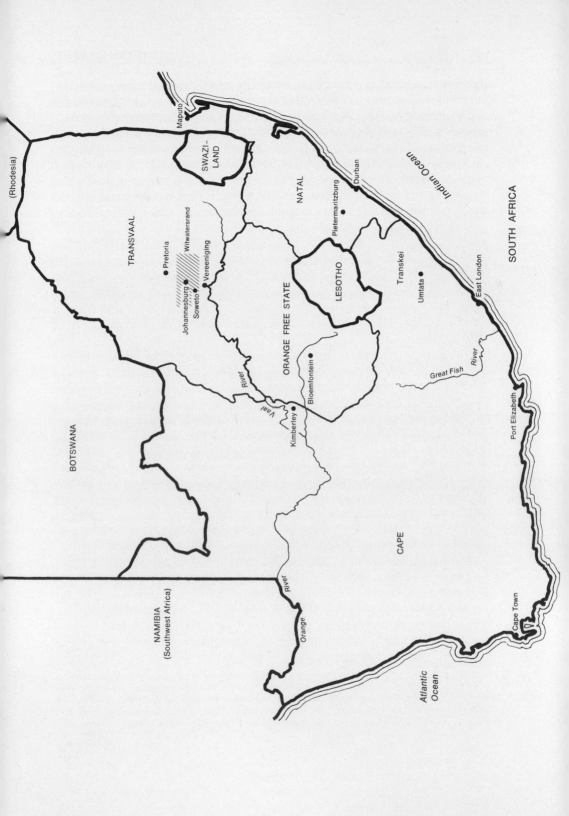

freshment station at Table Bay in 1652, one of the first European settle-
ments in Africa south of the Sahara and halfway to India. At the outset, the
European presence was small: after thirty-five years of settlement, only eight
hundred Europeans had come to the Cape, two hundred of them
Huguenots. In the vicinity of Table Bay and the immediate interior, the
European settlement encountered the Khoikhoi, a nomadic pastoral society,
and bands of hunter-collectors. Initially, the relationship between the
Company and Dutch settlers on the one hand and the indigenous society on
the other was essentially commercial—bartering for sheep and cattle. But
before the eighteenth century, many of the Khoikhoi, having lost most of
their cattle, entered the service of the Europeans as servile laborers. The
Company and the growing settler population also began using the slave
trade. Slaves were brought from Angola and West Africa, later from
Madagascar and East Africa, from Indonesia, Malaya, and elsewhere in
Southeast Asia. By the end of the eighteenth century, a slave population of
26,000, mostly in the western Cape, outnumbered the European settler
population.[24]

The European farmers practiced a mixture of commercial and subsistence
agriculture. Their farming methods were characterized by extensive use of
land and recurrent "trekking" after new farming areas. By 1795, the
trekboers, the nomadic European stock farmers, had pushed the colony's
boundaries to the Orange River in the north and face-to-face with the more
densely settled and better organized African (in this case, Xhosa-speaking)
societies in the east. Frontier conflict, growing population, and land
pressure had by the early nineteenth century left an increasing number of
Africans[25] squatting on the European farms. Many of the European settlers,
hoping to escape the pressures on the eastern frontier and the now English
administration, sought new farming areas deep in the interior. They also
sought to recreate the system of woonkaffers, African squatters, supplemented by the widespread "apprenticing of native children."

The pattern of racial admixture and African labor on European farms
was buttressed by a developing state role in land and labor questions. From
the early nineteenth century, the colonial administration regulated the
mobility and service contracts of Khoikhoi and African farm workers.
Throughout the century, the colonial and settler regimes helped forge a
labor framework—a medley of hut taxes, pass laws, and constricted African
reserves—that eroded African peasant society.

24. The Coloured population group in South Africa is a mixed racial group, drawing
primarily on these slave peoples, the Khoikhoi, and, to some extent, Europeans and Africans.
25. African will be used in this book when referring to the various Bantu-speaking groups;
black will be used as an inclusive term for Africans, Coloureds, and Asians.

The diamond discoveries at Kimberley in 1870 and the gold discoveries on the Witwatersrand in 1886 set South Africa on an industrial and capitalist path. But from the outset, the developing capitalist order reflected the prevailing racial lines and hierarchy. Ownership of the numerous and overlapping diamond claims was at an early stage concentrated in European hands; indeed, the diggers organized to block the growth of Coloured claimants. English and, to some extent, French and German investors ventured into the deep-level gold mining that would dominate the Witwatersrand and, after the Second World War, parts of the Free State. For the more skilled work, mine owners drew on the established mining communities in Cornwall and California; for the laboring positions, they drew on the peasant societies of South Africa, Mozambique, other territories in Central Africa, and, for a short while, China. The European farming community responded slowly to the developing markets for food; in some instances, more slowly than the African farming communities. But with state assistance—the Natives Land Act and other measures—white farmers gained control over both agricultural commodity and labor markets.

Capitalist development has gone a long way toward remaking South Africa. The Witwatersrand, whose mining camps housed perhaps 3,000 workers in 1887, encompassed in excess of 100,000 people by the turn of the century and by the 1960s, included 2.5 million people and a sprawling manufacturing and mining complex, stretching from Witbank in the east to Krugersdorp in the west. At the turn of the century, the great majority of the population in South Africa lived in rural areas, but by the sixties a majority of the Europeans, Coloureds, and Asians, and a third of the Africans lived in urban areas. Employment in the mining industry doubled, while gold output quadrupled; employment in manufacturing and commerce increased more than tenfold. Small-scale industry, the gold mines, and a few mining houses had been transformed into a vast complex of organizations and institutions: agricultural cooperatives, marketing boards, industrial councils, trade unions and labor federations, business and trade associations, and large manufacturing and parastatal enterprises.

But the race lines remain. Whites, who constitute only 10 percent of the labor force in gold mining, are entrenched in the most skilled positions and receive more than half of the total wages. On the average, white workers receive five times the wages of African workers. Africans are segregated in the work place, the urban townships, and the African "homelands"; their movements are circumscribed by a complex of pass and race laws that lead to the prosecution of more than a half million Africans each year. They are denied the franchise and trade-union rights; virtually every recognizable black leader has been banned, jailed, or exiled.

More than 70 percent black population in 1900

ALABAMA

Alabama

On December 14, 1819, Alabama became the twenty-second state in the Union and the eleventh established as a slave state.[26] During the preceding three hundred years, Spanish, French, and British flags had flown over the territory. In that period, European settlers displaced the indigenous population that had occupied more than half the territory and created a society that would depend on unfree black labor.

When Europeans began to map and trade with the interior, they found four major Amerindian groupings: the Cherokees in the northeast, Chickasaws in the northwest, the Choctaws in the southwest, and the Creeks in the center and southeast. Substantial European settlement, therefore, would have to await massive "land concessions" and forced removal of the Amerindian populations. They began on a small scale: in 1765 the Choctaws ceded to the British a strip of land between the Chickashay and Tombigbee rivers, while the Creeks ceded a narrow, twelve-mile strip along the coast. The state of Georgia in 1789, without apparent legal foundation, sold most of the present states of Alabama and Mississippi to "Yazoo" land companies. Increasing Amerindian concern with the alienation of land and increasing European pressure for areas of settlement were eventually joined in war. After the First Creek War of 1813–14, the Creeks were forced to cede most of their land in Alabama. Within three years after the war, Choctaws, Chickasaws, and Cherokees were also forced to make land concessions. Indeed, three-fourths of the state was now open to white settlement. By 1835, the Amerindians had given up or exchanged all their land in Alabama; the last remnants of the Cherokees and Creeks were removed forcibly, some fleeing to Florida and some taken in chains to the West.

The forced removal of the Amerindians brought land companies, a great European population movement from Virginia, the Carolinas, and Georgia —and slaves. Homesteaders took up land in the hills, the ridges, and tablelands; the planters and slaveowners, mainly from Georgia and South Carolina, took up the rich bottom lands near the major rivers and eventually occupied the fertile Black Belt. At the time of statehood, 1819, a third of the inhabitants were slaves; by 1860, at the outset of the Civil War, one of every two inhabitants was a slave.

---

26. This section on Alabama draws upon the following background readings: Albert Burton Moore, *History of Alabama;* Allen Johnston Going, *Bourbon Democracy in Alabama 1874–1890;* William Warren Rogers, *The One-Gallused Rebellion: Agrarianism in Alabama, 1865–1896;* Lucille Griffith, *Alabama: A Documentary History;* Carl V. Harris, *Political Power in Birmingham, 1871–1921;* J. Morgan Kousser, *The Shaping of Southern Politics;* Paul B. Worthman, "Black Workers and Labor Unions in Birmingham, Alabama, 1897–1904"; and Ethel Armes, *The Story of Coal and Iron in Alabama.*

Planter rule in Alabama was tempered by the presence of a large non-slaveowning farm population in central and north Alabama. But the white farmers did not question the white ascendancy or institution of slavery. The planter-controlled legislature placed increasing restrictions on manumission: an 1834 act required that freed slaves leave the state within twelve months; in 1860, manumission was barred altogether. The slave codes provided for a rudimentary pass system, barred meetings of five or more male slaves off the plantation, and established patrols to watch over the slave population and insure the enforcement of the slave codes.

The Civil War blocked the South's and Alabama's bid for regional autonomy and brought an end to the institution of slavery. It did not, however, except for a brief respite, bring an end to white rule and did not immediately bring an end to unfree labor. On a campaign of thoroughgoing white supremacy, with widespread intimidation and fraud, planters and small white farmers toppled the Reconstruction regime; and with similar methods, the planters in the Black Belt gained control of the Democratic party and the black vote, and mastered the defense of white supremacy.

The Democratic ascendancy in Alabama allowed the planter to retain his land and once again control his farm labor. Fearing that black labor would be drawn off to the higher-paying cotton-growing areas or that agricultural labor would prove inefficient without some form of compulsion, planters began reconstructing the framework of labor control. Wage contracts soon gave way in the Black Belt to sharecropping arrangements. The post-Reconstruction legislatures enacted lien laws that gave planters greater control over the cotton crop and, consequently, over the black sharecroppers. They also acted to prevent the flight of tenants: "false pretense" laws that provided criminal penalties for breach of contract; antienticement laws and special taxes on labor agents in Black Belt counties. Law was supplemented by a framework of extralegal violence that encouraged blacks to take out labor contracts and avoid independent farming or marketing.

Business enterprise in Alabama was built atop this foundation of white rule, planter ascendancy, and unfree labor. The first blast furnace was constructed in 1880 and opened the way to black and white urban employment. The population of Birmingham increased from just over 3,000 in 1880 to more than 26,000 in 1890 and 130,000 by 1910. In the mineral district, blacks found their way to the foundries and underground mining. They failed to establish a firm position, despite experience in the "plantation crafts," in the skilled trades or the developing mechanical crafts. Southern cotton mills, "savior of the poor whites," located outside the urban areas and drew largely on white, female, and child labor.

Capitalist development was not in any case very far advanced: in 1880 wage earners comprised only .8 percent of the population, hardly larger than the wage earning group of 1850. Even in 1900, wage earners were less than 3 percent of the Alabama population.

But three-quarters of a century of capitalist development transformed Alabama society. Though only one person in ten lived in urban areas in 1900, by 1970, six in ten lived there. Less than 15 percent of the population was engaged in agriculture; in the Black Belt in particular, production had shifted to large, mechanized farming units and to cattle and soybeans; cotton sharecropping had been virtually eliminated. More than half of the potential labor force was employed in manufacturing and commerce.

Three-quarters of a century of growth, however, had left race lines largely intact. Law, custom, and violence placed blacks at the back of the bus, in separate bathrooms, schools, parks, sports activities, and residential areas. Blacks were almost entirely excluded from the building, railroad, and engineering crafts; they languished in the foundries and mines, in the "nigger jobs." Black income was only 40 percent that of whites. In politics, whites held every state, county, and municipal office, while blacks remained disenfranchised.

When Rosa Parks refused her seat at the back of a Montgomery, Alabama, bus in 1955, she set off a period of protest, violence, and outside intervention that consumed Alabama for at least a decade and that left the racial order in shambles.

THE RELATED RESEARCH SETTINGS

My related settings are not strictly racial orders: the principal divisions have been religious, perhaps cultural, but not racial. Nonetheless, these societies have been caught up in some of the same historic processes and pose some of the same problems. In Northern Ireland and Israel, settler regimes were established, if not as direct agents of European colonial expansion, then at least as part of a more general expansion of world markets and intrusion on peasant societies. As in my primary research settings, settler societies posed questions of land alienation and ownership and, to a lesser extent, questions of labor control. In each case, a state, largely responsive to an identifiable ethnic group, tried to answer these questions in ethnic terms. The resulting divide left Protestants and Catholics, Jews and Arabs, segregated from one another and left the former in each case with disproportionate economic resources and social privilege and exclusive access to the state. The divide survives in Israel, despite substantial economic growth. In Northern Ireland, the divide survived three hundred years of Irish history, including the last half century of capitalist development in Northern Ireland, though it

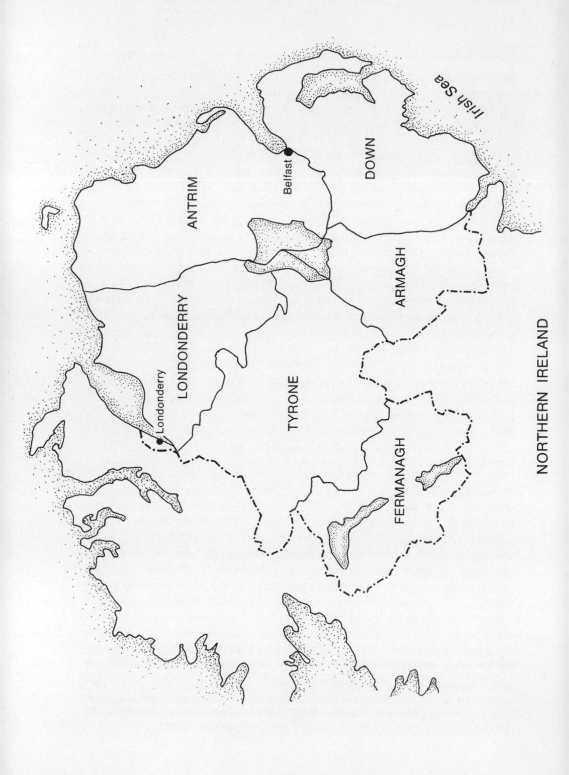

NORTHERN IRELAND

Irish Sea

DOWN

ANTRIM

Belfast

ARMAGH

LONDONDERRY

Londonderry

TYRONE

FERMANAGH

lost much of its formality in the face of political disorder and outside intervention.

These settings provide another test for my propositions, though only in relation to particular class actors—businessmen in Northern Ireland and workers in Israel. Still, they help establish the greater generality of the problem and help explain capitalist development in ethnically divided societies.

Northern Ireland

The division between English settlers and the native Irish predated the religious question.[27] The first Irish Parliament in the thirteenth century included no native Irish members and roundly condemned English settlers who adopted Irish hairstyles and dress. English settlers were barred from intermarrying with the natives, living by ancient Irish laws, or speaking Gaelic. But the principal divide in Irish history emerged in the interplay between religion—the split between the Church of Rome and the Church of England—and the land question.

The interplay began, ironically enough, under Catholic Queen Mary's reign. She began on a small scale what later became fundamental English policy for Ulster and the whole of Ireland: the displacing of the settled Irish population by English, mostly Protestant farmers. The Irish resisted English settlement, but after nearly a decade of struggle, the Earls of Tyrone and Tyrconnel, along with the leading Catholic chieftains from Ulster, fled to the Continent. The end to Gaelic political authority in Ireland opened the door to systematic English settlement in the area that is now Northern Ireland. The Irish farmers in Ulster lost all title to their land, which was given to English and Scottish "undertakers" who agreed to foster settlement by "loyal subjects" of the crown. The Ulster plantations, despite a small number of Irish grantees and, later, a limited Irish tenantry, established an English presence in Ulster. In 1630, the British population on the Ulster plantations exceeded British settlement in all of North America; eventually, 21,000 Englishmen and 150,000 Lowland Scots would join the colony in Ulster.

27. See Tony Gray, *Psalms and Slaughter;* Richard Rose, *Governing Without Consensus;* Denis P. Barritt and Charles F. Carter, *The Northern Ireland Problem;* Robert Kee, *Ourselves Alone;* Oscar Handlin, *Boston's Immigrants;* Ian Budge and Cornelius O'Leary, *Belfast: Approach to Crisis;* Michael Hechter, *Internal Colonialism: The Celtic Fringe in British National Development 1536–1966.*

Renewed Catholic resistance in the 1640s brought the slaughter of Protestants in the North and a challenge to English sovereignty in Ireland. The English forces, under Cromwell's personal command, took up the Lord's work and slaughtered the rebel forces and the Irish citizenry in turn. The horror at Drogheda and other battles in 1649 was matched only by the scope of land confiscation following the hostilities. The Act of Settlement left only 14 percent of the land, all west of the Shannon, in Irish hands; in Ulster, less than 5 percent remained.

Protestant Ulster resisted the Catholic rebellion under James II, standing alone among the Irish provinces, swearing allegiance to William of Orange and the Protestant cause. And Ulster, not Dublin, was aligned with the dominant forces of the period. The Protestant settlers at Londonderry withstood James's siege of 105 days; William's forces routed the Catholic armies at the River Boyne, sending James back to France and a rebellious Catholic population back to its earlier subjugation. But England and the Protestant settlers would settle for nothing less than the destruction of Catholicism in Ireland, by forced conversion, if possible, and, failing that, by rooting out the last vestiges of Catholic economic and political power. Between 1691 and 1793, the Irish House of Commons and the English Privy Council enacted the Penal Laws to insure that there would be no repeat of earlier rebellions. A bill to "Prevent the Further Growth of Popery," for example, barred Catholic education in Ireland, made Catholic minors eligible for adoption by Protestant guardians, barred Catholics from purchasing land or from leasing it for a period in excess of thirty-one years, prevented Catholics from bequeathing what little land they had to one son (thus increasing the number of small, uneconomic farming units), barred Catholics from voting or sitting in Parliament, and limited their right to travel within Ireland. Other legislation prevented Catholics from employing apprentices or becoming apprentices themselves and barred them from the legal and teaching professions and, above all, the priesthood.

The English settlers did not displace or eliminate the native Irish peasantry, though not for lack of effort: the potato famine took a million lives, and emigration to the United States and England took another million and a half. The Irish peasantry had been left destitute, some on marginal subsistence plots, some as tenants on English-owned land, and most as cottiers, labor tenants who for a small potato patch paid with their labor and their pigs.

The Anglo-Irish Treaty of 1921 brought partition—a Catholic government in Dublin and continued Protestant ascendancy in Ulster. Lord

Craigavon, the first prime minister in the six counties of Ulster, demanded a "Protestant Parliament for a Protestant people" and a "Protestant State." He abolished proportional representation and substituted in its place a system of voting and districts that insured Unionist party control at Stormont (the parliament in Ulster), Westminster, and in the various local councils. Constituencies were gerrymandered. The "company" or "property" vote insured additional voting strength for those, mostly Protestants, who owned highly rated property. The system was immensely successful: until recently, the Protestant Unionists regularly held 80 percent of the seats at Stormont and all twelve seats at Westminster.

Capitalist development in Ireland accompanied and reflected these currents in Irish history. With Catholics barred historically from landownership in Ulster, it was the Protestant community that responded to developing markets in England and that managed the changeover from tenancy to wage labor. The two principal developing industries, linen and shipbuilding, were Protestant owned and based in Ulster. Harland and Wolff, the principal shipbuilding firm, was founded in 1860 and by 1900 employed 9,000 workers. By 1875, the linen industry employed 50,000 workers. Protestant workers monopolized the artisan positions in the engineering industry and shipbuilding and dominated employment in all of Ulster.

In 1850, only a third of the male labor force was employed outside of agriculture, but by the time of partition it had risen to 43 percent and by 1951, to 60 percent. Economically, Northern Ireland now resembled other parts of Great Britain—Wales and Scotland, for example. Harland and Wolff had emerged as the largest shipbuilding yard in the world, and the engineering industry had grown from its dependence on textiles and shipbuilding to a more diversified involvement in equipment and aircraft manufacture.

When the British finally sent troops into violence-torn Belfast in 1969, the Protestant ascendancy was alive and well in Ulster. All the principal industries were Protestant owned and managed. Catholics traveled to work in these Protestant industries and Protestant areas only with great difficulty and at genuine peril. They were lower-paid than their fellow Protestant workers and more likely to face unemployment. The Ulster Unionists were firmly in control of the state. All the permanent secretaries and virtually all persons of consequence in the government were Protestants. And at Burntollet Bridge outside Derry, Protestant policemen stood by as Protestant militants beat and chased Catholic civil rights marchers.

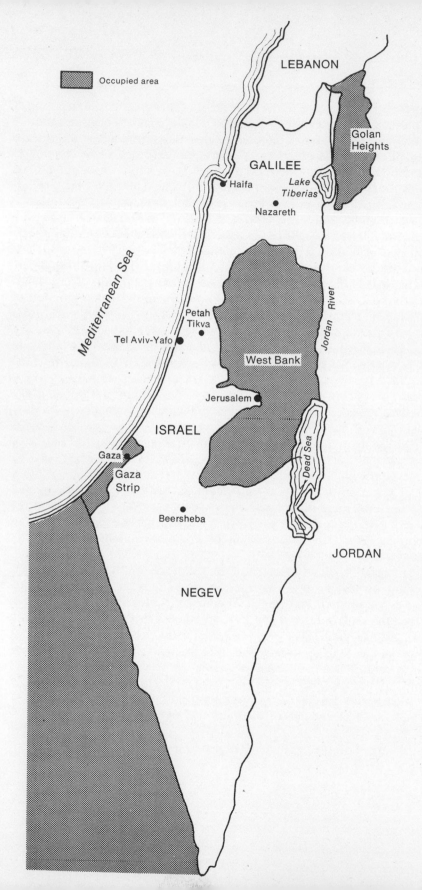

LEBANON

Occupied area

Golan
Heights

GALILEE

Haifa
*Lake
Tiberias*

Nazareth

Mediterranean Sea

Petah
Tikva

Tel Aviv-Yafo

Jordan River

West Bank

Jerusalem

ISRAEL

Dead Sea

Gaza

Gaza
Strip

Beersheba

JORDAN

NEGEV

Israel

The undermining of the Arab peasant society began well before large-scale Jewish settlement in Palestine.[28] The area came under the sway of the Seljuk Turks in the eleventh century, the Crusaders during the twelfth and thirteenth centuries, and the Ottoman Empire from the sixteenth. A population that had numbered in the millions at various times had sunk to 250,000 by 1800. Though the depopulation was reversed in the nineteenth century, the pressures on peasant society were undiminished. A disintegrating Ottoman Empire, under increasing pressure from Europe, sought new sources of public revenue at the expense of the Arab peasantry. It replaced the traditional and inefficient system of tributes with the Ottoman Agrarian Code of 1858, providing for individual titles and direct taxation. The system of tenure and taxation increased peasant indebtedness, abrogated common grazing areas, and provided a framework of land speculation that would facilitate later Jewish settlement.

The long-standing Jewish presence in Palestine, particularly in Jerusalem, had survived Herod and the Crusades and had posed no serious threat to the Arab community or peasant society. Large-scale Jewish settlement beginning in the late nineteenth century, on the other hand, contributed to a process that was limiting Arab tenancy and grazing rights and that opened up opportunities for intermittent wage labor. The First Aliya (wave of migration) between 1882 and 1904 brought Jewish settlers to colonies sponsored by Baron Rothschild. They had hoped to develop the colonies on the basis of "self-labor," Jewish labor, and consequently provide for increased Jewish settlement in Palestine. But within a decade, "cheap" Arab labor had replaced "dearer" Jewish labor; the Jewish settlers advanced to supervisory positions in the colonies or moved to their own farms, employing Arab workers in the process. The Second Aliya and Third Aliya brought renewed commitment to a Jewish economy in Palestine. By 1923, more than 100,000 Jewish settlers were working in the Jewish plantations, agricultural collectives, and Jewish cities, like Tel Aviv. But a disintegrating Arab peasant economy and increasing commercialization brought more and more Arabs into the Jewish sector as laborers. The Jewish labor movement insisted on 100 percent Jewish employment on the plantations and in

28. See S. N. Eisenstadt, *Israeli Society;* Michael Curtis and Mordecai Chertoff, eds., *Israel: Social Structure and Change;* Elia T. Zureik, "Transformation of Class Structure Among the Arabs in Israel: From Peasantry to Proletariat"; Elia Zureik, "Toward a Sociology of the Palestinians"; Santiago Quintana Pali, "The Arabs in Israel: A Class Formation Analysis"; Don Peretz, *Israel and the Palestine Arabs;* Abner Cohen, *Arab Border-Villages in Israel;* Jacob M. Landau, *The Arabs in Israel;* Israel, Central Bureau of Statistics, *Statistical Abstract of Israel, 1976;* Henry Rosenfeld, "The Arab Village Proletariat."

construction and conducted a campaign of picketing, strikes, and terrorism into the early thirties. It demanded that the mandatory authorities allot 50 percent of the employment in the railroads, post offices, and road construction for Jewish labor and establish a separate Jewish wage scale at a "civilized standard."

The limited capital investment in Palestine was dominated from the 1920s by the privately owned Jewish plantations, Jewish National Fund, and the Histadrut (Jewish general workers' union); British spending on railways and roads, though not under Jewish control, largely served Jewish commercial development. The scattered small-scale Arab industries and some wealthy Arab notables were no match for the private and collective capital investment brewing in the Jewish sector. For the Arab fellahin, Jewish settlement spelled increased pressure on the peasant economy and partial but still limited proletarianization. Arabs found marginal and unstable wage employment on the Jewish farms, in government service and in construction, and generally received half the Jewish wage rate for comparable work. The Arab civil disorders in 1929 and 1936 to 1939 were an unfocused and bloody response to these relationships and to the general course of Arab-Jewish contact.

Though the distinctions between Arabs and Jews in this period were formalized and pervasive, they were not managed by a state under Jewish control. The colonial administration had allowed large-scale Jewish immigration and land purchases, even granted considerable communal autonomy, but it had not allowed the political role played by settler communities elsewhere. Nonetheless, Jewish settlers in Palestine, even before the expiration of the British mandate, had their own army (the Haganah), elected governing body (Vaad Leumi), and political arm (the Jewish Agency). After partition, these institutions were integrated into a new Jewish state. Though the Arabs after 1948 were now only a minority in Israel, the Jewish state reflected the struggle in Palestine and the uncertain security situation in the region. Arab movements and political activity were circumscribed by the Israeli military administration in the Galilee and Little Triangle. Arab lands were threatened by the establishment of "protected areas" on the borders (1949), the Absentees' Property Law (1950), and the rising demand for new Jewish settlements. With the Law of Return (1950) and the Israeli Nationality Act (1952), returning Arabs were denied the citizenship rights automatically granted to new Jewish settlers.

The pace of industrial and agricultural development and the transformation of Israeli society in the three decades after independence was staggering: gross national product per capita (in 1970 pounds) nearly doubled by 1960 and increased threefold by 1975; gross domestic capital formation too doubled by 1960 and increased five and a half times by 1975; the quantity of agricultural production increased fivefold by 1960 and elevenfold by 1975. Israeli Arabs did not escape the pace of economic change. Immediately after partition, almost two-thirds of Israeli Arabs were engaged in agriculture, but by 1971, the number had fallen below a quarter. The urban population had almost doubled. More than two-thirds of Arab wage workers now commute each day to the Jewish cities, taking up a significant portion of the jobs in construction and manufacturing, forming, by some accounts, a rural or village proletariat.

But much has not changed. Jewish workers, through the state labor exchanges, have first claim on new job opportunities and dominate the most skilled and stable areas of employment. They control the labor councils, the national trade unions, and the Histadrut. The Israeli Arabs for the most part live outside the Jewish cities. They have little access to development funds or new private capital. And while the military administration of the Arab areas has been lifted, three decades of development have not altered the Jewish character of the Israeli state.

There are important differences among these settings, despite the comparability in racial or ethnic divisions and the processes that formed them. At the simplest level, there are differences in demographic ratios. Africans constitute almost four of every five persons in South Africa. Their predominance has been even more marked in the rural economy and gold mining; since the 1930s they have outnumbered whites even in manufacturing. In Alabama, blacks were a majority of the population in the Black Belt until the 1970s but never in the entire state. While blacks were a substantial majority in iron-ore mining and sometimes in coal mining, they were a minority in steel manufacture outside the foundries, a minority in secondary industry and commerce, and excluded entirely from textiles until recently.[29] In Israel and Northern Ireland, the subordinate groups were a substantial majority of the entire population until partition and, in both cases, became minorities almost overnight.

The various dominant groups have had radically different capacities to mold and control events in these settings. The European settlers in South Africa have had de facto autonomy as a society and control of state institutions from 1910. Jewish settlers in Palestine did not gain autonomy and state control until 1948. But in both cases, the dominant groups

29. See George Frederickson, "Industrial Development, White Labor, and Racial Discrimination" for a discussion of the implications of these demographic differences (unpublished paper, pp. 55–56).

exercised military and administrative control during the principal period of capitalist growth and increasing political disorder. Dominant groups in Northern Ireland and Alabama, even if they maintained their political autonomy during certain periods, lost it during periods of acute political crisis. The Stormont Parliament was dismissed at the height of the civil rights protests and sectarian violence; Governor Wallace, even as he stood in the schoolhouse door blocking the way of black school children, was superseded by the federal courts and United States Army.

These differences and others, however, provide opportunities rather than obstacles to our principal mode of investigation: the examination of class actors in developing, divided societies. We will be able to see, particularly in the conclusion, how differences in demography, state resources, and autonomy affect the durability of racial division.

PART ONE / FARMERS

CHAPTER 3

Commercial Agriculture and the Elaboration of the Racial Order

Racial domination is rooted in the precapitalist countryside.[1] Long before there were businessmen demanding controls on subordinate labor or trade unions constructing racial job barriers, there were dominant landowners and farmers.[2] Race differences were important to the organization of the farm kitchens and fields in the Cape Colony and Alabama Black Belt. There, as we should expect in racial orders, land and labor became race questions: land, because Europeans monopolized large expanses of farmland, while Amerindians, blacks, Khoikhoi, black Africans, and other subordinate groups struggled with paltry landholdings or highly restricted occupancy rights; labor, because subordinate groups were brought under rudimentary and sometimes well developed systems of unfree labor. Though racial discrimination was apparent in the formalities and prejudices that governed personal relations, it gained social and historical force through land confiscations, on the one hand, and indenture, slavery, *condiciones,* and squatting, on the other.[3]

What happens when a rural economy built on race, land alienation, and unfree labor becomes part of a developing capitalist economy? How will dominant landowners and farmers respond to the increasing commercialization and increasing mobility of labor? What role will they demand of the state? How will they respond to the ideas, new social relations, and groups emerging in the industrial areas?

---

1. *Precapitalist* for our purposes refers to a set of productive relations not involving wage labor. That farmers produce for distant markets or that the economy is part of a developing world capitalist economy is not the controlling criterion here; dependence on wage labor is. A plantation slave economy, for example, may be fully commercial, producing cotton for markets abroad, while productive relations remain precapitalist, in other words, dependent on slave labor. The corollary of this position, of course, is that capitalist relations become dominant not with increasing commercialization by itself but with the changeover from unfree to wage labor. See the discussion of this issue in Eugene D. Genovese, *The Political Economy of Slavery,* pp. 19–23.

2. *Dominant* and *subordinate* in this context refer to sections of the population in a racially divided society.

3. These various labor forms will be considered in much more detail in chapters 4 and 5.

TWO ROUTES TO CAPITALIST AGRICULTURE

There are vivid examples of rural development in nonracial settings—the English and German cases in particular—that should help us anticipate some answers before looking at the racial orders themselves.

The English Example: The Ridding of the Peasantry

The English countryside, partitioned by fences, stone walls, hedges, and trees with parcels for "customary tillage" and meadows for common grazing, gave way under the force of development. Enclosure of the common lands had begun as early as the thirteenth century but developed into a general movement only in the eighteenth. Some 300,000 acres were enclosed between 1710 and 1760 and 7 million between 1760 and 1843.[4]

The common lands were consistent with early cottage industries, like spinning and hand-weaving, that allowed workers to divide their time between wage labor and subsistence agriculture. Only with their enclosure did a full-blown wage-earning class emerge in the cities and countryside. The cottager and marginal farmer who depended upon the commons for pasture, firewood, and tillage found the traditional rural existence increasingly marginal and the resort to day labor an increasing necessity. They became part of an historic process, Hobsbawm observes, where "farms grew larger, farmers relatively fewer, and the villagers more landless."[5] By 1830, England had eliminated its peasantry[6] and created a class of wage workers selling its labor power to the factories and farms.[7]

It was not simply wage-labor, however, that infused the city and countryside. There developed what Barrington Moore calls an "osmosis between business and the landed aristocracy," though on the former's terms,[8] or what Hobsbawm calls, "the commercialization of rural life."[9] Landowners, certainly after the English Civil War, were no feudal excrescence. They had benefited from the expanding international trade in

4.   Barrington Moore, Jr., *Social Origins of Dictatorship and Democracy,* pp. 9–19; T. S. Ashton, *The Industrial Revolution, 1760–1830,* pp. 18–19; Arnold Toynbee, *The Industrial Revolution,* pp. 12–18.

5.   E. J. Hobsbawm, *Industry and Empire,* pp. 102–03; also see E. P. Thompson, *The Making of the English Working Class,* pp. 217–21.

6.   The use of the word *peasantry* in this work is consistent with John Saul and Roger Woods's definition of the term: rural laborers "whose ultimate security and subsistence lies in their having certain rights in land and in the labour of family members on the land, but who are involved, through rights and obligations, in a wider economic system which includes the participation of non-peasants" ("African Peasantries," pp. 104–05).

7.   See Ashton, *The Industrial Revolution,* pp. 78–87.

8.   Moore, *Social Origins,* pp. 36–37.

9.   Hobsbawm, *Industry and Empire,* pp. 28–29.

wool, the mining concessions for their coal and iron ore, the sale to the railways and towns of agricultural land at "non-agricultural prices," the development of turnpikes and canals, and the growth of both the local and national markets for food.[10] Their participation in the cash economy was irreversible, their association with the rising bourgeoisie both intimate and politically convenient. They demanded the enclosure of common lands and helped construct a rural economy built upon cash crops, large landholdings, tenancy, and wage labor.

The English example has brought in its wake theories of development, both Marxist and non-Marxist, that seek to generalize the experience. For both Marx and Polanyi, capitalism brings the rapid commercialization of all social and productive relations, the demise of the peasantry, and the transformation of all factors of production—land, capital, and labor—into commodities. The precapitalist economy—with its towns, guilds, trade monopolies, and rooted peasantry—gives way to a new order where, as Polanyi notes, "nothing must be allowed to inhibit the formation of markets," where no "incomes . . . [are] permitted to be formed otherwise than through sales."[11] This full development of exchange, Marx writes, presupposes the "dissolution of all fixed personal (historic) relations of dependence in production." The worker "carries his social power, as well as his bond with society, in his pocket."[12] The shackles of the traditional society, including vassalage and serfdom, are "exploded, ripped up." Individuals are left "free to collide with one another and to engage in exchange within this freedom."[13] In agriculture, capitalist development transforms the "feudal landlord into the landowner," the hereditary, unfree tenant into the modern farmer, and the "resident serfs, bondsmen and villeins who belonged to the property into agricultural day-labourers."[14] Marx concludes: "It is nothing more than the extension of wage labour, from the cities to the countryside, i.e., wage labour distributed over the entire surface of society."[15]

It is a reasonable presumption that dominant landowners in a racial order, if they followed the English lead, would become part of the rapid transformation of rural social relations, providing a distant variant on the "growth school."[16] They would respond to the developing markets for food

10. See J. T. Ward and R. G. Wilson, eds., *Land and Industry: The Landed Estate and the Industrial Revolution.*

11. Karl Polanyi, *The Great Transformation,* pp. 38–39, 69.

12. Karl Marx, *Grundrisse,* pp. 156–57.

13. Ibid., pp. 162–64.

14. Ibid., pp. 252–53.

15. Ibid., p. 277.

16. See the discussion of the "growth school" in chapter 1.

and labor by consolidating their landholdings and dismantling the traditional labor system: the mass of subordinate squatters or sharecroppers and
the mix of custom, poverty, obligations, and coercion that keep subordinate
laborers on the farms would look increasingly like so much excess baggage.
The dominant commercial farmer here needs to be free of the subordinate
peasantry. He needs to be free of labor controls—indeed, of the ideas that
justified them and the state machinery that gave them force.

It is a reasonable presumption as well that the rigid race lines associated
with the bondage of the subordinate section would fade with the rural labor
system itself and blend into the more contemporary problem of race in
capitalist society.

The German Example: The Plundering of the Peasantry

The Industrial Revolution came later to the petty states of Saxony, Bavaria,
Wurtemberg, and Prussia than to England. In England, the regime of the
guilds had given way to the free towns and manufacture before the
nineteenth century; a national market had emerged for agricultural as well
as industrial goods. But in Germany, even as late as 1850, guilds continued
to regulate manufacture, while the various kingdoms, archduchies, and
duchies imposed "fair" prices and regulated the quality of production.[17]
Toll stations and local regulation of manufacture and commerce placed
limits on the emerging national market; requirements in Prussia and other
jurisdictions for the registration and authorization of companies limited the
growth of manufacturing and banking enterprises.[18] Not until 1895 did the
workers in German industry outnumber those engaged in agriculture.[19]

But the differences in the English and German experiences were more
than generational. Feudal agriculture in Germany, as in England, gave way
under the pressures of expanding trade and the developing inefficiencies in
feudalism itself, but the transition to capitalist agriculture did not include,
as in England, an "enclosure movement" or a rapid dispersal of the
peasantry. There was certainly enclosure: the Junkers freely enlarged their
own holdings at the expense of the Prussian peasants. In Schleswig-
Holstein, the pattern of enclosure and wage labor resembled that experienced in England.[20] But enclosure was not common in western Germany; the fragmented estates, as well as the German peasantry, lingered on.
And free wage labor of the British sort was resisted throughout the length
of the territory.

17. E. J. Hobsbawm, *The Age of Revolution 1789–1848*, pp. 210–11.
18. David S. Landes, *The Unbound Prometheus*, pp. 197–98.
19. Ibid., pp. 187–88.
20. Maurice Dobb, *Studies in the Development of Capitalism*, p. 241.

The landowners increased production of commercial crops, not by the elimination but by the "plundering of the serf-peasants":[21] the rediscovery of long forgotten seigneurial rights and dues; the use of coercive measures to keep the peasantry near at hand. The Junkers also alienated peasant lands, transforming themselves from feudal landlords to capitalist farmers and their serfs to hired labor. But they managed this transition to commercial agriculture while evolving state coercive measures that foreclosed the "land-flight of the labourer."[22] In this sense, the German experience resembled that of the Baltic States, where emancipation of the serfs was accompanied by severe restrictions on the mobility of labor.[23]

The transition to capitalist agriculture in Germany—whether it involved the plunder of the peasantry or land expropriation with hired labor—was, in Barrington Moore's characterization, necessarily "labor repressive." It required that the peasantry, previously bound to the land and lord by custom, mutual obligation, economic necessity, and law, remain on the land for some substantial period, despite the breakdown of custom and peasant rights, spreading poverty, and the advance of economic alternatives. It required, therefore, strong state action to limit the labor market.[24] Plunder or land alienation alone, without the repressive machinery, would almost certainly have brought the flight of the peasantry.

The ability of landowners to construct the labor-repressive machinery depended to a large extent on the weakness of the emerging bourgeoisie, which in other circumstances would have demanded freer access to the rural labor force.[25] David Landes writes of a German bourgeoisie that bowed before the "*status quo* and sold its liberal birthright for a mess of chauvinistic pottage seasoned by commercial legislation and administration favourable to business enterprise."[26] As one moves east, Landes writes, "the more the bourgeoisie takes on the appearance of a foreign excrescence on manorial society."[27] Engels despaired that the German bourgeoisie would ever take up the progressive ideas necessary for the development of a free wage laboring class. The bourgeoisie, rather than seizing control of the government and fashioning a development strategy suited to its needs,

21.   Evgenii Preobrazhensky, "Peasantry and the Political Economy of the Early Stages of Industrialization," p. 221.
22.   Quoted in Dobb, *Studies*, p. 275. Also see Hobsbawm, *The Age of Revolution*, p. 182.
23.   Dobb, *Studies*, p. 275.
24.   Moore, *Social Origins*, p. 434. The concept of labor repression contrasts the reliance on "strong political methods" with reliance on labor markets. It is most appropriately employed for periods where both state action and markets are evident and threatening one another. Also see the discussion of this subject in chapter 8.
25.   In 1848, the Rhineland industrialists turned to Karl Marx to edit their journal, *Neue Rheinische Zeitung* (Hobsbawm, *The Age of Revolution*, pp. 158–59).
26.   Landes, *The Unbound Prometheus*, p. 8.
27.   Ibid., p. 129.

surrendered to events. It looked "around for allies with whom to share its
rule, or to whom to cede the whole of its rule, as circumstances may
require," Engels wrote. It looked to the "monarchy with its army and its
bureaucracy," the "big feudal nobility," the "little cabbage-Junkers," and
the priests. "With all these the bourgeoisie made pacts and bargains, if only
to save its dear skin, until at last it had nothing left to barter."[28]

The commercial farmers in Germany made the transition to capitalist
agriculture not by abandoning feudalism, but by restoring feudal rights and
dues and placing severe restrictions on the mobility of farm laborers. For an
extended period the farmers, faced with expanded agricultural markets,
demanded increased state vigilance over the labor market. The transition to
capitalist agriculture, consequently, was characterized by the lingering,
rather than wholesale transformation, of the rural class structure: the
peasantry did not quickly give way to wage labor in the cities and
countryside; the bourgeoisie proved weak, failing over an extended period
to place its stamp on the state or ruling political alignments; and the
landowners, while increasingly responsive to market opportunities, retained
their distinctive, "feudal" guise during an extended transition to capitalist
agriculture.[29]

It is a reasonable presumption that dominant landowners in a racial
order, if they followed the German example, would seek to extend and
perhaps elaborate the traditional labor system and the racial disabilities
associated with it.[30] The need to expand production of cash crops would be
met, not by the rapid displacement of rural labor and the resort to labor
markets, but by a three-pronged plundering of the subordinate peasantry:
first, by further restricting subordinate landholding and, consequently,
subsistence production; second, by intensifying subordinate labor services;

28. Frederick Engels, *The Peasant War in Germany*, pp. 12–13, 164–65.
29. I will not enter the debate on at what point agriculture can be characterized as capitalist.
It is almost certainly the case that wage labor was present in feudal Europe and also true that
labor had not universally lost its compulsory character even after wage labor was predominant.
For my purposes, it is sufficient to note, first, that there is an early point where compulsory
serflike labor is predominant and, second and more important, that there is a class of
landowners during the transition who insist on the compulsory character of labor even as wage
labor becomes more and more widespread and laborers become more and more mobile.
Whether this class of landowner is capitalist or precapitalist is not nearly so important to
establish as their origin in the precapitalist period and their role in the transition to capitalist
agriculture. See the discussion of these issues in Dobb, *Studies,* pp. 35–36; Ernesto Laclau,
"Feudalism and Capitalism in Latin America"; H. K. Takahashi, "The Transition from
Feudalism to Capitalism"; and Paul M. Sweezy and Maurice Dobb, "Communication—The
Transition from Feudalism to Capitalism."
30. This argument is closely related to the "neo-Marxist" position on growth and racial
domination presented in chapters 1 and 7, but in this case the argument does not have
distinctively Marxist roots.

and third, and most important, by increasing state control over the movements of subordinate farm laborers. Without the elaboration of the labor-repressive apparatus, subordinate rural laborers might escape the plunder by flight to subsistence agricultural areas, to other areas of dominant agriculture, or, worse, to the growing industrial centers—with uncertain consequences for the commercial farmer and the racial order.

Dominant landowners would make the transition to capitalist agriculture by underlining the role of race in the society and labor market. For landowners, the race lines are so intimately associated with their access to the state and their control over rural laborers as to be indistinguishable from them. After a long period of land consolidation and mechanization, they might well turn away from the race lines and the labor system, but during an extended transition to capitalist agriculture, dominant landowners would remain a distinctive and powerful remnant of the precapitalist period, insisting on the elaborated state role in the labor market and insisting on the racial order itself.

This chapter is about the probable affinity of commercial farmers in a racial order for the German experience. We shall discover, first, that the racial orders are part of a larger international political economy where landowners have conventionally opted for a lingering peasantry over wage labor and for labor repression over labor markets; second, that landowners in a racial order can draw on the lack of social obligations and commonalities across the dominant-subordinate divide to legitimize coercion and insure the viability of labor repression against market pressures; and finally, that racial orders discourage political alignments that under other circumstances might threaten the position of commercial farmers and the framework of unfree labor. These factors together should give dominant commercial farmers a wide latitude over an extended period to fashion the repressive and racial features of these societies.

LABOR-REPRESSIVE AGRICULTURE

Constraints on labor mobility are a routine response of landowners to the changing fortunes and opportunities of their farm laborers. Kautsky writes, for example, that landowners watch as "a powerful current of migration swells up among the poor peasantry," as "the relative weight of the rural population shrinks and its composition deteriorates." For a short period, they attempt to evolve "juridical constraints" against the flight of farm laborers. The traditional landowner, the increasingly commercial farmer, and perhaps the rising merchant class, conspire in a "new feudalism," a transitional phase of "feudal capitalist exploitation,"[31] a period, for Marx, where older labor forms linger on as remnants "in an entirely stunted form, or even travestied."[32]

Though serfdom was not universal across feudal Europe and though it rarely survived beyond the initial stages of manorialization,[33] various instruments for extracting labor services or tributes survived in parts of France until the Convention in 1793.[34] In Germany, compulsory labor services and feudal dues were intensified even as late as the early eighteenth century.[35] In Russia, the legal code of 1649 brought serfdom to the migratory peasantry.[36] Corvée labor—the exchange of labor time on the lord's land for the right to work a parcel of land—was intensified and extended during the nineteenth century, encompassing construction projects, brickmaking, and carting of the lord's produce;[37] even as late as 1835, serfs that left for industrial employment might be recalled to work on the lord's land.[38]

Still, as Kautsky argues, the transition to capitalist agriculture in Europe extends over a finite period: "[It] can not last long," because "the progressive march of industry destroys it."[39] But accompanying the decline of the peasantry, the traditional landowner, and labor-repressive policies in Europe was their extension to other parts of the world; indeed, to terrain historically hospitable to racial orders. For Immanuel Wallerstein and Andre Gunder Frank the decline of compulsory labor in the "core" economies and its rise in the "periphery" are two sides of the same coin. The growth of wage labor and tenancy in western and southern Europe was accompanied by "a slave class of African origin" and "a serf class" of "American Indians in the Western Hemisphere."[40] While coerced labor had become increasingly untenable in the emerging bourgeois economies at the

31. Jarius Banaji, "A Summary of Selected Parts of Kautsky's *The Agrarian Question*," pp. 38–40.
32. Marx, *Grundrisse*, p. 106.
33. Marc Bloch, *Feudal Society*, pp. 241–49.
34. Ibid., p. 196. Among the remnants of seigneurial rights, we should include *mainmorte*, the "dead hand" that prevented the serf from "alienating his tenure" and gave the lord the land as a seigneurial inheritance; the *terriers*, the periodic revision of the manorial rolls whose cost was assigned to the serf and whose preparation facilitated the collection of feudal dues; the *quit-rent*, the payment at the succession of a new toiler on the land that, in effect, legitimized the lord's claims; and the *banalités*, the lord's control of the mill, bakehouse, and sale of farm products that, in the final analysis, insured the lord's hegemony. See Bloch, *Feudal Society*, pp. 249–51; Sydney Herbert, *The Fall of Feudalism in France*, pp. 4–35.
35. F. Engels, "On the History of the Prussian Peasantry," in *The Peasant War*, pp. 158–59.
36. Eric R. Wolf, *Peasant Wars of the Twentieth Century*, pp. 51–52.
37. Ibid., pp. 52–55.
38. Ibid., p. 73.
39. Banaji, "Kautsky's *The Agrarian Question*," pp. 38–40.
40. Immanuel Wallerstein, *The Modern World-System*, p. 87. He also includes a yet larger "serf class" in eastern Europe.

core, land seizures, population transfers, violence, and compulsion proved both palatable and feasible in the periphery. Western Europe gained its bullion, minerals, and foodstuffs by transferring a technology that was "labor-intensive" and a social system that was "labor-exploitive."[41]

The relationship of the periphery to the core is less important for our argument than the increasing scope of labor repression. Coercive methods for organizing agricultural production and a labor force and later maintaining them in the face of expanding markets were as much a part of colonial history as Livingstone's expedition to the Zambezi and Magellan's circumnavigation of the world. Compulsory labor and tributes and restrictions on labor mobility—the stuff of lingering serfdom and labor repression in western Europe—were rapidly generalized across the face of Latin America, parts of North America, Africa, and Southeast Asia.[42] The later movement toward capitalist agriculture in these societies, therefore, encountered a countryside largely unfree, a class of landowners committed to coerced labor, and a local state structure embroiled in labor-repressive policies.

The hacienda in particular, with its *patrón* and *hacendados* (lord of the estate), *colonos* and *arriendo* (labor tenants), and *pongaje* and *condiciones* (labor services), most clearly underlined the role of coercion and compulsory labor services in the New World. A landowning class with little capital but a voracious appetite for land and labor was joined with a peasantry whose position in the villages and peasant economy had become, or had been made, increasingly marginal. The *colonos,* who never set eyes on a manor, demesne, or tithe farmer were nonetheless compelled to perform road and maintenance work, pay an array of fees, provide transport to market, and perform compulsory labor services, including planting, harvesting, and domestic work. In exchange for these services, the *colonos* received a fixed gratuity or fee and a small subsistence plot. They were obliged, however, to buy their supplies and market their meager harvest through the hacienda.[43] No wonder Hobsbawm concluded that the hacienda of La Convención province in Peru "will probably interest the historian of the

41. Ibid., p. 100.
42. To suggest that forms of compulsory labor reminiscent of feudal Europe were widespread in the periphery should not be confused with the more difficult proposition, not argued here, that a feudal mode of production was predominant. See Jack Goody, *Technology, Tradition, and the State in Africa,* pp. 1–20. We should also keep in mind that labor-repressive methods were not entirely foreign to the New World. See Rodolfo Stavenhagen's discussion of the Aztecs and Incas and the kingdom of Nupe in Nigeria, *Social Classes in Agrarian Societies,* pp. 43–46.
43. E. J. Hobsbawm, "A Case of Neo-Feudalism: La Convención, Peru," pp. 39–40; Eric R. Wolf, "Aspects of Group Relations in a Complex Society: Mexico," pp. 56–57.

European middle ages more than the typical economic historian of our century."[44]

The hacienda, however, was not confined to La Convención. The haciendas occupied, along with the Indian *communidades,* the full sierra region of Peru.[45] Before the rise of Allende in Chile, almost two-thirds of the arable land was organized in great *fundos,* hacienda-type agricultural units that replicated the social roles of *patrón* and peasant and the social relations of compulsory labor services.[46] The Indian communities of central Mexico and Guatemala were caught up in the steady expansion of haciendas. A "structure of privilege," reminiscent of La Convencíon, jeopardized the "free villages" and structured the relations between Indians and Ladinos. Before the First World War, there were over 8,000 haciendas, averaging about 3,000 hectares each; 475 of these estates ranged between 10,000 and 100,000 hectares.[47]

Associated with the hacienda was a class of landowners who resisted the developing markets in land and labor and depended increasingly on its access to the state. There was little room here for democratic reforms. "The landed upper class," Jeffrey Paige writes, "must rely on political power to prevent a free market in land, to protect itself against competition from small holders or plantations, to prevent expensive technological change from undermining its financial position, and to protect its huge under-employed labor force from the lure of higher wages in more efficient enterprises."[48]

Perhaps more immediately relevant for the racial orders are the plantations that brought commercial crops—sugar, tobacco, tea, and cotton—to the New World.[49] Such plantations in Peru, Guyana, and Hawaii now are capital and land intensive and depend almost exclusively on wage labor.[50] But plantation agriculture was not always organized around the labor market. With only scattered populations near the principal areas of cultivation and an accelerating demand for plantation workers, notions of free wage labor seemed, at best, inappropriate. The overriding issue was not whether these societies would resort to "non-market" mechanisms but only to which repressive form they would turn: slavery, indentured immigration,

44. Hobsbawm, "A Case of Neo-Feudalism," p. 48.
45. Julio Cotler, "The Mechanics of Internal Domination and Social Change in Peru," pp. 412–19.
46. James Petras, *Politics and Social Forces in Chilean Development,* pp. 26–63.
47. Wolf, *Peasant Wars,* pp. 3–17; Rodolfo Stavenhagen, "Classes, Colonialism, and Acculturation," pp. 239–46.
48. Jeffrey M. Paige, *Agrarian Revolution,* p. 17.
49. Plantations were important to the development of Natal in South Africa and the pre- and post-Civil War Black Belt in Alabama.
50. See the discussion of these issues in Paige, *Agrarian Revolution,* pp. 12–25; and Sidney W. Mintz, "The Plantation as a Socio-Cultural Type," pp. 43–44.

sharecropping, or some "contrived absence of alternatives to which the labor force could turn."[51] It was "the mechanism of labor force control," Mandle writes, that was the "key to plantation society."[52]

The development of the plantation economy in Guyana, for example, was characterized by successive forms of unfree labor. Slavery was abolished in 1838 and gave way to indentured immigration, primarily from India, but also from Madeira, Africa, China, and the West Indies.[53] The web of labor controls, a former magistrate in the colony observed, "had been so framed and its net, covering all possible offences, was woven so closely, that not even the smallest peccadilloes could escape its meshes."[54] In some parts of Brazil and the Spanish Caribbean, the abolition of slavery was succeeded by a mixture of hacienda and plantation agriculture. The former slaves were compelled by law and the absence of land and alternative employment to work subsistence plots on the plantation, while "donating" several days a week to the larger enterprise.[55] In other parts of Brazil and in large areas of the cotton South, plantation slavery was superseded by various forms of closely supervised sharecropping.[56]

The hacienda and plantation generated landholding classes that did not live by what Wolf calls the "dance of commodities," or at least not by the dance of labor. They relied instead on continuing or, indeed, accelerating state efforts to limit the scope of the labor market or their laborers' access to it. While plantation and hacienda owners responded to different product markets—distant in one case and more parochial in the other—both understood the necessity of retaining the peasantry and developing labor-repressive policies.

It should not be surprising if commercial landowners in racial orders, caught up in some of the same historic processes, came to a similar understanding of necessity.

THE VIABILITY OF THE GERMAN ROUTE: THE FURNIVALL EFFECT

The German case provides a difficult example to follow. Whether in the core economies of Europe or the peripheral economies of the Western Hemi-

---

51. Jay R. Mandle, "The Plantation Economy: An Essay in Definition," pp. 57–60; also see Ida C. Greaves, "Plantation in World Economy."
52. Mandle, "The Plantation Economy," p. 61.
53. Jay R. Mandle, *The Plantation Economy*, pp. 12–35.
54. Ibid., pp. 63–64.
55. George L. Beckford, *Persistent Poverty*, pp. 94–95.
56. Manuel Diégues Júnior, "Land Tenure and Use in the Brazilian Plantation System," pp. 106–15; Beckford, *Persistent Poverty*, pp. 280–85.

sphere and Africa, it demands a precarious balancing act: on the one hand, the plunder of peasant landholdings and labor; on the other, constraints on the mobility of rural labor. The balancing act, in addition, must be executed against a backdrop of increasing peasant resistance. With the squeezing of subsistence production, the breakdown of peasant rights and landlord obligations, and the spread of wage labor, rural laborers may repudiate their labor services or join in more serious collective resistance.[57] The act falters in the end if landowners cannot call on the state to legitimize and assist in the control of the rural labor force.

Not all states and societies, at all times, are up to the task. They may be overtaken by the rapid spread of commercial relations as the peasantry is drawn into the labor market and capital floods the rural areas; the "feudal capitalist" phase may be superseded by forms of agricultural production reminiscent of the English case or perhaps by other forms, like small holding. The labor-repressive alternative may fail for lack of capacity or will. The state must be able to regulate labor contracts and obligations and check the flight of labor from the rural areas; the society must provide the values—or the absence of values—that allow landowners and the state to plunder peasant society and elaborate the framework of unfree labor.

In a racial order, the balancing act is less likely to falter for lack of support from the state and society. Here, landowners operate within a milieu that supports a level of state coercion and plunder that even early-nineteenth-century Europe might have found distasteful.

In his classic work, *Colonial Policy and Practice,* J. S. Furnivall contrasts European societies, where "progress is conditional on the observance of certain social obligations" and "similar moral standards" constrain the landowner's domination of peasant society and his avarice, with the colonial settings, including the racial orders, where no such "social will" exists. The economic factor, "the test of cheapness," he writes, becomes the guiding force in these settings, "subject to no restraint but that of western law," consequently, to no restraint at all.

> These forces, liberated from the control of custom by the impact of the West, pursue their natural course, breaking down the social order, disintegrating native organic society into individual atoms, and, by thus depriving man of social protection against natural selfishness, operate more intensively, eliminating social values, and diffusing poverty.[58]

In these colonial settings, the absence of "social will" gave landowners

57. See James C. Scott, *The Moral Economy of the Peasantry.*
58. J.S. Furnivall, *Colonial Policy and Colonial Practice,* pp. 291–93; also see Paul A. Baran, "On the Political Economy of Backwardness," pp. 83–84.

and the state a latitude in repression that facilitated their plunder and control of peasant society. Furnivall wrote directly about the tropical economies, like Burma and Netherlands India, but his analysis might well have been applied to a broad range of colonial economies. In Angola, for example, vast land concessions were ceded to a relatively small number of Portuguese settlers. The African claimants to the land were moved about on the concession or forced on to reservations bordering the coffee estates. The "native work book" and forced labor became indispensable props of the "migratory labor estates." Paige is undoubtedly correct that without these "special privileges of land concessions and compulsory labor," the coffee estates would have collapsed, giving way to alternative forms of agricultural production.[59]

The racial orders were founded on the lack of "social will" between the dominant and subordinate populations. The history that led to the dispossession of peasant lands and the breakdown of peasant society, that included forced population transfers and slavery, and that left the dominant population in control of the state and the subordinate population virtually without rights did not readily foster commonalities—shared values or empathy—that might limit the scope of repression. The dominant landowner's plea for help was addressed to states not unfamiliar or uncomfortable with plunder or labor controls. Indeed, their pleas would be buttressed by a rationale and broad understanding in the dominant community as a whole that would lend legitimacy to such policies. Racist ideologies and practices that facilitate separate living patterns in other contexts would provide critical support for labor repression in this rural context.

The racial orders provide a coincidence of interests that enhances the attraction and viability of the German example. Commercial farmers in a racial order, consequently, may more readily opt for the German route to capitalist agriculture: labor-repressive policies are allowed, indeed encouraged, to run a course frequently constrained in other times and places.

LIMITING THE BUSINESS CHALLENGE:
THE VENDEE EFFECT

Landowners may respond to commercialization by elaborating state controls over the rural laboring population only so long as other groups in the society do not challenge their access to or control of the state. Democratic reforms, for example, that give some level of political influence to the rural

59. Paige, *Agrarian Revolution,* pp. 230–54.

population would threaten the whole repressive structure: given access to the state, no rational-acting class of agricultural laborers would long tolerate the land confiscations, forced labor, labor dues and services, passes, debt peonage, or other forms of labor control so important to commercial farmers. The principle was well understood throughout the colonial world. In Angola, the estate owners resisted any change in the political order that might have given the African majority a political voice, even if in the process they risked a full-fledged guerrilla war.[60] In Peru, landowners resisted any change in the Spanish literacy requirement that might admit the Indian population to the electorate.[61]

The most likely challenge, however, short of peasant revolution or democratization, comes from the emerging class of factory owners and entrepreneurs. They may have their own feelings on the proper role of labor markets and the state; they certainly will insist on reasonable access to the society's labor resources—in this case, bottled up in the rural areas. For Marx, "agriculture more and more becomes merely a branch of industry, and is entirely dominated by capital."[62] The merchant, urban industrialist, and, finally, the bourgeois farmer develop sufficient self-confidence to foresake the feudal monopolies and controlled labor force in favor of the market and free wage labor.

The challenge to the traditional rural economy, however, has been difficult to mount. The early bourgeoisie did not emerge as a bull in a china shop, smashing all in its path: it treaded very softly indeed. Rather than face the uncertainty of an open market and unknown competitors, the early industrialists and merchants sought to create monopolies and fence off their local markets.[63] They also sought to fence off their workers. In fourteenth-century and fifteenth-century Europe, few believed that a labor force could be organized without compulsion. The early industrialists, no less than the feudal landowner, believed in impressment of labor, prescribed wages, and restrictions on the movement of labor.[64] Dobb underlines the initial affinity of the bourgeoisie for feudal practices: "One feature of this new merchant bourgeoisie that is at first surprising as it is universal, is the readiness with which this class compromised with feudal society once its privileges had been won."[65]

The penetration of the bourgeoisie into the French countryside as early as the sixteenth century did not herald the dissolution of labor constraints; it

60.   Ibid., p. 254.
61.   Cotler, "The Mechanics of Internal Domination," pp. 420–23.
62.   Marx, *Grundrisse*, p. 107.
63.   Dobb, *Studies*, p. 89.
64.   Ibid., p. 231.
65.   Ibid., p. 120.

brought, instead, a refinement and restoration of the seigneurial structure.[66] This association with feudal methods and later with the crown produced what Moore loosely describes as the " 'feudalization' of a considerable section of the bourgeoisie, rather than the other way around."[67] The German bourgeoisie of the nineteenth century proved no more capable than the sixteenth-century burghers of freeing the feudal peasants. Like the continental bourgeoisie as a whole, it feared another 1789: better to compromise with the feudal classes and buy "gradual social emancipation" than risk the consequences of a more radical transformation.[68] Even in England, where the bourgeois ascendancy was more readily established, early mining concerns relied heavily on impressed or convict labor.[69] The bourgeoisie generally accepted the Tudor and Stuart legislation that penalized vagabondage and provided for compulsory work. And even after the reforms of 1832 and the repeal of the Corn Laws, the English bourgeoisie compromised with the lords and squires on control of local government.[70]

Forces in development itself, new areas of trade, new industries and methods of production,[71] steeled the European bourgeoisie and, ultimately, threatened the dominance of precapitalist landowners. Should we expect similar forces to strengthen the position of businessmen in racial orders and, consequently, to threaten the labor-repressive and racial framework?

Forces in development alone have not been sufficient to transform the rural economy, even in major areas of Europe: change has also depended on political challenges that at critical points aligned the emerging bourgeoisie with other powerful social groups—in particular, with a volatile, discontented peasantry. It was to this rural population that the Convention in 1793 felt compelled to turn.[72] The surge of revolutionary fervor may have come from the sans culottes in Paris, but, as Moore observes, "each surge succeeded as long as it could draw on active support from the countryside."[73] The counterrevolution in the Vendée, however, underlines what may happen when the bourgeois challenge to the *ancien regime* fails to enlist the support of the peasantry. In Val-Saumurois, the more tenuous hold of the nobility and clergy and the market orientation of the small peasants brought out the shared perspective of the bourgeoisie and peasants. Here the revolution took its course. But in Mauge, where commercialization was little developed, subsistence agriculture widespread, and the nobility well entrenched, the bourgeoisie and peasantry did not come together—with

66. Marc Bloch, *French Rural History*, pp. 124–26.
67. Moore, *Social Origins*, p. 109.
68. Engels, *The Peasant War*, p. 20; also see Landes, *The Unbound Prometheus*, pp. 190–92.
69. Dobb, *Studies*, p. 233.
70. Hobsbawm, *Industry and Empire*, pp. 106–07.
71. Dobb, *Studies*, p. 219.
72. Herbert, *The Fall of Feudalism*, p. 195.
73. Moore, *Social Origins*, p. 77.

nearly tragic consequences for the revolution.[74] The bourgeoisie on its own could not undermine the structure of seigneurial privilege or the position of landowners.

In France as a whole, however, the peasantry and bourgeoisie came together for long enough to destroy the web of aristocratic privilege. Whatever the parochial reasons that might have brought them together to make a revolution, their alignment made possible the dominance of new productive relations,[75] and the demise of unfree labor.

In racial orders, it is only with great difficulty that the bourgeois challenge to dominant landowners and unfree labor unites with the challenge of other major social groups, such as the subordinate peasantry. Their shared interest in dismantling the structure of rural control is very likely obscured by the racial lines that pervade the society, that place an enormous gulf between the dominant businessman and subordinate rural laborer. Their formal political alignment, even over a short period, runs counter to the principal conventions governing social and political relations; indeed, it would probably bring on a counter mobilization of the dominant society against such "mixing." Still, businessmen are not above taking advantage of the disorder that might follow on the rising of the subordinate peasantry. They might well reinforce some demands that free subordinate labor for the industrial areas or endorse demands that might restore economic stability. But they would formally align themselves with the challenge to the repressive framework only on highly selected occasions, with great caution, and, indeed, only with great difficulty.[76]

Without an alignment with other social groups opposed to the traditional labor system, businessmen could not easily raise wage labor and mobility to the level of accepted social principles; on their own, they can offer only a feeble challenge to the whole network of coercion that girds the racial order and the position of dominant landowners.[77]

In the absence of an effective challenge to the repressive framework, businessmen, rather than persisting in opposing the position of dominant landowners, may align themselves with the de facto power holders in society. Like the German bourgeoisie of the nineteenth century, they may

74. Charles Tilly, *The Vendée*, pp. 130–32.
75. "The peasant's role is thus essentially tragic," Wolf writes. "His efforts to undo a grievous present only usher in a vaster, more uncertain future" (*The Peasant Wars*, p. 301).
76. We will consider the conditions under which businessmen support changes in the repressive and racial framework in part II of the book. Among the conditions are the dominance of secondary manufacture over extractive industry, high levels of political disorder that threaten the business environment, and outside pressures that threaten the capacity of the state to control local events.
77. The peasantry, for its part, may have difficulty gaining broad social support; in any case, it may, like Zapata's bands in Morelos and the peasant communities in Russia, have difficulty shaping or controlling its own upheavals (Wolf, *Peasant Wars*, pp. 9–91).

join with the landed classes, yielding one "bourgeois position" after another.[78] Like the Brazilian or Chilean entrepreneurs of the twentieth century, fearing the instability of peasant protests and recognizing their own impotence, they may join in what Fernando Henrique Cardoso calls the "traditional order of political control"[79] or what Paul Baran calls the "feudal-mercantile order."[80] They join, consequently, the political alignment that supports labor-repressive agriculture and critical features of the racial order.

Commercial farmers, immersed in the racial divisions and unfree labor that characterized racial orders from their beginnings, should not readily reconstitute themselves as an agrarian bourgeoisie, ridding themselves of their subordinate peasantry and buying wage labor in the market. The English example in rural development seems remote from the historical experience of racial orders and perhaps singular even for Europe. Instead, there is good reason to believe that commercial farmers will succeed, at least over an extended period of time, in bottling up their subordinate rural labor force. Their success lies, in part, with the conventionality of the German experience: landowners throughout the Western Hemisphere and Africa have regularly and increasingly called on the state to help circumvent the market in rural labor. Their success also lies with characteristics of the racial order that reinforce labor-repressive policies: the lack of "social will" between the dominant and subordinate populations, which facilitates the dispossession and coercion necessary to labor control, and the racial divide itself, which keeps groups opposed to the framework of rural control from aligning with one another, groups that in other historical contexts have challenged the ascendancy of landowners.

Dominant landowners and farmers, therefore, can be expected to construct state policies fully consonant with their historic aversion to labor markets and their affinity for control of the subordinate population. They should, in the process, help elaborate the racial order itself.

78. See Baran, "On the Political Economy of Backwardness," p. 85.
79. Fernando Henrique Cardoso, quoted in Joseph A. Kahl, *Modernization, Exploitation and Dependency in Latin America,* p. 153.
80. Paul A. Baran, *The Political Economy of Growth,* p. 195; also see Petras, *Politics and Social Forces,* pp. 53–55, 58–61.

CHAPTER 4

South Africa: The Development of
Labor-Repressive Agriculture

We are often told of natives who are idle in the cities, but [I] can give the hon. Minister the assurance that there are hundreds of natives who are idle at the chromium mines, the iron mines and the platinum mines. These natives should also be brought back to the farms. As far as the cities are concerned, Proclamation No. 61 of 1947 gives the urban authorities the right to take steps against native vagrants. They have not taken steps in the past, with the result that the natives have been encouraged to remain idle. . . . [T]here should be people who are prepared to do everything in their power to persuade the natives to return to the farms. We must have a proper system of distribution with depots in all the various towns. I want to suggest that not the urban authorities but the Central Government should take over this policy of sending natives back to the farms. These natives should be recruited. A native who roams about without a pass and permit should be heavily punished, and we ought to have a proper system of distribution so that the people in Rustenburg, Standerton, Brits and other [farming] districts will know that on a particular day the natives will be brought there for specific farms.

Member of Parliament
6 September 1948[1]

INTRODUCTION TO COMMERCIAL FARMERS

South Africa has come a long way from the encapsulated way station at Cape Town; so too have its white farmers. The isolated *trekboer*,[2] indifferent to land titles and world market prices, has gone the way of the frontier; gone with the grazing disputes in the eastern Cape, the six-thousand-acre farms at a nominal twenty-four rix-dollars annual rent, and subsistence husbandry with self-sufficient shepherding, shoemaking, smithing, and wagon building.[3] He is now enmeshed in an elaborate array of market relations. His

1. *Hansard,* 6 September 1948, cols. 1617–18.
2. *Trekboer* refers to the farmer of largely Dutch origin who practiced a form of nomadic pastoral agriculture, extending the effective boundaries of the Cape Colony to the east and north (C. W. de Kiewiet, *A History of South Africa: Social and Economic,* pp. 10–20).
3. See J. F. W. Grosskopf, *Rural Impoverishment and Rural Exodus,* pp. 33–45; Francis Wilson, "Farming, 1866–1966," pp. 107–12.

maize makes its way not to the refreshment station at Table Bay but to distant markets in Europe and neighboring African states. Agricultural production in 1975 was six times the volume at the time of union (1910) and incalculably more than the rudimentary subsistence and wool production in the early Cape Colony.[4] Prices rise and fall, as they always have, with the vagaries of local droughts and pest infestations but also with the whims of international commodity markets and national marketing boards. His African laborers are no longer bound to the farms as slaves or as some feudal patrimony. Wage labor has replaced compulsory, unremunerated labor services on the one hand and grazing rights and garden plots on the other.[5]

That the white farmer has made a "successful" transition to capitalist agriculture there can be little doubt.[6] On the other hand, that this transformation of the countryside has "liberated" the African peasantry or undermined the traditional relationship between black and white remains doubtful.

During an extended transition to capitalist agriculture, lasting even into the contemporary period, white commercial farmers not only failed to rid themselves of the African peasantry, they repeatedly sought out new ways to keep African labor in the rural areas. That was no easy task: the impoverishment of the native reserves and the more efficient utilization of white-owned land closed off opportunities for African production; the mines and factories and some advanced sections of agriculture provided wage-laboring opportunities that dislodged African labor from the traditional labor framework. White commercial farmers, consequently, demanded state control over the work obligations and movements of African rural laborers, demands that rose in volume as Africans found their way to the labor market. The commercial farmers brought into the developing capitalist society a tenacious identification with unfree labor and race lines. The white farmer in 1920 and 1950, though by then deeply immersed in market relations, seemed no less committed than the Natal farmer of the Shepstone era to the control and domination of the African population.

By the late sixties, there was good reason to believe that the transition had run its course, giving way to a dependence on wage labor and labor markets, mechanized and intensive farming units, and a declining African labor force in the rural areas. Only at this point were white commercial farmers willing

4. In addition, two-thirds of current agricultural production is exported abroad (D. Hobart Houghton, *The South African Economy,* pp. 228, 241; see also appendix B, table C.2).
5. H. M. Robertson, "150 Years of Economic Contact Between Black and White," pp. 6–7.
6. Capitalist in this context refers to agricultural production based on free wage, rather than unfree, labor. Associated with the changeover to free wage labor is increasing agricultural production and commercialization—the sale of products in distant markets. See chapter 3, note 1 for further discussion of the issue.

to let go of their African laborers, to turn away, in effect, from labor-repressive agriculture.

That process bears little resemblance to the English example. The development of capitalist agriculture in South Africa did not bring a rapid transformation of rural social relations, with precapitalist landowners recreated as an agrarian bourgeoisie, buying and selling, committed to free wage labor and markets, and the African peasantry thrown into the labor market, denied access to the land and freed from compulsory labor services. Nor, as suggested by the "growth school," did development bring a declining attention to racial categories.

Mike Morris, a contemporary Marxist scholar, argues that agriculture in South Africa was organized along capitalist lines by 1920, "irrespective of the low degree of development of the productive forces." The African laborer "was no longer able to set the means of labour into motion because he was separated from them"; he "necessarily laboured with them under the organizational control of the farmer."[7] Some quasi-feudal labor forms may have lingered into the modern era, but they lingered as shells, barely reflecting the precapitalist economy that created them; they were increasingly overshadowed by wage labor and the landlessness of the African peasantry. The agricultural crisis of the thirties, however—the falling agricultural prices and flight of African farm workers—threatened "the very existence of capitalist agriculture,"[8] bringing on new efforts at labor control. The war and the continuing crisis in agricultural labor brought National party attempts to dam up the rural labor force. It is important, however, to see apartheid not as some "return to a 'feudal system' of extra economic coercion in the countryside." Apartheid, Morris writes, was "the outcome of a determinate class struggle, it signalled the victory of capitalist farmers over the direct producers (labor tenants); at the end of the phase of transition, it ushered in a new stage in the development of capitalist agriculture."[9]

Morris's analysis highlights a variety of issues central to our understanding of changing rural economy, including the shift from precapitalist to capitalist labor forms and the increasing disabilities imposed on African rural laborers. The attempt to identify a point in the twenties when South African agriculture was fully capitalist is less useful for our purposes, for it underemphasizes what is transitional and contradictory in the process: the simultaneous development of wage labor and compulsory labor services. It

7. M. L. Morris, "The Development of Capitalism in South African Agriculture: Class Struggle in the Countryside," p. 306.
8. Ibid., pp. 315–17.
9. Ibid., p. 338. Another important work in this field is David Kaplan's "Capitalist Development in South Africa: Class Conflict and the State."

neglects the struggle of landowners, steeped in traditions of unfree labor and racial domination, who sought to expand production and respond to markets for food, even create wage forms, while repeatedly seeking to circumvent the market in labor. It fails, therefore, to outline a process, similar in some respects to the German one, that led landowners and farmers to hold on to their "feudal baggage" in a modern world, with important consequences for the nature of the state and the place of unfree labor.[10]

This chapter describes the development of labor-repressive agriculture in South Africa—the changing labor forms, the elaboration of labor controls and racial disabilities. The next chapter considers the role of organized white agriculture in shaping racial and labor policies and managing its own extended transition to capitalist agriculture.

RACE AND LABOR IN THE PRECAPITALIST COUNTRYSIDE

The intermingling of black and white in southern Africa and the dominance of the latter over the former did not begin, as suggested by the Native Economic Commission in 1932, with "two economies," one rooted in a "native population . . . living under a primitive subsistence economy" and the other in a European population committed to commerce and the "money economy."[11] Black and white met on the South African frontier bearing different resources and ideas, to be sure, but not wholly different agricultural methods or attitudes to the market. Their meeting and the growth of commerce altered their relations and respective fortunes.

The European farmers in the Cape peninsula from the late seventeenth century and the eastern Cape frontier from the middle eighteenth engaged in a rudimentary form of commercial and subsistence agriculture, providing for their own consumption but raising cattle, sheep, and selected crops for the way station at Table Bay, bartering with Khoikhoi in the Cape interior or the Xhosa near the Fish River, in both cases, breaching the trading monopoly of the Dutch East India Company.[12] Their crude farming methods, destructive of the soil and land extensive, necessitated large farming units and the characteristic trekking after new farming areas. By the mid nineteenth century, white farmers in the eastern Cape, and later in the

10. I do not mean to imply that there is a return to a "feudal system," only that labor controls become a central part of the transition to capitalist agriculture.

11. Union of South Africa, *Report of the Native Economic Commission 1930–32*, U.G. 22, 1932, p. 3.

12. Richard Elphick, *Kraal and Castle*, pp. 151–62; Monica Wilson, "Cooperation and Conflict: The Eastern Cape Frontier," pp. 233–41.

Orange Free State, were able to sell the wool of their merino sheep in international markets.[13] But for the most part, European farming in this period was too unresponsive or too unproductive to meet new market opportunities. At the outset, the mining towns in Kimberley and the Witwatersrand were forced to go abroad for maize; by 1900, South Africa was importing substantial quantities of wheat, maize, meat, eggs, milk, and butter.[14]

African farming too was organized around subsistence production and trading, the latter developing as long-distance barter for cattle, dagga, and metals and, later, as agricultural production for the developing European markets. The Khoikhoi in the western Cape depended heavily on a form of nomadic pastoral farming that eventually brought them into bartering relations with the East India Company and free European farmers, relations that eventually would strip them of their cattle and their independent livelihood.[15] The Xhosa in the eastern Cape depended upon a more sedentary form of agriculture, with mixed tillage and pastoralism. They, too, along with other African groups, responded to trading opportunities. The Mfengu of the Ciskei and the Sotho of Basutoland joined in what Colin Bundy describes as a "virtual explosion of peasant economic activity" in the 1870s.[16]

The fundamental differences between the two forms of agriculture—and the starting point for the racial order—lay in the presumptions governing questions of land and labor. The European farmers, despite the caution of the East India Company and, later, the British Colonial Office, came to covet the "Hottentot" and "Kaffir" cattle and grazing lands. They also viewed the Khoikhoi, Malay slave, and African as an emerging class of servile laborers. They sometimes drew distinctions between the slaves, baptized slaves, and *swart vry burghers* (free black citizens) and held ambiguous attitudes toward the nature and legal status of the Khoikhoi— variously viewed as apelike or noble savages, as indigenous aliens or citizens.[17]

But if they recognized these legal and social distinctions, the white farmers had no doubts about the non-Europeans' place in the developing labor framework. Beginning in 1658, the Cape Colony joined directly in the

13. F. Wilson, "Farming, 1866–1966," p. 107.

14. Ibid., pp. 113–14; Sheila T. van der Horst, *Native Labour in South Africa*, p. 139.

15. Elphick, *Kraal and Castle*, pp. 23, 57–68.

16. Colin Bundy, "The Emergence and Decline of a South African Peasantry," pp. 373–76; also see F. Wilson, "Farming, 1866–1966," p. 114; and Monica Wilson, "The Growth of Peasant Communities," pp. 69–70.

17. I. D. MacCrone, *Race Attitudes in South Africa*, p. 7; see also Hermann Giliomee and Richard Elphick, *The Shaping of South African Society, 1652–1820*.

East African and Indonesian slave trade. By the end of the eighteenth century, slaves had taken over domestic service, the skilled trades, small-scale retailing, and the heavy farm work in the western Cape. The 26,000 slaves in the colony outnumbered the European freemen. (There were also between 1,000 and 1,500 free blacks and 14,000 Khoikhoi.)[18] Slavery had become an integral part of Cape society; by one account, it could not "be removed without sacrificing the Colony and perhaps the poor slaves themselves that are in it."[19] Still, while slaves were appended to the shops of Cape Town and the farms in the western Cape, their proportion of the total laboring population, including the "free" Khoikhoi and Africans, dropped as one moved east.[20] Slavery was never incorporated into a well-developed labor and agricultural system—like plantation slavery—that would dominate the interior. The slave trappings survived not in slave institutions, but in the presumptions that would govern race relations and farm labor.

The nomadic Boer farmers carried these presumptions with them into the African interior. They believed deeply in "colour inferiority";[21] manual labor in service of another was tainted by the "curse of Ham" and was properly performed by slaves, the Khoikhoi, and, eventually, the "Kaffirs." In effect, they supported the ideas and prejudices of a slaveholding class, without, at the same time, employing many slaves or creating an agricultural system suited to their use. C. W. de Kiewiet provides a summary of the process and its consequences:

> Slaves and droughts, Hottentots and isolation, cheap labour and land, combined to create the institutions and habits of South African society. The sons and daughters born to sturdy Hollanders and Huguenots learned to look upon the labour of the field and upon all hard physical toil as the functions of a servile race.[22]

Even before the eighteenth century, with the loss of their cattle and increasing poverty, the Khoikhoi began entering the service of the Company and of the European farmers as laborers. They received, in exchange, food and lodging, some tobacco, and security against attacks by settlers and

18. M. F. Katzen, "White Settlers and the Origins of a New Society, 1652–1778," pp. 204–5; Giliomee and Elphick, *The Shaping of South African Society.*
19. W. S. Van Ryneveld, 1797, quoted in André DuToit and Hermann Giliomee, *Afrikaner Political Thought,* "The Colonial Crisis, Labour and Slavery (1780–1840)," document 2.
20. Giliomee and Elphick, *The Shaping of South African Society;* Elphick, *Kraal and Castle,* pp. 178–79.
21. MacCrone, *Race Attitudes,* p. 100; G. V. Doxey, *The Industrial Colour Bar in South Africa,* p. 9.
22. De Kiewiet, *A History of South Africa,* p. 21.

other African groups.[23] The destruction of Khoikhoi society that followed
signaled the beginning of a process that would bring an end to the frontier
and create in its place a checkered, black-and-white mosaic in the South
African countryside—the first stage in a highly developed pattern of racial
domination and unfree labor.

By the mid nineteenth century, the African squatter—the "black serf " in
Wilson's characterization—was the central figure in this framework and the
backbone of white farming up until World War I. He left an African peasant
economy faltering in the face of internal disorder and European expansion.
He became a *woonkaffer,* resident African, cultivating the white man's land
and shepherding his cattle and sheep. His labor was available at the white
farmer's will, usually for two or three days a week, though rarely exceeding
two hundred days in a year. In exchange, the African might retain a few of
his cattle, build a hut, and cultivate a small garden plot; in some areas of the
country, the squatter might receive rations and a shilling a day for his labor
but such payments were by no means the rule. Indeed, in some cases,
Africans paid an additional "ground rent" for the privilege of squatting.[24]

That squatting brought black and white into a new intimacy was not
particularly troublesome at first, not even in the Transvaal and Free State,
where the "colour question" was so salient. The issue in the nineteenth-
century countryside was not segregation but labor. Under prevailing
conditions, where the cash economy was so little developed, African
squatting was the only way to insure an adequate supply of farm labor. Few
European farmers could afford wage inducements, while most could afford
to offer grazing rights to a few African families. In any case, white farmers
had convinced themselves that the peasant society was unresponsive to wage
inducements. The African squatter, barely at the edge of "civilization,"
would almost certainly squander these payments or, worse yet, seek out the
"leisure" of the "native reserves." One farmer verbalized this widespread
sentiment: "I consider that my labour is very cheap indeed, but if I paid
them what they are worth to me, they would all leave."[25]

Nor were white wage laborers, or even white squatters, an acceptable
alternative. This class of landless *bywoners* hovered at the bottom of white
rural society, unable to compete with the African laborer and unable to
establish an economic farming community.[26] Each passing crisis—the
rinderpest epidemic of 1896, the South African War, the droughts of 1918
and 1919—winnowed the white rural poor.

23. Elphick, *Kraal and Castle,* pp. 172–74, 178–81, 236–39.
24. Grosskopf, *Rural Impoverishment,* pp. 1–167; Morris, "The Development of Capitalism
in South African Agriculture," pp. 195–96; F. Wilson, "Farming, 1866–1966," p. 117.
25. Quoted in Margaret Roberts, *Labour in the Farm Economy,* p. 31.
26. De Kiewiet, *A History of South Africa,* pp. 192–93.

As long as local markets were little developed and European farmers little interested in distant ones, the system of African squatting would not necessarily bring, as it did for the Khoikhoi, the destruction of African peasant society. The African economy and white farming were not yet so intricately bound together in the early nineteenth century that, as the Native Economic Commission later suggested, "the latter is in entire conflict with the former, and must ultimately disintegrate it completely."[27] But increasing agricultural production in the middle and later nineteenth century, without substantial changes in agricultural methods, brought increasing concern over labor supplies. White farmers, previously content with two or three families on or near their land, began thinking in more grandiose terms. Complaints about the "shortage of labor" reverberated across the countryside, threatening the African's tenuous hold on his land and labor power.

In Natal, the white settlers and a stream of select committees deplored the "indolence" of African men and their reluctance to enter the ambit of white farming. As early as 1852, a commission of inquiry claimed that the African reserves allowed Africans "to follow idle, wandering, and pastoral lives or habits, instead of settling down to fixed industrial pursuits."[28] The white farmers, consequently, raised a continual clamor for the break-up of the reserves and the abrogation of tribal practices that kept Africans bound to the traditional peasant economy. The farmers failed to "disperse the reserves," but they created hut taxes and restrictions on landholding that Africans could escape only by living on white-owned farms.[29] In the Cape, commissions warned of a serious labor shortage in the western districts: the white farmers could not attract Africans away from the reserves or the colony's "frontiers" or prevent Africans from leaving for the gold fields, public works, and diamond mines.[30]

Alongside the system of squatting and labor services and the anguish over the shortage of labor, there developed what Francis Wilson calls "a thicket of pass and vagrancy laws."[31] At the outset of the nineteenth century, the Cape administration imposed limitations on the movement of the Khoikhoi. They were required to establish fixed places of residence and register with the *landdrost;* they might move from farm to farm or one administrative district to another only when in possession of a pass.[32] Though the

27. Union of South Africa, *Report of the Native Economic Commission 1930-32*, p. 3.
28. Quoted in David Welsh, *The Roots of Segregation*, p. 31.
29. Van der Horst, *Native Labour*, pp. 46-50.
30. Cape of Good Hope, *Report of the Select Committee, Supply of the Labour Market*, A.26-1879; Cape of Good Hope, *Report of the Select Committee on the Labour Question*, C2-1892.
31. F. Wilson, "Farming, 1866-1966," p. 117.
32. Van der Horst, *Native Labour*, pp. 8-10.

Khoikhoi were exempted in 1828 from such race-specific legislation in the Cape, they, like the Africans, were brought under the masters and servants laws. The 1856 act in the Cape imposed compulsory registration of contracts and criminal penalties for the servant's breach of contract. Amendments to the law in 1873 added special penalties for farm servants, including hard labor, spare diet, and solitary confinement. In the eastern Cape, legislation like the Glen Grey Act imposed new taxes and new patterns of land ownership, thus insuring an increased supply of African farm labor.

The Voortrekker Republics proposed labor controls that, had they been implemented, would have been the envy of Cape farmers. Africans, like the Khoikhoi in the early Cape, were forbidden to wander about the republics without a pass signed by an employer or official. Those without passes were to be uprooted and allocated to dispersed reserves near the white farming settlements. These restrictions, however, were never effectively implemented. In their place, white farmers substituted hut taxes, compulsory labor on public works, random violence, and a system for "apprenticing" African children.[33] After the South African War, Transvaal farmers took up these policies, taxing Africans in the subsistence economy and breaking up the reserves.[34]

White farmers were also concerned with the distribution of squatters, fearing that Africans would congregate on farms near the reserves or on farms that offered relatively attractive terms of service. A labor market that white farmers refused to let rule the question of availability certainly could not be permitted to rule the question of distribution. The very earliest Voortrekker regulations in Natal limited to five the number of African families that might reside on a white farm.[35] That principle was enshrined in the Transvaal Plakkers Wet (Squatters Law) of 1895 and virtually all subsequent legislation on the question.[36]

The black and white farming communities of southern Africa came together under the banner of the "labor shortage." For whites, agriculture emerged from the isolation and simplicity of the frontier fully embroiled in questions of labor supplies and "native policy." The Africans emerged squatting on the white owned land and, de Kiewiet notes, choking on their own.[37]

33.   Ibid., pp. 56–57; Leonard Thompson, "Cooperation and Conflict: The High Veld," pp. 435–37.
34.   Transvaal, *Report of the Transvaal Labour Commission: Report and Evidence,* Cd. 1894, Cd. 1896, 1904, pp. 13–15, 38–39.
35.   South African Institute of Race Relations, *Farm Labour in the Orange Free State,* p. 14.
36.   F. Wilson, "Farming, 1866–1966," pp. 117–18.
37.   De Kiewiet, *A History of South Africa,* p. 80.

FROM LABOR TENANCY TO WAGE LABOR:
THE STATE AND THE LABOR MARKET

I had little else to do and watched the while that I was there;—but I did not see a single white man at work. I heard their voices,—some Dutch, though chiefly English; but the voices were the voices of masters and not of men. Then I walked round the place with the object of seeing, and nowhere could I find a white man working as a labourer. And yet the Orange Free State is supposed to be one South African territory from which the black man has been expelled. The independent black man who owned the land has been expelled,—but the working black man has taken his place, allured by wages and diet.

Anthony Trollope
1878[38]

When land in the white areas was relatively plentiful and cheap and the market for agricultural products limited, squatting was an appropriate route to a rural labor force. The African squatter had all the marks of servility and cheapness consistent with the traditions of South African labor and the resources of the white farming community. But commercialization and rising land values began to undermine traditional practices in South African rural economy. The careless use and control of labor and land could not long survive the modernization of agriculture. The African squatter, as well as the white *bywoner,* increasingly was an anomaly.[39]

Indeed, the system of African squatting had become a mixed labor form even before the mines played havoc with land values and markets and before the system's legal demise in 1913. Farmers sought to shield their laborers from the hut and poll taxes and the allure of town life, but nonetheless money began to permeate African life on the veld. Rare was the farmer in the waning days of African squatting who could afford not to mix a few shillings and rations with rights to grazing and cultivation. In some instances, the European landowner and the African squatter engaged in a form of joint production, or "working on the shares," that limited the supervisory activity of the former and gave the latter a certain permanency and proprietorship over the white land. In mixed or pure form, however, the squatting system was suitable for only the most inefficient farming techniques; more important, it left Africans free, though resident on white land, to spend a large portion of their time producing for their own consumption.

In 1913, the government tried to eliminate African squatting and sharecropping and, some have argued, the commingling of black and white in the countryside. "Thus suddenly a firm line was to be drawn between

38. Anthony Trollope, *South Africa,* pp. 397–98.
39. De Kiewiet, *A History of South Africa,* p. 187.

white and black settlement," de Kiewiet writes. "The segregation of which men had been talking for a hundred years was to be undertaken at last."[40]

The Natives Land Act, however, was neither an enclosure movement nor a means of ridding European agriculture of its black peasantry. On the latter, the act made clear that it should not be construed as "restricting the number of Natives who, as farm-labourers, may reside on any farm in the Transvaal."[41] A few years later, the Natives Land (Beaumont) Commission reaffirmed that segregation was not at issue: "A very general impression prevails that the Act contemplates a segregation—complete or partial—of the Native races throughout the Union. The impracticality of such an idea makes it difficult to understand how it has come to be entertained."[42] Africans continued their migration to the European rural areas well after the act, even in the Free State, where between 1911 and 1921, the African population increased by 24 percent.[43]

The act sought primarily to dislodge Africans from their traditional tenancy arrangements in European areas and to increase the amount of labor provided to the European farms.[44] Some farmers, particularly in the Free State, chose to evict squatters and incorporate their land into more intensive units, free of inefficient African subsistence farming. There were, nonetheless, only limited attempts to create a rural proletariat and labor market. With increasing population pressure in the reserves, a consequence, in large part, of the act, and increasing numbers of Africans seeking work in the white areas, farmers found that they could demand more work of their farm laborers.[45] In Natal and the Transvaal, where existing tenancies were unaffected, and even in parts of the Free State, Africans faced pressures to renegotiate their tenancy arrangements and expand their labor services.[46] African rural laborers had few defenses against this formalization and intensification of the labor situation.

In the three decades after the Natives Land Act, the principal alternative to squatting as a way of organizing a rural labor force was *labor tenancy*. It

40. Ibid., p. 205.
41. Quoted in ibid., pp. 291–92.
42. Union of South Africa, *Report of the Natives Land Commission. Minutes,* U.G. 25–1916, p. 3.
43. Van der Horst, *Native Labour,* p. 292; Grosskopf, *Rural Impoverishment,* pp. 1–67.
44. Van der Horst, *Native Labour,* p. 291. Africans were prevented under the act from purchasing or renting land outside certain scheduled areas, while Europeans might not purchase or rent inside of them. Existing sharecropping and squatting arrangements could be maintained, except in the Free State, where all such rentals were prohibited.
45. The refusal of the government to act on the recommendations of the Beaumont Commission, especially the recommendation for more land in the scheduled areas, is discussed by de Kiewiet, *A History of South Africa,* p. 206 and Doxey, *The Industrial Colour Bar,* p. 166.
46. Union of South Africa, *Report of the Natives Land Commission,* p. 4; Van der Horst, *Native Labour,* p. 292.

began disintegrating almost before it started in the Cape and Free State, but in other areas of intensive agricultural production—the northern districts of Natal and most of the Transvaal—labor tenancy emerged pre-eminent.[47]

Labor tenants resided on white farms or nearby "labor farms" and agreed to perform no less than 90 days of service and, where designated by the state, up to 180 days. In some cases, labor tenants fulfilled their terms of service "at the will" of the white farmer, but such complete entrapment was a remnant of earlier squatting arrangements and did not characterize labor tenancy as a whole. Normally, the labor service was provided during a continuous period of four to eight months, leaving the tenant free to seek outside employment during the remainder of the year. In exchange for these services, the labor tenant received a small cash compensation, mealies and other rations, grazing rights for a few head of cattle or goats, a piece of arable land (traditionally an acre in size), and a small garden plot near the tenant's hut. Both the African and white parties to these tenancy arrangements understood that the cultivation and grazing rights represented a gesture rather than a genuine means of subsistence. That could be realized only by supplementing these meager cash and in-kind wages with outside employment during the nonservice period.[48]

Labor tenancy was, in one sense, a mere formalization and extension of the earlier quasi-feudal labor patterns. De Kiewiet, for one, believes there is little to choose between the labor tenant and the medieval serf: "There is the same exchange of labour services for the permission to cultivate the land and graze on the common, the same right to cut wood for fuel or building, the same tendency for the tenant's entire family to be bound by his 'contract.' "[49] The last pattern is particularly important for understanding the stability of the labor form and the immobility of the African population caught up in it. For, unlike conventional systems of wage labor, here the farm owner has a hold on the tenant's entire family, checked only by the most tenuous contract arrangements.[50]

47.   Morris, "The Development of Capitalism in South African Agriculture," pp. 295–96.
48.   This discussion relies primarily upon Edith B. Rheinallt Jones, "Farm Labour in the Transvaal," pp. 5–9; Roberts, Labour in the Farm Economy, pp. 39–42.
49.   De Kiewiet, A History of South Africa, p. 203.
50.   All members of the family could be called upon to perform labor services and, unless they performed to the satisfaction of the white farmer, could be evicted. Only when the farmer felt the service had been adequately completed could any member of the household gain a pass to seek work off the farm; if any member failed to return for subsequent periods of service— a son that preferred the work in town or on another farm, for example—the remainder of the family might once again face the prospect of eviction. That hold, along with some genuine advantages for the African tenant, gave the system a "sense of stability" missing in more modern labor forms. See Roberts, Labour in the Farm Economy, pp. 63–66; Union of South Africa, Report of the Native Farm Labour Committee, 1937–39, G.P. –S. 3396–1939-102, p. 18; Jones, "Farm Labour in the Transvaal," pp. 8–9.

But to view the labor tenant system as a simple extension of precapitalist agriculture is to neglect vital changes in labor practice, particularly the spread of *wage labor*. By the early 1930s, rights to grazing and arable land, the mainstay of any serflike relationship, provided a majority of tenant income only in the northern Transvaal. In other major farming areas—Natal and the western Free State—more than 70 percent of tenant income was derived from cash and in-kind wages (food, stock, clothing).[51] Morris quite properly concludes that white landowners no longer derived a substantial surplus from "direct feudal rent (i.e., as a labour rent for the land he [the African farm worker] tilled)"; they derived it instead "indirectly through the appropriation of the surplus value embodied in the agricultural commodities [the African farm worker] produced."[52]

The Native Economic Commission in 1932 also underlined the emerging contradictions within labor tenancy, particularly the growing conflict between the more commercial farmer and the traditional African labor tenant:

> Where land values have risen and intensive cultivation is coming in, it is no longer economically possible for the farmer either to give the grazing which the Native wants or to allow him to work any portion of the land according to his own primitive methods. In such areas therefore labour shortage is beginning to be felt owing largely to the farmers' inability to remunerate in the manner which Natives prefer. In other areas the number of cattle, which the Native is allowed to graze, is being severely limited. This again brings conflict between farmer and labour tenant.[53]

But we should not conclude, as Morris does, that such wage payments and growing commercialization brought South African agriculture into the capitalist mode of production, transforming quasi-feudal landlords into an agrarian bourgeoisie and serflike labor tenants into an agrarian proletariat. The labor tenant system was an adaptation by traditional landowners to rising land values and a growing demand for labor; they sought to formalize and expand the period of labor service, provide an opportunity for wage labor outside the tenant's contract, and, most important, minimize the time tenants spent producing for their own consumption. But these "reforms" were developed within the contours of precapitalist labor practice. This traditional landowning class, even with increasing dependence on wage labor, sought to elaborate the bonds that tied the African peasant to the

51.   Morris, "The Development of Capitalism in South African Agriculture," p. 304. Only in Natal, however, was the majority of total compensation paid in cash.
52.   Ibid., p. 305.
53.   Union of South Africa, *Report of the Native Economic Commission, 1930–32*, p. 55.

land and to his labor contract. For them, commercialization brought increased use of wage labor without a commensurate willingness to depend on the labor market.

The combination of new and old elements—wage labor, grazing rights, and compulsion—proved contradictory and unstable, however. Even as squatting was prohibited and labor tenancy was put on a more formal footing, new state action was needed to further limit the mobility of African farm laborers. In 1932, the Native Service Contract Act provided penalties to push farm workers into labor tenancy arrangements and penalties to keep farm workers from escaping them. The law provided that an entire African family might be evicted from a white farm if any member of the family failed to render the necessary labor services; it also allowed the government to "proclaim areas" where African adult males who failed to produce a three-month labor contract would pay a tax of five pounds per annum. Though no area was "proclaimed" under the act, the principle of taxation and labor contracts was later incorporated into the Native Trust and Land Act of 1936.[54] In addition to the tax provisions, the 1936 act barred all Africans from the white rural areas, except those formally registered as a "servant of the owner," a "labour tenant," or a "squatter." Labour Tenant Control Boards were created to distribute registered workers over the appropriate white farms; the government was given the authority to extend labor service contracts in specific farming areas.

When a proclamation was issued for the Lydenburg District of the Transvaal, extending the period of labor service from 90 to 180 days, African workers fled the area in favor of more leisurely labor arrangements. The white farmers in the district consequently asked that the proclamation be extended to all of the Transvaal; a few years later, the South African Agricultural Union asked that it be extended to all of South Africa.[55]

The system, nonetheless, continued its decline. The thirties brought recurrent droughts, rising costs, and growing claims by the mining industry on the agricultural labor force. What in the past had seemed a short-term or seasonal shortfall of African labor increasingly took on the appearance of a permanent labor shortage.[56]

More vehemently than ever, white farmers, characteristically, insisted that the state limit African labor mobility. They complained to the Farm Labour Committee of 1937–39 that the pass laws were not effectively enforced, that traveling permits were granted even when farm laborers lacked proper approval from their employers, that Africans under eighteen

54. Van der Horst, *Native Labour,* pp. 285, 293.
55. Ibid., p. 294; F. Wilson, "Farming, 1866–1966," pp. 141, 154; and South African Labour and Development Research Unit, "Farm Labour in South Africa: A Review Article," p. 127.
56. Morris, "The Development of Capitalism in South African Agriculture," pp. 315–17.

gained passes without written permission from the appropriate landowners, and that inadequate forms of identification "made it possible for Natives to desert with impunity."[57] In the late thirties, the South African Institute of Race Relations made an accounting of the Free State farmers' complaints and proposals:

> There should be a stricter enforcement of pass laws, and free movement of Natives should be further controlled by regulation; Native children should not be allowed to go to towns; Natives under eighteen years of age should not be allowed to leave the district without a pass from the Native commissioner, and this pass should not be given if the farmer requires his services at a wage which satisfies the Commissioner; Natives under twenty-one must be prohibited from seeking work in Johannesburg; there should be no recruiting on farms for mines or public works; only Natives from the Protectorates should be used on roads and public works, or, as one group of farmers expressed it, "our Natives" must not be used; refusal to accept work at "ruling rates" should entail strict discipline in a labour camp; a Native who cannot prove nine months' service during a year should be punished; wandering for more than three weeks should be considered as vagabondage and punished; a maximum wage should be fixed for each district and no Native should be allowed to leave the district; the Native should not be allowed to say what he does and what he does not want to do; he should not be allowed to sell his labour where he chooses; the amount of stock on European farms allowed to Natives should be allocated to European farms according to need.[58]

The complaints were not without effect. The Department of Native Affairs issued General Circular No. 22 of 1938, which sought to correct some of these difficulties arising from the workings of the labor market. The circular provided, among many technical details:

> 1. No travelling pass or permit to seek work may be issued to any labour tenant unless the period for which he is allowed to absent himself from his landlord's service is clearly indicated in the "Special Pass" issued to him by his landlord or on the reverse of his document of identification in the space provided.
> 2. Every travelling pass or permit to seek work, issued to a labour tenant, must be endorsed with a rubber stamp "Farm Labour Tenant, not to be employed after . . . ," with the date on which his leave expires recorded in the space provided.

57.   Union of South Africa, *Report of the Native Farm Labour Committee, 1937–39*, pp. 11, 24.
58.   South African Institute of Race Relations, *Farm Labour in the Orange Free State*, p. 41.

"This Circular," it concluded, "is being issued with the concurrence of the Secretary for Justice."[59]

By the end of the thirties, the Native Farm Labour Committee could find almost nothing worth salvaging in the labor system. It discovered that tenants and landowners alike found the system burdensome and uneconomic. Under prevailing forms of agricultural production, it concluded, there was no attraction in a system that "deprived the farmer of native labour for a considerable part of the year."[60]

World War II brought on a crisis in South African agriculture. The contradictions in labor tenancy, already apparent in the thirties, were exacerbated by wartime demand for agricultural products and the accelerating flight of African labor to the cities. But European farmers responded to the crisis, as they had in the past, not by generalizing market relations, but by insisting on even more elaborate state measures to control the African rural population.

The postwar Nationalist government responded with a combination of "reform" and "reaction": first, by abolishing squatting and labor farms and speeding the changeover to wage labor; second, by giving a new formality and scope to the pass laws and influx controls.[61] The Native Laws Amendment Act of 1952 developed the sometimes haphazard barrier between country and town into a veritable Berlin Wall. It provided for a system of labor bureaus that, in the absence of market mechanisms, allocated African labor in both urban and rural areas. Before an African male worker could leave his family and work in a proclaimed area, he needed the permission of the district labor bureau, which, in turn, needed the authorization of the regional labour bureau. Permission was not ordinarily granted, however, unless the white farmer consented.[62]

A survey of farms in the Albany and Bathurst Districts of the eastern Cape found that most allowed younger workers to leave for temporary periods but that a sizable number, about a third, were extremely restrictive: some insisted on substitute workers; some retained the right to recall the workers "at will"; and others simply refused to grant permission.[63]

"One cannot avoid the conclusion," Doxey notes, "that the root of the trouble lies in the fact that influx control and direction of labour, as

59. "General Circular No. 22 of 1938," annexure to Union of South Africa, *Report of the Native Farm Labour Committee, 1937–39.*
60. Union of South Africa, *Report of the Native Farm Labour Committee, 1937–39,* pp. 7–10, 11–18.
61. The principle that migration from countryside to town be controlled and limited, even under conditions of rapid industrial development, predates the Nationalist government. The Natives (Urban Areas) Consolidation Act of 1945 already provided that "rural" Africans be excluded from "proclaimed areas," in other words, the major cities.
62. Roberts, *Labour in the Farm Economy,* pp. 125–26.
63. Ibid., p. 83.

operated today, are not primarily or even chiefly concerned with the needs of the economy, but are regarded as an effective means of excluding as many Africans as possible from the urban areas and of perpetuating the migratory system."[64] Doxey might also have noted that the controls provided an effective means for retaining an African rural laboring population, even though it had lost its grazing and cultivation rights and depended primarily upon wage labor.

The changeover from squatting to labor tenancy to wage labor brought in each instance a diminished access of African rural laborers to subsistence production—to the traditional African farming areas, the reserves, and to grazing and cultivation rights on European farms. In each instance, the changeover was accompanied by an increasing reliance on wages, on the sale of labor power for cash or in-kind payments. And accompanying the change in labor forms were increasing opportunities for African workers to escape their traditional labor obligations by moving on to other farms or to jobs in the mines and factories.

But the changeover also brought, virtually in direct proportion to the declining access to land and increasing reliance on wage labor, accelerated efforts to formalize labor obligations and limit the market in labor. Commercial farmers and the state were intent after World War II, as they had been at the turn of the century, on maintaining an African peasantry, even though that peasantry no longer had significant access to the land and relied primarily on wages for its subsistence. The recurring agricultural crises, particularly in the thirties and forties, brought renewed efforts to find yet more refined ways of limiting the market.

Commercial landowners had moved well beyond the precapitalist labor practice that brought the Khoikhoi into the service of the Dutch East India Company or European farmers in the Cape Peninsula and that left the Xhosa squatting on European farms in the eastern Cape. But notions of unfree labor and racial domination, so important to the precapitalist countryside, did not fade as market relations began to permeate European agriculture. White South Africa, as we have seen, faced the transition to capitalist agriculture by elaborating state controls over the rural African population, by in effect reaffirming patterns of race domination and unfree labor.

64. Doxey, *The Industrial Colour Bar*, p. 175.

CHAPTER 5

The South African Agricultural Union: Managing the Transition to Capitalist Agriculture

ORGANIZED AGRICULTURE

The Political Connection

Commercial farmers followed the German route to capitalist agriculture because, in large part, there was a state willing and able to construct labor-repressive policies. The Natives Land Act (1913), Native Service Contract Act (1932), Native Trust and Land Act (1936), and Native Laws Amendment Act (1952) provided the critical tools for increasing agricultural production while retaining a large African laboring population in the rural areas: on the one hand, squeezing African landholdings and subsistence production and intensifying compulsory labor services; on the other, limiting African labor mobility and access to industrial or urban employment.

The basis for such sustained assistance to commercial farmers may lie in the development requirements of the state itself rather than in the political standing of the white farming community. Just as the state depends on the growth of revenue-producing industries, such as gold mining, it may support an expanding food supply from domestic sources. Each measure in the area of labor repression brought a declining reliance on inefficient, subsistence production and increasing reliance on intensive land uses and wage labor.

The policies, nonetheless, were developed within a political climate where commercial farmers had an extraordinary access to the state and where state officials seemed responsive to farming interests on a broad range of issues.[1]

---

1. This proposition is not an easy one to demonstrate, however; nor is it uncontested. One important study on the South African state maintains, for example, that mining interests were dominant before 1924 and in that year yielded their position to a "power bloc" organized by "national capital," capitalist farmers and manufacturing interests supported by a "petty-bourgeois" white working class. After the raising of the gold price and fusion of the major political parties in the early thirties, mining and foreign capital joined the dominant political

Between 1910 and the mid-fifties, the major governing parties depended principally on rural constituencies and political actors drawn directly out of agricultural occupations. The South Africa party government (1910–24), the Pact government and National party successor (1924–33), the United party fusion government (1933–39), and the postwar National party government (1948–) constructed policies that allowed farmers to maintain their African labor force, gain control over marketing, and divert resources from the developing and profitable gold-mining sector.

The South Africa party (SAP), the first governing party and the dominant force in South Africa for a decade and a half after Union, drew primarily on rural constituencies. More than half of its parliamentary members in 1910 were engaged in agricultural pursuits, including the presidents of the South African Agricultural Union and South African Planters Union and the director of the South African Cooperative Union. The SAP yielded power in 1924 to a coalition whose major member, the National party, displaced the SAP in the rural areas of the Free State, the central Cape, and Transvaal. Though lawyers were slightly more prominent than farmers among the Pact's parliamentary members (37 versus 32 percent), by 1929 farmers were again the largest bloc. During the early United party reign, beginning in 1933, farmers retained a third of the seats, still the largest bloc in parliament. Its members included the principal officers of the South African Agricultural Union, the Natal Woolgrowers, the Cape Agricultural Association, the Natal Agricultural Union, the Transvaal Agricultural Union, the Cane Growers Association, and the Co-operative Wine Farmers Association (KWV). The National party, out of power in the thirties and early forties, was even more dependent on white farmers: virtually all of its parliamentary members were elected in rural constituencies; almost two-thirds in 1943 were engaged in agricultural occupations. When the party came to power in 1948, half of its members in parliament were drawn out of agriculture.[2]

---

alignment. See Robert Davies, David Kaplan, Mike Morris, and Dan O'Meara, "Class Struggle and the Periodisation of the State in South Africa," pp. 6–20; also see my discussion of this issue in chapter 4.

Another study of the South African state—one that unfortunately has been sequestered and cannot be cited here—rejects the whole notion of "hegemony" and "power blocs," focusing instead on the state's need for "legitimation" and revenue. The latter requirement brought continuing state concern with the welfare of the mining industry; in effect, an alignment of mutual advantage that allowed the industry to reduce labor costs and white employment. According to this study, the 1924 Pact government, despite its rural and labor constituencies, did little to disrupt the profitability or employment patterns in the mining industry; nor did it seek to divert mining profits for the development of the agricultural sector.

2. Alfred William Stadler, "The Party System in South Africa, 1910–1948," pp. 200–262. A survey of contemporary political leaders (1968–69) shows that Afrikaans-speakers, mostly Nationalists, generally grew up in rural areas (59 percent versus 26 percent among English-speakers). See H. W. van der Merwe, M. J. Ashley, N. C. J. Charton, and R. J. Huber, *White South African Elites,* p. 107.

These governments did not ignore other interests in white society and, in particular, did not neglect the welfare of the gold-mining industry: even farmer-dominated governments could appreciate the revenue derived from a profitable and expanding gold-mining industry.[3] But government after government acted, often over the opposition and at the expense of mining and manufacturing interests, to insure the profitability of commercial agriculture.

Soon after the National party came to power in 1924, the Economic and Wage Commission warned against any change in the distribution of national income that might come at the expense of agriculture, suggesting that both white workers and the mines were taking an unreasonable share of the total.[4] By one account, the state began almost immediately thereafter to divert surplus income from the mining sector in order to subsidize both price supports on agricultural commodities and protection for indigenous industry.[5] It laid the foundations for cooperative agriculture and, eventually, producer control over the supply of commodities and over prices; it constructed import duties that effectively blocked further importation of sugar and wheat.[6]

After the rapid rise in gold prices in the early thirties, the United party government supported a further tilt toward white agriculture. In the period between 1933 and World War II, the state created the structure of marketing boards, export and import controls, and credit arrangements that granted farmers almost unlimited price-fixing powers and laid the foundation for mechanization after the war.[7] The tilt toward agriculture, along with the increasing diversification of the economy, was, in effect, financed by increased taxation on mining profits.[8] Under the United party government in the thirties, direct taxation of the gold mines provided one-third of state revenues; in the period between 1927 and 1939, direct expenditures on agriculture increased by 400 percent.[9]

When the National party came to power in 1948, it proved no less generous in its support for white agriculture. The price of maize was increased by 50 percent in three years, allowing the doubling of farm profits

3.   To that end, they allowed the mining industry to retrench its white labor force. They also helped construct the framework for cheap labor policies: pass law administration, African reserve areas, and, most important, the Chamber of Mines' virtual monopoly on the recruitment of foreign African labor.

4.   Union of South Africa, *Report of the Economic and Wage Commission 1925*, U.G. 14–1926, pp. 80–82.

5.   David Kaplan, "Capitalist Development in South Africa: Class Conflict and the State," p. 12.

6.   J. T. Tinley, *The Native Labor Problem of South Africa*, pp. 210–20.

7.   Hobart Houghton, *The South African Economy*, p. 58; Ralph Horwitz, *The Political Economy of South Africa*, pp. 148–54.

8.   C. W. de Kiewiet, *A History of South Africa*, p. 253.

9.   Davies et al., "Class Struggle and the Periodisation of the State," p. 18.

in this critical Nationalist stronghold.[10] National party ideology in its early construction recognized the pre-eminence of agricultural interests and resisted a new socioeconomic order based on the values of "Liberalists" and "Capitalists." The Nationalist opposition in 1943 supported the principle of marketing boards but under the full control of producers: "if we have a Control Board for the wheat industry . . . then let it be a Control Board composed of the wheat farmers and of the wheat farmers alone."[11]

Commercial and mining interests, even as they benefited from some aspects of state policy, recognized and criticized the tilt toward agriculture. Throughout the thirties, when the marketing and labor framework was elaborated in rural areas, the Association of Chambers of Commerce (ASSOCOM) complained of the lack of consultation: "The views of commerce and of the taxpayers in the towns are being consistently and persistently ignored." It protested the "indiscriminate relief " provided the farming community in distress and the proliferation of marketing boards that left the pricing mechanisms fully in the hands of the producers.[12] The Chamber of Mines too complained of the ability of farmer organizations in South Africa to limit the recruiting of African labor for the mines.[13] It bitterly protested the marketing bills, which granted farmers a "complete monopoly" and "simply aggravate the maladjustments which at present exist and which have been produced by almost identical control schemes."[14] They objected also to the import duties on wheat and other products, which increased the cost of production on the mines and endangered the "primary producer, the mining industry."[15]

Loosening the Political Connection

As long as commercial farmers headed down the German road, there was little choice but to cultivate the political connection. A supportive state apparatus was a precondition for expanding production while holding African workers in the rural areas. But the successful outcome of such an approach—the growth of agricultural production, the accumulation of wealth in white rural areas, and the complete dependence of African workers on wages rather than rights to the land—allowed commercial farmers to contemplate alternatives to labor repression. A South African

10. Francis Wilson, "Farming, 1866–1966," pp. 143–44.
11. *Hansard,* 19 January 1943, col. 77.
12. *Commercial Bulletin of South Africa,* May–July 1935; *Commercial Opinion,* May 1936; January–April 1937.
13. Chamber of Mines (Transvaal), *Twenty-Second Annual Report, Year 1911,* p. xliii; *Forty-Eighth Annual Report, Year 1937,* pp. 96–97.
14. Chamber of Mines (Transvaal), *Forty-Seventh Annual Report, Year 1936,* pp. 67–69.
15. Chamber of Mines (Transvaal), *Thirty-Third Annual Report, Year 1922,* p. 96.

Agricultural Union (SAAU) that demanded increasing state control over the labor market and elaboration of the racial order was able to shift gears in the postwar period, particularly in the late sixties. It now spoke less of labor controls and more of the need to be rid of an African peasantry. It was intent on developing a rural economy built on land consolidation, mechanization, and a reduced but better trained African labor force. Organized agriculture, after an extended transition to capitalist agriculture, stepped back from the labor-repressive framework and important elements in the racial order.

CAPITALIST AGRICULTURE AND THE DISPLACEMENT OF THE AFRICAN PEASANTRY

The Last Remnants: The Natal Labor Tenants

The struggle of white farmers in Natal to retain the labor tenant system points up the difficult transition to capitalist agriculture and, at the same time, underlines its triumph. Here, in the Vryheid and Newcastle areas of northern Natal and, to a small degree, in the eastern Transvaal and the eastern Cape, white farmers resisted pressure from the Department of Agriculture and the SAAU to give up precapitalist labor forms. They sought as late as the early seventies to continue employing extensive farming methods and African labor tenants. African families continued to live on "white land," receiving grazing for livestock and land for cultivation, while providing three-to-six-months labor service on the white farms. There remained in Vryheid and Newcastle, an officer of the Natal Agricultural Union observed, a small reminder of "feudalism."[16]

The Natal Agricultural Union (NAU) and the wool growers, consequently, offered a protracted and isolated defense of the system. When the other provincial agricultural unions failed in 1956 to nominate a full complement of representatives to the Labour Tenant Control Boards, reflecting their declining need for such labor and diminished interest in the question, the Natal Union stepped into the breach: it nominated the Natal representatives and suggested that it also be allowed to fill the other positions on the boards.[17] The government declined the offer but reassured the Natal farmers

16. When it is clear from the text that the quoted material is derived from the author's interviews, there will be no footnote citation. See Appendix A, "Notes on Method and Sources." On the question of labor tenancy, see G. G. Antrobus, "Farm Labour in the Eastern Cape, 1950–1973," pp. 11–22; also interviews with the officers of the Transvaal Agricultural Union.

17. *NAUNLU,* 20 April 1956, p. 7.

that the shift away from labor tenancy would not be accompanied by a flight of African labor. Only the infirm and the elderly, the Department of Native Affairs wrote the Natal Union, would be encouraged to return to the Trust Land.[18]

In 1960 the NAU, resisting government pressure and dominant opinion in the SAAU, presented a strong defense of the system. Its memorandum conceded two principles in capitalist agriculture: first, the "labor farm" that served "no other purpose by the owner than as a source of adequate labour for their farming or other operations elsewhere" was wasteful and un-economic; and second, the labor tenant system was "probably the least productive system of employment, in terms of manpower." But the NAU defended the system on other grounds. Labor tenancy, it wrote, satisfied the Zulus' need to own livestock and cultivate land and, consequently, created "a comparatively satisfied labourer." The system was well suited to the white farmer's lack of cash and to his attitude toward the cash economy. If farmer and laborer became mired in cash transactions, the competition with commerce and industry would undermine the rural economy. Better, in the NAU's view, to maintain the labor tenant system and provide a "clear division of labour between rural and urban areas" than to rely on markets and the wage economy.[19]

When the government announced in 1967 that the labor tenant system would end within three years, the Natal farming community was thrown into turmoil. The NAU attacked the government position as "quite unrealistic":

[S]uch a change-over must be of an evolutionary nature, synchronised with the financial ability of the employer to make the change, with the competence of the subsistence worker to adapt to a money economy and a new way of life, and with the government authorities to house and to generate employment for all the surplus Bantu who will have to leave the farms as the result of the change.[20]

The secretary warned that "revolutionary change" would disrupt "our farming operations" and the "excellent master/servant relations that exist on the vast majority of Natal stock farms."[21] At the annual NAU Congress, farmer delegates became somewhat hysterical: "Who will house the 100,000 Bantu when three years is up?" "What will prevent the Bantu from entering the reserves and remaining idle the entire year?" "What country can afford

18. "Statement of the Department of Native Affairs," quoted in ibid., 1 June 1956, p. 1.
19. "Memorandum prepared for the Committee of Enquiry into the Native Labour Tenant System," *NAUNLU,* 18 March 1960, pp. 1, 9–10.
20. *NAUNLU,* 20 October 1967, p. 3.
21. Quoted in *NAUNLU,* 28 July 1967, p. 1.

to carry such sloth?" "It is subsidized idleness—the white man's burden."[22]

In 1970, the government, SAAU, and NAU agreed to an evolutionary but final solution to the labor tenant problem.[23] For the white farmer's part, he would substitute only full-time wage laborers for any departing labor tenants or allow the positions to remain vacant; in effect, "pegging" and then reducing the number of labor tenants.[24] For the government's part, it would make "every endeavor" to "redistribute surplus Bantu on farms, to farms where there is a shortage of labour before accommodating such surplus Bantu in the homelands."[25] For the African tenant's part he would face the grim prospect of eviction, resettlement camps, intensification of labor services under existing tenancy agreements, or wage labor. For many, the choice was incomprehensible. Cosmas Desmond presents their feelings:

> One old man said, "Our great grandfathers were born in this area and now, at this stage of my life, we are forced to leave . . . there is no place for us to move." Other old people said that their sons were allowed to stay to work for the farmers, but they themselves were not wanted. Others, too old to work, were being evicted because their sons would not work for the farmers. One said: "The Whites first of all told us to get rid of our cattle. We did that, and now they are getting rid of us. We think it better for all of us that we die. . . . A dog was not treated like this."[26]

But the government remained confident of its direction. "I am convinced," the commissioner-general for KwaZulu claimed, "that when [African tenants] see the benefits of [the decision to bar tenant farming] they will accept it completely."[27]

The number of African labor tenants fell from 163,000 in 1964 to 27,585 in 1970. The government announced in 1973 that the Cape, Free State, and Transvaal were entirely free of labor tenants. In Natal, only 16,000 isolated labor tenants remained.[28]

The government and organized agriculture agreed, in effect, that wage labor and modern agricultural practice would rule the entire countryside, that not even in Vryheid, a small ranching section of Natal, would the traditional labor forms be allowed to linger.

22. Quoted in *NAUNLU*, 22 September 1967, pp. 11–12.
23. South African Agricultural Union (SAAU), *Report of the General Council for Submission to the Annual Congress 1969/70*, p. 59.
24. *NAUNLU*, 10 July 1970, p. 1.
25. *NAUNLU*, 4 September 1970, p. 1.
26. Cosmas Desmond, *The Discarded People*, p. 219.
27. Quoted in Francis Wilson, *Migrant Labour*, p. 91.
28. Colin Bundy, "The Abolishion of the Masters and Servants Act," p. 44.

Reversing the *Verswarting* of the Countryside

In 1937, there were only 6,000 tractors in South Africa; the rise in demand
for animal-drawn wagons and trolleys still overshadowed lethargic tractor
sales and manufacture.[29] The pace of change following the war proved
staggering, however. The one tractor for each 430 morgen of land became
by 1960 one for each 94 morgen. By 1973, the number of tractors reached
164,000. Agricultural production and efficiency also increased in the period
after the war, though not at the heady pace of mechanization. Wheat,
groundnut, fruit, and sugar output nearly doubled in the decade following
the war; average yield of wheat and maize in the same period increased by
50 to 60 percent.[30] Overall, the volume of agricultural production increased
threefold in the three decades after 1945.

Associated with the rapid increase in agricultural production following
the war were two other developments with important consequences for the
labor-repressive framework: first, the increasing interest in skilled African
laborers rather than the traditional concern with interchangeable, unskilled
labor tenants; and second, a concern with reducing the size of the African
rural laboring population.

Before the Commission on Bantu Education, at the outset of modern
National party rule, the SAAU suggested training in the practical arts, in
skills that could be readily translated into productive labor on the farm. But
it did not pursue the issue on a regular basis until the sixties. In May 1967,
the SAAU submitted a memorandum to the Commission of Enquiry into
Agriculture that lamented the inefficiencies in African and Coloured labor
("the most important single factor at present hampering efficiency in
agriculture") and proposed expanded vocational training in tractor operations and animal care.[31] In 1973 and 1974, the SAAU went further: it
insisted, against the tenor of state thinking, that organized training should
be provided for African workers in rural white areas.[32]

29. Republic of South Africa, *Second Report of the Commission of Enquiry into Agriculture*,
R.P. 84–1970, p. 144; F. Wilson, "Farming, 1866–1966," pp. 152–53; also see appendix B, table
C.2.

30. F. Wilson, "Farming, 1866–1966," p. 163; Houghton, *The South African Economy*, p.
232. Despite these advances, agricultural efficiency still lagged well behind that in the United
States and Europe. The Commission of Enquiry into Agriculture suggested that if a
conventional family farm from the midwestern United States were placed in South Africa, it
could achieve the same level of maize output only by employing ten times its normal labor
complement (Republic of South Africa, *Second Report of the Commission of Enquiry into
Agriculture*, p. 157).

31. SAAU, "Memorandum for Submission to the Commission of Enquiry into Agriculture," May 1967, pp. 91–2.

32. SAAU, *Report of the Annual Congress for the Year 1973/74 for Submission to the General
Council*, p. 64; SAAU, "Bantu Wage Policy," 1974, p. 5.

The new thinking about training, however, was inseparable from the consideration of a larger question: the reversing of the *verswarting,* or "blackening," of the countryside. Under the traditional labor framework, involving a mix of squatters, labor tenants, and wage laborers, the rural labor force grew larger and increasingly black.[33] By the early fifties there was little room for the white *bywoners,* small landowners, and some laborers that occupied the rural areas at the turn of the century. Outside the Cape, 98 percent of farm workers were African.[34] The Commission of Inquiry into European Occupancy of the Rural Areas found that 25 percent of the farms in the Free State were occupied solely by Africans, without any white supervision or presence; in four magisterial districts in Natal, 42 percent of the farms were operated in such fashion.[35]

While areas of protected white employment were emerging under the Mines and Works, Wage, and Industrial Conciliation Acts, the Africanization of South African agriculture proceeded almost unabated. Indeed, "civilized labor policies" were never applied, or even seriously considered, in agricultural employment; farm labor was regularly, almost mechanically, exempted from South Africa's major industrial laws. Though the development of the rural areas created a "poor white problem," the need for a large, African labor force guaranteed that the solution would come in the urban rather than rural areas.

But mechanization and wage labor changed the traditional equation for production and demography: increasing commercialization could now be accompanied by a static or declining African presence in the white rural areas. The white commercial farmer, freed of the conventional paraphernalia in labor tenancy—grazing and cultivation rights—could now turn away from part-time employment and family accommodations. The Commission of Inquiry into European Occupancy of the Rural Areas speculated: "If farmers were to introduce a system of *cash wages* and hire strong young labourers at a higher monthly wage, the number of Bantu in the rural White areas would greatly diminish." It hoped that 1,800,000 of the 2,400,000 Africans living on white farms could be encouraged or compelled to "return" to the homelands, leaving only the full-time wage laborer still residing in the white rural areas.[36] A later commission of inquiry reaffirmed the trend and the impact on the racial make-up of white rural areas. The

33. See appendix B, table C.1.
34. Southern Africa Labour and Development Research Unit, "Farm Labour," p. 96.
35. Union of South Africa, *Report of the Commission of Inquiry into European Occupancy of the Rural Areas,* G.P.–S.7029095–1959, pp. 19–20.
36. Union of South Africa, *Report of the Commission of Inquiry into European Occupancy of the Rural Areas,* p. 18.

solution to *verswarting* did not lie in grandiose schemes for segregating the races or special protection for uneconomic white farmers, the Commission of Enquiry declared, but in the more general consolidation and mechanization of agricultural units. "The blackening of White farms will therefore have to be combated by a reduction of labour and not by an increase of White farmers."[37]

The SAAU endorsed the Report of the Commission of Enquiry into Agriculture, particularly the recommendation that agricultural land not be further subdivided: "It is not South African Agricultural Union's policy . . . to support the development of an agricultural peasantry in our country."[38] The SAAU maintained, with an eye toward reducing the size of the African labor force, that mechanization should be introduced into "all aspects of production . . . from beginning to end."[39] As long as there was mechanization in planting but not harvesting or storage, the large, inefficient African labor force would remain in the white rural areas.

> The South African Agricultural Union has always advocated the policy of fulfilling a farm's minimum labour requirements by means of a nucleus of permanent, fulltime workers. These should live on the property, be well-trained and well-housed and, of course, paid at rates to compete with the wages offered by other sectors.[40]

Between 1955 and 1962 the number of Africans in the white rural areas, after a century of almost continuous growth, remained steady[41] and, after that, began an historic decline. Between 1960 and 1971, by one estimate, 438,000 Africans abandoned agricultural employment; between 1971 and 1973, an additional 248,000 made their exodus.[42]

South Africa, it seemed, was irretrievably on the path to a much reduced, more skilled, wage-laboring population in white rural areas. The implications for labor control and racial differentiation soon became apparent.

37. Republic of South Africa, *Second Report of the Commission of Enquiry into Agriculture*, p. 19.
38. SAAU, *Report of the Annual Congress 1971/1972*, pp. 19, 37.
39. The SAAU was not insensitive to the impact of modernization. "Now is not the time to throw blacks out of labor," one officer declared. Another stated, "We must find jobs for these people."
40. SAAU, "Memorandum for Submission to the Commission of Enquiry into Agriculture," p. 68.
41. Republic of South Africa, *Second Report of the Commission of Enquiry into Agriculture*, p. 141.
42. Data collected by Jill Nattrass, reported in Southern Africa Labour and Development Research Unit, "Farm Labour," p. 100.

THE ELABORATION AND EASING OF LABOR CONTROLS

What has evolved is that these laws were not the method to keep labor on the farms. This was a way to tell farmers that labor was a commodity, no different from fertilizer or anything else. If you want to keep your labor, you'll have to pay for it. Legislation can't help you keep your labor.

> Officer
> Natal Agricultural Union
> 1977

The SAAU, and most of organized agriculture, came out of the war more firmly committed than ever to the intensification of labor controls. It insisted on new barriers between the urban and rural labor forces and on a developed system of labor bureaus.[43] At the very least, it urged, the government should take chapter IV of the Native Trust and Land Act of 1936 more seriously, expanding its implementation to all four provinces:

> So far as farm labour is concerned the Native Trust and Land Act of 1936 affords the means to exercise effective control. Chapter IV permits the proclamation of defined areas and thus control by committees, but the effectiveness of the system depends upon its application to the whole Union.[44]

After the Nationalists came to power in 1948, the SAAU restated its "native labor policy," urging the government to establish labor bureaus and broaden the application of Chapter IV. Before the Tomlinson Commission (The Commission on the Socio-Economic Development of the Native Areas), it urged the government to divide the African labor force into two principal groups, agricultural and industrial.[45]

The Native Laws Amendment Act of 1952, following on SAAU policy, divided South Africa into "proscribed" urban areas and "non-proscribed" rural areas. It provided for labor bureaus in rural and African areas and strict control over labor mobility both between and within them. By 1954, 450 labor bureaus had been established; by 1957, 512; and by 1971, 797.[46]

The Natal Agricultural Union demanded, even after these initiatives, that the government redouble its vigilance over the "surplus populations illegally settled in the cities. It insisted that the Department of Native Affairs limit the recruitment of labor in farming areas and give greater force to pass

43. See discussion in M. L. Morris, "The Development of Capitalism in South African Agriculture: Class Struggle in the Countryside," pp. 335–37.
44. Quoted in ibid., pp. 336–37.
45. "Memorandum to Commission," quoted in *NAUNLU,* 10 October 1952, pp. 1, 5.
46. William Finlay, "South Africa: Capitalist Agriculture and the State," pp. 107–09.

law provisions, particularly those sections requiring the "farmer's consent" before an African laborer or tenant might seek alternative employment.[47] A decade and a half after World War II, the Natal union remained firmly committed to the 1948 SAAU "native labor policy":

> Once again it is desired to stress the necessity for the effective implementation of existing legislation aimed at stabilisation of the labour force and division of labour between town and country and in particular we mention the Natives (Urban Areas) Act, Chapter IV of the Native Trust and Land Act, Natives (Abolition of Passes and Co-ordination of Documents) Act.[48]

Even as Africans were burning their passes in 1960, the NAU asked the government to avoid any relaxation of the contract and pass regulations.[49]

Nor did the SAAU in this period relax its vigilance over the labor market. It opposed government-financed pension programs that might benefit Africans "still quite fit for work"[50] and drought relief that might give Africans "the impression that they need not work."[51] And "behind" these "natural pressures," the SAAU insisted upon a pattern of law and administrative practice that guaranteed the requisite farm labor. In 1964, the SAAU made representations to the minister of Bantu administration, requesting that Africans "endorsed out" of the western Cape be returned to their place of birth, "which often was a white farm."[52] A year later, it urged farmers to observe the labor regulations and asked the government to provide "the strictest possible control in regard to the enforcement of the Bantu identity book system and for better supervision over the movements of Bantu" and the "fastest possible consideration of court cases involving Bantu labourers."[53] In 1966 and again in 1967, it chastised the authorities for lax enforcement of registration and identity book requirements. "After due consideration of the entire matter," the SAAU Council concluded that "the enforcement of the relevant control regulations was a prerequisite for an effective control system, which was essential for our country."[54] But the government as well as the farmers were slow to respond to SAAU hopes for a "central labour organisation with regional or commodity branches"[55] or,

47. *NAUNLU,* 10 April 1953, p. 1; *NAUNLU,* 20 September 1957, p. 3.
48. *NAUNLU,* 18 March 1960, p. 10.
49. *NAUNLU,* 5 August 1960, pp. 7–9.
50. SAAU, *Report of the General Council 1956,* p. 21.
51. SAAU, *Report of the General Council 1965/6,* p. 75.
52. SAAU, *Report of the General Council 1963/4,* p. 68.
53. SAAU, *Report of the General Council 1964/5,* p. 73.
54. SAAU, *Report of the General Council 1965/6,* p. 77.
55. See SAAU, "Memorandum for Submission to the Commission of Enquiry into Agriculture," p. 70.

at the very least, an expansion and expanded financing of the existing labor bureaus.[56]

But by the late sixties, mechanization and the declining need for labor had begun to make themselves felt. White farmers and the SAAU began acceding to labor markets, recognizing their laborers quite literally as "commodities." The SAAU suggested that farmers, as much as the government, were responsible for lax enforcement of the pass laws and haphazard use of identity documents. By the early seventies, the SAAU had virtually stopped calling for an "effective labor control system." It spoke of cooperative recruitment efforts[57] but began soft-pedalling the labor bureaus and hardly mentioned labor controls and pass regulations. Indeed, when the government repealed the masters and servants laws and other laws affecting contracts and labor obligations, the SAAU reacted hardly at all: "As a result of complaints received in this regard, your Council investigated possible alternative measures, but came to the conclusion that the breaking of a service contract again being made a criminal offence, should be relinquished."[58] Despite the SAAU's role in creating the labor-repressive framework, it now deplored the use of "criminal penalties" in the labor market. "We thought it was ridiculous to arrest a man because of employment," the SAAU officer declared. "An unwilling laborer is far worse than an inefficient one. He can wreck your machinery. If he wants to go, let him go. . . . I don't believe in forced labor." The Council of the SAAU in 1977 decided that it would no longer subscribe to measures "to control or impair the movement of labor."[59]

For the provincial unions, the traditional labor framework had become, at best, a paper structure and, at worst, a drag on the agricultural economy. The officers of the Natal union were perhaps the most forceful on the question:

> We have little faith in the labor bureaus. Agriculture falls fairly far down as a preferred occupation. So in most areas, people don't use them. They just break the law. They just strike a bargain. Theoretically, you then send a card into the labor bureau. But it's a paper structure that doesn't work. The Bantu Administration Boards provide some enforcement. But before them—and now too—there is no real enforcement. The police are not interested in raiding farmers to see if they have unregistered labor.

56. SAAU, *Report of the General Council 1971/2*, p. 61.
57. SAAU, *Report of the General Council 1973/4*, p. 64.
58. SAAU, *Report of the General Council 1974/5*, p. 61.
59. Related in interview with officers of the Natal Agricultural Union.

The officers of the Transvaal and Cape unions indicated that they supported the repeal of the masters and servants laws and that their unions and farmers generally were less interested in the whole area of labor controls. Mechanization and "political changes," they said, brought new attitudes toward labor: "The people in South Africa realize more and more that we are working with people, not with animals or slaves." A Transvaal farmer observed, with a little regret, that he now faced his African laborer face to face in the market, "without controls," without labor bureaus, and without contracts. "If someone wants to go," he concluded, "there is nothing you can do to stop them."

THE LIMITS OF MODERNIZATION

Preserving a Rural Labor Force

The commitment to commodity relations and the free market, however, was framed by other aspects of the SAAU's African labor program that did not give way under modernization. While the SAAU had by the mid-seventies lost interest in strict enforcement of labor controls, it continued to insist that labor not move freely into the urban areas and that inducements be provided to discourage urbanization. That there was some inconsistency between relaxing labor controls and maintaining barriers to urbanization did not seem to bother the white farm community.

The SAAU, for example, tried to limit the role of Bantu Administration Boards, fearing that business and industry would otherwise gain influence over the allocation of farm labor:

> In considering this matter, your Council took the fact into account that the only function of the Labour Control Boards was to allocate labour to farmers and that these boards consisted of farmers in the vicinity. If the functions of the Labour Control Boards were taken over by the Bantu Affairs Administration Boards, it could mean that other interested parties would have a say in the allocation of labour to the agricultural sector, which should be avoided.[60]

One Transvaal farmer, while no longer able to compel labor services, still insisted on controlling access to urban employment. He sought, for example, to curtail an African bus service that allowed the wives of farm laborers to take jobs in town. In any case, under existing legislation, the farmer indicated, "women can go to work only if the farmer agrees and under the condition that they can be recalled at the need of the employer."

60. SAAU, *Report of the General Council 1975/6*, p. 79.

In 1971, the SAAU passed on to the government a recommendation of the Transvaal Agricultural Union that "well organised" transportation services in rural areas be reconsidered. The union felt that such services gave African farm laborers a misplaced opportunity to work in nearby cities.[61]

In the end, organized agriculture opted for commodity relations, the working of a labor market, but within a rural space. The officer of the Transvaal union described such a framework.

> There is nothing to keep the worker from moving from farm A to farm B. That has to do with relations on the farm, and wages are important. The voluntary movement of labor to the city, however, that is partly controlled. If the laborer can't show that he is properly employed, then he can be stopped. They are not allowed to go to the city. But he can move from farming community to farming community.

The SAAU also sought to preserve those aspects of the racial framework that made life for African farm workers relatively less encumbered than for Africans in urban areas. The SAAU and the provincial unions, for example, urged the government to subsidize black primary schools in white rural areas ("If you don't provide a school, perhaps a clinic as well, you are going to lose your labor") and supported the growth of postprimary education there as well.[62] The SAAU successfully resisted, as it turned out, any attempt by the government to limit to 3 percent the number of African workers who might be housed in family accommodations, the rule in industrial areas. After repeated representations on the issue, the SAAU received the following reply from the Department of Agriculture: "[In the case of pure farming operations], the Department will not insist on single labourers and housing compounds. The 3% rule is, therefore, not applicable."[63]

Ten years later, the SAAU resisted a government proposal that would have prevented "contract workers" from bringing their families to white rural areas, as the government had already done regarding "contract workers" in the cities. Though the government was careful to distinguish contract workers from "farm workers," the SAAU could "not see its way clear to support the proposed amendment." The union was acutely sensitive to the advantages in the labor framework that encouraged African workers to remain on the white farms.[64]

61. SAAU, *Report of the General Council 1971/2*, p. 63.
62. SAAU, *Report of the General Council 1974/5*, p. 37.
63. SAAU, *Report of the Annual Congress 1963/4*, p. 67.
64. SAAU, *Report of the General Council 1972/3*, pp. 56–57. The Riekert Commission in 1979 proposed that white farmers not be required to expel retired African laborers from their farms, and the SAAU seemed moderately supportive of the proposal. But the government rejected the recommendation, wanting to avoid any "large–scale squatting on farms" (*Financial Mail*, 22 June 1979).

Consolidating Landholdings: Support for Separate Development

The development of capitalist agriculture ultimately led commercial farmers to step back from labor controls, indeed, to step back from state structures that monitored and regulated the lives of African laborers. A large, bottled-up African peasantry was no longer a precondition for commercial agriculture under prevailing forms of production. But the very same developments also allowed commercial farmers to head off in a very different direction: to support the dislodging of "black spots," facilitating expanded mechanization and intensive uses of farmland. Here, commercial farmers were inclined to support racial policies central to contemporary forms of racial domination. Again, Natal, with its lingering peasantry, illustrates by counterexample the course of capitalist agriculture.

Natal: "It Is Not This Union's Function to Cut Up Natal."

In Natal, where black and white agriculture had historically been intermixed and where labor tenancy had been most enduring, separate development policies had a greater impact than in other parts of South Africa. Here the antiseptic terminology, such as "land consolidation," and crude terminology, such as "black spots," brought a sweeping restructuring of rural life. Thousands of black farmers and laborers were uprooted, some entering the employ of white farmers, some entering resettlement camps in the reserves, and some simply wandering back to the reserves or other "black spots." White farmers too faced an uncertain land and boundary situation and often had to scramble to reestablish a labor force.

The Natal Agricultural Union did not share the SAAU's unqualified enthusiasm for separate development. When the Tomlinson Commission in 1952 gave renewed attention to the reserves and land purchases, the NAU reacted in horror. The African, in its view, was not up to farming outside the white man's scrutiny:

> All our sustenance comes from the soil and the biggest squanderers of the soil is the Native. On this score this Union opposes any further acquisition of land until that which is already in his possession is correctly used. The wastage of natural resources in the locations will not stop at their boundaries if ignorance and wasteful practices are not combated.[65]

The government, despite these strong entreaties from Natal, proceeded with a program of land consolidation and population removals.

The Natal Union was not above trying to gain some advantage in a bad situation. It urged the government to give high priority to removing "black

65. *NAUNLU,* 24 October 1952, p. 6.

spots" and finding resettlement areas in the state lands of Zululand. But the government "cleaned up" only a few "black spots"—465 morgen in the first decade of consolidation—concentrating instead on the purchase of white farmland. The NAU warned, "The longer the areas of Bantu in exchange for European occupants are left the larger the population thereon grows and the more difficult their removal becomes."[66] In order to "safeguard the water catchment areas," particularly the fertile Drakensberg watershed, it urged the government to "depopulate" the area in favor of a more conservation-minded, white farming community. Finally, it recommended that the whites retain all the land they occupied in Zululand and that the pattern of landownership reflect the white farmer's association with the dominant white community. The NAU insisted, for example, that "all European-owned land . . . be linked by European-occupied corridors" and the "main lines of communication, both road and rail . . . be straddled by European-owned land."[67]

While the NAU won some concessions from the government, mainly the "safeguarding of the watershed," the Union did not alter the thrust of state lands policies. In 1970, the minister of Bantu administration and development reminded the NAU that while the department had a "gentleman's agreement . . . in regard to consultation on land exchanges in Natal," it was free to "go ahead in light of what [the minister] thought best," regardless of the NAU's opposition.[68] By 1972, the NAU was refusing to submit proposals for land consolidation; worse yet, it began speaking disparagingly of the whole enterprise. "There has been far too much loose talk about the essentiality of consolidation," the president of the NAU declared. "A little thought reveals that a combining into one block makes sense, but more than that breaches the validity of the concept."[69] The NAU told the government, "It is not this Union's function to cut up Natal."[70] The government's proposals would "move hundreds of thousands of people, with disruption to all," and to what end?[71] Finally, the deputy minister of Bantu affairs complained in Parliament, "The NAU came forward with certain proposals and we asked them for further proposals, but none was forthcoming." The Council of the NAU was blunt in its reply: "This was intentional on our part. As our President explained in a message in *Naunlu* on 9th June 1972,

66. *NAUNLU*, July 1967, p. 31.
67. P. C. Reyburn, "Natal," *Organized Agriculture*, March 1962, p. 28; see also *NAUNLU*, 12 June 1970, p. 3.
68. Quoted in *NAUNLU*, 26 June 1970, p. 1.
69. Quoted in *NAUNLU*, 15 September 1972, p. 3.
70. Ibid.
71. *NAUNLU*, 18 August 1972, p. 5; Natal Agricultural Union (NAU), *Annual Report 1971/2*.

it is Council's view that it is not for this Union to suggest which land should be acquired by the government in the execution of its policy."[72]

Cooperating in Land Consolidation

The government and the SAAU, on the other hand, moved hand in hand on the development of land-consolidation policies. "It has always been the Government's policy to acknowledge organised agriculture in this connection," the minister of Bantu affairs and development stated in 1962, "although the law does not demand that the Government should consult farmer organizations or divisional councils about the purchase of land."[73] Together, they helped sort out the "black spots" that should be "cleared," the land scheduled for purchase, the boundaries to be drawn, even the fences to be constructed.[74] While in the seventies the SAAU began to grumble about the slow pace of land consolidation and the need for "buffer zones" and economic farming units, it remained committed to the general principles of the policy and continued to cooperate in its implementation. In 1972 and 1973, the SAAU made concerted representations to the government, urging it to move rapidly on land purchases and to aim for "maximum consolidation" of the black and white areas.[75] Though the government had been more cautious and inconsistent than the SAAU would have preferred, the process of consultation and shared decision making remained fully intact. The officer of the Transvaal union commented on the extent of the cooperation: "We handle this [land consolidation] for the government. They contacted us in 1973 and 1974, and we contacted all our affiliates. I can assure you that the government will not sell one farm without contacting the agricultural union."

The European farmer, steeped in squatters, labor tenants, and "a thicket of pass and vagrancy laws," fought perhaps a century-long struggle to avoid the logic of wage labor. Wage and unfree labor never worked well together and, without growing state intervention, would have disrupted or transformed South Africa's rural economy. In the 1930s, white farmers demanded stricter control over the obligations and movements of labor tenants: they got the Native Service Contract Act in 1932 and Chapter IV of the Native Trust and Land Act in 1936. In the 1940s, white farmers demanded an impenetrable barrier between the rural and urban labor

72. NAU (Council), *Annual Report 1971/2*, p. 5.
73. Cited in *Organized Agriculture*, August 1962, p. 25.
74. SAAU, *Report of the General Council 1960/61*, p. 58; *1963/4*, p. 67; *1966/7*, p. 59.
75. SAAU, *Report of the General Council 1973/4*, pp. 39–41; see also SAAU, *Report of the General Council 1971/2*, p. 19.

forces: they got the Natives (Urban Areas) Consolidation Act in 1945 and the Native Laws Amendment Act in 1952. Above all, in 1948 they got a National party government. With the Nationalist ascendancy, they found a government committed to refining the system of labor controls and, in apartheid, an ideology consonant with the white farmer's ideas on race and unfree labor. This transition to capitalist agriculture has dominated the South African rural economy and racial order in this century.

The transition seemed to run its course only when the white farmer, dependent on wage labor and tractors, began to release his grip on the African rural laborer. Labor-repressive agriculture has not been dismantled: pass laws and labor bureaus still figure prominently in the lives of African laborers and white farmers alike; European farmers have not yet submitted themselves to an unfettered labor market. But the white farmer no longer requires and, more important, no longer demands that the traditional labor controls be refined and the enforcement mechanisms expanded. Indeed, with few complaints of "labor shortages" and growing demands for "economic farming," the SAAU has begun to yield on the traditional concerns of the white farming community: the masters and servants laws fell with hardly a whimper; the pass laws and the labor bureaus, the system of labor controls, are diminishing concerns for white farmers and the SAAU.

What impact will these changes have on the racial order? They probably will not lead European farmers to abandon their racism. A substantial majority of farm leaders from the agricultural unions, cooperatives, and marketing boards advocate rigid segregation on buses, in bathrooms, residential areas, and union membership. An overwhelming majority insist on the maintenance of a white Parliament and belong to the National party.[76]

European farmers probably will not abandon "grand *apartheid.*" Plans for consolidation and formation of African homelands are fully consistent with more intensive land uses and the dependence on wage labor. Indeed, the traditional black-and-white mosaic, characteristic of the South African countryside in the nineteenth century and first half of the twentieth, may be an impediment to capitalist agriculture. The change, however, does allow for two important developments in the rural economy that may affect the nature and survival of the racial order.

First, with the decline of labor-repressive agriculture and the loosening of the political connection, commercial farmers may themselves lose political standing and the ability to shape the racial order. There is evidence that the

76. These results are derived from a leadership survey conducted under the auspices of the Centre for Inter-Group Studies in 1968 and 1969. Hendrik van der Merwe was kind enough to provide me with office space at the Centre and access to the original questionnaires.

erosion has already begun. By the late sixties, the manufacturers' three-decade assault on the agricultural cooperatives had begun to bear fruit. The courts questioned the traditional privileges of the cooperatives, and the government established the first serious inquiry into the whole question of agricultural assistance and marketing. The SAAU correctly interpreted these developments as "a direct attack on the right of the producer to market his own produce and benefit from the savings."[77] The government went further, urging a cutback in the granting of "indiscriminate" aid and the entrenching of inefficiency.[78] Finally, even Afrikaner businessmen began questioning the level of state assistance and the size of the agricultural bureaucracy, suggesting that "industry as the greatest basic wealth creator deserves this preferential treatment and assurances from the authorities." The government decision in 1971 permitting the sale of yellow margarine, like similar decisions in western Europe and North America, signaled the political decline of commercial farming.[79]

Second, with the decline of labor-repressive agriculture and the spread of labor markets, white farmers may step back from some of their traditional concerns: they have less need of the conventional racial categories and repressive ideas and ideologies; they have less need of a state committed to controlling the movements of African laborers. The white farmers may not abandon the racial order, but their identification with it, so complete and profound during the past century, may lack the conviction and imperatives that accompanied the prolonged and tumultuous transition to capitalist agriculture.

77. *Georganiseerde Landbou,* February 1967, p. 7.
78. Republic of South Africa, *Third Final Report of the Commission of Enquiry into Agriculture,* R.P. 19–1972, pp. 100–03; see discussion of the Marais-Du Plessis Commission in A. W. Stadler, "Agricultural Policy and Agrarian Politics"; and Merle Lipton, "White Farming: A Case History of Change in South Africa," pp. 17–20.
79. David Welsh, "The Political Economy of Afrikaner Nationalism," p. 264.

CHAPTER 6

Race and Rural Economy in Alabama

In South Africa, white farmers settled in the western Cape, then pushed north toward the Orange River and east toward the Fish; later, they settled the high veld of the Orange Free State and the Transvaal and the valleys and coastal plains of Natal. In the process, they intruded on the pastoral and mixed farming communities among the Khoikhoi and Africans and brought a large slave population from Indonesia and East Africa. The European settlers created a form of subsistent and nomadic farming with limited trading and a class of servile laborers, slaves and servants at first, and later, "apprentices" and squatters. They responded to expanding commercialization by intruding further on the African subsistence economy, intensifying labor services and, most important, limiting labor mobility. Their path to capitalist agriculture was strewn with coercive state measures, including hut taxes, land expropriations, pass laws, and labor bureaus. The shift from squatters to labor tenancy to wage labor brought increasing efforts to circumvent the market in labor. In the process, commercial farmers established a close identification with a state-repressive structure and helped elaborate the racial order.

At the center of Alabama's post-Civil War agricultural economy were landowners and commercial farmers who, like their South African counterparts, depended upon a large rural laboring population and responded to the threat of labor markets by expanding the meaning of unfree labor. White slaveowners had monopolized landownership in a Black Belt across central Alabama and, in effect, the production and marketing of cotton. The Civil War and emancipation, however, had brought an end to slavery and, for a short period, threatened land patterns and labor supplies in the Black Belt. But landowners weathered Radical Reconstruction and, against an uncertain labor environment and growing demands of primary industries, evolved a variety of extramarket mechanisms for forestalling independent black farming and retaining black laborers and tenants. In the process, Black Belt commercial farmers helped to establish political control over the black population and to draw race lines in the society.

State and race weighed heavily upon rural society in Alabama, creating what Barrington Moore, Jr. in other contexts aptly labels a "labor repressive agricultural system." If Moore is correct in his analysis, the system should not easily give up authoritarian institutions in favor of democratic ones.[1] And if our analysis of the German and South African examples is correct, the system and society should not easily lose their racial character.

That analysis and projection are not uncontested, however. Stephen DeCanio, for one, points out numerous recorded instances in the post-bellum period of labor mobility, labor shortages, and planter competition for black farm labor. He notes that wages for farm labor tended to rise immediately after the war and perhaps even exceeded the value of black labor's marginal product. There were, of course, widespread efforts to intimidate blacks, collude on black farm wages, impose labor contracts, and force labor, and DeCanio does not neglect them: "The various repressive laws and acts of violence perpetrated against blacks were indeed wide-spread." But in the absence of evidence that wages were held down below the marginal productivity of labor, it is difficult to conclude that these measures were "instruments of economic exploitation in the labor market." We are left with an agricultural system that, for all its faults, was only lamely "labor repressive" and was incapable of providing the "basis of the Southern legal and social climate."[2]

An analysis that concentrates on wage levels or even on the effectiveness of control measures misses the dynamic underlying labor-repressive agriculture and the racial order. The mobility and "high" price of black labor and the attempts to limit mobility and reduce wages are two sides of the same process. It is not the *fact of control* alone that undermines democracy and exacerbates racial divisions. It is the *attempt to maintain control* in the face of a developing market for labor that has such profound consequences for society. Just as the antebellum South could not escape the low productivity of black slave labor[3] and the fact that a slave was not mere property but a "man held down by force,"[4] the postbellum South could not readily escape the contradiction between the black man's "freedom" and the landlord's contempt for it. That tension brought a recurrent planter insistence on coercive state measures and racial disabilities. That those efforts did not

---

1. See Barrington Moore, Jr., *Social Origins of Dictatorship and Democracy,* pp. 434–35.
2. Stephen J. DeCanio, *Agriculture in the Postbellum South: The Economics of Production and Supply,* pp. 13, 16–119, 170–71. For an excellent discussion of the literature on labor markets after the Civil War, see Harold D. Woodman, "Sequel to Slavery: The New History Views the Postbellum South."
3. Eugene Genovese, *The Political Economy of Slavery,* pp. 43–69.
4. David Brion Davis, *The Problem of Slavery in Western Culture,* p. 261.

eliminate the labor market, the lure of employment elsewhere, or independent black farming only insured that planters would not relax their vigilance over the racial order.

In this chapter, I describe the development of commercial agriculture after the Civil War and the construction of a labor framework, one that brought an historic association between the freedman, unfree labor, and the Black Belt. I examine the development of coercive mechanisms at the county and state governmental levels that narrowed the workings of the labor market. Finally, I consider the organization of commercial farmers, primarily in the Black Belt, which stood behind the racial order in the 1950s and 1960s, even as the rural economy moved away from cotton sharecropping and black labor and as the society faced increasing political disorder. In the end, with only remnants of a black peasantry, with mechanization and larger farming units, commercial farmers could afford to watch the dismantling of the racial order.

THE TRANSITION TO CAPITALIST AGRICULTURE

Agricultural Development

Agricultural development in Alabama after the Civil War was organized around a staple, inedible "money crop": cotton. In retrospect, that the South and Alabama turned to cotton does not seem very startling. Cotton was intimately associated with slavery and plantation life, and the northern and European cotton markets were as strong after the war as before. But there were serious impediments to the revival of cotton agriculture. Plantation owners had difficulty imagining that blacks with the collapse of the work gang and overseer supervision, would pick cotton or that blacks could comprehend the "responsibilities" and "freedom" of a labor market. The freed slaves, on the other hand, wanted their own land and were uncertain about cotton. They watched with some anticipation the work of Thaddeus Stevens and the federal land policies that had given freedmen land on the Sea Islands off South Carolina and on the coast, and in the area of the St. Johns River in Florida. They were reluctant, consequently, to return to the plantations or take out labor contracts.[5] Though white tenant farmers and small landowners showed some interest in cotton production, it remained a "cash crop," supplementary and subordinate to vegetables, hogs, and staple

5. Oscar Zeichner, "The Transition from Slave to Free Agricultural Labor in the Southern States," pp. 23–25.

crops like corn.[6] Neither did "coolie labor" or white immigrants show much interest in coming to Alabama to revive cotton's fortunes.

But cotton's fortunes were revived, though at the expense of the traditional organization of production and, to some extent, at the expense of the black man's freedom.[7] The system soon came to depend on family labor and varying forms of tenancy.[8] Cotton was no longer produced on large plantations but on smaller farming units, averaging just over 125 acres in size, under the control and supervision of large landowners, many of whom retained their land from the antebellum period.[9] By 1880, cotton production in the Black Belt had reached 275,000 bales, up from the 150,000 produced in 1870; and by 1890, it had reached 375,000 bales, just short of antebellum levels. Cotton production also picked up in the area south of the mineral district and the wire grass area in the southeast, but the Black Belt, with its dark soil and black population, with more than 40 percent of total cotton production, still remained the principal cotton-producing area.[10]

Cotton's revival came at the expense of other crops and a more diverse southern agriculture. In the absence of seasonal credit and a sound banking system in the South, farmers turned to merchants and "crop liens." The merchants and landlords almost always insisted on cotton production and gave credit only against a cotton crop.[11] Cotton's revival also came at the expense of merchants and industrial interests: the former, as landlords, established the pre-eminence of their liens, and the latter, as Black Belt representatives, helped eliminate the Office of Industrial Resources, limited internal improvements, and shifted their tax burden to manufacturers.[12]

The postbellum agricultural system, with its principal commercial crop, concentrated land ownership, small farming units, rudimentary mechanization, and crop liens, survived nearly a half century, until the boll weevil, exhausted soil, and depression began to take their toll. The first signs of decay emerged around World War I: the boll weevil entered the Mississippi

6. Albert Burton Moore, *History of Alabama*, p. 277.

7. This latter issue will be considered in more detail in the next section.

8. Roger L. Ransom and Richard Sutch, "The Ex-Slave in the Post-Bellum South: A Study of the Economic Impact of Racism in a Market Environment," pp. 131–34; also see appendix B.

9. Jonathan Wiener states: "What occured was not the 'downfall' or destruction of the old planter class, but rather their persistence and metamorphosis" ("Planter-Merchant Conflict in Reconstruction Alabama," p. 73). See also Jonathan M. Wiener, "Planter Persistence and Social Change: Alabama, 1850–1870."

10. Horace Mann Bond, *Negro Education in Alabama: A Study in Cotton and Steel*, p. 123; also see appendix B, table II.C.3 for the period after 1900.

11. Roger L. Ransom and Richard Sutch, "Debt Peonage in the Cotton South After the Civil War," pp. 644–45, 651–54, 656.

12. Wiener, "Planter-Merchant Conflict," pp. 80–89; Allen Johnston Going, *Bourbon Democracy in Alabama 1874–1890*, p. 111.

Black Belt around 1910 and reached cotton-growing and black farming areas of Alabama just two years later;[13] during the war, blacks began to take up employment opportunities in northern cities. Still, cotton acreage, production, and employment were maintained until at least 1930.[14] But the Depression years brought out the system's "decadence." One observer of the Georgia Black Belt wrote its epitaph:

> The decadence of this civilization is far advanced. The fertility of much of the soil has been mined away. Most of the fine old houses have fallen into disrepair. Many of the resourceful descendants of the more influential families have abandoned these rural areas, as have many of the more alert farm tenants. Poverty, illiteracy, undernourishment handicap most of those who remain.[15]

The boll weevil, agricultural depression, and now the federal government intruded deeply on the old relations and agricultural forms. The Agricultural Adjustment Administration (AAA) and Bankhead Cotton Control Act, for example, encouraged landowners to plow up thousands of acres of Black Belt land; in the interest of "soil conservation" and higher prices, they also encouraged them to get rid of their tenants and croppers.[16]

It is difficult to select the exact time when "decadence" becomes indistinguishable from "collapse" and a new form of agriculture takes over.[17] In the South as a whole, cotton production, which contributed almost half the value of agricultural products before the Depression, provided only one quarter by 1950.[18] In Alabama, cotton acreage declined during the Depression and continued downward even when the rest of Alabama's agriculture joined the general upswing during and after World War II.[19] Cotton production dropped precipitously during the Depression and again in the sixties.[20] By the early sixties, the farms provided barely 6 percent of total income; cotton accounted for a mere 1.5 percent.[21] The 3.5 million acres planted in cotton during the early part of the century, which

13. Bond, *Negro Education in Alabama*, pp. 226–27.
14. *The Blue Book of Southern Progress*, p. 120; see appendix B, table II.C.3.
15. Will W. Alexander, "Foreword," to Arthur F. Raper, *Preface to Peasantry*, p. xiv.
16. They also provided a very substantial inducement to turn croppers into wage laborers, but that issue will be discussed in the next section. See George B. Tindall, *The Emergence of the New South 1913–1945*, pp. 396–404, 409; Gunnar Myrdal, *An American Dilemma: The Negro Problem and Modern Democracy*, vol. 1, pp. 232–35, 255–61.
17. The researchers of the Georgia Interracial Commission wrote of the "collapse of cotton tenancy" in 1935, for example (Charles S. Johnson, Edwin R. Embree, and W. W. Alexander, *The Collapse of Cotton Tenancy*).
18. B. U. Ratchford, "Patterns of Economic Development," p. 220.
19. *Blue Book of Southern Progress*, p. 120.
20. See appendix B, table II.C.3.
21. Alabama Business Research Council, *Transition in Alabama*, p. 1.

had justified such awe and the appellation "King Cotton," shrank by 1970 to 563,000 acres—and most of them *outside* the Black Belt.[22] The system of cotton tenancy had given way to large units of production: Black Belt farms began increasing in size from the mid-thirties, suddenly increased by 50 percent during the fifties, and nearly doubled between 1963 and 1974.[23] The system had also given way to soybeans and cattle and, as we shall see, to wage labor.

Changing Labor Forms

Both the freedman and the former slaveowner faced an uncertain labor environment after the Civil War. The freedman was torn between an array of uncertain opportunities: moving to Mississippi, where wages were higher; accepting a wage contract on the plantation; trying his luck in the small cities; or simply waiting for land, supported in the meantime by pilfering and Union Army rations. The former slaveowner wanted to keep his labor but was uncertain about the terms and the emerging market in labor. In the confusion, he often turned to a variety of coercive measures. In Mississippi, Vernon Wharton writes, the landowners and employers turned to "irregular courts, the breaking up of crowds of Negroes waiting for boats, the arrest of emigrants on charges of vagrancy and of obtaining goods under false pretences and the beating and kidnaping of Negro leaders."[24] Across the Black Belt, landowners harassed labor agents, urged laws against vagrancy and laws for the apprenticing of minor children, prevented blacks from acquiring property, and, through violence and intimidation, forced blacks to take out labor contracts.[25]

Still, the mixture of markets, coercion, and uncertainty brought out a mixture of labor forms in the immediate postbellum period. Some landowners and blacks opted for the "standing wage system," a form of wage labor that allowed money payments only after a six-month or twelve-month period of service. The landowners, at least, preferred these "contracts" to daily wages that left black laborers free to move on before the cotton crop was picked. Others turned to a "part-standing-wage system," which provided for monthly money payments, supplemented by three or four acres of land for subsistence cultivation.[26] Perhaps the least enduring labor form was

22. Neal R. Peirce, *The Deep South States of America*, p. 267; see appendix B, table II.C.3.
23. University of Alabama, Center for Business and Economic Research, *Economic Abstract of Alabama, 1963*, p. 155; *1966*, p. 176; and *1972*, p. 197; also appendix B, table II.C.1–2.
24. Vernon Lane Wharton, *The Negro in Mississippi 1865–1890*, pp. 114–15.
25. Zeichner, "The Transition from Slave to Free Agricultural Labor," pp. 26–27; Wharton, *The Negro in Mississippi*, pp. 84–85.
26. Thomas J. Edwards, "The Tenant System and Some Changes Since Emancipation," pp. 20–21; also Woodman, "Sequel to Slavery," p. 551.

the "four-day plan": for access to implements and land two days a week, the black tenant was obligated to provide at least four days of labor services in the landlord's fields. By 1880, almost one-third of the former slaves were employed as wage laborers.[27]

The most enduring alternative, however, was a nonwage, dependent labor form: the share system. More than half of all black farmers in 1880 rented land by committing some share of their crop to the landlord; in the Black Belt and cotton areas, the percentage was undoubtedly higher.[28]

It may have been inevitable that the "free" black laborer would get caught up in some dependent labor form. He entered the labor market without experience as an independent farmer, with no capital or farm implements and virtually no political and civil rights. A small number, probably fewer than one in ten, managed to buy their own farms,[29] but most, without access to credit or land, preferred to enter into sharecropping arrangements. Here, black laborers seemed to escape the worst abuses of the gang system but, nonetheless, faced landlord supervision over most farming practices, including methods of cultivation and fertilizing, and oversight of the property and the "regularity of labor."[30] For the right to plant and cultivate a cotton crop, they paid the landlord somewhere between one-third and one-half of their crop, depending upon who provided the mules, fertilizer, and equipment.[31]

The dependent aspects were apparent in the generalized imbalance between landlord and tenant: on the one side was the land, capital, and state: to the other side was labor, circumscribed by its race, poverty, and political impotence. "Hence," Gunnar Myrdal writes, "a most inequitable type of tenancy fixed itself upon the South."[32] But the dependency also took specific forms: the weight of laws and credit arrangements that impinged on the cropper's freedom and remuneration. First, there were the "false pretense laws," used widely in Alabama, which required the faithful carrying out of labor contracts under threat of criminal sanctions. A sharecropper who abandoned his fields faced imprisonment and forfeited his entire interest in the crop.[33] Second, there were the "crop liens" and "lien

---

27. Ransom and Sutch, "The Ex-Slave in the Post-Bellum South," pp. 137–38.
28. Ibid.
29. Ibid. Wooman argues that wage aspects were important even within the share system by the turn of the century. That status represents a change in access to land and share in supervision over production but not an opening up of the labor market ("Sequel to Slavery," pp. 552–53).
30. Oscar Zeichner, "The Legal Status of the Agricultural Laborer in the South," pp. 420–21.
31. DeCanio, *Agriculture in the Postbellum South,* pp. 282–83.
32. Myrdal, *An American Dilemma,* p. 227.
33. The United States Supreme Court declared the Alabama law unconstitutional in 1911 (Zeichner, "The Legal Status of the Agricultural Laborer," pp. 42–45).

laws," also well established in Alabama, which usually encumbered the cotton crop and left the sharecropper at the mercy of merchants and landowners. "Fancy prices at the commisary, exorbitant interest, and careless or manipulated accounts," the authors of *The Collapse of Cotton Tenancy* conclude, "make it easy for the owner to keep his tenants constantly in debt." In the early thirties, their study found, a third of the tenants had debts of more than a year's standing. In Alabama, the average tenant's indebtedness was eighty dollars.[34] The combination of law and debt produced, by one account, a "preface to peasantry"[35] and, by another, a "system of peonage."[36] For Booker T. Washington, the labor framework "binds" the black man, "robs him of independence, allures him and winds him deeper and deeper in its meshes each year till he is lost and bewildered."[37]

The system of dependent sharecropping survived into the fifties, perhaps as a remnant into the early sixties, though its deterioration was apparent during the Depression. Already by 1920, blacks in the Alabama Black Belt, who made up 92 percent of farm tenants and sharecroppers, had begun leaving in favor of the mineral district and other urban areas.[38] By 1930, the relative and absolute position of sharecroppers had begun to slip across the cotton South; wage laborers, traditionally on the margins of the rural economy, began to figure more prominently.[39] The boll weevil, the inefficiencies of cotton tenancy, and the AAA had each taken their toll. The last encouraged a reduction in cotton acreage and number of tenants; the local program, under the control of the planters themselves, provided cash payments that mainly accrued to landlords rather than sharecroppers.[40] But cotton sharecropping gave ground not just to bugs and acreage allotments. The inefficiencies and enormous labor requirements of cotton agriculture contrasted sharply with the mechanization in other farm activities and crops. "Tractors and sharecroppers do not go together because of inefficiency in labor use," one author observed. "Either the tractor or the sharecropper must go."[41] With their AAA cash payments in hand and with rising demand for agricultural products during World War II, Black Belt landlords began their own transition to modern and capitalist farming. Tractors were introduced into cotton operations, particularly land breaking and

34. Johnson et al., *The Collapse of Cotton Tenancy,* pp. 9–12.
35. Raper, *Preface to Peasantry.*
36. Thomas D. Clark, *The South Since Reconstruction,* p. 93; Ransom and Sutch, "Debt Peonage in the Cotton South."
37. Quoted in Pete Daniel, *The Shadow of Slavery: Peonage in the South 1901–1969,* p. ix.
38. Bond, *Negro Education in Alabama,* pp. 228–36.
39. John Leonard Fulmer, *Agricultural Progress in the Cotton Belt Since 1920,* p. 171.
40. Johnson et al., *The Collapse of Cotton Tenancy,* pp. 48–52.
41. Fulmer, *Agricultural Progress in the Cotton Belt,* pp. 61, 171.

harrowing, but also planting and cultivating.[42] In the decade following the war, the number of tractors in the Alabama Black Belt increased threefold, from 2,153 to 6,404, and increased by almost 40 percent between 1959 and 1969. Cotton gave way to yet more mechanized and less labor-intensive farming operations: soybeans, cattle, and poultry. And the sharecropper and black population, they too gave way, sometimes leaving the soil for relief projects and the cities, sometimes making the transition to wage labor. The number of black tenants in the Black Belt decreased steadily from the mid-thirties; the Black Belt population began to drop precipitously in the fifties.[43]

LABOR REPRESSION: THE STATE AND THE LABOR MARKET

Both slavery and dependent sharecropping depended upon a state and political climate that facilitated controls over farm labor. In the antebellum period, those controls were incorporated into the "slave codes" and enforced by a "rudimentary state." The Alabama Slave Code of 1852 provided, for example, that a slave carry a pass when away from the plantation "or some letter or token from his master or overseer"; that no more than five slaves be allowed to "assemble together at any place off the plantation," with or without passes; and that patrols "disperse all such unlawful assemblies."[44] In the absence of effective state regulation and monitoring, the system depended on the slaves' illiteracy: the codes provided stiff penalties for anyone teaching a slave to "read, spell, or write."[45] State regulation came in the form of frontier-type police patrols. Poor whites, overseers, and slaveowners alike rode with these patrols, guarding against slave insurrections and punishing slaves who failed to abide by the codes.[46]

The state role in the labor market after the war was considerably more problematic. On the one hand, black labor was more mobile and less clearly hampered by lack of political rights and the smothering paternalism of the plantation; on the other hand, the state, at least for a short period, had slipped from "planter" control and had uncertain constitutional and

42. Ibid., p. 63.
43. Tindall, *The Emergence of the New South,* p. 432; see appendix B, table II.C.1–3.
44. "Alabama Slave Code of 1852," reprinted in Lucille Griffith, *Alabama: A Documentary History to 1900,* pp. 155–57.
45. Moore, *History of Alabama,* p. 377; Eugene Genovese, *Roll, Jordan, Roll: The World the Slaves Made,* pp. 561–62.
46. Genovese, *Roll, Jordan, Roll,* pp. 617–18; W. E. B. DuBois, *Black Reconstruction in America 1860–1880,* pp. 12, 27.

effective powers over the movements of "free" labor. Indeed, planters never managed to fetter the black man as chattel. DeCanio presents a persuasive compilation of cases where blacks refused labor contracts, responded to wage inducements, and moved away to take up nonagricultural occupations.[47] But the mobility and humanity of black labor did not keep planters from trying repeatedly to master the "labor problem," from using the state and the racial climate to limit the mobility of black labor. That the solutions continually fell short of the problem only heightened the need for vigilance.

The "black codes" provided the initial planter response to the labor market, though they soon fell before Reconstruction governments in Alabama and elsewhere. But while they survived, the black codes provided an insight into the planters' lack of regard for "free wage labor." Whether Alabama's codes were "one of the most severe in the south," as DuBois maintains, or "less severe than those in other states," as William Warren Rogers maintains, they certainly contained the standard provisions about vagrancy, apprenticing children, and enticing labor.[48] They allowed county committees, particularly in the Black Belt, to impose a "uniform system of labor" and inspect labor contracts.[49] After Reconstruction, the Bourbon governments, out of necessity, moved more cautiously on the labor question but, nonetheless, sought to take hold of the problem. The system of dependent sharecropping, Horace Mann Bond maintains, could not have been created without the "control over legislation in the State, and over the police power locally."[50] The post-Reconstruction governments first attempted to limit the freedman's opportunities off the plantation and outside the Black Belt. State action on land sales, credit, and marketing discouraged blacks from turning to independent farming; limits on relief and rations, as in Mississippi, discouraged blacks from remaining idle; and taxes imposed on labor agents in fourteen Black Belt counties sought to conceal employment opportunities available outside of Alabama.[51]

The state government also attempted to bind black laborers to their contracts and the land. The lien law of 1866 gave creditors, merchants and landlords in particular, first claim on the cotton crop, preceding the claim of the tenant farmer who planted and harvested it. By the late seventies, a series of amendments shifted these claims in favor of the landlords at the expense of both merchants and tenants: the landlord's lien was "superior to

47. DeCanio, *Agriculture in the Postbellum South*, pp. 51–76.
48. DuBois, *Black Reconstruction*, pp. 175, 487–88; William Warren Rogers, *The One-Gallused Rebellion: Agrarianism in Alabama, 1865–1896*, pp. 8–9.
49. Rogers, *The One-Gallused Rebellion*, p. 9.
50. Bond, *Negro Education in Alabama*, p. 121.
51. Going, *Bourbon Democracy in Alabama*, pp. 96–99; Wharton, *The Negro in Mississippi*, p. 96; Ransom and Sutch, "The Ex-Slave in the Post-Bellum South," pp. 139–44.

all other liens, for rent and advances made" to tenants.[52] In any event, landlords and tenants came to live with the system, the former because they gained some control over black labor, the latter because they gained access to credit markets.[53] The "false pretenses" law of 1885, amended in 1903, provided criminal penalties for breach of contract. It thus sought to circumvent the United States Constitution and federal laws against debt peonage and debt slavery. Under the law, laborers and tenants who received salary advances, as was customary in Alabama, and left their jobs prematurely were guilty, "prima facie," of "intent to injure or defraud their employers." All contract laborers, consequently, worked with a jail sentence, indeed with the prospect of convict labor, hanging over their heads.[54]

At the local level, the state—an amorphous collection of mayors, county officials, sheriffs, justices of the peace, judges, and election officials—became an agent of labor control or, at the very least, practiced a studied indifference to the impositions on black labor. During the immediate postwar period, local officials across the state, but particularly in the Black Belt, searched the homes of blacks, confiscating shotguns, muskets, and pistols.[55] They did little to forestall the individual and mob violence that drove blacks from "independent farming" and forced them to take out labor contracts.[56] The state's involvement in "debt peonage" and "dependent sharecropping," however, was more deliberate. In both cases, control over black labor was maintained through "local custom" and "local law enforcement." Four groups of "conspirators," Pete Daniel argues—the plantation owners, constables, justices of the peace, and plantation overseers—channeled black laborers to the white farms and forced them to remain there. Contrived and real debts, petty offences and frame-ups became instruments for organizing a labor force. Court records at the turn of the century confirm that "debt peonage" was widely practiced in Coosa and Tallapoosa counties, just north of the Black Belt. There is also suggestive evidence that the heart of the system was in Lowndes, Dallas, and other Black Belt counties; widespread intimidation and violence, however, successfully blocked investigation in these areas.[57] Debt, "false pretense"

52. Quoted in Wiener, "Planter-Merchant Conflict," p. 88.
53. Rogers, *The One-Gallused Rebellion,* pp. 12–17; Going, *Bourbon Democracy in Alabama,* pp. 93–95; Ransom and Sutch, "Debt Peonage in the Cotton South," pp. 653–54; Wiener, "Planter-Merchant Conflict," pp. 80–93.
54. Daniel, *The Shadow of Slavery,* pp. 66–67; Zeichner, "The Legal Status of the Agricultural Laborer," pp. 424–25. In *Bailey v. Alabama,* 211 U.S. 452 (1911), the United States Supreme Court declared the law unconstitutional.
55. Dubois, *Black Reconstruction,* p. 489; also see Wharton, *The Negro in Mississippi,* p. 88.
56. DuBois, *Black Reconstruction,* p. 674; Zeichner, "The Transition from Slave to Free Agricultural Labor," pp. 26–27.
57. Daniel, *The Shadow of Slavery,* pp. 43–64.

laws, and local officialdom were critical to sharecropping: they helped landowners keep their labor force through the growing season and encouraged laborers to "renew" their contracts. The courts and local constables could usually be counted upon to "enforce" both custom and law and ignore day-to-day "intimidation" essential to the working of the labor system.[58]

The question of labor control was inseparable from the question of the black franchise. Black Belt farmers retained their disproportionate influence at the level of state government and their monopoly over the local judiciary and county offices only by manipulating and limiting the black vote. Without that control, Black Belt whites believed, their ascendancy would be threatened and their black laborers set free. The franchise, therefore, became the first battleground for white supremacy and the labor framework.

In 1874, white voters in Alabama overthrew the Reconstruction and Republican regime, giving the Democrats control over both houses of the legislature and the governorship. Black voters were kept from the polls by widespread riots, shootings, and fraud;[59] in Mississippi, Wharton writes, "after each resulting riot Negro resistance to white domination in the surrounding area completely collapsed."[60] By 1880, Democrats were in full control of the elections and county governments.[61] The Black Belt became a crucible for voter manipulation: Democratic party control of the sheriffs, probate judges, and election inspectors left whites free to tamper with election returns and intimidate black voters. Of the ninety-two congressional elections between 1875 and 1891 contested because of voting irregularities, ten originated in Alabama, and most of these in the Fourth Congressional District—the Black Belt.[62] In seven cases where blacks and Republicans could not be driven from office, the governor abolished the counties and appointed Democratic officials to oversee elections and administer local government.[63]

Through such manipulations, black "voters" repeatedly helped elect the candidates of the white-supremacist Democratic party. Indeed, the pattern of fraud and intimidation proved more successful in Alabama than in any other southern state, save Georgia.[64] With the black vote well in hand, the Democrats beat off strong, successive challenges by the Alliance, the

---

58. See the discussion of this issue in another Black Belt setting in Allison Davis, Burleigh B. Gardner, and Mary R. Gardner, *Deep South,* pp. 225–29, 296–311.
59. Going, *Bourbon Democracy,* pp. 16–18.
60. Wharton, *The Negro in Mississippi,* p. 190.
61. C. Vann Woodward, *Origins of the New South,* p. 84.
62. Going, *Bourbon Democracy,* p. 38.
63. Ibid., pp. 33–35.
64. J. Morgan Kousser, *The Shaping of Southern Politics,* p. 28.

Jeffersonian Democrats, and Populists, all of whom made direct appeals for the support of black voters.[65] The Black Belt gave up the black franchise and its controlled black vote only after nearly losing these elections and only when persuaded that disenfranchisement would also adversely affect poorer whites. The Constitutional Convention of 1901, following the lead of most other southern states, proposed a literacy test, poll tax, property test, and grandfather clause. In the subsequent referendum, poorer whites in northern Alabama turned down the proposals; the black "voters" of the Black Belt, on the other hand, voted themselves and a large number of poorer whites out of politics.[66]

The 1901 constitution also included a legislative apportionment that counted the now nonexistent black voters and thus heavily favored the Black Belt whites. That apportionment survived unchanged, despite major population shifts in favor of north Alabama and the mineral district, until the federal courts intervened six decades later, in 1962.[67]

THE ALABAMA FARM BUREAU:
MAINTAINING RACIAL DOMINATION

To a considerable extent, Black Belt farmers had relied directly on the state to maintain the racial order and their class position. Legislators from the Black Belt, free to ignore the black and voteless majority of the population, regularly acted to prop up the position of Black Belt farmers, cotton, rural landowners, and whites—perhaps in that order. On simple economic questions, the legislators supported minimum taxes on farmland: both in the late nineteenth century, when they constructed and defended a tax structure favoring large property owners, and in the 1960s, when after seven years of difficult struggle with business and urban interests, they passed a constitutional amendment taxing farmland on 15 percent of its value but business and utilities at 25 and 30 percent, respectively.[68] On simple political issues, the legislators could be counted upon, whether in 1902 or 1962, to defend the Black Belt's disproportionate representation in the state legislature. No other issue in the 1950s, one researcher argues, more clearly set off the Black Belt and rural legislators from the remainder of the state.[69]

65. Rogers, *The One-Gallused Rebellion*, pp. 213–22, 237–43, 283–85.
66. Kousser, *The Shaping of Southern Politics*, pp. 60, 65, 229, 241; Woodward, *Origins of the New South*, pp. 341–42; V. O. Key, *Southern Politics*, pp. 545–46.
67. Peirce, *The Deep South States*, pp. 246, 293.
68. Sheldon Hackney, *Populism to Progressivism in Alabama*, pp. 139–41; and interview with an officer of the Alabama Farm Bureau.
69. Murray Clark Havens, *City Versus Farm? Urban-Rural Conflict in the Alabama Legislature*, pp. 30–31.

When civil rights issues resurfaced in the 1950s and 1960s, the legislature, with Black Belt legislators in the lead, sought to suppress black political organization and limit the black franchise. In 1956, the legislators in two Black Belt counties, Wilcox and Marengo, passed, over urban opposition, two bills limiting the rights of labor and civil rights organizations. They provided for a $100 a year organization license fee and a levy of $5 on each member.[70] In 1961 and 1963, Black Belt legislators provided the principal backing for the Un-American Activities Resolution. It provided for a permanent joint legislative committee to investigate individuals and groups "who seek to destroy the ideals of the citizens of the State of Alabama"— in the historical context, civil rights and voter registration organizations.[71]

Though Black Belt farmers depended heavily on legislative protection, they nonetheless forged their own political instrument and link to state and national governments: the Alabama Farm Bureau.

Organizing the Black Belt

A state Farm Bureau organization was established in Alabama in 1921 and from the beginning was intimately connected with the Agricultural Extension Service. The first president of the organization declared, "I went back to Alabama convinced that the extension service and the farm bureau must march forward hand-in-hand to a better agriculture and a more satisfying rural life, each in its proper place."[72] In fact, the relationship between the two organizations was so close that local observers and one author had difficulty disentangling them:

> The relationship between the two organizations has been so close that it is hard to tell whether the Farm Bureau was promoting education and legislation through the Extension Service, or the Extension Service was promoting these activities through the Farm Bureau. There was a time when the Extension Service in Alabama dominated the Farm Bureau and was charged with being a political machine which elected not only the legislature but the governor [Bibb Graves].[73]

70. Alabama Labor Council (AFL-CIO), *Proceedings of the First Biennial Convention of the Alabama Labor Council, AFL-CIO,* Mobile, Alabama, 31 October 1956, p. 15; Havens, *City Versus Farm?*, pp. 44–45.
71. Alabama Labor Council (AFL-CIO), *Legislative Report, 1961,* pp. 21–22, 30–35; *1963,* pp. 15–16, 18–23.
72. Quoted in Orville Merton Kile, *The Farm Bureau Through Three Decades,* p. 174.
73. Christiana McFadyen Campbell, *The Farm Bureau: A Study of the Making of National Farm Policy 1933–40,* p. 19.

The network of county agents—supported by private, state, and federal funds—and the network of farm bureaus provided the core for a growing and powerful farm organization.[74] In 1933, the Alabama Farm Bureau had 2,590 members, the strongest organization in the South but woefully weak by midwestern standards. The organizing campaign in the thirties, supported by efforts of the Extension Service, brought the membership to 41,014 by 1943 and 61,667 by 1948.[75] In 1973, Alabama Farm Bureau membership topped 155,000.[76] By the sixties, the Farm Bureau was not simply a collection of local committees but a major insurance company, real estate developer, and wholesaler.[77] And by all accounts, the Farm Bureau had established itself as one of the major political forces in the state.[78]

The Farm Bureau, both nationally and at the state level, has emphasized prices—rather than consumer cooperatives, for example—and, therefore, commercial agriculture. In Alabama that emphasis has inevitably brought the Farm Bureau to a preoccupation with cotton and the Black Belt. In the thirties, the Farm Bureau, together with the Extension, began a major organizing drive among cotton producers, in large part to gain control over the AAA cotton production control committees; in the forties, it helped producer representatives win out over processors on the Cotton Council.[79] The early emphasis on commercial agriculture and the Black Belt provided an inheritance that the organization has not easily abandoned. A Farm Bureau officer notes that even in the seventies, membership rates are highest in the Black Belt areas and that the organization normally "leans" toward the policy preferences of its Black Belt members. Though cotton production has declined and various commodity committees have grown up within the Farm Bureau, the organization remains strongest among Black Belt commercial farmers—beef producers, for example—and weakest among commercial farmers in north Alabama, like the poultry producers. In recent years, the Farm Bureau has been challenged by leaders emphasizing "small scale farming," who charge the Farm Bureau with bowing to "large landowners and the paper and pulpwood companies in south Alabama."[80]

74. See Orville Merton Kile, *The Farm Bureau Movement*, pp. 100–04.

75. Campbell, *The Farm Bureau*, pp. 94, 102.

76. Alabama Farm Bureau Federation, "Annual Report," given by President J. D. Hays, Fifty-second Annual Meeting, Alabama Farm Bureau Federation, Mobile, Alabama, 1973. Also, by 1973, membership took in a diverse lot of nonfarmers who were interested in insurance and other Farm Bureau benefits.

77. *Birmingham News*, 8 October 1967; 9 October 1967.

78. See discussion in *Birmingham News*, 11 October 1967 and discussion of this issue in chapter 10.

79. Campbell, *The Farm Bureau*, pp. 87–92, 132–33.

80. *Birmingham News*, 29 December 1971.

Defending the Racial Order

Though the Alabama Farm Bureau formally admits black members, it has
never given serious consideration to the interests of black (or white)
independent farmers or black tenant farmers. For the most part, blacks were
left to the whims of individual county organizations. In some cases, blacks
were segregated in meetings or forced to hold separate gatherings.[81] In a few
cases, blacks were admitted to separate black county farm bureaus; the last,
in Macon County, was not "phased out" until 1970. In any event, blacks
after 1937 were not counted in the apportionment of state delegates,[82] and,
one officer observed, "Delegates to the conventions were all white. As far as
I know, there has never been a black delegate to the State Farm Bureau
meetings and there are no blacks on the State Central Committee." Another
officer recalled a few black delegates, "but I've never been to a meeting
where there was an effort to elect a black. . . . You see, they trust the white
man to serve their interest in the Farm Bureau."

The Alabama Farm Bureau has resisted any attempt by the government
or the black tenants themselves to change the labor framework in the Black
Belt. When the AAA first established production control committees in the
1930s, the Farm Bureau initiated a vigorous campaign to organize cotton
producers and gain control of the program.[83] It also helped structure the
national marketing quotas to favor the old cotton states—Mississippi,
Alabama, and Georgia—at the expense of the newer cotton areas in the
West.[84] In the Black Belt, the Farm Bureau used its relationship with the
county agents (Extension Service) and influence over production control
committees to insure that cash payments and crop controls benefited its
members, in effect, landowners rather than tenants. The former gained the
lion's share of benefit payments and the latter the brunt of crop reductions.[85] Some of the displaced tenants eventually joined the Communist-
backed Sharecroppers' Union of Alabama and faced the hostility of Black
Belt officialdom and the violence of white landowners.[86] One tenant farmer
reflects on his court appearance:

> They didn't mention the union. They talked about that as much as
> they wanted outside the courtroom, but inside, it weren't spoken of.

81. Campbell, *The Farm Bureau*, pp. 24–26.
82. Ibid., p. 25.
83. Campbell, *The Farm Bureau*, pp. 85–87.
84. Ibid., pp. 127–28.
85. Myrdal, *An American Dilemma*, pp. 258–59; Johnson et al., *The Collapse of Cotton
Tenancy*, pp. 49–52.
86. F. Ray Marshall, *Labor in the South*, pp. 156–57.

They all knowed what it was, and that it *might* have been involved, but they didn't want to consider that *their* niggers would have anything to do with a union. They wanted that thing to perish—so they didn't ask me. Just a matter of a nigger done got into trouble tryin to destroy their way of life.[87]

When the Farm Security Administration in the late thirties began tampering with the traditional labor framework, the national Farm Bureau president, a former head of the Alabama organization, commented, "We thought the Farm Security Administration was to help tenants to become farm owners; we did not know it was to reform us."[88] The Farm Bureau joined with local white opinion in opposing a cooperative settlement in Wilcox County and later joined other sections of organized agriculture in crippling the entire program.[89]

Three decades later, the interconnected agricultural establishment—the Farm Bureau, Extension Service and county agents, and now the Agricultural Stabilization and Conservation Service (ASCS)—continued to reflect the traditional racial and labor pattern. The ASCS in 1966 employed no black professional employees and only two black clerks; at the county level, it employed 127 employees, only six of whom were black, and 22 field representatives, none of whom were black.[90] The county committees that control crop allotments and price supports—the core of the farm program and a critical base for the Farm Bureau—operated without effective black participation: the Civil Rights Commission in 1966 found no blacks among 201 county committeemen in Alabama.[91] At public hearings before the commission, black farmers claimed that they were given smaller acreage allotments than whites, and black tenants claimed that they "were evicted for refusing to sign over their allotment checks to the landlord."[92]

The Farm Bureau in the postwar period has pressed a number of non-civil-rights issues with, nonetheless, negative consequences for black workers and farmers. It has consistently opposed the introduction of a state minimum wage,[93] "labor union efforts to enroll farmers for the purpose of

87.   Theodore Rosengarten, *All God's Dangers: The Life of Nate Shaw*, p. 339.
88.   Quoted in Campbell, *The Farm Bureau*, p. 167.
89.   Ray Marshall and Lamond Godwin, *Cooperatives and Rural Poverty in the South*, pp. 32–35.
90.   Alabama State Advisory Committee to the U.S. Commission on Civil Rights, "ASCS Operations in Twenty-Six Alabama Counties," May 1967, p. 12.
91.   Ibid., p. 16.
92.   A Report of an Open Meeting by the Alabama State Advisory Committee to the U.S. Commission on Civil Rights, "The Agricultural Stabilization and Conservation Service in the Alabama Black Belt," April 1968, pp. 21–22.
93.   Alabama Farm Bureau Federation, *Farm Bureau Policies for 1967*, p. 72.

representing their interests,"[94] attempts to "repeal or modify" the "right-to-work" law,[95] and reapportionment.[96]

The Farm Bureau has consistently, throughout the entire civil rights period, opposed attempts by the courts, the federal government, and blacks to integrate Alabama society. With the *Brown v. Board of Education* decision on the near horizon, the Farm Bureau pointed to "the urgent need for the equalization of white and negro school facilities in order to maintain separate facilities."[97] And between 1956 and 1966, it annually iterated a simple but provocative demand: "We insist that segregated schools be maintained in Alabama."[98] When the integration issue moved from the schools to the lunch counters and ballot boxes, when business groups began to waver, the Farm Bureau remained implacable. In 1961, it fought to retain the literacy requirement for voting[99] and two years later opposed presidential proposals on public accommodations and equal employment opportunity: "We oppose the intent of the Civil Rights Bill now in Congress because it takes away civil rights and because through such legislation all Americans of all races could lose constitutional rights."[100] Though major business organizations across the state condemned lawlessness and, in effect, conceded important aspects of the racial order, the Farm Bureau continued to attack the Civil Rights Act of 1964 as "unconstitutional and an infringement on the rights of property owners." The Farm Bureau aligned itself with the most visible symbol of white supremacy and white southern resistance: "We commend Gov. Wallace for his efforts to defend our rights and voice the opinions of Southern citizens."[101]

"I don't find farm labor the big problem it used to be," the Alabama Farm Bureau officer observed. The cotton pickers have come and gone. The sharecropping is "not a significant factor any more. It used to be, you know, many years ago." Now, there are the small farms with one or two hired laborers and the big machinery—"one hundred horsepower tractors and better."[102] By the late sixties, the civil rights and voting rights bills had come and gone. White political power was under siege in Greene and Lowndes

94. Alabama Farm Bureau Federation, *Farm Bureau Policies for 1965*, p. 53.
95. Alabama Farm Bureau Federation, *Farm Bureau Policies for 1956*, p. 13.
96. Interview with officer of the Alabama Farm Bureau.
97. Alabama Farm Bureau Federation, *Farm Bureau Policies for 1953*, p. 11.
98. Alabama Farm Bureau Federation, *Farm Bureau Policies for 1956*, p. 17.
99. Alabama Farm Bureau Federation, *Farm Bureau Policies for 1961*, p. 52.
100. Alabama Farm Bureau Federation, *Farm Bureau Policies for 1963*, p. 29.
101. *Birmingham News*, 8 November 1964.
102. Interview with officer of the Alabama Farm Bureau.

counties. And, after the court-ordered legislative reapportionment, the president of the Farm Bureau warned, "The commercial-industrial-urban complex now dominates the legislature."[103]

Though the traditional labor framework, "King Cotton," and the racial order have seemingly passed into history, we should not neglect Alabama's rural economy and its impact on the pattern of racial domination. White landowners in Alabama's Black Belt reconstructed commercial agriculture after the Civil War, responding to markets for cotton in the South, New England, and abroad; but they also sought over an extended period to avoid a market in labor. The landowners turned to intimidation and mob violence, to local custom and officials, to state law. In each case, white landowners helped to elaborate the meaning of racial domination and to limit the freedom of black labor. Against a backdrop of increasing mobility of labor and a diminishing ability to control it, they tried to create a system of dependent sharecropping. The system, with all its contradictions, poverty, and racism, survived at least into the thirties and, in less potent form, until the late fifties and early sixties.

The Black Belt farmers, even as machines and new commercial crops took over, did not easily abandon the old ideas and politics. With the racial order under attack from within and without—from the civil rights campaigns, population movements, and the courts—with growing dissension between businessmen and farmers, they nonetheless stood by the state structure and politicians that they had helped create.

The end was unheralded. There was no advertisement in twenty-two Alabama newspapers, like one sponsored by the major business associations in 1965, announcing the demise of the racial order.[104] By the late sixties, the Farm Bureau and white farmers had unobtrusively given up the race question; without sharecroppers, with machines, beef and soybeans, they could afford to.

---

103. Alabama Farm Bureau Federation, "President's Report," Forty-seventh Annual Meeting, Alabama Farm Bureau Federation, Mobile, Alabama, 1968, p. 4.
104. See chapter 10.

PART TWO / BUSINESSMEN

CHAPTER 7

Business Enterprise in a Racial Order

The businessman's role in a racial order is, to say the least, ambiguous. The businessman pictures himself as preoccupied with business decisions and requirements, indifferent to the politics, racial conflict, and domination that swirl around him. If sometimes distracted from this managerial focus, he is at least confident that "the well tried laws of economics cannot be denied in the long run."[1] The businessman, however, adjusts to the requirements of a racially stratified labor force and the demands of the state. Racial segregation and practices that prevail outside the factory are transposed onto the work routine; racial barriers to geographic and occupational mobility or to trade-union representation are placed alongside other "givens" in management decisions. Indeed, the businessman sometimes appears not as an indifferent or reluctant practitioner of race discrimination, but as an active and enthusiastic supporter. Passes, criminal penalties for "breach of contract," antienticement laws, highly circumscribed trade-union rights, and a divided working class are the stuff of a controlled and cheap labor force.

Three schools of thought—growth, accommodative, and neo-Marxist—have sought to impose order on these options. The growth school, drawing on both Weber and Marx, asserts that an emerging industrial order is incompatible with the constraints, categories, and immobility of a racial order.[2] Capitalist development may coexist with remnants of colonialism, feudalism, or even a racial order, but, over the long term, must undermine them. At the micro level, the logic of growth depends upon the actions and ideology of an emerging business class. Conventional management practice is distorted by the costly duplication of facilities, restrictions on allocation of labor, and the limited productivity of workers in the subordinate racial section.[3] As businessmen insist on substituting "lower-cost factors of

---

1. *The Manufacturer*, May 1961, p. 11.
2. See the discussion of the "growth school" in chapter 1.
3. *Subordinate* and *dominant* in this work, unless another meaning is apparent from the context, refer to the less-privileged and privileged sections of the population in a system of racial domination: in South Africa, principally Africans and Europeans; in Alabama, blacks and whites. The terms will be extended later to nonracial systems of ethnic domination: in Northern Ireland, Catholics and Protestants; in Israel, principally Israeli Arabs and Jews.

production" for "dearer" ones,[4] these irrational (nonprice) barriers in the market look increasingly anomalous and, indeed, eventually give way.

The "growth" school is buttressed by a sociological literature that anticipates the growth of entrepreneurial and middle classes that have little patience with nonmarket social distinctions. Seymour Martin Lipset, for example, helped popularize the notion of "working-class authoritarianism," arguing, in effect, that the middle class shows greater tolerance for the rights of minorities and expresses less ethnic and racial prejudice.[5] His analysis was supported by later social survey findings indicating that middle-income and upper-income whites are most opposed to discrimination in housing, public accommodations, and other areas. "In direct and sharp contrast to low-income white views on civil rights are the more enlightened and even advanced attitudes of the affluent quarter at the top," William Brink and Louis Harris write. "These better educated and more privileged white people feel most deeply about the necessity to make progress to achieve equality for Negroes."[6]

That capitalist development and business behavior and attitudes undermine exclusory racial practices remains a powerful suggestion in this area of inquiry. It draws upon both a Marxist and classical economic foundation and surfaces incessantly in the protestations of businessmen[7] and political leaders.[8]

The accommodative school argues that businessmen, while preferring an unencumbered business environment, readily adapt and conform to the larger society's requirements and ideas. Herbert Blumer maintains that industrial practice "almost invariably adjust[s] and conform[s] to the pattern of race relations in the given society." If racial lines are drawn in the society at large, these lines are "followed in the allocation of racial members inside the industrial structure."[9] Ignoring these lines risks industrial unrest and political conflict.[10] The willingness of businessmen to accept or foresake race lines depends, therefore, on the depth of racial sentiment among workers and commercial farmers in the dominant racial section and on the commitment of the state to maintaining the racial and labor patterns. Where the sentiment and commitment are strong, businessmen adjust conventional business practice to meet the requirements of the larger society.[11]

4. Ralph Horwitz, *The Political Economy of South Africa*, p. 6.
5. Seymour Martin Lipset, *Political Man*, pp. 97–99, 120.
6. William Brink and Louis Harris, *Black and White*, pp. 133–36.
7. For an interesting example, see Michael O'Dowd, "South Africa in the Light of the Stages of Economic Growth."
8. E. Franklin Frazier, *Black Bourgeoisie*, pp. 131–45.
9. Herbert Blumer, "Industrialization and Race Relations," pp. 240–41.
10. Ibid., pp. 232–33.
11. See Henry W. Ehrman, *Organized Business in France*, p. 275, particularly the discussion of business associations and their adjustments to weak and strong political authorities.

A variant on this school maintains that all groups within the dominant racial section—industrial workers and commercial farmers, but also businessmen—benefit from the section's economic and political position and, therefore, easily adapt to the prevailing racial orthodoxy. They may differ on how social control is to be maintained;[12] they may argue on how the economic surplus derived from subordinate workers and the precapitalist peasant mode is to be distributed within the dominant racial section;[13] their actions, however, are mutually reinforcing on the issue of racial domination. Businessmen may defer immediate profits to prevent the "impoverishment" of dominant workers ("what common benefit there is in being white is likely enhanced by some intraracial 'benevolence'"),[14] or tolerate wage differentials that accrue to the advantage of dominant workers or labor controls that largely benefit commercial farmers.

The neo-Marxist school, while allowing for the accommodative side in business practice, emphasizes the role of the bourgeoisie in exploiting, indeed creating, a system of race domination.[15] For Oliver Cromwell Cox, racial antagonisms are among the "fundamental traits" of the capitalist system. "The interest behind racial antagonism is an exploitive interest," Cox writes, "the peculiar type of economic exploitation characteristic of capitalist society."[16] The businessman, far from decrying the limitations on mobility or the state role in the labor market, demands more elaborate controls over the subordinate population and, therefore, the elaboration of the racial order. He benefits from the development of a system that provides a ready supply of "cheap" labor and that limits the bargaining and political position of the racially subordinate population: workers are divided along race lines, while a large, if not the predominant portion of the working class is unorganized; businessmen are free to allocate and compensate subordinate workers, unfettered by collective bargaining or unwilling workers who may freely seek alternative employment.[17]

A number of Marxist writers, while underlining the racially exploitive features in business practice, allow for the changing composition of capital —the declining need of secondary-manufacture and transnational corpo-

12. Lawrence Schlemmer, "Employment Opportunity and Race in South Africa," p. 4.
13. David Kaplan, "Capitalist Development in South Africa: Class Conflict and the State."
14. Marcus Alexis, "A Theory of Labor Market Discrimination with Interdependent Utilities," pp. 301–02.
15. The racial order "may most adequately be explained," Frederick Johnstone writes, "as a class system—as a system of class instruments, produced, and determined by the specific class structure and system of production of which it formed a part" ("Class and Race Relations in the South African Gold Mining Industry, 1910–1926," p. 3).
16. Oliver Cromwell Cox, *Caste, Class, and Race: A Study in Social Dynamics*, pp. xxx–xxxii.
17. A similar pattern is evident in the use of "foreign workers" in the advanced capitalist societies of western Europe. See Manuel Castells, "Immigrant Workers and Class Struggles in Advanced Capitalism: the Western European Experience," pp. 46–53.

rations for the traditional race lines and labor controls.[18] Businessmen do not easily throw off a system of race domination that bolsters their hegemony in society and politics. Faced with changing labor requirements and markets, and with little personal stake in the traditional communal privilege, developing sections of capital may step back from the racial orthodoxy. Here, in late-developing capitalism, there may emerge some of the "disintegrating" forces that the growth school associates with capitalism itself.

To evaluate these schools, to establish some expectations about business enterprise before looking at our research settings,[19] I will first examine developing business practice in nonracial settings. Only by understanding conventional business practice can we avoid mystifying its consequences for racial orders. Do businessmen oppose artificial constraints in the labor market? How easily do they adapt to the values and policies of other groups in society? What role do they demand of the state in the labor market and work place?

If business enterprise has conventionally evolved both an ideological and practical opposition to socially or politically imposed market constraints, we might expect, as does the growth school, that businessmen will play down racial exclusions. If, on the other hand, business enterprise readily adapts to socially or politically imposed market constraints, or exploits them, there is little reason to anticipate the amelioration of racial exclusions. Businessmen may, as suggested by the accommodative school, introduce race lines into new contexts or, as suggested by the neo-Marxists, elaborate them even further.

The range of interests and goals associated with modern business practice allows for varied responses in social and political life. In an extreme case, Schumpeter observes, "there is no policy short of exterminating the bourgeoisie that could not be held to serve some economic or extra-economic, short-run or long-run, bourgeois interest, at least in the sense that it wards off still worse things."[20] But the range of business responses in a racial order is both finite as well as varied. In some contexts, business enterprise is intimately associated with labor-repressive policies. Primary

---

18. See Martin Legassick, "South Africa: Capital Accumulation and Violence," pp. 261–64; Anders Boserup, *Who is the Principal Enemy? Contradictions and Struggles in Northern Ireland,* pp. 12–14, 24–26.

19. This chapter was first drafted in the fall of 1974 and published in somewhat different form in 1976 (*Politics and Society* 6 [Fall 1976]) prior to my field research in Alabama, Northern Ireland, and Israel, but not South Africa. Though the chapter has been modified further in the present book, the expectations (or hypotheses) are essentially those that guided the work from the beginning. They have not been revised to conform with the findings.

20. Joseph A. Schumpeter, *Capitalism, Socialism and Democracy,* p. 56.

manufacturers,[21] particularly early in capitalist development, find constraints on labor mobility congenial; they foster an increased state role in the labor market and work place. Disabilities imposed on the labor force help the businessman to form a labor force; divisions in the working class help him to control the work place. In other contexts, business enterprise responds flexibly to market and labor constraints. Primary and secondary[22] manufacturers alike, particularly later in capitalist development, accommodate social conventions without serious protest. They readily adjust to the requirements of the state and other powerful groups in the society.

The conflict suggested by the growth school, between business enterprise and artificial constraints, is wholly imaginary. Business enterprise in the first instance uses or creates constraints on labor, and in the second, accommodates them. It is this logic which should govern business enterprise in a racial order.

THE LABOR-REPRESSIVE SIDE

Organizing a Labor Force

The labor market in an emerging capitalist order almost never responds spontaneously and generously to the needs of the new employers of labor. Would-be commercial farmers, industrialists, mine owners, and fragile national and municipal governments search out wage laborers for their factories, pits, shops, and work gangs. Sometimes an embryonic proletariat responds to the posting of rates; sometimes rising wage rates will lure peasants from their subsistence plots and precapitalist labor relationships.

21.   Primary industry or manufacture refers to business enterprises that normally extract or process a product without substantial fabrication or assembly. It is related, then, to a range of concepts employed by economists and organization theorists for characterizing economic development and organization. For our purposes, it is sufficient to note that such enterprises early in capitalist development normally depend on limited capital and technology and substantial inputs of unskilled labor.

Primary industry includes extractive enterprises, such as diamond, gold, coal, and iron-ore mining. It may include, as in Alabama before the turn of the century, iron manufacturers that operated well-developed iron-ore and coal mines, but only limited rolling-mill facilities. For our purposes, it does not include later-developing primary industries, like petroleum, that are capital and technology intensive and that employ relatively small inputs of labor. See James D. Thompson, *Organizations in Action*, pp. 108–09; Paul R. Lawrence and Jay W. Lorsh, *Organization and Environment*, p. 23; Charles P. Kindleberger, *Economic Development*, pp. 171–80.

22.   Secondary industry or manufacture (or indeed, simply manufacturing) for our purposes refers to business enterprises that depend on production processes employing substantial fabrication or assembly. These enterprises normally combine more advanced technologies, a smaller input of unskilled labor, and greater skill differentiation.

Very often, however, no wage rate, no matter how lucrative, will lead peasants to exchange precapitalist life for the exigencies of the capitalist labor market. The idyllic rationality of supply and demand and factory life frequently have little attraction to workers who find order and familiarity, as well as poverty, in traditional social relationships. This stubbornness leads the entrepreneur to the state. Free wage labor as a principle and the labor market as an institution do not provide a sufficient supply of wage laborers at a wage rate acceptable to the emerging bourgeoisie. The labor market must be nudged beyond its natural inclinations, free wage labor and laissez faire economics, notwithstanding.

It is difficult, nonetheless, to draw a hard and fast line between labor that is free in the conventional sense, driven by the "whip of hunger" and landlessness,[23] and labor that is forced, compelled by indenture, land expropriation, or law. But the extremes are easily distinguishable and analytically important: at one end, a labor force emerges with the decay of the traditional order and the attractions of the new; at the other extreme, it emerges under the force of political scrutiny, control, and manipulation. In the latter case, natural economic forces are so inadequate to the demand for labor and the political chicanery so widespread that the process can be characterized as "labor repressive."[24]

Capitalist development has rarely proceeded without this repressive side. Alongside such bourgeois inventions as the division of labor and joint stock companies, stand various political arrangements to insure a cheap and controlled labor force. The plantation economies in Latin America and cotton tenancy in the American South depended upon a variety of repressive measures, including debt peonage, intimidation, and constricted legal and political rights.[25] The primary industries early in capitalist development, particularly mining and the railroads, repeatedly turned away from the market in labor and toward the state. They helped create state migrant labor programs that provided fixed supplies of labor at fixed rates of pay and that placed severe restrictions on labor mobility and organization.[26] They created company towns and labor compounds that limited the wages and political leverage of industrial workers.[27] With the growth of workers' combinations, businessmen and business associations encouraged further

23. Max Weber, *General Economic History*, p. 277.
24. Barrington Moore, Jr., *Social Origins of Dictatorship and Democracy*, p. 434.
25. See Stanley B. Greenberg, *Politics and Poverty: Modernization and Response in Five Poor Neighborhoods*, pp. 21–24; Rodolfo Stavenhagen, "Classes, Colonialism, and Acculturation"; André Gunder Frank, *Capitalism and Underdevelopment in Latin America;* and Allison Davis, Burleigh B. Gardner, and Mary R. Gardner, *Deep South*, pp. 232–40, 296–311.
26. See Ernesto Galarza, *Merchants of Labor: The Mexican Bracero Story*.
27. See Harry M. Caudill, *Night Comes to the Cumberlands*, pp. 101–11.

state intervention. In England and the United States, they sought sweeping limitations on workers' "conspiracies" and restraint of trade,[28] the suppression of worker-based political movements,[29] and court and police intervention to halt work stoppages.[30]

Given this affinity of primary industries in particular for labor-repressive arrangements, similar enterprises in racial orders can hardly be expected to find such practices singularly abhorrent. A racial order provides no less, and probably more, opportunities for manipulating labor supplies and controlling a labor force. Racially subordinate workers face not simply class disabilities, but also the traditional race barriers to organization and movement and an expectation in the dominant racial section as a whole that such controls will be maintained. Their plight is exacerbated by the marked, perhaps unusual, vigilance of the state. In a racial order, the state that has customarily acted as an instrument of population and labor control[31] finds the administrative requirements of labor-repressive policies both workable and congenial. "Indeed," John Rex observes with regard to the South African case, these conditions seem to provide "the theoretically most perfect system of labour exploitation yet devised."[32]

Export firms with large proportions of unskilled workers—commonplace in the primary industries—should find such a labor framework particularly congenial. They are not concerned for the most part with investments in training and labor stabilization. Their labor is, in a neoclassical and Marxist sense, interchangeable and replaceable. Nor do they require rising wage levels and, therefore, a growing domestic market for their products. Coal, iron, and gold bullion often find few buyers in the local economy. Indeed, with an established international market price for their products, these firms cannot idly pass on wage increases to their international customers. Profitability depends on their ability to hold down or reduce costs at the most logical and vulnerable point—the mass of unskilled workers. For the export-primary manufacturer, this point becomes the controlling issue: How can the firm attract an adequate, perhaps increasing, number of workers at a constant or declining wage? Here, the state protects the firm

28. See E. P. Thompson, *The Making of the English Working Class*, pp. 238–46; 498–521; and Irving Bernstein, *The Lean Years*, pp. 206–15.
29. Thomas R. Brooks, *Toil and Trouble*, pp. 114–23; and Bernstein, *The Lean Years*, pp. 141–42.
30. Philip Taft and Philip Ross, "American Labor Violence: Its Causes, Character, and Outcome."
31. The state in both South Africa and the American South has played a decided role in this area. See Vernon Lane Wharton, *The Negro in Mississippi, 1865–1890*, pp. 80–96, 117–24; and Francis Wilson, *Labour in the South African Gold Mines, 1911–1969*, p. 3; also see the discussion of the state in chapter 17.
32. John Rex, "The Plural Society: The South African Case," p. 50.

from the workings of a labor market that might otherwise associate an increased supply of labor with rising wage levels. These firms turn to the state to attract labor out of the subsistence and rural economy, to hold laborers to their contracts, to subvert the market in labor.

Controlling the Work Place

The emergence of capitalist enterprise was, in large part, the assertion of ownership control over the work place. By no means was that control undisputed. The medieval guilds united workers in the same occupations, limited competition, and established standards of work.[33] In the early part of the nineteenth century, the Elizabethan Long Law still protected English workers in apprenticeships and guilds. The landed nobility, fearing the power of an emergent middle class, supported corporate bodies that assisted specialist workmen. The nobility, writes Morazé, hoped to encourage a "rise in the cost of labour" and, consequently, to limit the profitability of industry.[34] The advance of "liberty" in France more readily undermined the position of the guilds. Feudal labor regulations were washed away along with the vestiges of the ancien regime. In 1830 the minister of trade declared, "There is no law compelling a scale of wages to be fixed for any particular industry," and the government "positively cannot interfere in the matter" of contracts.[35]

It was on the issue of work place autonomy that businessmen established their pre-eminence, but it was here that businessmen were compelled to defend their gains. The workshop, momentarily freed from the guilds and labor regulations and placed firmly under the guidance of managers, became the battleground of atomistic entrepreneurs, organized workers, and, later, of organized business, trade unions, and the state. Though businessmen formed associations to press tariff legislation or to discourage price competition, the most aggressive and broad-based ones chose to defend "liberty" in the work place. When the National Association of Manufacturers in 1895 tried to interest businessmen in questions of home and foreign markets, the merchant marine, and canals and waterways, few businessmen (certainly not more than a thousand) seemed interested.[36] But when the NAM took the leadership in the open-shop movement, it emerged

33. H. H. Gerth and C. Wright Mills, eds., *From Max Weber: Essays in Sociology,* pp. 321–22.
34. Charles Morazé, *Triumph of the Middle Classes,* p. 201.
35. Ibid., p. 202.
36. Harmon Zeigler, *Interest Groups in American Society,* p. 111; and James Q. Wilson, *Political Organization,* p. 154.

as the largest and most powerful business association of its day. The NAM's fortunes continued to rise and fall with the need to defend the work place.[37] Similar concerns were important among British and French businessmen. In Britain, business groups emerged in response to the formation of the Trade Union Congress and union attempts to repeal the Criminal Law Amendment Act.[38] French business associations, angered by their forced capitulation to labor under the Popular Front government in the thirties and later under the postwar de Gaulle government, persisted in the struggle for the work place. "The bourgeois mentality of the French employers, large and small," Henry Ehrman writes, "is spontaneously inimical to the sharing of authority which is involved in all collaboration between the organizations of management and labor."[39]

For the contemporary businessman in most advanced capitalist societies, the work place is no longer a controlling issue. Management and labor have turned to institutional rules and accommodations. Together, Clark Kerr observes, they have reduced the market "to the irreducible minimum," limiting mobility between jobs and access to new ones, controlling promotions and layoffs.[40] But the imposition of order on the work place, even if it now offers some managerial advantages, was not sought by businessmen. They organized to forestall it; once labor-management relations were institutionalized, they sought to minimize their scope. Labor attitudes, the strength and type of trade unions, and favorable labor legislation remain important considerations in plant location. A mix of these factors favorable to business autonomy (and low labor costs) was instrumental in the movement of industry to the American South and to the south of the United Kingdom (away from the major coal fields).[41]

A racially divided working class, however, offers businessmen opportunities for autonomy that have been effectively extinguished outside the racial orders. A glimmer of these possibilities was apparent in the French case, where sectarian and ideological disputes within the French labor movement facilitated persistent intransigence in the business community. These divisions, however, are only a partial measure of those present in racial orders: the working class is divided by customary and legal distinctions; dominant workers can and probably will seek advantages at the expense of workers in the subordinate racial section.

37. Wilson, *Political Organization*, p. 155–56.
38. Stephen Blank, *Industry and Government in Britain*, p. 11.
39. Ehrman, *Organized Business*, pp. 427–28.
40. Clark Kerr, "The Balkanization of Labor Markets," p. 65; also see Earl Latham, *The Group Basis of Politics*, pp. 28–33.
41. R. C. Estall and R. Ogilvie Buchanan, *Industrial Activity and Economic Geography*, pp. 76–77.

Amid those divisions, businessmen may create some managerial opportunities. First, they may overwhelm trade unions that represent only a fraction of the work force or that demonstrate internal disunity.[42] This approach is particularly important in primary industries, where the question of controlling the work place is inseparable from the problem of general labor costs. In the absence of effective organization among dominant workers or of state regulations, management may challenge the prevailing racial division in the work place, substituting cheaper subordinate workers for dearer dominant ones. In primary industries, where skills are relatively undifferentiated and labor costs critical, the introduction of black labor and "undercutting" may prove endemic.

Second, businessmen may stabilize relations with organized workers in the dominant racial section while maintaining their autonomy in areas of (unorganized) subordinate employment. This approach is appropriate in secondary industry, where skill differences between the racial sections are important and widespread labor substitution impracticable or in primary industries that have failed to crush the racially dominant unions. In either case, the labor market and work place take on all the appearances of a dual labor situation: a primary organized area encompassing the more skilled, more prestigious, and better-paid positions and a secondary unorganized area involving the lower-paid, unskilled jobs.[43] The state, acting to secure and defend the position of dominant workers, need only legitimize this dominant labor-management quid pro quo. The seemingly inexorable intrusion of the state and unions into the work place is contained within the boundaries of the primary labor market.

Either approach—profiting from a divided working class or stabilizing relations with dominant workers—provides the businessman with a scope and freedom of enterprise rarely achieved in modern business practice.

THE ACCOMMODATIVE SIDE

Business Autonomy and Business Imagery

The notion that a growing business class will undermine a racial order draws heavily upon an idealized vision of business practice: resisting "irrational limitations on trading in the market,"[44] feudal and landed interests that

42.   It is this pattern of business autonomy and worker disorganization that may account for the findings in the United States that income inequality among whites is greatest in areas of most pronounced racism. See Michael Reich, "The Economics of Racism," pp. 110–13.
43.   See David M. Gordon, *Theories of Poverty and Underemployment,* pp. 50–51.
44.   Weber, *General Economic History,* pp. 276–77.

limit access to all the factors of production, guilds and trade unions that impose controls on the use of labor, and a state that attempts to regulate prices and the market in labor. Businessmen in this view display little patience with privilege or politics. They want a "work space" of their own, free from interference in the management process.[45]

This imagery reflects the triumphant tone and ideological position of the European business class prior to 1900 more than that of contemporary business practice. The bourgeoisie had harnessed steam, brought Napoleon III and Bismark to power, and was ascendant in London, Paris, and Berlin. Its political program—"the destruction of the old, conservative monarchies; the proclamation of freedom of enterprise and control over as much of public administration as needed to be preserved"—seemed complete.[46] This conception of a self-assertive, autonomous business class emerged even later in the unabashed conservatism of the southern textile industry[47] and the opposition to the Popular Front government by French employers.[48]

But single-minded intransigence in the face of threats to business autonomy, while consistent with the business imagery, is in large part unreal. Businessmen in primary and secondary industries have proved capable in numerous historical cases of adjusting to the most outlandish tampering with business prerogatives. The Confindustria openly praised governmental policies during the Fascist period. Prominent industrialists were members of the government, while others accepted executive positions in the governmental corporations.[49] In Vichy France, industrialists accommodated themselves to a "continuous and progressive fusion of officialdom and business,"[50] what General de Gaulle called "a social and moral order which had worked against the nation."[51] After the war, both French and British businessmen accommodated policies previously anathema to them, including nationalization.[52] The Conservative party made an historic and ready

45. Grant McConnell, *Private Power and American Democracy*, pp. 246–47.

46. Morazé, *The Triumph of the Middle Classes*, pp. x–xi.

47. It stood almost alone (with the National Association of Manufacturers) against the Keating-Owen Child Labor Act in 1916 and was supported only a year later by the Supreme Court: "The act in its effect does not regulate transportation among the States, but aims to standardize the ages at which children may be employed in mining and manufacturing within the States" (*Hammer v. Dagenhart*, 247 U.S. 251, 38 S. Ct. 529, 62L. Ed. 1101 [1918]; see also George Brown Tindall, *The Emergence of the New South, 1913-1945*, pp. 321–23; and Bernstein, *The Lean Years*, pp. 235–37).

48. Even after the agreement at Matignon, they opposed legislation restricting their right to hire and fire workers and the use of public employment exchanges; they engaged in wholesale firings of union workers (Ehrman, *Organized Business*, pp. 33–46).

49. Joseph LaPalombara, *Interest Groups in Italian Politics*, pp. 412–13.

50. Ehrman, *Organized Business*, p. 64.

51. Ibid., p. 348.

52. Ibid., p. 351.

adjustment to the Labour government programs.[53] By the mid-1960s, the major business associations had formed the Confederation of British Industry to affect a new relationship between government and business. What had emerged, Stephen Blank writes, was an industrial life characterized not by business autonomy, not by government intervention in the private sector, but by a "broad area between the public and private sectors in which the structure of authority is indistinct."[54]

The accommodation to "alien" ideas is understandable where a strident business ideology is tempered by persistent attack or vitiated by weak bourgeois impulses in the society at large. Schumpeter was struck by the entrepreneur's increasing unwillingness to defend the autonomy of business enterprise. "The typical bourgeois is rapidly losing faith in his own creed," he writes. "They talk and plead—or hire people to do it for them; they snatch at every chance of compromise; they are ever ready to give in; they never put up a fight under the flag of their own ideals and interests."[55] Perhaps Schumpeter exaggerates the businessman's cowardice and malleability. He highlights, however, a feature of bourgeois life not often stressed in its imagery: where business autonomy is challenged by other groups, ideologies, or the state, businessmen are frequently defensive; they can learn to live with both the welfare state and fascism.

That business enterprise modifies or ignores its own ideology in a racial order should prove no more surprising than these historic accommodations. The racial order makes demands on industry no more unpalatable or burdensome than the impositions of socialist and fascist governments— indeed, probably less. Businessmen can live with separate toilets and promotion lines, as they learned to live with pension programs and price regulations. Other groups in the dominant racial section—commercial farmers or workers—may be in a position to insist upon it. That "unrestrained freedom of enterprise" may secure the maximum wealth for the community as a whole[56] is a feeble response to other dominant groups that depend on the society's particularism and inequality.

These accommodations seem alien to an imagery that stresses business autonomy and rationalism. They are typical, nonetheless, of orthodox business practices in most industrialized nations.

Stability and Profit Maximization

Let us assume for the moment that the racial order throws up a series of

---

53. Samuel H. Beer, *British Politics in the Collectivist Age*, p. 218.
54. Blank, *Industry and Government*, pp. 3–5.
55. Schumpeter, *Capitalism*, p. 161.
56. Ibid., p. 75.

obstacles to the profit-maximizing firm:[57] labor mobility is impaired; the great mass of industrial workers lack training and adequate socialization for industrial life; management must consider, in addition to the normal exigencies of the work place and labor market, special protections for dominant workers, racial customs in wages and job placement, and segregation in the shops and offices. Can we assume that businessmen, faced with such tampering with management practice, will throw off these customary, legal, and political constraints?

We can, if businessmen follow certain basic rules: the firm must rely upon an internal standard and logic to guide its behavior; it must pursue a profit-maximizing strategy and opportunely jump at short-term advantages in the market and elsewhere. The business firm, then, is a self-contained actor. Its own standards and needs, not the priorities of other groups or the state, will determine how it will cope with a given environment.[58]

Businessmen moved by such logic should show little patience with the petty obstacles of a racial order. The firm should mercilessly test the limits of customary practice, hoping to narrow the scope of racial exclusions and barriers. It should take a permissive view of legal restrictions, while challenging those laws that impair its efficiency. Finally, the firm, using its access to the state, should attempt to dismantle statutory racial exclusions and challenge other social groups that seek to impose them.

This confrontation between the firm and the racial order, though plausible, is hardly necessary or likely. Firms conventionally foresake efficiency or short-term profits, while minimizing social conflict and maximizing stability. There is an "interdependence of organization and environment," James Thompson writes, that is "inevitable or natural" and "adaptive or functional."[59] Social conditions and customs, including race discrimination, affect management practice, but so do high transportation costs, "unfair" tariffs, excessive labor costs, and scarce mineral resources. Where these conditions prevail over long periods of time, firms will deal with them as *constraints;* where they vary, firms will deal with them as *contingencies.*[60] In either case, the environment becomes a regular part of business decision making. No firm, no matter how committed to its internal needs, can live with the uncertainty that comes with persistent social conflict.

57. We must set aside for the moment the argument of the first section that firms face opportunities as well as obstacles in a racial order.
58. James D. Thompson calls this approach a "closed-system strategy" (*Organizations in Action,* p. 406).
59. Ibid., p. 7. Thompson labels this strategy an "open" or "natural" approach.
60. Ibid., p. 23–24.

In numerous historical instances, firms have attempted to stabilize environmental conditions rather than overcome them in the interest of some higher business purpose. After an initial period of industrial turmoil, American managers and workers began emphasizing security and certainty. Industrial relations are now characterized by periodic negotiation, institutionalized grievance procedures, and rigid promotional ladders.[61] British businessmen no longer respond to changing market prices or demand in classical economic fashion; rarely do firms drastically increase or cut back production and employment. They keep their eyes, Andrew Shonfield writes, "firmly fixed on the long term."[62] The textile industry, for example, no longer follows the orthodox practices that produced a volatile employment and production situation; it now conducts a "much steadier policy." On the London Metal Exchange, stable price policies have proved contagious. Mineral producers are no longer content to live with fluctuating prices, gluts, and scarcity of mineral output. They prefer to establish contract prices and production quotas.[63]

Segregation and racially exclusive public policies are just so many constraints with which firms in a racial order must come to terms. Businessmen may decide that these constraints impose intolerable costs and must, therefore, be eliminated. But where business operates profitably and where attempts to tamper with racial practices elicit profoundly hostile public responses to capitalism and free enterprise, businessmen may simply place these constraints alongside other givens in management practice.

Race in the Labor Market

We might reasonably expect the capitalist market to eliminate race discrimination if product markets are competitive, employers are free to hire whomever they choose, and at least one firm has no "taste for discrimination." The nondiscriminatory firm hires subordinate workers in preference to dominant ones (who, because of their "taste for discrimination," require a higher wage); its cost structure and profitability compare favorably to those of discriminatory firms. Since, as Kenneth Arrow observes, "capital will flow to the more profitable enterprise," the less discriminatory firm expands at the expense of those that indulge their taste for discrimination. In the long term, only the nondiscriminatory firms "survive the competitive struggle."[64] The market, having been cleared of discriminating firms, is now

---

61. Kerr, "Balkanization of Labor Markets," p. 69.
62. Andrew Shonfield, *Modern Capitalism*, p. 360.
63. Ibid., pp. 364–65.
64. Kenneth J. Arrow, "The Theory of Discrimination," p. 10. This assumes that there are constant returns to scale and that firms are capable of expansion until the market is exhausted. See Joseph E. Stiglitz, "Theories of Discrimination and Economic Policy," p. 7.

free from wage discrimination.

Where the dominant workers themselves insist upon discrimination, the market produces segregation but still tends to eliminate discrimination. Dominant workers will demand a higher wage when compelled to labor alongside subordinate workers. That is the price of their prejudice. But "an income-maximizing employer," Gary Becker observes, "would never hire a mixed work force, since he would have to pay the W [dominant] member of this force a larger wage rate than members of W working solely with other W."[65] Employers, then, create a labor force divided into two equally cheap sections, one comprised exclusively of dominant workers and the other of subordinate workers.

Yet there are sound theoretical and empirical reasons to believe that real market forces do not translate simply into market equity. The basis for persisting discrimination, we shall see, can be found in the market itself and in the special features and profit opportunities in a racial order.

First, even classical economic models must presume that in the short term the market will reproduce inequalities based on productivity and skill scarcity.[66] Even in the long term, one cannot assume that the patterns of investment in human capital will break with past practice; indeed, it is likely that training opportunities will follow the same pattern of inequality that characterizes the society as a whole. The state in a racial order, as an agent of the dominant section or some group within it, will favor dominant workers and insist that businessmen follow its example.[67] It may exclude subordinate workers from apprenticeships; it may confine their education to "complementary rather than substitute skills."[68]

Second, short-term costs associated with incremental decisions place even the most beneficent long-term outcome in doubt. Arrow correctly observes that "marginal adjustments are punished, not rewarded."[69] The employment of additional subordinate workers, while substituting lower-paid

65. Gary Becker, *The Economics of Discrimination,* p. 56.
66. Albert Rees, *The Economics of Work and Pay,* p. 34; Gordon, *Theories of Poverty,* pp. 28–29.
67. Richard B. Freeman provides convincing data in this regard in his "Alternative Theories of Labor Market Discrimination: Individual and Collective Behavior," pp. 41–42. Business decisions, even in a racial order, are not always made in the context of entrenched inequality. Perceived differences in productive capacity are often normative assumptions rather than concrete differences. Apparent differences may readily evaporate under industrial experience. Indeed, there are points in all industrial societies, whatever the form of stratification, where workers meet on the basis of productive equality: where neither dominant nor subordinate workers are experienced in industrial employment, ambitious members of the subordinate section meet less skilled members of the dominant one; where workers grapple with radically new technologies or where jobs make few demands on skills and training.
68. Freeman, "Alternative Theories of Labor Market Discrimination," p. 40.
69. Arrow, "Theory of Discrimination," p. 20.

workers for more expensive ones, also yields higher wages for the remaining dominant workers. In addition, firms that opt for large-scale substitution lose their accumulated investment in laid-off dominant workers. These changeover costs are considerable, perhaps prohibitive. In fact, the integrating firm gains no substantial advantage over other firms until integrated firms come to monopolize the market (if they ever do). The substitution of subordinate for dominant workers in integrating firms eases the supply of dominant workers, thus rewarding the "hold out" firms. Only where the labor market is very tight can we expect the integrating firm to gain a genuine short-term advantage.[70]

Third, the monopoly of dominant workers over supervisory-foremen positions, a virtual law in racial orders,[71] insures that dominant workers will continue to receive a discriminatory wage. The foreman prefers to minimize the subordinate-dominant employment ratio and is compensated for his tastes: every additional subordinate worker increases the wage that must be paid to the foreman; each additional dominant worker reduces it. Thus, "W [dominant] worker," Arrow writes, "is worth more than his marginal product, while a B [subordinate] worker is worth less."[72] This wage pattern should prove endemic in a racial order.

Finally, employers who engage in "equal amounts" of discrimination have few incentives to alter the traditional labor patterns. In most multiracial economies, that situation would not arise, however, as employers rarely have identical utility functions, that is, the same ratio of dominant to subordinate workers. But racial orders belie common assumptions about such issues. The state or trade unions may impose a common ratio; businessmen may urge the government to impose uniformity. In either case, the effect is the same. Arrow writes: "Then each firm's labor force is the same, and the allocation of labor is efficient. The effects of discrimination are purely distributive. The most obvious implication then is that B [subordinate] workers are paid less than their marginal product, so that the W [dominant] workers and employers together gain."[73] By achieving a shared, if imposed, utility function, business enterprise avoids the long-term instability and short-term costs associated with labor substitution. Its profitability is unmarred by wage discrimination: "The entire effect is that of a transfer from B [subordinate] to W [dominant] workers."[74]

70.   Duran Bell, Jr., "The Economic Basis of Employee Discrimination," pp. 131–33.

71.   This employment pattern, Donald Dewey argues, was a "virtual 'law' " in the southern labor market. If the employer sought to challenge the law, he would have to pay, and perhaps pay dearly, for his disobedience ("Negro Employment in Southern Industry," p. 283).

72.   Arrow, "Theory of Discrimination," pp. 10–11.

73.   Ibid., p. 7.

74.   Ibid., p. 8.

Thus, few attributes of business enterprise or the labor market compel or urge a firm to minimize wage discrimination and inequality. Business enterprise rewards inherited or societally produced advantages in productive capacity. Even where dominant and subordinate workers must meet on the basis of productive equality, wage disparities are likely to persist. The market provides few incentives for a firm to alter wage and employment patterns. Changeover costs are high, the initial market advantage limited, while bonus payments to dominant workers may wipe out the immediate gains from substitution. Perhaps most important, where common utility functions are imposed, business enterprise can operate efficiently and profitably under conditions of wage discrimination. Firms may solicit or welcome industrywide agreements or government policies that fix employment ratios for all firms. Such an explicit racial determination, precluded in most industrial societies, is a common possibility in a racial order.

FROM REPRESSION TO ACCOMMODATION: THE IMPACT OF DISORDER

There is little in the conventional behavior of businessmen to substantiate the growth school. That business ideology supports market freedom and business autonomy, and opposes feudal and state meddling in the market, there can be no doubt. But the ideology, though important for establishing business hegemony in society, barely conceals the businessman's penchant for unfree labor, sometimes demanding the elaboration of the state role in the labor market, and sometimes incorporating or replicating the demarcations prevailing in the larger society.

Businessmen in primary industries, even as they oppose preindustrial constraints on labor mobility, develop their own aversion to free labor markets and learn to use the state in the organization and control of a labor force. As the neo-Marxist school pointed out, there is every reason to expect that business enterprise will use and invigorate race lines as part of a developing labor-repressive structure. Businessmen should make demands on the state and racial ideology in an attempt to draw labor out of the rural economy, to limit the mobility of subordinate labor, and enforce labor contracts. They should emphasize the racial divisions in the working class and certainly resist labor organization in areas of subordinate employment, perhaps using subordinate labor to undercut dominant wage scales and labor organization. That such policies reinforce the "cheap labor" aspects of the racial order should not be surprising: the limited spending power of subordinate workers has little impact on profitability and expansion possibilities, and the transiency and lack of training among subordinate workers suits the nature of work in primary industries.

Businessmen in secondary manufacture and commerce are less preoccupied than primary manufacturers with labor,costs; indeed, they have less need of the whole labor-repressive structure. Organizing a labor force, subverting the labor market, and controlling the work place are less important for them than gaining labor stability, accumulating investments in training, and expanding domestic markets. There is little reason to expect, therefore, that these businessmen will identify closely with the racial order or demand its elaboration.

Businessmen, however, have learned to live with both fascism and socialism. They can almost certainly learn to accommodate a racial order. Where commercial farmers and dominant workers insist on the traditional race lines, businessmen will take the course of least resistance, opting for accommodation over endemic political conflict. Dependent on the good-will of dominant consumers and the state, businessmen will learn to tolerate prevailing ideas on political practice and the utilization of labor. Even under ordinary market conditions—buying cheap and selling dear—businessmen will reproduce underlying themes in the racial order: segregation of the work place and inequality of income and status.

Is there anything to choose between the repressive side of business enterprise apparent in the primary industries and the accommodative aspect apparent within secondary manufacture and commerce? Businessmen in primary industries, particularly early in capitalist development, will almost certainly identify closely with the racial framework; businessmen in secondary industry and commerce, even if not closely identified, will very likely help reproduce it. It seems that as long as primary and secondary industries have only themselves and perhaps commercial farmers and dominant workers to contend with, repression can blend into accommodation without significant consequence. As long as the racial order can provide a reasonably stable and profitable business environment, the accommodative side can take in what is repressive and discriminatory in the society.

But accompanying the growth of secondary industry—indeed the process of capitalist growth—are increasing threats to the traditional business environment: protests from the subordinate section, intervention by outside powers, and challenges to the prevailing ideas and customs.[75] Escalating disorder and instability, we shall see, may turn a nuance into a genuine difference in approach to the racial order. The primary manufacturers that depend on the labor-repressive structure must come to the defense of the racial order. For them, the state manipulation of the labor market and work

75.   See the discussion of political disorder in chapter 1, note 71.

place have become conventional and indispensable aspects of business enterprise. They yield the racial order only at the expense of their labor supplies, wage scales, and autonomy. Secondary manufacturers and commercial interests, on the other hand, may adopt alternative approaches to the developing disorder. For them, the racial order is neither a precondition nor an indispensable part of business enterprise. How they respond—their posture toward the traditional race lines and state, toward the old ideas and political alignments—should prove a critical aspect of change in racial orders.

CHAPTER 8

South Africa: Labor Repression and
the Gold Mines

An industrial revolution in any country, as history has shown, creates tremendous problems, which at times appeared insoluble even where the population was relatively homogeneous. But, as history has also shown, the solutions were inherent in the situation itself. They arose from the higher standards of living, and all that flowed from them, brought about by technical advances.

South Africa Mining and
Engineering Journal
September 1960

POLITICS AND MARKETS

There is nothing unusual or bizarre in the South African businessman's defense of free enterprise and economic growth. In virtually all emergent capitalist societies, business spokesmen support ideas that justify business practice and legitimize the businessman's economic and political aspirations. These ideas reflect in some measure principles that govern capitalist development, especially notions of free wage labor and economic rationality.[1] They also represent a political and philosophic counter to the economic constraints demanded by established precapitalist and emerging working-class groups. Freedom of enterprise denies the landowner and commercial farmer's peculiar hold on rural workers and access to state protection and subsidies. It stands against trade-union efforts to limit the supply of labor and fix wage levels. That businessmen themselves tolerate or encourage trade monopolies or constraints on the labor market does not detract from the ideological and political stance of the business community: economic growth is an overriding public good that requires, if not free markets, then at least the removal of artificial barriers to the free exercise of business enterprise.

---

1. Max Weber, *General Economic History*, p. 277.

In South Africa, the conventional defense of freedom of enterprise emerges as an ideological attack on the prevailing system of racial domination; in effect, a South African variant on the "growth school."[2] The white public, some business spokesmen maintain, faces a stark choice between politics, on the one hand, and economics and markets, on the other. The evolving state vigilance over race questions—influx control and pass laws, restrictions on training and labor utilization—limits economic growth. It limits the autonomy and, therefore, the invigorating aspects of business enterprise. "I have always thought," declared the chairman of Anglo-American Corporation, the largest gold-mining house, "that the rapid economic development of South Africa would in the long run prove to be incompatible with the government's racial policies, and recent events have tended to confirm my opinion."[3] The president of the Transvaal Chamber of Industries claimed:

> The main problems are prejudice and purely political issues which, by their very nature, must conflict with economic issues. Civilization as we know it is built on an economic foundation, and policies to be progressive must of necessity have an economic basis. If they are founded on purely political emotional issues, they cannot make for economic progress.[4]

More analytic in its approach is an array of supportive scholars who see the intrusion of the state into economic decision making as "a pact against free market co-ordination of resource-utilization,"[5] and a pattern of serious "economic dysfunction."[6] South African business executives, beginning with the early mining magnates, are essentially market and cost conscious. If left to their own devices, Ralph Horwitz maintains, they would substitute "lower-cost factors of production," thus imperiling the privileged position of the white worker.[7] They would allow questions of income and land distribution to be resolved in the market;[8] instead, they are compelled to

---

2. See the discussion of the growth school in chapter 7.
3. *Optima* 24, no. 1, p. 4. The managing director of a large mining house offered a similar analysis of the conflicting positions and optimism about their resolution: "The economic forces are closely integrating. With the facade of separation overlying the whole situation, you restrict the free economic implementation. But inexorably, the economic ship carries on." Other business leaders confirmed that these racial impositions on economic matters are "inhibiting the natural growth of the economy" or are "prejudicial . . . to the expansion of business interests."
4. *Commercial Opinion*, April 1950, p. 407.
5. Ralph Horwitz, *The Political Economy of South Africa*, p. 7.
6. Pierre van den Berghe, *South Africa: A Study in Conflict*, p. 196.
7. Horwitz, *The Political Economy*, p. 6.
8. Ibid., p. 298.

abide by "administrative decisions of what the supply and demand *ought to be."*[9] But in the end, Horwitz maintains, "the South African economy is inescapably integrated in the pursuit of productivity. Economic rationality urges the polity forward beyond its ideology."[10]

Important sections of the business community have tried to soften the consequences of growth, arguing that white society would not be undermined in the process. The Chamber of Mines, as it sought to substitute black for white labor in the gold mines, maintained that the elimination of government restrictions would "promote efficiency and secure the maximum field for the employment of European labour."[11] White interests were safe in European hands, it maintained. The Chamber had "a full sense of its responsibility towards the [white] community."[12] The Federated Chamber of Industries declared that industrialists "subscribe to the concept of residential social segregation" and they, as other citizens, "are surely no less concerned with the 'fundamental issue of the Europeans preserving their White race and the Western European civilization' than any political party."[13]

But for a succession of white governments, the National party, most white trade unions, and the varied Dutch Reformed churches, the argument that white society would survive or benefit from unfettered economic growth seemed disingenuous. These white groups, not liberal academics and businessmen, as it turns out, are the most fervent adherents of the growth school. What are influx controls and job color bars if not the tools to keep businessmen from "swamping" or displacing white workers? The Mining Regulations Commission (1925) urged the reenactment of the Mines and Works Act and entrenchment of job color bars, because the mining houses follow a "deliberate policy, consistently pursued throughout the period under review, of displacing European in favour of cheap coloured labor."[14] Thirty-five years later the minister of labor declared that without the statutory color bar, the government "would not have the power of taking

---

9. Ibid., p. 314.
10. Ibid., p. 405. Though Pierre van den Berghe does not share Horwitz's optimism about South African capitalism, he is equally emphatic that business requirements clash with the priorities in a racial order. "A complex capitalist economy," he writes, "requires, perhaps above all else, a freely mobile labour force which is responsive to labour demand." This requirement can hardly be met where jobs are reserved for particular racial groups, where workers are channeled into various forms of migratory labor, and where workers, both white and black, are offered few incentives to produce more or pursue alternative areas of employment (*South Africa*, pp. 191–95).
11. Chamber of Mines (Transvaal), *Annual Report 1922*, p. 45.
12. Chamber of Mines (Transvaal), *Annual Report 1921*, p. 57.
13. *The Manufacturer*, December 1956, p. 5.
14. Union of South Africa, *Report of the Mining Regulations Commission*, U.G.36–1925, p. 18.

action against the ousting of white workers from spheres of employment to which, *inter alia* . . . employers would then be able to appoint Black workers in white positions to their heart's content."[15] At critical times, this opposition to business practice is presented as a choice between "material advantages" and "the continued existence of a separate white people."[16] A National party backbencher affirms his government's unyielding commitment to the latter:

> Capitalists and certain employers . . . for the sake of bigger profits and enriching themselves, want to disturb our traditional labour pattern and racial harmony here in South Africa. . . . But we say inexorably that the growth rate is not priority number one with us. If we had to choose between the growth rate and the position of the white worker here in South Africa, we would immediately and unambiguously tell them that we are giving preferences to the position of the white worker.[17]

These perspectives on economic growth and racial domination require some restrictive assumptions about business enterprise in South Africa: businessmen are committed to freedom of enterprise and free markets; their latitude in management and investment is constrained by a coterie of racial exclusions; they decry the expanding role of the state in society and the labor market; and finally, their actions, unless circumscribed by state intervention, tend to undermine prevailing racial practices. The gold mines in South Africa, the base for primary industry and principal motor force in capitalist development for nearly three-quarters of a century, lend little credence to these assumptions. The mining houses, we shall discover, demanded the elaboration of a state machinery that helped to create an African proletariat, limit African labor mobility, and maintain "cheap" migrant labor. They resisted the organization of African workers, using the state to enforce labor contracts, put down African work stoppages, and limit collective bargaining.

THE STATE AND THE LABOR FRAMEWORK

The labor market in South Africa has often proved a disappointment to the purchasers of African labor. Cape farmers in the 1880s complained of "a serious want of labour," particularly in the Western districts and the

15. *Hansard,* 18 May 1971, col. 7001.
16. *Hansard,* 18 May 1971, col. 7006; and 23 February 1971, col. 1480.
17. *Hansard,* 4 September 1970, cols. 3397–99.

sections removed from "native locations."[18] Similar complaints pervaded settler politics in colonial Natal.[19] A late-nineteenth-century traveler in South Africa exclaimed: "Every farmer, every merchant, every politician I had met and spoke with since I had put my foot on South African soil had sworn to me that the country was a wretched country simply because labour could not be had!"[20]

One might have responded to a sluggish supply of labor by raising wage rates; labor might have been attracted from other areas, other pursuits, or even from the subsistence economy. Settler farmers and businessmen, because of perceived impracticality or excessive cost, shunned that alternative. They turned instead to political remedies. Treaties with Mozambique at the turn of the century brought foreign contract laborers at negotiated, though fixed, rates of pay. Taxes were levied on "huts" in the tribal areas, encouraging African peasants to seek cash remuneration in the modern sector.[21] In Natal, tribal chiefs regularly provided African laborers for six-month compulsory service on road construction and maintenance, usually at wage rates substantially below those prevailing in the open market.[22] Salary inducements and wage competition were actively discouraged. The South African Native Labour Regulation Act of 1911 declared: "No person . . . shall by offering higher wages or greater benefits or other inducements, persuade or attempt to persuade any native who has been lawfully recruited to desert or repudiate having been so recruited or to break or repudiate any then existing and binding contract of service."[23]

These rudimentary examples of labor repression constitute the beginnings of what has become in our time the essence of *apartheid:* the use of race laws to control the mobility and proletarianization of African workers.[24] This section reviews some of the basic political elements in the South African labor environment.

Political Remedies for a Feeble Labor Market: Pass Laws and Influx Control

Pass laws and influx control predate the establishment of mines and factories in South Africa. In the Cape Colony, slaves were required to carry

18.   Cape of Good Hope, *Report of the Select Committee on the Labour Question,* C2–1892; and Cape of Good Hope, *Report of the Select Committee, Supply of the Labour Market,* A. 26–1879.
19.   David Welsh, *The Roots of Segregation.*
20.   Quoted in Francis Wilson, "Farming, 1866–1966," p. 120.
21.   Sheila T. van der Horst, *Native Labour in South Africa,* p. 111.
22.   Ibid., pp. 92–93.
23.   Quoted in Horwitz, *The Political Economy,* p. 81.
24.   See Harold Wolpe, "Capitalism and Cheap Labour-Power in South Africa: from Segregation to Apartheid."

travel documents, and for a short period in the early nineteenth century, the Khoikhoi were forced to take up fixed abodes and carry passes. When Africans began moving into the white settler areas of the eastern Cape, the pass laws were extended to them as well. In some areas the pass laws helped colonial administrators monitor the numbers and movements of Coloureds and Africans, while serving the labor-control requirements of white slaveowners and farmers. In other areas, however, these same regulations restricted the supply of African labor and raised the ire of white farmers.[25]

But the monitoring and "passport" functions of the Cape pass laws are a far cry from the draconian and pervasive pass and influx laws that characterize the capitalist era in South Africa. It is in the modern period, from 1875 to the present, that South African labor law begins to resemble the Elizabethan Statute of Apprentices writ large.[26]

In the mining districts around Kimberley and the Witwatersrand, pass laws became the principal vehicle for controlling desertion and labor turnover among African laborers. Formal labor control began in 1872 with the compulsory registration of labor contracts. Africans in the Kimberley district were obliged to produce their labor contracts on demand and to acquire a pass on the satisfactory completion of their work obligations. "Any person found wandering in a mining camp without a pass and unable to give a satisfactory account of himself," H. J. and R. E. Simons note, "ran the risk of summary arrest, a £5 fine and three months' hard labour or twenty-five lashes."[27] The vagrancy laws were amended a few years later to provide a six-month prison term with hard labor for any "idle and disorderly person."[28] Convict labor turned these labor-control mechanisms into direct measures for organizing a labor force in the diamond fields. At various times between 1873 and 1887, the Kimberley jails housed as many as 67,000 prisoners. The De Beers Mining Company, soon the dominant force in the mining industry, built a convict station for 3,000 to 4,000 convict-miners.[29]

Convict labor, vagrancy laws, and passes were soon supplemented by the principal labor-control arrangement at Kimberley: the closed compound system. African miners entered the compound at the outset of their terms of

25. Van der Horst, *Native Labour,* pp. 32–33; David Welsh, "The Growth of Towns," pp. 196–97.
26. See Guy Routh, "Industrial Relations and Race Relations," pp. 3–4. The Elizabethan law provided, W. Stanley Jevons writes, "any workman departing from his city, town or parish, without a testimonial from his previous employer or some officer, was to be imprisoned until he procured a testimonial; or if he could not do so within the space of one and twenty days, was to be whipped and used as a vagabond."
27. H. J. and R. E. Simons, *Class and Colour in South Africa 1850–1950,* p. 38.
28. Cited in ibid., p. 39.
29. Peter Kallaway, "Preliminary Notes Towards a Study of Labour on the Diamond Fields of Griqualand West," pp. 8–9.

service and left only at the expiration of their contracts. They received all their amenities in the compound and were protected from the abuses of alcohol, their own inexperience with industrial discipline, and "unscrupulous" enticements from competing employers.[30] Kimberley, as de Kiewiet observed, "was the cradle and testing ground for social and economic policy."[31] Pass laws and compounds would soon become the rule on the Witwatersrand.

With the Natives (Urban Areas) Act in 1923, the labor-control principles were extended to the developing industrial and urban centers. The act provided that in "proclaimed areas," African males "must carry and may be required to produce on demand either a permit to seek work or a duly registered service contract, in order to establish his right to be within the area."[32] To eliminate the "surplus" unemployed African population,[33] the act urged localities to establish Native Advisory Boards to register labor contracts. By 1937, with amendments to the act, the central government was able to mandate "influx" controls and separate African townships.[34] The government relaxed its enforcement of the pass laws during the war years, but in 1945 began, once again, to elaborate the "influx" controls.[35] The Natives (Urban Areas) Consolidation Act of 1945 provided for registration by the employer of "every contract of service entered into by a male African" and granted "the right to exclude any African female from entering" an urban area and "the right to prohibit any male African who is not in possession of a contract of service from remaining in the area for a period beyond fourteen days."[36]

The National party government sought to rationalize the system further. It substituted a single reference book for the myriad documents that Africans carried previously, the poll tax receipt and pass book, for example. That simplification, along with an elaborate system of labor bureaus, placed the African industrial worker under even closer government scrutiny and tighter regulations on labor mobility.[37] In the mid-sixties, the government

30. See Simons, *Class and Colour,* pp. 42–43; G. V. Doxey, *The Industrial Colour Bar in South Africa,* pp. 33–35.
31. C. W. de Kiewiet, *A History of South Africa: Social and Economic,* p. 90.
32. Quoted in van der Horst, *Native Labour,* p. 273.
33. Muriel Horrell, *Legislation and Race Relations,* pp. 2–3.
34. Ibid., p. 3.
35. David Welsh, "The Growth of Towns," pp. 198–99.
36. Doxey, *The Industrial Colour Bar,* pp. 169–70.
37. An unemployed African, unless considered permanently urbanized under section 10, could remain unregistered for only seventy-two hours in a "proclaimed" area. He must seek work through a government-run labor bureau that assigned the work locality, type of employment, and might select a specific employer. Each month, employers were to endorse their African employees' reference books and report within seventy-two hours any African job vacancies. The law, however, was haphazardly administered and failed to routinize the labor system (Doxey, *The Industrial Colour Bar,* pp. 172–74).

attempted to make up for lax enforcement and gaps in the legislation. With the Bantu Laws Amendment Act of 1964, employers could hire only those African workers assigned or sanctioned by a labor bureau. The act's provisions were extended to casual laborers, independent contractors, and Africans previously exempted as permanent residents of urban areas. Regulations promulgated four years later limited labor contracts to one year and required that employers "repatriate" African workers when their contracts expired. In 1971, the discretion and jurisdiction of local authorities were abrogated in favor of a fully centralized labor administration.[38]

In 1977 the government appointed a one-person commission (Riekert) to reexamine the system of influx control and pass laws, but its report and the government's subsequent white paper in 1979 left the labor framework intact. The Riekert report recommended the maintenance of influx control, though it proposed that the burden of control shift from arrests and criminal penalties to stricter enforcement of housing and employment restrictions for "illegal" urban workers. The government refused to lift the criminal penalties but did immediately quintuple the fine for employing unregistered African workers.[39]

The emerging labor environment, if pervasive and repressive, nonetheless grated against the inclinations of African workers and the forces in industrialization. Between 1921 and 1924, yearly convictions under these laws averaged 48,000; by 1948, the figure had climbed to 184,000; and by 1962, to 385,000. In the decade between 1965 and 1975, yearly prosecutions averaged 600,000.[40]

Business Autonomy: Suppressing African Labor Organization

In areas of dominant employment, businessmen exchanged their autonomy for orderly, institutionalized labor-management practice. They chose, in effect, to go beyond the period immediately after Union, which was marked by on-and-off negotiations between the Chamber of Mines and the white mine workers' unions and by periodic labor unrest, culminating in the great mine strike of 1922. The Industrial Conciliation Act of 1924 brought an historic accommodation between white labor and management: white workers' organizations were granted formal recognition and industrial councils were created to settle disputes, structure collective bargaining, and administer apprenticeship and benefit programs.

Unfortunately, white management and labor chose to "bury the hatchet" in the heads of the African industrial workers. "Pass-bearing" persons—

38. Section 10 Africans were exempted from the provisions on contracts. See Horrell, *Legislation and Race Relations*, pp. 39–40, 43; Francis Wilson, *Migrant Labour*, p. 162.
39. *Financial Mail*, 22 June 1979, pp. 1051–52.
40. Wilson, *Migrant Labour*, p. 164.

Africans—were not considered "employees" under the terms of the act.[41]
And under subsequent National and United party governments, the essence
of industrial conciliation remained unaltered: a well-ordered labor environment for white workers in mining, construction, and manufacturing; for the
African workers, whether in industry or agriculture, no trade-union recognition or bargaining.

The Struggle against "Labour Peace"

Black workers did not willingly yield the work place to management and
the state. The African presence in industrial life has been accompanied
by rage and strikes, messianic movements, and trade-union organization.

African mine workers in 1911, only five years after rural Africans in Natal
had raised shields and assegai against hut taxes, downed tools at the
Dutoitspan, Voorspoed, and Village Deep mines. Management, with the
connivance of organized white miners, readily responded with police and
mob violence, imprisoning African strikers under the masters and servants
laws. A boycott of concession stores in 1918 and a wave of small-scale
African strikes were followed by widespread arrests for breach of contract
and, subsequently, by the threat of a general strike. In 1920, 40,000 African
miners struck for higher wages, reform of the concession stores, and
elimination of the "colour bar." The government placed police cordons
around the twenty-two affected compounds; the mining houses introduced
white strikebreakers and mob violence.[42]

Clements Kadalie in the twenties and thirties organized the largest of the
mass-based African trade unions, the Industrial and Commercial Workers
Union of Africa (ICU). Nearly 100,000 Africans, drawn not just from the
Witwatersrand, Durban, and Cape Town, but from the northern Free State
and eastern and northern Transvaal, responded to the organization's
evangelical appeal. But the ICU's broad scope and aversion to strikes
prevented it from penetrating the work place. Employers declined to
negotiate with ICU representatives; the government registrar declared that
the ICU was not a "statutory trade union"; and the South African Trade
Union Congress, the most important trade-union federation in South

41. The Wage Act of 1925 offered some wage protections for unorganized white workers
and, after 1937, for African workers as well. Amendments to the Industrial Conciliation Act in
1937 permitted the minister of labor to extend industrial council agreements to African
employees, even though Africans could not be party to negotiations.
42. Simons, *Class and Colour,* p. 154, 207–28; Edward Roux, *Time Longer Than Rope,*
pp. 132–34.

Africa, refused to permit its affiliation.[43] The ICU was succeeded in the thirties and forties by periodic booms in African trade unionism and non-European trade-union federations. Employers, with only minor exceptions, declined to speak to African representatives; the state refused them recognition, allowing the African unions a hearing only before wage boards and investigatory commissions; and the white unions offered them only a reluctant coexistence.[44]

The African mine workers' strike of 1946 was, as Dan O'Meara observes, a "watershed event."[45] The strike stands out not simply because of its scale (76,000 Africans struck at least twenty-one out of forty-five mines, bringing gold production to a standstill on as many as twelve of them) or because of the enormous brutality in the government and Chamber of Mines' response (1,600 special constables held the mine compound under a state of seige). Work stoppages and repression are commonplace in South African industrial relations. The 1946 strike, however, was the first large-scale work stoppage organized by an African labor organization, the African Mine Workers' Union (AMWU). African trade unions and control of the work place, not simply wages or concession stores, were now at issue. In addition to the conventional insistence on regular wage increments and cost-of-living allowances, the AMWU demanded abolition of the compound system, pass laws, and formal "tribal" divisions on the mines. It also sought recognition of the AMWU as bargaining agent for African mine workers. The Lansdown Commission, whose recommendations had become central concerns of the strike, rejected the union's plea: Africans have "not yet reached such a standard as to appreciate the power of collective bargaining or other benefits of trade unionism." It warned, however, that the existing system of *indunas,* head boys, and police boys afforded little audience for collective African grievances and opinion.[46] Neither the commission's warnings nor the demands of the AMWU brought serious changes in the developing labor system.

43. This discussion relies upon the accounts of Simons, *Class and Colour,* pp. 361–68 and Roux, *Time Longer Than Rope,* pp. 153–76.

44. The Non-European Trade Union Federation disintegrated in the 1930–33 period; the Non-European Trade Union Coordinating Committee collapsed along with the African Mine Workers' Union; and the South African Congress of Trade Unions (SACTU) declined with the banning of the PAC and the ANC and the suppression of their underground organizations in 1964 (L. Douwes Dekker, D. Hemson, J. S. Kane-Berman, J. Lever, and L. Schlemmer, "Case Studies in African Labor Action in South and South West Africa," pp. 10–11; also see Edward Feit, *Workers Without Weapons*).

45. Dan O'Meara, "The 1946 African Mine Workers' Strike in the Political Economy of South Africa," pp. 147, 160.

46. Union of South Africa, *Report of the Mine Natives' Wages Commission,* U.G. 21–1944, pp. 36–37.

Virtually all the remnants of African labor organization were destroyed after Sharpeville in 1960.[47] But the banning of union leaders and the demise of the African labor federations did not dispel the specter of African work stoppages. More than 75,000 African workers participated in the illegal Durban strikes of 1973 and 1974.[48] These strikers were not miners, who could be herded easily into isolated compounds. The strikes spread through the manufacturing complex in and around Durban and engulfed the major textile, automobile, engineering, and construction industries. African workers stood outside their factories, in the streets, and on soccer fields, demanding a rand or two more a day. The state, however, remained committed to the "labour policy and the machinery which has been created, which has given us this great measure of labour peace in this country."[49]

The Unorganized Work Place

This "labour peace" was predicated on a legislative tangle that made it illegal for Africans to withhold their labor and virtually impossible for Africans to form labor organizations. Masters and servants laws, providing criminal rather than civil liability for breach of contract, were readily adapted to deal with African strikes. The Native Labour Regulation Act of 1911 provided fine and imprisonment where African workers refused to "obey any lawful command of his employer" or neglected to "perform any work which it is his duty to perform."[50] Though such laws fell into disuse or were repealed in twentieth-century Europe, they were further elaborated in South Africa. With the wave of African strikes during World War II, the government promulgated War Measure 145, which, in Margaret Ballinger's terms, made "all strikes of all African workers in all circumstances illegal."[51] Two years later, the government presented War Measure 1425, limiting gatherings on mining property to twenty persons.[52] Only in 1974, under the threat of international sanctions, did the government divorce

---

47.   What remained in 1973 was one major African union, the National Union of Clothing Workers with 17,000 members, and a cluster of smaller African unions with no more than 500 members each. Fewer than 20,000 Africans belonged to labor organizations (Hemson, "Black Strikes," annexure B).
48.   Muriel Horrell, Dudley Horner, and Jane Hudson, *A Survey of Race Relations in South Africa 1974*, p. 325.
49.   *Hansard*, 13 February 1973, col. 566.
50.   Doxey, *The Industrial Colour Bar*, p. 129.
51.   Cited in Roux, *Time Longer Than Rope*, p. 331.
52.   O'Meara, "The 1946 African Mine Workers' Strike," p. 153.

South African capitalism from some of the worst abuses of Dickens's times.[53]

In the absence of unions and legal strikes in the African labor market, the government has turned to various forms of representation, short of genuine collective bargaining. In 1939, the Departments of Labour and Native Affairs expressed concern about the spread of African unions that lacked any formal recognition or supervision and that too often fell under the control of "Europeans who seek to exploit their grievances for their own profit."[54] These departments proposed a series of informal rules that would have provided, in effect, "administrative recognition." The proposals, however, were rejected by the African unions themselves and, eventually, by the government. The latter felt that African workers were afforded adequate protection by Wage Act determinations and the vigilance of inspectors from the Department of Labour.[55] With the spread of African unions and work stoppages during World War II, the Departments of Labour and Native Affairs again proposed draft rules for registration of African workers' organizations and for consultation through local divisional inspectors of labor. Before losing office in 1948, Smuts proposed binding arbitration by government officials and, in the words of the Botha Commission, gave Africans "as far as practicable, the same rights without permitting them to take part in industrial councils formed by employers and European employees." Again, the African unions demanded full recognition as "employees" under the Industrial Conciliation Act.[56]

The National party-dominated Botha Commission proposed in 1951 "special measures" for the "control and guidance" of African unions.[57] But recognition of African unions, whether in statutory, administrative, or any other form, was no longer acceptable to the government. The Bantu Labour (Settlement of Disputes) Act of 1953 reaffirmed and tightened the exclusion

53. The Second General Law Amendment Act repealed masters and servants laws from the Cape of Good Hope, Orange Free State, Transvaal, and Natal that dated back to 1856. It also expunged sections of the Bantu Labour Act of 1964 that imposed criminal penalties for desertion, breach of contract, and failure to obey an employer. The right of African workers to strike is still radically circumscribed, even with the "reforms" provided by the Bantu Labour Relations Regulation Act of 1973 (Horrell, Horner, and Hudson, *A Survey of Race Relations 1974*, pp. 336–37).

54. From the Native Affairs Commission's Report 1939/40, cited in Union of South Africa, *Report of the Industrial Legislation Commission of Enquiry* (Botha), U.G. 62–1951, p. 199.

55. Union of South Africa, *Report of the Department of Labour,* U.G. No. 36, 1940, p. 5.

56. Union of South Africa, *Report of the Industrial Legislation Commission of Enquiry,* 1951, p. 200.

57. Ibid., p. 226.

of Africans under the Industrial Conciliation Act: it prohibited strikes by
African workers and provided penalties of one thousand rands or three
years in jail. Later legislation during the fifties barred the attendance of any
African representative at the proceedings of an industrial council or
conciliation board and forbade employers from checking off union dues or
union sick benefits for African employees.[58]

In the place of organization in the subordinate, African section of the
work place, the government and employers opted for "works" and "liaison"
committees. Though works committees date back to the Bantu Labour
(Settlement of Disputes) Act of 1953, neither the government nor employers
took any form of worker communication seriously until the Durban strike
of 1973. At the time of the strike, there were only eighteen functioning
works committees; even earlier, at the peak of "communications," there
were only forty. "To my disappointment, I must state today," the minister
of labour commented, "that I have over the years received no positive
reaction from employers to my request as to how the works committee
system may be improved." But with the Natal labor force in open revolt,
with communication taking place in the streets and soccer stadiums, the
government acted quickly to revive the committee system. The Bantu
Labour Relations Regulation Amendment Act (1973) encouraged employers and African workers to form "works committees"—plant level
"negotiating" bodies comprised of elected African representatives—or
better yet, "liaison committees"—plant-level bodies comprised of management as well as elected African representatives, with chairmen, in most
cases, selected by management. In the year following the bill's enactment,
employers established 182 works and 1,134 liaison committees.[59]

In mid-1979, the Commission of Inquiry into Labour Legislation
(Wiehahn) proposed that the government include Africans in the industrial
conciliation machinery: Africans would be permitted to join existing
registered unions that voluntarily opened their memberships to all race
groups; or they could form exclusively African unions that might be
registered with the state. However, important qualifications to the proposals
—including maintenance of extant closed-shop agreements, works and
liaison committees, and the union's right to exclude black workers, and
broader and more onerous registration procedures and restrictions on trade-
union political activity—seriously limited the scope of these "reforms." The
subsequent government white paper and legislation introduced further

58. Muriel Horrell, *South Africa's Workers*, p. 17.
59. Muriel Horrell and Dudley Horner, *A Survey of Race Relations 1973*, pp. 276–77;
Horrell, Horner, and Hudson, *A Survey of Race Relations 1974*, p. 332.

qualifications, which included barring the registration of multiracial unions.[60]

The labor-repressive framework helps businessmen organize a labor force and maintain control over individual laborers; it allows for the orderly evolution of labor relations in white areas of employment, while leaving businessmen free to exercise their autonomy in unskilled, African areas. In the end, it insures that African workers will realize neither the full advantage of their mobility and labor power nor the economic and political benefits that come from regular, organized influence over the work place.

DEVELOPING LABOR POLICIES OF THE CHAMBER OF MINES: ORGANIZING A LABOR FORCE

The gold-mining industry, because of its size and importance in the economy, because of the glitter and mystery that surrounds its output, stands out from other sections of South African society. Two other aspects, however, make the industry critical to an understanding of labor repression in the capitalist period: first, labor supplies that proved inadequate and unresponsive to an accelerating demand for labor; second, a low grade of ore and an international market price for gold that created endemic cost problems.[61] Together, these factors turned the gold-mining houses toward the race question and the state: first, to insure the availability of labor; second, to insure its regularity and cheapness. Coercion and discrimination, pervasive but formless on the nineteenth-century farms, became systematic and seemingly inviolable in the hands of the Chamber of Mines.

The Supply of African Labor

The Chamber of Mines from the outset understood that it could not organize a labor force and minimize labor costs while depending "upon the

60. Republic of South Africa, Department of Labour and of Mines, *Report of the Commission of Inquiry into Labour Legislation*, part 1, R.P. 47/1949; *Financial Mail*, 22 June 1979, pp. 1053–55.
61. Other aspects of the cost problem include: high transportation costs (the Witwatersrand in its earliest years was inaccessible by rail); protective tariffs and government-sponsored monopolies for domestic manufacture, particularly dynamite; high wages for skilled miners attracted from Europe, North America, and Australia; and the high cost of food, clothing, and basic services—efficiencies in gold production did not reduce maintenance costs for the mining labor force. See Doxey, *The Industrial Colour Bar*, pp. 42–43; and M. L. Morris, "Capitalism and Apartheid: A Critique of Some Current Conceptions of Cheap Labour Power," pp. 5–6.

ordinary arrangements for supply."[62] After some initial competitive give-and-take and ineffective forays into labor recruiting in the early 1890s, the mining houses reaped the advantages of collusion and the pass laws.

In 1897 the Chamber of Mines organized its own labor-recruiting organization, what was later called the Witwatersrand Native Labour Association. With the signing of the Anglo-Portuguese modus vivendi in 1901, it became the sole recruiting agent in Mozambique and the principal suppplier of African labor to the gold-mining industry. In 1912, the Chamber established the Native Recruiting Corporation, bringing African laborers from South Africa and the Protectorates under its labor monopsony. With control over the supply of labor, with its own inspectors, the Chamber was able to establish a standard contract, fix the quality of rations and the length of the working day, and, most important, affect a series of wage reductions for African workers. The Chamber of Mines and the Native Recruiting Corporation soon settled upon the "maximum average" as the simplest vehicle for fixing wages and preventing ruinous wage competition among the mining houses. The mines were not bound by a firm salary schedule; they were prevented, however, from offering African workers wage inducements that on the average exceeded wage levels on other mines.[63]

The mining industry also sought pass laws that would prevent a "large desertion of Natives, consequent upon the reduction of wages."[64] The Chamber in 1893 submitted draft pass regulations: "Elaborate measures are provided for securing identification, for preventing employers engaging 'boys' who cannot show a discharge from a previous employer, and generally for affording companies a reasonable guarantee that if they get labour from a distance they will reap the benefit of the outlay incurred."[65] The Chamber lobbied hard—"no opportunity of urging the advisability of their being passed as quickly as possible was neglected"—and in 1895, "the Chamber had the satisfaction of seeing them passed, practically without alteration."[66]

But the Kruger government was reluctant to extend the pass law provisions beyond a limited number of districts and was, from the Chamber's view, lax in administering the laws. A mine manager told the Industrial Commission of Inquiry (1897): "We have here the most excellent

62. Chamber of Mines (Witwatersrand), *Annual Report 1895,* p. 26.
63. Van der Horst, *Native Labour,* pp. 130–31; also H. M. Robertson, "150 Years of Economic Contact Between Black and White," pp. 15–19.
64. "Letter from Witwatersrand Chamber of Mines to State Secretary, Pretoria," Chamber of Mines (Witwatersrand), *Annual Report 1890,* p. 66.
65. Chamber of Mines (Witwatersrand), *Annual Report 1895,* p. 13.
66. Ibid., p. 14.

law, in my opinion—namely the Pass Law—which, if properly carried out, and efficiently administered, will enable us to get complete control over our kaffir labourers."[67] Memorials of the Chamber before the commission sought expanded application to cover all districts of the Witwatersrand, more staff for the Pass Department, and increased police, offices, and judicial commissioners to administer the law.[68] The commission and the Chamber even toyed with the possibility of "forced labour."[69]

After the defeat of the Boers, the British administration brought a new mood to the pass laws and the mining industry generally. The Transvaal Labour Commission (1904) set the tone for the decade. Labor shortages are the only "deterrent to the expansion of the industry," it declared. "It is therefore imperative to find means to enable the mines to work to their full capacity."[70] The new administration began immediate inquiries into the dynamite concession and other monopolies granted by the Kruger government. It also provided what the Chamber described as "far better provisions than formerly existed" for "regulating the procuring and engaging of native labourers."[71]

Unable to obtain sufficient African labor after the South African War, the Chamber of Mines began to encourage the importation of Chinese contract laborers. In 1903 the Chamber told the Transvaal Labour Commission that there was a "want of unskilled labour on the mines and throughout South Africa." The pool of African labor, unfortunately, was "almost quite exhausted." The Chamber posed an alternative: "We are convinced therefore that there is no other solution than to allow the importation of suitable unskilled labour from all available sources."[72] Sir George Farrar, a prominent mining magnate, also suggested to the same commission a limited form of "Asiatic" immigration: "It means that if Asiatic labourers unfortunately have to be brought into this country, they can be brought in under Government control, and only as unskilled labourers, prohibited to trade, prohibited to hold land, or compete with any white man, and that they should be carefully indentured and be repatriated

67. Chamber of Mines (Witwatersrand), "The Mining Industry," *Evidence and Report of the Industrial Commission of Enquiry,* p. 44.
68. Ibid., p. 489; see Chamber of Mines (Witwatersrand), *Annual Report 1896,* p. 6.
69. Chamber of Mines (Witwatersrand), "Testimony of the Chairman of the Chamber of Mines," in the "Mining Industry," *Evidence and Report of the Industrial Commission of Enquiry,* p. 8.
70. Transvaal, *Report of the Transvaal Labour Commission: Report and Evidence,* 1904, pp. 17–18.
71. Chamber of Mines (Transvaal), *Report of the Executive for the Years 1899, 1900, 1901,* pp. 5–8; also see Dennis Bransky, "The Causes of the Boer War: Towards a Synthesis," pp. 11–12.
72. Cited in the Chamber of Mines (Transvaal), *Annual Report 1906,* p. liii.

at the termination of the period of their engagement to the country from which they came."[73]

The Labour Importation Ordinance (No. 17 of 1904) legalized the first importation of Chinese labor: 1,055 "coolies" in June; 21,000 by the end of 1904.[74] The Chamber was assured its thirty shifts at fifty shillings a month. The slow return of African workers to the mines following the Boer War was "not, then, secured at the cost of rising wages."[75]

The end of direct British administration of the Transvaal in 1906 and the Act of Union in 1909 did not threaten the labor system in the Transvaal and surrounding territories. Indeed, the Union brought an immediate reaffirmation of developing practice in labor recruitment and pass regulation—the Native Labour Regulation Act.[76] Though the minister of native affairs barred further recruitment of African workers from Nyasaland and Rhodesia (these workers suffered particularly high mortality rates on the mines),[77] the government allowed the extension of the recruiting system in 1912 and proved capable of enforcing the pass laws. The Chamber felt that it should remind the National party in 1924 of some basic precepts in the South African political economy: "It cannot be too strongly emphasized that the Witwatersrand gold mining industry has been made possible by the low cost of native labour, and that its existence on a large scale depends on obtaining an adequate supply of that labour."[78] But the warning was hardly necessary. With new advances in antipneumococcal vaccine and the need for labor following the 1932 devaluation, the government gradually lifted the remaining restrictions on labor recruiting.[79] The Proceedings of the Chamber's Annual General Meeting in 1935 spoke of the "highly satisfactory supply of native labour."[80]

The Native Reserves and the Semiproletarianized Mine Worker

The native reserves—the near-subsistence African rural areas—are a requisite for African labor and cost minimization under prevailing forms of gold production. At the simplest level, the reserves provide manpower that can

73. Transvaal, *Report of the Transvaal Labour Commission*, p. 70.
74. Doxey, *The Industrial Colour Bar*, p. 58.
75. Robertson, "150 Years of Economic Contact," pp. 18–19.
76. Van der Horst, *Native Labour*, pp. 179–80.
77. Chamber of Mines (Transvaal), *Annual Report 1913*, p. lviii.
78. Chamber of Mines (Transvaal), Gold Producers' Committee, *Party Programmes and the Mines: A Business Statement*, 1924, p. 4.
79. Wilson, *Migrant Labour*, p. 113; see the statement by the Chamber of Mines (Transvaal), Gold Producers' Committee before the *Low Grade Ore Commission 1930–32*, Statement No. 7, pp. 7–9.
80. Chamber of Mines (Transvaal), *Proceedings at the Annual General Meeting 1935*, p. 13.

be dislodged from other pursuits; they provide workers that will, for whatever reason, tolerate the rigors of underground mining and the strictures of compound life. But at a more complex and important level, the reserves underwrite "cheap" labor policies. Because the reserves permit continued family agricultural production in the subsistence economy, the mining houses need pay only the subsistence and small cash requirements of their migrant laborers, expenses below, in effect, the cost of the workers' reproduction, below what would be necessary if the workers and their families became a permanent part of industrial South Africa. By urging the state to maintain the reserve areas—to regulate labor contracts, enforce pass laws and influx controls as well—the mining industry preserves "the low cost of native labour."

In the mid-twenties the Chamber of Mines took up a five-decade defense of the native reserves. The employers' side of the Economic and Wage Commission (1925) set out both the altruistic and economic motives behind these African rural areas: "They provide the most apt safeguard against unjust economic exploitation of the native, and they provide the best means of maintaining his morale in the difficult transition from primitive simplicity to the complexity of modern economic civilization." It was best that African participation in industrial life be limited "to intermittent periods of employment under sheltered conditions while the greater part of the native life is still passed in the nursery of his own tribal community."[81] Twenty years later, the Chamber pressed a similar theme, hoping to foreclose African trade unionism and labor stabilization:

> The culture of all these Natives is tribal and rural. Their contact with industrialism and industrial conditions is only recent, and they have little knowledge or understanding of the organization of industry. They are bound by the strongest ties to the traditions, customs and the authority of their respective tribes.[82]

Migrant labor and the mining compound, the Chamber argued, temper "the impact of what is to him a strange, bewildering world."[83] The alternative—labor stabilization—posed immeasurable cost problems, particularly family housing, social and medical services, and educational facilities. The Chamber warned that these costs "would place a dangerous strain on the already limited resources of the State and the gold mining industry."[84]

81. Union of South Africa, *Report of the Economic and Wage Commission 1925,* U.G. 14–1926, pp. 155, 157.
82. Chamber of Mines (Transvaal), *Tribal Natives and Trade Unionism,* 1946, p. 1.
83. Chamber of Mines (Transvaal), *The Native Workers on the Witwatersrand Gold Mines,* 1947, p. 3.
84. Ibid., p. 13.

But the system was under challenge. World War II brought rapid advances in the areas of secondary industry and urbanization. The Chamber's defense of "tribal life" appeared increasingly hollow as African shantytowns began encircling the white cities and African laborers began securing jobs in manufacturing. The Fagan Commission in 1947 heard spokesmen for secondary industry and commerce argue against the traditional labor system; the commission eventually made recommendations that, if implemented, would have weakened the migrant labor system.

The Chamber maintained its stand before the Fagan Commission and a later government inquiry into the "native areas," the Tomlinson Commission.[85] It stood steadfast for the continuation of migrant labor:

> The system of migratory labour has made it possible for the lowest commoner in the tribe to earn sufficient monetary remuneration with which to purchase trade goods and to meet his tax obligations while still retaining his traditional life in the Reserves. . . . Were it suddenly removed, the effect upon the Reserve population would be deplorable. The Native requires additional cash to meet obligations imposed upon him by European contact. . . . Thus the institution of migratory labour is at once a stabilizing factor in the National economy and the National social structure.[86]

The costs in any precipitous change, the Chamber argued, would be catastrophic:

> If, however, national policy were to encourage the process by insisting on a stabilised labour force for all industries, including mining, it would, in the words of the Witwatersrand Mine Native Wages Commission (Para-211), "bring about a catastrophic dislocation of the Industry and consequent prejudice to the whole economic structure of the Union."[87]

The Chamber reaffirmed its vigilance, even when the government and other entrepreneurs were shrinking away from the migrant labor system:

> The evils that exist have arisen as a result of rapid urbanisation of Natives employed in Commerce and Industry, a process which has

85. Union of South Africa, *Report of the Commission for the Socio-Economic Development of the Native Areas Within the Union of South Africa,* U.G. 61–1955, better known for its chairman, Professor F. R. Tomlinson. The Commission laid the basis for the present "homelands" policy (pp. 3–7).
86. Chamber of Mines (Transvaal), Gold Producers' Committee, *Statement of Evidence before the Natives Laws Commission of Enquiry,* 1947, p. 23.
87. Ibid., p. 38.

relieved them suddenly of all tribal restraint. The Industry endeavors to guard its Natives against undesirable and subversive influences and is largely successful in spite of many recent attempts on the part of those outside mine compounds to disturb the peace within.[88]

From 1960, after Sharpeville, when other industrial groups sought reform of the traditional labor framework, the Chamber defended the virtues of compound life, the levels of compensation, and the link with the African rural areas: "The preservation of links with the tribal background imparts both security to the individual worker and stability to the economy of his home territory."[89]

Wage Regulation and "Cheap Native Labour"

The Chamber of Mines has promulgated four not altogether consistent principles of African wage regulation: first, wage levels in the Witwatersrand gold mines are "not only adequate but generous";[90] second, "the Witwatersrand gold mining industry has been made possible by the low costs of native labour";[91] third, the gold mining industry would close down if substantial wage increases were granted to African workers;[92] and fourth, "any increase in the level of native wages would be followed" by a reduction in the "native labour available to industry in the Union."[93]

The Chamber, therefore, has opposed any attempt to uplift or regulate African wages. In 1890, before there was a South African state concerned with industrial wages, the Chamber wrote the Transvaal government and spoke of the "altogether abnormal and excessive" remuneration paid African workers and promised "strenuous efforts . . . to bring about a large reduction."[94] A survey by the Chamber revealed, to the surprise of none, that all twenty-five responding companies considered the prevailing wage rate too high.[95] The Mining Industry Board in 1922 accepted the evidence of the Chamber that "the mining industry in the Transvaal, like all industries of any magnitude in South Africa, is built upon the basis of cheap native

88. Ibid., p. 39.
89. Chamber of Mines (Transvaal and Orange Free State), *Annual Report 1960,* p. 57.
90. Union of South Africa, *Report of the Economic and Wage Commission 1925,* "Evidence of the Gold Producers' Committee of the Transvaal Chamber of Mines," Statement No. 2, p. 1.
91. Chamber of Mines (Transvaal), Gold Producers' Committee, *Party Programmes,* p. 4.
92. Representation of the Chamber of Mines, Union of South Africa, *Report of the Select Committee on the Wage Bills,* S.C. 14–1925, p. 91.
93. Van der Horst, *Native Labour,* p. 197.
94. Chamber of Mines (Witwatersrand), *Annual Report 1890,* p. 66.
95. Ibid., p. 65.

labour for unskilled work."[96] The board itself, consistent with the testimony of the Chamber, failed to recommend any legislation in this area.[97] When the basic outlines of the wage and conciliation bills were presented in 1924 and 1925, the Chamber acted vigorously to erect a fortress around the mining industry and preserve its wage structure. The Chamber raised a host of objections to the wage bill before it reached the select committee stage,[98] and when it reached the committee, the Chamber sought the "exclusion [of mining] . . . from the operations of the Bill."[99] The full weight of the legislation, the Chamber argued, should fall on unorganized "sweated" industries, the mining industry apparently not being among them.

The Chamber not only resisted minimum wages on the mines, it opposed amendments to the wage bill in 1937 that would have extended wage protections to African workers in secondary industry. Where Africans in these industries received wages "above the customary rates," the Chamber argued, there followed a "detrimental effect upon those industries which are primary producers such as mining and farming:"[100] African workers were attracted to town life rather than the mines, thus speeding the process of "detribalization"; the mining industry was forced to restrict output and close low-grade mines. Before the Lansdown Commission during World War II, the Chamber warned that even a "slight increase" in African wages would shorten the life of the productive mines and close three others.[101]

Only in 1972, with rapidly rising gold prices, uncertain supplies of foreign and migrant laborers, and new opportunities for training African workers, did the Chamber and the mining houses begin to reconsider African wage levels. Between 1911 and 1969, African mine wages remained constant in real terms.[102] But beginning in 1972, the mining houses increased African wages; indeed, at a rate almost double that of whites—38.1 percent compared to 20 percent between 1972 and 1974.[103] The African miner's wage, consequently, reached the princely sum of 29 rands a month; the white miner's wage averaged 475 rands. This shift must reflect, in light of the

96. Union of South Africa, *Report of the Mining Industry Board*, U.G. 39–1922, p. l2. The Chamber of Mines reported, "In almost every respect this evidence was endorsed in the findings of the Board" (Chamber of Mines [Transvaal], *Annual Report 1922*, p. 131).
97. Union of South Africa, *Report of the Mining Industry Board 1922*, p. 8.
98. Chamber of Mines (Transvaal), *Annual Report 1924*, p. 57.
99. Union of South Africa, *Report of the Select Committee on the Wage Bill*, p. 66.
100. Chamber of Mines (Transvaal), *Annual Report 1937*, p. 72.
101. Union of South Africa, *Report of the Witwatersrand Mine Natives' Wages Commission*, p. 20.
102. Wilson, *Labour in the South African Gold Mines*, p. 46.
103. Horrell, Horner, and Hudson, *A Survey of Race Relations 1974*, p. 281. In absolute terms, of course, white miners still received larger wage boosts than did the African gold miners.

Chamber's previous history, a new outlook among the mining houses. The Anglo-American Corporation began speaking of the need to move toward a "high-wage capital-intensive economy"; this position was seconded by the Johannesburg Consolidated Investment Company and, in more cautious terms, by the Chamber of Mines itself.[104]

The mining houses, however, have not determined to accept state wage regulation or to equalize African and white wages. In areas of African employment, even in newly developing semiskilled jobs, the mining houses are unilaterally creating wage scales well below those previously applicable to whites. The European gold miner, the director of one mining house observed, is overpaid: "The white has got a very warped situation. Why continue the warp [in African areas]? That's an obscenity." The manager of Anglo-American Corporation's gold-mining division declared: "The white rate is not the rate for the job or, in blunter terms, the job is not worth the wages being paid for it." The "solution," therefore, "does not lie in paying blacks the artificially high wages which have developed." In some professions, the higher rate might be applicable, "but to pay the same rate to white and black lorry drivers or to shunters or plasterers" or, indeed, to ventilators and mine workers "is not sensible."[105]

DEVELOPING LABOR POLICIES OF THE CHAMBER OF MINES: CONTROLLING THE WORK PLACE

None of the mining houses, certainly not the Chamber of Mines, has ever tolerated labor organization among African workers. They were not very enthusiastic about trade unions among whites either. After breaking the white mine workers' unions in 1922, the Chamber of Mines advocated "voluntary" conciliation, "free direct discussion between employer and employee." But with the passage of the Industrial Conciliation Act in 1924, the Chamber reluctantly accepted some limits on "managerial authority" in areas of white employment.[106] By 1937 the Chamber had come full circle, signing a closed-shop agreement with the Mine Workers' Union.[107]

The developing accommodation with the white unions left the Chamber

---

104. *Rand Daily Mail,* 2 September 1972; and Statement by the Chairman, H. F. Oppenheimer, Anglo-American Corporation of South Africa Limited, *Financial Mail,* 8 June 1973, p. 957; *Rand Daily Mail,* 6 September 1972; and *Rand Daily Mail,* 2 July 1974.
105. D. A. Etheredge, "Wages, Productivity and Opportunity," p. 7.
106. Chamber of Mines (Transvaal), *Annual Report 1924,* pp. 55–56; and Chamber of Mines (Transvaal), Gold Producers' Committee, *Party Programmes,* pp. 2–7.
107. Chamber of Mines (Transvaal), *Annual Report 1937,* pp. 64–65.

free to solidify its autonomy in areas of African employment. Here, the
Chamber refused even voluntary, "free direct discussion." Its emphasis,
instead, was on maintaining a controlled and disciplined African labor force
and the continued use of criminal penalties to forestall African work
stoppages. Before the Economic and Wage Commission (1925), the
Chamber observed: "[The] forced labour, the discipline, and the loss of
wages serve to convince [the African worker] of wrongdoing and to
demonstrate the unprofitableness of any failure, without lawful cause, to
observe the terms of his labour agreement."[108] Before the ink had dried on
the closed-shop agreement with white workers in 1937, the Chamber spoke
out against a minimum wage and trade unions for Africans, even if the
reforms were confined to secondary industry.[109] Indeed, the Chamber
intervened in a strike of African workers in the Johannesburg coal-
distribution trade, fearing that union recognition there might prove infec-
tious and spread to the mines.[110]

With the wave of strikes in 1942 and again in 1946, with the formation of
the African Mine Workers' Union (AMWU), the Chamber once again
turned to the traditional labor framework. First, it resisted the demands of
African workers and the recommendations of the Mine Natives' Wages
(Lansdown) Commission for increased wages and allowances.[111] Second, it
demanded, and got, strong state action to put down the work stoppages: the
United party government introduced War Measure 1425, prohibiting
gatherings larger than twenty persons on mine property; the police encircled
the affected mine compounds and arrested local and national union leaders.
Finally, the Chamber reiterated its long-standing position that the "native
population" was unprepared for collective action and vulnerable to "Com-
munistic" influences.[112] The Chamber issued a general circular to compound managers that forbade discussions with the AMWU;[113] union
organizers were victimized as a matter of course and of Chamber policy.[114]
The strike itself, the Chamber declared, "was provoked by agitators." By
contrast the "vast majority of our Native employees were neither interested
in the strike nor connected with the 'principles' on which it was said to be
based."[115]

108. "Evidence of the Gold Producers' Committee of the Transvaal Chamber of Mines,"
Union of South Africa, *Report of the Economic and Wage Commission,* 1925, Statement No. 3,
p. 2.
109. Chamber of Mines (Transvaal), *Annual Report 1937,* p. 72.
110. W. G. Ballinger, Correspondence with S. P. Bunting, 9 December 1941, Ballinger
Papers.
111. Roux, *Time Longer Than Rope,* p. 336.
112. Union of South Africa, *Report of the Witwatersrand Mine Natives' Wages Commission,*
pp. 36–37.
113. Roux, *Time Longer Than Rope,* pp. 336–37.
114. O'Meara, "The 1946 African Mine Workers' Strike," p. 159.
115. Chamber of Mines (Transvaal), *Proceedings at the Annual General Meeting 1946,* p. 4.

After the 1946 strike, the Chamber began to broaden its defense of the labor framework from policies that minimized labor costs on the mines to ones that provided for the welfare of African workers and the stability of society. Intermittent and migratory labor, the Chamber maintained, "is in harmony with the Native's own view."[116]

> Thus in the same way as the Native of the kraal prefers his spectacular and athletic tribal dances to the more sedate waltz of the Western world; and in the same way as his palate finds appetising many foods that would not appeal to the European, so too does he regard his traditional life of comparative leisure as preferable to the long span of years dedicated to hard work.[117]

Compound life and a controlled work environment were consistent with the African's work habits and capacity for organization. "Their contact with industrialism and industrial conditions," the Chamber observed, "is only recent, and they have little knowledge or understanding of the organisation of industry." In this milieu, "no proper conduct of a trade union is possible." The Africans' best interests were served, therefore, by the Native Affairs Department, inspectors from the various recruiting corporations, and the mine staff itself. "Every Native employee may go direct to the compound manager, who is always ready to listen to grievances without their passing through formal channels."[118]

Though the mining houses in recent years have considered alternatives to migrant labor and influx control,[119] they remain immovable on their autonomy in the work place. All operate within the traditional processes for communication and bargaining: African wages are set unilaterally, without consultation with African workers or even the white unions.[120] These

116. Chamber of Mines (Transvaal), Gold Producers' Committee, (Statement of Evidence), *Native Laws Commission of Enquiry,* 1947, Statement No. 2, p. 23.
117. Chamber of Mines (Transvaal), *The Native Workers on the Witwatersrand Gold Mines,* 1947, p. 1.
118. Chamber of Mines (Transvaal), *Tribal Natives and Trade Unionism, 1946,* pp. 1–6. The Chamber of Mines presented a similar position before the Industrial Legislation Commission of Enquiry (Botha): first, "The Chamber is thus opposed to the introduction of trade unions for Native employees in the Mining Industry"; and second, disputes are best handled "by the Department of Native Affairs in consultation with the employers and employers' organisation in this Industry" ("Statement of Evidence before the Industrial Legislation Commission of Enquiry," presented in the Chamber of Mines (Transvaal), *Annual Report 1951,* p. 120).
119. In my own survey, two of three managing directors of mining houses favored the easing of influx controls, and all three favored reduced dependence on migrant labor. See Appendix C, South African businessmen (I.A.), question 11.
120. All three mining directors in my survey set African wages without consulting the white unions or African workers; none had discussed wages with a works or liaison committee. See Appendix C, I.A., questions 4 and 6; also see *Management Responsibility and African Employment in South Africa.*

judgments depend upon the industrywide minimums established by the Chamber of Mines and an archaic communication network built around "tribal *indunas*." One mining house seemed content with these "tribal representatives" or at least constrained by the nature of their African labor force—"unsophisticated" and "tribal." The director observed: "It's not Soweto. They have their own tribal *indunas* and the evidence is that they are not ready to go away from that scheme of things." Two other mining houses, while allowing for new forms of collective bargaining sometime in the future, feared the consequences of a "premature" trade unionism. "We have to consider whether we will get responsible reaction," one director warned. "Frankly," the other concluded, "I don't think I'll be the first one to experiment with them."

POLITICAL DISORDER AND PERSISTING LABOR POLICIES

The political disorder in 1960—the slaughter at Sharpeville and the national emergency—brought, even within the mining industry, a reassessment of the traditional labor framework. Businessmen watched African protesters destroy their passes, the most visible symbol of labor repression. They watched the outflow of capital that followed the state of emergency. Although the mining industry financed a sizable percentage of its capital expenditures from working profits, it too was affected by the decline in "investor confidence." The president of the Chamber warned, "Clearly, every effort must be made to restore overseas investors' confidence in the inherent soundness of investment in gold mining, or the industry will be unable to maintain its rate of expansion."[121] At a Rand Mines Annual Meeting, one speaker observed, "South Africa is just one above Cuba as an investment."[122]

The Chamber cautiously joined with other business associations—Die Afrikaanse Handelsinstituut, the Association of Chambers of Commerce of South Africa, the South African Federated Chamber of Industries, and the Steel and Engineering Industries Federation of South Africa—urging the government to smooth the areas of greatest "friction." The pass laws, influx controls, and, to some extent, African trade unions were the core issues. A

---

121. Chamber of Mines (Transvaal and Orange Free State), *Annual Report 1960*, p. 50. The Chamber also worried about a decision of the Tanganyikan government to cancel a labor-recruiting agreement with the Chamber and an announced decision by the Zambian government to limit further labor recruiting (Wilson, *Migrant Labour*, p. 115).

122. Quoted in the *South Africa Mining and Engineering Journal*, no. 3513, 3 June 1960: 1357.

joint memorandum to the government included various proposals "to reduce the number of incidents of harsh methods."[123]

The Chamber of Mines—dependent upon migrant and largely foreign labor, removed from the political crisis in the cities—did not move from a critique of "harsh methods" to an assault on its own labor system. Indeed, the president of the Chamber contrasted the placid conditions on the mines with unrest in manufacturing and the townships.

> These men coming in their hundreds of thousands from many undeveloped parts of Southern Africa receive on our mines an introduction to Western ways of life free of the evils normally associated the world over with the transition from an agricultural to an industrial environment. They live in an ordered, protected society shielded from the hazards of township life.[124]

An editorial in the *South Africa Mining and Engineering Journal,* while acknowledging the political crisis, spoke favorably of conditions in mining: "About the only bright ray in the present situation in South Africa is that the gold mining industry continues to operate unimpeded either by the State of Emergency or events which have flowed from the disturbances that led up to it." It concluded, "This fortunate position arises from the Native labour system employed on the mines."[125]

The labor-repressive environment survived the disorders, instability, and the Chamber's modest venture into reform. Prime Minister Verwoerd condemned as "traitors" business leaders who thought more of profits than the white man's survival; the minister of finance threatened an investigation of irregularities in the stock exchange.[126] Calm was restored in the political arena—the African National and the Pan African Congresses were banned —and in the economic area—foreign investment and general economic activity were restored to pre-Sharpeville levels.[127]

Within six months after the initial disorders, the *South Africa Mining and Engineering Journal* could comment, "It was certainly quite remarkable to see how quickly South African politics could be forgotten once the idea of a higher gold price hove over the horizon once again."[128] By mid-1961, the mining journals had put Sharpeville and labor reform behind them.

Twelve years later, however, the unrest reached the mining compounds. On September 11, 1973, crowds of African miners, upset about changes in

123. The memorandum is considered in much more detail in the next chapter.
124. Chamber of Mines (Transvaal and Orange Free State), *Annual Report 1960,* p. 57.
125. *South Africa Mining and Engineering Journal,* no. 3506, 15 April 1960, p. 891.
126. *Hansard,* 20 May 1960, cols. 8326–27.
127. See the Nedbank Group, *South Africa: an Appraisal,* pp. 150–51.
128. *South Africa Mining and Engineering Journal,* no. 3534, 28 October 1960, p. 1059.

the wage structure, held the compound manager at Anglo-American's Western Deep Level Mine under siege. Twelve miners died in the police violence that followed. The mine manager confessed, "We may have made a mistake in our wage structuring. . . . Maybe in the African mind we have done them an injustice."[129] There was no way of knowing for sure, for the mining companies had no reliable system for bargaining or handling grievances. In early 1974, a number of mines, particularly Anglo-American's Welkom gold mine in the Orange Free State, were hit by violence and strikes. The "faction fighting" continued throughout the year and spread to Western Deep Levels at Carletonville, the ERPM mine at Germiston, and the West Rand Consolidated gold mine near Krugersdorp. Because of the violence and an array of wage issues, thousands of African miners refused to enter the mines; many sought repatriation to Malawi, Lesotho, or elsewhere.[130]

The labor system that had previously provided a "protected society" was now at the center of African unrest. A few of the mining houses and the Chamber of Mines began once again to reevaluate their dependence on labor-repressive mechanisms. Anglo-American urged the industry to recognize the changing labor requirements of South African mining: the development of a "high-wage capital-intensive economy." Its own approach "is aimed at moving farther and farther away from the traditional labor system which tended to regard Black workers as inter-changeable, unskilled labour units, and which tolerated an extremely high labour turnover."[131] Directors of other mining houses expressed cautious support for modifying, or at least humanizing, the labor-control mechanisms. "I think you need it," one director observed, "some sort of influx control, a benevolent one, if such is possible." But he concluded, "On the other hand, this one here is not benevolent and it's full of cruelty of a remarkable order." Another director seemed ready to abandon migrant labor altogether: "Oh, yes, I most decidedly would be delighted to have a fixed community—settled on a place, housing, and the chap doesn't like us, he leaves. If he likes us, he joins us and his family and the whole thing like that. I certainly would."

The Anglo-American Corporation announced that it was prepared to recognize "genuine African trade unions" and provide them with access to the compounds and with organizational assistance. The government, and very likely the white Mine Workers' Union, however, were adamant in defense of the prevailing system of "bargaining" and "communication": "The Government does not intend reviewing the organising of Bantu workers again, and believes that it is in the interests of all concerned that the

129.   Horrell and Horner, *A Survey of Race Relations 1973*, pp. 242–43.
130.   Horrell, Horner, and Hudson, *A Survey of Race Relations 1974*, pp. 289–91.
131.   "Chairman's Statement, Anglo-American Corporation of South Africa Limited," *Financial Mail*, 8 June 1973, p. 957.

status quo be maintained." Anglo-American stepped back from its proposal: while continuing to favor "recognising and dealing with any trade
union properly constituted and properly represented," the company would
not challenge government policy, particularly where other sections of
mining remained aloof or hostile.[132]

Such dabbling in reform has proved fanciful. The movement of Africans
into semiskilled positions, the increasing poverty of the "native reserves,"
and the new mines in the Orange Free State,[133] along with political disorder,
have enabled the mining industry to think about "benevolent" controls,
"fixed" communities, and "high-wage, capital-intensive" development. But
few in the industry think they are done with the labor-repressive structure.
The chairman of Anglo-American Corporation, as late as May 1974,
admitted that migratory labor is virtually a permanent feature of South
African gold mining: "When one considers the number of people involved,
and where they come from, one has to recognize that the problems are so
large, so complex, and so related to government policies both inside and
beyond South Africa's borders, that there is no realistic prospect of phasing
the system out in the foreseeable future."[134] Another director, one who
contemplated labor stabilization, concluded ruefully, "This stabilization is
purely hypothetical." The cost for infrastructure alone, the housing,
schools, and electricity, "would be tremendous." There is, after all, "no
political possibility."

Nearly a century after the first gold discoveries on the Witwatersrand, the
mining industry remains embroiled in the labor-repressive arrangements
that it helped create.

---

132. Horrell, Horner, and Hudson, *A Survey of Race Relations 1974,* pp. 291–92.
133. While the Chamber tried to preserve the labor system in the fifties, its most important
member, the Anglo-American Corporation, proposed some tentative steps toward stabilization
in the new Orange Free State gold fields. Sir Ernest Oppenheimer stated, "Personally, I am
convinced that it is in the interest of the Natives and of the mines to establish villages for
married Native people, and also to improve on the present compound structure and general
arrangements." In 1952, he proposed that approximately 10 percent of native laborers on the
Free State mines be housed in family accommodations. One hundred houses were to be
constructed; five hundred were planned. This modest scheme, however, was rapidly squelched
by the government: "The establishment on a mine of villages for Native married mine workers
with their families is wholly disapproved." Instead, the government reaffirmed its support for
the traditional position of the Chamber of Mines: "The continuance of the traditional policy
of the use of migrant labour on the gold-mines, accommodated in compounds, which has been
advocated consistently by the Gold Producers' Committee [of the Chamber of Mines] has the
approval of the Department of Native Affairs." Only highly skilled, indigenous South African
personnel, up to a limit of 3 percent, would be allowed family accommodations on the mines.
See Theodore Gregory, *Ernest Oppenheimer and the Economic Development of South Africa,*
pp. 574, 579–80.
   None of the mining houses, including Anglo-American, has taken full advantage of the 3
percent upper limit on family accommodations for African laborers.
134. "Chairman's Statement, Anglo-American Corporation," *Financial Mail,* 17 May 1974.

CHAPTER 9

Manufacturing and Commerce in South Africa: Accommodating the Racial Framework

Commercial agriculture and mining were at the center of the developing capitalist economy in South Africa. In this century, they posed a continuing threat to the African subsistence economy and, increasingly, provided the principal avenues for wage labor. They were the backbone of expanding commercial and market relations in South Africa and the principal sources of wealth and capital. Politics, at least until World War II, was largely in their hands, as was the labor-repressive framework.

To the other side stood a diverse lot of small-scale manufacturers and commercial ventures, with little capital, without substantial political influence. The Federated Chamber of Industries (FCI) represented secondary-manufacturing interests from 1917, and the Association of Chambers of Commerce (ASSOCOM) represented retail interests from as early as 1892. But the shops in the major ports and mining towns, even Hulett's sugar concern in Natal, were no counter to the scope of agricultural production and the concentration of capital in mining. The value of manufacturing output in the 1920s accounted for less than 13 percent of total production, trailing far behind that of mining and agriculture.[1] The FCI and ASSOCOM were no counter to the Chamber of Mines and the various farm-marketing organizations.

The interests of early manufacturing and commerce were elemental: markets in the latter case and "protection" in the former. The labor-repressive framework—the pass laws, the masters and servants laws, the native reserves—was the province of the primary producers. The small manufacturers and traders sought entry into an economy whose labor environment was largely given.[2]

1. D. Hobart Houghton, "Economic Development, 1865–1965," pp. 32–33; Belinda Bozzoli, "The Origins, Development, and Ideology of Local Manufacturing in South Africa," pp. 195–99; also see appendix B, table I.E.
2. The general weakness of manufacturing interests in the early years was evident in the struggle for "protection." The policy was introduced by General Smuts during 1921–22 and elaborated by the 1924 Pact government, an alliance of white workers and farmers (Bozzoli, "The Origins, Development, and Ideology," p. 213).

By the late thirties, the size of manufacturing and its labor force had changed radically. A manufacturing work force that in 1934 was split almost evenly between Europeans and Africans and did not exceed a quarter of a million had doubled in size by 1944. Two-thirds of the wartime labor force was African. A decade later the manufacturing labor force doubled again and 70 percent were Africans. By the mid-sixties, the contribution of manufacturing to the national economy exceeded that of mining and agriculture combined.[3] Manufacturing was emerging as a major, perhaps dominant, sector in the South African economy and a major employer of African labor.

The labor framework and racial order were increasing concerns: questions of migrant labor, native reserves, influx control, labor mobility, urbanization, and African unions could no longer be left to the Chamber of Mines and agricultural cooperatives alone.

The enthusiasm for race lines and labor controls evident in mining and commercial farming was not matched in the manufacturing and commercial sectors of the economy. At the ideological level, FCI declared, "[The] well tried and inexorable laws of economics should not be lightly disregarded."[4] Indeed, it rejected the mining industry's demand for repeated state participation in the labor market and work place: "The country's future prosperity demands that the problem of the Native in industry should be determined from an economic and not a political point of view."[5] At the policy level, FCI confirmed the traditional "necessity for strict control over the movements of idle and disorderly persons" but demanded reasonable access to the country's labor supply: "Each section must have free access to the country's resources, both human and material." It condemned the National party's policy of apartheid as "naive and over-simplified," particularly with respect to the "flow and availability of Native labour in urban areas."[6] ASSOCOM condemned "the impediment to the industrial growth of the country which restricts the creation of wealth to a section of the community" and the "restrictive labour laws" which prevented the employer from hiring "Natives in anything but the most unproductive and unremunerative capacities."[7] It urged the government to simplify the pass system "with the intention of achieving its ultimate abolition; this end will be achieved with the stabilisation of the Union's Native labour force."[8]

3. G.V. Doxey, *The Industrial Colour Bar,* p. 68; D. Hobart Houghton, *South African Economy,* pp. 228–29; also appendix B, table I.D.2, and table I.E.
4. *The Manufacturer,* December 1956, p. 5.
5. Ibid., February 1951, p. 31.
6. *F.C.I. News,* September 1948, pp. 7, 9.
7. *Commercial Opinion,* April 1947, p. 335.
8. The Johannesburg Chamber of Commerce, "Memorandum Submitted to the Commission of Enquiry into Laws Affecting Natives in or Near Urban Areas."

The ideological commitment to "economics" over "politics" and the insistence on "free access" to African labor supplies, however, has not under ordinary circumstances brought secondary industry and commerce into a serious clash with the racial order. On a narrow range of issues, where the costs of continuing race discrimination àre high and where the interests of primary producers are minimal, businessmen have challenged selected racial practices. They have, for example, opposed union- and state-imposed "job color bars," insisting on the right to hire and train African workers in a limited range of occupations. *But the resistance to job discrimination has been subsumed by a pervasive accommodation to custom and the needs of the primary producers.* That accommodation has come in two areas: the reproduction of racial segregation and hierarchy in the work place and, more important, the adaptation to the labor-repressive framework, after initial halting efforts to create a stable and urban African proletariat.[9] Businessmen in secondary industry and commerce have learned to live with the pass laws, migrant labor, and native reserves. Only during periods of serious political disorder and economic dislocation have businessmen renewed their search for other ways of organizing a labor force. And even then, they have quickly abandoned the issue when order was restored or when the government seemed strong enough to resist pressures for reform.

---

9. The voice of organized Afrikaner manufacturing and commerce, the Afrikaanse Handelsinstituut, did not share in the emerging orthodoxy of secondary industry. Unlike FCI and ASSOCOM, it talked little of labor stabilization: it reaffirmed the commitment of the Chamber of Mines, the agricultural cooperatives, and the National party to influx control and "macrosegregation" (A.J. Visser, "Great and Difficult Task of Nationalist Government" in *Volkshandel,* June 1948, translated by Jeffrey Lever). But Afrikaner enterprise in the immediate postwar period was more an aspiration than a major element in secondary industry. Afrikaner insurance companies, SANTAM and SANLAM, and wine producers, such as KWV (Kooperatieve Wijnbouwers Vereeniging) were established around World War I. But major industrial enterprise did not begin seriously until 1939, with the founding of the Reddingsdaadbond (Savings Association). Anton Rupert's Rembrandt Group produced its first cigarette in 1948. When the National party assumed power in 1948, Afrikaners, who were a majority in the European population, controlled only 6 percent of industry, 1 percent of mining, and 25 percent of commerce (David Welsh, "The Political Economy of Afrikaner Nationalism," pp. 253–60; Brian Bunting, *The Rise of the South African Reich,* p. 379).

While the mainstream of secondary industry and commerce was grappling with problems of labor supply, skill levels, and labor turnover, the Afrikaanse Handelsinstituut was still concerned with gaining a "corner of the market." "The Afrikaner," a feature article in its official organ stated in 1940, "will thus have to shift out of agriculture into other branches of production and, further, will have to gain a place in the ranks of the entrepreneurial classes in mining, commerce and industry." With limited entrepreneurial talent and capital and substantial financial dependence on Afrikaner agriculture, the aspirant Afrikaner bourgeoisie was reluctant to turn away from the traditional labor system. See W.F.J. Steenkamp, "The Afrikaner-Case First," in *Volkshandel,* March 1940, trans. J.L.; see also Dan O'Meara, "The 1946 African Mine Workers' Strike in the Political Economy of South Africa," pp. 165–66.

RESISTING JOB COLOR BARS

The Prime Minister desires it to be understood by all Departments of State that it has been decided as a matter of definite policy that, wherever practicable, civilized labour shall be substituted in all employment by the Government for that which may be classified as uncivilized. Civilized labour is to be considered as the labour rendered by persons, whose standard of living conforms to the standard generally recognized as tolerable from the usual European standpoint. Un-civilized labour is to be regarded as the labour rendered by persons whose aim is restricted to the bare requirements of the necessities of life as understood among barbarous and undeveloped peoples.

Circular No. 5
Secretary to the Prime Minister, Pretoria
31 October, 1924

The Prime Minister desires that the contents of my Circular No. 5 of 31st October, 1924 (a copy whereof is attached for easy reference) be again brought to the attention of all Government Departments and Provincial Administrations and that note be taken that it is the policy of the Government to give effect thereto.

Circular No. 5 of 1949
Secretary to the Prime Minister, Cape Town
28 March, 1949[10]

The State and the Allocation of Work

European labor in South Africa has never been content to enter the labor market without the protection of customary and statutory "colour bars." In some areas, such as construction and mining, specific occupations or trades have, as long as anyone can remember, been reserved for whites; others have almost invariably been performed by Africans—"Kaffir work" in the local parlance. In the skilled trades, the white artisan has conventionally worked with a "native assistant" or two, who must "carry and hold his tools, do the rougher parts of the work, and generally act as a sort of industrial valet to his master."[11] The prevailing wage structure, even without the formal allocation of work, has included discontinuities that leave whites on the upper side of the divide, in the better paid positions, and Africans on the lower, in the less remunerative jobs.[12]

A long procession of state commissions in the first quarter of this century resisted the tendency for these customary color bars to become law. The

---

10. Ballinger Papers, University of the Witwatersrand.
11. Transvaal, *Report of the Transvaal Indigency Commission 1906–08*, T.G. 13–1908, p. 42.
12. See Union of South Africa, Department of Labour, *Work Reservation*, p. 5.

Transvaal Indigency Commission (1906–08) opposed "any Government action which is designed to protect the white man against reasonable competition from the coloured races." Such policies, it warned "would have the effect of ensuring to the white man higher wages than would be economically justified."[13] The Mining Industry Commission (1907–08), even while trying to assure a place in industry for the white worker, opposed formal job reservation:

> But in our opinion any measure which seeks to place a permanent artificial barrier by legislation in the way of a coloured man improving his position according to his capacity is very difficult to justify or maintain. Further, we feel assured that no such measure could by itself be permanently effective in securing the ends desired so long as conditions are permitted to exist which cause natural laws and economic forces to be operating in the opposite direction.[14]

These sentiments were echoed in the Economic Commission (1914), the Relief and Grants-in-Aid Commission (1916), the Native Grievances Inquiry Commission (1913–14), and the Low Grade Mines Commission (1920). The last posed the issue in elementary terms: "From the point of view of abstract justice as between man and man, there is nothing to be said in [the color bars'] favour."[15] And, in what may have been the last official warning before "civilized labour policies" pervaded government and industry, the Economic and Wage Commission (1925) stated: "On general principles it appears to us to be unsound policy to exclude by legislation a class which has no representation in the legislature, from economic opportunities at present open to them, for the benefit of the politically privileged class."[16]

The warnings, however, did not forestall the increasing role of the state in the allocation of work. The Mines and Works Act of 1911 (and the reenacted and amended version of 1925) specified the number of whites required to supervise African miners and limited the issuance of "blasting certificates" to white miners. Thirty-two core occupations were thereafter reserved for white mine workers; an additional nineteen job categories were later included by agreement between the Chamber of Mines and the white

---

13.   Transvaal, *Report of the Transvaal Indigency Commission,* pp. 45–56.
14.   Transvaal, *Report of the Mining Industry Commission 1907–08,* 579–3/2/08–2000, p. 38.
15.   Union of South Africa, *Report of the Low Grade Mines Commission,* U.G. 34–1920, p. 29.
16.   Union of South Africa, *Report of the Economic and Wage Commission 1925,* U.G. 14–1926, p. 122.

unions.[17] When the allied Labour and National parties gained power in 1924 (the Pact government), "civilized labour" became a standard for the society at large and for state employment. Under Circular No. 5 of 1924, the government substituted white for African workers in the railways, harbors, post offices, and elsewhere. Between 1924 and 1933, white employment rose from 9.5 to 39.3 percent in the Railways and Harbours Administration; African employment dropped from 75 to 48.9 percent.[18] The newly created Department of Labour helped to structure the emerging wage machinery and to foster "protected" employment opportunities for white workers.[19]

When the National party again came to power in 1948, it reaffirmed Circular No. 5 and extended the "civilized labour" policies beyond mining and state employment. The Native Building Workers Act of 1951 provided for the training of skilled African tradesmen but at the same time barred African employment on any project outside of the "Bantu areas."[20] But the state-imposed "job reservation" in construction was only a hint of what was to come in the Industrial Conciliation Act of 1956. The minister of labour might now reserve jobs for a particular race group or fix the ratio of European to African employees in an industry, a factory, or in certain types of employment. The government was responding, the Department of Labour claimed, to the entry of Africans and Coloureds in "classes of work which had traditionally been performed by Whites," and to a fear that newly created segregated Coloured and Asian trade-union branches might undermine the position of the established white unions. "Work reservation is an attempt to create order out of chaos and to prevent racial friction," it concluded.[21]

More pervasive than formal government determinations were the negotiated reservations created by consenting employers and trade unions under the careful scrutiny of the state. It is common practice for industrial council agreements to establish ratios for "journeymen" (the Apprenticeship Act effectively excludes Africans from these positions) and "artisan assistants." Others simply, but effectively, exclude persons "not eligible for trade union membership"—in other words, Africans—from certain categories of employment. Before 1972, for example, Africans were barred from the top seven grades of employment in the steel and engineering industry. In 1972, Africans were permitted to enter the lowest of these, grade D, and in 1974,

17. Doxey, *The Industrial Colour Bar*, p. 117; H.J. and R.E. Simons, *Class and Colour in South Africa*, p. 234.
18. Sheila T. van der Horst, *Native Labour in South Africa*, p. 251.
19. C.W. de Kiewiet, *A History of South Africa*, p. 224.
20. Union of South Africa, Department of Labour, *Work Reservation*, p. 6.
21. Ibid., pp. 7–9.

grade C, provided employers adhered to the following conditions: first, no person eligible for union membership—in other words, a European—is displaced; no African supervises the work of a European; and in the event of a recession, preference in retention or hiring is given to European employees.[22]

In recent years, the government and trade unions have shown a willingness to relax these restrictions—assuming "friction" is minimized and control maintained. The prime minister told an annual conference of the Motor Industries Federation, "It should be clear that in terms of Government policy there is nothing to prevent employers, with the co-operation of the trade unions, taking the necessary steps to bring about improvements in the productive use of non-White labour."[23] The Post Office and the Postal Association reached an "honourable settlement" that permitted Africans to serve as postmen on a "temporary" and, later, on a permanent basis. This freer utilization of African labor followed state guidelines that provided "that each racial group should as far as feasible be served by its own people," and that where there was a shortage of white workers, Africans could be hired "to the extent of the shortage" and "on the distinct understanding that the position" of white workers was "not adversely affected in any way."[24] In 1972, the railways began hiring Africans as "train marshallers," a job virtually identical to "shunters" that, when in white hands, paid twice the salary. The government also encouraged O.K. Bazaars and Barclays Bank to hire Coloured women and urged employers in the steel, engineering, and motor industries to negotiate greater opportunities for African workers.[25] Despite strong protests by the white building-workers' union, an industrial tribunal in the construction industry began reexamining the existing job reservations. The chairman of the tribunal observed that "no developing industry should remain static" and that "necessary adaptations [of job reservations] should periodically be considered."[26]

In 1979, the Wiehahn Commission recommended that job reservations under the Industrial Conciliation Act be abolished, though it proved much

22. Republic of South Africa, "Agreement for the National Industrial Council for the Iron, Steel, Engineering and Metallurgical Industry." Also see Republic of South Africa, "Main Agreement for the Motor Industry."
23. *Rand Daily Mail,* 4 October 1973.
24. *Hansard,* 22 March 1972, cols. 3829–30.
25. *Hansard,* 1 May 1973, col. 5475 and *Hansard,* 4 September 1970, col. 3395; also see Dr. P.J. Riekert, "Increasing Productivity as a Condition of Economic Growth in South Africa," p. 8.
26. *Rand Daily Mail,* 15 March 1974. Still, in 1974, the minister of labour declared: "We do not hesitate to say at all times that as long as the National Party is in power, job reservation will be the law of South Africa" (*Hansard,* 23 February 1971, col. 1482).

more cautious in recommending changes in other color-bar provisions and practices: it put off making any recommendations with regard to the Mines and Works Act or the composition of apprenticeship committees and urged employers and unions to move cooperatively in changing negotiated job reservations; it endorsed practices that are formally color-blind, but nonetheless "safeguard" skilled labor and workers with "permanency of residence in an urban area."[27]

The state has moved from an earlier extended period (1911–70) when it insisted on strict protections for white workers to a contemporary period where it allows for "controlled employment" of Africans in formerly white jobs. Throughout these periods, however, businessmen in manufacturing and commerce have resisted the state role in the allocation of work.

Business Resistance: "The Whole System of Job Reservation in Industry Is Repugnant."

Manufacturing and commercial organizations opposed these particular forms of discrimination because, in large part, their position reflected that of industry generally—including mining. The Chamber of Mines had established racial-employment ratios in the 1890s[28] and acquiesced to the color-bar provisions of the Mines and Works Act of 1911 and the status quo agreement of 1918, but it insisted in 1922 on the right to "reorganize" underground work. "The mines are merely claiming the right," the Chamber observed, "which no one has ever dreamed of denying the farmer or the commercial men when revenue falls off, of retrenching employees and thus improving efficiency while economising expense and conserving the industry."[29] With a falling gold price and rising European wages, the Chamber of Mines challenged the power of the white unions and the legality of the Mines and Works Act.[30] Indeed, it raised questions about the entire system of job color bars:

> Surely, if ever a law needed a thorough thrashing out in the open House, it is one which can deprive three quarters of the population of the country of the right to earn a living in any way they are capable of doing! We would urge upon the Government our view that this measure is one of the gravest character and calling for the fullest possible consideration lest great injustice may result.[31]

27. Republic of South Africa, *Report of the Commission of Inquiry into Labour Legislation,* part 1, R.P. 47/1979, pp. 41–42.
28. Chamber of Mines (Witwatersrand), *Annual Report 1890,* p. 68.
29. Chamber of Mines (Transvaal), *Annual Report 1921,* pp. 133–36.
30. Francis Wilson, *Labour in the South African Gold Mines,* p.46.
31. Chamber of Mines (Transvaal), *Annual Report 1924,* p. 57.

The Chamber lived with the retrenched, but still protected position of white workers until the late sixties. It began then a decade-long attempt to buy African advancement by a "responsibility allowance" for the white worker's "co-operation in the rationalisation of artisans' work on the mines."[32] In 1977, the Chamber of Mines made special representation to the government urging that the Mines and Works Act be reviewed along with other color-bar legislation.

Manufacturing interests joined the attack after World War II, opposing National party proposals for formalizing the job color bars. The FCI declared in 1948, "The optimum allocation of resources requires that each worker shall be employed in the sphere and the capacity in which he is most productive." What was required was not more demarcations but "the progression of the Native in reclassified jobs."[33] When job reservations were added to the Industrial Conciliation Act and applied to the clothing industry in 1957, the FCI rallied to the companies and unions that stood against the government. It pointed with pride to "the solidarity of all organised industry behind the clothing manufacturer—a demonstration that total job reservation is regarded as unworkable in any type of manufacturing as it obviously is in the clothing industry." If that statement of solidarity was not sufficiently provocative, the FCI wrote, "while the Minister could impose job reservation, he cannot compel moral compliance thereto."[34]

Following the lead of the clothing manufacturers, the Industrial Council for the Iron, Steel, Engineering and Metallurgical Industry, in a major confrontation with the government, refused to cooperate in the imposition of a job reservation. The manufacturers declared: "The whole system of job reservation in industry is repugnant, and accordingly these interests are not prepared to accept, during the currency of a negotiated agreement, a superimposed job reservation provision."[35] The government, consequently, withdrew the legislative requirement for consent of the industrial council and unilaterally imposed a particularly restrictive form of job reservation. The council was forced to adapt its agreement and incorporate government policy.[36]

ASSOCOM pointed to the incompatibility between economic growth and restrictions on the use of African labor and raised the whole question to the

32. Joint Statement of the Chamber of Mines and the Federation of Mining Unions, *Rand Daily Mail*, 2 July 1973.
33. *The Manufacturer*, February 1951, p. 31.
34. Ibid., December 1957, p. 5.
35. Quoted in Ray Alexander and H.J. Simons, *Job Reservation and the Trade Unions*, p. 20.
36. Union of South Africa, Department of Labour, *Work Reservation*, pp. 22–23.

level of principle and ideology: "There is general agreement that if the barriers to the fuller employment of Native labour could be removed, our economic situation would be transformed within a comparatively short period."[37] At the time of Sharpeville, ASSOCOM reiterated this theme, suggesting that both economic growth and political stability hung in the balance: "If the full benefit of this process is to be obtained, then no barriers must be placed in the way of persons of any race utilizing present skills or acquiring and employing new ones."[38] ASSOCOM reiterated its position in the seventies, declaring "profoundly distasteful" a threatened job determination with respect to clerks: "Today's ban on clerks could be tomorrow's ban on messengers—and who in the business community can plan ahead with certainty under such circumstances? If the growth rate in the economy is to be maintained, it is essential that such uncertainty should be minimized."[39]

Only the Handelsinstituut, among the business associations, endorsed the white-labor policies and job reservations. "It is thus clear," it observed, "that where some white employers and certain trade unions do not consider the interests of the white employees, the latter are obliged to look to the government for job reservation as the only way to entrench the position of the white."[40] But by 1970, even the Handelsinstituut began to worry about the labor shortage in skilled areas, the restrictions on the prerogatives of management, and the need for freer utilization of labor. Its emphasis, like that of ASSOCOM and FCI, was on "practicality . . . reclassification of skilled work . . . training in white areas . . . and efficient utilization."[41]

At the company level, businessmen face a range of informal and formal job color bars, some imposed by the white trade unions, "the people themselves,"[42] and some imposed by the state. Companies, nonetheless, have tried to narrow the application of job reservations. Some companies,

37. *Commercial Opinion,* February 1949, p. 335.
38. Ibid., June 1960, p. 15.
39. Ibid., August 1970, pp. 4–5.
40. *Volkshandel,* November 1957, trans. J.L.
41. Ibid., June and July 1970, trans. J.L.
42. The director of one company observed:
   The government wouldn't stop us in B category. But the rest of the artisans would walk out. It is the trade unions which insist on these reservations. In 1963 to 1965, all the lorry drivers were white. . . . [pause] The boilermakers, electricians, and machinists will go last of all, maybe in ten or twenty years.
   I would like to see job reservation dropped. I'm really talking at the trade unions, not the government. We're being held back by the people themselves.

Another director described the maneuvering between job reservations and the white trade unions:

   The movement up of Africans is inhibited by the attitudes of the trade unions. We established a new plant—outside the coverage of the industrial agreement—with no

particularly those heavily dependent on African labor, negotiated or bought African advancement: "We were trying to establish the principle that if we were to concede anything wage-wise, the unions would have to admit that the white work force is inadequate for the job." Other firms applied for exemptions but, increasingly, turned their eyes away from infractions of the law. One company stood by, allowing its white labor force to dwindle below the mandatory 18 percent minimum and Coloureds to enter the "reserved" supervisory jobs. Job reservation "increasingly is being ignored," the director observed, but warned, if you are "too blatant about it, you'll get knocked." Another director suggested a more direct course: "We don't apply for exemptions, since we know we won't get them. We just break the law."

The black intrusion into formerly white jobs "is happening," a director observed. "It is like a snowball."

REPRODUCING THE RACIAL BARRIERS AND HIERARCHY

Racial Segregation

Before dawn, the long procession of commuter trains begins dumping its payload of African workers on the Johannesburg railway station's non-European platforms. The African commuters filter through the streets and onto the buses, finding their way to the white shops, factories, and homes. The lengthy, early morning procession is the product of residential segregation. The African township of Soweto stands far from the pleasant homes, lawns, and pools of the Johannesburg suburbs and the bustle of business and commercial concerns in downtown Johannesburg. It sprawls across the veld far outside the city, distinguished by the monotony of its structures, the dirt roads, and the pall of smoke and dust. The African resident of Soweto lives with these conditions and joins the procession because some functionary has stamped his identity card *African* and not *Coloured, Asian,* or *White.* That classification is the key to which bathroom door he enters, where he lives and works, what job he holds, how much he earns, and much more.

---

closed shop. This left us freer to act. But the arrangement did not last long. In the first place, the other employers were more restrictive than we. Secondly, our employment practices were starting to lead to a reaction among some of our employees. The Yster en Staal [a white union] was recruiting, involving the Department of Justice and the Department of Labour. We were faced with the possibility of job reservation. . . .

In 1969, we entered into a closed-shop agreement with the same unions. This effectively excluded Yster en Staal. The nine unions have worked out a flexible arrangement with us. This has become a more desirable arrangement than the independent situation where whites were more reluctant to accept change.

Segregation in South Africa is built into prevailing social theory and custom but also into law. Housing segregation is conditioned by the Natives (Urban Areas) Act of 1923, the Native Building Workers' Act of 1951, the Native Transport Services Act of 1957, and the Group Areas Acts of 1950 and 1957; job segregation, by the Factories, Machinery, and Building Works Amendment Act of 1960 and the Physical Planning and Utilization of Resources Act of 1967; union segregation, by the Industrial Conciliation Acts of 1924 and 1956; and social segregation, by the Reservation of Separate Amenities Act of 1953, the Population Registration Act of 1950, the Prohibition of Mixed Marriages Act of 1949, and the Immorality Act of 1927.

No section of the business community has challenged the prevailing forms of racial segregation. That the Handelsinstituut reaffirmed its commitment to segregation, "with an eye to the maintenance of order, welfare and civilization,"[43] is hardly surprising. But the easy adaptation to race lines is not confined to smaller-scale Afrikaner entrepreneurs. When the National party came to power in 1948, the FCI "accepted the need for residential segregation *within* urban areas."[44] It later gave specific policy meaning to that acceptance, supporting the Group Areas Act, the most disruptive piece of segregation legislation enacted in the Nationalist period. The FCI's secretary for non-European affairs states that the legislation would prcvide a "stable labour force of non-Europeans within easy transport from industrial centers."[45] Lest anyone doubt its commitment to segregation, the FCI later restated its position in more encompassing terms:

> Regarding the question of social equality the Chamber did on the occasion of the passage of the Group Areas Act, unequivocably state its belief in residential segregation. A similar principle is also now being applied by Government and Municipalities in the establishment of large Native settlements in areas adjacent to our cities and towns. We know that the vast body of industrialists as ordinary citizens do subscribe to the concept of residential and social segregation.
>
> Our purpose in making these observations is to highlight the fact that industrialists in their capacity as ordinary citizens are surely no less concerned with the "fundamental issue of Europeans preserving their White race and the Western European civilization" than any political party.[46]

Only a small minority of business leaders sampled during 1966 and 1967 opposed separate toilets or enforced separation in residential areas. Indeed,

43. See *Volkshandel,* May and October 1960, trans. J.L.
44. *F.C.I. News,* September 1948, p. 9.
45. Ibid., October 1955, p. 37.
46. *The Manufacturer,* December 1956, p. 5.

the survey turned up high levels of personal prejudice among both English and Afrikaner entrepreneurs.[47] Another survey conducted almost two years later found that barely half the businessmen in manufacturing and commerce supported the desegregation of buses and less than a quarter supported the desegregation of toilet facilities.[48] My own survey of businessmen conducted during 1973 and 1974 turned up precious little resistance to racial segregation. When asked about "aspects of the social environment" that "create difficulties for you in managing the company," virtually none of the directors referred to separate amenities, offices, or unions. Most felt, as one director put it, that the question is "social and cultural apartheid, which I think you have whether on the statute books or not."

The accommodation to racial segregation did not keep businessmen from commenting on the human and economic costs in such policies. One director pointed out the productivity losses inherent in the system of townships and commuter transportation:

> You know, these guys, apart from the fact that they have to walk for a long distance before they get to the first bus stop, when they get to the bus, they have to stand. When they get to the train, they've got to stand. So by the time the guy gets to work, he's leaning on his feet for hours. And he's thrashed and, you know, how big is his productivity?

Another pointed to the unfortunate conditions in the townships and the consequences for business practice:

> Oh, well, they come in with all sorts of head wounds and there's probably a little bit too much drinking amongst them. And we really have to look after them a little bit beyond the normal course of duty. Our surgery down here on Monday is full and I think that it is, I think, if in fact, if they had better social amenities, they'd probably be much more interested in producing well and earning money to spend on all these amenities.

But these cautions do not detract from the general acquiescence or support for segregation policies. Factories, offices, and stores have incorporated the appropriate separations in amenities and services. Despite considerable state activity in this area, businessmen have offered few representations before government commissions and made few public protests.

---

47. Heribert Adam, "The South African Power-Elite: A Survey of Ideological Commitment," p. 80.
48. These findings are based on the author's reanalysis of questionnaires included in the "Study of White South African Elites, 1966–69." Access to these materials was generously provided by the Centre for Inter-Group Studies under the directorship of Hendrik van der Merwe.

Income Inequality

The social distance between black and white in South Africa is no more striking than the enormous gap between their wages. The average wage of an African worker in the early seventies was barely 15 percent that of a white worker—less than 10 percent in mining, 17 percent in manufacturing, and 29 percent in commerce. Even where African and white workers performed identical tasks, such as bus driving, the African wage reached only 70 percent of the white's and sometimes did not reach half.[49] And while Africans garnered the lion's share of wage increases in the early seventies, the entire quarter-century since World War II has brought increased inequality. Between 1948 and 1973, the white worker's wage rose by a phenomenal 416 percent; African wages over the same quarter-century rose by only 36 percent.[50] The average wage increase for white workers, not surprisingly, far exceeded their productivity gains, while those of African workers fell below theirs.[51]

Businessmen in manufacturing and commerce, with more semiskilled labor and few compounds, operated with a narrower wage gap. They nonetheless extended the customary wage patterns into the developing sectors of the economy. They bargained with the white unions and lived with their terms, allowing the white workers, in effect, to set wage patterns in areas of black employment. They regularly pleaded poverty before the Wage Board and resisted minimum wages for specific industries and the nation. They created their own "dual wage structures," recognizing that "a white does a somewhat greater job than the black man does," and their own "pyramids," placing whites at the pinnacle and blacks at the base.

This easy accommodation to convention, however, was not accompanied, as in mining, by an elaborate defense of low-wage policies; nor did the manufacturing associations, in order to maintain and refine the wage system, make regular representations before commissions and government ministers.[52] They did not attempt to forge state structures that would control the proletarianization of African workers or ideologies that would justify the Africans' continuing dependence on the native reserves.

---

49. S. Biesheuvel, "The Black-White Wage Gap," pp. 1–5; Wilson, *Labour in the South African Gold Mines,* pp. 46–59. There also exist sharp disparities between black and white workers in the areas of paid leave, pensions, medical care, workmen's compensation, silicosis relief, and housing. Also see Sean Archer, "Inter-racial Income Distribution in South Africa," 1971.

50. The consumer price index was up by 147 percent in the same period. Muriel Horrell, Dudley Horner, and Jane Hudson, *A Survey of Race Relations 1974,* p. 235.

51. Biesheuvel, "The Black-White Wage Gap," pp. 12–13.

52. See the discussion of mining and "cheap" labor in chapter 8.

If anything, businessmen have offered a modest critique of low-wage policies, suggesting, in their place, productivity criteria and a concern with domestic markets. When South Africa and the economy were threatened by disorder in 1960, the FCI urged a reappraisal of the wage structure: "[It] is also incumbent on us—indeed it is our duty as employers—jointly with other commercial and industrial groups to examine afresh the wage levels of our native workers and to ensure that we as employers do not contribute to feelings of frustration due to inadequate wages."[53] During 1959 and 1960, ASSOCOM warned that the wage gap and the "low earnings of non-Europeans" endangered the growth of the national economy.[54] Again in 1973 and 1974, with strikes in Durban and elsewhere, businessmen publicly deplored conditions in the "sweated industries," particularly textiles, and in numerous instances raised African wages. Still, businessmen were cautious, urging that the wage structure of the future reflect productivity differences between black and white workers. Increases in African wages must be accompanied by increases in the "African's value to the employer, based on efficiency and length of service."[55]

Even the Handelsinstituut seemed ready to move toward productivity criteria and abandon "cheap" labor policies. In the sixties, it had supported increased wages in manufacturing but primarily as a way of encouraging development in the border areas and the displacement of African workers in the white areas: "The consequence of such a policy will be that fewer Bantu will be used to perform the same work and that higher remuneration and accompanying higher mechanization . . . will increase the replacement possibility of Bantus by immigrants from the European class."[56] By 1972, the position of the Handelsinstituut had become indistinguishable from the remainder of manufacturing and commerce. It lamented the acceleration of African and European wages since 1963 without sufficient advances in productivity. "Industrialists cannot continue to absorb cost increases due to scarcity of labour at the expense of investment returns and profits," it declared. "Faster labour training, less labour restrictions and better utilisation of labour are appropriate solutions."[57]

The modest critique of the wage structure had by the middle seventies become orthodoxy in the business community and outside. As the first wave of Durban strikes began to subside, the government raised questions about low-wage policies and the wage gap. The prime minister confessed, to the surprise of nearly everybody, that he found "lessons" in the disturbances.

53. *The Manufacturer,* May 1960, p. 5.
54. *Commercial Opinion,* September 1959, p. 17; December 1959, p. 6; and June 1960, p. 14.
55. The Johannesburg Chamber of Commerce, Addendum to the "Memorandum Submitted to the Commission of Enquiry into Laws Affecting Natives in or Near Urban Areas."
56. *Volkshandel,* October 1961, trans. J.L.
57. Ibid., October 1972, trans. J.L.

They contain a lesson for the Wage Board, a lesson for the workers and a lesson for the employers. We would be foolish if we did not all benefit from the lessons to be learned from that situation. . . . [In] the past there have unfortunately been too many employers who saw only the mote in the Government's eye and failed completely to see the beam in their own. . . . [E]xperience tells me this, that employers, whoever they may be, should not only see in their workers a unit producing for them so many hours of service a day; they should also see them as human beings with souls.[58]

The government announced that narrowing the wage gap was official policy and, indeed, had been official policy for some time. It criticized employers who bemoaned their inability to pay increased wages when confronted by the Wage Board and readily granted them when faced with a walkout of African workers.[59]

CONTESTING AND ADAPTING TO THE POLITICAL MARKET

Creating an Urban Working Class

Only two years after the formal inauguration of apartheid, the FCI prepared a major policy statement on "The Native in Industry," questioning some of the most sacred assumptions in the labor-repressive framework. The government, the FCI declared, must come to terms with the mass of "detribalised natives." Otherwise it would face "a menace rather than a constructed [sic] factor in industry."[60] It must recognize "that, in order to gain the maximum productivity of the Native, a stable Native force is required and that facilities should be created to give that stability to the detribalised urban Native."[61]

58. Quoted in Muriel Horrell and Dudley Horner, *A Survey of Race Relations 1973*, p. 283.
59. *Hansard*, 13 February 1973, cols. 566–67.
60. Quoting Report of the Board of Trade, "The Native in Industry," *The Manufacturer*, February 1951, p. 33.
61. Ibid. The commitment to new facilities did not carry over into an industry commitment for employer-financed housing. The government, for example, proposed that industrial enterprises, unable to house their own workers, pay a special levy to underwrite the costs of government housing schemes. All the major groups in manufacturing and commerce, including the Handelsinstituut, protested the policy. The FCI and ASSOCOM even boycotted government-sponsored committees on "native housing." The Handelsinstituut argued that while the wage structure in gold mining necessitated compounds, the native worker in industry could well afford an economic rent. ASSOCOM specifically denied that housing methods in the primary sector could be transferred to modern industry; it deplored any government attempt to compel "industry in urban areas to provide housing for Native employees" (*Volkshandel*, December 1949, trans. J.L.; *Commercial Opinion*, December 1948, p. 273).

The prime minister condemned the industrialists' intrusion into political affairs and later warned that even if economic realities had to be considered, "the natural desire for economic gain could not be allowed to take precedence over other more vital considerations; for example, it would be fatal for the Europeans to allow black spots of millions of natives to encircle the European cities."[62] The FCI, consequently, stepped back from a direct political encounter with the government.

> In pursuance of these objectives it becomes a function of the Chamber [FCI] to collaborate with the Government of the day on all matters which have an industrial bias, to give praise where praise is due and to criticise any action which will militate against the interests of industry and the national economy. But it is not a function of this Chamber to appraise the relative merits or demerits of any democratic political party or ideology.[63]

The FCI, however, continued in less strident terms to urge labor stabilization. Manpower "must be within easy reach of our factories," it commented, "and we must therefore recognise that the Native, who forms the bulk of the labor force of the country, must be given a permanent niche in our industrial centres."[64] The FCI's memorandum before the Tomlinson Commission doubted that any natural economic advantages existed in border or reserve areas. It urged the government instead to recognize the organic suitability of the African for manufacture:

> It has resulted in the realisation that Natives possess a natural aptitude for the performance of repetitive tasks which are the basis of mass production manufacture. The factor of monotony and consequent fatigue, so important a problem in mass production, is virtually non-existent as far as the Native is concerned, especially if he is employed on machines with rhythmic motions.[65]

In 1959, the FCI again submitted memoranda reaffirming its commitment to an urbanized labor force and continued economic expansion "based in all respects on sound economic considerations." It took particular exception to lower wages prevailing in "perimeter" industries that "undermine the position of the already established industries."[66]

ASSOCOM took the opportunity provided by the Tomlinson Commission to make a sweeping attack on the labor system. The government

62. *The Manufacturer,* August 1951, p. 23.
63. Ibid., March 1951, p. 5.
64. Ibid., January 1953, p. 13.
65. Ibid., June 1953, p. 15; and July 1953, p. 39.
66. Ibid., November 1959, pp. 9–13.

and the white community at large, the association wrote, "has not yet brought itself to accept the Native as a permanent, integral feature of modern urban life." Legislation proposed by the minister of native affairs to inhibit migration was apparently part of that unreality. But, the association submitted, "this migration of Natives to the cities should be allowed to continue"; it should of course be guided, but not controlled. This labor force would ultimately prove more productive and better prepared to purchase manufactured goods. "The Association would urge most strongly that, however desirable may be the economic development of the reserves, nothing whatever should be done to intervene, through controls over personal movement, or by other artificial means, to restrain Natives from migrating from the reserves to industry, commerce and other forms of employment in the rest of the Union."[67]

Only the Afrikaner sections of secondary industry and commerce remained outside this critique of the labor system. Afrikaner businessmen proposed, contrary to the considered opinion of the FCI and ASSOCOM, that the government pursue border industry rather than urban development and "cheap" labor rather than labor stabilization. "The only way in which this apartheid policy will naturally take shape," however, "is by establishing economic drives," in other words, "abundant cheap labour."[68] The Handelsinstituut told the Tomlinson Commission that the state should "suspend minimum wage agreements" and allow the white investor to operate profitably in both border and reserve areas.[69] Such investment could be underwritten or conducted jointly with state capital, but only with the "economic incentive of lower wages" would the necessary private capital enter the field. Even then, it might be necessary to convert "strategic lines of connection [verbindingslinies] . . . into white 'fingers' [inlopergebiede] in order to give whites an opportunity to establish industries and to attract labour from the native hinterlands."[70]

It should not be surprising that infant Afrikaner industries, with a tenuous hold on the market and limited access to capital, would find border industry development and "cheap" labor policies attractive.[71] Nor should it be surprising that the major developed sectors of manufacturing and commerce would be critical of such policies, seeing them as attempts to avoid a settled working-class population in the cities and as a threat to their established market position.

67. *Commercial Opinion,* April 1952, pp. 455–71.
68. *Volkshandel,* March 1951, trans. J.L.
69. Ibid., March 1953, trans. J.L.
70. Ibid., June 1956, trans. J.L.
71. Ibid., March 1957, trans. J.L.

In the late sixties and early seventies, the government introduced sweeping legislation to structure and control the movement of African labor and the location of industry. The Physical Planning Act of 1967 sought to prevent the expansion of African labor-intensive firms in the Witwatersrand and surrounding industrial areas; new labor regulations sought to expand the system of labor bureaus, freeze African employment in the western Cape, and expand the use of migrant rather than settled African labor.

The ASSOCOM and FCI presented a joint memorandum to the government opposing the Physical Planning Bill.[72] They criticized the bill as "permissive in character" and a "haphazard and fragmentary approach to the decentralisation of industry." The physical planning concept failed to take into account burdensome administration costs, the impact on labor mobility and supplies, and the general consequences for a "free enterprise economy."[73] The FCI later attacked the Physical Planning Act and associated legislation as a "sticky web of restrictive legislation," an "administrative and legal straitjacket," and an attempt to "throttle and intimidate industrial enterprise."[74]

This time the government stepped back. Exemptions from the restrictive provisions in the legislation were freely granted. And in 1971 the Riekert white paper set a higher black-white labor ratio, one well above the government's initial goal for "whitening" the cities. The emphasis now was on "practical apartheid." The Handelsinstituut warned, as other associations had much earlier, that the "apartheid ship might land on the economic rocks." It urged a policy of separate development that depended "in the first place on economic practicality and a sufficient tempo in practice."[75]

The accommodation of business and the state was now virtually complete. The National party government for its part had modified the labor ratios and streamlined the labor bureau system to meet the complaints of manufacturers. But for their part, businessmen accommodated the full complement of labor-repressive policies; influx control, migrant labor, and physical planning no longer produced the memoranda and protests of an earlier day.

Some firms now emphasized the flexibility in the prevailing labor system and the ability to gain adequate supplies of labor. A Durban textile manufacturer observed, "We've had no problems obtaining labor from any reasonable surrounding area." Even the Physical Planning Act, perhaps the

72. *Commercial Opinion,* June 1967, p. 6. It was secondary industry that felt the brunt of the legislation and that eventually resisted the law's application.
73. *F.C.I. Viewpoint,* September 1970, pp. 17–20.
74. Ibid., April 1968, pp. 5–6.
75. *Volkshandel,* June 1970, trans. J.L.; July 1973, p. 9, trans. S.B.G.

most direct tampering with management prerogatives, was now seen as a "paper tiger." One director stated: "It's not in effect. If we want more labor, we usually have a case which the government is willing to accept." The director of a major paper company had similar success in circumventing these labor "constraints": "We made representation and the government saw our predicament. The problem has been overcome. For the most part, we have been able to expand our operations freely."

Other companies had begun to see the benefits in the labor framework, some because it provided incentives to limit the size of the labor force: "Like petrol rationing, it's good for us," one director observed. "We are forced to keep numbers down." Others noted that it insured a ready, continuous supply of labor:

> You must appreciate that we have a twenty-four-[hour] . . . continuous process. . . . It's seven-days-a-week production. So if you have a breakdown, and you have them hostelized [migrant labor in single-sex dormitories], you can call out any number at any time and you know they're available. This is purely seen from a management point of view. If they were urbanized, and looking at all the distances they have to travel to get to work and that sort of thing, you can imagine the problems that arise then.

Others feared the instability that might follow on the lifting of labor controls. A director of a major department store, one that would almost certainly benefit from labor stabilization, explained his ambivalence:

> [It's] slow and it's cumbersome. It's quite obviously, from a business point of view. . . . If someone comes to you and says, "I'd like a job," and you've got a job waiting for the man to take, it's infinitely easy to say, "Sure, start right now," than "Go back to your kraal and speak to your chief" and all that sort of nonsense.
>
>   Ideally, I'd like to see the abolition of influx control, because I believe that any labor should be—black, white, I don't care what color he is—should be free to find his own job without artificial control. But as things are in the homelands at the moment, there are so few opportunities for employment that this influx could be quite serious.

The director of an engineering firm summarized these responses and captured the accommodative side of business practice: "We've been here long enough to deal with it."

African Trade Unions

Employers in all sections of the South African economy exercised an enormous authority over Africans in the work place. In the extractive industries, like gold mining, and the heavily black labor-intensive industries, such as textiles, employers fixed African wage rates and established conditions of employment with only slight reference to collective bargaining or statutory minima. In a minority of firms, African wages were established together with unions that bar African participation. Though the rare union used this opportunity to press for African advancement, African wages were normally a secondary issue or worse, an afterthought. In most cases, management left the initiative in African wages almost entirely to the unions, though it appreciated the conflict of interest involved. "To put it bluntly," one director observed, "the unions here don't know their ass from their uppers. They recognize the need to labor totally, but also the threat of the black man. I don't believe they pushed hard enough for the blacks in the last negotiations." In a few cases, firms relied upon the African liaison or works committees, but even here, the communication was elementary and indifferent. The practice in a major state-owned enterprise was illustrative: "It's not really a negotiating body. I might go down and see them together with, like a personnel manager—and we might be the only whites—to listen to the representation and so on. Come back, make a study of it. Most of the time they give us notices on what they're going to talk about." Often, the works committees were presented with a fait accompli or offered an opportunity to make technical changes that did not affect the basic wage concessions made with the white trade unions. "We don't negotiate [wages]," a director of a textile company noted. "We talk about it."

Nonetheless, employers in manufacturing and commerce have at various points been willing to exchange or modify this authority in favor of collective bargaining arrangements that might insure greater labor stability. After World War II, while the Chamber of Mines was bemoaning the "tribal native's" lack of sophistication and capacity for organization, the FCI turned to African trade unionism.[76] Its Ad Hoc Labour Legislation Committee decided in 1946 that there was "no alternative to the recognition of Native Unions on the same basis as Unions comprising members of other races." The committee took note that negotiations with African unions was in any case an emerging pattern in industry in the Transvaal and Cape: "The

76. Afrikaner business, though not unrelentingly hostile to some form of native representation, shared the Chamber of Mines' fear of African trade unions. At the outset of National party rule, the Handelsinstituut observed:

> The nonwhite trade unions unfortunately pose the potential dangers due to the possible disturbance to sound labour relationships by communist agitators. The withholding of all rights and unfair treatment of nonwhite labour creates a fruitful source for communism. Too much power can, again, be abused by the underdeveloped and sometimes very incorrectly informed native labourer (*Volkshandel,* November 1948, trans. J.L.).

idea of collective bargaining has taken root and is growing. In the opinion of the committee, it follows that legislation should expressly encourage collective bargaining, especially in the absence of channels of political expression."[77]

In 1951, when the government was reexamining the labor system, the FCI reiterated the need for African trade unions, though it remained flexible on the form they should take: "The progression of the Native in the manufacturing field will be accompanied by an increasing demand to participate in the negotiation of wages and they should be allowed to organize their own trade unions subject to such regulatory machinery as may be considered necessary."[78] The unruly work place, it argued, should give way to more orderly labor-management relations—at the very least, to industrywide collective bargaining with unions that represent both skilled and unskilled workers.

As the political and economic fabric was unraveling in 1960, both the FCI and ASSOCOM floated trial balloons on African trade unionism. The FCI's "Statement of Principles" noted, "whilst immediate action was needed, from a long-term point of view there was also a need for extending to the Natives some trade unions, or branch unions under the supervision of established unions."[79] ASSOCOM's "Statement of Policy" stated, "It is believed, however, that collective bargaining is an essential element in the ultimate achievement of an adequate level of wages."[80] Even as the unrest was subsiding and as business organizations were moving away from other demands, the FCI posed a provocative query: "Could there be any moral objection to Bantu representatives appearing before industrial councils to plead the case of their own people instead of having to do so through some European official as mouthpiece?"[81] That the five-organization memorandum,[82] "Proposals to Ease Racial Tension," did *not* mention African trade unions suggests that the FCI and ASSOCOM stood alone on this issue. The remaining organizations—the Chamber of Mines, SEIFSA (a major force in the manufacturing sector), and the Handelsinstituut—were willing to support selective reforms in the administration of the pass laws and influx controls, but not African trade unions. One month before signing the joint memorandum, the Handelsinstituut warned that such tinkering

77. Federated Chamber of Industries, "Report No. 3 of the Ad Hoc Labour Legislation Committee: Native Trade Unions," pp. 1–2.
78. *The Manufacturer,* February 1951, p. 33.
79. Ibid., May 1960, p. 2.
80. *Commercial Opinion,* June 1960, p. 15.
81. *The Manufacturer,* November 1961, p. 21.
82. See the discussion of the five organization memorandum in the next section.

with the labor environment threatened to "bury apartheid" and, consequently, "protection" for whites "in the long term."[83]

By the early seventies the accommodative side of business practice,
apparent for the Handelsinstituut and SEIFSA, had become the predominant approach to the work place. Not even the Durban strikes of 1973 and
1974 could resurrect the earlier business interest in "Native unions." True,
the Natal Employers' Association (NEA) proposed a general minimum
wage ("the very low wages of some employers has proved the undoing of
others") and some "machinery to enable [the African] to negotiate for
himself in a meaningful manner." It questioned the appropriateness of
criminal penalties or influx control as a way of containing African work
stoppages: "[We] want our own labour back as soon as possible—the same
trained labour. It is of no help to us to see it imprisoned—endorsed out."[84]
The Chambers of Commerce also questioned the conventional exclusion of
African workers. "Two facts stand out starkly in the South African scene,"
the president of the Durban Chamber of Commerce observed: one was the
"complete inadequacy of Wage Board determinations" and the other "the
tremendous contrast between the machinery for collective bargaining
provided for white workers, and the appalling lack of it for Africans."[85]
ASSOCOM, while supporting government proposals immediately after the
strikes, informed the government that it fully anticipated the de facto
recognition of African trade unions.[86]

But virtually every section of manufacturing supported government
action to suppress African trade-union organization and new legislation
that might forestall it. In 1973, the NEA advised its member companies,
representing a broad section of Natal manufacturing, not to negotiate with
striking workers or their representatives.[87] It also urged the government to
act under the security laws against the organizers of African unions.[88] When
the NEA had the opportunity to meet with the minister of labour and
comment on draft legislation, it failed to advance its earlier concern with
negotiations in a "meaningful manner." Instead, it sided with SEIFSA in
opposing stronger works committees and supporting the more "manage-
able" liaison variety.[89] When the second round of strikes came in 1974, the

83. *Volkshandel,* May 1960.
84. L.D. Thorne, "Lessons to Learn," mimeo, 27 February 1973, pp. 1–2.
85. *Natal Mercury,* 1 February 1973, p. 13.
86. Horrell and Horner, *The Annual Survey of Race Relations 1973,* p. 277. All three
commercial concerns in my survey supported the unionization of African workers. One
director commented: "We've no objection. They should have fair representation like everyone
else. I'm not a labour man. But as a business manager, they must have means of saying what
has to be said."
87. *Rand Daily Mail,* 6 February 1973.
88. Interview, L.D. Thorne, director, Natal Employers' Association.
89. *Natal Mercury,* 1 February 1973, p. 2.

NEA reaffirmed its support for the state labor framework: "Certainly the majority [of the member firms] were agreed that it was too early to condemn this system [of committees] as an ineffective tool of management."[90] The alternative—African trade unionism—while facilitating communication might threaten the employers' "absolute control of the situation."[91]

The principal employer opposition to African unions emerged in the steel, iron, and engineering industry. SEIFSA responded to potential African strikes by providing preemptive wage boosts for Africans while, at the same time, opposing any recognition of African trade unions.[92] The director of SEIFSA declared: "We don't believe there's any place in this system for Black unions. If unions are operative, obviously management may be prepared to listen. But we are a highly organized industry and conditions of employment of Africans are prescribed."[93] The director's position had hardened by the time of the 1974 strikes: "In this industry there will be *no* —and you can underline *no*—negotiations with African trade unions."[94]

When the government first proposed draft legislation providing for the weaker "liaison" committees only "where no [stronger] works committee exists," SEIFSA tried, successfully as it turned out, to alter the legislation.[95] SEIFSA appointed a subcommittee to consider the legislation and recommended an increased emphasis upon "communication" through liaison committees. Other firms and associations (including the NEA) supported the SEIFSA initiative. "The original legislation would have channelled us into these works committees," one director pointed out. "The employer would have lost the initiative. The employers wanted other alternatives." The later bill provided for works committees "in respect of an establishment in which no liaison committee exists." The employer, consequently, was guaranteed representation on the committee and a voice in the selection of the committee's chairman.

After enactment of the legislation, employers rushed to establish liaison committees before a statutory deadline that left the initiative with African workers: after the deadline, employees might opt for works or liaison committees by referenda. SEIFSA urged its members immediately to establish liaison committees and to discourage African workers from

90. Natal Employers' Association, *Monthly Bulletin,* February 1974, pp. i–ii.
91. Ibid., p. iii.
92. *Rand Daily Mail,* 1 March 1973.
93. *Financial Mail,* 30 November 1973, p. 921.
94. Horrell, Horner, and Hudson, *A Survey of Race Relations 1974,* p. 317.
95. This discussion of SEIFSA and the draft legislation is based upon the Steel and Engineering Industries Federation of South Africa, *Monthly Bulletin,* May 1973, p. 5; and interviews with major Transvaal-based engineering and paper companies. Also see the discussion of works and liaison committees in chapter 8.

choosing the works committee alternative: "Where any request for a works committee is received from the Bantu employees, the employer should use his good offices and endeavour rather to establish a liaison committee."[96] In a few cases, branch plants failed to register liaison committees in time, leaving African workers free to choose the stronger works committees. One company decided to victimize these recalcitrant African workers.

But we don't want to be patronizing about it. We will ask the employees on the liaison committees on where they want this school money to go. I'm not sure what we will do about the works committee. I'm not going to sit down with their chairman on it.

[The works committee] was the result of subversive activity. We have been open with them and they decided on a works committee. I think they have taken a wrong decision. They don't get any communication or feedback. They are certainly not going to be able to get out of us what the liaison committees are achieving. I wouldn't want to call it a white backlash . . . but there is some resentment. It's all because our manager at Springs wasn't on top of the situation. If he'd gotten a liaison committee set up before July, the legislative deadline, we could have gotten it accepted by the government and wouldn't have all this trouble.

Among the twenty-five firms included in this survey, only two faced functioning works committees; the remainder dealt with liaison committees that rarely negotiated wages and that remained under firm management control.

This bent for liaison committees reflects a continuing management interest in its control of the work place, even in secondary industry, and a continuing resistance to African organization. "I don't like it," the director of a chemical company exclaimed. "I just like to be the master of my own place." That mastery, as it turns out, comes down to a question of power— and political power at that.

The minute you deal with trade unions, you're dealing with power. Unions are groups which have positions to defend which can become involved, generally, with the overall efficiency and effectiveness of an operation. . . . If you start making a multiracial or a black trade union, there is going to be competition which isn't going to be responsible.

For other companies, mastery comes down to a question of labor control, not unrelated to questions of political power. The director of an engineering company stated:

96.   Quoted in L.C.G. Douwes Dekker, "Are Works Committees Trade Unions?" p. 21.

[The Bantu] knows if he has a job, he damn well wants to keep it. He wants to behave himself because he doesn't want to find himself back in a tribal land.

I do not relish the thought of having a foreign negotiating situation —white labor, black labor, and employers. I think the prime minister has a point: he has no objection to collective bargaining as long as it takes an evolutionary form. The blacks are not at present sufficiently responsible. They would be led by the nose by agitators.

And the director of one of the largest chemical and explosives operations in South Africa observed:

We place a high premium on stability in explosives. If we find stones in our explosives, its a bloody disaster. We need a large measure of control over our work force. . . .

We are paternalistic enough to think we must protect our Africans from organizations which purport to protect his interests. I have respect for Anna Scheepers but not for the Johnny-come-latelies who are now fomenting trouble.

Finally, the director of a major auto manufacturing company captured the accommodative and political side of such mastery.

Well, I don't think that the Bantu has already reached that level of development in industry that he can really understand this fine relationship between management and labor. I think it's a question of development. It's not illegal for a black man to form a union, but it's just not recognized in terms of the Industrial Conciliation Act. And the history of this country has shown quite adequately that, although there have been a number of Bantu trade unions, they have not been very successful. For a number of reasons: first of all, because of internal corruption; secondly, because they've become instruments in the hands of certain political faction groups, and for that reason they have not been successful.

Though recognition of African unions is not by itself illegal, the director indicated that he will negotiate with Bantu trade unions only when "it becomes government policy in this country to negotiate with them."[97]

97. One company has waged a continuing battle to deny recognition to both the Metal and Allied Workers Union and an independent African trade union (affiliated with the registered Coloured union). When African workers at one plant struck over the recognition issue, the company fired 220 employees, though all but 65 were eventually reinstated.

It is difficult to tell at this point how employers may react to the highly qualified trade-union rights granted Africans during 1979. The Federated Chamber of Industries pointed up the difficulty of designating permanent urban residents as "employees" under the Industrial

Political Disorder and the Challenge to Accommodation

Sharpeville

The political turmoil surrounding the African protests and the murders at
Sharpeville in the spring of 1960 brought severe economic dislocations to
South Africa: the net outflow of private capital reached 152 million rands
and foreign reserves fell 132 million rands; the stock market, gold share
index, and retail sales plummeted.[98] Businessmen in manufacturing and
commerce, some of whom had nearly forgotten their discomfort with
apartheid, began searching for alternative labor forms.

Almost immediately after Sharpeville, the executive committee of AS-
SOCOM unanimously adopted a "Statement of Policy" that questioned the
labor system. The statement underlined the "frustration" that had
"motivated the unrest to which the Union has been subjected" and
proposed expansion of African "consuming ability," the "free" development of "Bantu areas," collective bargaining for African workers, and
increased employment opportunities. It indicated that "natives should be
permitted to acquire freehold title in urban Native townships," and "whilst
complete freedom of movement may not be practicable in existing South
African conditions, the trend should be in the direction of progressively
relaxing restrictions to the utmost extent possible."[99]

The government was not favorably disposed to the timing or substance of
ASSOCOM's statement: The prime minister charged that ASSOCOM's
intervention was part of an organized campaign against the state. Nor did
the other business associations, particularly the Chamber of Mines and
Handelsinstituut, rush to associate themselves with ASSOCOM's remarks.[100] The FCI, however, issued its own "Statement of Principles" that
condemned "lawlessness," requested better communication with African
leaders, and reiterated its position on the "permanency of the completely
urbanised Natives," without further details on pass laws or influx control.[101]

Conciliation Act while denying the designation to migrants who may occupy the same jobs in
the same work place. The directors of SEIFSA, and a member of the Wiehahn Commission,
proposed that migrant workers be "phased into the trade union movement" but only after
bilateral agreements are concluded with foreign and "independent" homeland governments
(Republic of South Africa, Department of Labour and of Mines, *Report of the Commission of
Inquiry into Labour Legislation*, p. 31). Individual employers have in practice adopted
conflicting positions on the new legislation, some willing to negotiate with bona fide African
unions but many using the new registration procedures to create "company" or "cooperative"
unions (*Financial Mail*, 16 November 1979, p. 699; 23 November 1979, p. 825; *The Star*, 24
November 1979).

98. *Financial Mail*, 25 June 1976, p. 1111.
99. *Commercial Opinion*, June 1960, pp. 14–15.
100. Ibid., June and July 1960.
101. *Supplement to the Manufacturer*, May 1960, p. 2.

When it became evident that the political unrest and consequent economic instability would not readily subside, the five major business associations —the Handelsinstituut, ASSOCOM, FCI, SEIFSA and the Chamber of Mines—joined in a general critique of the labor system. These "suggestions and comments," their memorandum read, were submitted "jointly" and "in a spirit of patriotism." The memorandum focused on the crux of the labor-repressive system: pass laws and influx control. The laws and their manner of enforcement, it stated, create "(a) a feeling of insecurity among the Bantu; (b) an undue restriction of freedom of movement of the Bantu; (c) unnecessary interference with Bantu family life; (d) considerable friction between the police and the Bantu." In their place, the memorandum proposed an identity document for urban Africans and an end to criminal prosecutions for contravention of the pass laws. "Such an arrangement would enable the Government to announce to the world the withdrawal of the present reference book carried by the Bantu and the issue to all sections of the population of identity documents."

The joint memorandum also proposed major changes in the qualifications for permanent urban residence and exemptions from the pass laws, offering as a presumption that "the number of this type of Bantu would increase over the years." Among the new procedures for winning exemption from the pass laws were support by an African's current or previous employer and five years of "lawful" and "law-abiding" residence in an urban area. The memorandum suggested, against the grain of the traditional labor framework, that "a Bantu should have the right to transfer from one employer to another in the same urban area without forfeiting his right to be in that area" and that "the wife and unmarried children of any urban Bantu" should be permitted to live and work in the urban areas.[102]

The immediate effect of the joint memorandum was electric. The impact might have been substantive, however, had not all the business associations, excepting ASSOCOM, backed away from the document. The FCI began immediately to emphasize the "friction" in the existing administration rather than modification of the labor framework. It advised the government that the international business community was "not asking for a change in policy" but "a more elastic implementation."[103] On the first anniversary of Sharpeville, the FCI abandoned the political confrontation altogether. "Various outside interests," it observed, "including one of our industrial magazines, have been counseling organised commerce and industry, especially of late to make their collective weight felt in the political field."[104] But

---

102. "Proposal to Ease Race Tension," *Commercial Opinion,* July 1960, pp. 6–7.
103. *The Manufacturer,* September 1960, p. 5.
104. The "industrial magazine" was almost certainly the *Financial Mail* or *Commercial Opinion.*

the FCI had made its accommodation: "We must underline this point, namely, that we have to work within the compass of what Parliament determines."[105] The Handelsinstituut had abandoned the political struggle almost before it started: "The Afrikaanse Handelsinstituut can accept the policy of separate development and strive for close feeling and co-operation with the government and its departments in order to watch over the interests of the businessman and to be helpful to the authorities with sober and practical advice."[106] A year after Sharpeville, it was emphasizing the "Buy South Africa" campaign and likening South Africa's struggle to that of the turn-of-the-century Boer Republics.[107]

Only commercial interests continued to point out the economic costs of apartheid and the need for more than symbolic change.[108] In July 1961, more than a year after Sharpeville, ASSOCOM stated: "The abolition of influx control and job reservation, with positive action to develop the Bantu area would reduce the danger of unrest and lead foreign investors to take a more optimistic view of our future." It circulated a statement by the president of the Johannesburg Chamber of Commerce warning, "If the Republic is going to be a viable state, separate development in all spheres will have to depend more on the natural inclinations of people and less on repressive legislation."[109] Finally, ASSOCOM printed a speech before the Cape Town Chamber of Commerce, underlining commerce's isolation from the government and the remainder of the business community.

> Government spokesmen seem intent on falsely presenting the importer as the villain of the piece in order to divert public attention and anger away from the very grave consequences of Government folly and irresponsibility. . . .
>
> May I state my personal view of what brought about the crisis in our balance of payments and of what in consequence the future seems to hold. Between the ban on the free movement of White men's money outside the Republic and the ban on the free movement of Black men's persons inside the Republic, there is a direct link of effect and cause. Unfreedom encompasses the Black man's person, the Coloured man's opinions and the White man's money. The interconnection was inevitable but the tragedy was, and is, that so few White Men recognize it.[110]

105. *The Manufacturer,* May 1961, p. 11.
106. *Volkshandel,* October 1960, trans. J.L.
107. Ibid., May 1961; December 1961, trans. J.L.
108. *Commercial Opinion,* September 1960, pp. 9–15.
109. Ibid., July 1961, pp. 11, 40.
110. Ibid., September 1961, pp. 7–8.

These were traumatic events. It was a period when manufacturing and commercial needs were clearly articulated, the tensions between these needs and the labor-repressive system exposed, and when business associations found themselves at the center of political controversy. The protests of secondary industry, however, did not carry the day. The National party government refused to grant the legitimacy of these claims or of their claimants. The labor-repressive arrangements—influx control and pass laws —remained intact. Business journals now spoke less of "folly" and "irresponsibility" and more of "cooperation," "trusted partners," and "accommodation."[111]

Soweto

The 1976 disorders in Soweto—indeed, in Guguletu, Cape Town, the University of the North, Bophuthatswana, and elsewhere—were more intense and the government response more violent than the 1960 disorders surrounding Sharpeville. The waves of protests, which began in June with the burning of schools and bottle stores, by the end of August included work stoppages, particularly on the Witwatersrand. In September, the strikes spread to the western Cape, engulfing the textile industry and thoroughly disrupting commerce in Cape Town itself. By the end of the year, the marked decline in long-term credits and the outflow of capital were inescapable.[112]

Even before the first wave of disturbances had ended, businessmen began to wonder aloud whether they were facing another Sharpeville. The *Financial Mail* wrote: "After Sharpeville the economy plunged into one of its dark periods. Is the same going to happen now?"[113]

There was something similar to the aftermath of Sharpeville in the business community's immediate response to the disorders. Soon after the June riots, the Transvaal branch of the FCI pointed out in a memorandum to the prime minister that order and stability would follow only on the removal of the "broad basis of discontent." As it had done sporadically over three decades, the FCI urged the government to give a sense of security and permanence to the large urban black population, emphasizing the need for housing and "civic self-government in the townships."[114] Such a policy, it argued, was consonant with traditional business goals and the maintenance of white power.

---

111. *The Manufacturer,* January 1966, p. 14.
112. William N. Raiford, "International Credit and South Africa," pp. 69–76.
113. *Financial Mail,* 25 June 1976, p. 1111.
114. Transvaal Chamber of Industries, "Memorandum to the Honourable B.J. Vorster, Prime Minister," 29 July 1976, p. 2; also *Financial Mail,* 20 August 1976, pp. 633–34.

The thought most basic to our submission is the need to ensure a stable, contented urbanised Black community in our metropolitan and industrialised areas. In this context a stable "middle class" is most important.

Our prime point of departure should be that this "middle class" is not weakened by frustration and indignity. Only by having this most responsible section of the urban Black on our side can the Whites of South Africa be assured of containing on a long-term basis the irresponsible economic and political ambitions of those Blacks who are influenced against their own real interests from within and without our borders.[115]

A few companies sounded a more alarming note. Anglovaal's chairman, for example, pointed to the "gloom" and "pessimism" that pervaded "the atmosphere of business in South Africa today" and suggested that businessmen take up a more broadly political role: "The growing feeling of crisis had surely reached the stage where private enterprise must reexamine its role in society and question to what extent the scope of its activities should be extended in order to protect the economic structures that had been built up over the years."[116]

ASSOCOM stood alone, however, when it combined feelings of pessimism with a call to restructure the racial order. As in 1960, however, ASSOCOM came into direct conflict with the state. The prime minister warned ASSOCOM against any proposals for "a new socio-economic order that would do away with the private enterprise system, and destroy the democratic rights of the electorate."

Change must come through political processes . . . [T]he Government cannot abdicate its basic responsibilities and principles to business and other groups. . . . You cannot ask me to accept policies rejected by the electorate and in which I do not believe.[117]

The response of the major sections of manufacturing and mining, however, was modest in comparison to 1960—but so was the crisis.

The state had demonstrated in 1960 that in spite of international opinion and declining business confidence, it was quite capable of restoring order and prosperity. Measures to insure domestic security and prevent the repatriation of funds by nonresident investors, many of which were enacted

115. Transvaal Chamber of Industries, "Memorandum to the Honourable B.J. Vorster, Prime Minister," p. 2.
116. Basil E. Hersov, "Anglovaal, Chairman's Review," *Financial Mail,* 5 November 1976, p. 488.
117. Quoted in *Comment and Opinion,* 29 October 1976, pp. 11–16.

during the Sharpeville aftermath, provided reassurances that were not available in the "dark days" of 1960. Though some businessmen gave in to the "gloom," most continued to emphasize the accommodative side of business practice. The Chamber of Mines remained silent. SEIFSA expressed unrelenting optimism in the economy and recommended harsh measures against striking workers. While the Transvaal branch of the FCI presented a memorandum to the government, the parent body chose private consultation and cautious pronouncements on political questions: "Politics is not our business; our business is the business of business." It specifically rejected any intervention by the Chamber on legislative questions: "Whether [FCI] should go as far as to say this and that law should be changed to suit industrialists is a different matter."[118]

When the business community finally assembled in Johannesburg to tackle the problems raised by the unrest, they avoided the major flash points, such as African trade unions, voting rights, influx control, pass laws, and separate development. They opposed job discrimination and settled upon self-help programs, housing, and "the adoption of free enterprise values by urban Blacks."[119] Accordingly, they established the Urban Foundation to promote a higher quality of life in the black urban centers.[120] Their object was stability and perhaps their motives were humane, but the *Star* properly observed, "There is nothing in the businessmen's programme that clashes with State policy."[121]

Manufacturers and retailers have never been closely identified with the racial order. The labor system did not help them organize a labor force or maintain production; if anything, it limited their access to labor supplies and prevented labor stabilization. They played little part in creating the state mechanisms or racist ideologies that have governed capitalist development in South Africa. They did not insist on pass laws, influx control, or labor bureaus; they had little use for the native reserves and the whole framework for semiproletarianization and "cheap" labor. Indeed, secondary industry and commerce have consistently opposed job color bars and, less consistently, the system of labor controls.

Nonetheless, there has developed a broad area of accommodation between these developing sectors of the economy and the racial order. In

118. *Financial Mail*, 22 October 1976, p. 303.
119. This discussion draws upon the *Rand Daily Mail*, 1 December 1976; *Financial Mail*, 19 November 1976, p. 697; and 3 December 1976, pp. 889–91.
120. Urban Foundation, *Proceedings of the Businessmen's Conference on the Quality of Life of Urban Communities*.
121. *The Star*, 1 December 1976.

some respects, the state has moved to accommodate the more pressing needs of industry, limiting the application of job color bars and the Physical Planning Act. But in most other respects, business itself has come to terms with the constraints and opportunities in the racial order, even in areas where business associations have historically contested state policy. The racial segregation and inequality that characterize the society have been readily reproduced in the work place. Business associations here have managed to find the silver lining in policies that limit the influx of African workers to the cities and that deny African workers the right to organize and withhold their labor. Though manufacturers did not construct these policies —and might well live without them—they, like the Chamber of Mines, have used them to restrain African wages and insure continuing business autonomy at the work place.

The broad accommodation to the racial order has broken down in the last two decades only when the African population has called the prevailing hegemony into question and when economic dislocations have threatened the business environment. In 1960, after Sharpeville, manufacturers and retailers rediscovered their interest in a stable, urban working class and expressed their impatience with state meddling in the labor market. Though in 1976, after Soweto, businessmen were less intent on such reforms and less willing to chance a direct clash with the state, they raised questions about the quality of African lives and the role of discrimination. They questioned the ability of the prevailing state structures and ideas to provide for the economy and stable growth.

CHAPTER 10

Businessmen in Alabama: Elaborating, Accommodating, and Unraveling the Racial Order

"Segregation is a Wooden Leg"

The South today is somewhat comparable to a robust young man who wears a wooden leg as a result of a childhood accident. Except for this one handicap, the young man is sound of mind and limb, capable of leading a perfectly normal life. . . .

In fact, there is every reason to believe that this young man, with proper therapy, can ultimately overcome his handicap completely and become a superior citizen. The speed of his recovery hinges on the effectiveness of the therapy. . . .

In fact, the leg is getting so much attention that the rest of the young man is being virtually ignored. The fact that the South is pacing the nation in many fields of industrial, scientific, and civic progress is being lost in the increasing barrage of segregation news. . . .

We think it is in the interest both of the nation and of the region to have more discussion of southern progress and to have less careless talk about the wooden leg.

Manufacturers Record
May 1956

SOUTHERN INDUSTRIALISM

An odd collection of authors and politicians gathered around the idea of southern industrialism. Whatever else they differed on and however else they evaluated the consequences of industrialism, they all pictured the process as confounding and, ultimately, transcendent. Industrialism, they argued, unleashes forces that shatter traditional social structure and practice and impose new values and ways of thinking. With industrialism comes prosperity, opportunity, and choice. The opportunists among them hoped to sit atop the new order, while others at the bottom hoped simply to share in the economic bounty. Some looked to industrialism as an escape from the South's traditional poverty and racism. Even some opponents of the New South believed, no less than the most zealous apostles, that industrialism wreaks havoc on the old ways.

The idea that industrialism creates new opportunities was current before Henry W. Grady proclaimed the New South at the New England Society in New York. The Reconstruction regimes supported industrial progress in principle and created state agencies to encourage and underwrite it—in Alabama, the Bureau of Industrial Resources. The corruption and enormous state debt associated with railroad development sometimes obscures the hopes and beliefs current in the Freedmen's Bureau and among blacks: industrialization promised blacks opportunities for advancement that would certainly be denied them in the countryside.

It was Henry Grady, however—and, to some extent, Booker T. Washington—who lent force and legitimacy to the idea. Grady led the way, calling on the South to honor speculation and accumulation, to defer to a new breed of men, cloaked in romance and nostalgia, yet committed to "progress." Grady and other spokesmen for the New South, C. Vann Woodward writes, "were preaching laissez-faire capitalism, freed of all traditional restraints, together with a new philosophy and way of life and a new scale of values."[1] With the "Atlanta Compromise," Booker T. Washington told the corporate world and white southerners that blacks would take their chances with capitalist growth and the businessman. They would put aside politics and emphasize industrial education, thrift, patience, and friendly relations with their employers. But Washington was not simply moderating black aspirations; he was identifying the fate of black Americans with an idea and class that promised their own kind of revolutionary transformation.[2]

That is precisely what the Southern Agrarians feared. These southern writers based at Vanderbilt University, W. J. Cash wrote, "were mouthpieces of the fundamental, if somewhat only subterranean, will of the South to hold to the old ways."[3] If customary practices were to be retained, the South would have to resist "progress" and "stop the advances of industrialism, or even undo some of them"; "it must find the way to throw it off."[4] The South would have to insist on the traditional values—"honor, courage, generosity, amiability, courtesy"[5]—and on the traditional agricultural forms, variously the plantation and yeoman farming. The "agrarian order" was threatened by science, materialism, and the "Chamber of Commerce of its county seat."[6]

    1. C. Vann Woodward, *Origins of the New South,* pp. 145–57, esp. p. 148; and C. Vann Woodward, *Tom Watson, Agrarian Rebel,* pp. 88–91, 165.
    2. Booker T. Washington, *The Future of the American Negro,* pp. 76–79.
    3. W.J. Cash, *The Mind of the South,* p. 390.
    4. Twelve Southerners, *I'll Take My Stand,* pp. xix–xx; see discussion in William H. Nicholls, "Southern Tradition and Regional Economic Progress," pp. 189–91.
    5. Cash, *The Mind of the South,* p. 392.
    6. Twelve Southerners, *I'll Take My Stand,* p. xix.

Nonetheless, strong intellectual currents in the South insisted on industrialism—and its consequences. For William H. Nicholls and others in the North Carolina "progressive" tradition, the "old ways" did not conjure up romance and lost wars but simple impediments to southern economic progress. Industrialism was nearly smothered by "agrarian values," a "rigid social structure," and "monolithic political structure." A persistent industrialism, buttressed by "wise leadership," ultimately would throw off these values and structures, including, although Henry Grady was ambiguous on this point, "white supremacy."[7] With industrialism would come new industrial centers and a new middle class that, once freed of the "hidebound rural society," would introduce a new flexibility into social relations. With the expansion of wealth, the poor whites would no longer fear economic competition from black tenants and workers, removing a principal source of racial antagonism. The South's "economic progress," consequently, would "steadily" weaken the "race oriented traditions."[8] For Broadus and George Sinclair Mitchell, there is a force in the evolution of the factory that "destroys separatism, and invites and forces national and world consciousness."[9] The dominance of manufacture over agriculture inevitably brings a moment, "briefer" in most cases and "longer" in the case of the South, where there is a "revolution in our whole social habit and procedure."[10]

And then there was Birmingham, the "Pittsburgh" of the New South, yet for Martin Luther King, Jr., the "most segregated city in America."[11] A century of southern industrialism and a "new breed of men" seemed only to elaborate the framework of racial domination.

Capitalist development in Alabama in its early stages depended upon primary industries and textile manufacturing that did not undermine the developing labor system in rural areas or the racial hierarchy. Indeed, it depended upon industries that could and did take advantage of the racial milieu, using the state[12] machinery to help create and control a black working class and highlighting racial divisions and prejudices to limit trade unionism and break work stoppages. Increasing development brought secondary manufacture and commercialization—and a declining business

7. Nicholls, "Southern Tradition and Regional Economic Progress," pp. 191–92; also see Clarence H. Danhof, "Thoughts on the South's Economic Problems," p. 65.
8. William H. Nicholls, *Southern Tradition and Regional Progress,* pp. 58–68, 180–81; Nicholls, "Southern Tradition and Regional Economic Progress," pp. 194–95.
9. Broadus Mitchell and George Sinclair Mitchell, *The Industrial Revolution in the South,* p. ix.
10. Ibid., p. 114.
11. Martin Luther King, Jr., *Why We Can't Wait,* pp. 47–50.
12. *State* in this context refers not to the "state" as a federal unit but to the administrative, legal, coercive apparatus operating only within Alabama.

dependence on black labor, race lines, and the racial state. Businessmen in manufacturing and commerce, nonetheless, mainly accommodated prevailing racial practices, recreating the racial hierarchy and segregation in the work place and buttressing the racial order.

The contrast between their accommodation and the earlier complicity of primary industries became apparent only after black protests and outside pressures raised the costs of maintaining the racial order. Then, businessmen in these emerging sectors of the economy, little dependent on the racial framework, chose to abandon certain customary racial practices and propose alternative ways of organizing Alabama society. The business challenge to the racial order, however, came only with the changing composition and needs of business in Alabama and with the rise of political disorder that accompanied and played on these changes.

CAPITALIST DEVELOPMENT IN ALABAMA

Primary Manufacture and the Rural Economy

Small-scale manufacturers before the Civil War did not seriously contest the ascendancy of planters and their labor system or, for that matter, the racial ideas and practices that buttressed it. Manufacture began in Alabama with a scattered lot of small enterprises that for the most part serviced the rural and slave society: forges, bloomeries, blacksmith shops, and even a few blast furnaces and rolling mills.[13] At the outbreak of the Civil War, there were barely a dozen cotton mills, employing perhaps a 1,000 workers, many of them slaves, and only a few factories producing cotton gins. The largest was owned by Daniel Pratt. He accumulated capital that later proved critical to the development of coal and iron mining but before the Civil War managed to combine manufacture and plantation agriculture, slave and free labor.[14] Still, in 1860, less than 1 percent of the population was employed as wage earners in manufacturing.[15] This incipient capitalism was badly serviced by Mobile and Montgomery, towns largely oriented to cotton interests, and by a disconnected railway system supported by individual subscription, in Ethel Armes description, "trembling on the verge of collapse and utter extinction."[16]

---

13. Lucille Griffith, *Alabama: A Documentary History to 1900,* pp. 197–200; Ethel Armes, *The Story of Coal and Iron in Alabama,* p. 186.
14. Griffith, *Alabama,* pp. 194–96; Albert Burton Moore, *History of Alabama,* p. 284.
15. Holman Head, "The Development of the Labor Movement in Alabama Prior to 1900," p. 12.
16. Armes, *The Story of Coal and Iron in Alabama,* p. 105.

These small enterprises operated within an economic and political milieu that was not, in any case, hospitable to manufacture. The white subsistence farmers, the slaves, and meager towns offered only a limited market for manufactured goods; the small planter class offered a market for cotton-related manufacturing—cotton gins, for example—but not for a broader range of locally manufactured goods. Planters, in any case, resisted the growth of a manufacturing class that might support protective tariffs and northern capitalist interests. They did not wish to see resources diverted from land and slaves or their own wealth taxed to subsidize railroad construction.[17] Alabama voters in 1840 opted for macadamized (layered stone) roads rather than railroads. "It is hard for a man who has lived in Alabama seven years to account for the deep and widespread suspicion and want of confidence in such investments," a contemporary observer wrote. "They seem to be afraid to subscribe to [railroads], or to have anything to do with them."[18] Up to 1860, at the onset of war, Alabama planters were disinclined to underwrite internal improvements. Alabama capitalists asked in frustration, "What becomes of the twenty-five million dollars which our commerce distributes annually among the planters of Alabama?" There was, they concluded, "a lack of public spirit, no foresight, an utter indifference to the future."[19] Those that survived and prospered, like Daniel Pratt, settled, Eugene Genovese writes, for a "modest industrial expansion within the context of planter control."[20]

Though the Confederate Congress gave little encouragement to Alabama industry and though the war destroyed virtually every furnace, rolling mill, forge and foundry, and long stretches of railroad lines in Alabama, manufacturing emerged from the ashes. The provisional, Reconstruction, and "conservative" governments in Alabama identified themselves with industrial expansion and took up those railroad subscriptions that the planter-controlled governments had treated with such reserve. The Louisville and Nashville Railroad and the Alabama and Chattanooga Railroad, each with their entourage of politicians, land speculators, and railroad officials, vied for state favors and state endorsement of railroad bonds. Governor George S. Houston, himself an industrialist, railroad company director, and friend of Birmingham mining interests, helped L & N win

17. Mitchell and Mitchell, *Industrial Revolution in the South*, pp. 4–5; Eugene Genovese, *The Political Economy of Slavery. Studies in the Economy and Society of the Slave South*, pp. 24–25, 164–65.
18. Armes, *The Story of Coal and Iron in Alabama*, pp. 105, 116.
19, Quoted in ibid., p. 122.
20. Genovese, *The Political Economy of Slavery*, p. 193. Genovese also suggests that the acquiescence to planter control offers the prospect of a "Prussian road to industrial capitalism, paved with authoritarianism, benevolent despotism, and aristocratic pretension" (ibid., p. 207). Also see my discussion of the same subject in chapter 3.

access to the rich mineral region in north Alabama.[21] Later, Governor Thomas Goode Jones would resist the growth of Populist forces, drawing heavily on the support of railroad and mining interests.[22]

Faced with so prominent a business presence, it is difficult not to conclude with C. Vann Woodward that the members of post-Reconstruction governments "were of middle-class, industrial capitalistic outlook, with little but a nominal connection with the old planter regime"; they, not the Reconstruction governments, Confederates, or planters, "laid the lasting foundations in matters of race, politics, economics, and law for the modern South."[23]

The glare from railroad politics, however, may obscure a pattern of capitalist development in Alabama that failed to establish the pre-eminence of capital over land or undermine the racial framework, a pattern that, on the one hand, failed to challenge the use of unfree labor in the rural economy and, on the other, the extension of unfree labor into the urban, capitalist one. That pattern included: first, the "reconstruction" of Black Belt commercial farming and the continued political importance of large landowners; second, the development of a textile industry dependent on and compatible with Black Belt agriculture; and third, the emergence of primary industries—coal and iron-ore mining and iron manufacture—in north Alabama.

The Black Belt and cotton did not go the way of the slave plantation: planters in the post-Reconstruction period managed to recapture their labor force, retain their land, and construct lien laws at the expense of merchants.[24] With cotton production moving back up to pre-Civil War levels, farmers came to believe once again that the development and wealth of the South could be organized around cotton and unfree labor.[25] The Constitution of 1875, fashioned under Black Belt scrutiny, eliminated the Bureau of Industrial Resources, prohibited the state from carrying out internal improvement projects or even advancing credit for them, and fixed a corporate profit tax equal to the individual rate.[26] Though the Black Belt spokesmen did not urge a complete repudiation of the state debt or cut off of land sales to mineral interests, they did manage a fairly consistent

21.   Horace Mann Bond, *Negro Education in Alabama. A Study in Cotton and Steel,* pp. 43–46; Woodward, *Origins of the New South,* pp. 8–11.
22.   Sheldon Hackney, *Populism to Progressivism in Alabama,* pp. 15–18.
23.   Woodward, *Origins of the New South,* pp. 20, 22.
24.   Bond, *Negro Education in Alabama,* pp. 122–23; Jonathan M. Wiener, "Planter-Merchant Conflict in Reconstruction Alabama," pp. 73–94; see the extended discussion of this issue in chapter 6.
25.   Clarence H. Danhof, "Thoughts on the South's Economic Problems."
26.   Allen Johnston Going, *Bourbon Democracy in Alabama 1874–1890,* p. 111.

criticism of manufacturing interests that threatened labor supplies and cotton production.[27] Moreover, they managed after 1870 to shift a large percentage of their tax burden to the mineral district in the north.[28]

Alabama and the Black Belt, nonetheless, shared the South's general enthusiasm for textile manufacture. No less than white southerners elsewhere, the Alabama public became "an informal chamber of commerce to advance the industry":[29] bring the "factories to the fields" and uplift the South's poverty-stricken whites. In a rash of nearly unrestrained enthusiasm, the Alabama legislature allowed localities to remit corporate taxes; it also refused to regulate the hours of adult males and repealed laws limiting child labor in selected cotton-mill areas and later, under pressure from mill interests, in the entire state.[30] "Mill fever" created mill towns across Alabama but particularly in the Piedmont area. The number of cotton spindles increased from well under 100,000 in 1880 to over 400,000 in 1900 and doubled again by 1910.[31]

The interest in textile manufacture, paradoxically enough, only underlines the importance of the Black Belt in Alabama's industrial development. In the first place, growth of textile mills and cotton production were complementary: mills in the Piedmont, "alongside the field" by one account,[32] drew on cotton production in the nearby Black Belt and even in upland counties like Cherokee and Calhoun. In the second place, and more important, textiles and cotton did not compete for the same labor. After some speculation in "coolie," immigrant, and even native white workers, Black Belt farmers settled down with their traditional black laborers. Despite the Civil War, emancipation, and Reconstruction, the Black Belt retained its share of Alabama's black population: 39.1 percent in 1860 and 38 percent in 1900.[33] The textile mills, on the other hand, turned to white labor; more specifically, the mills recruited labor on the tenant farms and in the hollows and relied increasingly on the labor of children and women.[34] The number of men employed in the Alabama mills between 1885 and 1895 increased by 31 percent, while the number of women increased by 75

27. Armes, *The Story of Coal and Iron in Alabama,* pp. 216–17; William Warren Rogers, *The One-Gallused Rebellion. Agrarianism in Alabama, 1865–1896,* pp. 92–93; Going, *Bourbon Democracy in Alabama,* pp. 110–13, 116–19.
28. Bond, *Negro Education in Alabama,* pp. 132–34.
29. Mitchell and Mitchell, *The Industrial Revolution in the South,* p. 11.
30. Going, *Bourbon Democracy in Alabama,* p. 113.
31. United States Department of Labor, *Labor in the South,* p. 9; Woodward, *Origins of the New South,* pp. 131–34.
32. Contemporary report, cited by Griffith, *Alabama: A Documentary History to 1900,* p. 621.
33. Bond, *Negro Education in Alabama,* p. 128.
34. See Mitchell and Mitchell, *The Industrial Revolution in the South,* pp. 30–32, 54–56.

percent; the number of boys under eighteen increased by 81 percent and the number of girls, by 158 percent.[35]

Textile manufacturers and planters coalesced to protect their ideas and their labor supplies against the market, labor unions, north Alabama, and Birmingham.[36]

At the crossroad of the North and South Railroad coming up from Montgomery and the Alabama and Chattanooga Railroad coming down from the Northeast, amid coal seams and Red Mountain iron ore, Birmingham developed, an enclave of speculation and industrial enterprise that recalled not mint juleps and plantation paternalism but the routine and grind of northern heavy manufacturing. Here, the Elyton Land Company and Henry Fairfield DeBardeleben layed out the boundaries and street plans and drew up the bylaws of Birmingham and the surrounding iron and coal towns. Along with mining capitalists like Colonel James Withers Sloss, they brought out high-quality coking coal in 1878 and built the Alice Furnace in 1880. They also helped introduce into the region the L & N railroad, almost fully owned by eastern and foreign capitalists, and the Tennessee Coal, Iron and Railroad Company (TCI), 95 percent of whose stock shares were held in New York, Massachusetts, and Europe. Before the turn of the century, TCI consolidated sixteen of the various coal and iron companies under its ownership, including 76,000 acres of coal land, 460 coke ovens, two blast furnaces, and seven and a half miles of the Red Mountain iron-ore seam. The whole collection, under threat of collapse in 1907, passed into the hands of the United States Steel Corporation.[37]

All the forces anathema to the Old South congregated in Birmingham. Immigrant workers, comprising nearly a quarter of the white population of the city, came to work in the coal mines and make pig iron; and free blacks too, unhampered by the traditional forces of social control, came to work and live in the burgeoning city. Birmingham grew from "a staring, bold,

35. Woodward, *Origins of the New South,* p. 226.
36. They also coalesced against new textile mills that threatened a local monopoly over labor. One firm even in the 1970s tried to discourage the local community from recruiting new industry. The officer of the firm observed:

> There tends to be a tendency on the part of the industrial development groups in these small towns to try to bring in more industry than the labor supply will take care of right at the particular time. And that's caused some problems in this area right now.
> We went through a period in the past of trying to counsel industrial development groups against this sort of thing. But as a matter of reality, we wound up in almost every instance being, not necessarily condemned, but at least criticized for being antigrowth and antiprogress.

37. Carl V. Harris, *Political Power in Birmingham, 1871–1921,* pp. 15–19; Armes, *The Story of Coal and Iron in Alabama,* pp. 332–36, 425–27, 516–23; United States Steel Corporation, Tennessee Coal and Iron Division, *Biography of a Business,* 1960, p. 22.

mean little town"[38] with 3,086 people in 1880 to 26,178 in 1890 and, with incorporation, 130,000 by 1910. More than half the coal miners and almost two-thirds of the iron and steel workers were black; approximately 40 percent of the residents of Birmingham were black, the largest percentage of any large city in the United States.[39] Little wonder that one Black Belt newspaper urged Birmingham to tear down its furnaces, fill the coal mines with dirt, and disperse its populations to plant cotton.[40]

Industrialism and capitalism were firmly planted in Alabama soil by the end of the nineteenth century. The total amount of capital invested increased from almost $10 million in 1880 to $46 million in 1890 and $70 million in 1900.[41] Textile production was booming; iron production had risen from a mere 11,000 tons of pig iron in 1872 to 8 million tons in 1900;[42] railway mileage had increased from under 1,000 miles before the Civil War to 4,197 in 1900.[43]

But capitalist development up to the turn of the century had proceeded under the watchful eye of Black Belt planters, sometimes in sectors fully complementary and dependent on cotton production, at other times as primary extractive industries confined to a modern capitalist enclave in north Alabama. The consequences of that pattern will be apparent in the norms governing labor practice, emphasizing unfree labor and race domination, and the labor-repressive policies and segregation that characterized the urban industrial economy in its first half century.

The New South

It is difficult to pinpoint the time or period when Alabama escaped the dominance of planters and primary industry. George Tindall suggests World War I: "The most significant effect of the war on the South was to create situations of dynamic change in an essentially static society."[44] With the help of English investors and a Canadian engineer, Alabama began to convert its water resources into electric power, emerging as the South's principal producer by 1926.[45] Textile production, measured in numbers of cotton spindles, continued to grow at the heady pace witnessed in its early

38. Harris, *Political Power in Birmingham,* p. 234; also quoted in Woodward, *Origins of the New South,* p. 136.
39. Paul B. Worthman, "Black Workers and Labor Unions in Birmingham, Alabama, 1897–1904," pp. 55–58; Harris, *Political Power in Birmingham,* pp. 20–22, 34–35.
40. *Selma Times,* reported in Going, *Bourbon Democracy in Alabama,* p. 47.
41. Head, "The Development of the Labor Movement in Alabama Prior to 1900," p. 200.
42. Harris, *Political Power in Birmingham,* p. 16.
43. Griffith, *Alabama: A Documentary History,* p. 521.
44. George B. Tindall, *The Emergence of the New South, 1913–1945,* p. 53.
45. Ibid., pp. 72–73.

days: doubling between 1900 and 1910 and once again between 1910 and
1930.[46] United States Steel, now assured that its takeover of TCI would not
produce antitrust action, invested $11 million at the new Fairfield Works
outside Birmingham.[47] Other traditional indicators of southern industrialism and Black Belt ascendancy also began to change. During the
war, there was a substantial drop in the numbers of children working in the
textile mills, and there were the first inklings of a "Great Migration" that
would eventually alter the rural labor pattern.[48] Clarence H. Danhof is
probably correct, however, that the war and the spurt in economic growth
principally destroyed the "proposition that the Old South was a viable
system in the modern world." They did not so much create a new form of
industrialism as set off a "search for a new rationale of the old system, for
the causes of the South's predicament, for a new system, or for methods of
accelerating the emergence of the New South that had been proclaimed
several generations earlier."[49] In 1920, after all, only 22 percent of Alabama's population lived in urban areas, and only 5 percent were wage
earners. Alabama was still organized around agriculture, textiles, and
primary industry.[50]

But World War II and the subsequent two decades brought rapid
economic growth and important changes in the nature of southern industrialism. The traditional patterns, for example, were almost completely
subverted. Agriculture represented a declining share of total production and
employed a declining portion of the labor force. Across the entire South, the
agricultural labor force began dropping in the thirties, from 43 percent of
the total labor force in 1930 to 22 percent in 1950. Cotton cultivation in
particular began a rapid decline in this period; by 1950 it accounted for only
a quarter of cash farm receipts.[51] In Alabama, the number of farm tenants
began to drop precipitously after 1940; one third of all farmers quit the rural
areas between 1954 and 1959 alone. Beginning in the mid-sixties, Alabama
witnessed a major shift to larger, more labor-efficient units of production.[52]
The rapid growth of the textile industry came to a halt in the thirties.
Between 1930 and 1965, Alabama lost some 300,000 cotton spindles;

46.   Richard L. Rowan, *The Negro in the Textile Industry*, p. 21.
47.   Tindall, *Emergence of the New South*, p. 59.
48.   Ibid., p. 322.
49.   Danhof, "Thoughts on the South's Economic Problems," pp. 10–11.
50.   Donald B. Dodd and Wynelle S. Dodd, *Historical Statistics of the South 1790–1970*,
pp. 2–3.
51.   B.U. Ratchford, "Patterns of Economic Development," p. 220.
52.   Alabama Business Research Council, *Transition in Alabama*, p. 2; University of
Alabama, Center for Business and Economic Research, *Economic Abstract of Alabama*, 1963,
p. 155; 1966, p. 176; 1972, p. 197; also see appendix B, table II.C.2. This material is discussed
in more detail in chapter 6.

employment in the same period dropped from 53,000 to 38,000.[53] And while price mechanisms that discriminated against TCI were lifted in 1948, steel production and employment failed to "take off." The numbers of workers in steel manufacture in 1950, 48,000, remained unchanged a decade and a half later. Employment in iron-ore and coal mining in the same period dropped from 22,000 to just under 6,000.[54] Primary industry was clearly a declining sector of Alabama's industrialism.

While agriculture, textiles, and steel declined, other sectors were fast developing. The construction of dams near Muscle Shoals and the development of the Tennessee Valley brought electric power and water resources to the northern portion of the state. An enormous expansion of wartime investments brought a boom across the South, but particularly in states like Texas, Louisiana, and Alabama. Mobile was nearly overrun by the construction and growth of shipyards and the doubling of its population in four short years.[55] During the war years, nonagricultural employment increased from 405,000 in Alabama to 633,000, and while there was a lull after the war, it increased from 663,000 in 1951 to 818,000 in 1964. Increases in manufacturing employment were particularly marked between 1960 and 1965.[56]

Manufacturing was also more diversified and dispersed. New technologies developed in the late twenties and early thirties allowed the paper industry to use southern pine, opening the way for International Paper and Scott Paper near Mobile. Ten thousand workers were employed in the paper industry in 1950; that figure jumped to 37,000 by 1965. Employment also increased in the lumber, metal-fabricating, chemical, and garment industries.[57] Jefferson County, including the city of Birmingham, was a declining center of manufacture, producing 43 percent of the total value in manufacturing in 1939 but only 33 percent in 1958.[58] In that same period, Mobile, Decatur, and Gadsden emerged as substantial urban centers; the percentage of the population in urban areas jumped from 30 percent in 1940 to 40 percent in 1950 and 58 percent by 1970.[59]

53. Rowan, *The Negro in the Textile Industry,* p. 21; University of Alabama, Center for Business and Economic Research, *Economic Abstract of Alabama,* 1966, p. 26.

54. H.H. Chapman, *The Iron and Steel Industries of the South,* p. 378; University of Alabama, Center for Business and Economic Research, *Economic Abstract of Alabama,* 1966, p. 26.

55. Tindall, *The Emergence of the New South,* pp. 699–701.

56. James G. Maddox, *The Advancing South: Manpower Prospects and Problems,* p. 224; appendix B, table II.D.

57. University of Alabama, Center for Business and Economic Research, *Economic Abstract of Alabama,* 1966, p. 26; Herbert R. Northrup, *The Negro in the Paper Industry,* pp. 14–15.

58. Alabama Business Research Council, *Transition in Alabama,* p. 69.

59. William C. Havard, "The South: A Shifting Perspective," p. 14; appendix B, table II.B.1.

In the period after the Civil War, the South entered a phase of industrialism characterized by a strong agricultural sector in the Black Belt, an allied textile industry that did not challenge the traditional place of cotton or agriculture, and an enclave of primary industries: coal and iron-ore mining and iron manufacture. That pattern survived the nineteenth century and a good part of the twentieth. It did not, however, survive the increasing pace and changing course of industrial development associated with World War II. The new pattern of industrialism included a much smaller role for agriculture; a growth of secondary industry, commerce and service occupations, including government, and a dispersed and growing urbanism.

Economic growth and the changing pattern of industrialism did not immediately undermine prevailing racial practices: businessmen in manufacturing and commerce readily accommodated the customary demarcations and norms that predominated in the rural economy and the primary extractive industries. Only after these demarcations were challenged by the subordinate population and the federal government did businessmen question the costs of accommodation and consider new ways of organizing a labor force.

COAL AND IRON: DEVELOPING LABOR-REPRESSIVE POLICIES

Labor-repressive policies are not a contemporary issue for Alabama's primary industries. Businessmen in mining and steel manufacturing go about organizing and keeping their labor force in very much the same way as businessmen in secondary industry and commerce: their black workers are for the most part free to move between jobs, move North, or refuse employment without fear of imprisonment or police harassment. Criminal penalties for breach of contract are barred by the United States Constitution, and the issue of passes died with the Civil War and the coming of emancipation.[60] Businesses do not now boast of manipulating race differences in the labor force or inflaming racial prejudices. It would have been injudicious, therefore, to ask businessmen, as I did trade-union leaders, "Do you believe management has ever taken advantage of racial differences among the [steel] workers?"[61]

There are, nonetheless, historical answers to this and other questions concerning labor repression. During early capitalist development, munici-

60. A rudimentary pass system existed in the antebellum period. See the discussion of this question in chapter 6.
61. Because labor repression is not a contemporary issue in Alabama, it was not possible to explore these issues through the interview material.

pal, county, and state officials attempted to place controls over the developing black working class and recreate forms of unfree labor. Convict labor, laws against vagrancy and labor recruiting, and police action against multiracial unions and strikes were commonplace in the South and were particularly important to Alabama's industrial development. Mining and iron interests, as we shall see, urged the state to elaborate these repressive mechanisms.

Organizing a Labor Force

With the overthrow of Reconstruction, convict labor in Alabama came into its own and, at the same time, took on its racial character. By 1877, virtually all the convict laborers in Alabama were black. Mining entrepreneurs, taking their first cuts at the "Big Seam," were not loath to take advantage of a business opportunity, whether in minerals or labor. The Pratt Mines, for example, one of the more important in the Birmingham area, signed a five-year convict lease with the state government in 1882. Indeed, in 1887, all the state convicts (approximately 1,000) were leased either to the Pratt Mines or two plantations. When convict leases were put up for bid in 1887, the mining companies dominated the bidding, and TCI, now in possession of the Pratt Mines, won an exclusive ten-year contract with the state government.[62] The mining companies were not restricted to state leases, however. Between 1891 and 1913, Jefferson County leased all its able-bodied convicts to TCI, the Sloss-Sheffield Steel and Iron Company, and the Pratt Consolidated Coal Company. In fact, counties all over Alabama financed their prisons and other services through convict leases held in the mining districts; local courts and their court officials enlarged their fees by pursuing petty offenders, most of them black, and sending the "guilty" off to the mines. Carl V. Harris estimates that between 1906 and 1911, an average of 1,500 state and county convicts were employed by the coal companies each year. Though the mines could not be mined by convict labor alone, the mining companies viewed the system as "remunerative" and a healthy insurance against unionism. The white workers worried that the convict leases depressed wages and working conditions and undermined the organization of free laborers.[63]

Agricultural interests, otherwise loath to see black labor drift to the mining districts, helped administer the system of convict labor. Their reasons were simple enough. The well-publicized hardships at the mines, the

62. Going, *Bourbon Democracy in Alabama,* pp. 176, 178–79.
63. Harris, *Political Power in Birmingham,* pp. 202–04; Hackney, *Populism to Progressivism,* pp. 144–45, 265–66.

cruel treatment and high death rate,[64] were thought to leave a "healthy" impression on the minds of rural black laborers. Much more important, however, was the revenue question. State and county governments became dependent on the revenue from these leases to finance penitentiaries and other government services. In 1890, 6 percent of Alabama's total state revenue came from convict leases held primarily in the mining district.[65] Governor Joseph F. Johnston defended the system, despite evident abuses, in strict fiscal terms: "The lease contract with the Tennessee Coal, Iron and Railroad Company expires with the year 1897. The state receives from this source about $11,000 per month which cannot yet be dispensed with."[66] Convict labor was not dispensed with until 1928.

The executives of the iron and mining companies were anxious that the "social regulation" of "free" blacks not come at the expense of their labor supplies.[67] They, no less than the other white residents of Birmingham, hoped that the end of plantation discipline would not create indiscipline in the mines and cities. But they opposed the application of the county fee system in the Birmingham area, an arrangement that encouraged deputies to arrest blacks for petty offenses. The system, they claimed, "demoralized" black labor and threatened labor supplies. For similar reasons, the executives tried to forestall prohibition in Birmingham. The top executives of TCI and other major coal and iron companies signed an open letter that said, in part, "new labor, such as we need, will not come to a prohibition district" and that "large numbers of our best workers would leave."

But businessmen, particularly during periods of labor unrest or labor shortage, were enthusiastic advocates of vagrancy laws and labor agent registration laws. As Carl Harris points out, businessmen helped create a public impression that blacks were prone to idleness and crime and, at the same time, attempted to elaborate the state and local government regulation of vagrancy. Thus, in 1891, they supported a Birmingham city antivagrancy ordinance that proscribed any individual with "no visible means of support" who "lives without employment" or "habitually neglects his employment"; the businessmen also backed state ordinances in 1903 and 1907 that seemed to enhance control over black labor.[68] In 1910, the Chamber of Commerce declared:

Negroes are allowed to loaf throughout this district, especially in the cities. The remedy for this is for the county and city officials to enforce

64. Going, *Bourbon Democracy in Alabama,* pp. 182–83.
65. Ibid., p. 179. Mining companies easily outbid farmers for these leases and, hence, provided the bulk of the revenue.
66. "Governor's Message," quoted in Griffith, *Alabama: A Documentary History,* p. 523.
67. This discussion relies primarily on Carl Harris's excellent discussion of "Social Regulation" in Birmingham's early history (*Political Power in Birmingham,* pp. 186–216).
68. Ibid., pp. 198–201.

the vagrancy law, which they can do by spending only one-hundredth as much energy as is spent in hunting down craps shooters. Should the vagrancy law be enforced the idle negroes would seek employment, which would insure better results at the mines, furnaces and other industries.[69]

In 1918, during a period of "acute labor shortage," a large number of businessmen successfully lobbied the city commission for stricter anti-vagrancy laws and the personnel to enforce them.

Businessmen also attempted to discourage labor agents from "enticing" laborers, particularly black ones, from their jobs or the mining district. In 1912, the executives in mining and iron persuaded the city commission to increase the tax on labor agents to $2,000. And during World War I, the coal companies induced the Birmingham city commission, over the objection of the white labor unions, to raise the tax to $2,500, add an agent's bond of $5,000, and vigorously pursue labor agents without licenses.[70]

Control of the Work Place

Accompanying him [Van A. Bittner, UMW representative] came a band of northern negroes and northern whites, who went from camp to camp throughout the mining districts, negro organizers and white organizers speaking from the same platform arousing passions, inflaming feelings, and for the first time bringing to the Alabama miners, of whom more than 70% are negroes, the news that they were underpaid and ill-treated.

> *Citizen's Report on the 1920 UMW Strike*
> *Presented to the United States Coal Commission*
> *by the Alabama Mining Institute, 1923*

Alabama's pioneer capitalists in the mining district depended on black labor and those in the Piedmont depended on white native labor as bulwarks against trade unionism. The mill operators proudly proclaimed the virtues of "native labor," its "abundance" and its affinity for the "open shop." A promotion bulletin in the twenties declared: "There has never been a strike or other labor disturbance of consequence, because the native labor in the textile industry is not subject to those disturbing influences common in sections where the foreign element dominates the industrial field."[71] The mining companies hoped, particularly after the mine strike of 1894, that blacks would give them less "trouble" and that the society's preoccupa-

69. Quoted in ibid., p. 211.
70. Ibid., p. 226.
71. Alabama Power Company, Commercial Department, *The Textile Industry in Alabama,* no pagination.

tion with race questions would provide an added check against labor organization.[72]

To help insure the loyalty of their black employees, the mining companies initiated a concerted social welfare program that would later serve as a model for similar "open-shop" campaigns. TCI, now under United States Steel ownership, improved housing conditions, corrected commissary abuses, and organized a comprehensive welfare and educational program.[73] The companies also subsidized itinerant preachers and publications for black workers that railed against the United Mine Workers and called for "work and individual betterment."[74] For Booker T. Washington, this welfare capitalism was the hope of black Americans: "Welfare work of the Tennessee Coal, Iron and Railroad Company . . . is an outstanding example of what can be done to improve the living and social status of the Negro industrial worker."[75] For the steel and mining executives, welfare capitalism brought other benefits:

> In his adherence to this prime essential of liberty the Alabama coal operator has the cooperation and active support of the Negro. The Negro is primarily a free agent and hence a non-union man. . . . You appreciate, I am sure, the measure of the Negro's contribution to non-union Alabama. . . . We should carry our "welfare work" for the Negro beyond the confines of any single mining village and apply such principles to all deserving Negroes wherever found, and thus have the Negro understand that he is to have justice and opportunity.[76]

The paternalism at TCI should not obscure the more explicitly racist contrivances for undermining labor organization: specifically, the recruitment of black strikebreakers, the use of black convict laborers, and the fanning of racial prejudices.

Convict labor, for example, was a hedge against unionization, and employers were not shy about its purpose. The president of TCI, soon after the U.S. Steel takeover, wrote: "The chief inducement for the hiring of convicts was the certainty of a supply of coal for our manufacturing

72. Darold T. Barnum, *The Negro in the Bituminous Coal Mining Industry,* p. 20.
73. Sterling D. Spero and Abram L. Harris, *The Black Worker,* p. 247.
74. Ibid., pp. 137–38; F. Ray Marshall, *Labor in the South,* p. 74.
75. Quoted in Marshall, *Labor in the South,* p. 74.
76. Speech by executive of DeBardeleben Coal Company, quoted in Spero and Harris, *The Black Worker,* p. 363. Little wonder, however, that after the "open shop" gave way to the multiracial United Mine Workers, the Mine, Mill and Smelter Workers' Union, and the United Steelworkers, the mining companies began hiring fewer black workers. See Sally Furse, "History of the International Union of Mine, Mill and Smelter Workers in the Jefferson County Area," p. 18; Barnum, *The Negro in the Bituminous Coal Mining Industry,* p. 26; and Richard L. Rowan, *The Negro in the Steel Industry,* p. 41.

operations in the contingency of labor troubles."[77] He was undoubtedly reflecting TCI's and the other mining companies' use of convict labor during the intense labor struggles from 1905 to 1908. In this period, TCI paid double the normal rate for convict leases and hired 1,950 convicts from Jefferson County alone. After the UMW was thoroughly routed in 1908, TCI's bids fell to customary levels.[78] But convict labor was not always sufficient, and employers turned to black strikebreakers. In the Gulf Coast ports, including Mobile, employers called on the ready supply of black "rabbit" labor to break the white screwmen's and longshoremen's unions.[79] In the mining district, usually during periods of labor difficulty, employers called on the state to use the antivagrancy laws and create a pool of black strikebreakers.[80]

While preaching welfare capitalism to black workers and leaders, coal and steel company officials were fanning racial prejudices in Birmingham and Alabama. The company response to the 1908 mine strike is the principal case. TCI, despite its "New Deal" for black workers, made sure that the white public did not lose sight of the "social equality" inside the United Mine Workers. Promanagement columnists reacted in horror to the women's auxiliary where "fair girls" mingled freely with blacks and meetings where "ignorant Negro leaders" addressed "assemblies of white women and children as social equals."[81] In the end, the specter of "idle negroes" and "social equality" mobilized the state and public opinion against the union. The governor banned public meetings, sent in the Alabama National Guard, and threatened to strengthen the antivagrancy laws. Declaring that "the integrity of our civilization" is at stake, he ordered the miners' tent villages cut down. "White men," he proclaimed, could not be left "to live in tents or in camps in Alabama" under the control of the UMW.[82]

77. Quoted in Harris, *Political Power in Birmingham,* pp. 203-04; also see Going, *Bourbon Democracy in Alabama,* p. 187.
78. Harris, *Political Power in Birmingham,* p. 204; Herbert G. Gutman, "The Negro and the United Mine Workers of America," p. 112.
79. Spero and Harris, *The Black Worker,* pp. 185-88.
80. Harris, *Political Power in Birmingham,* pp. 200–01. Both the UMW and the Alabama mining companies opposed attempts by labor agents to recruit blacks to break strikes in Arkansas, Oklahoma, Kansas, and Illinois. A handbill circulated in Birmingham read:

Wanted! Colored coal-miners for Weir City, Kan., district, the paradise for colored people. Ninety-seven cents per ton September 1 to March 1; 87 ½ cents per ton March 1 to September 1, for screened coal over seven-eighths inch opening. Special train will leave Birmingham the 13th. Transportation advanced. Get ready and go to the land of promise (Spero and Harris, *The Black Worker,* pp. 210–11).

81. Nancy Ruth Elmore, "The Birmingham Coal Strike of 1908," pp. 57–59; Richard A. Straw, "The Collapse of Bi-racial Unionism: The Alabama Coal Strike of 1908," p. 109.
82. Straw, "The Collapse of Bi-racial Unionism," pp. 107, 112; Harris, *Political Power in Birmingham,* pp. 221–22. Also see Herbert R. Northrup, *Organized Labor and the Negro,* p. 163.

The companies were no less reluctant to raise the race issue in the steel strike of 1918[83] and the mine strike of 1920–21. The company explained its predicament in the latter strike by noting that "southern Negroes . . . are easily misled, especially when given a prominent and official place in an organization in which both races are members."[84] The company was determined to oppose the UMW, which associated "the black man on terms of perfect equality with the white man."[85]

When unions in the thirties made another major effort to organize white and black workers in the primary industries, employers did not hesitate to use the race issue. The Fairfield city council, made up primarily of TCI employees, refused to lift a city ordinance that prohibited mixed meetings. Despite strong entreaties from the Amalgamated Association of Steel Workers, the council resolved to maintain and enforce the ordinance against the union.[86] The Congress of Industrial Organizations encountered similar obstacles when organizing rubber workers in Gadsden. A city ordinance passed in 1936 provided fines and imprisonment where "three or more persons, some of whom are white and some Negroes . . . hold either a public or secret meeting in which is advocated a movement looking toward destruction of the governments of the United States, the State of Alabama or the city."[87] A union organizer recalled how "thugs" broke up the union meeting in 1936: "They said that was the reason, because the colored and white were meeting together, but it wasn't, it was because we were trying to organize the union."[88]

ACCOMMODATING THE COLOR LINES

The primary industries in Alabama, like mining and steel, supported state racial measures to help create and control a labor force; they exacerbated racial differences among workers and in the society and helped mobilize public opinion and the state against multiracial organization. In the period when labor-repressive measures were possible, roughly 1874 to 1936, the primary industries had the field to themselves. Secondary industry and

83.   Spero and Harris, *The Black Worker*, p. 248.
84.   Quoted in Northrup, *Organized Labor and the Negro*, p. 163.
85.   Quoted in Tindall, *The Emergence of the New South*, p. 337.
86.   *Birmingham Post*, 9 September 1933. The union, however, was careful about its commitment to "social equality": "Our union, of course, is not seeking to elevate the negro, but experience teaches us that if the negro is not unionized side by side with the white worker, he will be used as a strikebreaker to kill the union movement."
87.   Marshall, *Labor in the South*, p. 190; Charles L. Phillips, "A History of the United Rubber Workers in Gadsden, Alabama, 1936–1943," pp. 59–60.
88.   Alice Hoffman and Jack Spiese, "An Interview with Ruben Farr," p. 22.

commerce began to play an important role in Alabama's industrialization only after convict labor and antivagrancy laws had passed from the scene and after the National Labor Relations Act had entered. Nonetheless, even as more diverse industrial interests emerged in the thirties, important aspects of the racial order were still intact. Both primary and secondary industry easily incorporated race lines into conventional management practice, and they easily accommodated the political alignments underlying the racial order. They gave up on customary racial practices only after concerted civil rights protests and actions by the federal government brought political and economic disarray.

"Colored" and "White" Work: "We Either Had Black Jobs or White Jobs. We Were Like South Africa."

The iron and steel industry has employed both black and white workers since the beginning. It has maintained, however, a formal racial allocation of jobs: blacks to the blast furnaces, iron-ore mines, and unskilled jobs; whites to the trades. In the mid-thirties, 81 percent of common laborers in the industry were black.[89] With mining jobs less clearly differentiated by skill, companies have proved less adept discriminators. They nonetheless have been able to approximate the conventional pattern: 77 percent of black miners were hand coal loaders.[90]

That the primary industries created discriminatory employment patterns is hardly surprising: these patterns seem fully consonant with their general racial practices during early capitalist development. That virtually every business in Alabama, no matter when established, adopted these patterns is of more general interest.[91]

A small number of companies, all with large foundry operations, have opted for a disproportionately large black labor force. Openness to black employment, however, should not be confused with a commitment to black job opportunities. The federal courts held that one of these companies up until 1961 "formally maintained exclusively black jobs and exclusively white jobs." Up until 1963, "black employees constituted about half the work force of the company, but only three blacks earned more than any white production worker, and few if any jobs had racially mixed staffing." And after the court ordered job desegregation, the company opened "black jobs"

89. Rowan, *The Negro in the Steel Industry,* pp. 28–30, 36.
90. Herbert R. Northrup, "The Negro and the United Mine Workers of America," p. 317.
91. Of the sixteen directors interviewed in Alabama, all indicated that their plants up until the mid-sixties maintained separate black and white jobs; eleven maintained separate seniority lines for blacks and whites. (Three firms had no seniority lists.) See appendix C, Alabama businessmen (I.B.), question 9.

to white workers, while failing to advance blacks into formerly "white jobs."[92] Another company claimed that blacks did not want to worry themselves about "millimeters and centimeters and scales and stuff"—the skilled positions—and were anxious and available for the "dirty jobs." Another maintained that black labor and menial work were synonymous: "I doubt if three hundred of them were white, because making pipe was largely a routine manual labor—hot, dirty jobs." But "this was the place to be," he added. "This was nigger heaven." The company described its black labor force:

> There again, keep in mind what we were employing: people that, generally speaking, were country blacks. What we did as long as we could, we didn't hire these alley niggers in Birmingham. They didn't want to work. But there was a period at the end of World War I when mechanization on the farm and the switch from cotton to cattle in Alabama made surplus a tremendous amount of country blacks. All they needed was work, and they had no education. That's who we hired. We put the word out if we wanted employees to our own people that we are going to be hiring. And they'd go home over the weekend, and they'd put the word out at the country church. And along about Tuesday we'd have the finest-looking specimens out there you ever saw. And that's who we hired.

Firms that hired black workers and yet had few of the stereotypical "nigger jobs" still normally managed not to offend Alabama traditions. The paper companies in south Alabama overcame weak local resistance to employing black labor but segregated blacks within their operations. International Paper beginning in the 1920s and Scott Paper in the 1950s routinely assigned blacks to the woodyard, recovery, maintenance, and menial jobs. The paper machines were reserved for white workers.[93] The rubber industry in north Alabama also confined blacks to laboring and service jobs.[94] One company with "Yankee" management "right down to the personnel level" segregated black workers in the reclaim department and janitorial jobs. When there were job openings, the personnel manager

92. *Pettway v. American Cast Iron Pipe Company,* 494 F. 2d 211 (1974): 218–19, 227–29. ACIPCO proudly publicized its good relations with "colored" employees. One employee, quoted in a company promotional publication, recalled: "I especially remember the annual Colored 'Y' banquets attended by Mr. Egan ACIPCO's founding chairman. He loved to hear Negro spirituals and we would sing them for him. There was a lot of close fellowship in those days."

93. Herbert R. Northrup, *The Negro in the Paper Industry,* pp. 33–35; *Stevenson v. International Paper Company, Mobile, Ala.* 352 F.Supp. 230 (1972): 241; *Watkins, Elijah v. Scott Paper Co.* 6 EPD: 5856–57.

94. Herbert R. Northrup, "The Negro in the Rubber Tire Industry," pp. 470–71.

"would go out to the gate and he'd say, look at the first fifty in line and pick ten big ones, the biggest ones he could find," the company officer recalled. "He'd say, 'You fellows come on with me.' They'd go in and the department foreman responsible for those jobs would put those ten guys on the job"— blacks in one area and whites in another. The officer described the policy: "I don't believe [company name] as a corporation gave a damn one way or the other. If you asked 'em, they'd probably say, 'We don't believe in discrimination,' and I'm sure that that has been a corporate policy from day one. Local situation dictates and that's probably how it was done here."

Companies readily accessible to the white public—commercial enterprises through consumers and the utilities through the Public Service Commission —employed few black workers.[95] In commerce, the few black employees were placed out of sight and presumably out of mind: in the warehouses, stockrooms, and cleaning jobs and not as sales persons. "The colored did not meet the public," one officer explained. The utilities faced explicit oversight by a white-controlled public agency and sought to conform to its expectations: "This was a traditional pattern in the community. . . . [We] have always had to be very sensitive to the community, being a regulated utility, sensitive to what could happen to you in the Public Service Commission. We try not to deviate too much from a community pattern."

The pattern of separate job areas was firmly entrenched by promotional and seniority lines. In some cases, like Goodyear Tire and Scott Paper, the unions and management jointly agreed to "lock" blacks into separate departments; but in other cases, particularly the textile and garment factories, separate promotional lines developed without sign of white workers' organizations. The results were similar in both situations: no matter how long blacks worked for a company, there was no escaping the discrimination at the point of entry. Even after formal job discrimination became illegal in 1964, the federal courts had difficulty unraveling the consequences of seniority and "job-bidding" arrangements. The courts found in the case of United States Steel that "most LOPs [lines of progression] were segregated, with the black-only and few racially-mixed lines containing, not surprisingly, most of the less desirable jobs and none of the highest paying ones." And once in a line of progression, life was virtually "preordained."[96] Similar arrangements were maintained in the

95. See Alabama State Advisory Committee to the United States Commission on Civil Rights, Dothan Open Meeting, 29 July 1966, p. 81–85.

96. *United States v. United States Steel Corporation,* 371 F. Supp. 1045 (1973): 1052, 1055. It is interesting to note that LOPs were important in the steel mills where there were skilled positions, a large number of white workers, and the United Steelworkers. In the iron-ore mines under the same overall management, where there was less skill differentiation, few white workers, and the Union of Mine, Mill and Smelter Workers until the late forties, plantwide seniority was the rule.

major paper companies and at Hayes International. At the latter, the courts found ten seniority divisions, each with one to seven lines of progression; 122 of the 145 blacks were employed in two of these divisions.[97] Virtually every company with large numbers of black workers maintained them in "dead-end" jobs. At one company, management and the unions created a seniority list for the crafts; "laborers," on the other hand, "were in a single [separate] seniority unit." For two of the companies with foundry operations, separate seniority arrangements had clear implications. One director noted: "We don't have that [plant-wide seniority] because there's nothing that you learned in the foundry that is applicable when you go into the machine department. So you can stay thirty years in the foundry and you go to the machine job, you're just like starting over." Another observed that blacks on the ramming station had "no place to get promoted to: when you're a rammer . . . that's the end of the line."

Some companies abandoned any pretense. The Goodyear Tire Corporation, in agreement with the union, maintained separate seniority lists for black and white male employees (and a separate list for females as well).[98] One foundry operation, unlike most other companies with a large black labor force, used a system of plantwide seniority but constructed a segregated bidding process: "But we had two bid boards. We had one that the black jobs were bid off on and another one that the whites have bid on. And just through mutual understanding, the whites always bid on the white one and the blacks always bid on the black one, and that's the way it went."

Segregating the Work Place: "It Was Just a Thing That Went Back to Slavery."

Businessmen in Alabama, without apparent discomfort, imposed Jim Crow on the work place.[99] The early industries that provided housing as well as bathrooms and water fountains invariably set aside separate black and white areas and provided white employees with more spacious, better equipped houses.[100] Modern industrial facilities, even those built in the fifties and early sixties, continued Alabama traditions in separate bathing houses, cafeterias, toilets, and drinking fountains. One company assigned black workers badge numbers between 0 and 900 and white workers, 901 to

---

97. *United States v. Hayes International Corporation,* 415 F.2d 1038 (1969): 1040.
98. *Local No. 12, United Rubber, Cork, Linoleum and Plastic Workers of America, AFL-CIO v. National Labor Relations Board,* 368 F.2d 12 (1966): 14.
99. All sixteen directors stated that their companies were fully segregated before the passage of the Civil Rights Act. See appendix C, Alabama businessmen (I.B.), question 10.
100. John C. Howard, *The Negro in the Lumber Industry,* pp. 65–66; Furse, "History of the International Union of Mine, Mill and Smelter Workers," p. 5.

1399. For virtually every businessman, that was the price—indeed, a small price—for doing business in Alabama. An officer described the logic of the situation:

> [The company] looked at what the local situation was and I think that any company that goes into a local area. . . . [pause] I mean you just can't go in and change feelings that have built up over years and years and years just because it happens to be just a little cheaper. You've got to take the impact on the people themselves into consideration.

Another company officer maintained that the law gave it no choice in the matter: "You've got to bear in mind that we are doing business in the state of Alabama and we agreed in our contract with the United States government to live up to all laws of the United States and all states and territories in which we do business."

Most companies, however, simply never questioned, maybe never wondered about, the segregation of the work place: it was "not unusual"; it was "customary."

In no instance that I could discover did management before the 1960s, drawing on cost calculations, business norms, or some abstract concept of justice, choose to desegregate the work place or break down job discrimination. Change came only when black civil rights organizations grew impatient with southern employment practices or, more often, when changes in law or federal policy forced it. An officer of a major food chain was frank about the forces at work:

> Professor, that's an embarrassing question. That's a bad question. You know damn well it changed in 1965. . . . [We changed in 1965] because we were forced to, yes. And the feelings, the feeling of the community was changing. . . . Let me clarify "change." We have always worked the black man but not as much in force until the government started to put the heat on us.

The "heat" came in the form of "constant pressure": the Maritime Commission ordered the breakdown of job barriers at the dry docks; the Interstate Commerce Commission ordered the desegregation of facilities in Louisville and Nashville Railroad stations;[101] a Presidential Executive Order required changes on the part of federal contractors, like Hayes International; and the Equal Employment Opportunity Commission (EEOC) filed complaints against most major corporations in Alabama. "That [EEOC] complaint charged us with just about every form of racial discrimination that is possible to charge a company with, and they were right," one director

---

101. *Birmingham Post-Herald*, 10 January 1956.

recalled. "Finally we came up with a conciliation agreement that we signed with the federal government, or with the EEOC, eliminating all of the things that were considered to be racial discrimination." Another company faced a series of demands for change, first because of the "president's edict," and second because "we had the EEOC on our backs to put some of these blacks. You know we don't have any. It's hard to argue with them about why you don't have any." Finally, the company was brought before the federal courts and ordered to end racial discrimination in hiring, promotion, and its employee-consultative scheme. In the end, virtually every major manufacturing establishment had to face the federal courts. They ordered changes in hiring practices, lines of progression, or seniority at United States Steel, Hayes International, Goodyear Tire, Scott Paper, International Paper, and Southern Bell Telephone.[102]

One officer concluded: "We know what it is like to be occupied."

POLITICAL DISORDER

You know, it was something you never really gave much thought to. You had a pattern that you had lived with all your life and there was no great urgency to do anything about it, even if you had wanted to. In my particular case: if I got something I know there ain't nothing I can do about it, I don't worry about it.

*Officer, Textile factory
1975*

102.   Unions often resisted changes in seniority. On occasion, a consent decree required that management override union contract provisions controlling seniority or lines of progression. Management sometimes moved so slowly that the courts were forced to intervene to speed the process (*United States v. Hayes International Corporation:* 1043; *Pettway v. American Cast Iron Pipe:* 227–28). At the individual level, white employees were able to register their protests only through erratic forms of "banditry." When bath houses were desegregated, white employees sometimes boycotted them and went home in their soiled work clothes. "White" and "colored" signs were mysteriously painted over water fountains and bathroom doors during the night. And on occasion, there was violence. An officer recollects the experience at a company in north Alabama:

You don't go out there and change it by persuasion. You change it by a battle. And that's exactly how it was changed. It was a battle all the way.

Now we took the signs down and left the two drinking fountains there. That didn't solve the problem because whenever a black tried to use the white drinking fountain, they first of all handled him on the spot. And then we handled the person that handled him on the spot. . . . Then they, the whites, got smart. There's no sense, you don't need to do it in there; you can do it out in the parking lot. Well, that's where it happened.

When we integrated the locker rooms, we ran into the same thing. . . . The first one that got in there, he lived one hell of a life. He'd find live snakes in his locker; he found his clothes shredded; he found his locker busted; he found his towel torn up. The first time he tried to get into the shower, he found himself being tripped. He found all kinds of harassments. We had nothing to do with those. We tried to stop it. It occurs because that's the way the people felt.

Southern Comfort: Land, Capital, and the Racial Order

If businessmen were dissatisfied with the Alabama business environment in the mid-fifties, they did a very good job of concealing their discomfort. There was no business outcry against restraints on labor utilization or irrational barriers in the marketplace and society.[103] They did not decry the dominance of rural legislators or the denial of the franchise to blacks. Even in retrospect, off the record, within the confines of their own offices, businessmen did not recall that the racial order created any "impediments" or "difficulties" for their enterprises. One business officer worried that Birmingham was "a sleepy, self-satisfied, nice southern town" and generated only a limited consumer market. But the same officer noted, "You accepted the society the way it was." For businessmen, racial domination "really was a way of life," was "accepted operational procedure" or, simply, the "pattern of the South." One officer remembered, "I really don't think . . . from 1950 through 1960 that we thought about it as causing us any particular problems. I suppose you could say it was a drifting with the prevailing tide of the area." Another officer concluded, simply and nostalgically, that the fifties was a "beautiful time."

Alongside the businessman's apparent accommodation to prevailing social practice is a not very reluctant acquiescence to the role of rural politicians and the Alabama Farm Bureau.[104] The affinity of the Chambers of Commerce and the Associated Industries of Alabama on the one hand and the Alabama Farm Bureau on the other is hardly in question.[105] Trade-union leaders since the CIO days have attacked the "reactionary association" of business and farm interests and the state Labor Council has come to view them as inseparable. At times, it also lumped them together with the White Citizens Councils of Alabama. "This year [1964]," the chairman of the Labor Council warned, "you will see these reactionary groups join forces with the Farm Bureau, the big mules in industry, the Dixiecrats, and with other anti-labor conservatives in the state."[106] Businessmen have not

103. Twelve of the sixteen directors interviewed found no problems for business in the "social environment." Only one pointed to racial customs or policies. See appendix C, I.B., question 8.
104. Eleven of sixteen directors felt that the Alabama Farm Bureau was probusiness. Only one thought it was antibusiness. See appendix C, I.B., question 16.
105. Donald Strong described the situation in the mid-fifties in these terms: "Until recently, it would not have been a great over-simplification to describe Alabama politics as a clash between poor farmers and black-belt planters allied with business leaders" ("Alabama, Transition and Alienation," p. 447). Our concern here is the latter alignment; the conflict between poor farmers and the Black Belt was considered in chapter 6.
106. Alabama Labor Council (AFL-CIO), *Special Convention of the Alabama Labor Council, AFL-CIO,* Birmingham, 21 March 1964, p. 3; see also Alabama Labor Council (AFL-CIO), *Legislative Report, 1959,* pp. 4–5; and discussion in chapter 15.

found the association embarrassing or the presumed influence unhelpful. The Alabama Chamber of Commerce confessed that "by and large we have the same position," and individual businessmen described their interests as "parallel" or "for the most, in agreement." One officer claimed, "The Farm Bureau does a hell of a job" and "We're in bed very close." The officer of the Associated Industries of Alabama indicated that his organization was allied before reapportionment with south Alabama and with the Black Belt, which were "very conservative" and probusiness: "Your landowners, your bankers . . . kind of a big industry, you might say." Land and business, he concluded, go "hand in hand."

There is no certain way of distinguishing whether businessmen are following the lead of Black Belt farmers or vice versa; or, indeed, whether businessmen and farmers simply share a broad range of strategic interests. How does one sort out these explanations when both groups oppose repeal of the "right to work" law, a state minimum wage, and increased unemployment compensation? How does one distinguish when the Farm Bureau is so deeply involved in the insurance business and investments in urban areas and businessmen so much involved with marketing agricultural products and producing farm implements? Business and farm groups have come apart on the question of ad valorem taxation, the former preferring a nondiscriminatory tax structure and latter wanting a lower percentage assessment for farmland. But both groups agree that ad valorem taxation is an exceptional issue.

Businessmen themselves, however, had no difficulty pinpointing the dominant political influence in the alignment. On the question of ad valorem taxation, after all, businessmen failed to pass a nondiscriminatory tax over Farm Bureau opposition. "They just beat us every time," the officer of one Alabama utility observed. The officer of another elaborated: "The Farm Bureau is without question, because of its county agent system, its ties into the state legislature and state agencies, has more influence than any other group in the state of Alabama. When [we] want to work out our problems, we generally go through the Farm Bureau." Business deference to farmer and rural interests was also apparent in the business response to the reapportionment issue.[107] The Alabama Constitution of 1901 had apportioned the legislature and, even then, had weighted the apportionment in favor of the Black Belt. Six decades later the disproportion bordered on scandalous. In Lowndes County, at the heart of the Black Belt, one state senator represented 2,057 white voters (the black population, comprising four of every five persons in the county, was disenfranchised); in Jefferson

107. Six officers interviewed opposed reapportionment of the state legislature, two favored it, and eight were unsure. See appendix C, I.B., question 14.

County, including Birmingham, one senator represented 130,000 registered voters.[108] Faced with a court order in 1962, the Alabama legislature sought to fashion new districts. But the courts in 1965 found parts of the plan unacceptable—an attempt to maintain disproportionate rural representation and cutup urban districts—and proceeded to draw new district lines itself. The major business associations and large numbers of individual businessmen stood with the farmers in their efforts to preserve malapportionment. The officer of one company commented:

> The legislature basically was run by the farmers, so to speak, the country folk, for years. And this is one thing that reapportionment did: it took the power from the farmers and put it in the urban areas. . . . I kind of felt like the farmers knew more about the economics and how to get things done than some of our legislators did. They understood some of the economics a lot better than some of my local folks do.

"Frankly," another officer observed, "I think the folks in south Alabama, I think those farmers know more about running the damn state than we do."

Black Belt farmers and rural legislators used their position to maintain Alabama's racial framework. They resisted school desegregation, contrived tuition grant schemes to resegregate white children in private schools, refused to lift franchise restrictions,[109] and attempted to suppress black political organization in rural areas.[110] Businessmen deferred to farmers on these questions.[111] Or at least they did until other demands and events disrupted the calm and the alignment.

Protest and the Unraveling of the Racial Order

The Montgomery bus boycott in 1955 began a process that Alabama did not escape for at least ten years and not until the racial order began unravel-

---

108. Neal R. Peirce, *The Deep South States of America*, pp. 246–47.

109. In 1957, the state legislature passed a law allowing county registrars to destroy voting records and hence limit federal intervention in voting questions (*Montgomery Advertiser*, 12 December 1959).

110. State legislation and state court orders barred the National Association for the Advancement of Colored People (NAACP) from Alabama between 1956 and 1964 (*Montgomery Advertiser*, 25 September 1964); other legislation provided for a state "Un-American Activities" committee to investigate civil rights organizations (Alabama Labor Council [AFL-CIO], *Legislative Report* 1961, p. 22). Also see discussion of farm politics in chapter 6.

111. Whether or not farmers dominated the alignment, they still deferred to businessmen on selected issues. Business groups, for example, wanted the level of corporate taxes placed in the state constitution and "frozen"; the farmers, though not the trade unions or education groups, agreed.

ing.[112] In Montgomery, the bus boycott was followed in successive years by the dynamiting of black churches and the closing of city parks to avoid court-ordered integration. In 1961, "freedom riders" attempted to integrate the Greyhound and Trailways bus stations. The unchecked violence of "mobs of bat-swinging, brick-and-bottle tossing white men, women, and teen-agers" brought martial law and six hundred federal marshalls to the streets of Montgomery.[113] "These federal officers will be withdrawn," the attorney general of the United States said, "as soon as state authorities show by their actions that they intend to preserve law and order in Alabama."[114]

When "freedom riders" arrived in Birmingham in 1961, they received no less violent a reception. Indeed, Birmingham brought demonstrating children, firehoses, and police dogs to the national attention. While city commissioner and director of "public safety" Eugene "Bull" Connor stood aside, white mobs beat demonstrators senseless and bloody. The police waged pitched battles with black demonstrators, arresting 2,800 blacks, including Dr. Martin Luther King, Jr., Reverend Ralph Abernathy, and Reverend Andrew Young of the Southern Christian Leadership Conference. In the end, the Sixteenth Street Baptist Church was bombed and four black children killed. Arthur Hanes, mayor of Birmingham, told a Mobile audience during these events, "The South is the last bastion of race pride and it is the last stronghold of true nationalistic feeling. Accordingly, it is the target of left-wing abuse. They say the Civil War was fought one hundred years ago but I tell you that the Civil War is just starting."[115]

Business concern with the course of events came slowly and unevenly. On the one hand, the president of the State Chamber of Commerce in 1958 called on the Congress to pass a constitutional amendment overriding the Supreme Court school integration decisions: "Now that the country is torn with strife from within and beset from without by the greatest danger that has ever confronted it, the Congress should rebuke this Supreme Court that has overstepped its bounds and exceeded its authority."[116] On the other hand, the president of the Birmingham Chamber of Commerce *privately* asked the head of the United Steelworkers to endorse the Supreme Court decision: "I'll tell you what I think you ought to do, you ought, as head of the biggest union in the state, you ought to enforce this law. I think the Steelworkers can do it."[117]

112.   This discussion of civil rights activities is based upon a reading of the *Birmingham News, Birmingham Post-Herald,* and *Montgomery Advertiser* for the 1955–65 period; also Peirce, *The Deep South States,* pp. 286–90.
113.   *Montgomery Advertiser,* 21 May 1961; 26 May 1961.
114.   *Birmingham News,* 22 May 1961.
115.   Quoted in the *Mobile Register,* 30 August 1963.
116.   *Birmingham News,* 20 November 1958.
117.   Reported by Ruben Farr in Hoffman and Spiese, "An Interview with Ruben Farr," p. 49.

The major manufacturing firms kept the events at a distance.[118] Many officers commented, in retrospect, that "had you not read it in the newspapers, you would not have ever known that it was going on downtown." The director of a textile company observed," Birmingham and Montgomery, that is another world." The director of a large foundry operation recalled, "Actually, it never did amount to what the press blew it up to amount to." Few of these manufacturing firms or their principal business associations believed that the demonstrations had any impact on their production or sales. One firm noted that there was resentment—"You could feel it in the air"—but that the events and aftermath had not "in any way affected production or relationships." An officer of the Associated Industries of Alabama, the principal association for manufacturing, believed the impact was overrated: "I don't think it hurt anything. May have scared folks for a while, but I don't think it hurt anything."

These manufacturing firms refused to become involved, at least publicly, in local affairs, noting "that wouldn't be characteristic of our company." The officer of a major national company recalled, "We have never gotten involved in civil rights issues in terms of being out front." He pointed to a statement of the company president that using economic power to bring about social change would be "quite beyond what a corporation should do."[119]

Firms more directly involved with the economy of Birmingham and Alabama began to worry about the adverse publicity and troubling economic signs. Though Birmingham's economy had paced the South in the early fifties, it now began to trail behind more "progressive" southern cities like Atlanta and Memphis. Retail and wholesale trade began to stagnate after 1958. Unemployment rose in 1956 and in the rest of the country two years later; but when the rest of the country and major southern cities recovered in the early sixties, Birmingham did not follow.[120] The Birmingham Chamber of Commerce began to wonder out loud how the city would "live down" the events surrounding the "freedom riders."[121]

In 1962, the civil rights movement began to exact a more direct toll from Birmingham businessmen: organized boycotts of local merchants seriously

118. Eleven of the sixteen directors claimed that the protests had no direct effect on their operations. Only four recalled that the protests disrupted their operations. See appendix C, I.B., question 15.
119. Only one company officer seemed actively to support the prevailing race arrangements and local politicians. The officer had been appointed to local office as a "representative" of blacks because his company had employed so many of them. He opposed the change in Birmingham government that eventually brought down Eugene "Bull" Connor.
120. Mary Phyllis Harrison, "A Change in the Government of the City of Birmingham: 1962–3," pp. 6–7.
121. *Birmingham News,* 5 July 1961.

cut into retail sales. "It's pretty difficult to boycott U.S. Steel," one department store officer commented. "It's easy to boycott a retail store." The head of one downtown department store noted, "It's on and it's hurting." The Chamber appealed to the civil rights protestors to not "seek to punish business concerns for community practices beyond their control."[122] The department and grocery store chains found themselves caught between boycotts and pickets by "colored groups" and the "KKK" and saw a deteriorating public image of Birmingham. "When the demonstrations hit," the officer of a department store remembered, "we had a great fear of what might happen to Birmingham, and I think the fears were born out, because Birmingham just got murdered, if you will, during the next few years, and it was a national image." He thought for most people outside Alabama, Birmingham conjured up images of "dusty streets and police dogs and firehoses and open, pitched warfare downtown."

That imagery posed a more concrete threat for a number of companies, particularly the state utilities. A major utility, with prominent buildings and equipment "necessarily located in the center of the city," worried about the "state of race relations" and "our investment in inner city real estate." For another utility with large capital requirements, the problem was a simple and immediate issue, the pricing of its securities:

> I remember being in New York in an information meeting back about 1963 or 1964, on sale of securities. The day we had the major or worst . . . rampage of demonstrators through Birmingham, that made the headlines in the *New York Times,* the morning that we had our information meeting with the investment banking group in New York. That was very difficult, very awkward, very hard to explain, a most unpleasant meeting.
>
> It is hard to know [whether it affects the rate] because unless another issue goes out that very day, you don't know what had to do with the market [and] what had to do with the prejudice against the company's ability to. . . . [pause] At the time, we were afraid it was going to hurt the pricing of securities. We were unable to perceive that it did, but then again, we don't know.

Businessmen who ordinarily remained aloof from politics, who in the past seemed comfortable with the racial order and the prevailing political alignments, were drawn into the "heat" of the "kitchen." The "freedom riders" brought in their wake calls from the business community for "law and order," condemnation of the "invasion of nonresident racial agitators," and urgent appeals that the president remove federal marshalls from the

122. *Montgomery Advertiser,* 30 March 1962.

state. But it also brought out the first signs of business resistance to the course of white politics. One local business group in Montgomery offered a highly qualified, modest criticism of individuals whose lawlessness was "triggered by extreme provocation";[123] another was more certain about the target of its criticism: "We do not under any circumstances approve or condone mob action on the part of any faction."[124] The State Chamber of Commerce, however, published a strong attack on the white mobs in Anniston, Montgomery, and Birmingham:

> Directors of the State Chamber deplore and condemn the recent acts of lawlessness and mob violence in several localities within the State by a very small group of people. Such acts can never be justified, even in the face of unwarranted and extreme provocation. They damage the good name of our State and create an image harmful to its best interest and its business and industrial development.

Among the Chamber's directors were officers of Hayes Aircraft, Avondale Mills, Southern Bell Telephone, Alabama Power Company, and Gulf State Paper Corporation.[125]

During 1961 and 1962, the Birmingham Chamber of Commerce explored ways of "reforming" the commission form of government that was the base for Public Safety Director Eugene "Bull" Connor and Mayor Arthur Hanes. The Chamber's intentions were not very well disguised: it hoped, under a cloak of municipal reform, to remove the principal defenders of traditional racial practices in Birmingham.[126] An officer of the Chamber enlisted the support of the Bar Association, then turned around and endorsed the Bar's recommendation for a strong mayor-council form of government.[127] Relations between the Chamber and the local government deteriorated. "Members of the Birmingham City Commission have taken exception to the Chamber's position," the president of the Chamber observed. "Any semblance of co-operation has ceased to exist."[128] Though the Chamber could not recruit anyone on a list of twenty-four "prominent citizens" to publicly join the reform effort, a broad-based committee of "average citizens" carried the campaign to a successful conclusion. The first elections under the new form of government were held in the spring of 1963,

123. "A Resolution," Montgomery Chamber of Commerce, *Montgomery Advertiser,* 31 May 1961.
124. "To Our Fellow Citizens," Rotary Club of Montgomery, *Montgomery Advertiser,* 31 May 1961.
125. *Birmingham News,* 26 May 1961.
126. This discussion relies primarily on Harrison, "A Change in the Government of the City of Birmingham," pp. 23–59.
127. *Birmingham Post-Herald,* 30 October 1962.
128. Ibid., 27 March 1963.

and racial "moderates" were the apparent victors. But the commissioners and "Bull" Connor refused to vacate office. It was during this period, when Birmingham had no effective government, that the civil rights campaign reached its peak.

Faced with political uncertainty, an effective boycott of Birmingham merchants, and "chaos" in the streets, the Chamber decided to take the political lead.[129] A major officer formed what was called a "subcommittee" of the Senior Citizens Committee to circumvent the politicians and carry on direct negotiations with black civil rights leaders. The committee claimed to represent companies employing somewhere between 50 and 80 percent of the Birmingham labor force; it declined, however, to disclose its membership, except to say that the downtown merchants were not involved.[130] In fact, the committee included representatives from the Alabama Power Company, Southern Bell Telephone, the banks, and the United States Steel Corporation.[131] Because the downtown merchants feared possible reprisals from white customers, they did not attend even these private meetings. The Chamber officer commented, "Remember, the merchant, he has to deal with people and most of them are whites and most of them are against the Negro." The merchants, however, met among themselves and secretly with a Chamber representative.

The committee finally concluded an agreement with the civil rights groups that provided for a phased desegregation of public accommodations, new employment opportunities for blacks, release of demonstrators from prison, and continued meetings between the Senior Citizens Committee and civil rights groups.[132] The state legislature adopted a resolution to investigate the Senior Citizens Committee to determine "who the members of this citizens committee are, what they have agreed to, and what their private interest into the matter are."[133]

Nonetheless, it was the merchants that were out on the limb. They alone agreed to desegregate their facilities and hire black employees. "No other form of industry or business was willing to move," the head of one of the department stores recalled. "Frankly, I went to several of the banks and

129. An officer of the Chamber of Commerce, Sydney Smyer, reports a secret meeting with the president of the United States. The president made clear that the alternative to some business initiative was federal troops. See Howell Raines, *My Soul is Rested: Movement Days in the Deep South Remembered,* pp. 163–65.
130. *Montgomery Advertiser,* 11 May 1963.
131. The committee composition was provided by a former officer of the Birmingham Chamber of Commerce. Andrew Young, a former officer of the Southern Christian Leadership Conference, recalls a meeting with business leaders in 1963 that created a committee of 100 to negotiate "the end to apartheid" in Birmingham (Statement by Ambassador Andrew Young, Johannesburg, South Africa, 21 May 1977, appendix D).
132. *Birmingham Post-Herald,* 11 May 1963.
133. Ibid., 15 May 1963.

implored them to put on black tellers the same week that we put on black sales people. I felt that this was something that had to be done citywide. And I went to the president or chairman of the board of several of the very major banks in Birmingham and was given a polite 'No.' "

With the civil rights demonstrations at Selma, Alabama, in 1965, the business community in Alabama gave up on the racial order. For them the murder of Viola Liuzzo, the burning of more churches, the antics of Sheriff James Clark and his Dallas County posse, and the violent confrontation at the Edmund Pettus Bridge marked the end of an era.[134] Nineteen local Chambers of Commerce, including those in Birmingham, Mobile, and Montgomery, plus the state Chamber of Commerce, the Alabama Bankers Association, the Associated Industries of Alabama, and the Alabama Textile Manufacturers Association, took out joint, full-page advertisements in twenty-two Alabama daily newspapers, the *Wall Street Journal,* and *U.S. News and World Report.* The advertisement proclaimed in no uncertain terms, in bold letters, "First, we believe in the full protection and opportunity under the law of all our citizens, both negro and white." It called on all Alabamians to abide by the Civil Rights Act of 1964, including the public accommodations provisions and, we must assume, Title VII, which barred discrimination in employment. With events in Selma fresh in mind, it stated, again in bold letters, "We believe in the basic American heritage of voting, and in the right of every eligible citizen to register and to cast his ballot." And it concluded with a statement of faith not irrelevant to the point of this book: "WE BELIEVE THAT AN EXPANDING ECONOMY WILL BENEFIT ALL OF OUR PEOPLE. This will provide more jobs and greater income, thus raising the standard of living for all of our citizens— both Negro and White."[135]

An "expanding economy" has been remaking Alabama society since the Civil War, changing, as the business community suggested, the fortunes of black and white but also the nature of racial domination. In the period after Reconstruction, the "expanding economy" included: a dominant agricultural sector in the Black Belt based on cotton production and black labor; a textile industry based neither on cities nor black labor; and an enclave capitalist economy based on coal mining and iron manufacture and, to a large extent, black labor. Race did not lose meaning in this historic context. Black Belt planters and textile manufacturers struggled to reconstruct some essential principles in antebellum race relations. In north Alabama, outside

134. For an excellent discussion of these events, see David J. Garrow, *Protest at Selma: Martin Luther King, Jr. and the Voting Rights Act of 1965.*
135. *Birmingham News,* 15 April 1965.

the paternalism of the plantation and the mill town, capitalists used the prevailing norms and the state to create and control their labor force in the mines and foundries. Through vagrancy and labor-agent laws and convict leases, they hoped to limit the freedom of the free wage laborer. By playing on the specter of "social equality," they mobilized the state and public against multiracial working-class organization.

The "expanding economy" carried Alabama beyond the simple "racism" and primary capitalism of this period, but not beyond the racial order itself. Agriculture and cotton were in decline, as were the large class of black farm laborers bound to the land. Industrial interests had become more diversified, with different labor requirements and different markets. Yet the "expanding economy" seemed to accommodate and entrench traditional racial practices. Businessmen in all sectors of the economy almost painlessly imposed racial discrimination and segregation on the work place: blacks were ensconced at the bottom of the job hierarchy, in "nigger" and "dead-end" jobs, in separate toilets and bath houses. Businessmen remained comfortable with the racial order and the political alignment that maintained it.

But businessmen in manufacturing and commerce who accommodated the racial framework were not fully dependent upon it and, indeed, could consider other ways of organizing a labor force. The "freedom riders" and boycotts—as one businessman put it, the "chaos in the streets"—forced businessmen in these developing sectors to reconsider their accommodation and their political options. Faced with a growing imagery of firehoses and police dogs and the array of federal marshalls, civil rights laws, and court orders, these businessmen slowly, painfully, groped for change and ultimately insisted upon it. The racial order collapsed under pressure from businessmen, pressure made possible by changing patterns of industrialism and a declining reliance on labor-repressive policies and made necessary by sustained black political unrest.

CHAPTER 11

Religion and Business Enterprise in Northern Ireland

GROWTH AND POLITICAL CHANGE IN ULSTER:
A FAMILIAR DEBATE

It may seem curious to focus on business enterprise in Northern Ireland. Everything we know about Irish history tells us that religious, not class, factors rule the Irish scene. The evidence is written on the walls of Shankill and Falls roads, in the consciousness of Protestants and Catholics alike. Protestant craftsmen as well as Protestant farmers swore allegiance to William and Mary; the Catholic landed gentry, not just Catholic laborers and tenants, remained loyal to James II. Even with the rise of factories, tenements, and business cycles, workers showed more interest in July 12, the anniversary of the Battle of the Boyne, and in the Easter Uprising than in May Day.

A considerable social science literature now confirms that sectarian rather than class issues are etched deeply into Ulster's contemporary consciousness. In Richard Rose's "Loyalty Survey," for example, middle-class and working-class Protestants express virtually identical levels of support for the Northern Ireland Constitution; middle-class and working-class Catholics are equally adamant in their opposition to it. But *within* the middle class and *within* the working class, Catholics and Protestants differ by as much as 36 percentage points.[1] Ian Budge and Cornelius O'Leary's survey in Belfast lends credence to these observations: "Simply from the overall relationships between party support and religion, and party support and class, it is certain that religion exercises a greater effect than class."[2] After reviewing these and other works on Northern Ireland, Arend Lijphart draws a number of stark conclusions : "The occupational differences between Protestants and Catholics are not so large that religion could serve as a surrogate for class" and "political attitudes and opinions correlate much more highly with religion than with class." He concludes, with Conor Cruise O'Brien, that "the

---

1. Richard Rose, *Governing Without Consensus*, p. 281.
2. Ian Budge and Cornelius O'Leary, *Belfast, Approach to Crisis*, p. 221.

application of the idea of class struggle to Northern Ireland is not intended as a descriptive-analytical model but as a normative ideal and a call to action."[3]

Highlighting sectarian conflict and the depth of religious beliefs does not enable us to ignore class issues, however, any more than our earlier emphasis on racial differences in Alabama and South Africa enabled us to ignore the role of commercial farmers and businessmen. It leaves unanswered, after all, my basic question: What happens when a society well ordered along ethnic or, in this case, religious lines undergoes increasing commercialization and industrialization? What impact does an emerging bourgeoisie, drawn largely from one side of the religious divide, have on the traditional religious barriers and hierarchy?

Moreover, it is difficult to ignore a historical and contemporary debate in Northern Ireland that addresses my basic question: a debate that depends on some of the same theoretical props that buttressed earlier arguments about race relations, particularly in South Africa and Alabama, and draws on familiar conclusions about capitalist development and business behavior and their impact on preclass or "archaic" social differences.

Northern Ireland, for example, has produced its own variant on the "growth school," no less provocative and simple than the ones advanced in Alabama and South Africa: the advance of modern industry and the accumulation of wealth break down barriers between individuals and groups and create new identities. The businessman, for his part, challenges the arbitrary divisions that stand in the way of efficient management practices and the outmoded forms of political authority and social constraints that intrude on the market and work place.

It is a comfortable model for liberal capitalists. Communal peace, in the end, comes not with imposed political solutions but with accelerated economic growth. *Northern Ireland Progress,* the official journal of the Northern Ireland Chamber of Commerce and Industry, recounted the assumptions that underlay its and the government's position in the mid-sixties:

> Looking back at Captain O'Neill's policies over the past six years, it is clear that there has been an assumption that rising standards of living would ease some of the longstanding community tensions. The success of the 'new Ulster' concept depended on every section of the community making a contribution; with greater opportunities for all, there would be less cause for defensive attitudes which produce

3. Arend Lijphart, "Review Article: the Northern Ireland Problem; Cases, Theories, and Solutions," pp. 91–93.

religious discrimination. To some extent, the policies have proved successful, though the battle for economic progress is an unending one.[4]

After the civil rights protests and violence of the late sixties, the new Northern Ireland Community Relations Commission pointed the way toward ending discrimination and religious conflict: "We have no doubt that the most important contribution that could be made to solving the problem of discrimination in the private sector would be to increase the total number of jobs available. Community relations will improve more easily in terms of extra slices of a bigger cake."[5] Tony Gray, after recounting more than five hundred years of religious bigotry and cruelty, concludes, with other liberal capitalists, "If there were two cars and a boat to every household in Northern Ireland, most of the bitter sectarianism would vanish overnight." With new investment and economic growth, "people will tend to think less and less about religion and politics and more and more about keeping up with the Faulkners."[6]

The challenge for the growth school is to explain how industrialization and increased prosperity in this century have managed to leave so vast a gulf between Catholics and Protestants in Northern Ireland.

Though no formal school has emerged emphasizing the accommodative side of business practice, the discussions of deep religious cleavages and the affinity of middle-class and working-class Protestants contain an implicit argument to that effect. Too much history predates capitalist development in Northern Ireland for businessmen to ignore sectarian lines: the siege of Derry and the Easter rebellion intrude on the labor market and shop floor. Indeed, businessmen, as part and parcel of the Protestant ascendancy, can reasonably be expected to produce the religious hierarchy in the work place.[7]

The orthodox Marxist position is derived from Marx's own experience with the Irish question in England and Ireland. He emphasized the animosities that separated the Irish and English sections of the working class and the Catholic and Protestant peasantry and the willingness of landlords and capitalists to exploit them. Religion in this context was not so much an opiate as an oft-turned handle for stirring up communal strife and undermining the effectiveness of class struggle. Still, Marx believed that the development process contained its own solution to the Irish question, taking

---

4. *Northern Ireland Progress* 19, no. 4 (April 1969): 6.
5. Northern Ireland Community Relations Commission, *First Annual Report, 1971*, p. 16.
6. Tony Gray, *Psalms and Slaughter*, p. 234.
7. See discussion in chapter 7.

both England and Ireland beyond sectarian divisions. With the death of the Irish-Catholic Church, Marx wrote, Catholic and Protestant tenants would unite against "landlordism," bringing down the English aristocracy in Ireland and laying the basis for proletarian revolution in England itself.[8]

Had Marx foreseen the vitality, or at least longevity, of Catholicism and Protestantism in Ireland, he might have given greater emphasis to the continuing manipulation of sectarian differences. The "Orange Machine," encompassing the dominant Protestant landed and business interests, sought in this century to crush political and labor impulses that cut across the religious lines. At the turn of the century, "Independent Orange" political and labor leaders violated two cardinal principles in Ulster politics: first, they questioned the beneficence of continued Unionist party rule; and second, they dared to appeal beyond the sectarian barriers. Calls for "workers and toilers" to "fight against the intrigues, political machines and confiscation" were met by government attempts to breed violence across the Falls Road divide and distrust of Protestant and Catholic strike leaders.[9] Above all, Independent Orangeism brought a renewed vigilance on the part of the Unionists against "home rule" and "home rulers." In 1910, the Independent Orangemen were brought to task:

> Orangemen must vote for every supporter of the Government, for it is only by doing so that they can prevent the Nationalists and priests from becoming masters of this country. . . . The Sloanites [Independent Orangemen] are prepared to betray their fellow Protestants.[10]

Independent Orangemen counterattacked in the immediate postwar period, accusing the Unionists of furthering "home rule" by "connecting the Union with privilege and ascendency."[11] But Edward Carson, Unionist leader, High Tory, defender of British rule in India, lawyer for Irish landlords and errant imperialists like Leander Starr Jameson, led a successful counterattack against Independent Orangeism and the Belfast labor movement:

> What I say is this: these men who come forward posing as friends of labour care no more about labour than does the man in the moon. Their real object and the real insidious object of their propaganda is to mislead and bring about disunity among our own people and in the

8. Karl Marx, "Letters on Ireland, 1867–1870," pp. 158–71.
9. J.W. Boyle, "Belfast and the Origins of Northern Ireland," pp. 134–37.
10. Quoted in Eamonn McCann, *War and an Irish Town*, p. 145.
11. W.J. Stewart, quoted in Geoffrey Bell, *The Protestants of Ulster*, p. 69.

end, before we know it, we may find ourselves in the same bondage and slavery as in the rest of Ireland, in the south and west.[12]

In the interest of Union, Carson and other Unionist leaders encouraged Protestant workers to expel "disloyal elements"—the radical Protestant labor leaders and Catholic workers—from the factories and docks of Northern Ireland. In the end, the Union Jack flew proudly over the Harland and Wolff shipyards.[13] By 1929, with the abolition of proportional representation, the Unionists had checked the advance of Independent Unionism and the labor candidacies. Protestant voters heeded the Unionist message: "BEWARE OF INDEPENDENTS: UP ULSTER: SCATTER YOUR ENEMIES: HONOR YOUR FRIENDS."[14]

Theories of business enterprise emphasizing the manipulation of divisions within the working class must consider that at least some of the "divided" may be willing, self-interested participants in the religious stratification. Protestant workers, not just landlords and businessmen, profited from religious discrimination and segregation. The Protestant ascendancy translated into Protestant jobs in the major industries, Protestant positions within the civil service and local council staffs, and council housing in working-class Protestant districts. Protestant workers, like the advanced sections of Northern Ireland industry, felt little attachment to a united Ireland; there was, in Anders Boserup's terms, "no affinity of nationality, no affinity of interests in economic terms." They feared association with a state that was, in fact, "politically reactionary and dominated by the Catholic church."[15]

Other Marxist writers give less attention to business interest in maintaining Orange rule and manipulating religious differences and more to the changing nature of capitalism itself. Early capitalism in Northern Ireland, Boserup writes, is a "traditional 'clientist' form of a capitalist social formation" where economic questions may remain dependent on a political and ideological struggle, where, in effect, religious questions still pervade market decisions.[16] The emergent bourgeoisie rose up within the Orange Order, acting to reinforce both Orange rule and the British connection; in this context, it might well have fanned religious prejudices. But modern capitalist forms have little use for Irish history. The economic sphere has an autonomy here that frees corporations from the Orange entanglement and

12. Quoted in ibid., p. 71.
13. McCann, *War and an Irish Town,* pp. 155–56.
14. Ibid., pp. 192–93.
15. Anders Boserup, *Who is the Principal Enemy? Contradictions and Struggles in Northern Ireland,* p. 6; also see McCann, *War and an Irish Town,* pp. 122, 170.
16. Boserup, *Who is the Principal Enemy?* pp. 2, 10–12.

opens up the market to bourgeois notions of achievement and efficiency. The change is captured in the shift from family-owned businesses to modern corporations. Boserup writes:

> In the long run this transition from family-based to public companies . . . is bound to weaken the Orange system decisively. The new industries are not dependent upon the cooperation of the establishment in those communities where they settle down and, because they are not so tied to the local community, they also do not have the same political ambitions as the old ones. For the same reason they have a less personalized relation to employees and have been less prone to discriminate in employment.[17]

Why should a DuPont or a Ford care whether its employees are Catholics or Protestants? As long as the company has an adequate labor force and a stable business environment, why should it care who rules in Derry or Newry?

This chapter uncovers a different facet of a similar process, one that emphasizes manufacturing and the accommodative side of business enterprise without a strong tradition in primary industry and labor repression. Northern Ireland industrialism was not built on "cheap" Catholic labor or low-paying, labor-hungry extractive industries. And while the linen industry employed a relatively undifferentiated, unskilled labor force, it did not for the most part draw on the Catholic rural areas or Catholic labor. Labor repression was a muted theme here. No major sector of Northern Ireland industry based its business enterprise on the manipulation and control of Catholic labor mobility and the proletarianization or suppression of Catholic political and trade-union organization. The state itself, though closely integrated into the Protestant ascendancy, never encompassed an elaborate machinery for the control and regulation of Catholic labor.

That is not to deny the close indentification of emerging business interests with the Protestant regime and Protestant domination in Ulster. Manufacturers were wary of any political arrangement in Ulster or all of Ireland that threatened their access to markets in England or subjected them to the tyranny of the Catholic peasantry or the Irish Church to the south. They were hardly loath to use the state to aid accumulation and limit working-class organization; they turned an intimate association with the dominant Unionist party into regular influence over state affairs. But they did not turn the state in Northern Ireland into a vehicle for circumventing the market, for organizing and controlling a Catholic labor force.

17. Ibid., p. 13.

The dominant theme in Northern Ireland industrialism is the thorough-going accommodation to the framework of Protestant domination. Manufacturers readily tailored hiring and work patterns and plant location decisions to reflect the thinking and interests of the dominant Protestant community. Though that accommodation may have come more easily for the small-scale, "clientist" firms early in capitalist development, the larger manufacturing operations, even the multinationals, have managed to leave the Protestant ascendancy undisturbed. Until the late sixties, the major secondary manufacturers and commercial concerns never questioned public policies that fostered job discrimination in private and public employment, the allocation of council housing, and the granting of the local franchise.

The Catholic civil rights protests, the sectarian violence, and subsequent British intervention brought a remarkably rapid retreat from the Protestant ascendancy. Though the manufacturers and the state were critical props for the Protestant cause in Ulster, both, oddly enough, were able to consider alternatives to the traditional Protestant hegemony: the former because its long-standing accommodation only concealed a steadily diminishing interest in the religious cause; the latter because it was closely identified with secondary manufacturing and commerce, rather than Protestant workers or landowners, and because it never administered the subjugation of the Catholic laboring population.

DEVELOPMENT OF MANUFACTURE: LINENS, SHIPBUILDING, AND ENGINEERING

Had the River Lagan remained "a meandering line," barring "vessels of any considerable Burthen passing up or down, except at very high Spring Tides,"[18] had the linen industry collapsed in the North as it had in the South or gone the way of Irish meat and wool export industries, and had Belfast remained a small market and port town of 13,000, we would have no test of our principal propositions. But a straight cut from the Quay at Garmoyle opened up the River Lagan and the port of Belfast; the linen industry crawled out from under the heavy hand of the landlord-supported Linen Board and, with the development of flax spinning and the power loom, the linen trade became the "natural business of Ireland."[19] Ulster was rapidly escaping the society of peasants and landlords still dominant in the South

18. Petition of the Belfast Chamber of Commerce, 12 November 1783, quoted in The Northern Ireland Chamber of Commerce and Industry, *Year Book 1977*, pp. 4–5.
19. Budge and O'Leary, *Belfast*, p. 19; W.H. Crawford, "Ulster Landowners and the Linen Industry," pp. 129–39.

and emerging as a "modern industrial and commercial centre with all the dynamism, self-confidence and abject popular misery of early capitalism."[20] The town of Belfast grew by leaps and bounds, reaching 50,000 even before the Victorian era and 350,000 by the era's close in 1901.[21]

The city reflected the development of what are still Ulster's two principal industries: linen and shipbuilding. In 1836, 2,000 workers were employed in Belfast's linen industry; by 1862, 15,000; and by 1875, 50,000.[22] Shipbuilding and marine engineering began in an unassuming manner: first with a wooden-ship-building company in the late eighteenth century, iron-sailing-ship construction by 1840, and, by 1860, the founding of Harland and Wolff on Queen's Island (Belfast). Before the turn of the century, the dry docks, shipyard, and engineering works sprawled over seventy-six acres and employed 9,000 workers.[23] The infant engineering industry grew up with textiles, particularly the repair and manufacture of spinning mills. With the development of marine engineering and shipbuilding, engineering emerged as a major industrial sector. It moved beyond ship repair and ropemaking to fans and armaments.[24]

The principal secondary industries of Northern Ireland were in place before 1900. The substantial growth, however, came in this century. By 1950, Harland and Wolff was the largest shipbuilding yard in the world, employing more than 20,000 workers. Ulster's engineering industry encompassed, in addition to shipbuilding, important fan and ventilation equipment manufacture, some light engineering (cables, control gear, etc.), and an aircraft industry.

Ulster's industrial development, however, was concentrated in a small number of industries whose major markets were abroad. All of these industries—linens, shipbuilding, and engineering—began experiencing difficulties after World War II. Ocean liners and aircraft carriers were no longer in great demand, and newly reconstructed yards in Germany and Japan seemed better able to handle the rising demand for tankers. In 1962, Harland and Wolff, Northern Ireland's single largest employer, laid off 8,000 of its 23,000 employees. With an unstable demand for the Comet and Seacat, employment in the aircraft industry fluctuated between 4,000 and 8,500 workers. After 1950, the linen industry collapsed. Foreign competition, traditional management practice, new synthetic fabrics, and increased cotton manufacture contributed to the decline of Ulster's first major

20. Boserup, *Who is the Principal Enemy?* pp. 3–4.
21. Emrys Jones, "Belfast," pp. 90–91.
22. Budge and O'Leary, *Belfast*, pp. 21, 73.
23. Ibid., pp. 73–74.
24. E.R.R. Green, "Business Organization and the Business Class," pp. 111–14; Budge and O'Leary, *Belfast*, p. 75.

industry. Between 1958 and 1964, a third of the plants closed their doors, leaving 27,000 workers, almost half of the 1950 labor force, without jobs.[25] High unemployment now seemed inescapable. In the late sixties, when unemployment in England barely topped 2 percent, the Northern Ireland rate had risen above 7 percent. The international recession in the mid-seventies forced the unemployment rate up to 10 percent.[26]

Growth and marginality are special problems for Northern Ireland because Protestants have shared disproportionately in the former and Catholics in the latter. Virtually all the major industries, including Harland and Wolff, Sorroco, Short Brothers and Harland, and Mackie, are Protestant managed and owned. Indeed, the major industrial complex in Northern Ireland falls along the Lagan Valley around Belfast, where Catholic residence is sparse in comparison to the remainder of Ulster; within Belfast, the principal industrial section, including the Queens Island complex, is nestled in a district where Catholic workers travel at their own peril. The Catholic working class, consequently, lives on the margins of Northern Ireland manufacture. In the Belfast region, where Catholics constitute a quarter of the population, unemployment in 1975 fell below 8 percent for the population as a whole, but in heavily Catholic areas of Belfast, like Falls Road, and Catholic border towns, like Newry, unemployment sometimes exceeded 20 percent.[27]

This chapter addresses the question of capitalist development and religious stratification in Northern Ireland by focusing on two groups within the business community: the managing directors of the principal Protestant-owned firms, and the major associations representing industrial and commercial interests in Northern Ireland.

BUSINESSMEN AND THE POLITICS OF THE PROTESTANT ASCENDANCY

The business community in Ulster has maintained a close historical identification with the Protestant ascendancy and government of Ulster. The Belfast Chamber of Commerce stood steadfastly against the recurring demands for home rule in Ireland, affirming, again and again, the necessity of the English connection. It opposed home rule bills in 1886, 1893, and

---

25. M.A. Busteed, *Northern Ireland,* pp. 9–11; Northern Ireland, *Report of the Joint Working Party on the Economy of Northern Ireland,* 1962, Cmd. 446, pp. 4–7, 46–47, 69.
26. Rose, *Governing Without Consensus,* p. 67; Northern Ireland, *Social and Economic Trends in Northern Ireland,* 1976, p. 19.
27. Northern Ireland, *Religious Tables, Northern Ireland,* 1975, p. 2; Northern Ireland, *Social and Economic Trends,* p. 21; Bell, *The Protestants of Ulster,* p. 29.

1912. In 1888, it wrote, "This meeting deplores the agitation which now exists for loosening the ties which render Ireland, in all respects an integral part of the United Kingdom." The Chamber feared that commercial prosperity would "receive a sudden shock from any legislation" that imperiled "the connection between this country and Great Britain."[28] The Chamber and the business community was no less committed on the question when the demand for home rule shifted from the Daniel O'Connells to the Eamon De Valeras. Indeed, there is only a bit of exaggeration in the claim that the business community supported and financed the Ulster Volunteer Force in 1913, thus insuring the intractability and political viability of the North.[29] When a bill for partition was offered in 1920, the Belfast Chamber accepted the principle:

> Then came the Bill of 1920, which maintained a common fiscal system for the whole of the United Kingdom, and secured to Northern Ireland its connection with Great Britain and its own Government. This, the Chamber reluctantly decided to support as the least harmful method of conferring enlarged powers of self-government upon Ireland under existing conditions.[30]

After partition, the Belfast Chamber devoted its publications and time to building the connection between the six counties of Ireland and Protestant Great Britain: it spoke incessantly of the "lack of customs barriers" between them and reminded its fellow Irishmen of materials, capital, and markets to be found only in England.[31]

The government of Ulster was not left to the politicians and landlords, however. "When the home rule Bill became law," the Belfast Chamber wrote, "the Chamber assisted directly in the establishment of the Government of Northern Ireland, which is now energetically functioning throughout Six Counties."[32] The first cabinets between 1921 and 1937 were dominated by the business community: among seven cabinet ministers under James Craig, one was a landlord and another a solicitor, but one was a company director, and three were former presidents of the Belfast Chamber of Commerce.[33] The first minister of finance was a two-time president of the Belfast Chamber.[34] James Craig himself, the first prime minister and the architect of the Protestant ascendancy, besides presiding

28. Quoted in Bell, *The Protestants of Ulster*, p. 95.
29. Ibid., p. 94.
30. *Belfast Chamber of Commerce Journal* 11, no. 1 (April 1933): 12.
31. Ibid., 1, no. 3 (June 1923): 35; also see J.W. Boyle, "Belfast and the Origins of Northern Ireland," p. 189.
32. *Belfast Chamber of Commerce Journal* 11, no. 1 (April 1933): 12.
33. Bell, *The Protestants of Ulster*, p. 100.
34. *Belfast Chamber of Commerce Journal* 1, no. 4 (July 1923): 57.

over a business-oriented cabinet, was himself a wealthy industrialist and defender of "wealth creation."[35]

The Unionist government, with the full backing and, to a large extent, participation of the business community, set out the framework for the Protestant ascendancy. First, the gerrymandering, "company vote," and abolition of proportional representation limited Catholic representation on the local councils and at Stormont. What was accepted practice immediately after partition still ruled electoral politics in the mid-sixties, when civil rights demonstrations finally called the whole system into question. In Londonderry, as late as 1969, a heavy Catholic majority was able to elect only eight of twenty councillors; in Omagh, a Catholic majority could elect only nine of twenty-one councillors.[36] These "electoral arrangements," the report on the disturbances in Northern Ireland asserts, produced "unfair results" and reflected a "determination to achieve and maintain Unionist electoral control."[37]

Second, government policy reinforced the segregation of Catholic and Protestant residential areas. In Belfast, Londonderry, and elsewhere, residential segregation preceded partition and Unionist religious policies. The Irish were segregated on the plantations—"outside the city walls," perhaps in the "Irish Quarter." In any event, "social intercourse" with the "mere Irish" was discouraged.[38] During the Victorian period, an impoverished Catholic peasantry sought out the crowded working-class areas of Belfast and Derry. But the influx brought in its wake recurring riots, a transfer of Catholic and Protestant populations, and the progressive diminution of the mixed areas. A riot report in 1886 declared: "The extremity to which party and religious feeling has grown in Belfast is shown strikingly by the fact that the people of the artisan and labouring classes . . . dwell to a large extent in separate quarters, each of which is given up almost entirely to persons of one particular faith and the boundaries of which are sharply defined."[39]

But partition and Unionist policies brought a worsening of residential segregation; bitter rioting between 1920 and 1923, the Special Powers Act of 1922, and the displacement of Catholic and Protestant populations helped mold Belfast into its present intractable and clearly demarcated form. After the war, Unionist-controlled local councils insured that two centuries of increasing segregation would not be disrupted by new social welfare and

35. Bell, *The Protestants of Ulster*, p. 38.
36. The Campaign for Social Justice in Northern Ireland, *Northern Ireland: The Plain Truth*, pp. 19–22.
37. Northern Ireland, *Disturbances in Northern Ireland*, Report of the Commission appointed by the Governor of Northern Ireland, Cmd. 532, 1969, p. 60.
38. Busteed, *Northern Ireland*, p. 41; Michael Hechter, *Internal Colonialism*, p. 184.
39. Emrys Jones, *A Social Geography of Belfast*, pp. 190–91; see also T.W. Moody and J.C. Beckett, *Ulster Since 1800*, pp. 96–97.

housing programs. Protestants and Catholics were provided council housing in their respective areas; a disproportionate share of council housing was given over to Protestants. The report on civil disturbances (1969) states: "The principal criterion however in such cases was not actual need but maintenance of the current political preponderance in the local areas."[40]

Only in education did the postpartition Unionist government attempt to break down some of the traditional religious barriers. But secular education foundered on the intense commitments of each group to its own doctrines, clerics, and classrooms. Protestants entered the public system when religious instruction was made mandatory in 1930; Catholics remained adamant, however, choosing to maintain separate church schools.[41] This educational segregation gave a permanence and rigidity to religious divisions that tried the patience even of the business community. In my interviews, businessmen regularly—and I think honestly—lamented the system of separate education: "A lot of us are very much opposed to it"; "The greatest tragedy of Northern Ireland is separate education"; and "Our educational system does nothing to change it."

The business community in Northern Ireland did not, after its first encounter with Protestant rule, step back and question religious segregation. The separation of Protestants and Catholics in the schools never had the support of the government or the business community. But housing policies and electoral manipulations developed with the connivance, or at least indifference, of prominent businessmen and business associations. At times in the fifties, the Northern Ireland Chamber of Commerce and Industry (NICCI) urged more housing construction and efforts to relieve slum conditions,[42] but such reform proposals stand out against a backdrop of almost unrelieved accommodation to segregation policies.

Today, the accommodation to the Protestant ascendancy is apparent in business insistence on "economics" and disinterest in politics. One director maintained that, at least for his firm, there was "no politics at all"; the firm was simply "not interested" in such issues: "I don't think big firms like Short Brothers, Mackey and ourselves would get involved in politics. We want to get on with it. I doubt if manufacturing would. . . . Anybody who employs a lot of workers can't afford to." A former officer for NICCI claimed that the organization was "never political"; it relied instead on "pure economics."

40. Northern Ireland, *Disturbances in Northern Ireland,* p. 61; also see Campaign for Social Justice, *Northern Ireland,* pp. 20–22, 26–28.
41. Dennis P. Barritt and Arthur Booth, *Orange and Green,* pp. 30–31.
42. *Northern Ireland Progress* 4, no. 4 (April 1954): 4; ibid., 5, no. 4 (April 1955):3.

But such claims are certainly disingenuous, and the businessmen themselves appreciated the fact. At a general level, businessmen wanted a stable business environment, and they fully expected the governments at Stormont and Westminster to accept responsibility for it. The CBI officer declared: "What we have said and said consistently: We exist in a political world and we look to government for stability. In short, the sooner they get this bloody mess together the better." At a more specific level, businessmen wanted an intimate association with political leaders, one that enabled them to exercise influence on the issues of the day and to "explain how the wealth-creating mechanism works, and the ways it should be supported and encouraged."[43]

Businessmen and the Unionist government at Stormont had, in fact, forged a close personal and political association. Past officers of the NICCI were particularly insistent on this point.

> We were in constant touch with all the ministers. One of the good things about the Stormont government, the local contacts were very good. If there were any questions, you get the answers that afternoon, practically direct access to any minister.
>
> Under the old system, there was close liaison between business and the government. We were on a first-name terms with all the members of the government. That would have been right up to the beginning of direct rule. We tended to have a smallish clique at the center of things and they knew everybody.

The Confederation of British Industry officer was no less intimate with Protestant leaders: "We were on first-name terms with the ministers. It was very good. They were anxious to get on. They too believed in wealth creation."

ACCOMMODATING DISCRIMINATION IN EMPLOYMENT

Thinking out the whole question carefully . . . I recommend those people who are Loyalists not to employ Roman Catholics, ninety-nine per cent of whom are disloyal. . . . I want you to remember one point in regard to the employment of people who are disloyal. There are often difficulties in the way, but usually there are plenty of good men and women available, and the employers don't bother to employ them. You are disenfranchising yourselves in that way. You people who are employers have the ball at your feet. If you don't act properly now before we know where we are we shall find ourselves in the minority instead of the majority.

Viscount Brookeborough,
Prime Minister, 1943–63[44]

43. *Business Letter,* NICCI, no. 24 (4 April 1977), p. 1.
44. *Londonderry Sentinel,* 20 March 1934, quoted in the Campaign for Social Justice, *Northern Ireland,* p. 33.

The linen industry, the starting point for capitalist development in Northern Ireland, was associated from the beginning with the Protestant ascendancy: both the Linen Board and the government hoped that linen manufacture, like cotton textiles in the American South, would provide avenues for dominant employment and ownership.[45] Linens did indeed provide opportunities, but also a pattern that now pervades modern industrial life in Ulster. The major manufacturers and largest employers engage precious few Catholics: Harland and Wolff, perhaps 500 Catholics out of a total labor force of 10,000; Mackie, 300 Catholics out of 4,500 employees; and the aerospace industry, where Short Brothers and Harland is the dominant firm, 800 Catholics out of 8,500 employees.[46] The engineering industry as a whole, providing the "cream of skilled work," has been inhospitable to Catholic job-seekers. As an officer of the Engineering Employers' Association put it, "The dominant community is keen to keep that."[47]

But the exclusion of Catholic workers, so apparent in shipbuilding, engineering, and, at an earlier point, textiles, is only one facet of a more pervasive pattern. There is a hierarchy in Ulster's political and economic life that gives Protestants a preferred access to the work place. Catholics, who constitute 31 percent of the population in Northern Ireland and 25 percent of the labor force, hold only 10 percent of the managerial positions in larger firms (18 percent in smaller firms) and only 12 percent of professional positions.[48] Indeed, Edmund Aunger points out, "the median Protestant is a *skilled* manual worker" while the "median Catholic is a *semi-skilled* manual worker."[49] But the hierarchy goes beyond the statistical median. At the upper end of the hierarchy there are both Protestants and Catholics, but the latter are concentrated in service occupations—teachers and shop-keepers that cater to segregated communities, for example—while the former are concentrated in finance and industry. At the lower end, there are both Protestant and Catholic manual workers and, given the predominance of Protestants in the working population, probably more of the former. But Protestant workers predominate in the prestige industries, like engineering and textiles, which provide year-round employment and avenues for advancement; Catholics predominate in less reputable areas, like construction and dock work, which provide irregular employment and fewer areas for advancement. Even on the docks, the mainly Protestant Amalgamated Transport and General Workers' Union handles cross-Channel boats where

45. Crawford, "Ulster Landowners," p. 117.
46. Northern Ireland, *Religious Tables,* table 9, pp. 50–51; interview with officer of Northern Ireland Chamber of Commerce and Industry.
47. Also see Northern Ireland, *Religious Tables,* table 8, p. 46.
48. Ibid., table 8, p. 45.
49. Edmund A. Aunger, "Religion and Occupational Class in Northern Ireland," p. 4.

traffic and work is regular during the entire year; the mostly Catholic Irish Transport and General Workers' Union handles the much less regular deep-sea traffic.[50]

The exclusions and the hierarchy conspire to make unemployment largely a Catholic problem. That situation prevailed at the onset of industrialization: the Irish census of 1891 showed a predominance of Catholics in the workhouses of Ulster.[51] And that situation prevails today: the 1971 census in Northern Ireland found 7 percent of Protestant men out of work—high by British standards—but fully 17 percent of Catholic men—high by almost any standard.[52] The problem is apparent in Belfast, where unemployment in Falls, a Catholic working-class community, is twice that in Shankill, a Protestant working-class stronghold.[53] And it is apparent in the Bogside in Derry, where a third of Catholic men sit idle and where the industrious emigrate to the South or to England.[54] Though it is conceivable that economic growth could cut into Catholic unemployment rates, industrial expansion has generally come in Belfast and the Lagan Valley, not in the border towns or in areas of high Catholic unemployment.[55]

The government of Northern Ireland was in no position to challenge the structure of Protestant-Catholic inequality. It, no less than employers in the private sector, reflected and served the dominant hierarchy and population. Few Protestants in Ulster, before the civil rights marches, would have tolerated a government that legislated against religious discrimination. Rose found that more than two-thirds of his Protestant respondents opposed "a law making it illegal to refuse a job or rent a house to a Catholic because of his religion."[56] Few Protestants would have urged the government to alter a pattern of recruitment and hiring that left virtually every position of consequence in the hands of Protestants. In 1959, every permanent secretary and every assistant secretary, save two, were Protestants. In 1969, there was one Catholic assistant secretary in the Ministry of Finance but none in the Prime Minister's Department, the Ministry of Health and Social Services, Ministry of Education, or, indeed, in any other ministry.[57] The one government agency charged with acting against religious discrimination, the

50. Aunger, "Religion and Occupational Class," pp. 11–12; Barritt and Carter, *The Northern Ireland Problem*, pp. 140–41.
51. Bell, *The Protestants of Ulster*, p. 19.
52. Aunger, "Religion and Occupational Class," p. 9.
53. Bell, *The Protestants of Ulster*, p. 29.
54. McCann, *War and an Irish Town*, pp. 22–23.
55. Northern Ireland, *Report of the Joint Working Party on the Economy of Northern Ireland*, p. 85; Dennis P. Barritt and Charles F. Carter, *The Northern Ireland Problem*, p. 106; and Northern Ireland, *Social and Economic Trends in Northern Ireland*, p. 21.
56. Rose, *Governing Without Consensus*, p. 481.
57. Barritt and Carter, *The Northern Ireland Problem*, p. 96; Campaign for Social Justice, *Northern Ireland*, pp. 4–5.

Community Relations Commission, emphasized voluntary changes and soon collapsed in impotence.[58]

The initiative for governmental action to end employment discrimination came only after British authorities imposed new directions on the unruly province. In 1973, the Working Party on Discrimination in the Private Sector of Employment, with representatives from the Northern Ireland Regional Council of CBI, NICCI, and the Northern Ireland Committee of the Irish Congress of Trade Unions, endorsed the principle of non-discrimination. Its recommendations for breaking down the religious barriers, however, reflected all the caution one would expect from parties to discrimination. The Working Party rejected quotas, "benign (reverse) discrimination," or criminal sanctions, like fines or imprisonment: these would "most likely . . . provoke sectarian hostility in industry and thus be counter productive." It emphasized, instead, a clear statement of principle and a Declaration of Intent: "We propose that the Government should invite representative organizations of employers and Trade Unions to sign, and to recommend their members to sign, a Declaration of Intent to observe the principles of full equality of employment opportunity."[59] Three long, bloody years passed before even these modest recommendations became law. The Fair Employment (Northern Ireland) Act of 1976, enacted at Westminster, took the course of least resistance: it barred discrimination in principle but, for the most part, followed the recommendations of the Working Party. Religious discrimination was now prohibited in Northern Ireland, but the prohibition was qualified by exemptions and timetables. Employment as teachers, clergymen, and domestics, for example, was placed outside the act's coverage; for a period of two years, firms with fewer than twenty-five persons and, for an additional year, firms with fewer than ten persons were also exempted from the act. In any event, employers and trade unions alike rushed to declare their good intentions.[60]

Business Imagery: "Let Me Have the Man That Can Do the Job."

Business imagery in Northern Ireland leaves little room for the Protestant-Catholic divide. Businessmen, whether associated with established business organizations or Protestant-owned firms, scoffed at the old shibboleths—

---

58. See Northern Ireland Community Relations Commission, *Second Annual Report,* 1 January 1971 to 30 April 1972.

59. Northern Ireland, *Report and Recommendation of the Working Party on Discrimination in the Private Sector of Employment,* 1973, pp. 12–13.

60. United Kingdom, *Fair Employment (Northern Ireland) Act 1976,* chapter 25, 1976, pp. 26–27.

the concern with "disloyalty" and the slogans, such as "Protestants, employ Protestants."[61] They insisted that modern business practice emphasizes, above all else, profit making and rational and efficient management. "As far as we are concerned," a CBI officer declared, "bugger it. We want to get on with it. Profitability. That's what we care about. We have enough problems without this on our backs. And it is totally irrelevant in a modern scene." The modern business does not "care a damn where a chap comes from," he said. It wants to know whether the man or woman can perform the job. A managing director of one of the largest firms was emphatic on this issue: "My board is made up of Scotsmen and Englishmen. They don't give a hoot whether a man is a Protestant or Catholic. They want to get a [x][62] out in time. That's what they care about."

The imagery of Northern Ireland business includes a vision of professional management hoping to break down parochialism and archaic personnel practices. While "hiring and firing" were conventionally left to the shop floor and untrained personnel officers—"at a low level," one company officer noted, where prejudice is given free rein—professional management shifts the focus to a "higher level" where "enlightened" attitudes limit the scope of prejudice. An officer of the NICCI observed: "It used to be that most of the firms were primarily family businesses, the family linen business. In the old days, the managers were provided mainly from the family. Now, most firms have a proper middle-level management team. They say, 'Let me have the man that can do the job.' "

To some extent, the imagery reflected the attitudes and practices of firms with foreign connections.[63] Why should a DuPont or General Electric, or even a British Leyland for that matter, stand in the way of Catholic employment or advancement? But the imagery now pervades top-level management in the established and Protestant business associations and firms as well. They, like their foreign counterparts, are part of a business climate that scorns constraints in the labor market and barriers to efficient production.

Accommodating Discrimination: "They Know Jolly Well It Would Be Difficult to Work Here."

The imagery, however, is not particularly consistent with actual business practice in Northern Ireland. True, these firms and associations signed,

---

61. Sir Joseph Davison, Orange Grand Master of Belfast, *Northern Whig,* 28 August 1933, cited in Campaign for Social Justice, *Northern Ireland,* p. 34.
62. The (x) represents the product of this particular company.
63. See Barritt and Carter, *The Northern Ireland Problem,* pp. 103–5; McCann, *War and an Irish Town,* p. 211.

some with considerable ceremony, the declaration of intent and principle; they insisted that self-conscious discrimination against Catholic workers has no place in their plants and organizations. A past officer of NICCI, for example, refused to recognize the problem: "I don't know of any firm at all practicing discrimination on any side." Similar views were expressed by a CBI officer: "We subscribe to the Declaration of Fair Employment. But a firm that discriminates? I don't know of them." But all these businessmen, despite their intentions and self-perceptions, accommodated discriminatory business practices: some did so reluctantly, but most did with little personal discomfort and little inclination to alter conventional practice.

For some of the smaller firms in Northern Ireland, hiring, and therefore discrimination, was a prerogative of the family or, in some cases, the local Orange Order. In either case, Catholic workers faced extraordinary barriers to industrial employment.[64] But even in the larger Belfast firms, the processes for hiring and promotion were often highly personalized and sectarian. Though employers could select apprentices by their own criteria, they often ignored modern personnel techniques in favor of traditional patronage methods. The owner, for example, might have responded to the pleas of a sheet-metal worker with twenty years' service: "I've got a boy coming along. Can you put in a word for him?" Or the mother who brought her son along: "You're a Shankill Road man. Can't you do something for him?"[65] In the shipyards, even as late as 1970, a department short three workers might turn to the foreman who knew "three blokes at the pub."[66] Such patronage arrangements, no matter how well intended, insured that the traditional employment patterns would be replicated. But, as one officer lamented, it was the "course of least resistance."

Few businessmen, however, viewed these patronage arrangements as the heart of the problem. They looked instead to the shop floor and the attitudes of Protestant workers. An NICCI officer observed: "When you have firms on Shankill and Falls Roads, then it comes from the shop floor. The workers will insist that no bloody Catholic come in. Management will say we want to hire but it comes from the shop floor. . . . [It] is discrimination by the workers themselves." The employer, in other words, was forced to operate within the constraints established by the workers; as the NICCI officer put it, "whatever the labor force will tolerate." If you operated within certain areas, "there is no way an employer can employ anyone except that particular religion." A large engineering firm, caught between

64. Boserup, *Who is the Principal Enemy?* pp. 8–9; Barritt and Booth, *Orange and Green,* 1972, p. 28.
65. Cited in interviews with Engineering Employers' Northern Ireland Association and NICCI.
66. Interview with officer of Northern Ireland Committee of the Irish Congress of Trade Unions.

two communities, believed that widespread residential segregation and the political climate precluded any substantial move toward integration:

> The situation in the plant is directly related to the level of political activity in the city at any point in time. One section of the factory is near the Catholic area—the painting section. We hired at once five Catholics for the night shift. There were forty on staff, so they made up 12 percent. At that time, there was a great deal of unrest in the city. One by one, these Catholic guys quit. I went down to the night shift one night and the foreman told me the boys were kicking the mickey out of them. They were exploding acetylene bombs. Two left because of direct intimidation. There is one left.

When the firm attempted to get the shop steward committee, all Protestants, to sit down with a committee of priests from the neighboring Catholic parish, "some of the hotheads in the factory" intervened to undermine the dialogue. Another officer described his own factory as a "Protestant stronghold." The company had "no bar" against Catholic workers, but its traditional hiring practices, location in East Belfast, and the attitudes of Protestant workers effectively precluded Catholic employment: "It demands a great deal of physical courage to cross over the bridge." Even a limited program to train and bring in Catholic apprentices failed to change tradition: "But it didn't happen. We didn't get the influx. Pressure, I guess. I can't say. In the present state, it's not fair to ask one to go into a stronghold of another."

The notion of "stronghold" is apparent in the summer months when Protestant workers bring the siege at Derry and the Battle of the Boyne down to the shop floor. An Engineering Employers officer described the pattern:

> This is something quite extraordinary. Employees have ways of declaring this is a Protestant firm. I don't think you would believe what you see in July. Great orange arcs over the machines. Union Jacks everywhere. Vanguard flags. Quite incredible. But you can imagine it is extremely intimidating if you are a Catholic.

Few of the firms risked tampering with these celebrations, despite their obvious impact on prospective Catholic workers. The Engineering Employers Association recommended that all *new* firms ban flags from the work place: "The flags might get caught in the machines." But it did not urge, for fear of Protestant worker reaction, that well-established firms alter the practice. A German-owned firm that banned all party flags, including those of the Vanguard party, faced a one-month strike. The Engineering Employers officer noted, "They didn't repeat the policy."

Resisting Change: "The Legislation and the Working Party Were
Overdone."

That employers faced strong pressures from the shop floor to maintain
traditional practices is difficult to deny. Whatever their commitment to the
imagery of nondiscrimination and meritocracy, employers were constrained
by the bigotry and violence that swirled about the factory and that set the
mood for the work place. The imagery might still have proved credible,
however, if businessmen had actively sought to limit the scope of religious
discrimination. They could, for example, have supported legislation barring
religious discrimination in employment, thus limiting management's ability
to accommodate discrimination and the worker's inclination to create it.
But management was not very interested in the issue. Though the *Northern
Ireland Progress,* the voice of the Northern Ireland Chamber of Commerce
and Industry, eventually supported franchise and housing reforms in the
mid-sixties, it made no mention of employment issues. In 1966, the Irish
Congress of Trade Unions presented a reform package, including changes in
the employment field, but the business community was nowhere to be
found. The proposals died for lack of a second.[67] Only when the violence
became intolerable[68] and the British government insistent, did the business
community begin to grapple with problems of employment discrimination.
  But grappling was hardly commitment. The business members of the
Working Party on Discrimination, though roundly opposed to discrimination in principle, proposed a very modest tack, rejecting imposed legal
solutions that might cause "sectarian hostility." The *Northern Ireland
Progress* seconded the Working Party's emphasis on voluntary compliance
and civil, rather than criminal, penalties.[69] The Northern Ireland Regional
Committee of the CBI declined to join with the Irish Congress of Trade
Unions in support of even these modest legislative proposals.[70] When the
recommendations were eventually embodied in the Fair Employment
(Northern Ireland) Bill, the NICCI proved very cautious: "In our opinion
the Bill could make difficulties for employers and it should be studied
carefully."[71] The NICCI officer, even after the bill became law, expressed
little enthusiasm for the legislative solution: "The legislation and the
Working Party were overdone. Sometimes legislation has opposite of the

---

67. Interview with Irish Congress of Trade Unions; also Bell, *The Protestants of Ulster,*
p. 92.
68. See the next section, "Political Disorder in Ulster."
69. *Northern Ireland Progress* 23, no. 8 (August 1973): 7.
70. Interview with Irish Congress of Trade Unions.
71. *Business Letter,* NICCI, no. 10 (16 May 1975), p. 3.

intended effect. . . . The general view was that people appreciated that there was discrimination on account of religion. But nobody thought legislation would improve it. We in fact felt that the employer with professional managers was making change."

POLITICAL DISORDER IN ULSTER

The Catholic Civil Rights Protests and Protestant Response

In 1968, the three-centuries-old Protestant ascendancy came unstuck. A subordinate Catholic population, which for a half century had supported an ineffective nationalist opposition party, turned to the streets. It first joined and then moved beyond the moderate civil rights organizations, such as the Campaign for Social Justice and the Northern Ireland Civil Rights Association, and challenged the symbols and reality of Protestant domination. In Caledon, Catholic protestors seized a council flat, calling attention to the eviction of Catholic families and the ready availability of flats for even single Protestants; civil rights marches followed in Coalisland, Dungannon, and Londonderry—the last ending in a well-publicized and portentous clash between the Royal Ulster Constabulary (RUC) and the demonstrators. Attempts to impose the Public Order Act and bar future demonstrations in the walled city of Londonderry brought only more demonstrations and closer scrutiny from the outside world, particularly from Westminster.[72] With the new year, civil rights protests took on a new intensity. Civil rights marchers on a trek from Belfast to Londonderry were harassed, pummelled, and assaulted; they only occasionally gained the protection of the RUC and the Ulster B Special Constabulary. At Burntollet Bridge, just outside Londonderry, the marchers were attacked with stones and cudgels while the police watched indifferently. Subsequent police assaults on the Bogside area in Derry set the stage for the crisis and disorder we now associate with Northern Ireland. The annual march of Apprentice Boys of Derry, well rooted in Protestant traditions, brought new confrontations: in the Bogside, Catholic residents threw up barricades and pummelled the RUC with stones and petrol bombs; in West Belfast, the Catholics commandeered buses and erected barricades; in Falls Road, Catholics were driven from their homes, and in many cases the houses were burned; and finally, in Londonderry and Belfast, six thousand British troops and barbed wire were introduced to restore "peace" and separate the warring communities.[73]

72. Northern Ireland, *Disturbances in Northern Ireland*, pp. 13–16, 68–69, 114–15.
73. Rose, *Governing Without Consensus*, pp. 105–12.

The seventies belong to the Irish Republican Army (IRA), the Ulster Volunteer Force (UVF), and the British Army. In 1968 and 1969, almost no one in Northern Ireland died because of civil violence; more died because of drownings and suicides. But in 1972, almost five hundred people died because of violence, exceeding all other causes of sudden death, including road and home accidents. Two hundred and forty-five people died because of violence in 1975.[74]

The fatalities in the Bogside and West Belfast are only one measure of the forces that threatened to undo a half-century of Protestant ascendancy: legitimate political authority was questioned and eventually undermined; the economy of Northern Ireland slowly but inexorably ground to a halt.

The Unionist government, under Captain Terrence O'Neill, though weighed down by a heavy baggage of antipopery, "Ultra" constituencies and Protestant traditions in Ulster, attempted serious electoral and housing reforms. In late 1968, immediately after the initial marches and police encounters, the government made the following proposals: an ombudsman to handle complaints of discrimination, a point system for allocation of council housing to guard against discrimination, and a development commission to replace the Protestant-controlled Londonderry Corporation.[75] But these reforms, by all accounts, were very late, failing to stem the tide of Catholic discontent and failing to bring along significant Protestant support for the government. Without support from the Catholic community and with growing dissatisfaction in working-class Protestant areas and within the civil service, the O'Neill government collapsed.

Its successor, under continued pressure from Westminster, had no choice but to carry on with the reform program. The Downing Street Agreement brought "one man, one vote" to local as well as Parliamentary elections, a Community Relations Commission, and guarantees of equal employment opportunities in statutory bodies and local authorities.[76] In October 1969, the B Specials were disbanded. The Unionist government, however, did not draw strength from such reforms, and the IRA violence was undeterred. The growth of an "Ultra" opposition within Unionist ranks threatened the unity of the Protestant cause and the capacity of the government to carry out the reforms and maintain order.

The government moved in two directions simultaneously: pressing ahead with the reform program and imposing "internment without trial." Like the O'Neill government, it collapsed under the strain.

With renewed demonstrations and bloody conflict in 1972, the British government suspended the Stormont Assembly and imposed direct rule.

74. Northern Ireland, *Social and Economic Trends in Northern Ireland*, pp. 46–47.
75. Northern Ireland, *Disturbances in Northern Ireland*, p. 115.
76. *Northern Ireland Progress* 21, no. 5 (May 1971): 3–4.

The Protestants of Ulster could no longer be trusted to bring about just relations between the religious communities and establish order; in short, they could no longer exercise the Crown's authority in the North of Ireland. New elections brought fragile alliances but neither order nor a strong government. In 1974, the Ulster Workers' Council conducted a fifteen-day general strike. The "power-sharing executive" at Stormont, recognizing the lack of public support and its inability to exercise legitimate political authority, resigned.[77]

The Northern Ireland economy was sluggish in 1968; so too was the British economy. But the events of October 1968 and August 1969, the accelerating sectarian violence, and the crisis of political authority turned sluggishness into what businessmen and government officials have come to view as a continuing crisis. Tourism, promoted successfully in the sixties, began falling off by the end of the decade and evaporated by 1972.[78] New job promotions—an index of economic activity and growth—remained steady between 1968 and 1972 and fell off precipitously thereafter, particularly in 1975. Indeed, in 1975 there were half as many new job promotions as in 1968. More important, however, was the changing composition of new job promotions and the declining capacity of Northern Ireland to attract outside investment. In 1968, 44 percent of new job promotions came from outside investment, 52 percent from expansion, and 4 percent from new internal investment. But by 1971, outside sources had almost completely dried up, falling to 16 percent and, by 1975, to 10 percent. Virtually all new job promotions after 1971 came from the expansion of already established firms.[79]

For two years after the initial disorders, these figures contrasted with the NICCI's emphasis on "business as usual." But in 1971, the NICCI set out the dimensions of the crisis: Northern Ireland was losing exports; orders were dropping; there was a lack of business confidence; new industries would not locate in the North; unemployment was rising; capital was not forthcoming; productivity was dropping; and businesses were regularly disrupted. With some melodrama, it warned: "Time is running out."[80]

The Business Response: Economic Decline and Political Reform

Before the bloody events began in 1968, the business community rarely spoke of discrimination, injustice, or the need for political reforms. It

---

77. See discussions in Bell, *The Protestants of Ulster*, pp. 121–31; Martin Wallace, *Drums and Guns: Revolution in Ulster*, pp. 44–61; and Robert Fisk, *The Point of No Return*.
78. Northern Ireland, *Social and Economic Trends*, p. 57.
79. Ibid., p. 14; see also "Ulster," *The Economist*, 29 May 1971, pp. xv–xvi.
80. *Northern Ireland Progress* 21, no. 10 (October 1971): 3–4.

seemed content with bland assurances that the problems were not very serious and that, in any case, the Unionist government had events well in hand. "We are attacking our problems with some success," the NICCI declared in 1965.[81] With the first inklings of trouble in 1966, the NICCI expressed regret over the "unflattering" publicity but felt assured that these events "will ultimately be seen as a momentary interruption, perhaps a very small interruption, in the story of Northern Ireland's progress."[82] It felt no sense of urgency and made no demands for reform.

But when the government moved cautiously in 1967 to bring about selective changes in the franchise and more decisively in 1968 to bring about basic changes in the local franchise and the allocation of council housing, the business community moved with the government. The NICCI commended the O'Neill government for emphasizing the "positive side" of change, for moving beyond the "parochialism" of Ulster life and taking "the broader view of affairs." It commented: "Politicians, like businessmen, must move with the times."[83] After the troubled street scenes in October and November 1968, a group of thirty-two businessmen published a letter of support for O'Neill. They sided, at this point, not with a broad program of social and political reform, but with "all who in the present situation call for peace and harmony as against conflict and discord."[84] The NICCI also reaffirmed its identification with the O'Neill government and its interest in political reform: "There may be room for debate about the specific changes necessary in Northern Ireland, and about the timetable for reform, but the civil rights demonstrators are at least pushing at a door which is already opening. They are not trying to withstand the tide of recent history in Northern Ireland."[85]

Identification with the government and its "opening door" policies remained firm, even when O'Neill took his case to the Protestant constituencies and lost. The NICCI lauded O'Neill's broadcast appeal for support "as a turning point in Northern Ireland's affairs"; in uncharacteristic fashion, it urged businessmen to wade into the political fray:

It is not the business of this Chamber to become involved in party politics, or in the internal differences of one party. But something can be said of businessmen's attitudes, which have been made increasingly clear during the events of recent weeks, and a likely outcome of Capt. O'Neill's broadcast is that more businessmen will seek to make their voice heard by active political participation. The business community

81. Ibid., 15, no. 6 (June 1965): 5.
82. Ibid., 16, no. 8 (August 1966): 7.
83. Ibid., 17, no. 6 (June 1967): 6–7.
84. Quoted in ibid., 18, no. 12 (December 1968): 5.
85. Ibid., 18, no. 12 (December 1968): 5–6.

has not been immune from the changes which have occurred in Northern Ireland life in recent years, and in many instances has set the pace for change.[86]

Businessmen, after all, had no difficulty with the choice O'Neill gave them between a "happy and respected province, in good standing with the rest of the United Kingdom" and a "place continually torn apart by riots and demonstrations, and regarded by the rest of Britain as a political outcast."[87] The business community and the Protestant middle-class backed O'Neill with "coupons" from the *Belfast Telegraph,* at the polls, and in the party caucus, while O'Neill's own constituents gave him only a weak plurality against the Reverend Ian Paisley, the most vocal opponent of O'Neill's "new liberal Unionism."[88]

In 1969, after O'Neill's resignation, the NICCI stood firmly behind the "one-man, one-vote" principle in local elections and stated: "The sooner the new Minister can act on this matter the better."[89] It commended the new minister, Major Chichester-Clark, for moving forward in this area and urged him to carry on with new public building programs and the point system for allocating council housing.[90]

The NICCI, while proposing political reforms, tried to minimize the economic costs and the effects on British and foreign investors. The Council of the NICCI adopted a resolution to remove "any impression that industrial and commercial life had been seriously curtailed in Northern Ireland by the recent disturbances." It emphasized the minimal losses to production: only .5 percent of total productive capacity was lost; only one of twenty-three firms suffering damage was still out of operation.[91] The NICCI still pointed out the "possible dangers to the economy of the country if there should be an adverse development of the situation" and assured the government of "full support of the Chamber in healing divisions in the community."[92]

But events were not hospitable to business confidence and cautious political involvement: with violence endemic in the life of Northern Ireland, the NICCI feared that "industry and business interests, fundamental to the life of the community, are pushed on one side by the wild men."[93] The

86. Ibid., 19, no. 1 (January 1969): 3–4.
87. Wallace, *Drums and Guns,* pp. 44–47.
88. Gray, *Psalms and Slaughter,* pp. 217–18; Wallace, *Drums and Guns,* pp. 47, 60; F.W. Boal and R.H. Buchanan, "The 1969 Northern Ireland Election," pp. 79, 83; Louis Gardner, *Resurgence of the Majority,* pp. 11–14.
89. *Northern Ireland Progress* 19, no. 4 (April 1969): 6.
90. Ibid., 19, no. 6 (June 1969): 5–6.
91. Ibid., 19, no. 10 (October 1969): 6.
92. Ibid., 20, no. 2 (February 1970): 8.
93. Ibid., 20, no. 9 (September 1970): 5.

NICCI spoke openly now of bad economic prospects and the failure of simple optimism to stem the decline:

> Until early August the business position tended to follow the U.K. pattern; we were in a business recession. . . . In August the position worsened. Law and order rapidly deteriorated and many people felt that the continued optimism which had been displayed in official circles was no longer appropriate.[94]

The situation in Northern Ireland, the Chamber asserted, had "radically changed": the "outrages" had become general; there was every prospect of a "catastrophic and lasting effect."

In 1971, the NICCI restated its commitment to the full reform program, including such controversial measures as turning the RUC into a civilian police force and the disbanding of the B Specials.[95] There was no longer room for half-measures. A business community that for years was blind to discrimination and that choked on phrases like "politics" and "injustice" demanded unqualified political reforms:

> Many Roman Catholics consider that they have not been able to share in community life as they should. This must be rectified. Although recent Government legislation, as clearly stated in the Government White Paper, "A Record of Constructive Change" (Cmd. 558) should have gone a long way to meet the legitimate demands of the majority, yet it is clear from a recent statement that doubts still remain amongst responsible members of the minority.
>
> Talks must have as their aim the removing of any injustices so that all citizens in the Province have equal opportunities and equal rights —and also equal responsibilities—and with the emphasis being placed on more jobs and better housing.[96]

But the economic and political situation seemed inescapably desperate. Eighty industrial companies had suffered bomb damage between August and December of 1971: nine had not resumed production, and seven had gone out of business entirely.[97] Rather than muttering against all odds that "business carries on as usual," the NICCI despaired: "The situation today is that industry and commerce are the chief targets of the bombers."[98] With "Bloody Sunday," the resignation of the government, the suspension of Stormont, the imposition of direct rule and the prospect of more strikes, the business community was reeling. On the one hand, it reminded Protestant

94. Ibid., 21, no. 11 (November 1971): 3.
95. Ibid., 21, no. 5 (May 1971): 3-4.
96. Ibid., 21, no. 10 (October 1971): 5.
97. Ibid., 22, no. 1 (January 1972): 2.
98. Ibid., 22, no. 3 (March 1972): 5.

workers that more disruptions would "further damage ... the economy" and prospects for "jobs and orders";[99] on the other hand, it demanded that the politicians do something, almost anything, "to get us out of this mess."[100]

Businessmen in manufacturing and commerce in this century were closely identified with the Protestant ascendancy in Northern Ireland. They insisted on the English connection and eventually on the partitioning of the six counties; they lent support to the first Unionist party government, and many joined the cabinets to help defend Orange rule and draw the religious lines. At the societal level, businessmen did not resist the disenfranchisement of Catholic voters and the segregation of Catholic housing. At the work place, businessmen accommodated the sentiments of the dominant Protestant community, giving Protestant workers a privileged access to employment and promotional opportunities. Catholic workers, consequently, survived on the margins of Northern Ireland's industrial development, outside of shipbuilding and engineering and, to some extent, outside the major industrial areas.

The increasing political disorder—the Catholic civil rights campaign, the police, IRA and UVF violence—and the economic downturn cast a shadow over the half-century Protestant ascendancy in Northern Ireland. But the dismantling of explicit religious discrimination came at the hands of what would normally be considered conservative forces. The Conservative and Labour parties at Westminster insisted upon reform. The dominant Unionist party, allied with the Conservatives, met the pressure from below and outside with modest reforms in housing and franchise. It could afford reform. With a majority Protestant population, its political dominance was not threatened ipso facto by an expanded franchise. Though it administered a largely Protestant civil service, it was not weighed down by a state apparatus for controlling the movements of Catholic workers. Businessmen in secondary manufacture and commerce, who had largely accommodated the religious order, supported political reform: the disarming of the Protestant private armies, the granting of one man, one vote, and a point system for the allocation of council housing. Businessmen too could afford reform: they employed few Catholic workers and had never seriously depended upon a Protestant-dominated state to control the proletarianization of Catholic workers.

Reform, in the end, was not a "radical position," the Engineering Employers officer observed. Businessmen "were hardly speaking against the men of property"; they "were siding with the existing governments at Stormont and Westminster, both Conservative."

99. Ibid., 22, no. 4 (April 1972): 5.
100. Interview with officer of NICCI; see also *Northern Ireland Progress* 22, no. 5 (May 1972): 5–6.

PART THREE / WORKERS

CHAPTER 12

Trade Unionism in a Bounded Working Class

The role of the dominant section in the course of capitalist development is not confined to its ownership of land and capital and its manipulation of a subordinate laboring population.[1] Commercial farmers and businessmen share the stage with a working-class population that at least the latter has helped assemble. English-speaking and Afrikaans-speaking workers in South Africa and white workers in Alabama had, in some instances, left impoverished and proximate farming communities and, in others, the mines and factories of more industrialized and remote parts of the world. They took up prominent positions in the mines and iron works, in the textile mills and construction. They became integral parts of cities like Birmingham and Johannesburg. And they, like workers elsewhere in the industrialized world, formed organizations, trade unions in particular, to advance their interests.

Here, as in previous chapters, we must ask: What role will these dominant class actors and their organizations play during capitalist development? How will they react to the increasing prominence of businessmen and the increasing proletarianization of the subordinate population? How will they protect their interests in a labor market riddled with racial divisions and antagonisms? How will the organizations of dominant workers affect the race lines in the work place? Among workers generally? In the society? What role will they demand of the state?

There are a number of conventional responses to these questions. One emphasizes the racism of white workers and the inclination, particularly of artisan unions, to adopt racially exclusory practices. "The illusion of the 'primitive savage,' " G. V. Doxey writes, "cuts sharply across the reality of emerging, urban industrial workers" in South Africa. Organized white workers were determined to resist the "primitivism" that "had been admitted to their ranks" and that "constituted a threat" to "white civilization."[2] In the United States, the early craft and railway unions conventionally barred black workers from the trade unions and industrial

---

1. *Subordinate* and *dominant* refer here, as elsewhere in the book, to the sections of the population in a racially divided society.
2. G.V. Doxey, *The Industrial Colour Bar*, pp. 4–5, 196–97.

employment, lending credibility to such characterizations. The pattern was apparent in the virulent racist response of the California Federation of Labor (AFL) to the influx of Mexican workers: "If we do not remain on guard," the Federation declared in 1928, "it is not going to be our country"; government institutions would be dominated by "a mongrel population consisting largely of Mexicans."[3] The racism was also apparent in the general lethargy of the American Federation of Labor in the face of widespread racial discrimination among its construction unions and other international affiliates.[4]

Booker T. Washington and many conservative black leaders[5] had little difficulty choosing between the racism of the early artisan unions in the South and the "opportunities" offered by liberal capitalists. They urged black workers escaping the rural economy and dependent sharecropping to shun the white-dominated labor organizations; indeed, to emphasize "punctuality, reliability, dependability, loyalty," to engage in strikebreaking, and to form separate "colored artisan" unions that might undermine the position of the white trade unions.[6] They understood what by now has become conventional wisdom: white working-class organizations "protect their mostly white membership from potential workers, many of whom are black."[7]

A variation on this response concentrates on a privileged element within the working class as a whole, which occupies the best paid and more skilled and secure positions and, by one account, constitutes an "aristocracy of labor." These privileged workers of the dominant section have little in common with the mass of unskilled, subordinate workers. They identify instead with the bourgeoisie and, indeed, collaborate in the "extraction of surplus value," in exploiting "the majority of the working class."[8] By participating as supervisors in the productive process, others have argued, they forfeit their affiliation even with the already narrow "white working class."[9] Sections of the dominant wage-earning group emerge as a "petty-bourgeois" element, fully allied with sections of capital against the interest of subordinate workers.[10]

3. See Stanley B. Greenberg, *Politics and Poverty*, p. 191.
4. See Louis L. Knowles and Kenneth Prewitt, *Institutional Racism in America*, pp. 22–24; and William J. Wilson, *Power, Racism, and Privilege*, pp. 107–8.
5. By no means was black leadership unanimous in this advice. See chapter 15.
6. See the more extended discussion in Greenberg, *Politics and Poverty*, pp. 179–87.
7. Knowles and Prewitt, *Institutional Racism*, p. 22.
8. Robert Davies, "The White Working-Class in South Africa," p. 49.
9. Howard Simson, "The Myth of the White Working Class in South Africa," pp. 196–97, 202–3.
10. Robert Davies, David Kaplan, Mike Morris, and Dan O'Meara, "Class Struggle and the Periodisation of the State in South Africa," pp. 10–13, 19–20.

Another, very different response emphasizes the increasing importance of industrial and general unions which are necessarily expansive and hostile to racial divisions in the society. The Steelworkers' Organizing Committee and the United Automobile Workers, for example, challenged the narrow hold and the racial practices of the Amalgamated Association of Iron, Steel and Tin Workers and the Mechanics Educational Society of America, respectively. They organized the full range of occupations in heavy industry, no matter how menial or low paid. But these unions also emerged as spokesmen for working-class political action and greater equality in the society at large. They supported a national minimum wage, national health insurance, and legislation to end racial discrimination in housing and voting. Their viability as unions depended upon their opposing sectional advantage in the work place and the society.[11] The Gasworkers, Seamen, and other unions in England, while continuing to rely on strikes and collective bargaining, sought protection by "legal enactment." Their viability also depended on the inclusiveness of their organizations, the steady expansion of franchise rights, and the legal commitment to minimum standards in wages, hours, and working conditions.[12]

One set of responses emphasizes the racism and narrowness of labor organization among dominant workers and the willingness of privileged sections to seek their own advantage at the expense of subordinate workers. The other emphasizes the necessary expansiveness of the emerging industrial and general workers' unions and their need to break down barriers, including racial ones, in the labor market and society.

But while these responses accurately reflect aspects of trade unionism within a racially divided labor force, they provide insufficient and, in some important respects, inaccurate answers to our primary questions and an inadequate analysis of trade unionism in racial orders. Above all, they fail to identify the processes in working-class life that should bring about an elaboration of the racial order.

The artisan unions, as already suggested, should identify closely with the racial order: there is a consonance between their own efforts to establish a monopoly of skills and the racial barriers that legitimize and facilitate the exclusion of subordinate, unskilled workers. But their exclusory practices are narrowly focused and do not require the elaboration of a state machinery to control the movements and proletarianization of subordinate workers. But dominant workers in mass industries, with little "job control" and skill scarcity, face different risks and imperatives. Their position is

---

11. See Irving Bernstein, *Turbulent Years*, p. 454; also see discussion of this position in chapter 15.
12. Sidney and Beatrice Webb, *Industrial Democracy*, p. 263.

threatened by the willingness of employers to substitute "cheaper" sub-ordinate workers and the precariousness of multiracial organization in a racial order. Some may, nonetheless, take the conventional route, opting to break down racial barriers and organize on a broad multiracial basis. But that path, as we shall see, is strewn with barriers to effective organization. Many should opt to organize on a racially exclusive basis and depend on the state and society for job protection.[13] They need and may demand a state machinery that maintains vigilance over the work place and labor market: erecting rigid job barriers, segregating industries, limiting the pro-letarianization of the subordinate population, and providing subsidized opportunities for dominant employment.

THE BOUNDED WORKING CLASS

To understand the role of dominant workers during capitalist development, we must be clear at the outset about their position in the productive process and labor market. In each of the racial orders, the dominant wage-earning population at some point constituted a full-fledged working class, made up of artisans and well-paid workers, to be sure, but also of unskilled and semiskilled workers in extractive industries and manufacturing and govern-ment service. We must not mistake the dominant worker's privilege as a member of the dominant section for his class position. Social status and political privilege do not necessarily translate into privilege or status in the labor market, though they may.

It is tempting, for example, to view dominant workers prima facie as "an aristocracy among the working class,"[14] set off from the subordinate working population. They are in this view well situated in the productive process, facing few of the uncertainties of the labor market and exhibiting many of the pretensions of the "better" classes. Like the "sober respectable artisans" described by Thompson and Hobsbawm, these privileged workers receive regular and decent wages, social security from their own friendly societies, respect at the work place and, to some extent, outside of it.[15] They escape the "world of extreme hardship, illiteracy, very widespread de-moralisation" that characterizes the life of unskilled workers.[16]

13. The affinity of general and industrial unions for exclusory practices and growing state control of the subordinate population is not the expectation, however, with which I began. At the outset of this project, and even after the South African field research, I believed that industrial unionism was necessarily inclusive. The Alabama and Israel research forced me to reexamine the basis for my earlier position.
14. F. Engels, *The Condition of the Working-Class in England,* p. 35.
15. E.P. Thompson, *The Making of the English Working Class,* p. 769; and E.J. Hobsbawm, *Labouring Men,* p. 273.
16. Thompson, *The Making of the English Working Class,* p. 814.

That the working class in nineteenth-century or even early twentieth-century Britain was divided into two distinct sections—sober artisans and laborers—was doubted by few contemporaries. Lenin spoke of the " 'upper stratum' of the workers, providing the principal membership of the trade unions, co-operatives, and religious sects, and the 'lower stratum of the proletariat proper.' "[17] While Marx joined many of the spokesmen of "new model unionism" in the International Working Men's Association, he warned the delegates against their privilege and against conspiring in the "wage system." The labor aristocrats, he stated, should "act as the champions and representatives of the whole working class," should "enlist the non-society men in their ranks" and "convince the world at large that their efforts, far from being narrow and selfish, aim at the emancipation of the downtrodden millions."[18] Employers and artisans too accepted the distinction. The employer believed, Hobsbawm writes, that "workers could be divided into two groups: the 'artisans', in possession of special skills or qualifications, and the mass of 'common labour', which could be hired, fired, or interchanged at will, without making any appreciable difference to efficiency."[19] And the artisan himself, while recognizing the ambiguities in his status, insisted upon the class and economic distinctions that separated him from the stratum of laborers.[20]

The racial orders have, in fact, included dominant workers who "could be hired, fired, or interchanged at will," who were hardly "sober" or "respectable," who lived with "extreme hardship, illiteracy and very widespread demoralisation." Their position diverged radically from that of other dominant workers who established their own skill scarcity, job security, and wage standards. The dominant wage-earning population should be viewed, therefore, as a *bounded working class*, including in varying proportions an "aristocracy among the working class" and a "lower stratum," but both set off from the subordinate wage-earning population of the "proletariat proper."

In a racial order, there is a powerful presumption that labor organizations within the bounded working class will confine their appeals and political work to the dominant section of the population. They may adopt a narrow, artisan approach, focusing on skill scarcity and apprenticeships; or they may adopt the strategies of general and industrial unions elsewhere: joining broad political issues and employing the customary baggage of strikes,

---

17. V.I. Lenin, *Imperialism,* p. 105.
18. Cited in David Fernbach, "Introduction," in Karl Marx, *The First International and After,* p. 18; G.D.H. Cole, *A Short History of the British Working-Class Movement, 1889–1947,* pp. 192–93.
19. Hobsbawm, *Labouring Men,* p. 322.
20. Ibid., pp. 275, 296.

collective bargaining, and work rules. They may define their relation to capital in conventional class terms of property and exploitation. In a racial order, however, such narrow or broad appeals are conventionally contained within the confines of the bounded working class.[21]

We will consider two forms of organization within the bounded working class: the artisan unions and the industrial and general workers' unions. They by no means exhaust the organizational options available. We might have referred, for example, to the anarcho-syndicalist approach of the International Workers of the World (IWW), or the early Confédération Générale du Travail Unitaire (CGT), or even the revolutionary "proletarian internationalism" of the International Socialist League in South Africa.[22] But anarcho-syndicalism was not very important to the organization of dominant workers in the racial orders. Dominant workers relied primarily on labor unions that preached "job control" or collective bargaining, that raised bread-and-butter issues or collectivist and socialist goals within the framework of nonrevolutionary political action.

ARTISAN UNIONS: CREATING POCKETS OF PRIVILEGE

Controlling the Supply of Labor

Artisan unions emerged at critical points in industry where groups of workers in skilled or strategic positions were able to formalize by organization their scarcity or importance. They made a special claim to status in the industry and to protection from the competition of unorganized and unskilled operatives. In Britain, the "new model" unionism of the mid-nineteenth century brought a little less Owenism and Chartism and much greater emphasis on apprenticeships, "vested interests of the craftsmen in his trade," entry restrictions, and "friendly benefits."[23] A few decades later, "new model" unionism also became important in Italy, particularly with the formation of a national federation of typographical workers and the diffusion of local hatters' organizations. The hatters, typographical workers, and other craft organizations established "price lists" for their labor,

---

21. The presumption that organizing efforts will be confined to the bounded working class does not necessarily preclude broader appeals. But the presumption affects the nature of the appeal and the prospects for success.

22. See A. Lerumo, *Fifty Fighting Years: The South African Communist Party 1921–1971*, pp. 37–45.

23. Sydney and Beatrice Webb, *The History of Trade Unionism*, p. 217; Hobsbawm, *Labouring Men*, p. 350.

conditions of apprenticeship, and identification cards.[24] In France, the hatters and printers formed similar organizations but also local federations of crafts, called the Bourse du Travail, which combined the functions of the labor exchange and workers' club with a view toward controlling the local market for labor.[25]

The exclusive artisan unions were a declining force in British industry before the outbreak of war in 1914. Capitalist enterprise was turning toward mechanization, a large group of semiskilled operatives, and a less clearly bifurcated wage structure. The small class of highly skilled artisans and large class of undifferentiated, low-paid, and unskilled workers—many of them women and children—seemed more and more inappropriate to the new industries and even to many of the old.[26] Artisan unions survived, nonetheless, in the building industry and printing; their monopoly position was maintained in some parts of the iron and steel industry. Others "diluted" their crafts. The traditional artisan unions both in Britain and the United States maintained artisan organizations in some sectors while steadily expanding their jurisdiction over industrial groups of lesser skill. "The craft unions of the thirties" in the United States, such as the Machinists and Electricians, and the artisan unions of early twentieth-century Britain became "both craft and industrial in varying proportions."[27]

At the outset, these unions established their positions in industry and among other working-class organizations by controlling the supply of labor, by adopting what H. A. Turner calls a "closed" approach or what the Webbs describe as the "Device of Restriction of Numbers."[28] By focusing upon and creating this narrow monopoly, the artisan unions could avoid the strike, except as "a last defense against some fundamental attack on their right to exist . . . or on their mode of operation."[29] They could, consequently, insulate themselves to a large extent from other workers and the state. Until changing patterns of industrialization forced some dilution of the crafts, the artisan unions faced no imperative to expand the size of their organizations: "Their interest lies rather in the opposite direction," Turner writes, "of limiting the intake of labour to the jobs that they control, and thereby restricting also the membership of the union itself."[30] They did not

24. Daniel L. Horowitz, *The Italian Labor Movement*, pp. 37–38.
25. Val R. Lorwin, "France," pp. 321–26.
26. Hobsbawm, *Labouring Men*, pp. 293, 300–01.
27. John T. Dunlop, "Structural Changes in the American Labor Movement and Industrial Relations System," pp. 108–9; also see the discussion of the "special trade sections" in French industry in Val R. Lorwin, *The French Labor Movement*, p. 151.
28. H.A. Turner, *Trade Union Growth: Structure and Policy*, p. 138; Webb, *Industrial Democracy*, pp. 560–61.
29. Turner, *Trade Union Growth*, p. 208.
30. Ibid., p. 242.

require alliances to bolster their bargaining or strike position. They deferred to other organizations and other workers to raise questions of broad social policy.[31] Indeed, the artisan unions discouraged expanded state activity that might impinge on traditional trade-union functions, such as controlling the supply of labor or providing death benefits.[32]

The Narrow Racial Exclusions

It is difficult to imagine that artisan unions would not find the racial order enormously congenial. Unions that ordinarily focus upon entry barriers to jobs and union membership should have little difficulty working within a labor framework that insists on privilege and barriers in the labor market. Where artisan unions encounter unskilled, physically distinctive, and socially stigmatized workers, they will almost certainly develop policies that discriminate against them.[33] The race lines further limit access to skilled positions and help legitimate the artisans' job monopoly in the larger dominant public.

Artisan unions in a bounded working class may be able to maintain a more effective monopoly over their skills over a longer period of time than unions in nonracial settings. Their job control depends not only on their "natural" skill scarcity but on race barriers that exclude large numbers of workers from this section of the labor market. New technology and mechanization need only displace skilled workers if management is free to substitute workers of lesser skill. And where artisan organizations are, nonetheless, forced to dilute their crafts, they may be in a better position to impose limits on the downgrading, particularly where the downgrading comes up against the boundaries of the bounded working class. The Webbs' confidence that controlled entry to the trades would dissolve before the "incessant revolutionising of industrial processes" and that "only an infinitesimal number of Trade Unions actually succeed in limiting the number of persons who become candidates for employment"—perhaps appropriate to Britain and the United States—may be misplaced in a racial order.[34]

The consonance of job control and racial discrimination produces a rigid, perhaps enduring barrier in the labor market but only a limited effect on the society as a whole. By establishing an effective monopoly in a corner of the

31.   James Q. Wilson, *Political Organizations*, p. 139; J. David Greenstone, *Labor in American Politics*, pp. 365–67.
32.   Abraham L. Gitlow, *Labor and Industrial Society*, pp. 29–30.
33.   See Wilson, *Political Organizations*, p. 126; see Orley Ashenfelter, "Discrimination and Trade Unions," p. 96.
34.   Webb, *Industrial Democracy*, p. 713.

labor market, the artisan union is, ironically, freed from the broader questions in race domination. The skilled worker in the bounded working class cannot be easily displaced by employers intent on substituting cheaper, lesser skilled workers; nor is he easily dislodged by processes in development or "swamped" by the increasing influx of subordinate workers into industry. There is little need for a state, therefore, that will continually intrude in the labor market on the side of dominant labor, that will protect dominant workers from the acts of employers and the competition of subordinate workers. The artisan unions should be content with a state that facilitates apprenticeships and licensing and that leaves the artisan unions free to exercise their job control.

INDUSTRIAL AND GENERAL UNIONS: THE DIALECTICS OF RACE DOMINATION

Preventing Undercutting

Working-class political and labor activity in England began on a rudimentary level, often allied with the middle class against the remnants of feudalism. But food riots soon mixed with labor disputes and a "wage movement pure and simple";[35] the "astonishing mass conversion to Protestant sectarianism" began to encompass "labor sects" and working-class congregations;[36] and enthusiasm for the Reform Bill of 1832 gave way to the People's Charter, Chartism, and the first genuine working-class political movement.[37] By the mid-nineteenth century, the European working class had its own views on political economy and, increasingly, its own organizations.

The industrial and general workers' unions emerged quite suddenly, sometimes with only a minor stimulus. Hobsbawm notes, "Unions, previously almost unknown, become universal overnight."[38] The impediments to organization—"the deadweight of tradition," "irregular labour," and the "craftsman-labourer pattern"— crumbled before the sheer force of industrial unionism. In Britain, at the very end of the nineteenth century, the dockers' strike and the organization of the Gasworkers' Union brought thousands of unskilled workers, previously considered inhospitable to

35. George Rudé, *The Crowd in History*, pp. 126–33.
36. E.J. Hobsbawm, *Primitive Rebels*, pp. 128–39.
37. See Rudé, *The Crowd in History*, pp. 179–91; Asa Briggs, "Chartism's Geographic and Economic Divisions," pp. 72–75.
38. Hobsbawm, *Labouring Men*, pp. 171–72.

organization, into the trade-union movement.[39] Between 1892 and 1912, while craft-union membership doubled in size, general unions increased almost threefold and industrial unions almost sixfold. In 1914, only one in twelve trade union members belonged to local craft organizations.[40]

The Confédération Générale du Travail Unitaire (CGT) in France, though encompassing both craft and industrial unions in its early years, later insisted that unions organize exclusively along industrial lines: craft organization and syndicalism did not exist comfortably together in the same confederation. The surge of industrial unionism, however, came only in the mid-thirties with the sitdown strikes, the Popular Front government, and the Matignon Agreement. The surrender of management and the new industrial legislation brought a miraculous growth in union membership: the CGT, for example, grew from one to five million members within a year.[41] With the passage of the Wagner Act in the United States, also in the mid-thirties, industrial unions, which had suffered under recurring waves of labor "injunctions," police repression, and company unions, gained a foothold in the mass industries. The CIO brought industrial organization to the steel, automobile, and rubber industries.

The industrial and general workers' unions incorporate workers in developing manufacturing who exercise little job control, whose skills are readily available and whose positions are readily undermined by the availability of "cheaper" substitute labor. The effectiveness of these organizations depends in large part, then, on their ability to fix the price of labor, establish a "rate for the job," and prevent undercutting—Turner's "open" approach and the Webbs' "Device of the Common Rule."[42]

In the absence of job monopolies, these unions are necessarily expansive. Large numbers of workers and coverage over a range of occupations are critical to collective bargaining, strikes, and political action. The "view that wages could and should be raised at the employers' expense, not that of the other workers and would be more likely to be so raised if trade unionism became general," Turner writes, "seems implicit in their organizing policy."[43]

These unions are also inescapably political. Their ability to organize broadly or fix a common rate at the work place depends heavily on the legal framework and the economic climate. They have never had the luxury, as have the artisan unions, to "not allow any political matter to be discussed

39. Webb, *The History of Trade Unionism*, pp. 404–07.
40. Hobsbawm, *Labouring Men*, pp. 180–81.
41. Lorwin, "France," pp. 341–42.
42. Turner, *Trade Union Growth*, p. 138; Webb, *Industrial Democracy*, pp. 560–61.
43. Turner, *Trade Union Growth*, p. 161.

at all nor entertained among us."[44] The widespread use of child and female labor threatened the precarious economic position of factory operatives; legal opinions, like the *Taff Vale* case in Britain and the *Danbury Hatters'* case in the United States, threatened the legal and financial standing of the unions; and injunctions and victimization threatened their right to withhold labor.[45]

The politics of industrial and general unionism, however, has ranged broadly between business unionism and syndicalism. In some cases, politics meant little more than lobbying for industry-specific legislation. Cotton workers sought legal limitation on the use of female and child labor in the textile factories; the seamen's federation sought safety regulation for British merchant shipping.[46] Some unions have supported labor legislation with a broader impact on wage standards. The miners and cotton operatives in Britain supported legal regulation on hours of work and working conditions;[47] the AFL-CIO, since the Second World War, has supported full employment policies and minimum-wage legislation. Many unions, however, have not been willing to settle for such wage and industry-specific concerns. They have attempted to broaden the franchise and labor's influence over political leaders. The "new unionists" of the British socialist movement sought to exploit the democratic social structure, demanding an expanded franchise, labor representation on town councils, and, eventually, the formation of the Labour party.[48] In the United States, labor's interest in party politics went hand in hand with the rise of industrial unionism.[49]

Finally, a few broad-based unions rejected both the narrow path of the craft unions and the "empirical socialism" of the industrial unions. Their political involvement was much broader, apocalyptic, and revolutionary and focused on what was then called "syndicalism." "Direct action" and the "general strike," the tools in syndicalist political action, avoided the limitations in existing political institutions and the conventionality of the established trade unions. Syndicalism was important within the CGT before Matignon,[50] in major sections of the British trade-union movement at the turn of the century,[51] and provided the impetus for the spectacular but short career of the Industrial Workers of the World.

---

44. Ibid., p. 181.
45. See Hobsbawm, *Labouring Men,* p. 182.
46. Turner, *Trade Union Growth,* p. 181.
47. Webb, *The History of Trade Unionism,* p. 313.
48. Ibid., pp. 412–18.
49. Greenstone, *Labor in American Politics,* pp. 364–65.
50. Lorwin, "France," pp. 238–39.
51. Cole, *British Working-Class Movement,* pp. 321–25.

Elaborating the State Racial Apparatus

The economic pessimism of the manual group is at the bottom of its character-
istic manner of adjusting the relation of the individual to the whole group. It
prompts also the attitude of exclusion which manual groups assume towards
those regarded as "outsiders."

Selig Perlman,
A Theory of the Labor Market, *1928*[52]

The multiracialism of industrial unionism, suggested at the outset of this chapter, follows from a simple but compelling scenario: unions organized in the dominant section that cannot create job monopolies based on skill scarcity must organize on a broad basis and attempt to fix a "rate for the job." Their ability to forestall the substitution of cheaper,[53] perhaps subordinate labor, their effectiveness in collective bargaining, and the power of their strikes depends, in the end, on their skill in reaching beyond the bounded working class, to somehow win over the incorporate subordinate workers.[54] If industrial unions are to insure a rising wage standard within industry, they must help insure a rising "common rule" in the society at large. They cannot focus exclusively on the bounded working class without undercutting their own position and standards. Indeed, the greater the wage gap between organized workers in the dominant section and the un-organized outside of it, the greater the employer's incentive for labor substitution and undercutting.

It is a plausible scenario. And certainly in industries where subordinate workers are present in large numbers, where they are employed in positions alongside dominant workers, and where there is little skill differentiation, unions would be hard pressed to organize on any other basis. Nonetheless, we should not underestimate the difficulty of open industrial unionism[55] in a racial order and the likely costs. Multiracial industrial unions are organized against the tenor of the society: often against the inclinations of

---

52. Selig Perlman, *A Theory of the Labor Movement,* p. 241.
53. Michael Reich and his associates state, for example, that "employers actively and consciously foster labor market segmentation in order to 'divide and conquer' the labor force." Their effectiveness is apparent, at least by inference, in the depressing effects of black job-seekers on white wages (Michael Reich, David M. Gordon, and Richard C. Edwards, "A Theory of Labor Market Segmentation," p. 361; Michael Reich, "The Economics of Racism," pp. 110–11; also see Victor Perlo, *Economics of Racism, U.S.A.,* pp. 4–10).
54. Ashenfelter, "Discrimination and Trade Unions," pp. 96, 110. The ratio of black to white wages is also increased by unionization in industrial sectors (while reduced in craft sectors).
55. Open industrial unionism refers to labor organizations that do not exercise a job monopoly based upon skill scarcity or strategic importance in the productive process and that, instead, attempt to bargain collectively for a large proportion of the employees in an industry regardless of race.

the dominant workers directly involved, and almost always against the prevailing sentiments in the dominant section and the general direction of state policy. Without the support of the state, industrial unions in nonracial settings have found it very difficult to gain employer recognition or to insure the effectiveness of their strikes. Industrial unions may, nonetheless, choose to live with their marginality and ignore the costs: the ostracism, charges of race mixing, the strikebreakers, and political repression.

Or they may decide to take advantage of opportunities in a racial order that sometimes permit an exclusive industrial unionism.[56] Set against the ambiguities and indeed improbability of multiracialism are a variety of approaches that enable dominant workers to create artificial skill scarcity, limit undercutting, and reduce the supply of subordinate workers. Each, as we shall see, requires an elaborate state machinery for policing employers and the labor market and controlling the movements of subordinate workers.

The industrial unions may help erect barriers around areas of dominant employment, limiting the entry of subordinate workers, thereby preventing undercutting. Though the reserved positions may prove only marginally different in skill content from other positions, minor differences can be exaggerated into inviolable demarcations. The reserved jobs can acquire special privileges and levels of remuneration. Dominant workers here, consequently, can fix a "civilized" rate of pay without fear that an influx of cheaper, subordinate workers might displace them. The divvying up of jobs on a racial basis against the inclinations of employers or the forces in the labor market, however, depends on the continuing support of dominant society and perhaps the regulative powers of the state.

Industrial unions may insist upon segregation, or parallel development, in an industry. However, if capital is mobile and the state indifferent, investment will flow to the unorganized, subordinate section within the industry; income and employment will fall in the dominant section.[57] Industrial unions will opt for segregation, therefore, only where the union and state can restrict the movement of capital or where the union "rate for the job" can be imposed on the nonunion sector. Both policies protect employment in the dominant section while creating unemployment among subordinate workers.[58] Both policies, however, require that strong coercive measures rule the market.

---

56. Exclusive industrial unionism refers to labor organizations that do not exercise a job monopoly and that attempt to bargain collectively and organize broadly within an industrial space cleared of subordinate workers.

57. Kenneth J. Arrow, "The Theory of Discrimination," pp. 17–18; Gary S. Becker, *The Economics of Discrimination*, pp. 22–27, 56.

58. Joseph E. Stiglitz, "Theories of Discrimination and Economic Policy," p. 9.

With strong support from the dominant section, industrial unions may be able to insist on a radical segregation of the capitalist mode of production —that is, the exclusion of subordinate workers from specific industries or the exclusion of subordinate workers from industry itself. Both approaches allow industrial unions to concentrate on fixing wage levels and organizing broadly but within a working space cleared of subordinate workers. Such policies, probably more than others we have considered, require an elaborate repressive network and structure of race domination that allow severe controls on the rural economy and the movements of subordinate workers. Ultimately, they must enlist the support of commercial farmers who also have a stake in the limited proletarianization of the subordinate population.

Industrial and general unions should support broad social welfare policies that, in this context, exacerbate inequalities between the racial sections. With rigid barriers separating dominant and subordinate industrial workers, the unions can allow a rising "Common Rule" within the dominant section and ignore or take advantage of lower standards in the subordinate one. They should support, for example, a legislative framework granting unions recognition and the right to strike and protecting workers from victimization, providing unemployment compensation, social security, and health care; they will not insist, however, that the programs reach beyond the bounded working class. As long as racial barriers remain high, poor or deteriorating standards in the subordinate section do not affect the standards of dominant workers. Indeed, to the extent that these programs enhance the labor productivity of dominant workers and retard that of the subordinate ones, market mechanisms will reinforce "artificial" racial barriers.

The success of exclusive industrial unionism depends on the continuing legitimacy of racially exclusory policies in the society at large. The barring of subordinate workers from specific jobs, the segregation of the work place and industry, in the absence of marked skill or productivity differences, must be buttressed by nonmarket, non-trade-union interventions—the racism of the dominant public, the support of other interests within the dominant section, and ultimately, the state. Without those interventions, industrial unions must opt for oblivion or the ambiguities in multiracialism.

There is considerable certainty and consistency in the position of artisan unions in a racial order. Their exclusory policies and job monopolies sit comfortably with the race barriers that divide up the working class and society. Together, race lines and skill scarcity create a rigid barrier in the labor market, one that should be apparent early in capitalist development and that should prove enduring despite developing pressures to dilute industrial skills. But the strength of the barrier and their job monopoly enable artisan unions to focus narrowly, to play down questions of undercutting or "swamping" and, therefore, to make only limited demands on the racial order and state.

But there is little certainty or consistency in the position of industrial and general workers' unions. They may move between two extremes: open industrial unionism against the general thrust of dominant society and state policy; exclusive industrial unionism with the elaboration of the racial order and state racial apparatus. Which course they pursue and when depend on a mix of factors, by no means idiosyncratic, but with an uncertain relationship to the level of development. Among the factors are the extent of racial integration in industry prior to unionization; the extent of pro-letarianization of the subordinate population; the degree of skill differentia-tion in industry; the relative political standing of other groups in dominant society, such as commercial farmers or primary manufacturers; and the willingness of the state to protect dominant employment, control the movements of subordinate labor, and limit the employer's freedom of enterprise. In combination these factors can yield contradictory results: a high level of integration in an industry, with a continuing influx of subordinate labor and a limited state and societal interest in regulating the industrial labor market, may bring multiracial, open industrial unionism; but the same level of "mixing" and "swamping" in the presence of a strong societal interest in safeguarding dominant labor and a strong state racial apparatus may allow an exclusive industrial unionism—with the full panoply of job protections and segregation policies.

Trade unionism in a bounded working class suffers, it seems, from a touch of Tom Watson, the Georgia populist. He too lived with the racial divisions and the ambiguities of a racial order, and, like the industrial unions, C. Vann Woodward writes, held "attitudes as completely contradic-tory and extreme as possible." The ambiguity drove him first to organize black and white tenant farmers—"You are kept apart," he warned them, "that you may be fleeced separately"—and later to despise and disen-franchise the black man—"The white people dare not revolt so long as they can be intimidated by the fear of the negro vote." There is perhaps a bit of schizophrenia or opportunism here but also dialectical processes that lead a Tom Watson, and industrial unions, to both multiracialism and the racial order.[59]

59. C. Vann Woodward, *Tom Watson, Agrarian Rebel,* pp. 220, 237.

CHAPTER 13

The Artisan Unions in South Africa: Pockets of Privilege in a Bounded Working Class

There's only one class here, first class . . . and last, for the wogs.

British immigrant to South Africa, 1973[1]

The diamond diggings at Kimberley and gold mining on the Witwatersrand brought the Cornish miner and the African peasant into the same modern, productive framework. Together they washed diamonds and crushed stones. They joined in a process that cut a gaping hole into Griqualand West and blasted out the underbelly of Johannesburg. Some workers, black and white, brought their own shovels and pickaxes; some laid claim to the diamonds and gold that hid beneath the surface. But soon these miners would work or supervise machines they could not own and receive wages for labor they could no longer control. The flow of diamonds to Amsterdam and gold bullion to Zurich followed on the heels of proletarianization, the emergence of a working class, in South Africa.

Capitalist development and proletarianization represented an enormous upheaval: luring African peasants from their kraals and European-owned farms and English-speaking workers from the British mines, countryside, and cities, indeed, from as far away as Australia and California; substituting a new technology and work organization for the subsistence and serflike conditions prevailing in the South African rural areas; and stirring together a seemingly endless variety of languages, cultures, skills, and experiences.

But the upheaval and emerging production relations had little impact on racial divisions that characterized European settlement in southern Africa from the seventeenth century. Assumptions that ruled the Colonial Office, the Kaffir Wars, and Afrikaner farms were reconstructed for use in the mines and workshops. "In South Africa we have not got a homogeneous population," the longtime leader of the Labour Party, Colonel Creswell,

---

1. Quoted in John Stone, *Colonist or Uitlander?* p. 204.

observed. "We have two races separated by the wide gulf of history and civilization; a gulf of difference in material wants which are considered necessary for life."[2]

But more than historic assumptions stood between European and African workers. They were separated by two fundamentally different patterns of labor recruitment and proletarianization. One drew on European labor, much of it skilled or experienced in mining operations. The newly consolidated diamond syndicate and highly capitalized deep-gold-mining enterprises paid dearly for skills considered scarce in southern Africa and some considered scarce even in Europe.[3] The other pattern drew on the African peasantry, but these workers, unlike their European counterparts, had few industrial skills that might command high rates of pay. Behind each African wage earner stood a fragile, peasant economy and the weight of labor-repressive legislation. The former, while supplementing African mine wages, provided an erratic but increasing supply of labor to the mines.[4] The latter, representing a mixture of taxes, pass laws, masters and servants ordinances, contracts, and compounds helped insure the availability and stability of African labor. For the European worker, and most observers at the time, those arrangements spelled "cheap labor."

The European worker might, nonetheless, as the Simons suggest, have affirmed his "class outlook" and resisted the early trappings of a bounded working class.[5] He might have ignored his own advantages in the labor market, including the limited supply of European workers and his virtual monopoly over skills indispensable to mining operations. He might have ignored differences in language, culture, and organizational experience. Rather than resort at the outset to "protectionist" strategies, the European worker might have challenged the vast complex of constraints that undermined the economic and bargaining position of the African laborer. He might, consequently, have attacked the farmer's reliance on masters and servants ordinances and hut taxes and the mining company's use of "closed compounds" and pass laws. The European worker, though employed in volatile and uncertain enterprises, though only weakly organized and politically marginal, could have aligned himself with international class

2. Quoted in Guy Routh, "Industrial Relations and Race Relations," pp. 7–8.
3. G.V. Doxey, *The Industrial Colour Bar in South Africa,* pp. 22–23; Robert Davies, "Mining Capital, The State and Unskilled White Workers in South Africa, 1901–1913," p. 46; Sheila T. van der Horst, *Native Labour in South Africa,* p. 81; C.W. de Kiewiet, *A History of South Africa. Social and Economic,* p. 91.
4. For discussions of this relationship, see Harold Wolpe, "Capitalism and Cheap Labour-Power in South Africa: From Segregation to Apartheid"; and Peter Harris, "Industrial Workers in Rhodesia, 1946–1972: Working Class Elites or Lumpenproletariat?" pp. 147–56.
5. H.J. and R.E. Simons, *Class and Colour in South Africa 1850–1950,* pp. 94–95.

principles against the Colonial Office, the Afrikaner farmer, the mining houses, the tenor of colonial and settler thinking, and his own short-term, and probably long-term, economic interests.

For the European worker, that alignment seemed more than a little fanciful. He accepted, instead, as did his employer and general European opinion, that the working population was divided rigidly between a European sector encompassing the most skilled and stable employment and a "native" sector encompassing the least skilled and marginal. While competition might exist within these sectors, in the "area between them one did not sink and the other did not rise."[6]

The racial division of labor and the hierarchy provided the initial outlines for a bounded working class in South Africa. They were fashioned by businessmen, the Colonial Office, and the European workers; they depended on genuine differences in skill scarcity, patterns of labor recruitment, wages and material expectations, and probably the racism of European settlers.[7] They shaped proletarianization and working class organization even after the European wage-earning population included men and women of little skill and industrial experience, after changing patterns of industrialization opened up opportunities for semiskilled African and European workers, and even after sections of the African population gained industrial skills of their own and began moving into areas to which one "did not rise."

The development of a bounded working class in South Africa and the emergence of organizations within it had a profound and continuing influence on the nature of the racial order. Artisan organizations were established early in the process and helped create an array of racial job demarcations in the labor market but had a limited impact on the state and racial structure. Organization among Europeans of lesser skill brought some attempts at multiracialism on the margins, but principally featured concerted efforts to elaborate the structure of race domination and the state racial apparatus. The exclusive industrial unions, first on the mines, later in government service and in some parts of secondary manufacture, demanded that the state reserve occupations for white workers, provide employment for "civilized" workers at "civilized rates of pay," suppress African labor organization, and limit the proletarianization of African workers.

6. De Kiewiet, *A History of South Africa,* p. 95.
7. The asserted gulf between higher and lower orders of civilization may have been, as Doxey suggests, a racist contrivance. "Traditional prejudices" act on real and imaginary differences between racial groups and gain "overt expression" in an array of racial demarcations and exclusions. The British worker, newly arrived on the mines, no less than the Boer farmer, gave ready acceptance to these distinctions. Doxey, *The Industrial Colour Bar,* pp. 4, 196; also Phyllis Lewsen, ed., *Selections from the Correspondence of John X. Merriman, 1905–24,* p. 243.

THE ARTISAN UNIONS

The organization of the developing European working class in South Africa began on a rudimentary level, drawing on diverse traditions of British and European labor and incorporating some traditions indigenous to South Africa. At Kimberley, the European diggers formed committees that attempted, among other things, to place controls on African and Coloured claimants and laborers.[8] But they remained largely unorganized as laborers until 1883, when the companies attempted to search white miners for errant diamonds, as they had always searched Africans. The white miners turned to strikes, demonstrations, and riots: they would not be reduced to the "Kaffir's level." Soon afterward, in 1891, the white miners formed a chapter of the Knights of Labor and vowed to wage "perpetual war and opposition to the encroachment of monopoly and organized capital." The Knights of Labor provided a short-lived exercise in organization but a number of lessons that would influence future efforts at labor organization. Its struggle was waged on two fronts, against the traditional foe, De Beers and other mining concerns, and against "cheap labour competition," in this instance, the developing African proletariat.[9]

But before the turn of the century, labor organizations with more modest goals, with direct ties to the "new model" unionism in Britain, were established in the coastal cities and on the Witwatersrand. As in Philadelphia and London, the typographical workers were among the first to organize, taking in Coloured artisans in Cape Town but only Europeans, largely English-speaking, in the Transvaal.[10] Before the South African War, the Witwatersrand Mine Employees' and Mechanics' Union took in a range of traditional craftsmen, lobbied for the eight-hour day, safety measures, and workmen's compensation, and defended the moderate intentions of South Africa's fledgling trade-union movement.[11] Soon after the war, the boilermakers, bricklayers, carpenters, iron moulders, printers, and other craftsmen formed the Witwatersrand Trades and Labour Council. It too spoke of the sober working man and the limited needs of the "trade societies."[12] Nonetheless, the artisan unions joined with organized mine workers and socialists in the Labour Party and the S.A. Industrial Federation, helping elect Labour candidates to municipal councils in Johan-

---

8. Van der Horst, *Native Labour*, pp. 72–73.
9. Simons, *Class and Colour*, pp. 37–46.
10. Ernest Gitsham and James F. Trembath, *Labour Organization in South Africa*, p. 14; T.C. Rutherford, "African Workers and the South African Typographical Workers," p. 138.
11. Simons, *Class and Colour*, pp. 56–57.
12. Ibid., p. 98.

nesburg and Durban, provincial legislative assemblies, and Parliament, lending limited support to mine workers during the 1922 Rand strike.

With the collapse of the strike and the S.A. Industrial Federation, the artisan unions set off on their own, forming the Associated Trade Unions of South Africa. They accepted the industrial conciliation framework as the best method of insuring the security of trade-union organization and establishing "cooperative control" over industry.[13] They accepted, above all, the framework set out by the Apprenticeship Act of 1922, which allowed the unions and management to regulate jointly the training and supply of apprentices and to exclude Africans for at least a half century from the trades in European areas.

The artisan unions created a series of job monopolies that took on a kind of ahistoricism. Despite major changes in productive relations—the shift from primary to secondary manufacture—and despite enormous changes in the composition of the labor force, artisans were able to retain control over their privileged sections of the labor market. Their monopoly, of course, did not preclude change in the labor framework: other pockets of privilege were created by the state; the growth of semiskilled work in manufacturing forced some dilution of the crafts and selective training of African workers; other types of unions emerged in state enterprises and secondary industry. But amid these transformations, the artisan unions were able to maintain their skill scarcity and organizational form and managed to retain and, in some cases, expand their memberships.[14]

They focused over the next fifty years on two sets of issues with consequences for the racial order: the role of the African worker in the labor movement and the scope of state-imposed job reservations.

The artisan unions argued, not for the liquidation of the African proletariat and the suppression of African trade unions, but for the organization of African work under the control and "guidance" of the dominant trade unions. For them, African workers were a complementary labor force, performing the less-skilled and more menial jobs to be sure, but not necessarily competitors to be barred from industry. Indeed, with their job monopolies secure and the barriers to entry sufficiently high, artisans might well have benefited from expanding industrialization and African proletarianization. (The same relationship obviously did not hold for dominant workers of lesser skill, but that issue is discussed in the next chapter.) The unions therefore supported policies that permitted the development of African labor organization, as long as it took an "evolutionary" form under the firm guidance of the registered trade unions.[15]

13. Ibid., p. 321.
14. See appendix B, table I.F.
15. Unions that were registered under the Industrial Conciliation Act of 1924.

Later, when the shortage of European artisans threatened an influx of Africans into the trades, a number of artisan unions began considering more direct forms of organization, ones that might protect the extant position of European artisans and insure the viability of the artisan unions themselves.

The artisan unions, with some important exceptions, opposed an expanded state vigilance over race lines in the labor market. Heightened state attention here directly threatened the artisan unions' own role in reserving work for dominant workers. By limiting access to certain skills and fixing a "rate for the job," the unions set off sections of the labor market for Europeans and protected them from African competition and undercutting. But state action might achieve a similar result without the necessity of strong craft organizations. Appreciating the threat, artisan unions struggled, sometimes with considerable fervor, to limit the scope of state action. By focusing on a specific and narrow racial exclusion, the artisan unions, ironically, ended up resisting the elaboration of a state racial apparatus and the proliferation of race lines in the labor market.

THE TRADES AND LABOUR COUNCIL AND THE AFTERMATH: AFRICAN WORKERS AND JOB RESERVATION

In 1925, the minister of labour, himself a member of the Labour party, invited the diverse elements of South Africa's labor movement to join together in a single labor organization, soon to be named the Trades and Labour Council (T and LC).[16] With some exceptions, particularly in the

16.   The T and LC watched, despite its initial honeymoon with the Department of Labour, the steady deterioration in relations with the state. The National party cast the first stone, rejecting the nomination of W.H. Andrews, head of the T and LC, to the Low Grade Ore Commission; the T and LC rejoined by attacking the Riotous Assemblies Bill as a threat to the trade-union movement and criticizing Pirow, the then minister of labour. By 1933, the T and LC could hardly gain an audience with the new government of Hertzog and Smuts. The chill began to threaten all aspects of labor-government cooperation: agreements were slow to be gazetted, T and LC nominees to the International Labour Organization were rejected, and closed-shop agreements were abrogated. Only the onset of World War II brought a respite from the inexorable slide. Shorn of its artisan and "Christian-National" unions after the war, the T and LC launched a bombastic attack on the Nationalist program. Its chairman declared: "A serious problem arises from the threat to the very existence of the Trade Union Movement coming from the tyrannical and oppressive laws our Government has passed in recent years, and from the constant campaign of disruption, slander and abuse directed by certain reactionary politicians against the Trade Union Movement." In 1952, the T and LC would join the Labour party, United party, and the Torch Commando in a "united front" against the government. It remains among the T and LC's most honorable and final acts. South African Trades and Labour Council (T and LC), *Annual Report and Balance Sheet, 1931,* pp. 6, 9–13; *Report of the Third Annual Conference, 1933,* pp. 15–16; and *Report of the Ninth Annual Conference, 1939,* pp. 26, 76–77; also T and LC (1949), *Minutes of the Second Annual Conference, 1951,* p. 4; and *Minutes of the Third Annual Conference, 1952,* pp. 547–48.

Cape, they came—including the Mine Workers' Union and the Transvaal artisan unions. There also came some of the unions that grew up in manufacturing in the late twenties and thirties, unions that fit less comfortably within the bounded working class. While in 1928 the T and LC rejected the membership of the amorphous African general workers' union, the Industrial and Commercial Workers' Union,[17] it included a number of multiracial (European and Coloured) industrial unions, including the Garment Workers' Union in the Transvaal and, later, a number of smaller African unions.

But the Trades and Labour Council became the arena where each division in the labor movement, where the logic of the bounded working class, was dramatized. The artisan unions and others debated, sometimes violently, the role of the Labour party, whether the T and LC should form a "political wing" of its own, and the appropriate attitude toward the Cape Federation.[18] But two issues, African workers and job reservations,[19] are particularly important for our purposes.

The artisan and open industrial unions differed on the role of African workers in the late thirties and regularly until the early seventies, with only brief respites during the Second World War and during the late fifties: the artisans argued for "evolutionary" or "parallel" forms of African organization; the open industrial unions urged the inclusion of Africans as "employees" under the Industrial Conciliation Act or, barring that, recognition of African trade unions, with full bargaining rights. But on the issue of job reservation, the two brands of trade unionism joined forces against the state, the artisans because state vigilance threatened their own role in protecting European workers, the open industrial unions because job reservations threatened to exclude many of their members. Both insisted on the "rate for the job," though one reached the principle through skill scarcity and the other through inclusive organization. But for both the rate became the means for guarding against competition and cheap labor.[20] On the issues of African workers and job reservations, the artisans and open industrial unions split and came together, shaping the labor movement's response to African proletarianization and the developing racial policies of the state and society.

17.   See the discussion of African labor organization in chapter 8.
18.   South African Trades and Labour Council (T and LC), *Report of the Third Annual Conference, 1933,* pp. 47–54.
19.   "Job reservation" in the South African context means the setting aside of specific jobs for specific racial groups. The Industrial Conciliation Act of 1956 allowed the minister of labour to fix racial quotas for specific jobs, companies, or industries.
20.   See Jeffrey Lever, "White Organized Labour and the Development of Non-White South Africans," pp. 50–51.

Artisan Unions Versus the Open Industrial Unions

As long as few Africans were organized in unions, the role of African workers was not seriously contested.[21] The Conference of the T and LC as late as 1936 unanimously, and almost without discussion, accepted proposals to organize African workers and to remove discriminatory legislation.[22] But by 1937, a number of small African unions had joined the T and LC. The fragile unanimity began to crumble. The Furniture Workers Industrial Union attacked T and LC representatives for neglecting African workers; the Amalgamated Engineering Union protested the organization of "low-paid" workers in its plants; and the South African Typographical Workers' Union resisted proposals to organize African unions.[23] The issue increasingly dominated the proceedings of the T and LC and led to persistent clashes between artisan and open industrial unions.

By the late thirties, the artisan unions had launched a major assault on the African and open industrial unions but also had proposed a limited form of African representation under the "trusteeship" of the "responsible" unions.[24] In 1940, the president of the T and LC, representing the Reduction Workers, affirmed the vague consensus of earlier years but urged the conference to look to some "evolutionary form": "Many Moons would pass before a statutory recognition was applied in the sense that they, the mixed, industrial unions wanted."[25] In 1947, the president, this time a member of the Typographical Workers' Union, urged the established unions to organize African workers in separate or parallel unions, if not for the sake of the "natives," then for the protection of white workers.[26]

---

21. "Open industrial" refers to the unions that offer few entry barriers (e.g., apprenticeships, "blasting certificates," or training) and that admit all workers eligible for trade-union membership. (Africans until very recently were legally excluded from membership in trade unions registered under the Industrial Conciliation Act and still may not join white or mixed registered unions.) Some of these unions, like the Garment Workers, organize over a broad range of occupations, but others, such as the Distributive Workers, represent a narrow range. But both organize workers who are easily displaced by cheaper African labor and whose positions are protected by expansive organization and the "rate for the job." The term does not strictly apply to unions that have organized all the occupations in an industry. (See chapter 12.)

All of the open industrial unions in this study included at some point European members; most also included Coloured and Asians; some created parallel or closely associated African unions; and a few used loopholes in the law to incorporate African workers.

22. T and LC, *Report of the Sixth Annual Conference, 1936*, pp. 83–87.

23. T and LC, *Report of the Eighth Annual Conference, 1938*, pp. 29–33, 67–68, 83.

24. See the "Presidential Address," T and LC, *Report of the Ninth Annual Conference, 1939*, pp. 7–8.

25. T and LC, *Report of the Tenth Annual Conference, 1940*, p. 64.

26. T and LC, *Report of the Fourteenth Annual Conference, 1947*, pp. 11–12.

The issue of African workers, along with the others before the Council, left the open industrial unions—the Garment Workers, Textile Workers, Leather Workers, and Distributive Workers—to one side. To the other side stood the artisan and exclusive industrial unions—the Amalgamated Engineering Union, Woodcutters, Bricklayers, Municipal Employees, Boilermakers, Electrical Workers, Reduction Workers, Typographical Workers, Engine and Firemen, Mine Workers, and Bank Officials.[27]

By 1950 the acrimonious division between them had left the T and LC in shambles and the open industrial unions isolated. (The role of the "Reformers" is discussed in the next chapter.) The principal artisan unions, as well as the exclusive industrial unions, had withdrawn from the Council, taking more than 50,000 affiliated members with them.[28] The National party government excluded T and LC representatives from the ministerial committee on new industrial legislation and banned many of its most prominent leaders. By the end of 1953, thirty-three union leaders had been forced to resign from trade-union offices, including the secretaries of the Garment Workers, Food and Canning Workers, and Building Workers.[29]

But when the government proceeded with new industrial conciliation legislation, splitting the mixed Coloured and European unions and providing for job reservations in industry, the artisan unions sought to reconstruct some unity in the labor movement.[30] A Trade Union Unity Committee was formed in 1954 under the guidance of the Typographical Workers, Boilermakers, and other artisan unions. It combined despair—"capitalism," not the trade-union movement, was "responsible for the integration of the non-Europeans in economic life of South Africa"—with opposition to the specifics of the Industrial Conciliation Bill. A Cape Town Conference in 1954 opposed segregation of the unions (and the segregation of their funds), job reservation, limits on the right to strike, the Industrial Tribunal, and the wholesale meddling in trade-union affairs.

Most of the tattered remnants of the established trade-union movement, excepting the exclusive industrial unions and artisan unions in state employment, came together in 1955 to form the South African Trade Union Council (SATUC, later TUCSA).[31] The open industrial and artisan unions

27.   See the card votes, T and LC, *Report of the Eleventh Annual Conference, 1941,* pp. 66–67; *Report of the Thirteenth Annual Conference, 1943,* pp. 28–29; *Report of the Fourteenth Annual Conference, 1944,* p. 45.
28.   T and LC (1949), *Report of the Second Annual Conference, 1951,* p. 4.
29.   Brian Bunting, *The Rise of the South African Reich,* p. 349.
30.   A number of the artisan unions, particularly those with branches in the Cape or Natal, included Coloured and Asian members.
31.   The remaining African unions joined SACTU (the South African Congress of Trade Unions) or simply remained in "communication" with SATUC (Muriel Horrell, *South Africa's Workers,* p. 20).

"sank their differences and personal opinions," the new president declared, "for the good of the cause."[32] They came together, however, on the latter's terms. From 1954 to 1961, the Trade Union Council remained under the careful guidance, first, of the Boilermakers, then the Typographical Workers, and finally, the Amalgamated Engineering Union.[33] The leadership spoke less of principle and more of bread-and-butter trade unionism. It insisted that the trade unions, not the government, had the responsibility to "safeguard" the position of white workers.[34] And it welcomed the assurance of the minister of native affairs that "the process of apartheid . . . will be implemented in such a way that nobody will in any way or at any stage suffer damage economically."[35]

The Trade Union Council, however, consistent with its earlier position, refused the invitation of the minister of labour to participate in the Industrial Tribunal and help promote the new job reservations.[36] When the government in 1957 sought to impose the first job reservation on the clothing industry, the TUC declared,

> The reservation of occupations for white workers will not secure their jobs for the 7,000 whites employed in that industry. On the contrary, their work and their wages and conditions depend on the continued employment in the industry of the 35,000 non-white workers whose occupations have now been reserved for whites.[37]

The TUC, consequently, backed a paralyzing strike in the garment industry and the "public fund" for workers "thrown out of work by the Determination."

Until 1961, under artisan leadership, the Trade Union Council maintained a cautious distance from the African unions. In 1957, a few African unions, formerly in "communication" with the TUC, agreed to participate in a TUC-sponsored Liaison Committee.[38] Two years later these unions formed the Federation of Free African Trade Unions (FOFATUSA) and expanded their liaison. But in 1962, the executive committee of TUCSA (formerly TUC) urged the conference to take away the African nationalists' thunder by admitting African trade unions to the Council. Despite the

---

32. South African Trade Union Council (SATUC), *Report of Proceedings,* First Annual Conference, 1955, p. 44.
33. In 1962, eight years after the organization's founding, a leader of an industrial union became president of the Trade Union Council.
34. See Ray Alexander and H.J. Simons, *Job Reservation and the Trade Unions,* pp. 29–31.
35. Quoted in SATUC, *Report of Proceedings,* First Annual Conference, 1955, p. 44.
36. SATUC, *Report of Proceedings,* Third Annual Conference 1957, pp. 31–33.
37. SATUC, *Report of Proceedings,* Fourth Annual Conference 1958, pp. 20–1.
38. SATUC, *Report of Proceedings,* Third Annual Conference 1957, p. 45.

opposition of the Iron Moulders, a coalition of artisan and industrial unions carried the motion.[39]

African unions did not rush to TUCSA's banner, however. Six joined in 1963; their combined membership was a thousand workers.[40] Though TUCSA expressed disappointment at these results, it established a standing African Affairs Committee, assigned additional organizers to FOFATUSA, and began organization work, particularly in sections of the engineering industry.[41]

Under pressure from the government, the Amalgamated Engineering Union disaffiliated from TUCSA, raising the specter of the T and LC collapse. The disaffiliation also brought a new caution on the part of the artisan unions. The Typographical Union, the Iron Moulders, Electrical Workers, and the Building Trades Workers warned that their members were in a rebellious mood. Rutherford of the Typographical Union led the attack: "I say that someone has rocked the boat. The boat was drifting along quite nicely; it was getting to its destination for the benefit of all the workers in the country. As I see it the position to-day, we have to back-pedal to some extent, if we do not want a very serious position to develop." He proposed that TUCSA divide into two wings, one for registered unions and the other for any union that wanted to affiliate. Compton of the Iron Moulders declared: "We believe that if a man is a moulder, or a production moulder, that his rightful home is in his craft union." But acceptance of the principle did not alter the facts in the present situation: "Are we going to be leaders without an army, or are we going to accept that we have to back-pedal in order to preserve conditions of the membership?"[42]

For three years, TUCSA watched the accelerating disaffiliation of artisan unions. Quick on the heels of the Amalgamated Engineering Union were the S.A. Diamond Workers' Union and the Motor Industry Employees' Union of South Africa; by the end of 1968, the Electrical Workers, the Amalgamated Society of Woodworkers, Johannesburg Municipal Transport Workers, the Typographical Workers, the Amalgamated Union of Building Trade Workers, and others had joined the exodus. In a two-year period, TUCSA had lost virtually every artisan union, 90,000 union members, and an estimated 21,000 rands in annual revenue.[43] The minister of labour was undoubtedly correct when he said, "TUCSA which wants to

39.   Trade Union Council of South Africa (TUCSA), *Report of Proceedings*, Eighth Annual Conference 1962, pp. 9, 43, 144–45, 161–64.
40.   TUCSA, *Report of Proceedings*, Ninth Annual Conference, 1963, pp. 6, 124–27.
41.   Ibid., pp. 29–30.
42.   TUCSA, *Report of Proceedings*, Twelfth Annual Conference 1966, pp. 183–90.
43.   TUCSA, *Report of Proceedings*, Fifteenth Annual Conference, 1969, p. 353.

be so un-South African, or certainly those officers in TUCSA, or those holding executive positions, who want to be, they can continue to be so, but their own supporters will reckon with them in a suitable way."[44]

Under an avalanche of disaffiliations and government reprisals, TUCSA stepped back from its initiative, urging the African unions to disaffiliate voluntarily; soon after, it reimposed and entrenched a constitutional clause barring membership by African unions.[45] It substituted for the old policy a weak statement of principle: "The Unions must prevent the exploitation of the workers, not members of the registered unions."[46]

In 1971, TUCSA began the process all over again. It appealed, as it had done periodically over two decades, for "an amendment of the definition of 'employee' in the Industrial Conciliation Act so as to include the African worker." The government, as it had done time and again, rejected the proposal out of hand.[47] Having made the pro forma attempt to alter the legislation, TUCSA began a three-year program to bring African workers into, or under the control of, the trade-union movement.[48] But once again few Africans responded. In early 1976, the National Union of Clothing Workers, the largest of the African unions, rejected the idea of a separate African coordinating body and affiliated with TUCSA.[49] Only four other smaller unions followed suit, virtually all of them captives of larger registered unions.[50]

In September 1976, the Boilermakers, one of the few remaining artisan unions in TUCSA and a long-time supporter of African trade unionism, disaffiliated. "We support the recognition of African trade unions," its secretary stated, "but we are just not prepared to see our members—particularly Coloured members—threatened by unorganized labour when

44. The government was more than a little involved in creating the atmosphere for these disaffiliations. The minister had placed direct pressure on the Amalgamated Engineering Union and threatened to create whatever mechanisms were needed in the situation (TUCSA, *Report of Proceedings,* Special Conference 1967, pp. 5–6).

45. TUCSA, *Report of Proceedings,* Special Conference 1967, pp. 13–14; *Report of Proceedings,* Fourteenth Annual Conference 1968, pp. 21–22; *Report of Proceedings,* Fifteenth Annual Conference 1969, pp. 392–93.

46. TUCSA, *Report of Proceedings,* Special Conference 1969, p. 166.

47. TUCSA, *Report of Proceedings,* Eightenth Annual Conference 1972, pp. 18–19.

48. It did not proceed, however, by incorporating already existing African unions or, for that matter, forming new ones. In 1972, it conducted a well-publicized canvass of the affiliated unions on the advisability of organizing African workers. In 1973, TUCSA urged its members to organize "parallel" African unions. This initiative proceeded with caution, guided by responsible unionism and the "under the wing" principle. In 1974, TUCSA once again voted to reopen its membership to the African unions. (Interview with president of TUCSA, 1973.)

49. *Financial Mail,* 27 February 1976, p. 649.

50. Ibid., 3 September 1976, p. 826 and 17 September 1976, p. 1019. One study found that independent unions had one paid organizer for every 330 members and parallel unions had one for every 2,300 members (ibid., 19 November 1976, p. 702).

there is serious unemployment among them. TUCSA's attitude did nothing to help us in this battle."[51]

Throughout this period, from the formation of the T and LC in 1930 to the struggles in TUCSA in the seventies, the artisans consistently supported policies that allowed the unions to maintain their control over certain skills, their monopoly in some corner of the labor market. To that end, the artisan unions opposed state-imposed job reservations and supported limited forms of African trade unionism that left African workers under the control of the established unions. The open industrial unions stood with the artisans in the mid-fifties when the government banned the leadership of the left-wing unions, instituted job reservations, and split the mixed unions. But in other periods, they pressed for a more expansive trade-union movement: in the forties, their efforts brought the break up of the T and LC; in the sixties and early seventies, the withering of TUCSA.

Artisan Versus the Exclusive Industrial Unions

A number of white, mostly Afrikaner, artisan unions in state employment and construction allied themselves with those in the T and LC opposed to the open industrial and African unions—against the Communists and "Kaffirs."[52] But these unions also allied themselves with white industrial unions, like the Mine Workers and Yster en Staal Unie from within the T and LC and the Blankewerkersbeskermingsbond (White Workers Protection Society) and Die Spoorbond from outside. The Blankewerkersbeskermingsbond had organized exclusive industrial unions with varying success in the garment and leather industries and in commerce; Die Spoorbond had organized unskilled and semiskilled railroad workers from the early thirties. After withdrawal from the T and LC, the white railway unions formed the Federal Consultative Council of the S.A. Railways and Harbours Staff Associations; the exclusive industrial unions and a few artisan unions created a Coordinating Council, the Ko-ordinerende Raad van S.A. Vakverenigings.

51. Ibid., 24 September 1976, p. 1124. The Boilermakers elected to rejoin TUCSA in 1979 (*Rand Daily Mail*, 3 October 1979).

52. "Exclusive industrial" refers to unions that offer few entry barriers to membership (e.g., apprenticeships, "blasting certificates," or training) but nonetheless limit membership to Europeans. None of these unions has organized an entire industry, but some, like the Yster en Staal Unie and the Mine Workers' Union, have organized all the European workers; others, like Die Spoorbond, have organized the Europeans in the lesser-skilled positions. All of these unions have organized workers who are readily displaced by cheaper, African labor and whose positions are protected by various exclusory practices.

All of the exclusive industrial unions of any consequence have been based in industries where the state has played an important role in protecting white labor or in state employment where the state has played a more direct role. It is of no little consequence that most of these industries from the late twenties were employing increasing numbers of Afrikaner workers.

The Confederation of Labour, formed in the mid-fifties, gathered up these various strands of white and Afrikaner trade unionism.[53] It incorporated artisan unions that had battled the Communists in the T and LC, unions born of "civilized labour policies" on the railways and in municipal governments, and unions, like the Mine Workers, that "reformers" had won away from their old leaders. Until the late sixties, the affiliated unions maintained a broad consensus on apartheid: first, on the application of job reservations and the suppression of African political and trade-union organizations; and second, on the government's program for developing "native reserve areas."

But in the late sixties that broad consensus splintered. In 1968, the leadership of the Artisan Staff Association and the Federal Consultative Council on the railways (including the railway artisan unions) began questioning various Coordinating Council, and perhaps state, policies: the rate of African advancement, the communication mechanisms available to African workers, and the hard-line position on job reservation. It also challenged the *verkrampte* politics of the Mine Workers' Union, Blanke Bouwerkers, and others affiliated with the Council.[54]

Despite the growing doubts of the artisan unions, the Confederation of Labour remained committed to apartheid. Immediately before the Durban strikes in 1973, the retiring president of the Confederation rejected all prevailing ideas on African representation, including mixed or parallel unions, and even spurned the proposal of the Artisan Staff Association, a member of the Confederation, for a Bantu Labour Council to defend the interests of African workers. White workers, he indicated, would not tolerate the mixing and the inevitable "chaos."[55] The proposal by the Artisan Staff Association in 1974 for a government commission on black trade unions was repudiated by key unions in the Coordinating Council and much of the leadership in the Confederation. The Yster en Staal Unie urged the government to rid the country of mixed trade unions; and the S.A. Association of Municipal Employees asked the government to block overseas assistance to the black unions.[56]

53. The South African Confederation of Labor included at the outset three federal bodies: the Coordinating Council, the Federal Consultative Council, and the South African Federation of Trade Unions. The last included a variety of artisan unions and soon disbanded. The Federation of Mine Production Workers later affiliated to the Confederation (including the Mine Workers' Union), as did a number of individual unions.

54. Horrell, *South Africa's Workers,* pp. 40–42; also see discussion in TUCSA, *Report of Proceedings,* Special Conference 1969, p. 16.

55. Reported in Muriel Horrell, Dudley Horner, John Kane-Berman, and Robin Margo, *A Survey of Race Relations in South Africa 1972,* p. 335.

56. Muriel Horrell, Dudley Horner, and Jane Hudson, *Survey of Race Relations 1974,* pp. 317–18. The Confederation unions in 1979 nonetheless voted, with some important exceptions, to support the recommendations of the Wiehahn Commission. The Yster en Staal Unie and the Mine Workers' Union were among those still opposed to African trade unionism.

By 1975, the gap between the Coordinating Council and the S.A. Railroads and Harbors Staff Associations became unbridgeable and the railway artisan unions withdrew their affiliation from the Confederation of Labour.[57] A former leader of the railway artisan unions, J. H. Liebenberg, declared:

> We are going through times in South Africa when everyone must stand up and be counted. But the Confederation has shot its bolt because it won't even think about the role of Black workers.
>
> It can't give attention to productivity because it won't talk about Black labour. It won't have dialogue with Blacks, but if Black workers are not considered the White workers will suffer.[58]

Similar view were expressed by the head of the Artisan Staff Association on the railways:

> So Blacks have to be upgraded. We feel mature enough to discuss this without pulling any punches. But I get the impression that the *Raad* sees Black advancement as a big bogeyman, and they shy away from it: The Black man is knocking at the door all the time. We can't wish him away.[59]

When the Coordinating Council resisted even the government's lame proposals for African representation before industrial councils, the railway artisans set out on a separate path.[60] In 1976, the South African Footplate Staff Association urged the Amalgamated Engineering Union to join with it in a new association, the South African Central Labour Organization (SACLO).[61] Soon after, the Artisan Staff Association on the railways, with 22,000 members, expressed interest in the new organization.[62] The artisans seemed intent on a path that distinguished them from both the exclusive industrial unions in the Confederation of Labour and the open industrial unions in TUCSA.

The artisan unions had established job monopolies and the institutional framework for regulating access to their skills and relations with employers.

57. Muriel Horrell and Tony Hodgson, *A Survey of Race Relations 1975,* pp. 208–09.
58. Quoted in the *Financial Mail,* 4 April 1975, p. 22.
59. Ibid.
60. Ibid., 5 March 1976, p. 737.
61. Ibid., 14 May 1976, p. 551.
62. Ibid., 25 June 1976, p. 1108. In 1979, leaders of the Artisan Staff Association and the Coordinating Council differed on the core recommendations of the Wiehahn Commission: the former supported recommendations allowing some Africans to join trade unions; the latter opposed them (Republic of South Africa, Department of Labour and of Mines, *Report of the Commission of Inquiry into Labour Legislation,* part 1, R.P. 47–1979, p. 20).

They had effectively excluded African workers from the trades. And despite enormous changes in productive relations, the size and racial composition of the working class, and the nature of the labor movement, they had retained that labor framework and their privileged market position into the contemporary period. With their market position secure, the artisans could leave questions of African proletarianization and mobility, the suppression of African trade unions, and the growth of the state racial apparatus to the industrial unions, whose interests were more directly involved.

CONTEMPORARY TRADE-UNION PRACTICE: ADAPTATION AND JOB CONTROL

The artisan unions' stance toward management, the state, and African workers depends upon their continuing ability to limit the supply of labor. Some artisan unions still organize only journeymen and employ a five-year apprenticeship; some organize a variety of "tradesmen," but "not operatives or fellows who come in the back door"; and some have begun to include a few occupations not "properly" apprenticed.[63] Yet others, drawing on their traditional crafts, have included "people who came in as a result of the fragmentation doing aspects of skilled artisan work," people who might more properly be considered semiskilled.[64] But both the narrow craft organizations and those with marginally diluted skills draw on the traditional framework of control. The Apprenticeship Act still rules the market: "It's one of the best apprenticeship acts in the world," a Boilermakers officer observed. They still negotiate through an industrial conciliation machinery that allows artisan unions, even the diluted ones, to negotiate Africans out of the skilled areas and establish a "rate for the job."

Protecting Employment

Despite their enormous control over access to skills and employment, the artisan unions believed that management gave high priority to advancing

63. See a discussion of these trends in other settings in John T. Dunlop, "Structural Changes in the American Labor Movement and Industrial Relations System," p. 109.
64. One artisan union, the Typographical Workers, handled these changes by weighting the votes cast by various members: journeymen cast a full vote in union deliberations, while lesser-skilled workers cast a proportionately diminished vote. When organizing in the mining industry, the Boilermakers limited itself to specific trades, like welding and boilermaking; but in shipbuilding and engineering, it represented an extraordinarily broad range of skilled and semi-skilled occupations. Its racially mixed registration, a political disadvantage in some circles, gave the union an organizing edge denied other unions in these industries.

African workers into more skilled positions[65] and believed that they would attempt to undercut white labor if given the opportunity. "The employers endeavor to dilute the work of the artisan in order to create job opportunities, so they say, for the Bantu population," a Motor Industry Employees officer noted. "We like to believe that quite often the purpose is high profits; obviously, because these people are earning lower salaries than the white artisans." Other artisan unions shared his skepticism. A Building Trade officer claimed, "The employers want to fragment. They want to do away with all the trades, water the trades down to where there is practically nothing left for the artisans. So it goes to the Bantu, goes to the cheaper rate of pay all the time."

Still, only slightly more than half of the officers of artisan unions in my survey believed that African workers constituted a threat to the position of white workers. Four saw no threats at all, and three worried more about divisions within the working class.[66] Most of the artisan unions continued to oppose state job reservations as a way of protecting white workers.[67]

Nonetheless, virtually all of the artisan unions had initiated other forms of job reservation. The trade unions, not the government, instituted the pervasive negotiated arrangements that reserved specific jobs for trade-union members, established ratios of white to African labor, and instituted stringent criteria to protect white jobs against African encroachment. The Amalgamated Engineering Union, for example, took credit for one form of negotiated exclusion: "In our agreements, interdicted six years ago, 1966, I think it was, we put into our agreement a clause that only persons eligible for trade-union membership could be employed on certain classes of work. Those were the five top classes of work, the five top rates." The Boilermakers' Union, party to the same agreement, claimed that such exclusions were essential to counteract the influx of nonunionized African labor.

It was a job reservation, but it was a job reservation slightly different to the accepted form of job reservations. We said, "Look, we are

---

65. Eleven of sixteen officers of artisan unions believed that "advancing black workers" was a priority of managment. Four identified other priorities. See appendix C, South African workers (II.A.), question 4.

66. See appendix C, II.A., question 6.

67. Of the sixteen officers of artisan unions interviewed, eleven believed that state-imposed job reservations were ineffective or opposed them outright. Four favored their imposition. See appendix C, II.A., question 10. A small section of the artisan unions, mostly in government employment, had long advocated government-imposed job reservations. A few unions, like the Artisan Staff or Footplate Staff Association, even now insisted on job reservation's "regulatory" and "temperizing" effects, even as they recognized the declining value in such reservations. Other artisan unions, like the Blanke Bouwerkers, insisted that "the principle is right," only the government had shown little diligence in its applications.

getting to a stage, as you can imagine, that unions were going out of existence with this terrific inflow of Africans coming in all the time, because there's nothing left for the unions at all." So we had to say, "Well look, this is where they're going to stop, now."

When the Boilermakers, the Amalgamated Engineering Union, and other unions agreed to modify these restrictions, they gained in return specific job guarantees: no union member (or person eligible for membership) could be replaced by an African employee; no union member could be supervised by an African employee; in the event of a recession, job preference would be given to union members; and changes in work practice would require prior consultation with union representatives.[68] The motor-repair industry agreement adopted a different tack, though the exclusion was no less definitive. The number of "body shop assistants" (Africans) that could be employed in any shop was fixed by the "ratio clause," while the Apprenticeship Act reserved employment in the skilled mechanic positions for whites and some Coloureds. The Motor Industry Employees' Union in the Transvaal extended the act's effective prohibition against the training of Africans into a more general exclusion of Coloured and Indian workers as well: white members were barred from training black apprentices. In fact, the union suspended a few members bold enough to try.[69]

While the mining industry and state agencies fall outside the principal industrial legislation, artisan unions here too have established formal and informal arrangements that extend the color bar. An understanding between the Underground Officials and the mine owners provided, "no nonwhite will be a supervisor of the white, and we also have an agreement that they will not specifically displace a white man to make a job for a nonwhite." On the South African Railways, the unions, in conjunction with the government, introduced a "work allocation committee." The government agreed to request a change in work practice when a staff shortage developed in an area of "white employment." The railway artisans took credit for the committee and a committee decision to allow "artisan assistants." The concession was limited, however, as it precluded the possibility of further advancement by Africans and Coloureds on the railways: "Now after a reasonable period the Coloureds could then go in terms of our existing legislation, they could go and qualify for artisan status. The same applies to Indians." The interviewer asked, "On the railways?" "No. They could never on the railways but I mean we could continue using them as artisan assistants. But, as I say, they could ultimately qualify and then go and work outside."

68. Republic of South Africa, "Agreement for the Iron, Steel, Engineering and Metallurgical Industry."

69. Horrell, *South Africa's Worker*, pp. 102–03; *Financial Mail*, 21 November 1975, p. 740.

African Trade Unions

The artisan unions, secure in their trades and concerned with control of specific jobs rather than an industry, continued to support limited forms of African trade unionism. Only three of the union officers insisted on the existing framework of "communication"—works or liaison committees—and only three proposed full incorporation of African workers under the existing industrial legislation. The remaining nine artisan unions supported some partial incorporation or a separate African trade-union framework.[70] What they wanted ultimately were racially segregated African unions governed by "moderate" leaders, under the guidance of the white unions or the state.[71] The officer of the Underground Officials observed:

> I don't think they'll call them unions, but I do feel that the Industrial Conciliation Act should allow organization so as to create consultation and communication channels with the non-European. To me it is not to their advantage to think of the union as a multiracial problem, because the intimate contact that must come about will lead to the exact position which in our national life has led to what they call petty apartheid. Within the union ranks, if you have a multiracial affair, you will get that same friction developing and the union will be more busy trying to smooth the difficulties between members instead of fighting their employer or the state.

Some of the railway unions preferred the existing liaison committees but, if they proved unacceptable to African workers, would accept other forms of communication. The Footplate Staff officer commented:

> I'm not going to say a trade union as such, as we know it in the western sphere of civilization . . . the trade union is not necessarily the solution. The reason I say that, his background, the way he looks at it from his point of view. . . . we don't know his attitudes. Every worker should have the right to organize. But we never had similar views from the Bantu himself. On the whole, we don't know his exact views on this matter, if they want it. If he wants a union and feels it is the solution to his own problems, let him have it. But let it be his own. Don't let white people, Coloured, and Asians get mixed up in it.

The Motor Industry Employees, fully protected under existing legislation and trade-union practice, supported a limited form of recognition.

70. See appendix C, II.A., question 5.
71. See note 62 and the discussion of the Wiehahn Commission in chapter 8.

I believe there should be communication. I believe there should be consultation. Whether fully fledged unions are going to be the answer, I would hate to guess at this stage. I think it would depend entirely on whether those in charge of the union or at the head of the union are responsible people. This is as far as I would like to go.

But some artisan unions, particularly those with semiskilled workers, wanted to go further. "We want them all members of this one union," the Typographical Workers officer declared. "Our argument is that we have been a mixed union for so long—white, Coloureds, and Asians—that we can accommodate the Bantus as well and have one printers' union." In 1973, despite an earlier reluctance on this issue,[72] the Typographical Workers' Union asked privately that the government allow organization of African workers in the printing industry. The Building Trade Workers hoped in the future to organize the growing numbers of skilled African construction workers. "That is our only salvation," its officer declared. Without real trade unionism, the African worker is "footloose," his spokesmen "responsible to nobody." But "you take him into trade unions, then he can be protected and we can see what is going on." Until recently, the Boilermakers had argued tenaciously for organizing African workers. More than any other artisan union, it had seen the changing nature of the labor force and the consequences for the trade-union movement. "You see, the only way that the union movement can survive a fall in South Africa," the Boilermakers officer declared, "is to organize the blacks; otherwise, it will go out of existence."

The Iron Moulders also argued for the unionization of African workers but with a rigid theoretical dogmatism that, in effect, precluded any movement in that direction. During TUCSA's recurrent internal turmoil, the Iron Moulders argued that the Industrial Conciliation Act should be amended and that Africans should be admitted to "proper" craft unions. Its general secretary told TUCSA Conferences throughout the sixties and early seventies that his union did not want two iron moulders' unions or any "artificial form of trade unionism."[73] He reaffirmed that "the fight should be to get everybody in this country, the government included, to believe in the necessity for all people to have the right to join trade unions that would cater for them as workers in a particular field."[74] But "let us be quite blunt," the officer stated:

---

72. TUCSA, *Report of Proceedings,* Twelfth Annual Conference, 1966, p. 183, and *Report of Proceedings,* Fourteenth Annual Conference, 1968, pp. 514–16.
73. TUCSA, *Report of Proceedings,* Twelfth Annual Conference, 1966, p. 183.
74. Ibid., p. 181.

My union would open its ranks tomorrow to the African. It has always been their policy. And they say anybody that does my job must belong to my union and get the rate of pay. But the government says, "They will not be ever allowed to come in your union." Now we will never agree that a man comes and does our job who can't belong to our union or can't belong to a union. It is logical. Otherwise you are going to be undermined by the employer.

Since the government, and most of the artisan unions, would not allow African membership in the unions, the Iron Moulders felt compelled by their own logic to support a variety of exclusory policies, including job reservations.

"Parallel" African unions were the product of this ferment. The Boilermakers and the Typographical Workers organized affiliated African organizations; the Confederation of Metal and Building Unions (CMBU), representing most of the major unions in the iron and steel, engineering, and construction industries, announced the formation of "parallel organizations to represent Africans." The CMBU declared flatly that the existing works committee system was a "danger to our membership because there is no effective control over their activities."[75] Though the "parallel unions" were at odds with official policy, they were nonetheless a moderate response to the problem of African organization. They would focus on the select class of semiskilled African workers, "the 80,000 or 100,000 who had graduated to the semiskilled level," who "are quite capable of acting in a responsible manner regarding trade unions," and not on the "labouring class," who "are incapable of absorbing the normal day to day affairs of trade union members."[76] They would dwell on bread-and-butter questions and, perhaps most important, remain "under the wing" of the registered artisan unions.

In any event, despite the great ferment on the issue, eleven of the sixteen artisan unions had no plans to organize African workers; only five were presently organizing among African workers or had plans to do so.[77]

The Framework of Race Domination

The artisan unions care a great deal about the racial exclusions that have enabled them to limit access to their skills. But for the most part, the artisan

75. Position quoted in Muriel Horrell and Dudley Horner, *A Survey of Race Relations in South Africa 1973*, p. 270.
76. President of the CMBU, "Black Representation—What is the Answer?" *People and Profits,* July 1973, p. 20.
77. See appendix C, II.A., question 5. By the end of 1979, with the growth of "independent" African unions and the granting of qualified trade union rights to African workers, there were new efforts to establish and register "parallel" African unions (*The Star*, 24 November 1979).

unions have not pressed the government either to elaborate or dismantle the framework of race domination. Indeed, while four of the officers of artisan unions felt that apartheid undermined the position of the trade unions and two thought that it was supportive, fully half thought it irrelevant.[78]

The occasional artisan union had risen to defend race legislation, like the Natives Urban Areas Act of 1923[79] and the Pegging Act in 1946,[80] and a few among the artisan unions today, like the Blanke Bouwerkers, still insist on it. But most have hardly addressed the issue. In the seven TUCSA conferences between 1967 and 1973, the artisan unions offered only four resolutions: one technical matter affecting only registered trade unions, two questions on general business practice, and only one issue of importance for workers as a whole.[81] In recent years, the artisan unions have pressed the government, with little success, for improved coverage under the Workmen's Compensation Act and for the institution of a national, contributory provident fund. But rarely have artisan unions risen to address questions of homelands policy, migrant labor, the pass laws, or other measures that the industrial unions and the African workers themselves seem unable to avoid.

Instead, artisan unions, even those which have criticized the framework, emphasized its impermanence or irrelevance. The Boilermakers officer noted: "I'm fully convinced that apartheid is on its way, except that we'd be left with something like you've got in the United States—a sort of apartheid that would be applied by the people, not by legislation or anything like that." The Typographical Workers officer counseled patience:

> Well, of course, [apartheid] undermines trade-union interests. But at the same time to do away with it overnight, I think it would have dreadful complications in this country. I think it is something that has grown for so long, the breakdown will have to be gradual. I can't see them doing away with it overnight.

Others practiced a studied indifference to state policies, excepting those that had a specific, identifiable effect on white workers or trade-union members. T. C. Rutherford, longtime leader of the Typographical Workers' Union and TUCSA, declared at the outset of the Nationalist period:

> [The] Trade Union Council as such has not the slightest interest in party politics. This is proved by the fact that the Council is not

78. See appendix C, II.A., question 8.
79. T and LC, *Report of the Eighth Annual Conference, 1938,* p. 83.
80. One artisan leader declared: "Our social instincts will not permit us to buy property next door to an Indian and hobnob with them. While we want to help the Indians, we will not do so at our expense" (T and LC, *Report of the Sixteenth Annual Conference, 1946,* p. 43).
81. Compilation by the author.

opposed to the prohibition of the use of trade union funds for party
political purposes. For that reason, too, the Council has no views on
"apartheid." . . . The Council is concerned with the application of
apartheid in any manner that may only prejudice the economic
interests of the workers.[82]

And a Footplate Staff officer concluded in 1974: "I can't see a field where
it would affect us."

These officers reflected an indifference born of security and job control
that has allowed most artisan unions now and in the past to step back from
the racial order. The artisan unions have used specific racial exclusions to
powerful effect, but even within the bounded working class, they have not
been among the central actors demanding the elaboration of the racial
framework.

---

82. SATUC, *Report of Proceedings,* First Annual Conference, 1955, p. 44.

CHAPTER 14

Forging a Bounded Working Class: Exclusive and Open Industrial Unionism

Make no mistake about it—colour equality whether brought about in the "gradual" way favored by the United Party liberalists, or in the quick, violent way of the Communists, means the end not only of European Civilization but of the White man in South Africa.

> Mine Workers Union
> Die Mynwerker
> *17 February 1950*

The industrial unions have operated on the margins of the bounded working class, indeed, at its most ambiguous point. Unlike the artisan unions, they did not attempt to organize workers whose skill scarcity, security, and wages were all consonant with their position in the racial hierarchy. Here, the unions faced racially "privileged" workers who lived daily with the insecurities of the labor market and the prospects of undercutting. They worked in industries where workers did not easily turn to skill scarcity or apprenticeship training, where the "cheap, African worker" was no hypothetical figure but a genuine presence and "threat." Labor in these sectors of the economy, black and white, was largely interchangeable and competitive. Industry, at least before new rigidities were introduced into the market, employed Africans and Europeans as drill sharpeners on the mines, laborers and gangers on the railroads, and as steam-press operators in the garment factories.

The dominant unions and workers faced some difficult choices. They might have ignored the race lines and the privilege of European workers and organized on a broad basis. Some, like the Garment Workers, took that route, living with the consequent isolation, strife, and political repression. Most others chose to organize only among dominant workers. But that route could protect European workers only if the unions could erect rigid racial barriers and persuade the employers of labor to heed them. That route demanded, ultimately, that unions maintain an extraordinary vigilance over the race question. It also demanded that the state buttress the racial barriers in the labor market, controlling the movements of African labor and

311

providing employment for European labor. Virtually all of the exclusive industrial unions were organized in the state sector (such as the railways and the municipalities), the quasi-state sector (such as the iron and steel industry), and in those sections of the private sector (such as mining) where the state had traditionally established protected positions for European workers.

The open industrial unions never escaped the marginality that characterized their origins.[1] They emerged during the twenties and thirties in private manufacturing and commerce, where there was little alternative to open industrial unionism: Europeans, Coloureds, and Africans were employed in unskilled and semiskilled positions, and the state showed little willingness to separate them. But the unions were themselves isolated within the trade-union movement and increasingly overshadowed by artisan and exclusive industrial unionism.[2] The surge in manufacturing during World War II and afterwards, which might ordinarily have enhanced their position in the labor market and in the bounded working class, served only to compound their marginality. Industrial growth was accompanied by the "Christian-National" organizing drives in the garment, textile, retail, and leather industries, the banning of trade-union leaders, the promulgation of job reservations, and, ultimately, the exodus of European workers from the lower reaches of these industries.

The exclusive industrial unions played a critical part in shaping the racial order. Early in this century, they identified their own marginality in the labor market with the fate of the dominant section as a whole, sometimes enlisting the state in the defense of their position. They began on a small scale, urging the state to reserve specific occupations in gold mining but failing to impose a "white labor policy" on the industry as a whole. But with the influx of poorer, Afrikaner workers into the cities and industry, the mine workers joined with others in the dominant section and demanded state protection and state policies that would guarantee the future of a white working class in South Africa. "Civilized labour policies" brought large numbers of white workers into state employment and sections of private manufacture. But they also brought exclusive industrial unions on the railways, the iron and steel industry, and municipal employment. They, along with the established unions in mining, would insist on continuing state vigilance over white laboring conditions. With the influx of Afrikaner workers to the cities in the late thirties and black labor during and after World War II, the exclusive industrial unions joined other forces in the

1. See chapters 12 and 13 for definitions of "open" and "exclusive" industrial unionism.
2. See the discussion of this issue in chapter 13.

white section demanding the elaboration of the racial framework,[3] in this instance, the expansion of white employment policies, the use of state-imposed job reservations in the private sector, the suppression of African trade unions, and the banning of "Communist" trade-union leaders. They also demanded state policies, framed in only rudimentary and racist terms at that time, which would limit the entry of Africans into the white, industrial economy.

DEVELOPING LABOR ORGANIZATION AND THE STATE

The organization of white mine workers from the 1890s was forged amid rising concerns about the future of white labor in the mines and the reservation of "white work." While white labor occupied the positions at the top of the skill hierarchy, they were not spared the competition of African workers who dominated employment at the bottom. The mining companies substituted "cheaper" African for "dearer" European labor in a range of occupations and insisted that white gold miners supervise increasing numbers of African workers. In 1893, only nine years after the Struben brothers' gold discovery on the Witwatersrand, white miners lobbied the Volksraad, urging legislation that would bar Africans, Asians, and Coloureds from blasting operations on the mines. Indeed, the "blasting certificate" became then, and for the next eighty years, the symbol of the white miner's defense against undercutting. Before the turn of the century, the positions of bankman, onsetter, and hoist operator were set aside for white miners, and before the Act of Union, managers, engine drivers, mechanical engineers, boiler attendants, liftmen, mine overseers, shift bosses, and surface foremen were added to the list. In the interest of "public health and safety," and certainly in the interest of continued white employment in the mines, these job reservations were incorporated into the Mines and Works Act of 1911 and its reenactment in 1926.[4]

But the mine workers and their leaders in the early years of this century went much further, recommending strong measures to encourage white employment in the mines and the exclusion of Africans from European industry. In 1908, the president of the Trades and Labour Council told the Mining Industry Commission:

3. See the excellent discussion of these emerging alignments in Dan O'Meara, "Analyzing Afrikaner Nationalism: The 'Christian-National' Assault on White Trade Unionism in South Africa, 1934–1948."
4. Ray Alexander and H.J. Simons, *Job Reservation and the Trade Unions,* pp. 3–5; Francis Wilson, *Labour in the South African Gold Mines 1911–1969,* pp. 7–11.

If this country is to be a white man's country and a home in a British Colony for white people, then we must take seriously into consideration our attitude to the coloured question. I would strongly advocate a principle whereby certain territories are set apart for the natives of this country; and with respect to the Indian coolie and the Chinese, I would absolutely exclude them altogether.

The Mining Industry Commission itself, uncharacteristically captive of European labor, challenged the role of capitalist enterprise in the development of a "white South Africa":

The true function of the mining industry in the economy of the State is not primarily to yield the greatest possible profit to those whose capital has been embarked in mining enterprises. . . . The mines might conceivably be yielding large profits, and the exploitation of the mineral wealth of the county might be proceeding at a great rate under conditions which would contribute but little to the maintenance and growth of a white population, and not at all to the growth of a white working population.[5]

The Commission proposed a more limited exploitation of the mineral wealth and advanced prima facie the attraction of policies that "make the industry more dependent upon the services of white men and less upon those of coloured men than is at present the case."[6] It sought, consequently, to dismantle the labor controls, including the recruiting monopoly, passes, and masters and servants laws, that facilitated African employment on the mines.

The mine workers' interest in entrenching white labor and the mining companies' interest in reducing costs, often at the expense of white employment, brought recurring and accelerating violence to the mines. In 1907, the Chamber increased the number of rock-drilling machines and, consequently, the number of black laborers supervised by each white miner. Rather than supervise their own retrenchment, white miners walked off their jobs.[7] A major strike in 1913 began with a minor protest about the number of mechanics on one mine and spread to mining centers across the reef. British workers, now joined by Afrikaners who had entered the mines as strikebreakers in 1907, attacked the Rand Club, a favorite haunt of the mine owners, and set fire to Park Station and the offices of the *Star*. The government and the Chamber of Mines, advised that the military could not

---

5.   Transvaal, *Report of the Mining Industry Commission 1907–08*, 579–3/2/08–2000, p. 22.
6.   Ibid., p. 27.
7.   Ernest Gitsham and James F. Trembath, *Labour Organization in South Africa*, p. 28.

hold Johannesburg, agreed to a settlement.[8] They recovered some of their losses a year later, however, with a massive military intervention during the railway and general workers strike. The government declared martial law, arrested the strike committee, and deported its leaders.

But labor, with the mine workers at the center, was now an important force in local politics. The Labour party won control of the Johannesburg City Council in 1918; a "joint board of control," half council members and half union representatives, governed Johannesburg during the municipal workers strike of 1919. For one day, a similar board took over the affairs of the Durban City Council.[9]

With renewed Chamber attempts after World War I to lower operating costs and retrench white labor, the Mine Workers' Union became embroiled in the last major European strike in South Africa. The walkout that began in the coal mines spread to the gold fields, the Victoria Falls Power Company, the engineering industry, and the municipal governments in Johannesburg, Benoni, and other towns, eventually encompassing 30,000 white workers.[10] The government responded with military forces brought from all over South Africa; air force and artillery units brought down the red flag over the Benoni Trades Hall and forced the surrender of workers' battalions at Boksburg and Fordsburg.[11]

On the workers' side, 153 people were killed, 534 wounded, 110 persons charged with "high treason."[12] The governing South Africa party, for its part, suffered substantial losses in the Transvaal Provincial Council elections and two years later in the Parliamentary elections. The Chamber proceeded with its original plans for retrenching an estimated two thousand white jobs. The number of whites employed on the gold mines did not again reach the immediate postwar levels until the mid-thirties; the ratio of black to white workers on the mines did not sink again to wartime levels until the late thirties.[13]

While the artisans were establishing their job monopolies and mine workers were fighting the retrenchment of white labor, impoverished *bywoners,* the marginal white tenants in South African agriculture, began finding their way to the cities. Some took up the rock-drilling machines left idle by striking white miners in 1907; others competed with African workers for the unskilled and semiskilled positions in small-scale manufacturing;

8. Ivan L. Walker and Ben Weinbren, *2000 Casualties,* pp. 35–41.
9. Gitsham and Trembath, *Labour Organization,* pp. 4–46.
10. Walker and Weinbren, *2000 Casualties,* p. 125.
11. Gitsham and Trembath, *Labour Organization,* p. 50; Norman Herd, *1922: The Revolt on the Rand,* pp. 27–34.
12. Walker and Weinbren, *2000 Casualties,* pp. 125, 151.
13. Appendix B, table I.D.1; Wilson, *Labour in the South African Gold Mines,* p. 157.

and yet others sank into unemployment.[14] "At the base of white society had gathered, like a sediment, a race of men so abject in their poverty, so wanting in resourcefulness, that they stood dangerously close to the natives themselves."[15] More than a few observers at the time questioned whether this poor white class would survive the competition. The African worker, with a "subsidiary source of livelihood in the produce of his tribal lands," one report declared, would surely monopolize the most menial and lowest-paid industrial positions. The unskilled white worker, for his part, scorned the working conditions and the salaries associated with "Kaffir work." The Transvaal Indigency Commission in 1908 wrote: "So long as these conditions continue, any man who has to depend for his livelihood on his power of earning wages, and who has not the knowledge or the training to qualify him for doing skilled or semiskilled work, is almost certain to become indigent."[16] That indigence and the propinquity of black and white threatened the "colour division."[17]

Some of the poorer whites were attracted to the mines and the Mine Workers' Union; fully half of those arrested during the Rand Strike of 1922 were Afrikaans-speaking. But others, perhaps the bulk, were drawn into manufacturing and government employment under the aegis of "civilized labour policies." The Pact government[18] established a Department of Labour to advance the cause of "civilized labour" ("persons whose standard of living conforms to the standard of living generally recognized as tolerable from the usual European standpoint") at the expense of the uncivilized ("persons whose aim is restricted to the bare requirements of the necessities of life as understood among barbarous and undeveloped peoples.")[19] It sought with the Wage Act of 1925 to guarantee civilized rates of pay and white employment in areas not protected by collective bargaining agreements.[20] The Railways and Harbours Administration began substituting white for African labor, displacing 15,000 Africans in the process; and in the Free State, Natal, and Transvaal, the departments of public works

14.   G. V. Doxey, *The Industrial Colour Bar*, pp. 80–83, 107; C. W. de Kiewiet, *A History of South Africa: Social and Economic*, p. 165; Transvaal, *Report of the Transvaal Indigency Commission, 1906–08*, T.G. 13-1908, pp. 27–29.
15.   De Kiewiet, *A History of South Africa*, pp. 181–82.
16.   Transvaal, *Report of the Transvaal Indigency Commission 1906–08*, pp. 22–26; J. F. W. Grosskopf, *Rural Impoverishment and Rural Exodus*, pp. I–161–4.
17.   See *Report of the Carnegie Commission: The Poor White Problem in South Africa, 1932*, p. xx.
18.   The Pact government was an alignment of National and Labour parties or, as Robert Davies observes, settler bourgeoisie and working class ("The White Working-Class in South Africa," pp. 44–45).
19.   *Circular No. 5*, 31 October 1924.
20.   Union of South Africa, *Report of the Select Committee on the Wage Bill*, S.C. 14-1925.

began hiring only white workers for unskilled positions. While private employers moved more slowly, they too discovered, with the inducement of tariff protection, the virtues of civilized labor: whites began entering semiskilled positions previously held down by Africans or positions created solely for the purpose of absorbing white labor.[21]

Though African workers on the gold mines outnumbered whites by almost nine to one in 1930 and while Africans outnumbered whites by more than three to one in the population as a whole, here, in government employment, manufacturing, and commerce, Africans were barely in the majority.[22]

It was among this white working-class population that a range of exclusive industrial unions began to make headway. Die Spoorbond drew initially on railway workers disgruntled with the English-speaking leadership of the staff associations but soon attracted, as the secretary observed, workers from "all grades," with "interest especially from the Afrikaans-speaking workers." Though the railway administration resisted industrial unionism and at one point canceled Die Spoorbond's check-off facilities, the union after World War II won the right to organize a wide range of unskilled and semiskilled workers. The secretary recalled:

> Then there was a new subdivision of workers in 1948 and Die Spoorbond again got recognition with a substantial share of the workers on the railways. I'll say at that time the potential was 22,000, but it included the lowest-paid workers—that is, the ordinary labourer and furthermore, some general grades, the plate layers and gangers and all motor vehicle drivers on the South African Railway.

A group of three hundred white ISCOR (Iron and Steel Corporation) workers broke away from the artisan—and English-dominated—Boilermakers' Union in 1936 and formed the Yster, Staal-, en Verwante Nywerhedeunie. Unlike many of the artisan unions at the time, the Yster en Staal Unie reached out to the emerging Afrikaner working class. It grew up with and thrived on "white labor policies." Later, with its position in a state-owned enterprise secured, the Yster en Staal Unie expanded into allied industries, such as plastics, automobile, cement, pulp and paper, and became the dominant exclusive industrial union in the private sector. The officer of the union commented:

> The union is organized on an industrial basis with a very wide registration. In fact, we are the biggest single trade union in South

21. Sheila T. van der Horst, *Native Labour in South Africa*, pp. 248–49.
22. See appendix B, tables I.D. 1–3.

Africa, extending into twenty industries. We also have the widest registration. And we are active in all the industries for which we have registration, unlike some of the other unions, like the Boilermakers.

There also grew up a number of industrial unions that responded to different labor traditions and that sought to organize more broadly among African, Coloured, and European workers. The garment unions opened their doors, first to the influx of barely literate Afrikaner women, and then the rising tide of Coloured and African, mostly female, factory workers. They weathered wage-cutting efforts and major strikes in 1931 and 1932, police harassment, the "Christian National" union challenge, and bannings under the Suppression of Communism Act. Despite their own trials, the garment unions assisted other industrial unions, like the Tobacco Workers' Union, Sweet Workers' Union, Food and Canning Workers' Union, and the Radio, Television, Electronic and Allied Workers' Union.[23] The garment unions, nonetheless, stood almost alone. The industrial unions in allied industries, like textiles, did not emerge as important forces in the trade-union movement. The open industrial unions elsewhere, like the Distributive Workers, never secured sufficient membership to establish an industrial council and often had to rely on the generosity of the Wage Board and the good offices of employers.

The contours of a bounded working class were by now apparent. Artisan unions, comprised largely of Europeans, with Coloureds and Asians in Cape Town and Durban, but no Africans, were entrenched in industry, regulating their own apprenticeships and skill scarcity under the Apprenticeship Act. The European mine workers, organizing workers of somewhat lesser skill, had struggled over most of the century to prevent the displacement of white labor. In the end, their tenure on the mines depended upon the reservation of mining occupations, including blasting, under the Mines and Works Act. A poor white class, drawn largely out of the rural economy, gained a foothold in mining and took up many of the unskilled and semiskilled positions in developing manufacturing and state agencies. Their position in the labor market, however, depended upon state policies that subsidized the employment of "civilized labour" and European industrial unions that insisted on continuing state vigilance over the race lines. They over-

23. See Anna Scheepers, "The Garment Workers Face the Challenge," pp. 123–32; Solly Sachs, *The Choice Before South Africa*, pp. 68–73, 168–73; Letter to J. de V. Louw, Liquidator: Act 44 of 1950, from E.S. Sachs, 9 October 1950, Ballinger Papers; Delia Hendrie and Dudley Horner, "The People and Workers of the Cape Peninsula: A Sketch," pp. 23–33; John Mawby, "Afrikaner Women of the Garment Union During the 'Thirties and 'Forties."

shadowed a number of multiracial unions in manufacturing that sought to challenge the developing presumptions in the bounded working class.[24]

CONTEMPORARY TRADE-UNION PRACTICE: MAINTAINING APARTHEID POLICIES

Protecting White Employment and Standards

Though the 1922 Rand strike and the violent struggle over the displacement of European labor had become distant memories, the exclusive industrial unions still feared undercutting. All the union officers in my survey believed that management placed a high priority on advancing African labor, often at the expense of the European position in industry.[25] (None of the officers of open industrial unions believed that.) Though the three exclusive industrial unions in state employment did not identify threats to the position of European workers, those organized at least in part in the private sector —the Mine Workers' Union and the Yster en Staal Unie—identified "cheap, African labor" as a continuing problem.[26] (None of the open industrial unions mentioned African workers as a threat to their members' position.) The officer of the Postal Association, even after describing the protected position of white postal workers, outlined the classic problem of privileged workers without job control:

> Now, on account of the bigger supply of labor, of nonwhite labor, than the supply of white labor, the nonwhite workers can be obtained at lower wages, and if it is done uncontrolled, it means that the white man's wage will be forced down and the standard of living will have to be lower on account of stronger competition for the job from the nonwhite side.

The open industrial unions, worrying more about disunity in the working class than "cheap black labor," have consistently opposed state measures, including job reservations, to protect white workers from undercutting. They opposed them in testimony before the Botha Commission, the Industrial Tribunal, and the courts, and when the first job determinations were issued, in concerted union and political action. While the artisan

---

24. There were also at this point a number of smaller African unions, and while often allied with the open industrial unions, they were not a part of the bounded working class.
25. See appendix C, South African workers (II.A), question 4.
26. See appendix C, II.A, question 6.

unions and employers in the engineering industry resisted the application of job reservation there, the Garment Workers' Union sued the government and struck on the issue. Two decades later, when the government came to the Natal garment union to approve an exemption from the reservation, the officer wrote back, "We never supported job reservation and we don't care who works in the industry which our agreement applies for. We have no racial differences." The Garment Workers were joined by the National Union of Distributive Workers, who had called on workers to oppose this "pernicious Industrial Conciliation Bill which, if passed, will mean the end of free trade unionism as we know it today."[27] The application of the act had not led to a mellowing of the union's opposition. "You must remember one thing, that the colour bar is anti-working-class," the officer declared. "The essential feature of the colour bar is anti-working-class, not anti-race."

The exclusive industrial unions, on the other hand, helped create the system of job reservation and, even after years of declining application, still supported it: four out of five of the union officers favored a continuing state role in reserving white work; one thought job reservation had become an ineffective tool for protecting white workers.[28] The Mine Workers' Union, for example, despite recent changes in work practice in the gold-mining industry, insisted that the "blasting certificate" remain a white privilege. The Yster en Staal Unie was willing to accept only minor changes in the application of job reservations and only under the close scrutiny of the trade unions.

> We are prepared to allow the Bantu in. But let me tell them when and where we are doing it. . . . [We] do it on a technical basis where it is not practical to maintain the reservation. . . . The union has laid down the policy. Nine times out of ten, the employer has created a shortage because he wants the Bantu in at a lower rate.

Through informal agreement with the government, the Postal Association had maintained areas of protected employment. It had in recent years allowed some African employment in formerly white areas, but reluctantly and under controlled conditions:

> [It] was felt that the department could not cope with the work on account of the staff shortage, and they were forced to employ nonwhites. . . . Although in the beginning my association's attitude was: we understand your problem, but we don't agree with you,

27. South African Trade Union Council (SATUC), *Report of Proceedings,* First Annual Conference, 1955, p. 48.
28. All five of the open industrial unions opposed job reservation. See appendix C, II.A, question 10.

because we believe that if you paid the person a better wage, you'll get the white person. That was, of course, a pure trade-union point of view. I suppose any trade union would have adopted that attitude.

But even such modest lapses should be handled with caution, the Yster en Staal warned: "Experience has proved that once dilution or infiltration has been permitted it is almost impossible to turn the clock back."[29] If the government turns to the "rate for the job" rather than "job reservations" and civilized labor policies, "there will be no place for the Whites in industry, because they cannot compete in the labour market with people who have a far lower standard of living."[30]

The insistence on job reservation among the exclusive industrial unions was set alongside more sweeping proposals for the exclusion or isolation of African labor. The Mine Workers' Union, for one, has kept the larger goal before the Chamber of Mines and the white public. As late as 1957, it urged white workers to wipe the phrase "Kaffir work" from the white man's dictionary: "No work is dirty work." If the white man is to survive, he must recognize that the struggle today is no longer between a "small group of armed Voortrekkers" and a "mass of barbarians"; it is a "struggle to learn, a struggle to work, a struggle about the future of the *volk*."[31] The union decried the growing concern with "productivity" and "black advancement" and warned: "We maintain, if whites want to remain in power in this country, it is absolutely essential that we learn to manage without the 'boy.' We must also as a starting point accept that there is no such thing as Kaffir work and white man's work."[32]

While continuing to emphasize job reservations, the leadership of Yster en Staal Unie spoke, almost wistfully, of more extensive demarcations: "It must also be remembered that the White workers do not take kindly to working shoulder to shoulder with non-Whites doing the same type of work, and for this and other reasons it is necessary to keep the races apart wherever possible, preferably under separate roofs, where they have to do the same type of work."[33] Because of the union's resistance to further

29. *S. A. Werker*, January 1965, p. 3.
30. Ibid., September 1965, p. 13.
31. *Die Mynwerker*, March 1957, p. 4, trans. S.B.G.
32. Ibid., October 1957, p. 4, trans. S.B.G.
33. *S. A. Werker*, December 1971, p. 16. This position is similar to one suggested by Die Spoorbond:

> First of all, the laborer group on its own, we have accepted that 15,000 positions be permanently transfered to the Bantu. Before, you know, it was on a temporary basis. . . . We say alright, transfer the whites there and give this all to the nonwhites, so then we won't have any clashes. We don't want any clashes. . . . That's the main point by apartheid, is to avoid clashes, you know.

African advancement, the ISCOR management had considered creating separate "racial teams" within plants or, more probably, racially separate plants: the Newcastle works near the "Zulu homeland" on an African basis; the Pretoria works with an unusually large percentage of white employees.[34]

The officer of Die Spoorbond best summarized the exclusive industrial union's fear of undercutting and its commitment to varied and effective forms of job protection: "If there is no legislation, no job reservation and no apartheid, it means handing over what we have wrought to the nonwhites. So the white man has a right and he wants protection from being swamped."

African Trade Unions

The organization of African workers does not by itself threaten the position of artisans whose skills are scarce and whose job control is almost complete. The citadels of electricians and iron moulders will not automatically fall before the rush of organized semiskilled and unskilled African workers. But African trade unionism almost certainly threatens the position of the European mailman, truckdriver, foundry worker, or miner whose position depends on organization at the work place and access to the state. Indeed, African trade unions might in time, as white labor organizations themselves have done, take a political course. And for many of the exclusive industrial unions, that is the rub.

"All European workers, men as well as women, know that full legal recognition of Native trade unions amounts to suicide for White South Africa," the Mine Workers' Union declared. "For the workers know instinctively that trade unionism is the most efficient form of organization and is potentially a *most powerful weapon.*"[35] Even as the state clamped down on African trade unions in the fifties, the Mine Workers' Union reminded its members and the public of the larger implications in the issue: "Precisely because the Bantu is not sufficiently developed, it can easily happen that he is allowed to be led by a few political agitators. In other words: the Bantu union is not primarily used to achieve better working conditions and better wages but to exercise political pressure."[36] Partnership, the union warned, was "a fool's paradise." It was a threat when the Communists were active in 1946 and also now, as "Leftists and the capitalists and their press" were joined in an "unholy alliance" to "break

34. See Mike Morris and Dave Kaplan, "Labour Policy in a State Corporation: A Case Study of the South African Iron and Steel Corporation, Article Two," pp. 7–8; also author's interview with ISCOR officer.
35. *Die Mynwerker,* 24 August 1949, p. 7.
36. Ibid., 24 August 1956, p. 4.

the White unions."[37] Neither the "faction fights" nor the Durban strikes of
the seventies had dissuaded the Mine Workers' Union. Its officer declared:
"I feel here they, the Africans, should not have any say—especially in the
gold mines. . . . I will fight it all the way."[38]

The Yster en Staal Unie denied that African workers have the "mental
preparation" for democratic and strategic organizations, like trade unions.[39]
Failure to heed that reality, its officer declared, would bring catastrophe:

> You can't put a dangerous weapon in the hands of a child and expect
> him not to have an accident. This would have led to an exploitation of
> the Bantu worker. The Bantu worker would have been the first hurt.
> You would have had a revolution among the white workers, and you
> would have a bloody economic catastrophe.

The Postal Association, while experiencing little of the political turmoil
apparent in the private sector or the labor movement in an earlier period,
reiterated the concerns of exclusive industrial unionism:

> That, of course, is a purely political question. If I see it against the
> general background at the moment, I think it would be a dangerous
> thing for the economy as such. As I see it, if you were to, say, give the
> control of the industrial councils . . . they would be able to dictate a
> wage for the nonwhite worker which is not in keeping with his
> performance; shall I say for racial or for political reasons. And that, in
> my opinion, would be the quickest way of destroying our economy.

Only Die Spoorbond among the exclusive industrial unions seemed to
waver on this issue. Before the Botha Commission, it opposed "integrated
trade unions": "It's a question of ten to one, and you know what the
consequence of ten to one is." But it suggested then, and believed two
decades later, that some form of "Bantu trade union" is acceptable when the
government "feels the Bantus are far advanced enough so they can have
trade unions."[40]

The open industrial unions, standing at the edge of the bounded working
class and dominant society, have sounded the discordant and largely

37. Ibid., 12 July 1972, p. 2.
38. *Financial Mail,* 25 July 1975, p. 310; and author's interview with officer of the Mine
Workers' Union.
39. *S.A. Werker,* June 1966, p. 3.
40. The president of the Coordinating Council repeatedly dissented from the major
recommendations of the Wiehahn Commission. Commissioner Nieuwoudt cautioned that
African unions would "make unreasonable demands" and that their activities were "bound to
spill over into the political and social spheres, leading to untenable pressures." Whites would
be "swamped, with concomitant erosion of the vested rights of other groups" (Republic of
South Africa, Department of Labour and of Mines, *Report of the Commission of Inquiry into
Labour Legislation,* part 1, R.P. 47/1979, p. 20).

ineffectual note on this issue. "They're people like me. Why can't they belong to their trade unions?" the Leather Workers officer asked. "Why can't they belong to our trade unions?" At the 1973 annual TUCSA Conference, the Natal Garment Workers' Union asked the same question and led a stormy call for African unionization. The leader warned: "Don't vote for it if you're not going to do it, because I'm going to do it. Don't wear a mask for the outside world." All of the officers of open industrial unions favored full incorporation of African workers and four stated that they were already organizing separate or parallel unions.[41]

But the bounded working class had left little room for such initiatives. The Distributive Workers had organized African workers and "tried to get them into the negotiating room," its officer recalled. But the union crumbled under "government bannings." When it revived the parallel African union in 1975 and sought "the same facilities as are extended to NUDW officials regarding access to premises," it faced virtually complete management indifference and, it seems, pressure from the Department of Labour.[42] Only the Garment Workers' Union of South Africa, drawing on extraordinary leadership and an earlier loophole in the law permitting the participation of African women, seemed able to sustain labor organization among African workers. "Our union, having been under the leadership of Mr. Sachs," their officer explained, "has taught never to oppose or take away the rights of any human being to earn a living."[43]

The State and Racial Framework

Only the open industrial unions in the bounded working class challenged the racial boundaries and the state structure that has maintained them. They opposed petty and general apartheid, resisted, and felt the brunt, of political repression, and repeatedly supported extended health care and minimum-wage legislation.[44] Indeed, TUCSA's preoccupation with general, as opposed to union-specific, issues was accompanied by the open industrial

41. Three of the exclusive industrial unions opposed any form of African trade-union organization; two were willing to entertain some partial or separate forms. None had plans to organize African workers. See appendix C, II.A, question 5.

42. *Financial Mail,* 4 June 1976, pp. 821–22.

43. It is difficult to tell whether the Wiehahn Commission recommendations and subsequent "labor reforms" will make a difference. Some parallel African unions closely allied with existing white and mixed unions have sought registration, but most of the independent African unions seem skeptical of proposals that place such severe restrictions on trade union organization. See the *Financial Mail,* 29 June 1979, pp. 1142–43; 6 July 1979, p. 34.

44. SATUC, *Report of Proceedings,* Third Annual Conference, 1957, pp. 42–43; Trade Union Council of South Africa (TUCSA), *Report of Proceedings,* Ninth Annual Conference, 1963, pp. 9–11, 53.

unions' incessant prodding. And during earlier periods, when political repression was less widespread, some of the industrial unions maintained a loose affiliation with the Labour party[45] and, at one point in the fifties, joined with the Labour and United parties and the Torch Commando in a united front against the National party government.[46]

In recent years, not even the open industrial unions have provided a sustained critique of the prevailing framework of racial domination, offering little more than a tiresome parade of letters. When the government introduced legislation in 1967 barring mixed membership in political organizations, TUCSA sought the "total exclusion" of trade unions from the definition of groups, while showing little interest in the effect on "political parties" and other political organizations. An effort by African unions to "oppose the Bills on the grounds that they infringed upon the basic human right of free association and organisation, and not take a stand restricting our opposition solely to matters affecting trade unions" was voted down at the TUCSA conference without debate.[47]

For the exclusive industrial unions, the apartheid framework was the key to their trade-union practice and the survival of a white working class. In the absence of genuine job control, only the state, not industrial councils or apprenticeships, could bar the way to African economic advancement. Job reservations provided some protections, as did the suppression of African trade-union organization and political leaders, but only separate development promised ultimately to relieve the pressure on the bounded working class, to limit African proletarianization. There was nothing fanciful or academic in "growth points," "border industry development," or "homelands," the Yster en Staal Unie declared.[48]

> Our policy is conservative, protective for all races. We support separate development and we believe that if South Africa is granted time to fully develop this policy the members of all races will be happy and able to earn a decent living. . . . The liberalistic trade unions have pledged themselves to oppose the idea of separate trade unions, job reservation and border industry development, while we strongly support these measures because we consider them essential for the orderly arrangement of race relations as well as for protection to the way of life we are used to.[49]

45. The Garment Workers actually maintained an "on and off again" relationship with the Labour party. See the South African Trades and Labour Council (T and LC), *Report of the Ninth Annual Conference, 1939*, pp. 92–96; and the *Report of the Twelfth Annual Conference, 1942*, pp. 23–24.
46. T and LC (1949), *Minutes of the Third Annual Conference, 1952*, pp. 47–48.
47. TUCSA, *Report of Proceedings*, Thirteenth Annual Conference, 1967, pp. 50, 199–200.
48. *S.A. Werker*, January 1972, p. 5; September 1965, pp. 10–11.
49. Ibid., December 1963, p. 3.

The Mine Workers' Union was, if anything, even more determined to maintain the racial order: "The fact is and remains that the preservation of our white domination in South Africa lies in absolute forced separation."[50] Segregation at the mine face and in the union, however, paled before the union's determination to resist a political rapprochement between black and white. During the Sharpeville crisis, the Mine Workers' Union staunchly defended the "Republic" ("Yes, we want to contend that the choice for the whites of South Africa is not one between a Republic and a monarchy but between a white Republic now or a non-white Republic in a number of years"),[51] the pass laws ("Pass books are not to aggravate the Bantu but to prevent a great stream to the cities for work"), and the basic outlines of separate development: "The solution lies in that the whites in this country must stand together for a strong government to lead the Bantu to self-government in his own territory. There can be no speaking of political rights for the Bantu in the White territory."[52] The intervening decade had not altered the union's fundamental identification with apartheid policies: "I am one hundred per cent for apartheid, and it supports trade unions," the officer declared. "As far as the homeland is concerned, they must send the Bantu back to the homeland as quickly as possible and get our towns clean. . . . I feel, if we can send the Bantu to his homeland, it will be a wonderful thing. . . . [The government] will send the Bantu back to the homeland; that will happen, or out."

THE WANING OF EXCLUSIVE INDUSTRIAL UNIONISM

Capitalist development brought Europeans of varying skills and industrial experience into the mines, factories, and cities of South Africa. It also brought African labor out of the rural economy. Some of the Europeans formed artisan unions and soon won control over their scarcity and apprenticeships, barring Africans from skilled work in the process. Other Europeans, however, did not easily insure their scarcity or guard against the entry of "cheaper" African labor. They nonetheless won two historic victories.

First, the mine workers, while failing to turn the gold-mining industry into a haven for white labor, managed by the mid-twenties to reserve a range of critical occupations for Europeans and, along with the Labour party and the emerging Afrikaner working class, managed to generalize "civilized labour policies" to manufacturing and state employment. Unions, drawing heavily upon unskilled and semiskilled Afrikaner workers in railways,

50. *Die Mynwerker*, 2 March 1956, p. 4, trans. S.B.G.
51. Ibid., 29 July 1960, p. 4, trans. S.B.G.
52. Ibid., 19 August 1960, p. 4, trans. S.G.B.

municipal employment, and the steel industry, turned increasingly to state protection. Die Spoorbond and Yster en Staal Unie, with the Mine Workers' Union, laid the basis for exclusive industrial unionism.

Second, with the growth of manufacturing and the African working class following World War II, the exclusive industrial unions won revisions of the labor framework—splitting up the mixed trade unions, limiting African trade unionism, and establishing the principle of job reservation in industry. Against the apparent currents in capitalist development, they supported policies that they hoped would slow or reverse African proletarianization, that would "clean" the towns and provide for a European industrial economy.

But the same forces that brought Africans and Europeans together in a capitalist framework and European workers to demand increasing state protection also brought the decline of exclusive industrial unionism and, with it, waning pressure for the elaboration of apartheid policies. The exclusive industrial unions were a declining force in industry and state employment by the seventies and perhaps earlier. Die Spoorbond, which had once included almost 35,000 railway workers, now found few Europeans willing to work with pick and shovel or push trollies. With the shortage of Europeans in more skilled positions, the leadership of the union had urged its members to take "more responsible work with the result that the force of [European] laborers . . . diminished to, today, less than three thousand." The Postal Association too had accepted a declining membership, encouraging its members to do a "bonus walk" during the transition. The Durban Municipal Employees' Society had traded its acquiescence to a declining European labor force for a closed-shop agreement. And despite the historic position of the Mine Workers' Union and some bold rhetoric, it too had accepted a narrower European role in underground mining. The advance of the Reduction Workers and others into management status had further isolated the European mine workers in the industry. Only the Yster en Staal Unie, with aggressive organizing efforts across a number of industries, had managed to combine assertions about white labor policies with a stronger position in the labor market.

/The exclusive industrial unions, which for at least half a century had demanded the increasing elaboration of the state structure and the racial order, were a declining factor in capitalist development.[53] The unions themselves had not abandoned their commitments to apartheid. But with the upward advance of European labor—the emergence of managers, technicians and, indeed, "aristocrats of labor"—exclusive industrial unionism mattered a great deal less than it had during earlier periods.

53. Their impotence was reflected recently in the president of the Coordinating Council's lone dissent on the major recommendations of the Wiehahn Commission; also, in the widely reported estrangement of the white mine workers and Nationalist government.

CHAPTER 15

Trade Unionism in Alabama:
Breaking Down and Formalizing the Racial Barriers

During the course of capitalist development in Alabama, white workers helped impose race lines on the emerging labor market and factories. For some of Alabama's most prominent black spokesmen, that seemed to be the way of such "poor whites." Booker T. Washington at the Tuskegee Institute and William Councill at the State Normal School at Huntsville counseled Alabama blacks against cooperation with white workers and trade unions. The white unions, they stated, drew a color line while preaching a "sort of impersonal enmity" toward the "best white people," the employers "who give our race employment and pay their wages."[1] It was difficult, after all, to ignore the growing restrictions on black artisans after the Civil War,[2] the sixty strikes against the employment of black workers between 1880 and 1900,[3] and the white working-class riots in St. Louis and other cities in 1917 against the encroachment of black workers.[4] Washington and Councill identified the hopes of Alabama blacks with industrial expansion and the New South, unbridled by working class organization and aided by the "patience," "industry," and "loyalty" of black field hands and factory workers.[5]

It is also difficult, however, to ignore the experience of the fledgling general and industrial unions: the Knights of Labor, the United Mine Workers of America, and the Mine, Mill and Smelter Workers. While Washington, Councill, and a host of black ministers toured the mining camps and the black residential areas of Birmingham, urging cooperation with the "better class" of whites, these unions set about organizing both

1. See the discussion of Booker T. Washington and William Councill in Horace Mann Bond, *Negro Education in Alabama: A Study in Cotton and Steel*, pp. 205–14; and Paul B. Worthman, "Black Workers and Labor Unions in Birmingham, Alabama, 1897–1904," p. 60.
2. Booker T. Washington, *The Future of the American Negro*, pp. 78–79.
3. C. Vann Woodward, *Origins of the New South 1877–1913*, pp. 222, 360; Sterling D. Spero and Abram L. Harris, *The Black Worker*, p. 162.
4. Elliott M. Rudwick, *Race Riot at East St. Louis, July 2, 1917.*
5. Bond, *Negro Education in Alabama*, p. 208; Woodward, *Origins of the New South*, pp. 357–58.

white and black workers. The Knights had established white "assemblies" in Mobile and Birmingham by 1879 and, within six years, eight black "assemblies" across the state.[6] Even as Jim Crowism encroached on the franchise and streetcars at the turn of the century, the United Mine Workers organized white and black together in one union. It openly preached racial solidarity, and by employing black organizers, electing blacks to local and national union offices, and mixing black and white strikers, "cheek by jowl," in tent colonies outside Birmingham,[7] it challenged the most sacred principles of the racial etiquette. The Mine, Mill and Smelter Workers, following the lead of the UMW and the more radical Western Federation of Miners, forced questions of racial solidarity on the iron-ore mines and eventually on the post-World War II CIO organizing campaign in Alabama.[8]

Perhaps it was here, in the mines and mass industries, that trade unions struck at the foundations of the racial order. For some of the most perceptive observers of American trade unions and black workers, industrial unions had no other choice, save their own destruction. The United Mine Workers organized where skill levels were rudimentary, where blacks and whites worked the same jobs, and where failure to organize the entire labor force almost certainly spelled ruin. "The fact that the United Mine Workers was an industrial union from its start," Herbert Gutman writes, "made the notion of exclusion difficult to justify."[9] Sterling Spero and Abram Harris believe that the structure of industrial unions precludes "race prejudice and craft snobbery." The International Ladies Garment Workers in the North and the United Mine Workers in the South drew not on a narrow conception of "job control" but upon a "broad social philosophy" and expansiveness in organization.[10]

But these opposing emphases—on racism and exclusion on the one hand and expansiveness and solidarity on the other—fail to explain trade unionism in a bounded working class.

Craft unions, we shall discover, are easy enough to understand and both perspectives get them right. Unions that daily emphasize skill scarcity and exclusions find racial lines both congenial and functional. The craft unions in Alabama, like the artisan unions in South Africa, organized early in capitalist development and, except in a small number of trades, excluded blacks from a privileged corner of the labor market. Though the white

6. F. Ray Marshall, *Labor in the South,* pp. 22–23.
7. Herbert G. Gutman, "The Negro and the United Mine Workers of America."
8. Sally Furse, "History of the International Union of Mine, Mill and Smelter Workers in the Jefferson County Area."
9. Gutman, "The Negro and the United Mine Workers," p. 83.
10. Spero and Harris, *The Black Worker,* p. 347.

craftsmen vehemently defended their racial privilege, they demanded little of the state,[11] outside of licensing and "union rates" on government contracts. They were not party, except as spectators, to the bitter labor and racial strife that enveloped mining and manufacturing at the turn of the century and during the late thirties and forties. When the racial order began unraveling in the early sixties, the craft unions stood with the state political leaders against the civil rights movement and the federal government, but their concern was more for the inviolability of their apprenticeships than for the framework that kept blacks voteless and impoverished.

Both perspectives rightly emphasize different aspects of industrial unionism. White workers in major industries, like textiles, steel, and rubber, certainly expressed a virulent racism, and their labor organizations formalized a broad range of racial exclusions. But it is also true that, as an active participant in the labor movement put it, among the "institutions or groups in the state of Alabama," only the trade unions "promoted integration and joint activity on the part of the different races."[12] Against the prevailing mood of the society and the racial prejudice of workers and capitalists, industrial unions preached racial solidarity.

Both perspectives, however, miss the dialectical processes underlying industrial unionism in a bounded working class.[13] The industrial unions organized in the racial order at its most ambiguous point: among white unskilled and semiskilled workers, otherwise considered "privileged," who exercised little job control in the craft sense and whose security and standards were continually threatened by "cheap black labor," strikebreakers, and the manipulation of the race issue by employers. In some industries, where skills were little differentiated and blacks were present in large numbers, industrial unions attempted to incorporate all workers, regardless of race. But the continuing repression and divisions that accompanied multiracial organization in Alabama drove others to exclusive industrial unionism. While craft unions had exercised a specific exclusion at the point of entry to the job market, the exclusive industrial unions gained control over employment conditions by elaborating racial barriers in the work place and society. In the absence of skill scarcity, they were forced to maintain a vigilance over those barriers that lent formality and intensity to the racial order.

The influx of black and white labor into the mining districts in the late nineteenth century and the dislodging of black labor from the rural areas in

---

11.   The state in this context includes the administrative, legal, and coercive framework shaped at the Alabama (state) rather than national level.

12.   Interview with Attorney Jerome Cooper, representing the Steelworkers' Union.

13.   See definition of the "bounded" working class in chapter 12.

the thirties and forties brought, simultaneously, multiracialism and attempts to formalize racial barriers.

The racial framework in Alabama, however, was not the product of such ferment. The industrial unions were never able to enlist the support of the state. Politicians and officials, allied with commercial farming and frequently with mining and railway interests, would countenance neither formal recognition of the unions nor white labor policies. The open industrial unions, consequently, never generalized their own halting multiracialism beyond the unions themselves. The exclusive industrial unions, while formalizing race barriers in the labor market, were never able to convert their vigilance into a state preoccupation with protecting white labor.

When the racial order was challenged in the early sixties, most of the open industrial unions avoided the race question, fearing that the issue would splinter the unions. But the exclusive industrial unions came to the defense of the racial order. They feared the demise of a legal framework and climate of opinion that had limited black labor mobility and that had permitted the formalization of racial barriers in the unions and at the work place.

THE BOUNDED WORKING CLASS IN ALABAMA

The rough contours of the bounded working class were visible after the Civil War along with the first appearance of mines, mills, and new towns. White workers soon occupied all but the "plantation crafts," while blacks took up the laboring jobs in the coal and iron-ore mines and foundries. In the textile industry, backbone of the New South, even the laboring jobs were closed to black workers. The racial divisions and hierarchy were apparent at the outset of proletarianization, well before there were strong craft or industrial organizations.

Exclusion from the Crafts

With the abolition of slavery, black craftsmen faced the labor market and the racial order unaided by the slaveowners' political power and social standing. They retained their position in some of the slave crafts— bricklaying and plastering and, to some extent, carpentry and painting—but failed to establish positions as mechanics and skilled construction workers. Plumbing, printing, and skilled machine operations developed with little or no black participation.[14]

14. Spero and Harris, *The Black Worker*, pp. 159–60; Herbert R. Northrup, *Organized Labor and the Negro*, pp. 18–19.

With the rise of craft unions in Alabama and the South toward the end of the century, the pattern was given an organizational form and a new formality. The craft unions surrounded their trades with a certain mystery and craft rules, such as apprenticeships, that insured their fraternity and skill scarcity. For black workers in a racial order, such job control had clear and ominous implications. Between 1900 and 1940, the number of black carpenters and bricklayers in the South changed hardly at all; the number of black painters and plasterers increased, but the percentage of blacks in the trade dropped or remained constant. In the same period, blacks were effectively excluded from plumbing, electricity, and the railway crafts.[15]

In Mobile, the white carpenters formed their first local in 1867, but the second was not formed until 1885, followed a year later by a black local. The painters and decorators organized a local in 1887; the bricklayers and plasterers, in 1891; the plumbers, in 1899; and the electrical workers and stonecutters, in 1900. A similar array of building unions was formed in Montgomery in 1900. In Birmingham, a small lodge of the Amalgamated Association of Iron and Steel Workers (120 employees) organized in 1880, followed by the typographical workers in 1886, the machinists in 1888, and the boilermakers a year later. They, along with the painters, carpenters, tailors, and jewelers, formed the Birmingham Trades Council in 1889. With the depression in the early 1890s, the Council became virtually moribund, held together only by the work of the musicians' and printers' unions. But by 1900, the Council and craft unionism in Alabama were firmly established: 6,000 workers and thirty-one locals were represented on the Council; two years later, even excluding the 8,000 affiliated miners, 12,000 workers and sixty locals were represented.[16] Outside of mining and iron and steel, black workers were confined to separate "colored" carpenters' locals in Mobile and Montgomery. By 1905, there were black locals in Birmingham for barbers, brickmasons, and carpenters and an integrated local for plasterers. Nonetheless, only 212 of Birmingham's 2,425 skilled craftsmen in 1901 were black.[17]

The Black Proletariat and Primary Industry

Industrialism and urbanism were not very far advanced in the immediate post-Civil War period. Just over 6 percent of the population lived in urban

15. Northrup, *Organized Labor and the Negro,* pp. 18–19.
16. Marshall, *Labor in the South,* pp. 24, 45–46; Carl V. Harris, *Political Power in Birmingham, 1871–1921,* p. 44; Holman Head, "The Development of the Labor Movement in Alabama Prior to 1900," pp. 113–17.
17. Worthman, "Black Workers and Labor Unions," pp. 61, 69–70.

areas; with almost 30,000 residents, Mobile was the largest city, and Birmingham did not yet exist.[18] The factory system had not yet advanced beyond cotton spinning and cotton gin manufacture, small iron works, and blacksmiths. For Alabama, like the South, the principal economic problem after the war was the organization of an agricultural labor force.

Industrialization in Alabama began with a conjunction of minerals (iron ore, coal, and limestone) and black labor. They met initially in response to the rising demand for iron and mine labor during the Civil War: coal was mined in the Birmingham area and furnaces built at Selma, Tuscaloosa, and other parts of north Alabama; black slave labor was used for the heavy work in the collieries and foundries, while Confederate soldiers were detailed as mechanics, foremen, and skilled operatives.[19] The Civil War experience was not lost on Henry DeBardeleben, Truman Aldrich, and James Sloss, the principal speculators in Birmingham minerals. They turned, almost from the beginning of their mining operations, to black labor and black convict leases. By 1890, 800 convicts, over two-thirds of the state total, were leased to mines in the Birmingham area.[20] Heavy industrialization and black labor were now inescapable. By 1900, 10,000 black miners worked in the collieries, more than 50 percent of the total labor force and a yet larger percentage of the more difficult underground jobs. Black miners remained a majority of the labor force in the coal mines until 1940.[21] In the iron and steel industry at the turn of the century, black workers comprised almost two-thirds of the labor force. They were particularly prominent in the blast furnaces and as common laborers, the dirtiest and hottest work in the steel plants and iron-ore mines and, by all accounts, the lowest-paying and most difficult jobs in the industry.[22]

There were three basic patterns of proletarianization and organization in Alabama: first, steel and iron, where blacks were a large percentage of the labor force, dominating the most difficult and menial work in the foundries and blast furnaces, but where union organization was confined to the rolling mills and crafts until the CIO organizing campaign; second, coal and iron-ore mining, where blacks were a majority—often an overwhelming majority —of the labor force, and where organization took in both black and white workers; and third, coal mining and, later, paper making and shipbuilding,

18. Lucille Griffith, *Alabama: A Documentary History to 1900,* p. 178; see appendix B, tables II. B.1–2.
19. Bond, *Negro Education in Alabama,* p. 125.
20. Allen Johnston Going, *Bourbon Democracy in Alabama 1874–1890,* pp. 176–80.
21. Northrup, *Organized Labor and the Negro,* pp. 156–57; Darold T. Barnum, *The Negro in the Bituminous Coal Mining Industry,* p. 26.
22. Worthman, "Black Workers and Labor Unions," pp. 57–58, 75; Richard L. Rowan, *The Negro in the Steel Industry,* pp. 28–29, 36.

two industries important to south Alabama, where blacks and whites were organized in separate locals or unions.

Until the thirties, the labor force in iron and steel manufacture was essentially unorganized. The Amalgamated Association of Iron, Steel and Tin Workers had formed a lodge in Birmingham as early as 1880 and maintained contracts until 1909. But it organized exclusively in the rolling mills and skilled positions and chose, despite a flexible policy on the part of the national union, to exclude black workers. It never gained a substantial foothold in the industry and was continually threatened by the encroachment of black workers and strikebreakers. Only with the formation of the Steelworkers Organizing Committee (SWOC) did white and black workers band together in one union. Nonetheless, it took a national agreement between John L. Lewis and the president of the United States Steel Corporation, five years, and a major organizing campaign at Tennessee Coal and Iron (the U.S. Steel subsidiary in Alabama) and smaller plants in north Alabama before a majority of the workers joined the union in 1942.[23]

In the iron-ore mines, where there were few skilled positions and blacks comprised 75 to 80 percent of the labor force, the pattern was different. There, the Mine, Mill and Smelter Workers, an offshoot of the Western Federation of Miners and the militant IWW, organized the entire labor force from the beginning. Its first efforts in 1918 were crushed, but after a series of violent strikes in 1933 and 1936, it won recognition at TCI's iron-ore mines. The union, however, never escaped its black and radical roots. It was continually harassed by the Ku Klux Klan, white authorities, and many of its white members; contention over alleged Communist leadership led key locals at Muscoda, Ishkooda, and Wenonah in 1949 to join the United Steelworkers and the CIO to expel the union in 1950.[24]

The organization of coal mining, like that of iron and steel, dates back to the first years of heavy industrial development in Alabama. But the unions in coal mining did not follow the lead of the early iron and steel unions and organize only among whites and skilled workers. The Knights of Labor had organized both black and white assemblies in the mining district; the United Mine Workers of Alabama, founded in 1893, had organized along industrial lines, with blacks and whites in separate locals. But Jim Crow did not survive very long in the mines. The multiracial UMW, now affiliated to the national union, grew to 11,500 members by 1904 and 18,000 by 1908. The

23. Marshall, *Labor in the South,* pp. 182–88; George B. Tindall, *The Emergence of the New South 1913–1945,* pp. 514–15; Head, "The Development of the Labor Movement in Alabama," pp. 113–15.
24. Furse, "History of the International Union of Mine, Mill and Smelter Workers"; and Marshall, *Labor in the South,* pp. 182–83.

1908 miners' strike, however, left the union in ruins. Though the National Recovery Administration offered the UMW a brief respite during the war, labor organization among the coal miners did not recover until 1933.[25] Then, with strong support from the national union and the federal government, the UMW began organizing again in Alabama. Within a matter of months, 18,000 workers were enrolled in eighty-five locals. Within a year, after widespread strikes and violence, the UMW reached agreements for recognition with 90 percent of the operators. Only Charles De-Bardeleben, one of the founders of the industry, successfully held out against the union.[26]

Black workers were a major factor in paper making from the thirties on, though confined to the woodyards and selected menial jobs in the mills. The paper machines and skilled maintenance jobs were entrusted only to whites. Labor unions were a major factor too: the United Papermakers and Paper Workers (more accurately, its forerunner before merger) organized a local in Mobile in 1933. But the rigid segregation of work was matched by a similar pattern in labor organization. The UPP generally issued charters for white employees in the paper mills; the International Brotherhood of Pulp, Sulphite and Paper Mill Workers organized black employees throughout the plant in one local and white employees in the pulp mill and yard in another.[27]

In shipbuilding, most of the skilled workers, an unusually large percentage of the work force, were organized under the Metal Trades Department of the AFL. That placed the labor force, including a growing number of black workers, in the hands of the Machinists, Electrical Workers, Plumbers, and Boilermakers, particularly the last union. The Boilermakers organized black workers in "auxiliary locals" and granted them almost none of the rights of membership, including apprenticeships. With the CIO organizing campaign in 1938, most black workers on the Gulf Coast turned to the International Union of Marine Shipbuilding Workers. Still, in 1964, blacks comprised 43 percent of the operatives and 83 percent of the laborers in the southern shipbuilding industry. Only 16 percent of the craftsmen were black.[28]

25. Head, "The Development of the Labor Movement in Alabama," pp. 56–57, 94; Harris, *Political Power in Birmingham,* p. 45; Worthman, "Black Workers and Labor Unions," pp. 81–82; Herbert R. Northrup, "The Negro and the United Mine Workers of America," p. 319.

26. Tindall, *The Emergence of the New South,* p. 506; Marshall, *Labor in the South,* pp. 143–45.

27. Herbert R. Northrup, *The Negro in the Paper Industry,* pp. 4–5, 33–37; Marshall, *Labor in the South,* pp. 212–13.

28. Northrup, *Organized Labor and the Negro,* pp. 213–15, 225–27; Lester Rubin, *The Negro in the Shipbuilding Industry,* p. 99.

White Industrialization

The cotton textile mills were located from the 1880s in the Piedmont section amid a large pool of impoverished white farmers and sharecroppers.[29] That was their strength and appeal. White families, women and children in particular, flocked to the mill towns, content to work in an industry that promised salvation for the South and security for white workers. For a half century, the textile industry employed an increasing number of spindles and white textile workers and rivaled the iron and steel industry in total employment and value of production.[30]

Unions were not very important in Alabama's textile industry. White employer and employee developed an affinity of interest that seemed to fend off working-class enmity for the bourgeoisie. "There was no cleavage between owners and operatives," Broadus and George Mitchell write. "They did not see themselves as employers and employees, but as companions in the same boat on rather desperate seas. If anything besides joint economic effort were needed to weld them into one, the presence of the free blacks accomplished it."[31] Certainly the promoters of the industry in Alabama congratulated themselves on the purity of their labor force and the "harmony of feeling which exists between employer and employee."

> Textile mill labor in Alabama is exclusively open shop. There has never been a strike or other labor disturbance of consequence because the native labor in the textile industry is not subject to those disturbing influences common in sections where the foreign element dominates the industrial field.[32]

Though the Textile Workers Organizing Committee had begun organizing southern mill towns in the late thirties in Alabama, even separate black and white locals—a first for the CIO—could not save the union. Only after World War II would the International Ladies Garment Workers' Union make inroads in north Alabama, and not until the late fifties would the Amalgamated Clothing Workers of America begin effectively to organize white workers in north and east Alabama.

Other industries in Alabama, like rubber tire, for example, lacked an historic identification with the "poor white problem," but depended,

29. Alabama Power Company, Commercial Department, *The Textile Industry in Alabama,* no pagination.
30. Richard L. Rowan, *The Negro in the Textile Industry,* p. 21; W.M. Adamson, *Industrial Activity in Alabama, 1913–1932,* p. 76.
31. Broadus Mitchell and George Sinclair Mitchell, *The Industrial Revolution in the South,* pp. 31–32.
32. Alabama Power Company, Commercial Department, *The Textile Industry in Alabama.*

nonetheless, on white labor. These industries were located principally in north Alabama, where white labor was plentiful but where no sense of "companionship" brought employer and employee into carefree harmony. Bitter labor violence flared in Gadsden and other north Alabama towns during the Depression, much of it surrounding the organization of the rubber tire industry. In 1943 a virtually all-white local of the United Rubber Workers won recognition in Goodyear's Gadsden plant. It set the stage for the triumph of the CIO and white industrial unionism in north Alabama.[33]

UNDERMINING WHITE LABOR

Who was behind that [disenfranchisement]? I felt to an extent it was the rich white man and the poor white man, both of em, workin to take the vote away from the nigger—the big man and a heap of the little ones. The little ones thought they had a voice, but they only had a voice to this extent: they could speak against the nigger and the big man was happy for em to do it. But they didn't have no more voice than a cat against the big man of their own color.

Nate Shaw, quoted in All God's Dangers, *1974*[34]

That black workers posed a threat to the security and standards of white workers in Alabama was no idle prejudice of the white trade unions or working class. They were a threat. Unorganized and socially marginal, blacks were available at lower wages and as strikebreakers. There is a classical economic explanation for these roles: the living standards of formerly unfree labor and the conditions of black farm labor in the South. But the roots of the threat also reach outside the labor market. Individuals and groups cultivated the black workers' marginality and the social divisions and between black and white workers.

Black ministers and political leaders, for one, urged black workers to shy away from labor organizations and strikes. Blacks should align themselves with the employers: "Make friends with . . . the employer," they were urged. "Take whatever wages the company offered."[35] In Birmingham, itinerant black ministers, sometimes paid by the employers, called on workers to avoid the unions that discriminated against blacks and stand with the employers who provided job opportunities.[36] Both in Alabama and nationally, black leaders urged capitalists and black workers to take

---

33. By 1944, one-sixth of Gadsden's population were members of the CIO. Marshall, *Labor in the South*, p. 227; Charles L. Phillips, "A History of the United Rubber Workers in Gadsden, Alabama, 1936–1943," pp. 18–19, 35, 66.

34. Theodore Rosengarten, *All God's Dangers: The Life of Nate Shaw*, p. 35.

35. Worthman, "Black Workers and Labor Unions," p. 60.

36. Spero and Harris, *The Black Worker*, pp. 137–38.

advantage of these divisions in the working class. Booker T. Washington told employers that the black worker by nature and history held no "impersonal enmity to the man by whom he is employed."[37] Black labor, he wrote, will not disrupt the work place: "You should remember that you are in debt to the black man for furnishing you with labor that is almost a stranger to strikes."[38] Marcus Garvey, like Washington and other leaders, urged blacks to side with the "white capitalist" and hold their wages below that of whites.

> It seems strange and a paradox, but the only convenient friend the Negro worker or laborer has in America at the present time is the white capitalist. The capitalist being selfish—seeking only the largest profit out of labor—is willing and glad to use Negro labor wherever possible on a scale reasonably below the standard union wage. . . .
> If the Negro takes my advice he will organize by himself and always keep his scale of wage a little lower than the whites until he is able to become, through proper leadership, his own employer; by doing so he will keep the good will of the white employer and live a little longer under the present scheme of things.[39]

Alabama employers were hardly reluctant converts to the virtues of "cheap," unorganized black labor. In almost every strike on the mines between 1894 and 1918, employers dipped into the pool of black labor; indeed, black employment in the coal mines and steel industry increased with each successive strike. At Mobile and New Orleans, employers turned to unorganized, mostly black "rabbit" labor to break strikes by screwmen and longshoremen.[40] A number of companies began substituting black labor as a defense against the white worker's increasing interest in labor organization. The Tennessee Coal and Iron Company created a number of all-black mines in the late 1890s and, after the U.S. Steel takeover in 1907, began a system of thoroughgoing paternalism for black employees. After a strike by white workers in 1893, the Louisville and Nashville Railroad hired only black brakemen, switchmen, and firemen in the Birmingham division.[41]

Neither were employers reluctant converts to the race issue and the advantages in the state racial apparatus. During the multiracial strikes in 1894, 1908, and 1919, employers decried race mixing and appealed to the

37. Booker T. Washington, "The Negro and the Labor Unions," p. 757.
38. Quoted in Woodward, *Origins of the New South*, p. 364.
39. Quoted in Spero and Harris, *The Black Worker*, pp. 135–36.
40. Head, "The Development of the Labor Movement in Alabama," pp. 95–100; Spero and Harris, *The Black Worker*, pp. 185–88; Barnum, *The Negro in the Bituminous Coal Mining Industry*, p. 20.
41. Worthman, "Black Workers and Labor Unions," p. 58.

sensibilities of the white public and the authorities. In each instance, they were able to rely on the National Guard, convict labor, and antivagrancy laws.[42]

The threat of black labor and undercutting affected some white workers more than others, however. Skilled workers, for one, established strong, exclusive trade unions by the turn of the century and escaped the most bitter, racially divisive labor turmoil of this century. Racial discrimination, as we shall see in the next section, served their control over jobs and skills. But their early success insulated them from both black preachers that pushed "cheap," unorganized black labor and employers that played on racial differences in the labor movement. Indeed, there is little evidence in my own survey that leaders of craft unions worried about such issues. None of the leaders could recall any attempt by management to exploit or fan the race issue; none seemed troubled by the continuing differences between black and white workers.[43]

The industrial unions, on the other hand, without job control or skill scarcity, never escaped these issues. If they organized only the white section of the working class, they were threatened by the black's lower wages and availability and the employer's willingness to substitute black for white labor. If they organized the entire labor force, regardless of race, they were threatened by their members' own prejudices, the reluctance of black workers, and the employer's willingness to use the race issue. Leaders of the industrial unions, even in the seventies, believed that management fostered prejudice and racial divisions in the labor force.[44] In the steel industry, the union leadership reflected the long and troubled history of such issues. "The company can take credit for the racial prejudice that grew up in the mill," one leader observed. "It is one of their gimmicks to control the work force." Another leader of the United Steelworkers, active during the early CIO organizing days, described the process: "When we began to organize, [management would] tell the colored people, 'Well, all the union wants is a little money—you paying dues.' And they'd take a white group and say, 'Listen, you stay out of the union. We're going to make a supervisor out of you some of these days.' " Similar sentiment and processes were evident on the dry docks, where racial conflict accompanied organization during and after World War II. "The company was just playing one against the other," the leader of the Marine and Shipbuilding Workers' Union recalled:

42. See the discussion of this issue in chapter 10.
43. See Appendix C, Alabama workers (II.B), questions 10, 14, and 21.
44. Eight of the officers of industrial unions stated that racial divisions caused problems for the union. (One did not know whether they did, and three stated that race did not pose a problem.) Eight also believed that management used the race issue. (Two did not know whether it did, and two believed that management did not use the issue.)

"They'd take somebody on an extra dirty job and say to the white, 'What the hell. They [the blacks] have some . . . they would be glad to have this job.' And to the colored they'd say, 'The white would be glad to have this job.' They just play one off against the other. That was before we was organized."

In the garment and textile industries, where plants were more dispersed, often outside the large urban areas, unions faced a management and public sentiment that freely played with these issues. While many of the industrial unions faced the race question in the thirties or immediately after World War II, for the Amalgamated Clothing Workers and the International Ladies Garment Workers' Unions it was a recent problem. A leader of the former union observed:

> [It] would create the kind of problem that it just created for us in a small town where, because the blacks had the courage, that the company put the pressure on and tried to divide the people and things of this kind. And there's nothing more dangerous than prejudice in a situation like that. And [you] know any, a smart employer or smart lawyer, can take advantage of prejudice.

The leader of the latter union described how management "robbed" him by use of the race issue during a Black Belt organizing drive.

> I've had a campaign backfire on me a couple of years ago in Evergreen, Alabama where—I can't document it, but it's been an undercurrent—where the whites were supposed to be saying that there will be a black union. The blacks would be the officers. They'll take over. And I had the thing won up until about two weeks prior to the election and then the whole thing turned on this black issue.

Though the officer could not firmly document management's responsibility for the "black issue," he concluded, "I think you can see the writing on the walls."

But even in the absence of employer efforts, industrial unions must grapple with divisions between black and white workers. In some cases, like the Steelworkers or Autoworkers, the leadership worried that the race question would "destroy the union." Black and white members split on the election of national union leadership, the *Brown* v. *Board of Education* decision, and the Brewer-Wallace gubernatorial election. "They kept us diluted," the UAW officer lamented. "We couldn't get off the ground in politics as long as that racial issue was there." Some watched race questions take over from labor questions within the union. A leader of the Communication Workers observed that every time "you went to a local meeting" during the late fifties and sixties "you always caught hell because of what the labor movement was doing" on civil rights issues. "For a long period of time, I think most people, all of their free time away from the job was devoted in some sort of a way to either thinking about, planning, or actually working against the blacks."

ORGANIZING OR EXCLUDING THE BLACK WORKER

Artisan Unions: "The Blacks Have Historically Been Afraid of Electricity."

Artisan unions in Alabama had little difficulty establishing a scope of organization consistent with the bounded working class and norms of the racial order: racial exclusions were no less congenial for them than exclusions based on craft. It was difficult, nonetheless, for the labor movement at the turn of the century to ignore the black barbers who formed their own locals, the plasterers who joined integrated locals, or the brickmasons and carpenters who were given charters despite the objections of local white artisans. After all, Samuel Gompers himself had warned the AFL's first Birmingham organizer, "The Negro workers must be organized in order that they may be in a position to protect themselves and in some way feel an interest with our organized white workingmen, or we shall unquestionably have their undying enmity."[45]

But "job conscious" trade unionism and "local autonomy" would soon enshrine as principle what the artisan unions found congenial in any case. They were not anxious to organize unskilled workers of any ethnic or racial variety or expand access to their skills. Race discrimination became part of the pattern. The plumbers, electricians, sheet-metal workers, elevator constructors, iron workers, railway craftsmen, and boilermakers excluded black workers.[46] With apprenticeship training, control of licensing boards, "father-to-son" relationships, "auxiliary locals," and the occasional strike, artisan unions turned this area of the labor environment into an essentially white affair.[47]

Until passage of the Civil Rights Act in 1964, those boundaries remained largely undisturbed. A half century of industrialization failed to dislodge the traditional privileges; in fact, by creating new areas for skilled employment,

45. Quoted in Worthman, "Black Workers and Labor Unions," p. 62; also see pp. 69–71.
46. Marshall, *Labor in the South,* p. 48; interview with officer of Birmingham Building and Construction Trades Council; Northrup, *Organized Labor and the Negro,* p. 214.
47. Three of the five craft unions in my survey were open only to whites before 1964; two accepted black members in separate locals. See appendix C, II.B, question 2.

it probably extended them. The union leadership, even in the mid-seventies, had little difficulty with the traditional employment pattern: for the electricians, "the blacks have historically been afraid of electricity"; for the printers, "colored people just didn't involve themselves with white people, not in this part of the country"; and for the iron workers, it was the "hardest work in the construction industry."

The integration of these unions came only in the sixties, when the federal courts, the Tennessee Valley Authority, the Equal Opportunity Commission, and the civil rights movement began impinging on the apprenticeship system and the "sense of fraternity." "We had to try to make the best of a bad situation," the officer of the Electrical Workers' Union stated. "By a bad situation, I mean it was something that we were being forced into, and anytime that you force anyone into something, it, of course, to begin with, it is a bad situation."[48]

The Industrial Unions: Difficult Choices

The vast "reserve army" of black labor and convicts and the nature of mass industry forced some hard choices on the industrial unions. A few of the

---

48.   One officer of a craft union indicated that the international union ordered desegregation; the others indicated that the pressure came from the courts or the federal government. See appendix C, II.B, question 2.
  The officer of the Carpenters and Joiners described the first tentative steps in a "bad situation":

> So we went out there and talked to these boys that were working for these black contractors. And we got thirteen who were apparently carpenters to come into my office at night and we told them what the problem is:
>
> > Now look, we are not going to try to pull the wool over your eyes. We are going to tell you straight from the mouth, going to tell it like it is. We have got a civil rights movement on here. We need some blacks in this union and we can't get 'em. We don't know how to get 'em. We aren't having any luck. We want you guys in the union and here is the wages and here is the benefits and these are the advantages of being in the union. Do you want in the union?
>
> When a member comes in this union, he stands up and follows these people and the chairman of the meeting administers an oath to him which is written in ritual which we use to run our meetings. Now here we had thirteen blacks coming in which at the time just, the people in the South, "Oh, hell, this is a disaster. Not going to be anything left for the whites. . . ," they thought. "Well, hell, the blacks are taking over. They are moving in. We have been invaded."
> The members just wouldn't stand. They resented the hell out of this many blacks. Now you could bring one in here, occasionally with some white fellows, and they wouldn't pay any attention to it. But the leadership at that time, and I was president of this local at the time, and I had to do the initiation. But I didn't say anything about them not standing up, even though they were out of order and should have stood up. I initiated the blacks and we came in. . . . The blacks were standing facing me with their backs to the people, and they never knew the difference.

unions were not up to the conflicting pressures. The Amalgamated Association of Iron, Steel and Tin Workers attempted to organize the iron and steel industry without including black workers. Its strikes proved ineffective, and the union collapsed in 1909.[49] Faced with these grim prospects, the industrial unions turned to two organizational options: organize black and white together in one union or attempt to gain control over black labor supplies and black workers.

Option One: Multiracialism

The United Mine Workers and the Mine, Mill and Smelter Workers' Union chose the first option; their lead was taken up in later years by the Congress of Industrial Organizations (CIO) and the International Longshoremen Workers' Union (ILWU).

The Mine Workers' Union of Alabama was organized in 1893 along industrial lines, with black and white workers in separate locals at the Pratt Mines and a racially mixed local at Hewitt.[50] It later affiliated to the United Mine Workers of America and took up the national objective: "Unite in one organization, regardless of creed, color or nationality, all workmen employed in and around the mines." The union had little choice. Blacks, who comprised more than half the labor force, worked alongside white miners in the same occupations and work places. There was little skill differentiation in the mines—more than half the workers were hand coal loaders—and little salary differential between the hand coal loaders and the machine operators.[51] By 1904, the UMW had organized between 6,000 and 7,000 black miners in Alabama and had forced its racial policies on the Birmingham Trades Council, the state AFL, and even some employers.[52] After a series of tumultuous strikes, it had signed an agreement with TCI in 1898 that "provided for no discrimination against Negroes."[53] Within the state UMW, blacks were ordinarily elected vice-presidents, and sometimes presidents, of locals, even where a majority of the members were white. To insure continued black participation in the union, a number of positions were explicitly reserved for black members: vice-president in district organizations and locals and three of eight positions on district executive

49. Head, "The Development of the Labor Movement in Alabama," pp. 113–15; Marshall, *Labor in the South,* p. 182.
50. Marshall, *Labor in the South,* p. 95.
51. Northrup, "The Negro and the United Mine Workers," pp. 316–18. Moreover, black miners from Alabama and the South were regularly recruited by mining companies to break strikes in Illinois, Ohio, Kansas, Colorado, and, later, West Virginia.
52. Harris, *Political Power in Birmingham,* p. 45; Worthman, "Black Workers and Labor Unions," pp. 67, 77.
53. Marshall, *Labor in the South,* p. 73.

committees.[54] The union also insisted on integrated district meetings, forcing city officials and merchants in Birmingham and Selma to swallow traditional racial principles.[55]

The International Union of Mine, Mill and Smelter Workers organized black and white workers on the iron-ore mines, a section of primary industry where wages were lowest and black workers were most firmly entrenched. Like the Mine Workers, the union insisted on integrated locals and a racial allocation of leadership positions.[56] The constitution, for example, provided that there be an equal number of black and white officials.[57] The "UMW formula," as it came to be known, governed leadership selection in the Alabama CIO during the forties and fifties and in the merged AFL-CIO until the mid-sixties. The CIO elected blacks as "vice-presidents at large," positions "understood to be preserved for blacks and women at that time."[58] In the state AFL-CIO, blacks were formally elected to three vice-presidents at large for the Southern District and three for the Northern District.[59]

If the UMW and the Mine, Mill and Smelter Workers provided models of interracial organization, they also offered all too clear examples of how difficult and tenuous such organizational strategies can be. The Mine, Mill and Smelter Workers, even with 80 percent black members, was forced to put a "southern" face on its interracial solidarity: the union segregated its meetings—blacks in the pews and whites in the choir loft—and established segregated picket lines. Despite these concessions to local sensibilities, the union could not escape accusations of "communism" or the antipathy of the Birmingham press: "What the arming of people who nurse their own racial grievances could lead to must be left to the imagination."[60] Nor could the union escape the Klan element in its own ranks, which threatened union solidarity and encouraged raids—successful, as it turned out—by the United Steelworkers.[61]

54. Worthman, "Black Workers and Labor Unions," p. 68.
55. Ibid., pp. 79–80.
56. The UMW leadership formula (white president and black vice-president) was used, according to my survey, in four of the twelve industrial unions; five had entirely white leadership; two had black leaders in separate locals; and one had black and white presidents. See appendix C, II.B, question 2.
57. Worthman, "Black Workers and Labor Unions," pp. 75–76; Furse, "History of the International Union of Mine, Mill and Smelter Workers," pp. 8–9.
58. Interview with the former legislative director, Alabama Labor Council; also see Alabama State Industrial Union Council (CIO), *Proceedings of Fifteenth Constitutional Convention*, April 1954, p. 210.
59. See Alabama Labor Council (AFL-CIO), *Proceedings of the Biennial Conventions of the Alabama Labor Council,* 1958 to 1964.
60. Quoted in Furse, "History of the International Union of Mine, Mill and Smelter Workers," p. 13.
61. Ibid., p. 20.

The United Mine Workers, even as it preached racial solidarity, maneuvered amid community pressures that threatened the union's survival. Traditional social presumptions demanded segregation. Even "on a worktrain with their dirty mining clothes on together," a black organizer for the UMW commented, black and white workers kept to themselves.[62] Beyond these presumptions, the union still faced hostile employers, unions, black leadership, and a state that watched over questions of "social equality." During every mine strike between 1894 and 1908, white mobs attacked black strikers and organizers; the state acted to protect mine property and the racial order. The governor declared in 1908: "You know what it means to have eight or nine thousand niggars [sic] idle in the state of Alabama, and I am not going to stand for it."[63] When the UMW sent organizers into Alabama some twenty-five years later in a successful attempt to revive the organization, the AFL leadership accused the union of advocating "social equality between the whites and the blacks."[64] The UMW was careful, however, to place whites at the head of "pit" committees that negotiated with white employers, and it often pointed out that "social equality" need not follow on "equal pay for equal work."[65]

Option Two: Controlling Black Workers

Other industrial unions in Alabama opted for the second path: control over, rather than solidarity with, black workers. Some of these industrial unions paid respect to multiracialism; indeed, some even took up the "UMW formula" for electing black leadership. The Steelworkers, for example, challenged an ordinance enacted in the city of Fairfield, home of TCI, that prohibited racially mixed meetings.[66] It went on to organize both the production and maintenance people, "where, if we had to strike," one of the principal organizers commented, "we could make it effective."[67] But the steel union reflected the skill and wage disparities and segregation that

62. Richard L. Davis, black organizer and member of the UMW Executive Board, quoted in Worthman, "Black Workers and Labor Unions," p. 59.
63. Quoted in Richard A. Straw, "The Collapse of Biracial Unionism: The Alabama Coal Strike of 1908," p. 112.
64. Quoted in Marshall, *Labor in the South,* p. 152.
65. Northrup, *Organized Labor and the Negro,* pp. 166–67; Marshall, *Labor in the South,* p. 152; Straw, "The Collapse of Biracial Unionism," p. 108. The United Automobile Workers too, following the strong lead of the international union, organized black and white workers in the aircraft industry on the basis of racial equality. But it began late in the process (mid-fifties), on a small scale, where there were very few blacks—perhaps 10 percent of the labor force. And, as we shall see later, even under these circumstances, the union faced grave difficulties during the civil rights period.
66. *Birmingham Post,* 19 September 1933.
67. Interview by author with former officer of United Steelworkers; also see Alice Hoffman and Jack Spiese, "An Interview with Ruben Farr."

characterized the industry. White leadership was entrenched at the top and in the principal locals; the union lent formality to "lines of progression" that gave whites a virtual monopoly over the best paid and most skilled jobs. In two plants, black workers abandoned the Steelworkers in favor of an AFL affiliate that promised to break the traditional employment pattern.[68] But the pattern and the union's hold were not broken in the principal locals at TCI. In local 1013, one of the biggest in the South, blacks have held only a tenuous position on the grievance committee, and segregation has pervaded the local leadership structure. A union officer observed:

> Blacks and whites still sit on separate sides of the hall but the five main officers of the local are all white, even though blacks constitute almost 40 percent of the local. Blacks have about 30 percent of the committees but not in the principal leadership and they know that a challenge would lead to their total exclusion from the leadership of the union.[69]

Other industrial unions were able to bring along or control black workers with a less obvious nod to multiracialism. The Rubber Workers and the Communications Workers organized along industrial lines but neglected black workers employed at the periphery of the industry. In the former case, the union allowed blacks their own shop stewards but otherwise denied them leadership positions in the union and membership on the grievance committee.[70] In the latter case, the union acknowledged blacks as marginal workers—"janitors, maids and laborers"—and organized them separately.

> What we did, I would meet with the black people in one of the black members' houses. So we had stewards and they had black stewards and we'd meet. I'd go to one of their houses, once a week, and hold a meeting with them in their living room—serve refreshments, go to the kitchen, eat cake and coffee.

The International Brotherhood of Pulp, Sulphite and Paper Mill Workers maintained formally segregated locals—one for white workers in the pulp mill, recovery operation, and yard, and one for blacks in all sections of the plant. The structure of the union largely reinforced traditional segregation in the factory and white control of the industrial union.[71] Not until 1970,

---

68. Northrup, *Organized Labor and the Negro*, p. 183.
69. Interview with officer of United Steelworkers; also see Fay Hansen, "Political Conflict and Consensus in a Local Union," pp. 28–29.
70. Interview with the United Rubber Workers. This issue would ultimately end up in court and is discussed in the next section.
71. Northrup, *The Negro in the Paper Industry*, pp. 36–39.

after repeated entreaties by the federal government and the international, did the union merge its locals at Scott Paper in Mobile.[72]

FORMALIZING RACIAL BARRIERS IN THE WORK PLACE

The work place was not a critical issue for the artisan unions. By limiting access to skills and employment, they at the same time isolated the race question and subsumed it under other exclusory practices, such as apprenticeships, licensing, and union cards. They did not need, consequently, to erect racial barriers in the work place (wage gaps, "colored and white" jobs, or lines of progression) nor to develop racist ideologies to justify them.

For the industrial unions in Alabama, hiring was largely a management prerogative. White workers sometimes walked off the job when blacks entered traditionally white areas: one researcher counts three such instances in Alabama before 1900;[73] Birmingham's white bricklayers, carpenters, machinists, and telephone linemen and Walker County cotton-mill workers struck over black employment around the turn of the century;[74] and white workers as late as 1956 protested the employment of black "doffers" at Avondale Mills.[75] But rarely were industrial unions able to "settle" the race issue through organization and strikes alone.

Reserving White Work

"Colored" and "white" jobs were commonplace before unionization in Alabama. The industrial unions, however, struggling for recognition in a society hostile to labor organization and among white workers uninterested for the most part in racial solidarity, chose to live with the distinction.[76] The racial division of labor was a given, customary and unavoidable. "We took whoever the company hired," an Amalgamated Clothing officer recalled.

---

72. Ibid., pp. 116–17; *Watkins, Elijah et al. v. Scott Paper Company* 6EPD (1973): 587. Though these mergers across the South sometimes undermined black union leadership—indeed, many of the black locals resisted the change—at Scott Paper, the black local was large enough to protect its position in a single multiracial union. As Herbert Northrup points out, "The shoe is on the other foot."

73. Head, "The Development of the Labor Movement in Alabama," p. 225.

74. Worthman, "Black Workers and Labor Unions," p. 59.

75. *Birmingham News,* 3 September 1956.

76. Eleven of the twelve industrial unions organized workers in separate black or white jobs. The one that did not was organized in an industry without black workers. See appendix C, II.B, question 11.

"You had to [organize] on the basis of the people that were in the plant."
If blacks were the janitors and maids and not the production workers, as in
garments and textiles, the union was in no position to throw over the
pattern. The United Automobile Workers faced a similar situation in the
more urban and more highly skilled aircraft industry:

> It was traditional in the South. They're what you call "nigger jobs."
> I'll tell you the truth: the workers are happy with that arrangement.
> That's what they've been taught is right. Generation after generation,
> they are taught that blacks are dirty and no good. It's bound to have
> an effect. The company could have hired whoever they wanted to.
> Even in the fifties, we just organized who they hired.

Even in the coal-mining industry, where the union was committed to
interracial solidarity, black workers were concentrated in the hand-loading
positions, while whites dominated machine operations and monopolized
supervisory jobs.[77] Today, the UMW in Alabama seems little conscious of
the earlier struggles. The leadership acknowledges that blacks are barely
evident in the more skilled mining occupations, such as machine operators,
section repairmen and electricians, and completely absent from the bull-
dozers and other equipment in the fast-growing surface mines.[78]

The Union of Marine and Shipbuilding Workers, CIO, was caught
between its own precarious position in the Alabama dry docks and the
racism of its white members. Immediately before World War II, when the
union won recognition, blacks were confined to the "black department"—
the dockhands, steeling, and painting. Only occasionally did blacks work as
caulkers or chippers and never as welders. The last was white work. Twelve
black welders were brought on to the night shift in 1943 only after the Fair
Employment Practices Commission and the War Manpower Commission
brought pressure on the Alabama Dry Docks. Antiblack rioting in Mobile
and an extended work stoppage at the dry docks, however, brought an end
to the experiment. Blacks moved up to the "North Yard" and worked the
full range of jobs on segregated shifts.[79] The union failed to protect even
these small gains, however. The officer observed: "We had to reduce
ourselves from around forty thousand to four or five thousand or less after
the war and the specialist lost out. The blacks went back into their
department, the black department, and got locked in." The union, after all,

---

77. Northrup, "Negroes and the United Mine Workers," p. 317.
78. Interview with officer of the United Mine Workers.
79. Tindall, *The Emergence of the New South,* p. 715; Northrup, *Organized Labor and the
Negro,* pp. 225–27; interview with the officer of the Union of Marine and Shipbuilding
Workers.

"is run by the membership," and, the officer added, "The whites outnumber the blacks."

The "big four" on the railroads—the Brotherhood of Engineers, the Order of Railway Conductors, the Brotherhood of Locomotive Firemen and Enginemen, and the Brotherhood of Railway Trainmen—went beyond custom; the Railway Brotherhoods, particularly the trainmen and firemen, excluded blacks from their "fraternity" and drew a firm racial barrier at the laboring grades. Their position was different both from the craft unions established in Alabama at the end of the nineteenth century and the industrial unions that struggled through the twentieth. They had strong collective bargaining rights from 1900; the trainmen and firemen, however, were not apprenticed and in the South, and Alabama, shared their crafts with large numbers of black workers. The firemen and trainmen, consequently, regularly addressed the "Negro question." Concerted campaigns were developed at national conventions to eliminate blacks from the railroads. Through a complex of work rules, quotas, terrorism, seniority arrangements, "bumping rights," priority arrangements for "promotable" white firemen, "full crew legislation," and other ingenious devices, the white unions were able to reduce drastically the number of black workers. During World War I, the railway unions enlisted the U.S. Railroad Administration in these schemes; during World War II, the railway companies and unions successfully shielded these practices from the Fair Employment Practices Commission.[80]

In 1942 a black fireman in Alabama, B. W. Steele, challenged the agreement between the Brotherhood of Locomotive Firemen and the Louisville and Nashville Railroad Company. The Alabama Supreme Court, though noting that the percentage of black firemen in the district had dropped from 98 percent when Steele was first hired to 20 percent at the time of the FEPC hearings, refused to throw out the agreement. The U.S. Supreme Court later reversed the state court.[81]

Separate Lines of Progression

Though most of the industrial unions inherited their "nigger jobs," they later helped forge a labor framework that entrenched them. Rules for the work place—separate lines of promotion, black and white seniority lists, and departmental seniority—gave white workers security and control over the best jobs; they gave black workers security in the "dead-end" jobs.

---

80. Spero and Harris, *The Black Worker*, pp. 284–315; Northrup, *Organized Labor and the Negro*, pp. 48–75.
81. Howard W. Risher, Jr., *The Negro in the Railroad Industry*, pp. 64–65.

These work rules became conventional practice in rubber, steel, and paper and were used extensively in coal mining, aircraft, retail trade, shipbuilding, dry docks, garments, and textiles.[82]

Local 12 of the United Rubber Workers in Gadsden, Alabama, negotiated an agreement with the Goodyear Tire Company that took cognizance of custom and locked blacks in the reclaim department in perpetuity. Though black workers might accumulate seniority, like white workers, it did not entitle them to bid on white jobs in the manufacturing section. Not until 1962 did the union merge the black male and white male (and white female) seniority rolls and create a system of plantwide seniority. The federal courts declared, "As a matter of custom and interpretation during this period, Negro employees with greater seniority had no rights over white employees with less seniority, and vice versa, with respect to promotions, transfers, layoffs, and recalls."[83] The union leadership did not include blacks on grievance committees during this period; in fact, a union officer recalled, "Actually the first contact we had with the black people was in 1960." When black workers attempted to contest the discriminating seniority procedures, the union maintained that "no contract violation exists." It agreed to process their grievance only after intervention by the union's international president, the President's Committee on Equal Employment Opportunity, the National Labor Relations Board, and the United States Court of Appeals.[84]

The national agreement between the United Steelworkers and the United States Steel Corporation provided that local union committees and local management work out their own seniority arrangements: at the Fairfield Works outside Birmingham, that meant departmental seniority. Management conventionally prefers to limit seniority to "like work" and had, in any event, maintained separate black and white seniority lists prior to unionization; the white-dominated locals too were content to leave blacks in separate "lines of progression." One Steelworker official commented, "There was collusion going on. . . . Both groups in some instances were hoping it would stay like it was." In 1962, responding to the President's Executive Order 10925 and *Whitfield* v. *United Steelworkers,* the local parties agreed to pool the lines of progression.[85] The courts provided further relief in 1973, instructing the company to pay for past discrimination. The

---

82. Seven of the eleven industrial unions (out of a total of twelve) negotiated separate seniority for whites and blacks. See appendix C, II.B, question 6.

83. *Local Union No. 12, United Rubber, Cork, Linoleum and Plastic Workers of America v. National Labor Relations Board* 368 F.2d 12 (1966):14.

84. *Local Union No. 12 v. N.L.R.B.*: 15–19; Herbert Northrup, *Negro Employment in Basic Industry: A Study of Racial Policies in Six Industries,* pp. 473–75.

85. *United States v. United States Steel Corporation* 371 F. Supp. 1045 (1973): 1055–56.

union's responsibility was confined to a small local that had "held the lines of promotion apart again so that the blacks would bear the brunt . . . of the layoffs."[86]

At Scott Paper Company outside Mobile, management in the early sixties, after prodding from the company's head office and federal officials, attempted to break down the pattern of black and white jobs and seniority arrangements. In this instance, the union, management, and the courts sought to maintain "lines of progression": the advanced paper machines, all agreed, demanded some restrictions on job bidding. But in 1962 management systematically transferred blacks into some thirty white lines of progression; further, in 1969, it unilaterally insisted that black workers carry their plant seniority with them into the new positions. The members of the formerly black local of the Brotherhood of Pulp, Sulphite and Paper Mill Workers welcomed the mangement initiative. The white locals, however, rejected or ignored it.[87]

The industrial unions took their chances with plantwide seniority only where there were very few black workers. The Communications Workers won "seniority across the bargaining unit" at Southern Bell Telephone. Blacks were confined to positions as janitors and maids before the passage of the Civil Rights Act of 1964 and were somehow left out of the seniority system. A union officer observed: "They could have gone into a janitor's job at a higher pay, but for all practical purposes, there was no line of progression. You hire in as a janitor; you work for fifty years; you retire as a janitor." Members of the Electrical Workers at Alabama Power Company also exercised broad seniority rights and were free to bid on jobs at any plant in the state. But janitors did not have bidding rights. Laborers were incorporated into the agreement only after the Laborers' Union threatened to organize the small number of black workers into a separate union.[88]

THE FRAMEWORK OF RACE DOMINATION

Building Up the State Structure

The framework of race domination in Alabama included the franchise laws and local officialdom that had kept blacks voteless from the turn of the century; the system of apportioning voters that had given Black Belt

---

86. Interview with attorney for the United Steelworkers.
87. *Watkins v. Scott Paper Co.*: 5857–61; interview with the officer of the Pulp, Sulphite and Paper Mill Workers.
88. Interviews with the officers of the Electrical Workers' Union and Laborers' Union.

planters control of the state legislature; the system of dependent sharecropping, with its lien, false pretense, and antienticement laws, its debt arrangements, and local courts and county officials, that sought to bind black rural labor to the land; the convict lease system and antivagrancy and labor agent registration laws that had helped industrialists organize a labor force; the local and state governmental repressive apparatus that facilitated strikebreaking and limited multiracial labor organization.

White workers had little role in creating that framework, however. The artisans who regulated their own scarcity had little need of it.[89] The ~~exclusive~~ *open* industrial unions who drew on black and white workers sought to lift restrictions on organizing and broaden the franchise; the exclusive industrial unions seemed content to formalize their control at the work place—creating white and black jobs and lines of progression—without forging state job protections and white labor policies.

From the late thirties, with the growth of the CIO in Alabama, the open industrial unions began chipping away at the racial framework. In 1942, the Alabama CIO warned, "The poll tax fight still looms up as one of the greatest issues in the South." It still loomed well into the fifties and sixties: in 1957, the Labor Council and other state labor organizations resisted an attempt by Black Belt representatives to reestablish the cumulative feature of the poll tax; in 1965, even as the state was forced to comply with new federal civil rights laws, Black Belt state senators successfully defeated a labor-backed amendment to repeal the poll tax.[90] The Labor Council also opposed the apportionment of legislative seats that favored Black Belt counties at the expense of the urban and industrial areas, joining a suit that took the issue away from the state legislature.[91] Finally, the Labor Council challenged the institutions of labor and political control in the Black Belt. It opposed "local bills" for Marengo and Wilcox Counties requiring that labor organizers register with the Board of Revenue and pay a license fee and similar legislation requiring that civil rights organizers register with county

---

89. The artisan unions have lobbied for legislation that furthers their job control, such as repeal of the "right to work" law or, at least, passage of an agency shop bill (requiring payment of union dues where a labor contract is in force.) They have also supported candidates, like Eugene "Bull" Connor and George Wallace, who "respected their picket lines and their 'rates' " (interview with the officer of the Birmingham Building and Construction Trades Council).

90. Alabama State Industrial Union Council (CIO), *Proceedings of the Fourth Constitutional Convention,* May 1942, p. 23; Alabama Labor Council, Railroad Brotherhoods of Alabama, and the United Mine Workers of America, *Joint Legislative Report, Regular Legislative Session 1957;* Alabama Labor Council (AFL-CIO), *Legislative Report 1965,* p. 11.

91. Alabama Labor Council (AFL-CIO), *Proceedings of the Fourth Biennial Convention, 1962,* p. 8.

officials.[92] The Labor Council in 1961 opposed the state "Un-American Activities" bill that provided for "a Permanent Joint Legislative Committee to study, investigate, subpoena, analyze, and interrogate the activities of persons, groups and organizations who seek to destroy the ideals of the citizens of the State of Alabama under the color of protection afforded by the Bill of Rights for the Constitution of the United States and the Constitution of the State of Alabama."[93]

Though the exclusive industrial unions benefited from a system that limited the proletarianization of black workers and tolerated union work rules, they were never able to construct an elaborate state defense of white labor and white laboring organizations; indeed, the state, closely identified with Black Belt planter interests and supported by textile, steel, and mining companies, had shown little regard for the views of organized white labor. It played an active role in crushing the industrial unions, protecting black strikebreakers, and fostering low-wage policies.[94] In the post-World War II period, Alabama was among a minority of states with no minimum-wage law; its unemployment compensation at one point was the lowest in the nation and was one of only three requiring employee contributions; the legislature quickly passed a "right to work" law and forbade state employees from joining trade unions.[95]

Dismantling the State Structure

While none of the unions depended heavily on the state racial structure, virtually all were threatened by the political disorder that brought it down. The exclusive industrial unions in particular, however, with few protections outside their own work rules and job demarcations, faced a precarious labor environment: social and political changes promised increasing mobility of black labor and increasing challenges to their formal racial barriers.

George Meany's support for the NAACP and his attack on the White Citizens' Council brought a rash of heated protests from white workers in Alabama, particularly from members of the United Steelworkers. Members of Birmingham locals wired the AFL-CIO, "If you continue to favor integration and contribute funds from the treasury to destroy our way of life

---

92. Alabama Labor Council (AFL-CIO), *Proceedings of the First Biennial Convention of the Alabama Labor Council,* Merger Convention of the Alabama State Federation of Labor and the Alabama State Industrial Union Council, Mobile, Alabama, 1956, p. 15; also interview with officer of the State Labor Council.

93. Alabama Labor Council (AFL-CIO), *Legislative Report 1961,* p. 22.

94. See the discussion of business and planter interests, chapter 10 and chapter 6.

95. Alabama Labor Council (AFL-CIO), *1967 Legislative Report and Voting Records,* pp. 6, 16; *Legislative Report 1961,* pp. 4–5.

we will band together with other locals in the South and fight for what we believe to be our rights."[96] The leadership tried to quiet the protests. "Without the union we wouldn't have made the progress we have made," Ruben Farr, the union's district director, responded. Privately, the union shied away from issues, like school integration, that might "tear up the union, or destroy it."[97] The leadership of the United Automobile Workers, an explicitly open industrial union, supported racial integration even as it faced serious pressure from white members to take a different course.

> When they really started integrating the schools, we began to have some trouble. At the Hayes International local, some members wanted to picket the schools, and wanted me to come out against integration. They wanted me to picket the schools. They put up pickets around Ramsey and Phillips High. I told them, "I'm not going down," and they told me that "we are going to take care of you around election time." I was reelected, but it had its toll. I didn't win by much and there was a lot of hard feelings among the membership. The Ku Klux Klan was active in the membership, and when I served on the biracial committee, the Ku Kluxers were ready to tear the council down.

Most of the other industrial unions with black members sought to avoid the UAW example. "We would not allow the race issue to come up," the Marine and Shipbuilding Workers officer reported. "We tell the blacks to go to the NAACP, 'Take it to them.' Or tell the whites if they bring something up, 'You go to the Klan.' That was it. We are here to deal with working conditions." When several black members attempted to bring these issues before a Laborers' Union local, the leadership cut off discussion. "We are not getting involved in that because we're here for one purpose and one purpose only: that's to make the best living that we can with our hands."

These open and some of the exclusive industrial unions were vulnerable to "raids" by the new southern, all-white unions and the Klan. Birmingham and Alabama were apparently the base for such groups. The Klan effectively infiltrated the Rubber Workers local in Tuscaloosa and Steelworkers locals in Birmingham.[98] Groups of workers threatened to withdraw from the Communications Workers and the Steelworkers;[99] independent unions—the Southern Fabricating and Steel Workers, and Southern Aircraft Workers, and the Association of Western Pulp and Paper Workers—challenged the established unions at Butler Manufacturing, Hayes International, and Scott

96. *Birmingham Post-Herald*, 24 February 1956.
97. Hoffman and Spiese, "An Interview with Ruben Farr," p. 49.
98. Ray Marshall, *The Negro Worker*, pp. 46–48.
99. *Birmingham Post-Herald*, 6 April 1956.

Paper, respectively.[100] Though a Southern Crafts, Inc. was formed in Birmingham, it had an uncertain membership and never seriously challenged any of the artisan unions.

The dissension in the labor movement soon moved from the local to the state level, threatening to undermine the State Labor Council. The locals, first in small numbers but then in a mass movement, began to disaffiliate from the Council. They complained about a new per capita tax but also about the integrated seating at conventions, the state organization's refusal to repudiate AFL-CIO support for the Civil Rights Act of 1964, and the failure to endorse Governor Wallace's presidential bid. With the final consolidation in 1958 of the AFL-CIO in Alabama, the Council membership had reached 107,000; by 1965, the affiliated membership had dropped to 56,000. A state labor organization that had encompassed almost 60 percent of AFL-CIO members in 1958 now represented fewer than a third.[101]

The building trades were the first to disassociate: the craft unions had already demonstrated some disenchantment with the Council's bias toward the "industrial type of union"[102] and had strongly endorsed Wallace on a number of occasions as a "friend of labor."[103] But the disaffiliation of the construction unions was overshadowed by the massive defection of larger industrial unions: the Rubber Workers local at Gadsden, the large Communications Workers local in Birmingham, virtually all the Steelworkers locals, including the largest local at TCI, and the Paper Workers in Mobile.[104] They stood with Wallace and segregation, not because of good rates or highway construction—important for the building unions—but because Meany and the federal government challenged their position in Alabama society and because George Wallace defended, albeit unsuccessfully, a racial order that had allowed them to segregate their unions, create white jobs, and entrench their status in an elaborate set of work rules. That the racial framework was largely the product of other interests in Alabama society was less important for them than the immediate consequences of its demise.

100. *Birmingham Post-Herald*, 21 May 1956; Northrup, *The Negro in the Paper Industry*, p. 114.
101. George Gustavus Kundahl, Jr., "Organized Labor in Alabama State Politics," pp. 69, 93.
102. Interview with the officer of the Mobile Construction and Building Trades Union.
103. Interview with the officer of the Birmingham Building and Construction Trades Council; also see Hansen, "Political Conflict and Consensus in a Local Union," p. 16.
104. Interviews with the officers of the Alabama Labor Council, Communications Workers and United Steelworkers; Hansen, "Political Conflict and Consensus in a Local Union," p. 47.

CHAPTER 16

The Histadrut: Bounded Working Class and the Jewish Ascendancy

The same process which leads to sweating in another country gives a tendency in this country to eliminate those who require a higher standard of life. In another sphere it is an exemplification of Gresham's 'Law of Currency'. In certain circumstances bad money will drive out good. In this competitive wage-production system in a situation such as we have in South Africa the lower civilization will gradually drive out the higher civilization.

Colonel Cresswell, Minister of Labour, South Africa, 1925

In the workers movement of the world we cannot find such an example. Wherever we find two different standards of living prevailing among the workers, those living at the higher standard are forced to confine themselves to special branches of work. But we have not seen an example of an organised and better-paid worker acquiring work that is done in the same place by unorganised cheaply-paid workers, and at the same time preserve his high standard of living and his social conquests.

David Ben-Gurion, Jewish Labour,[1] 1935

Jewish settlement in Palestine brought the development of a full-blown bounded working class, with Jews laboring in the orchards and construction, with Jews doing "all the work, from the least strenuous, cleanest, and most sophisticated, to the dirtiest and most difficult"[2]—yet separate from the Arabs. It did not emerge as an accidental consequence of colonial policy or the organization of a labor force for industry. The conception of a bounded working class was an integral part of Zionist and Jewish settler designs for Palestine.

A union for Jewish workers, such as the Histadrut, was not a necessary part of that original design. It is difficult, nonetheless, to imagine a separate Jewish economy and class structure developing amid the Arab fellahin[3] without an organization to manage the boundaries.

---

1. David Ben-Gurion, *Jewish Labour,* pp. 22–23.
2. A. D. Gordon, "People and Labor," p. 374.
3. *Fellahin* are Arab tenants or peasant farmers.

Some in the Zionist settlement and Histadrut hoped to avoid the boundary problem. "Now all that should be rightly asked of us," Golda Meir told the Anglo-American Committee of Inquiry, "is that by our coming into the country nobody must suffer."[4] The Jewish community asked only that it be allowed to accumulate capital and encourage Jewish immigration and that the employment opportunities arising from development accrue in the first instance to the Jewish community in Palestine. The intent was progressive ("Never before has the white man undertaken colonisation with that sense of justice and social progress which fills the Jew who comes to Palestine")[5] and nonexploitive ("We cannot accept the South African method: the nonprofessional work to the natives and the professional work to the Europeans.")[6]

But the Histadrut could not avoid a preoccupation with the boundaries between Jews and Arabs, between those "living at the higher standard" and "the unorganised cheaply-paid workers." It insisted on areas of protected employment for Jewish labor and on the corollary, the exclusion of Arabs from Jewish enterprises; the barring of Arab workers from the Jewish trade unions and labor exchanges; the fixing of "civilized" rates of pay and Jewish employment quotas in the British-administered railways and posts. The Histadrut helped formalize the distinctions between Arabs and Jews in the mandatory period and afterwards, giving effect to the distinctions in the labor market and demanding that the state too honor the boundaries. After Independence, it gave Jewish workers a pre-eminent position in the labor market and labor institutions.

The Histadrut emerged as the strongest organized force in the *yishuv*[7] and played a central part in the development of Israel, overshadowing the role of organized manufacturers' and farmers' associations, for example. While trade-union leaders were being deported from South Africa and jailed in Gadsden, Alabama, labor leaders like Ben Zvi, David Ben-Gurion, and Chaim Arlosoroff were joining the Jewish Agency, Zionist, and Vaad Leumi executives. They would shape Jewish-Arab relations from the centers of power in the yishuv and Israel. The bounded working class here, more than in any other setting we have examined, is intimately associated with the developing framework of ethnic domination.

---

4.   *Public Hearings Before the Anglo-American Committee of Inquiry,* Jerusalem, 25 March 1946, p. 78.
5.   Berl Katznelson, "Reaction v. Progress in Palestine," p. 8.
6.   David Ben-Gurion, "Opening Address" before General Federation of Jewish Labour, Fourth Histadrut Convention, February 1933, trans. Ester Lazar, pp. 14–15.
7.   *Yishuv* refers to the Jewish community in Palestine before partition.

CREATING A BOUNDED WORKING CLASS

The Jewish people in Israel make a curious, perhaps historically anomalous dominant section. The Jews themselves did not come to the Ottoman Empire or Palestine to advance the cause of British imperial policy or to construct a racial order.[8] They had barely achieved civil equality in Germany, France, and Great Britain when the pogroms became a regular feature of eastern European life. The halting assimilation of prominent Jews in France and Germany was balanced by the pauperization of Polish Jewry and the persistent slaughter of Russian Jews in and outside the pale of settlement. They came to Palestine, and later to Israel, as outcasts, to find work and escape persecution. Few among the Jewish settlers thought that Zionism would bring a "new Poland—with this change, that the Arabs will have the position of the Jews and the Jews that of the Poles, perhaps with the addition of a more gentlemanly attitude toward the minority race."[9]

The Jewish settlers of the late nineteenth and early twentieth centuries found in Palestine what some of them called, "Arab feudalism": a mix of seminomadic bedouin tribes, Arab *effendis* (large landowners), occasional day laborers, merchants, and the largest group, the Arab tenantry and peasant farmers.[10] Though Arab society in Palestine seemed precapitalist, the breakdown of peasant agriculture and the development of at least occasional wage labor was well advanced by the twentieth century. Arab villagers, like those elsewhere in Egypt and Syria, were losing out to commercialization. The use of individual land titles from the mid-nineteenth century and land sales, some stimulated by Jewish settlement, brought increasing pressure to sell village lands and diminishing access to previously unoccupied pasture land. The abrogation of communal lands, the growth of direct taxation, and peasant indebtedness forced increasing numbers of Arabs into the labor market.[11]

To the Jewish settlers, the Arab worker seemed only partially proletarianized, "steeped in ignorance and poverty, subjected to the domi-

---

8. It is certainly possible, however, that the British Colonial Office itself viewed the Zionist settlers in that role. See Abdul-Wahab Kayyali, "Zionism and Imperialism: The Historical Origins," pp. 98–99.

9. Berl Katznelson, "The Political Future of Palestine," p. 206.

10. Chaim Arlosoroff, "The Economic Background of the Arab Problem," pp. 3–10; also see Abner Cohen, *Arab Border-Villages in Israel,* pp. 2–8.

11. Palestine, *Report of the Commission on the Palestine Disturbances of August, 1929* (Shaw), 1930, p. 124; and Endriss E. Khalidi, "Palestinian Arab Villages in Israel," p. 23; Walter Laqueur, *A History of Zionism,* pp. 214–15; David Hurwitz, "The Agrarian Problem of the Fellahin," pp. 49–62; Elia Zureik, "Toward a Sociology of the Palestinians," pp. 5–7; also see chapter 2.

nation of an oppressive feudal society."[12] He vacillated between the subsistence economy and the Jewish sector or worked full time in the colonies while his family remained in tenantry. In either case, the Arab worker demanded less than a "civilized standard" for his labor and threatened to displace the fully proletarian, Jewish worker.[13]

Despite frequent references to a "dual economy"—one section Jewish, progressive and cooperative, and the other Arab and feudal—Arab labor penetrated the Jewish sector almost from the beginning.[14] In the first Jewish settlements at Rishon-le-Zion, the initial commitment to "self-emancipation" through "self-labor" gave way within twenty years to a Jewish supervisory staff in Baron de Rothschild's colonies and a small number of property owners employing mostly Arab laborers.[15] At Petah Tikvah in 1908, there were perhaps thirty Jewish workers among 1,000 to 15,000 Arabs. Even on Jewish national projects, like the tree nurseries of the Herzl Forest, the construction of the Jewish suburb of Jaffa (now Tel Aviv), and the Haifa Technion, employers relied heavily, sometimes exclusively, on Arab labor. Eighty to 90 percent of state employees under the mandate were Arabs. Before the wave of riots in 1936–39, Arabs constituted almost half the workers in the building industry and more than half the laborers in

12. General Federation of Jewish Labour in Eretz-Israel, *Report on Histadruth Activities in Palestine,* 1947, p. 16; also see Abraham Revusky, *The Histadrut: A Labor Commonwealth in the Making,* p. 36.

13. Even in the early 1960s, Arab workers continued to live in the villages and gain part of their livelihood from agriculture, though an increasing percentage spent part of the year working for wages (Henry Rosenfeld, "The Arab Village Proletariat," pp. 15–16; also see Khalidi, "Palestinian Arab Villages," pp. 20–22).

14. Zionist leaders also admitted that Jewish investment and settlement might have affected the Arab sector as well. Chaim Arlosoroff responded angrily to the Shaw Report:

Zionism should plead guilty of having stimulated within the sphere of its activities, all the processes which accompany the awakening of a stagnant Oriental economy. Zionism should plead guilty of having set in motion, within the boundaries of Palestine, a dynamic force such as no other Middle Eastern country has enjoyed to the same relative extent, while in the process of 'capitalisation' and Europeanisation. It should plead guilty of having had a hand in the breaking up of the large estates. It should plead guilty of having created, over night, a market for the produce of intensive farming—vegetable-growing and dairying. It should plead guilty—even if it be established that, on this account, a number of Arab tenants had to be moved from one village to another—of having pumped into certain sections of Arab agriculture so much capital (in form of money spent on land purchases and compensation paid to tenants) as to enable them to develop intensive mixed farming and the laying out of plantations ("Land, Immigration and the Shaw Report," p. 186).

15. Walter Preuss, *The Labour Movement in Israel,* pp. 19–20; Revusky, *The Histadrut,* p. 14, and Noah Lucatz, "Histadrut as a Nationalist and Socialist Movement, 1882–1948," pp. 20–23.

Jewish-owned orchards. Indeed, immediately before the war, Arabs made up more than half of the wage earners in Palestine.[16]

The "cheapness" and availability of Arab labor gave the yishuv, as they saw it, two alternatives: either accept the logic of the labor market and evolve into a small "economic aristocracy, monopolizing the occupations that require superior skills and intelligence"[17] or create, in effect, a bounded working class, a full-fledged Jewish working class with laboring opportunities that would open the way to large-scale Jewish settlement.

For important elements in the Second Aliya (1904–14),[18] particularly the followers of A. D. Gordon and the Hapoel Hatzair (Young Workers), the commitment to productive labor was the essential principle and spirit in Zionism. The lack of connection to the soil and productive occupations in the Diaspora and the early settlements had proved the source of malaise in the Jewish community and anti-Semitism across Europe. Gordon wrote, "We have become accustomed to every form of life, except to a life of labor —of labor done at our own behest and for its own sake."[19] In Palestine, the commitment to the "life of labor" became a commitment to the "conquest of work," *kibush haavoda*. The principle was set out in every issue of Hapoel Hatzair's paper: "The necessary condition for the realization of Zionism is conquest by Jewish labour of all occupations in the country."[20] Through the life of labor, Gordon wrote, the Jewish worker "would gradually transfer the centre of activity in all collective life from the sphere of the capitalist to that of the worker."[21]

For Ber Borochov and the Poale Zion (Workers of Zion), the commitment to Jewish labor had to be combined with a commitment to "proletarian struggle." Like the Gordonists, they believed that the national experience of the Jewish people, what Borochov called the "conditions of production," set the Jewish working class apart from other working-class groups and made their work experience remote from "nature."[22] But the simple example of Jews performing, even with dignity, the most menial jobs would not bring about the "assimilation" of the capitalist class and the reorganization of work. The capitalist left to his own devices would displace

16. Ben-Gurion, *Jewish Labour,* pp. 11–13; Samuel Kurland, *Co-operative Palestine,* pp. 85–86, 100; Svi Sussman, "The Policy of the Histadrut With Regard to Wage Differentials," pp. 42–47.
17. The Executive Committee of the General Federation of Jewish Labor, "Memorandum Submitted to the Palestine Commission of Inquiry," p. 3.
18. *Aliya* (plural, *aliyot*) refers to a wave of Jewish immigration to Palestine.
19. Gordon, "People and Labor," p. 372.
20. Quoted in Preuss, *The Labour Movement,* p. 28.
21. A. D. Gordon, "Nationalism and Socialism," quoted in Lucatz, "Histadrut as a Nationalist and Socialist Movement," p. 59.
22. Ber Borochov, *Nationalism and Class Struggle,* pp. 61–69.

Jewish workers and recreate the anomalies of work in Europe: "There was a danger that a community would arise in Palestine in which a class of Arab wage-earners would confront an upper-class of Jewish capitalists and the social cleave would be intensified and sharpened by national distinctions."[23] The interest of both Jewish and non-Jewish capitalists in cheap labor stands against the fundamental interest of the emerging Jewish working class in performing all forms of work and normalizing the work experience in the *yishuv.*[24]

The commitment of the Jewish settlers to establishing a Jewish laboring community, despite the growing numbers of Arab wage laborers, had important consequences for Jewish-Arab relations and the emerging framework of Jewish domination.

HISTADRUT AND THE LABOR ASCENDANCY

The Histadrut, though a labor organization from its founding in 1920, emerged in the conflict of competing Jewish labor parties, particularly the Hapoel Hatzair (Young Worker) and the Palestine Poale Zion (Workers of Zion), later reconstituted as Ahdut Haavoda (Working-Class Union). The former emphasized its "constructionist" goals, sometimes called practical Zionism, and deplored dependence on socialist doctrine and international socialist organizations. The latter, while involved with constructionist projects in Palestine, emphasized the emerging class struggle in Palestine and the connection with working-class movements in eastern and western Europe. On the ideological plain, these differences led the parties down separate paths; but at the practical level, the parties developed parallel institutions for recruiting party members and serving the newly arrived immigrants, including labor exchanges, agricultural settlements, and welfare societies.

It was this ruinous competition among the practical party institutions, as well as the growing impatience of newly arrived ("unaffiliated") immigrants, that led to the establishment of the Histadrut. The parties maintained their integrity as mobilizing institutions while yielding most of their trade-union and service functions to the General Federation of Jewish Labor (the Histadrut).[25]

23. Jewish Socialist Labour Confederation Poale-Zion, *The Jewish Labour Movement in Palestine,* 1928, p. 10.
24. Borochov, *Nationalism,* pp. 146–50.
25. For discussions of the parties and the establishment of the Histadrut, see Preuss, *The Labour Movement,* pp. 56–61; and Laqueur, *A History of Zionism,* pp. 304–08.

The Histadrut, its founders stated, would be open to "all [Jewish] workers subsisting on earnings of their own work and not exploiting the labor of others"; it would "persist in conducting the struggle of hired workers for improved labor conditions until the complete liberation of the working class." The founders were also determined that the Histadrut go beyond struggle to "constructionist" work, supporting "enterprises in all branches of agriculture and industry in city and village," labor cooperatives and colonization, "revival of the Hebrew language," and "organization and expansion of labor immigration."[26]

Within a decade of its founding, the Histadrut was the dominant labor organization within the *yishuv*, establishing the largest labor exchanges, dispensing health care, and organizing the orchards and workshops, along with the building, railway, and postal workers. In time, particularly after statehood, its workers' committees would become the primary influence on the plant floor, its national trade unions and economic committee would dominate national wage and income policies. Histadrut agencies, perhaps uncharacteristically for a labor organization, would also become a major source of investment and employment for Jewish workers.[27] Before statehood, 85 percent of Jewish workers belonged to the Histadrut; in 1971, 80 percent of Jewish and 50 percent of Israeli Arab workers were members.[28]

The Histadrut also dominated the organization of private interests, certainly within the *yishuv* and, for a long period, in Israel as well. Private capital has had a checkered career in both the world Zionist movement and the colonization of Palestine. Baron de Rothschild's turn of the century experiment in plantations, though important to the emerging labor pattern

26. "Statutes of the General Federation of Jewish Labour in Palestine," in Kurland, *Cooperative Palestine,* p. 265. The struggle of hired labor was, of course, a bit premature, as the Jewish working class in Palestine in 1930 comprised little more than 10,000 agricultural workers, 1,500 railway and port workers, and 2,500 construction workers (Preuss, *The Labour Movement,* p. 110). "This is the only nation," a former general secretary of the Histadrut observed, "where there is a union before there were workers."

27. Virtually all of Israel's Jewish workers and over 40 percent of the Arab workers receive full medical attention under Kuppat Holim, a trade-union rather than state-run comprehensive health scheme. More than a fourth of all workers are employed not by private or state-owned industries, but in farming and industrial enterprises organized under Histadrut's Hevrat Ovidm. It is responsible for cooperative enterprises (e.g., bus and taxi cooperatives) and acts as holding company for Histadrut enterprises, such as the Workers Bank, Solel Boneh (Israel's largest construction company), and Koor (an industrial holding company). While the Histadrut is now firmly rooted in industrial enterprises and Israel's cities, it has always included large numbers of agricultural laborers and membership from the *moshavim* (agricultural cooperatives) and *kibbutzim* (agricultural collectives) (Preuss, *The Labour Movement,* pp. 219–221; Peter Y. Medding, *Mapai in Israel: Political Organization and Government in a New Society,* pp. 16–17).

28. Irvin Sobel, "Israel," p. 190; also Dr. Joseph J. Lador-Lederer, "In the State of Israel," p. 195.

in Palestine, never generated the anticipated commercial agricultural development or attracted other forms of private capital. The "money Jews" in England, France, Germany, and Russia shunted aside Herzl's appeals for support and investment; indeed, he found support almost exclusively among Jews who gathered at places like the Working Man's Club in the East End of London and the parade route in Vilna.[29]

What bourgeois influence existed in Palestine came with the short-lived ascendancy of the middle class in the Fourteenth and Fifteenth Zionist Congresses (1925–27) and the Fourth Aliya (1924–31). But the attempts of the Zionist Congress to impose businesslike standards on the colonies collapsed. By 1933 Labor Zionism gained control of the movement in both Palestine (with almost three-quarters of the votes) and in the Zionist Congress, where it emerged as the largest faction. The substantial middle-class element in the Fourth Aliya brought an ephemeral urban prosperity, followed by the collapse in 1926.[30] The middle class that was willing to risk its future in Palestine came principally with "its name and pretensions" but little real capital, Berl Katznelson observed. "To us came, not middle class property, but a property-less middle class."[31]

Virtually all the land in Israel is now owned by the government or the Jewish National Fund; only in the citrus plantations does private ownership play an important role. The private sector in 1960 was responsible for just under 60 percent of net domestic product, but even here, the Histadrut maintains substantial stock holdings.[32]

The organization of private-sector interests has never been particularly auspicious. The Farmers' Association waged a persistent, and to some extent successful, struggle against organized Jewish labor on the plantations; it failed utterly, however, to alter the basic direction of colonization and economic development. Its pleas to the Jewish Agency and the mandatory authorities that immigration be limited to "plain Jews" rather than better organized Hehalutz members,[33] proved fruitless. Indeed, the Farmers' Association never gained a position of prominence within the institutions of the Jewish community.[34]

In its early years the Manufacturers' Association, founded in 1925, could not bind its own members to a labor agreement; in fact, important firms in

29. Laqueur, *A History of Zionism*, pp. 97–125.
30. Ibid., pp. 316–17; Preuss, *The Labour Movement*, pp. 78–79.
31. Quoted in Dan Giladi, "The Economic Crises During the Fourth Aliya (1926–27)," p. 166.
32. S. N. Eisenstadt, *Israeli Society*, pp. 79, 91.
33. The Hehalutz was an organization in Europe that trained young Jews on farms and in urban communes to prepare for manual work in Palestine.
34. Anita Shapira, "The Struggles for the Employment of Jewish Labour," pp. 26–28.

the private sector remained outside the association.[35] The bourgeois parties did not gain legitimacy and standing in the *yishuv* and did not win a substantial political role until well after Independence. The Revisionists under Jabotinsky made limited incursions into the Histadrut's control of labor exchanges and Jewish agricultural organizations, but lost out in the Zionist Congress, the labor movement, and Jewish institutions in Palestine.[36] The General Zionist party—drawing upon the Manufacturers' Association, the Citrus Growers' Association, and merchant groups—failed miserably in the 1949 Knesset elections, gaining only 5 percent of the vote. In 1951 the party tripled its poll and for a three-year period served in the government; its fortunes, however, declined thereafter, or at least until the seventies. For almost all of the post-Independence period, the various labor parties—Mapai, Rafi, Mapam, Ahdut Haavoda, and the Communists—garnered over half the total votes and played the major role in the governing coalitions and within the Histadrut.[37]

The Histadrut, consequently, had been relatively free to nurture its socialist and nationalist experiment, with important consequences for the labor framework and ethnic relations.

PROTECTING EMPLOYMENT: JEWISH LABOR POLICIES

Jewish Labor and "Civilized Rates"

The Arab penetration of the Jewish sector, particularly the colonies in Judea, and the Arab predominance in state employment under the mandate created a precarious situation for the Jewish settlements. Less costly Arab workers were displacing Jewish workers in the plantations and construction. The British authorities put out public works through a bidding system that guaranteed contracts for the lowest-priced contractors, ones who generally offered wages and working conditions acceptable only to the Arab fellahin.[38] By the end of the Second Aliya (1914), most of the Jewish workers had made their way out of the colonies, shifting the areas of settlement from Judea to Galilee. Others settled in Jewish cities, like Tel Aviv, where the building industry was expanding and contracting collectives provided opportunities for Jewish labor. But the depression of 1926–28 left a pall over

---

35. Preuss, *The Labour Movement*, p. 87.
36. Laqueur, *A History of Zionism*, pp. 367–68.
37. Eisenstadt, *Israeli Society*, pp. 294–97.
38. Preuss, *The Labour Movement*, p. 91.

the *yishuv*. A third of the total Jewish labor force and more than half of the Jewish workers in Tel Aviv were out of work.[39] The Histadrut responded, first, by demanding a greater share of the work in the areas of mixed Jewish-Arab employment. It organized contracting collectives and won, after applying political and communal pressure, contracts for a number of major roads. More important, however, was the Histadrut claim for a given percentage of state employment for Jewish laborers at a "civilized wage."[40] The labor leadership insisted initially that the state accept "Jewish wage-rates as a legitimate expression of the modern standard of life of one section of the citizenry of the country."[41] Since the authorities would not promulgate a minimum wage at a "civilized standard," the Histadrut proposed that half of all jobs be reserved for Jewish workers[42] at "wages prevalent in the Jewish labour market" and "under conditions befitting their cultural background."[43] At the time of partition, Jewish workers received nearly double the Arab wage rate for the same job.[44]

In the immediate post-Independence period, state policy still reflected these wage disparities and their justification. A memorandum in 1949 suggested that a "certain proportion" be preserved "between productive capacity and standard of living on the one hand, and the level of wages on the other." In addition, government ministers suggested in the First and Second Knesset that variations in "living conditions, the level of prices," and the payment of various fees, like union dues and insurance funds, justified "local fixing of the nominal wage."[45] In 1952, however, the state formally abolished discrimination in public institutions.

Second, the Histadrut demanded "one hundred percent Jewish employment" in the Jewish sector, turning increasingly to strikes and violence to drive Arab labor out of the plantations. Here was the front line in the *kibush haavoda*. "Arab labor is bound to penetrate even building and industry if no dyke is built against it in the plantation," a labor spokesman

39. Laqueur, *A History of Zionism*, pp. 288–91; Preuss, *The Labour Movement*, pp. 25, 64; Shapira, "The Struggles for the Employment," pp. 2–3; Giladi, "The Economic Crises," p. 170.
40. Preuss, *The Labour Movement*, p. 113.
41. General Federation of Jewish Labour, Executive Committee, "Letter of the Central Committee of the Palestine Jewish Labour Party on Jewish and Arab Labour to Sir John Hope-Simpson, H. M. Special Commissioner, July, 1930," in *Documents and Essays*, pp. 102, 113.
42. This figure was based on the Histadrut's calculation that Jews constituted 50 percent of the labor force "subsisting on their labour income alone."
43. General Federation of Jewish Labour, Executive Committee, "Letter of the Central Committee of the Palestine Jewish Labour Party on Labour Policy in Public Works," *Documents and Essays*, p. 113; Giladi, "The Economic Crises," p. 189.
44. Interview with Ruvin Katzav and Jusuf Khamis, Arab Department of Histadrut.
45. In the 1949–52 period, Arab workers received 35 to 70 percent of what Jewish workers were paid for the same work (Yoram Ben-Porath, *The Arab Labor Force in Israel*, pp. 62–65).

declared.[46] Jewish workers struck the Kinneret National Fund Farm in 1910 and soon after, the tree nurseries at Ben Shemen. With widespread Jewish unemployment in the late twenties and early thirties and increasing employer resistance to Jewish labor, the strikes became more pervasive and violent. Ben-Gurion noted: "The Zionism of the employers did not make them feel duty-bound to employ Jewish labour; neither could we depend upon the employers' national conscience."[47] At Petah Tikvah and surrounding colonies, the struggle for Jewish labor took on the "proportions of a civil war." Pickets surrounded the groves while Jewish workers' delegations demanded the exclusion of Arab labor. Even more violent strikes followed in 1930 and 1931, with farmers' committees turning to unorganized Jewish and Arab workers.[48]

But the pickets and recurring violence were an ineffective way to insure the continuing exclusion of Arab workers from the Jewish sector. The labor exchange became the principal tool for monopolizing the supply of Jewish labor and imposing the monopoly on Jewish employers. The institution would outlast the growing strife of the twenties and thirties and structure Jewish and Arab employment opportunities for three decades after partition.

Institutional Exclusions: The Labor Exchanges

When the unity conference created the Histadrut in 1920 out of a divided labor movement, it also sought to create a unified Histadrut labor exchange. It sought on one hand to incorporate the petty exchanges of the Poale Zion, Hapoel Hatzair, and other labor organizations, and on the other hand, to negotiate exclusive labor contracts with private employers, Jewish enterprises, and, to some extent, the mandatory government. But for a decade and a half, as the record of strikes suggests, the Histadrut exchange could neither incorporate all the competing labor exchanges nor force employers to accept the Histadrut's Jewish labor monopoly.[49]

The farmers' committees and the Farmers' Association were still able to employ Arab labor, using the Revisionist labor bloc (under Jabotinsky) and orthodox Jewish workers' labor exchanges to break the Histadrut's near monopoly of Jewish labor. The blue-and-white flag, "Ha-Tikvah," and the anniversary of Herzl's death were set against the red flag, the "Interna-

46. Kurland, *Co-operative Palestine*, p. 92.
47. Ben-Gurion, *Jewish Labour*, p. 21.
48. Kurland, *Co-operative Palestine*, pp. 86–88; Shapira, "The Struggles for the Employment," pp. 10–13.
49. Kurland, *Co-operative Palestine*, p. 54.

tionale," and the First of May. Violence developed at Kfar-Saba and other colonies, as well as in the streets of Tel Aviv.[50]

But in 1939, the Jewish Agency intervened and established a General (Jewish) Labor Exchange, involving the Histadrut, Hapoel Hamizrachi, the Federation of Yemenite Workers, the Agudat Israel workers, and the Federation of Spanish-Jewish Workers. The General Labor Exchange, dominated by the Histadrut, successfully resisted a 1939–40 campaign of the Farmers' Association and agricultural committees in the *moshavim* to boycott Jewish labor.[51]

After Independence, the General Labor Exchange was slow to respond to the demographic changes that removed much of the Arab population from the reach of the Jewish economy. The Histadrut itself affirmed the United Nations resolutions on nondiscrimination: "The Executive Committee of the Histadrut has accepted the principle of the equal right of the Arab worker to seek employment in the Jewish economy."[52] But the General Labor Exchange maintained an exclusively Jewish registration while allowing separate exchanges for Arab workers. The first Arab labor exchange was established in Nazareth in 1949. By 1958, eight others were functioning,[53] but only three were in rural areas, where the great bulk of the Arab population was concentrated. They distributed relief work and, with the military administration, regulated the flow of Arab workers into the Jewish sector but played almost no role in finding employment for Arab job-seekers. "Indeed," one economist observes, "they were cut off from the general network of labor exchanges, which objected to Arabs entering the Jewish labor market."[54] During an economic downturn in the latter half of 1956, pressure exerted by unemployed Jewish workers and Jewish labor exchanges brought some substitution of unemployed Jewish for previously employed Arab workers.[55]

In 1959, the General Labor Exchange and the government labor exchanges were consolidated and organized under the State Employment Service. The process was now rationalized: both the employers and the employees were required, with minor exceptions, to utilize the state

50. Shapira, "The Struggles for the Employment," pp. 12, 21–23; and interview with Aharon Becker, former general secretary, Histadrut.
51. Kurland, *Cooperative Palestine*, pp. 54–55.
52. *Israel Labour News* 3, no. 1 (21 November 1948).
53. Ibid., 3, no. 6/7 (5 January 1949).
54. Ben-Porath, *The Arab Labor Force*, pp. 52–53.
55. Don Peretz, *Israel and the Palestine Arabs*, p. 127. During recessionary periods, Arab unemployment is normally double the Jewish rate (19.4 percent and 9.0 percent, respectively, in 1967). During high-growth periods, 1970 for example, unemployment is uniformly low for both groups (3.2 percent and 3.4 percent, respectively) (Elia T. Zureik, "Transformation of Class Structure among the Arabs in Israel: From Peasantry to Proletariat," p. 53).

exchanges. Further, discrimination on the basis of religion, nationality, or race was prohibited.[56]

But technical provisions of the Employment Service Law insured that Jewish workers would have first claim on available employment. Under the law, Jewish and Arab workers must register at the labor exchange closest to their residence; and each labor exchange must give first preference to local workers.[57] But as Jewish workers live and work in the industrial centers and areas of new state, Zionist, and Histadrut investment and Arab workers live primarily in rural areas or Arab villages where new industrial development is scanty and hardly encouraged,[58] the effect is fully discriminatory: Jewish workers are first to take up employment opportunities in the dynamic sectors of the Israeli economy; Arab workers must commute on a daily basis to the major Jewish cities and take their place in line behind the local Jewish workers.[59]

The impact of such "technicalities" on Arab life emerged dramatically in the Arab town of Nazareth, site of the 1976 Arab civil disorders. Though Nazareth gained population from the evacuation of surrounding villages after Independence, new industrial development has been channeled to a new Jewish city of Upper Nazareth. Here, recent Jewish immigrants have settled and, through a separate Jewish labor exchange, monopolized the principal employment opportunities arising from the construction of an auto assembly plant, textile factory, and candy factory. Until 1967, all the workers in these plants were Jewish, while more than half of the Arab working population in Nazareth sought work in more distant Jewish cities, like Haifa (one hour away) and Tiberias (thirty minutes away). Now, almost half of the labor force in Upper Nazareth is comprised of Arab workers, but only because the labor exchange has exhausted its supply of local, Jewish job-seekers and has turned to other areas, including Arab Nazareth.[60]

The network of state labor exchanges fits comfortably within a pattern of Jewish and Arab proletarianization, where Jewish workers reside in the developing cities and Arab workers in villages, as a kind of "rural-dwelling proletariat." The former depend wholly on wage labor, and the latter, while maintaining ties to the land and traditional social relationships, also depend largely on wage labor. But because of the structure of the labor exchanges and proletarianization, Jewish workers gain a preferred access to the labor market. Histadrut leaders, as we shall see, have not been anxious to alter the

56.   Noah Malkosh, *Histadrut in Israel,* p. 54; Porath, *The Arab Labor Force,* p. 54.
57.   Ernest Stock, *From Conflict to Understanding,* p. 56.
58.   Interview with Yeruham Meshel, general secretary, Histadrut.
59.   Interview with Yitzak Ben-Aharon, former general secretary, Histadrut.
60.   Stock, *From Conflict,* p. 26; interview with Shimmone Matan, Histadrut.

functioning of labor exchanges or the patterns of proletarianization and investment.[61]

EXCLUSIVE TRADE UNIONISM

The Histadrut might have responded to the persistent undercutting and displacement of Jewish labor by organizing across the boundaries of the bounded working class. Some in the yishuv, like the Communist party, the "Faction," and the Gdud Haavoda (the Labor Brigade) suggested various forms of intercommunal working-class solidarity. Within the Histadrut, some posed questions about the practicality of trade unionism in a bounded working class: "We are not obliged to organize the Arab workers, but we must come to the realization that so long as the Arab worker remains unorganized the problem of the Jewish worker will find no solution."[62]

But the Arab worker remained largely outside the purview of the Histadrut. The Christian (Orthodox) Workers' Union in Jaffa enrolled about 300 Arab members, while the Arab Carpenters' Union managed 150, but both had died out by the mid-thirties.[63] In Tel Aviv and Jerusalem, only the Railway Workers' Union seemed to carry on from year to year. Attempts to organize Arab camel, bakery, and wood workers bore little fruit.[64]

More common than joint or cooperative trade-union organization was the occasional joint strike, joint bargaining stance, or Arab strike with tacit Histadrut support. In 1931, 3,000 Jewish and Arab automobile drivers conducted a one-week strike that resulted in favorable government legislation on income and fuel taxes. The Histadrut itself supported strikes by Arab boatmen in Haifa (1932), Arab workers at the Jewish-owned Nesher cement factory (1932), 800 Arab workers at the weaving workshops in Migdal (1932), Arab workers at the Spenney mineral water factory at Acre (1932), 500 Arab workers at the Iraq Petroleum Company (1935), and 800

61. Indeed, the lower cost of semiproletarianized Arab labor is more than offset by the Jewish labor preference of the labor exchanges—which, in any case, was their original purpose. See Khalidi, "Palestinian Arab Villages," pp. 23–26; Shulamit Carmi and Henry Rosenfeld, "The Origins of the Process of Proletarianization and Urbanization of Arab Peasants in Palestine," pp. 470–85; Rosenfeld, "The Arab Village Proletariat," p. 16; Khalil Nakhleh, "Anthropological and Sociological Studies on the Arabs in Israel: A Critique," pp. 50–51.

62. Quoted in Kurland, *Cooperative Palestine*, p. 29.

63. General Federation of Jewish Labour, Executive Committee, *A Report Prepared for the Fourth Convention*, February 1933.

64. General Federation of Jewish Labour, Executive Committee, *A Report Prepared for the Third Convention*, July 1927.

Arab workers at the Karaman cigarette factory in Haifa (1935).[65] Immediately after the war and before partition, Jewish and Arab workers joined in a number of well-publicized, though not particularly successful, work stoppages. In 1946, for example, there were strikes of government employees, the Haifa municipal workers, and Arab and Jewish workers at Socony-Vacuum Oil Company. Of the 58,506 working days lost during the third quarter of 1946, 8,540 days involved joint Arab-Jewish strikes. The joint strike of the Histadrut and the Palestine Arab Workers' Society at military bases across Palestine was one of the more successful of these ventures.[66]

Only in Haifa, and principally among the Union of Railway, Posts and Telegraph Workers, did the Histadrut encourage continuous organization of Arab and Jewish workers on a cooperative basis, or what Ben-Gurion called "co-partnership."[67] Here, there was little choice, however: Arabs outnumbered Jewish workers in the railways and posts in the mid-twenties by more than six to one;[68] Jews and Arabs constituted a mixed labor force in areas of state employment and in a growing "international sector."[69] In this context, the Haifa Labor Council (the local branch of the Histadrut) provided organizational assistance from 1923 to Arab workers. It encouraged the Railway Workers' Union to organize Arab carpenters and tailors. When organized Arab workers in Haifa resisted the general wave of riots in 1929, the Histadrut established an Arab workers' club with a Christian Arab at its head. This club and the Haifa branch of the League kept Arabs at work during the 1936–39 disturbances despite considerable pressure from the Arab nationalist movement.

In 1927, some Arab workers broke away from the joint union to form an Arab Railwaymen's Union. But between 1932 and 1936 the two unions created a joint committee to make representations to the government. The civil disorders that came at the end of this period, however, brought a temporary halt to this experiment in Jewish-Arab solidarity. Intermittent cooperation emerged again during the war and for the major post office strike of 1946.

65. Preuss, *The Labour Movement,* p. 119.
66. *Labour in Palestine* 1, no. 8 (22 August 1946); 1, no. 18 (11 November 1946); and 2, no. 4 (18 August 1947); General Federation of Jewish Labour, *Survey of Histadrut Activities,* p. 70.
67. Ben-Gurion, *Jewish Labour,* p. 39.
68. General Federation of Jewish Labour, *Survey of Histadrut Activities,* p. 18; Anita Shapiro, "The Ideology and Practice of the Joint Jewish-Arab Labour Union in Palestine," pp. 20–25; and General Federation of Jewish Labour, Executive Committee, *Report Prepared for the Third Convention.*
69. Shapiro, "The Ideology and Practice," p. 24.

Before the State: Separate Paths

The unity conference that created the Histadrut resolved "to promote comradely relations with Arab workers in Palestine" but deferred specific action to the Council and to later conferences.[70] These early discussions, particularly within the governing party of the Histadrut, the Ahdut Haavoda, included proposals that soon became unpalatable even to their sponsors. Ben-Gurion urged the party to recognize that "comradely relations" were an essential condition for "our redemption as free, working people" and that the Jewish labor movement "stands at the head of the movement for the liberation and the rebirth of the peoples of the Near East." He proposed that the Jewish labor movement help form parallel Arab unions and that the merger of the respective labor movements remain a serious, if distant possibility.[71]

The emphasis by the mid-twenties, as the economic downturn began to spread across the Jewish sector, turned to parallel or auxiliary unions for Arab workers. In 1925, the Third Council of the Histadrut declared: "The railway workers' union can be strengthened only when it contains within itself all the workers of the railway, post and telegraph, irrespective of race and nation." But two years later both the Third Council and the Third Convention affirmed that the railway workers' union should remain "an autonomous element with the general Histadrut."[72]

The Third Convention laid out a framework for the organization of Arab workers—an Arab auxiliary of the Histadrut, the Palestine Labor League. It was to be an international organization, comprised of two "national autonomous sections" and governed in two official languages, Hebrew and Arabic. The Jewish section, however, should maintain an "organic" tie to the Histadrut. "From the organizational point of view, all the Jewish sections belong to the 'General Federation of Jewish Labour in Palestine' [Histadrut] which continues to exist as before."[73] A report for the Fourth Convention in 1933 indicated that the Histadrut "is the main section of the League," and that "other national sections are allowed to unite themselves in autonomous national sections."[74]

70. Kurland, *Co-operative Palestine,* pp. 35, 265.
71. Shapiro, "The Ideology and Practice," p. 2.
72. General Federation of Jewish Labour, Executive Committee, *A Report Prepared for the Third Convention,* trans. E.L.
73. Preuss, *The Labour Movement,* p. 77; General Federation of Jewish Labour, Executive Committee, *A Report Prepared for the Third Convention,* trans. E.L.
74. General Federation of Jewish Labour, Executive Committee, *A Report Prepared for the Fourth Convention,* trans. E.L.

But the Histadrut's interest in even this auxiliary organization was short-lived.[75] The merger of Hapoel Hatzair and Ahdut Haavoda into a single Labor party, Mapai, reflected a growing concern about economic opportunity in Palestine and the Arab violence of 1929. The Mapai leadership no longer spoke of international unions; it mentioned only the need for contact between Jewish and Arab workers.[76] The Fourth Convention of the Histadrut in 1934 offered only ritualistic commitments to further organization in the international and Arab sectors: "The convention decides that in one of the councils to come the problems of organizing the Arab worker will come under thorough discussion."[77] Interest and moral and financial support waned by 1933 and utterly evaporated with the disorders of 1936.[78] A left-wing member of the Histadrut Executive Committee described the apparent lethargy:

> I have been a member of the Executive Committee for two years now and nobody has found time for dealing with this question [the Arab-Jewish problem]: four years of riots, three years of pause, two years of World War. Nothing has moved the Executive Committee. For two years, there exists a Committee for Arab Affairs: it has not once been assembled. This slogan of solidarity is daily abused by us. I give up any talking about Arab Federation, but I want a simple thing accomplished: at least cooperation with the Arab worker. . . . We live almost as in heaven, while the earth might be collapsing under our feet.[79]

After the State: Limits on Incorporation

After partition in 1949, the Jewish labor movement faced an altogether less threatening labor situation. A labor force that had posed continuing problems of "swamping" and "undercutting" was now relatively homogeneous. The Arab fellahin were still unorganized and poorly paid, but after 1948 they formed only a fraction of the potential labor force.[80]

75. By 1946, there were 37,500 Arab trade unionists. None of these workers were directly affiliated with the Histadrut; only 4,500 belonged to the Palestine Labour League, the Histadrut's Arab auxiliary. The remainder of the organized Arab workers were split evenly between a left-leaning organization, the Arab Workers' Society of Jaffa, and a right-leaning one, the Palestine Arab Workers' Society (*Labour Palestine* 1, no. 4 (18 July 1946).
76. Shapiro, "The Ideology and Practice," p. 19.
77. General Federation of Jewish Labour, *Fourth Convention of the Histadrut,* Second Session, January 1934, p. 111, trans. E.L.
78. Shapiro, "The Ideology and Practice," pp. 32–33.
79. General Federation of Jewish Labour, *Fifth Convention of the Histadrut,* April 1942, trans. E.L.
80. Arabs constituted 15 percent of the total population in 1949.

Accordingly, the Histadrut moved cautiously, despite concerns about security, to incorporate the Arab proletariat.[81] The process was slow, beginning first with Arab membership in affiliated trade unions and Histadrut health and welfare institutions and ending in 1965 when Arabs voted for the first time in Histadrut elections and when the Histadrut erased, over the opposition of Ben-Gurion, the term "Hebrew" from its title.[82] But three decades after it began, the process of incorporation included important limitations: Arabs moved slowly, almost imperceptively, into the governing labor parties within the Histadrut; Arabs were effectively excluded from the local labor councils; and most important, Arabs from the occupied territories were denied membership in the Histadrut and affiliated trade unions.

Incorporating Israeli Arabs

The Histadrut after partition offered, as it had in the past, "its fraternal greetings to the Arab workers" and resolved "to achieve the full cooperation of the Arab worker in the upbuilding of the State under conditions of complete social and civic equality and on raising the economic and cultural standard of the Arab worker."[83] But when pressed by Mapam for either an integrated union or one based on national sections, the leadership of the Histadrut proved reluctant. Lavon responded for Mapai:

> It is true that the question of organizing Arab workers is to be discussed. But I believe that we should go on with the constructive work and when the time comes, discuss and determine on this question, which is not simple at all. In the meantime, the League and the Fellaheen unions are sufficient for us to do whatever we can and have to do.[84]

At the very same convention, the Histadrut resolved to open its doors to the massive influx of immigrant Jewish workers and break down social and economic barriers in the labor market: "The Histadrut will see to it that trade unions remain open; it will fight against all selfish and profiteering

---

81. Yitzak Ben-Aharon, former general secretary of the Histadrut, observed:

   The major block to change in the Histradrut in the 1950s was the military regime in the Arab sector. . . . The Histadrut wanted absolute equality for the Arab workers, but this could only be done under normal wage and market conditions. So the whole problem of Arab workers joining the Histadrut is tied up with the abolition of the military regime.

82. Nahum Sharon, "The Histadrut in 1966," p. 35.
83. *Israel Labour News* 3, no. 23 (12 May 1949).
84. General Federation of Jewish Labour, *Seventh Convention of the Histadrut,* 24–30 May 1949, trans. E.L.

tendencies." These barriers, it resolved further, "stand in absolute opposition to the very character of the General Federation of Labour and its tasks."[85]

The first step toward incorporation of Arabs came in 1952: the Histadrut Council urged full and equal participation in the affiliated trade unions, though not in the Histadrut itself. That decision placed the trade-union movement behind demands for equal wages and working conditions.[86] It did not, however, open up the labor exchanges to Arab workers; nor did it bring Arabs into the Histadrut conventions or labor councils, where policy is made. "The point then," Aharon Becker, former general secretary, observed, "was that we had to have a Zionist sentiment to have membership in the Histadrut."

In their "fraternal greetings" at the Eighth Histadrut Convention in 1956, the Arab guests demanded full membership in the Histadrut and the labor exchanges; they sought new work opportunities for Arab workers and clinics in Arab villages. Mapam supported these demands. But again the Histadrut and Mapai leadership was cautious. A Mapai spokesman and head of the Arab Department in the Histadrut stated: "We all recognize the necessity of equality and of raising living standards and a lot has been done. Yet the question is complicated and should not be artificially aroused. Things must develop gradually."[87] In an article in the *Jerusalem Post,* he commented further, suggesting that "the problem . . . is not only an economic one." Consideration must be given to "conflicting tendencies and loyalties," the need to build consciousness, and the continuing role of landowners, elders, and Moslem religious leaders. "This means that the Histadrut has to reconcile itself to slow progress, and voluntarily forego immediate achievement of its full aims."[88]

In 1956, Arabs who served in the Israeli Army, essentially the Druze Arabs, were granted full membership rights. In February 1959, the Seventy-first Council of the Histadrut decided, and the Ninth Convention reaffirmed a year later, that Arabs should be admitted to the Histadrut on the basis of full equality. "Every Arab worker can join the organized workers' institutions," Aharon Becker declared. "This right is conditioned by his readiness to obey the Histadrut regulations and his loyalty to the state of Israel."[89] The Mapai Central Committee declared "that the move was in accordance

85. *Israel Labour News* 3, no. 23 (12 May 1949).
86. General Secretary's Report, cited in *Israel Labour News* 6, no. 21 (7 November 1952).
87. General Federation of Jewish Labour, *Eighth Convention of the Histadrut,* 18–29 March 1956, trans. E.L.
88. Reprint from the *Jerusalem Post, The Histadrut,* Supplement, 17 February 1956.
89. General Federation of Jewish Labour, *Ninth Convention of the Histadrut,* 3–5 February 1960, trans E.L.

with Mapai's policy of advancing the status of Arab workers with the Histadrut, parallel with their integration into the life of the nation."[90]

Before the 1959 decision, very few Arabs had responded to the Histadrut concessions: only 6,427 Arabs had joined the trade unions, for example. But by 1969 that figure had increased to 31,254.[91] In 1965, Arabs voted for the first time in Histadrut elections: 90 percent of those eligible cast ballots; and for the first time in any Israeli election, Arabs were fully incorporated into party lists rather than separate "Arab lists."[92] The Alignment and Mapai leadership were full of praise for the integrative process and accomplishments: "We still have to organize the unorganized workers, though one-third of the Arab population has joined the Histadrut. A clear process of Arab labor force integration in the country's economy can be seen."[93]

There is little question that between 1952 and 1966 the Histadrut made a number of integrative moves and substantially expanded its services to the Arab community. But incorporation came up against important limits, suggesting that despite the radical demographic changes after partition, the notion of a bounded working class had not lost its significance.

Limits on Party Participation

Arab membership in the Histadrut did not automatically open up membership in the political parties that governed it. Indeed, only at the factory level can one attain a position of influence within the labor movement without active involvement in a political party. The local labor councils, which at one time administered the labor exchanges and now control strike funds, appoint union secretaries, and create bargaining units, are elected on a party basis. The executive councils of the national trade unions are elected on a party basis, as are the executives of the Histadrut itself and the major associated labor institutions.

The governing Labor party (then Mapai), however, did not welcome Arab participation in 1959, or in 1965 for that matter. In the summer of 1976, the party of Labor Zionism recognized, "Now that we have the state we cannot maintain the separateness of the earlier period," and opened up the party to Arabs with full membership rights.[94] But there were Arab branches of the Labor party only in Nazareth, Acre, and Umm al Fahem. Of the 300,000 Labor party members, only 4,000 to 5,000 were Arabs; there

90. Quoted in the *Jerusalem Post,* 16 January 1959.
91. Moshe Allon, "The Histadrut in the State of Israel," p. 137.
92. Jacob M. Landau, *The Arabs in Israel,* pp. 178–81; Jacob M. Landau, "The Arabs and the Histadrut," p. 15.
93. M. Bartal (Mapai), General Federation of Jewish Labour, *Tenth Convention of the Histadrut,* 3–7 January 1966, trans. E.L.
94. Interview with Aharon Becker.

were forty to fifty Arabs in the Conference and ten in the Center, the principal governing body of the party.[95]

The late decision of the Labor Alignment to include Arabs was reflected in the limited Arab involvement at all levels of the Histadrut. Arabs have long been involved in the Haifa Labor Council and have gained reasonable representation in Acre. But Arabs were entirely absent from the Council in the largest city, Tel Aviv.[96] Only in the early seventies did the Labor party offer significant Arab representation in the executive councils of the principal mixed unions, the Construction Workers and Teachers. The Histadrut leadership, however, remained almost fully Jewish. The head of the Arab Department within the Labor party observed: "If you look at the general secretaries, the Executive Committee of twenty-one members, there are no Arabs. Under the secretary, a body of 301 members, that is the Active Committee, there are a few Arabs. In a body of 3,000, there are some Arabs, but very few."[97]

Limits on the Local Councils and Proletarianization

Histadrut rules provide that workers vote in the local councils closest to their residences. Their votes give Arab workers, who normally live a considerable distance from industries in the Jewish cities, some role in the service-delivery functions of the labor councils, particularly the clinics and insurance funds but little say at the work place or in the major industrial areas. Since Jewish workers live and work in the Jewish sector, the labor councils in the major cities, excepting perhaps Haifa, remain under Jewish control.[98]

There were three ways to lessen the discriminatory impact of residential voting for labor councils and local preference in labor exchanges: first, change the regulations; second, provide housing for Arabs in Jewish cities; or third, encourage industrialization in Arab areas. But neither the Histadrut nor the Labor party has shown any willingness to change the labor framework—a mix of regulations, patterns of investment, and proletarianization—that has guaranteed Jewish labor job security and protection from Arab competition.

The leadership stated, first, that Arabs did not want to live in Jewish cities, any more than the Jews want them there. "The people do not want to

95.   Interview with Ranan Cohen, Arab Department, Labor party.
96.   Interview with Ranan Cohen; interview, Katzav and Khamis.
97.   Interview with Ranan Cohen.
98.   Interview with Matan. Mr. Matan pointed out in correspondence that the trade unions, as opposed to the labor councils, allow Arabs a role at the work place: "Every Arab, a Histadrut member, has the full right to elect and be elected to the trade union to which he belongs in his place of work as well as to the general elections of his union, apart from the general elections for the Histadrut Convention once in four years."

live with the Jews in Tel Aviv," a Labor party official claimed. "To work there four days is very nice, but after that, they think they would feel better in their own village where they can be with their families. Tel Aviv or Haifa is a foreign town."[99] His views were shared by a former general secretary of the Histadrut and a Labor party member of the Knesset: "But the Arab has almost no interest to settle in the city. They prefer to live in their own communities. They don't want to bring their families to the Jewish civilization. These people are Muslims and they do not want to live with the infidel."[100]

But neither was the Histadrut leadership interested in diverting new investment from the Jewish sector in order to bring jobs to the Arab villages and towns. A former general secretary who guided the Histadrut through the crucial decade following incorporation emphasized the problem: "It is not so simple to invest money. But which do we prefer? Do we provide work for the new immigrants or do we locate among people who already have work? It is a matter of priority; it's a question of time too."[101] Policy, not time, was the issue for the present Histadrut leadership, however. The general secretary described his views on Arab industrialization:

> I recently had a meeting with Arab students on the problems of coexistence between Jews and Arabs in Israel. They claim that the Histadrut is not doing enough to create industry in the Arab villages. And this is what I responded to them: Why not create an Arab Zionism? We came to this land without money, without industry, without skills. We built it up. I told them, the problem is, you're waiting for a miracle.[102]

Limits on Non-Israeli Arabs

When Israel annexed East Jerusalem after the 1967 War, it opened its doors to the Israeli Arabs working and residing there. The Jerusalem Labor Council enrolled only 250 new Arab members in the first year after the war, but by March 1969, had brought in another 4,500, 40 percent of the salaried workers in East Jerusalem.[103] It threatened a strike against the Arab-owned National Bus Company and won an eight-hour day, a weekly day of rest, and annual holidays for its Arab workers. Similar strike threats and ultimatums brought reluctant concessions from the Hotel Owners' Association in East Jerusalem.[104]

99. Interview with Ranan Cohen.
100. Interview with Ben-Aharon.
101. Interview with Becker.
102. Interview with Meshel.
103. Landau, "Arabs and the Histadrut," p. 19.
104. *Jerusalem Post,* 4 March 1969; 10 March 1969; and 21 March 1969.

Histadrut efforts here, nonetheless, followed the conventional priorities of Jewish labor activity. The Jerusalem Labor Council acted first to ensure equality of Arab and Jewish wages in the Jewish sector (West Jerusalem). It acted in East Jerusalem and Arab enterprises, the general secretary of the Histadrut noted, "according to the economy's capacity and the workers' needs."[105] On the eve of 1969, the Jerusalem Labor Council estimated that another eighteen months would be needed to equalize wages between the branches in the two parts of the city.[106] The need to equalize wages in the Arab and Jewish sectors drew on a time-worn rationale. The secretary of the Jerusalem Labor Council commented:

> We are trying to ensure that we won't arrive at a situation where the Jewish labourer will disappear to be replaced by the Arab. We must avoid becoming merely a managerial class of people, and this could easily happen in the building trade if wages for Jews and Arabs aren't equalized.[107]

The Histadrut and the Labor party decided not to organize Gaza and West Bank Arabs, even though many of them commuted to work in the Jewish and Arab sectors in Israel. The issue reached the Histadrut executive but proved too "political" and volatile.[108] Ben-Aharon backed away from his momentary advocacy of Arab branches in the occupied territories: "What Mr. Ben-Aharon said was that we are considering opening clubs in the territories. The clubs would deal with education and information only, not with organization of workers."[109] His successor as general secretary confirmed that the issue was a political rather than a trade-union question and should be resolved at a "higher level."[110] That higher level, involving the Labor party and the military government for administered areas, formally barred economic and trade-union activity in Gaza, the West Bank, and the Sinai. Only in East Jerusalem and among the Druze population on the Golan was trade-union organization permitted.[111]

But the Histadrut had not only chosen to neglect organization of Arab, often "illegal" workers from the occupied territories; it had failed to insist on barriers against their becoming a "real part of the working economy,"

105. Ibid., 8 August 1967.
106. Ibid., 26 December 1968.
107. Ibid., 25 August 1969. The Labor party branch in Jerusalem had no Arab members (interview, Ranan Cohen). Arabs were excluded, the Prime Minister's Office notes, because citizenship had not followed annexation. Almost all Israeli Arabs in East Jerusalem carry Jordanian passports.
108. *Jerusalem Post,* 2 August 1974.
109. Ibid., 12 October 1972.
110. Ibid., 19 November 1972.
111. Ibid., 20 October 1967.

against their taking up the most menial jobs in the unorganized sectors of
the economy.[112] Large numbers of "illegal" Arabs had come to Jerusalem
and other Jewish cities, but many found their way to the Arab sector.[113]
"This is something you should see," Ben-Aharon said. "Arab manipulators
bringing in illegal Arabs from the occupied areas, undermining the position
of Israeli Arabs."[114] The government and the Histadrut, however, devoted
few resources to their control. In Jerusalem, for example, the employment
service assigned only two employees to this task.[115] The director of the Arab
Department of the Histadrut noted: "Officially, there are about 50,000
workers. Still the border is open. They come each morning to Beersheva and
Tel Aviv and Jerusalem. They have to find a job. They are not organized.
We can't control this situation; we cannot, nor can the Labor Department."[116]

The Histadrut seemed satisfied that with the Jewish worker's position in
the labor market secured, unorganized "illegal" workers in the Arab sector
would pose little threat to Jewish living standards and employment. Ben-
Aharon observed: "It is not a question of undermining the Israeli labor,
because there is no real unemployment."

The Israeli case provides an example of trade unionism in a bounded
working class writ large. Here, settlers planned to create a Jewish working
class in Palestine, where Jews would perform the most menial as well as
commercial occupations, where Jews would work the soil and work with
their hands. In labor, they would repudiate the perverse occupational
structure of eastern Europe that had left them isolated from other working-
class communities and vulnerable to persecution. In labor, Jews would find
dignity and establish collectivist and wage-laboring experiments no longer
remote from "nature." But the "conquest of labor" in the Palestine context
also included barring the way to Arab laborers who were being dislodged
from precapitalist relations and who too were beginning to take up laboring
opportunities in the Jewish sector. The Histadrut chose not to organize
across the boundaries of the bounded working class but to erect barriers to
Arab penetration of the Jewish sector. It called on the British authorities to
set aside a fixed percentage of jobs for Jewish workers at "civilized rates" of
pay. Through informal means (strikes and violence) and institutional
mechanisms (the labor exchanges), it sought to establish "one hundred

112. Interview with Katzav and Khamis.
113. Interview with Meshel.
114. Interview with Ben-Aharon.
115. *Jerusalem Post,* 13 August 1969.
116. Interview with Katzav and Khamis.

percent Jewish labor" in the Jewish-owned plantations and enterprises, in construction, industry, and the Jewish national projects. It sought to impose those barriers on the market and British mandatory authorities, on the Zionist institutions in Palestine, and, through its organic ties with the Jewish political leadership, on the Israeli state. Though Jewish workers after Independence no longer had to fear "undercutting," the Histadrut helped construct a framework that excluded Arabs from the national and local governing councils of the Histadrut and gave Jewish workers first claim on the labor market.

There is no shortage of explanations for the nature of Israeli society and the Jewish state: the work of Theodor Herzl, the pogroms in eastern Europe and holocaust in Germany, the intercommunal strife of the thirties and the security situation since 1948, the British colonial penetration of Palestine and alienation of Arab lands, the nature of settler regimes, and more. The bounded working class and Jewish labor organizations, however, should figure prominently among these explanations.

CONCLUSION

CHAPTER 17

Capitalist Growth and Persistent Racial Domination

At the outset of this book, I noted the perplexity of a contemporary world that had anticipated the passing or diminution of racial and ethnic conflict and domination, only to witness the resurgence of ethnic turmoil in western Europe and North America and the intractability of such conflicts in the Middle East, southern Africa, and Southeast Asia. I focused, in particular, on four settings where race or ethnic lines were evident and vivid prior to capitalist development and where these lines were later reproduced and elaborated—a century of developing capitalist relations notwithstanding. This perplexity led to the primary question of this work: What impact does capitalist development have on patterns of racial domination?

Most of the book was devoted to disaggregating the problem, focusing on particular class actors in particular historical situations. How did dominant farmers, businessmen, and workers shape the racial barriers? In the first part of this chapter, I will underline and interweave the critical patterns that emerged through the major sections of the book: first, in the behavior of the class actors; second, in the conjuncture of class action at particular points or periods in capitalist development; and third, in the growth of the state racial apparatus. This reconstruction attempts to make sense of these patterns as an explanation of development in specific settings and as theory. In the second part of this chapter, I will focus on this reconstruction as an alternative to the modernization literature and orthodox Marxist conceptions of growth and transcendence and the ahistorical explanations of persistent racial stratification. I hope to show how capitalist development as a historic process carries forward and elaborates racial distinctions, even as it creates contradictions that in some settings allow for the blurring of race lines and in others provide for persistent racial domination.

GROWTH AND THE RACIAL STATE

We propose state interference and state control on a large scale.
National Party M.P., South Africa, 1943

I have always said I am an Orangeman first and politician and Member of this Parliament afterwards. . . . [All] I boast is that we are a Protestant Parliament and Protestant State.

                              Unionist Party Prime Minister. Northern Ireland, 1934

The Period of Intensification

Capitalist development brought, along with wage labor, factories, and cities, the intensification of racial discrimination. The dominant[1] class actors during early capitalist development within the racial orders—indeed, those most closely identified with the "modern" economy and state—insisted on the race lines: dominant landowners responded to the pervading commercialization and increased mobility of farm labor by circumventing markets in labor and elaborating the labor-repressive and racial framework; businessmen in the primary, extractive industries used the framework of racial domination to help organize and control a labor force, to keep the labor force divided and, at least in the areas of subordinate employment, unorganized; the artisan unions associated race and skill scarcity and effectively excluded subordinate workers from privileged sections of the labor market; the industrial unions, at least where subordinate workers did not dominate employment in an industry from the outset, used race lines in the work place and society to set off and protect areas of dominant employment. These actors inaugurated a period of intensification, a period where racial domination was given a "modern" form and where repressive features were elaborated and institutionalized.

At the simplest level, the emerging class actors introduced conventional racial patterns into new settings, the factory and city in particular. Though the paternalism apparent in the countryside did not easily translate into a labor-management pattern and while ambiguity existed in some areas of secondary manufacture, the sense of hierarchy and presumptions about servile labor proved transmittable.[2]

But at other levels, the transfer built on and elaborated the structure of racial domination. The principles that both landowners and squatters used to organize production gave way to contracts, extended labor obligations, and institutional arrangements that controlled the distribution and mobility of subordinate labor. The mine owners' willingness to honor the racial canons did not by itself organize a labor force. For that, they created new and more elaborate institutions of control and repression: pass laws,

---

1. Consistent with the preceding sections of the book, *dominant* refers to a privileged section of the population in an ethnically divided society.
2. This part of the argument is consistent with the accommodative view set out in chapter 7.

compounds, convict leases, and vagrancy laws. They insisted that race lines be drawn more sharply, thus dividing the working class and labor market. Workers at the pinnacle of the bounded section insisted that skill differences correspond with the traditional racial hierarchy, but those at the bottom insisted on much more: only a continuing vigilance and generalization of race lines would preserve their status and areas of protected employment. Dominant businessmen and workers lent intensity to the racial order, introducing race lines into emerging capitalist relations and elaborating the repressive mechanisms associated with racial domination.

The period of intensification, however, represented, in large part, the ascendancy of commercial farmers during the transition to capitalist agriculture. Businessmen and workers responded to notions of unfree labor and markets nurtured in the precapitalist countryside and championed by the commercial farmers. That they took up such issues with so little discomfort is less testimony to the repressive features in extractive industries or manufacture and the preciousness of markets than the historic role of commercial agriculture. Dominant farmers bottled up their farm laborers during an extended transition to capitalist agriculture and, in the process, urged their ideas and methods on the whole society. Here, notions of white domination—*baasskap* and racism—were granted legitimacy and given social support; the absence of "social will," the lack of community between black and white, were enshrined as political principle. Here, political parties that championed racial domination and repression found their principal constituencies.

The period of intensification also brought the elaboration of the state racial apparatus. The growth of the state itself is not particularly surprising. "Modernization," nation building, and capitalist development conventionally bring the elaboration and growth of the state machinery: the formation of armies, regulation of police forces, the growth of bureaucracies and government staffs, and the ascendancy of tax collectors. Without them, Charles Tilly writes, claimants to the nation fail to win over the peasants' "land, goods, or labor"; they fail to gain control of the food supply, forge common loyalties, and organize the means of production.[3] In postcolonial settings in particular, there may develop what one scholar labels the "overdeveloped apparatus of the state."[4] The colonial authorities created bureaucratic states, reminiscent of state structures in seventeenth-century Europe but not of structures derived from the colonial societies themselves.

3. Charles Tilly, "Reflections on the History of European State-Making," pp. 19–24, 51–73.
4. Hamza Alavi, "The State in Post-Colonial Societies: Pakistan and Bangladesh," p. 61.

"Formulas, regulations, and laws," central administration, and tax collection came at the expense of the peasantry and, to a large extent, at the expense of the rudimentary, indigenous state.[5] There might have been "some shrinkage of effectiveness" in the aftermath of colonialism, Crawford Young points out, but the trend has been toward the further elaboration of the state. The growth of an interconnected bureaucracy and military— Young's "authoritarian formula" or Alavi's "military-bureaucratic oligarchies"—not "praetorianism," characterized state formation in the postcolonial societies.[6]

No less than other emergent nations and economies, the racial orders developed a capacity to collect taxes, raise armies, and police the countryside; they too created structures to manage class antagonisms. But the state bureaucracies and political leadership in the racial orders, particularly during the period of intensification, also emerged fully bound to the ideas and functions necessary for racial domination. In some respects, the state was elaborated as a simple instrument of class needs: employing dominant workers and maintaining vigilance over the bounded working class; intervening in the labor market; helping organize the subordinate labor force for agriculture and industry. This simple instrumentalism bred the conventional state processes—formalization, militarism, and bureaucratization— but realized here as the enormous weight of the state in the labor market. The state racial apparatus, however, evolved beyond mere labor repression. The state during the period of intensification came to represent the racial organization of society. It reflected the racial and political climate necessary to class formation but, in turn, began representing and managing the increasing formalization of race lines.[7]

The state racial apparatus encompassed the quite ordinary bureaucratic institutions—the post office and highway departments—that, in this con-

5. James C. Scott, *The Moral Economy of the Peasantry*, pp. 92–98.
6. Crawford Young, *The Politics of Cultural Pluralism*, pp. 79, 519–28; Alavi, "The State in Post-Colonial Societies," p. 59.
Samuel Huntington feared that the developing nations in Africa and Asia would fail to create such a state machinery, that political mobilization and economic change would not be matched by the "development of stronger, more complex, and more autonomous political institutions." Where the "state lagged behind the evolution of society"—"praetorianism" in Huntington's terminology—emergent nations would slip into "decay"—increasing violence and corruption and an evident lack of "moral consensus and mutual interest" (Samuel P. Huntington, *Political Order in Changing Societies*, pp. 10–11, 85). At least on the question of the state, however, Huntington's fears seem ill-founded.
7. For Leo Kuper and M. G. Smith, the state in plural societies becomes the essential regulative power and coercion that makes the racial organization of society possible. Indeed, they write, the "state precedes and constitutes society" (Leo Kuper, "Plural Societies: Perspectives and Problems," p. 17). But while properly emphasizing "statism" and the association with racial domination, they fail to take account of process and history. The elaboration of the state racial apparatus is in large part a consequence of this period of intensification.

text, served as avenues for the employment of dominant workers. It also included ordinary officialdom: at the upper reaches, those closely identified with the formulation of racial policies, and at the lower levels, the petty officers—the clerks, county executives, inspectors, registrars, and sheriffs—who in the aggregate effectuated the policy. It involved the entire extended legal and judicial system—the justices of the highest court and the justices of the peace—who adjudicated and enforced the race and labor laws. It involved the agents of economic development and regulation: the marketing boards and extension services that fostered the commercialization of dominant agriculture; the investment corporations, state enterprises, and state banks that fostered dominant employment and accumulation; the labor exchanges and industrial conciliation machinery that guaranteed dominant workers first claim on the labor market. It included the social welfare agencies, which provided social security for dominant workers and social regulation for subordinate ones. It included, not surprisingly, the police, national guard, and military forces; also the secret police and a network of spies and informers; the prisons and prison guards; it included the agencies of labor control, the array of petty officials who gave implicit force to the system; the bureaucratic agencies that formalized what previously was an individual and sometimes random tyranny. It included all the institutions of legitimization and socialization: the schools, colleges, perhaps the government press, radio, and television. And finally, it included the politicians and political parties. They grew up with the state racial apparatus and came to manage it. Their fate, identity, and ideology were intimately bound up with the survival and continuing elaboration of the racial order.

The state racial apparatus was, in large part, a product of this period of intensification: the attempt by various class actors, but particularly commercial farmers, to elaborate the labor-repressive framework. Labor control as a state function, race lines and categories as state charges, and racial domination as a state ideology were each elaborated in this period.

There is, nonetheless, good reason to believe that the state apparatus represents more than this particular convergence of class interests. In the first place, such bureaucratic machinery, independent of the needs of class actors and the requirements of the racial order, develops its own momentum and areas of autonomous action. The civil servants and managers that command it weigh heavily on civil society, in some contexts responsive to the needs of particular class actors, but in others, Marx suggests, gaining "abnormal independence."[8] For social theorists, like Weber, who give greater attention to problems of superstructure, bureaucracies conventionally establish their mastery of society.[9]

8. Karl Marx, *German Ideology*, quoted in Henri Lefebvre, *The Sociology of Marx*, p. 157.
9. See Anthony Giddens, *The Class Structure of the Advanced Societies*, pp. 124–27.

Second, and more important, state functionaries and a succession of governments rose above instrumental interests to help organize the dominance of commercial farmers and maintain the class alignments that underlay racial domination in its modern form. In reconciling what were often bitter and regular conflicts between class actors, the racial state emerged not just as a "political organizer of hegemony" or as a "condensation of a balance of forces," as Poulantzas suggests,[10] but as an increasingly autonomous agency representing the interests of the dominant section as a whole.

There was no small difference, for example, between the interests of commercial farmers and mining executives: though both supported labor-repressive policies, the former sought to bind subordinate labor to the land; the latter sought to transport the same labor to the mines. Nor is it easy to underplay the conflict between dominant workers, on the one hand, attempting to protect their employment and wage standards, and businessmen, on the other, helping to forge "cheap labor" policies and undercut labor organization. Those differences were continually debilitating. That each class actor belonged to the dominant section and therefore made legitimate claims against the racial state only compounded the conflict. The racial state emerged, consequently, as a kind of "Bonapartism" writ large. It stood "above" and "against civil society," not just at certain critical historical moments, such as a Louis Bonaparte (Napoleon) in mid-nineteenth century France and Kerensky in republican Russia,[11] but as a necessary and predictable institutional arrangement during the period of intensification.

Finally, the idea of racial domination came to structure state activity, to some extent, independently of the class forces that helped propagate the original idea. "Once an ideology arises," Eugene Genovese properly points out, "it alters profoundly the material reality and in fact becomes a partially autonomous feature of that reality."[12] In the hands of the state bureaucracy and political elites, ideas—once convenient, perhaps crass rationalizations —emerged as well-developed, legitimizing ideologies that provided the basis for state identity. State officials saw themselves as the "true" embodiment and protectors of the racial order, struggling to restrain sectional interests that had lost sight of the state's original purpose.[13]

10. Nicos Poulantzas, *Classes in Contemporary Capitalism*, pp. 98, 157.
11. Karl Marx, *The Eighteenth Brumaire of Louis Bonaparte*, pp. 122–23; I. Lenin, *The State and Revolution*, pp. 245–46; also see an important discussion of "Bonapartism" in the African context, Colin Leys, *Underdevelopment in Kenya*, pp. 207–12.
12. Eugene D. Genovese, *In Red and Black: Marxian Explorations in Southern and Afro-American History*, p. 32.
13. It is at this point that the state officials and the bureaucratic machinery appear to act autonomously with their own conceptions of order and the public interest. See the discussion of the "organic-statist tradition" in Alfred C. Stepan, *State and Society: Peru in Comparative Perspective*, pp. 29–33.

The state racial apparatus, consequently, emerged as a product of the period of intensification and as an important element shaping the further elaboration of the racial order.

South Africa

The intensification of race discrimination in South Africa took place over an extended period, roughly 1890 to 1960, demarcated by the efforts of commercial farmers, businessmen in primary industries, and industrial workers to expand state control over the African majority. Even before the growth of mines and towns, dominant farmers had evolved rudimentary pass laws and a system for insuring a "fair" distribution of African squatters. But with industrialization, particularly on the Witwatersrand from the 1890s, and expanding markets in labor and food, commercial farmers turned to a range of repressive measures: limitation on African landholdings and increased taxation of the peasant, near-subsistence economy; by the 1930s, formalization of labor contracts and the pass laws, expansion of labor services, and state regulation of labor tenancy; and after World War II, the development of new forms of influx control and a network of state-run labor bureaus.

From the mid-1890s until Sharpeville in 1960 and somewhat later, the mining houses helped construct a labor framework that provided increasing numbers of African workers, while circumventing the market in labor. Before the turn of the century they insisted upon state-supported labor-recruiting monopolies and the development and effective implementation of pass and masters and servants laws; during the first six decades of this century, they insisted on state efforts to maintain reserve areas and limit the proletarianization of African workers, and enlisted the use of state power to crush African labor organization and limit African wage demands. The mining houses expanded production and employment between 1910 and 1970 without granting African miners a real increase in wages.

The organization of dominant workers, particularly in mining and later in the steel industry and railroads, brought increasing efforts to protect and subsidize white employment. The industrial unions were among the first to support the limited entry of African job-seekers into white areas—in effect, the exclusion of Africans from the capitalist mode of production—and remained into the post-World War II Nationalist period among the staunchest supporters of grand apartheid. The white mine workers before the turn of the century insisted on formal reservation of "white work," particularly the blasting ticket, and struggled, often unsuccessfully, to impose that formula on the industry and the state. Along with newly urbanized Afrikaners in the twenties and thirties, these dominant workers supported state policies that subsidized the employment of "civilized labor" in state enterprises and in the private sector. After War II, they sided with other elements within the National party alignment supporting expanded "job reservation," the splitting of mixed unions, and a yet more elaborate framework to limit the urbanization and proletarianization of African workers.

The elaboration of the racial order and the development of the state racial apparatus in this period proceeded under the ascendancy of commercial farmers. Between 1910 and the early Nationalist period, 1948–56, commercial farmers constituted the largest single bloc in Parliament and, particularly, in the governing parties; their constituencies and their concerns provided the principal issues for the state. Though state officials did not neglect the labor requirements of the mining industry and, in some periods, the interests of white workers, in other critical areas, they leaned heavily toward white agriculture, often at the expense of other class actors in the dominant section. Perhaps after 1924 (the Pact government), but certainly after 1933 with the precipitous rise in the gold price, the state diverted the surplus from mining in order to subsidize prices of agricultural commodities. In the thirties, it created the marketing boards, export and import quotas, and credit arrangements that gave farmers almost unlimited price-fixing powers and expanded what commercial interests called "indiscriminate relief" for the farming community. And above all, for our purposes, it provided the repressive framework, particularly the Native Service Contract Act and the Native Trust and Land Act, that helped farmers retain their African laborers against market forces and other interests in the economy. When the National party came to power in 1948, it increased the price of wheat by 50 percent over three years and created the labor bureaus and new controls on urban migration.

The commercial farmers' hegemony transcended their dominance in Parliament and public policy matters, however.[14] They propagated the presumptions that governed relations between the Europeans and Africans —the social distance, hierarchy, and control. Their intrusion into the African subsistence economy—the alienating of land and the dislodging of labor—emerged as a primary principle in organizing the agricultural and industrial labor forces. Their aversion to markets in labor was readily adopted by the nascent mining industry and trade unions. And their

14. *Hegemony* refers, in Antonio Gramsci's formulation, to the dominance of a group in both "political" and "civil society"—the exercise of "direct domination" through the state and indirect domination through " 'spontaneous consent' . . . caused by the prestige (and consequent confidence) which the dominant group enjoys because of its position and function in the world of production" ("The Intellectuals," p. 13). A crisis of hegemony occurs when a group loses its grip on the state machinery or, more important, its ability to command "spontaneous consent," when the ruling ideas and normal presumptions are no longer generally persuasive.

dependence on the state to help organize and control the African labor force was generalized as the repressive state structure and denial of political rights to the African majority. Though racial domination in the period of intensification was a product of class formation at the onset of capitalist development, it drew heavily on ideas nurtured in the precapitalist countryside and articulated by commercial farmers during the transition to capitalist agriculture.

The construction of the apartheid framework followed on these developments but at the same time represented a crystalization of forces contained in the period of intensification. The racial state became the centerpiece of National party ideology and policy. Only the state, and party, could embody the destiny of the Afrikaner *volk,* uplifting it, insuring its control of the economy, and guaranteeing "that the position of the European race and the European civilization be maintained and safeguarded."[15] The leaders of the Nationalist opposition in 1943 told Parliament, "We propose state interference and state control on a large scale."[16] Apartheid ideology provided for a continuing state vigilance over the race line. At one level, the state would intervene in the labor market to protect the unskilled and semiskilled white worker, "seeing that a quota system is introduced for commerce and industry . . . and into each particular occupation";[17] laying "down that some industries shall be white and other industries black."[18] At another level, the state should provide for the further "evolution" of the African reserves. The new Nationalist prime minister told Parliament in 1948 that apartheid would "call into being institutions for [Africans] in their own reserves, and to promote and further develop institutions of their own which will enable them to have a large measure of self-government and which will enable them at the same time to retain their own national character."[19]

Apartheid also provided a legitimizing ideology that divorced the system of racial domination from its rural origins. It rooted the system instead in modern philosophic traditions that play down the individual and individual rights and that emphasize community and the *volk.* With a kind of Hegelian logic, apartheid insisted that the individual finds meaning only within his own *volk* and that he joins an alien *volk* only at the expense of his identity and morale.[20]

---

15.   D. F. Malan, quoted in *Hansard,* 19 January 1943, col. 61.
16.   *Hansard,* 19 January 1943, col. 82.
17.   Ben Schoeman, quoted in *Hansard,* 19 January 1943, col. 84.
18.   Malan, *Hansard,* 19 January 1943, col. 80.
19.   Malan, quoted in *Hansard,* 16 August 1948, col. 218.
20.   See A. James Gregor, *Contemporary Radical Ideologies,* pp. 236–54; and Heribert Adam, *Modernizing Racial Domination,* p.16.

Apartheid also provided the ideas and institutions that allowed a broadening of the coalition underlying the traditional hegemony. Under the apartheid umbrella stood a variety of emergent class actors caught between the opportunities and problems of developing capitalism and their traditional ties to the rural and Afrikaner community. Afrikaner intellectuals, advocates, *predikants,* and journalists became the exponents of the "poor white problem" and the carriers of the new ideology; incipient Afrikaner entrepreneurs drew on the pooled resources of the farming community and the white working class; and Afrikaner trade-union leaders used "Afrikaner sentiment" to draw industrial workers away from the "liberalist" and Communist unions. To weld these class actors together as a political and ascendant force, the National party leadership rejected as an ideological position the domination of one class by another and emphasized instead national sentiment realized in the racial state.[21]

Alabama

The attempt to reconstruct cotton production in Alabama's Black Belt after the Civil War ushered in a period of intensification, lasting from 1875 until roughly the Depression. Against a backdrop of formally free labor, higher contract wages in the cotton states to the west, and new employment opportunities in the mines and iron industries in north Alabama, white landowners attempted to recapture their labor force. Though forms of wage labor and labor markets emerged during this period, landowners increasingly turned to the state machinery to subvert them. In particular, they sought to develop a legal and coercive framework that would tie poor blacks—and whites—into a system of dependent sharecropping. The combination of lien laws, false pretense laws, intimidation, control, then elimination of the black franchise, and control of county governments worked with particular force in the Black Belt, forging the black freedmen into a dependent, black peasantry.

Developing manufacturing interests in Alabama—coal and iron-ore mining, iron and steel manufacture, and textiles—readily took up the presumptions and opportunities current in the countryside and among commercial farmers. The textile industry developed alongside Black Belt agriculture, emphasizing employment of unorganized, "native" whites without challenging the white landowner's first claim on black labor. The

---

21. Schoeman, *Hansard,* col. 82; also see David Welsh, "The Political Economy of Afrikaner Nationalism," pp. 252–63; and Dan O'Meara, "Analysing Afrikaner Nationalism: The 'Christian-National' Assault on White Trade Unionism in South Africa, 1934–1948," pp. 63–64.

iron and mining executives reproduced with some ambiguity the conventional racial hierarchy and turned without apparent discomfort to the panoply of repressive mechanisms: convict leases, vagrancy laws, and antienticement ordinances. Where white workers attempted to organize unions, businessmen did not hesitate to recruit black strikebreakers; and where blacks and whites attempted to organize together, employers did not hesitate to use the race question to mobilize public opinion and the state against "social equality."

By the turn of the century, the artisan unions had established their control over a privileged section of the labor market in Birmingham, Mobile, and other cities. But the industrial unions, whether organized on a multiracial or white basis, failed to gain recognition before the 1930s. In large-scale industries, like iron and steel, both white industrial unions and artisan unions proved ineffective, failing to organize the entire labor force and failing to block the use of black strikebreakers. Those industrial unions that won recognition in the thirties and forties—the Paper, Pulp and Sulphite Workers, the Rubber Workers, and United Steelworkers, for example— organized blacks "under the wing" of the white working class into separate or auxiliary locals or as "full" members on the periphery of the unions. After winning recognition, these unions helped divide the labor force into black and white sections and entrenched the demarcation through "separate lines of progression." Only the United Mine Workers and the Mine, Mill and Smelter Workers consistently challenged the racial conventions.

The period of intensification was organized under the political ascendancy of commercial farmers. They successfully resisted a genuine black presence in politics, helping to overthrow the Reconstruction regime by 1875, opposing the multiracial appeal of the Populists in the 1890s, and eventually spearheading the disenfranchisement of black voters in 1901. With the black vote in tow or eliminated, commercial farmers gained firm control of local government in the Black Belt and, using massive intimidation and fraud, gained a somewhat more tenuous hold on the state government. The Constitutional Convention in 1901 entrenched for the next six decades the Black Belt's disproportionate influence and control in the state legislature. The incipient working-class movement, on the other hand, did not threaten its position: the artisan unions settled for their apprenticeships; the white industrial unions could not gain a foothold in industry; the multiracial industrial unions were crushed under the prevailing racial conventions. The iron and mining industries, rather than forge a new hegemony based on markets and economic growth, settled for an enclave and export-oriented capitalist sector. They did not challenge the prevailing ideas on race domination or the political ascendancy of the Black Belt but used the norms controlling race and labor issues to help organize and control their own labor force.

The period of intensification in Alabama brought the development of the state racial apparatus: the local law enforcement agencies, the county governments, and justices of the peace; the legal framework that limited black labor mobility and black trade-union and political rights; the coterie of politicians who emerged out of white politics and who stood to lose by changes in the labor or racial framework, who helped forge political alignments between the "big mules" in Birmingham and the Black Belt planters. But the state machinery in Alabama did not strictly approximate its counterpart in South Africa: with the defeat of Confederate armies, Alabama was once again entangled in a national federal structure. The state lacked a substantial revenue base and exercised only limited control over the economy as a whole. Though the state bureaucracy and public works and, later, state-regulated utilities provided some opportunities for dominant employment, there was no opportunity for the growth of major state productive enterprises. State officials necessarily tailored the framework of labor control and the racial barriers to nationally established constitutional standards, even if at some points those standards were permissive or blind to southern racial practices.

Unlike South Africa, the growth of the state racial apparatus in Alabama was not accompanied by the development of an ideology that helped legitimize and broaden the class alignments behind racial domination. White Alabamians, commercial farmers, and the political elite never carried their justification for racial barriers beyond the "white supremacy" of the immediate post-Reconstruction period and the simple racism of the Jim Crow era beginning at the turn of the century. Racial domination was its own justification. But lack of ideological development and limits on the state racial apparatus played an important part in the unraveling of the racial order in a later period.

The Related Settings: Northern Ireland and Israel

The development of industry and the emergence of Protestant businessmen in Northern Ireland[22] did not bring on a period of intensification, as we have

---

22. Because I have concentrated on a single set of class actors in each of the related settings, it is difficult to reconstruct these periods and crises. My primary intent was to further understanding of business enterprise and trade unionism, respectively, not of Northern Ireland and Israel. Nonetheless, I will suggest some patterns of development that follow from those analyses.

formulated it.[23] That is not to deny that industrial development created disabilities for the Catholic population. Businessmen in the principal industries of Northern Ireland located their facilities in Protestant areas and employed an almost uniformly Protestant labor force. In areas of mixed employment—like small-scale manufacture in areas proximate to both communities—Catholics were generally employed in the less skilled and less stable positions. Protestant businessmen called on the state to maintain the political connections and markets in Great Britain, rather than in the Catholic republic to the south; they supported the limitations on the Catholic franchise and the development of a Protestant civil service; they resisted, particularly in the twenties, the growth of nonsectarian labor and political organizations that questioned the conventional Unionist-Protestant-business ascendancy. Indeed, businessmen did not simply accommodate these early patterns, they helped create and implement them: businessmen dominated the early Unionist party cabinets after partition.

But businessmen based largely in shipbuilding, engineering, and textiles rather than in primary extractive industries did not need and did not help create a labor-repressive framework. With few Catholic workers, they had no need of a state machinery for monitoring and controlling the movements of Catholic labor. They had no interest in Catholic reserve areas, migrant labor, or state maintenance of a semiproletarianized Catholic population.

The state that lacked a strong repressive side also lacked autonomy. While Northern Ireland had its own parliament and administrative structure after 1921 and legislated and administered Catholic disabilities over that period, it was still dependent on events and actors at Westminster. As in Alabama, the state relied on national political institutions for fiscal policies, revenue sources, transfer payments, and economic development. State officials and political leaders were not free to legislate the Protestant ascendancy without outside scrutiny and later, as we shall see, not free to protect their position through accelerated coercive and violent means.

In Israel, the pattern of mixed capitalist and collective economic development, under the ascendancy of the Jewish labor movement, brought the intensification of discrimination against the Arab population. In the Palestine period, the Histadrut had sought to limit Arab employment in the Jewish sector and in British mandatory agencies; it had attempted to create quotas and "civilized" wage rates for Jewish employment; it excluded Arabs from the Jewish trade unions and labor exchanges. But after partition and

---

23. The discussion here is confined to businessmen because of the focus of the earlier research.

with the establishment of the Jewish state, the Histadrut's petty discrimination became state discrimination on a large scale. The state takeover of the labor exchanges and state economic development policies insured that Arabs would remain outside the developing sectors of the economy and within an institutionalized, secondary labor market.

Labor Zionism, which had advanced the *kibush haavoda,* the conquest of labor, in the Palestine period, now justified the development of a state structure that was fully identified with the dominant Jewish population and maintained the Israeli Arab population in a semiproletarian and dependent status. Other forces in Israel and the Middle East that contributed to the elaboration of the Jewish state only strengthened and legitimized the discriminatory labor framework.

THE CRISIS OF HEGEMONY

The period of intensification gave way to forces in capitalist development that have called the framework of racial domination and the racial state into question, producing a continuing crisis of hegemony. The crisis emerged in the interplay of three factors: first, the increasing prominence of businessmen in secondary manufacture and commerce; second, the increasing political disorder originating with the subordinate section and external sources; and third, the persistence of the state racial apparatus.

Businessmen in all sectors had conventionally accommodated a broad range of racial barriers in the labor market and society, and manufacturers and retail interests proved little different. They recognized primary and secondary labor markets, segregated the work place, and created income inequalities; they learned to live with repressive structures that limited the mobility of subordinate labor. While they sometimes questioned policies that limited training opportunities or the stability of semiskilled labor, they conventionally deferred to other class actors with more direct interest in these issues and to the state that had become identified with them.

Still, businessmen in manufacturing and commerce had not turned to racial barriers and the state racial apparatus as principal or indispensable tools for organizing and controlling a labor force. Their accommodation to the racial order helped reproduce it in a modern, industrial context, but their accommodation should not be confused with necessity. These businessmen could live with other ways of organizing society and another kind of state machinery. Their flexibility, on race and labor questions, unimportant in earlier periods of capitalist development when primary industries were dominant, became increasingly important as secondary industry began to dominate the economy. Later in the process, commercial farmers and mining companies too began to question or lose interest in aspects of the traditional racial framework; the former as they moved to mechanization, more economic farming units, and wage labor; the latter as they mechanized and diversified their investments. Even white workers, securely ensconced in the upper reaches of the job hierarchy or in protected positions, considered allowing some exclusory practices to pass into disuse.

The difference between this emerging accommodation and the earlier complicity became politically relevant and a challenge to the traditional racial framework only after the subordinate population raised the costs of continuing repression. Then class actors who no longer viewed the racial framework and racial state as a precondition for business practice could grapple with alternative ideas and political reforms. But conversely, only after capitalist development had taken the society beyond the period of intensification could the subordinate challenge bring out the uncertainty and disunity within the dominant section. Only then could these dominant class actors consider responding by other than renewed or elaborated repressive measures.[24]

This apparent questioning of the racial framework did not necessarily signal the abandonment of racial differentiation but, instead, a turning away from traditional conceptions of domination and perhaps the assertion of manufacturing over commercial farming interests. The traditional hegemony had given way with industrialization to "mere dominance," in Gramsci's terms, the exercise of "coercive force alone."[25] What had been appropriate in a colonial context or necessary for the destruction of subsistence agriculture or the organization of a labor force for the white farms and mines seemed inappropriate in a universe of expanding markets and growing resistance to forced labor and the denial of political rights. The faint glimmer of paternalism and reciprocity apparent in the rural economy and the mining compounds and the gloss of legalism in modern political life hardly disguised the simple brutality and force that now lay at the center of the capitalist economy. "Direct domination" by the racial state was apparent not simply at crisis points, when "spontaneous consent had failed,"[26] but regularly as the state became the principal force in the racial order.[27]

24. The analysis here can take account of the disorder that is associated with the crisis of hegemony but cannot explain its rise as a function of capitalist development. That explanation requires a broader conceptual framework, one more sensitive to problems of proletarianization generally.
25. Antonio Gramsci, "State and Civil Society," p. 276.
26. Antonio Gramsci, "The Intellectuals," p. 12.
27. Even the slave South, it seems, was better able, Genovese writes, "to contain those antagonisms on a terrain in which its legitimacy [was] not dangerously questioned" (*Roll, Jordan, Roll: The World the Slaves Made*, pp. 25–26).

What businessmen hoped to create was a society and political framework that allowed the reproduction of capitalist relations yet lent an ethical quality to intergroup relations, a social order that could enlist the subordinate population in its own subordination. At minimum, that meant deemphasizing racial categories and the racial character of the state: the former lacked an ethical basis and the latter, legitimacy. It also meant dismantling a state racial apparatus that failed to serve developing labor requirements and that daily exposed the system's principal vulnerability—its illegitimacy and utter reliance on force. Businessmen, in effect, had come to understand Gramsci's notion of hegemony: force must be tempered by consent; arbitrary state action by the police and political administration must yield to law; the narrow interests of dominant groups must be seen as the "motor force of a universal expansion, of a development of all the 'national' energies." The bourgeoisie, whatever its role in organizing production, hoped to establish its "ethical-political hegemony in civil society" and "domination in the state,"[28] wished to rise above "every compromise and condition, to become the arbiter of the Nation."[29] It hoped the state would forsake its racial character and emerge as an "educator," reflecting a seeming moral consensus and helping legitimize class relations.[30]

But these aspirations in sections of the business community clashed with the fundamental interests and ideas embodied in the state racial apparatus. The bureaucracies, state officials, and dominant politicians yielded the traditional racial hegemony only at their own peril. Bureaucracies that had grown accustomed to intervening in the labor market and factory, to administering and controlling the lives of subordinate black workers, did not easily become "educators." The ideology and prejudice that had justified racial domination, permeating the media, schools, and society as a whole, did not immediately begin crumbling with the crisis of hegemony. The police and military apparatus did not readily wither away; nor did the public employees who worked under the white labor policies, or the politicians who sat atop the racial state apparatus and whose survival depended on continued white political domination. They stood by the traditional racial hegemony, even when the class alignment that had helped build that state racial apparatus gave way, even when the subordinate population challenged the state's effectiveness and legitimacy.

28. Antonio Gramsci, "The Modern Prince," pp. 160, 182; Gramsci, "State and Civil Society," pp. 246–47, 258–60.
29. Antonio Gramsci, "Notes on Italian History," p. 105.
30. Also see Huntington, *Political Order in Changing Societies,* p. 10; James O'Connor, *The Fiscal Crisis of the State,* pp. 6–9, 40; Tilly, "Reflections on the History of European State-Making," pp. 79–80.

Whether the racial order persisted in the process of development depended on this clash between the subordinate population and the racial order and the clash between the racial state and an aspirant bourgeois hegemony.

South Africa

The elements in the crisis of hegemony emerged initially out of developing forces within the economy: the increasing importance of manufacturing and commerce; the stagnation of the white trade-union movement; and the mechanization, increasing productivity, and declining African labor force in white agriculture. Some of these trends were apparent after World War II and others as late as the early seventies. But by then it was evident that the economy had moved well beyond the mixture of gold mining, white industrial unionism, and dependent black farm labor that had given South Africa the period of intensification.

The changing economy was apparent in the shifting political fortunes and positions of class actors and in their shifting identities; in effect, a peeling away of the class basis for the racial framework. For most of this century, white commercial farmers sought to circumvent the labor market, but now they no longer needed, and no longer demanded, the refinement of the labor-repressive framework. The farmer's political standing, however, declined along with the need for the labor controls. By the late sixties, the agricultural cooperatives had come under attack from the state and even from Afrikaner businessmen. The white trade-union movement, always splintered by ideological and racial differences, had by the seventies fallen on particularly difficult times. Against a backdrop of declining white membership, both of the major trade-union federations split over the issues of African labor and African trade unions. The Chamber of Mines, long the dominant business organization in South Africa, now shared center stage with a range of important associations, like the Federated Chamber of Industries, the Association of Chambers of Commerce, and the Afrikaanse Handelsinstituut, representing a broad range of manufacturing and commercial interests.

In the absence of political disorder, however, businessmen in these emerging sectors largely accommodated the racial framework, and to a lesser extent, the state reciprocated by accommodating certain business requirements. Despite fundamental changes in the capitalist economy and class relationships, there was no apparent crisis, no serious grappling with new ideologies or alternatives to the traditional racial hegemony.

But in 1960, then in 1973 and 1976, the African population disrupted the prevailing accommodation. Civil disorders, marches, strikes, and terrorism intruded on the apparent calm. The subordinate population and the outside world ultimately would not leave the private sector to its conventional business practice. At each point, businessmen in manufacturing and commerce supported changes in racially exclusory practices against the general tenor of white opinion and state policy. Many reluctantly concluded, against a backdrop of disorder and international pressure, that the ruling ideas—apartheid in particular—could not insure a proper business environment or satisfy international opinion and, most important, could not legitimize the dominant relations of production.

But businessmen by the middle seventies had put forward only feeble proposals to establish their own hegemony against the traditional dependence on race lines and repression. They reiterated some long-standing rhetoric on the value of economic growth and supported proposals to create an African entrepreneurial and middle class with "Western-type materialistic needs." But they did not support proposals that might alter the racial character of the state and society, except at the margins.

In the end, the African and external resistance was not sufficiently imposing. However widespread and sustained were the township disorders of 1976 and 1977, there was little evidence that the African resistance by itself, or in conjunction with the existing array of outside parties, could overthrow "legitimate authority" in South Africa.

In the end, the state seemed fully capable of containing the disorders. State officials maintained their commitment to the essentials of the racial framework and the continuity of the state racial apparatus. And under the circumstances, they could hardly do otherwise. The racial order had brought, along with repressive policies, an elaborate state machinery for monitoring and controlling the movements of black labor. State officials and the political leadership did not easily relinquish the labor bureaus, pass law administration, Bantu Administration Boards, aid centres, transit camps, police, informers, prisons, courts, and more. Despite the rising opposition of secondary industry and commerce, they had not renounced the rising costs of pass law administration, at least 112,825,237 rands annually, by one estimate.[31] Nor had they abandoned a migratory labor system that continued expanding despite its costs and the opposition of major sections of the business community.[32] The state machinery, above and beyond its race and labor control functions, constituted the white community. More than a fourth of all white workers in 1970 were employed directly

---

31. Michael Savage, "The Challenge of Change and Some Arithmetic of Apartheid," pp. 12–17.
32. Study by Jill Nattrass, reported in the *Financial Mail,* 19 September 1975, pp. 1116–18.

by the state and another 10 percent by the parastatals (corporations wholly or mostly owned by the state); half of all Afrikaner workers were employed in the public or semipublic sector.[33] The state, through the Iron and Steel Corporation, the Industrial Development Corporation and other parastatals, maintained control over major sectors of the economy, such as iron and steel, phosphates, and gas from coal, and substantial ownership in others, such as engineering. Its investment as a percentage of gross domestic fixed investment reached 53 percent in 1976, up from 35 percent in 1950.[34]

Even if state officials and the government had been able to relinquish some racial functions—administration of the pass laws and labor bureaus, for example—they could hardly have relinquished the white bureaucracies that accompanied them. Nor in searching for a new hegemony beyond racism could they have afforded to endanger white control of institutions that employed a very large percentage of the white community and that directed government investment into the white sector.

Capitalist development had brought the intensification of race disabilities and ultimately the crisis of hegemony. It had not through the seventies, however, even with changing class relations and changing labor requirements, managed to undermine the racial order.

Alabama

The class foundations for the period of intensification in Alabama began shifting almost as soon as they appeared together at the turn of the century. Cotton acreage, the number of cotton spindles, and the number of tenants in the Black Belt continued to expand up until the Depression but then began a decline from which "King Cotton" never recovered. Though other commercial crops picked up from cotton, the shift away from sharecropping and unmechanized, small units of production fundamentally altered the traditional rural economy. The primary industries—coal mining and iron and steel manufacture—never "took off" as many of the New South apostles had hoped and expected. Indeed, after World War II, employment in steel stagnated, while employment in coal and ore mining dropped to a fraction of prewar levels. Manufacturing and commercial sectors, on the other hand, generated an increasing and dominant percentage of employment and income particularly during World War II and after 1960.

The economy now was dominated by businessmen in industries that had not contributed to the period of intensification, that had not helped create

33. See Hermann Giliomee, "The Political Economy of the Afrikaner," pp. 26–27.
34. William N. Raiford (prepared by), "International Credit and South Africa," p. 25.

the framework of racial domination. Debt peonage, lien laws, and the convict-lease system had passed into disuse, been abolished, or been declared unconstitutional before secondary manufacturing and commerce generated 50 percent of total employment.

But even without these roots in the racial order, businessmen in secondary industry and commerce managed a thoroughgoing accommodation to the race lines. They created separate white and "nigger" jobs, even separate industries. They channeled blacks to the dirtiest, lowest-paying dead-end jobs and locked them in by creating segregated lines of promotion. They assigned blacks to separate changing rooms and fountains and, where the company provided housing, to separate residential areas. Moreover, businessmen did not challenge the Black Belt's continuing ascendancy in politics. The Alabama Farm Bureau remained, even through the sixties, the principal political force in the legislature, setting the tone on both labor and race questions.

When the "freedom riders" reached Montgomery and Birmingham and when violence and boycotts threatened business activity, both businessmen and the white politicians were forced to consider the difference between accommodation and necessity.

For their part, the white politicians and officials at the local and state governmental levels "stood in the schoolhouse door," prepared to defend the traditional race lines and the autonomy of the racial state. But ultimately, they had little more to stand on than their racial privilege. Without a firm class basis, without a philosophy or ideology, without substantial economic resources, and without ultimate control over the National Guard, they could not withstand the forces demanding change. Despite the bold rhetoric of a "Bull" Connor and George Wallace, local police were neutralized and state military forces "nationalized"; state laws controlling segregation and the franchise were declared unconstitutional, and federal registrars were introduced to enroll black voters. The Farm Bureau during this time reiterated its support for customary segregation in education, and a collection of artisan and industrial unions, including the major locals of the United Steelworkers, Rubber Workers, and Communications Workers, supported Wallace's resistance to federal intervention.

For their part, the businessmen, first a few, then in mass, abandoned the racial order and the racial state. The Chambers of Commerce helped overthrow the hard-core racist government in Birmingham, negotiated with civil rights leaders, directed compliance with the public accommodations laws, and eventually, along with all the major business organizations in Alabama, declared their support for "the basic American heritage of voting." They insisted against the tenor of the dominant society that the welfare of both black and white lay in a new hegemony—with the ascendancy of businessmen, markets, and economic growth.

The Related Settings: Israel and Northern Ireland

Development in Israel did not generate a crisis of hegemony: virtually none of the necessary ingredients were present in the postpartition period. Though there were protests by Israeli Arabs, the small size of the community (15 percent of the population after 1948), its concentration, and the internal security situation all militated against widespread and sustained disorder. The Jewish state and military structure seemed intact and confident of its ideology and Jewish character. And most important, for our purposes, the private manufacturing sector, nearly overshadowed by state and Histadrut investment activity, was in no position to contest the hold of Zionism on the dominant Jewish community and the state.

In Northern Ireland, on the other hand, the configuration of ingredients was entirely reversed. The disorder was widespread and sustained, threatening the normal functioning of the society and economy over a decade. The inability of local police forces and politicians to contain the violence brought the disbanding of the local police network and the introduction of British troops. The disruptions gained momentum from 1967 to 1971, effectively precluding new outside investments in Northern Ireland.

Businessmen, conventionally associated with Unionist-Protestant rule in Northern Ireland and themselves responsible for widespread employment discrimination, watched the developing disorder with increasing apprehension. When the extent and impact of the violence and the British commitment became apparent, businessmen demanded an end to the "Orange rule" that they had helped create: businessmen supported "one man, one vote," a point system to insure an equitable allocation of council housing, the disbanding of the B Specials, and "justice" for the Catholic minority. In the end, they called on all the communities in Northern Ireland to recognize that the solution to sectarian conflict and historic grievances lay in renewed economic growth.

CLASS FORMATION AND RACIAL DOMINATION

This reconstruction of the process suggests a general proposition: identifiable forces in capitalist development carry forward and elaborate patterns of racial and ethnic domination. The endemic racial and ethnic turmoil in modern political life—the violence at the Burntollet or Edmund Pettus

Bridge or the stone throwing and rioting in Nazareth or Soweto—cannot be dismissed as throwbacks to "archaic" identities or as remnants of precapitalist social relations. Nor can they be viewed as reactions to rapid growth, urbanization, and new values. Racial conflict and domination, whatever their origins in precapitalist relations, are modern social and political constructions. The "modernizers," the emerging class actors who shaped and dominated these settings, helped forge the state racial machinery, turning the traditional racial pattern into a system of labor control.

Racial domination, it should also be apparent from the reconstruction, is essentially a class phenomenon. By understanding the developing class relations in these settings, we can understand much of the specificity and the dynamic in developing race relations. Racial domination is not an amorphous, all-encompassing relationship between groups distinguished by physical characteristics but, for the most part, a series of specific class relations that vary by place and over time and that change as a consequence of changing material conditions. South African race relations, for example, can be characterized generally by the subordination of the African majority and the dominance of Europeans or, alternatively, by a range of class-specific policies, such as mining compounds, land alienation, native reserves, pass laws, labor bureaus, influx control, migrant labor, and job reservations. Each should be understood in the context of the class actors and alignments that urged it on the state. Even the evolution of elaborate ideological constructions, like apartheid, should be considered in light of the class actors who demanded the destruction of African peasant agriculture, control over African proletarianization, and protection for European workers.

To insist on the role of class formation is not to deny race or ethnicity an ontological status of its own. Racial categories are real, not simply surrogates for hidden, material forces: the dominant racial section does not dissolve into the bourgeoisie and the subordinate population into the proletariat; racial prejudice and group sentiment cannot be dismissed as superstructure or false consciousness. Race and ethnic groups are rooted in shared historical experiences, language facility, kinship ties, affinity in values and modes of behavior. But the affinities and commonalities that hold groups together and suggest group sentiments do not tell us enough about the dynamics of the groups or their relationships with other actors and the state. When and under what conditions will these sentiments become salient for group members? Will sentiment take a political form? And how will sentiment translate into relations of dominance? Jews and Arabs, for example, brought identities and historical experiences to Palestine that were only partially rooted in their respective material conditions. But it is difficult, nonetheless, to make sense of their evolving relations and the Jewish ascendancy without understanding the Jewish settlers' precarious position in the labor market, the undermining of Arab peasant agriculture, and the specific mechanisms used to guarantee Jewish employment.

To insist on the importance of class formation is not to assert that every event and nuance has a class character and can be explained by continuing reference to class interests. It is possible, as we discovered in our own reconstruction of the development process, that conflicts in the material world create or influence institutions and ideas whose class character becomes increasingly obscure. State practices, intimately associated with the articulated needs of class actors, persist well after the period when these actors dominated the developing economy and demanded state control of the subordinate population; state functionaries and political leaders retain their positions despite the dissolution of class alignments that brought them to power; ideas that justify group domination and labor repression continue to order group relations, though many of their adherents now seek new bases of hegemony. In Alabama, for example, Public Safety Director Eugene "Bull" Connor and Sheriff James Clark and registrars across the Black Belt faced the civil rights challenge virtually on their own: the landlord and his coterie of dependent sharecroppers had already given way to cattle, large farming units, mechanization, and wage labor; the businessman in manufacturing and commerce had long ago given up on vagrancy laws and convict labor and would soon discover "free markets" and the bounty in economic growth.

In insisting that these dominant class actors are critical to the persistence and intensification of racial disabilities, we are not asserting, at the same time, that the process unfolds without contradictions. We should not substitute for the "growth school" an alternative model that proposes an equally simplistic and linear relationship between growth and increasing race and ethnic discrimination. Capitalist development certainly brings a period of intensification that leaves an indelible impression on the society and state, but it also creates contradictory processes that sow disunity in the dominant section, increase the efficacy of subordinate protest, and give force to competing ideologies. There is no certainty that the contradictions will prove debilitating, as they were in Northern Ireland. There, businessmen in manufacturing and commerce who had helped construct the Protestant ascendancy eventually allied themselves with Catholic demands and a program of "reform." In other settings, however, such as South Africa, the contradictions brought about endemic instability and some anguish about the ruling ideas, but few serious threats to the racial state and the essentials of the racial framework.

The primary patterns in our reconstruction—particularly the conclusion that these dominant class actors are largely responsible for the persistence and intensification of racial disabilities—contradict virtually all reputable thinking on the question, from theories of "primordialism" to theories of "plural societies," from the modernization literature to orthodox Marxist and Leninist thought.[35]

The most common ahistorical, nondevelopmental theories of persistent racial and ethnic conflict emphasize alternative processes that cannot explain our reconstruction. The emphasis on the strength of "primordial" identities— the "givens," the "common biological origins"—captures the emotive aspects of race conflict apparent in these settings and suggests some reasons for the durability of such attachments. But the literature fails to take account of the class interests that are so tightly bound up with racial sentiment and practice; it is indifferent to the contradictory processes in development that in some settings and periods give force to racial categories and in others confound them.

The literature on plural societies alerts us to the importance of the state in the relationship between the dominant and subordinate sections of the population, but it too fails to capture many of the fundamental processes apparent in our reconstruction. First, by making political domination the "antecedent condition" ordering relations between the racial sections, it must ignore the apparent relationship between economy and society. Among our most compelling findings was the impact of changing patterns of agriculture, industrialism, and class formation on patterns of race relations. Second, by focusing almost exclusively on racial sections, it misses the class differentiation and shifting class alignments within sections of the population that shape the racial framework.

The modernization literature, on the other hand, is sensitive to problems of economy and society, but by assuming that growth overcomes diversity, that "modernization" transcends traditional identities, it gets the result and process wrong. Modern state structures, mass communication, mobility, literacy, new patterns of status, and inequality were all evident in these settings, yet the traditional racial hierarchy and divisions survived and developed over extended periods. Moreover, those actors most closely identified with the emerging capitalist order helped "modernize" racial domination, using racial divisions to circumvent the labor market, placing the imprimatur of race on state institutions. Racial stratification, rather than "peeling off" with "modernization," was incorporated into the developing labor market and modern state.

---

35. This literature was first considered in chapter 1.

Nor does the orthodox Marxist emphasis on the transformation of labor into a commodity, suggesting that capitalist relations "explode" or "rip up" the traditional bonds between people, come much closer to forecasting the outcome. On the one hand, it underestimates the tenacity of those traditional bonds, particularly among dominant workers. On the other hand, it underemphasizes the commercial farmers and primary manufacturers' interest in limiting the labor market and proletarianization. These class actors, integral to the developing capitalist order, helped insure that the labor market would reflect the traditional racial patterns and that the state would monitor and control the movements of subordinate workers.

To the extent that the modernization and Marxist literatures emphasize nonlinear transformations—the heightening of racial and ethnic identities and tensions *in the short term*—they come closer to describing the reconstructed process, but not close enough. First, they incorrectly associate upsurges of ethnic conflict with "backward" areas, with groups retaining links with the countryside, or with individuals who seek solace or advantage in less instrumental and more enduring social relations. On the other hand, they assume that the "modernizers," identified with the developing state structures and new sources of wealth, will seek to rationalize social relations and create new "overarching loyalties" and eventually take the society beyond these outbursts of tradition. But it should be evident by now that the latter too may seek advantage in the traditional social divisions and try to incorporate them into emerging market and political relations.

Second, how long is the short term in these nonlinear transformations of society? How long before "backward areas" are incorporated into the larger capitalist network? How long before the "modernizers" establish their dominance over the state and before communication and mobility break down traditional group loyalties? In our settings, racial and ethnic barriers were elaborated over three-quarters or, in one case, an entire century, of development. The racial and ethnic orders survived well past this period, diffusing only after external factors buttressed indigenous manufacturing and commercial interests and undermined the autonomy of the state and society. There is little here to warrant the optimistic phraseology of the modernization literature—the "pulverization" and the "sweeping away"—or the patience of countless spokesmen of the subordinate populations who identified themselves with capitalist growth and who waited for their slice of the expanding pie.

To relieve our perplexity about enduring racial and ethnic conflict in contemporary settings, we turned to the forces within capitalist development itself. By focusing on problems of class formation, we were able to identify processes that associated growth and the intensification of racial disabilities, that brought labor repression over markets, that turned "primordial" sentiment into state ideology, and that brought disunity to the dominant racial section and threats to the stability of the racial order.

Still, it is possible that developing capitalist relations within these societies carry forward the race and ethnic lines and conflicts while world market forces intrude on the indigenous political economy, threatening to eradicate them. External factors—the international community, the national state, credit markets, diffuse labor markets, and liberal ideology—all contributed to the undermining of racial domination in Alabama and the Protestant ascendancy in Northern Ireland. These same forces on a wider scale, while not yet decisive in South Africa and Israel, exacerbated the internal contradictions, encouraging subordinate resistance and encouraging some class actors to seek out alternative ways of organizing society. Over some indefinite period, the external factors could shift the balance against the current European and Jewish regimes.

But even then, we would not have escaped our problem. The racial orders, products of the plantation economies and settler societies of a colonial past, might eventually yield before world market forces and their own contradictions, but the forces in capitalist development that we have identified probably are not limited to these settings. Commercial farmers employing Mexican, Amerindian, Asian, Turkish, Dagomba, or some other distinctive group of farm laborers may evolve racist and coercive mechanisms to shield their workers from the lures of the labor market. Businessmen may recruit laborers from distant regions or countries—euphemistically termed "guest workers"—and reap the advantages of divisiveness in the labor force or the cost and political advantages in semiproletarianized or migrant labor; they certainly may adapt management practice to incorporate the prejudices and conventions prevalent in the community and among their labor force. And workers, threatened by the insecurity of the labor market and work place, may act to protect their skills and jobs against workers of lesser skill and standards, particularly against those workers recruited from other societies and cultures. Contained in each of those processes are the germs of racial or ethnic exclusion and demands for state action.

APPENDIX A

Notes on Method and Sources

FARMERS

South Africa

The strength and political importance of organized agriculture give a ready focus to field research in this area. While business opinion in South Africa is represented by five major associations and labor opinion by two or three major federations, farm opinion is expressed by only one overarching farm organization, the South African Agricultural Union (SAAU). It takes in all the major cooperatives and commodity organizations and represents the thousands of local farmers' associations, the district agricultural unions, and the four provincial unions. Because of its strength and organizational scope, the SAAU is regularly consulted by a broad range of officials. On agricultural questions, the deference to the SAAU is almost complete: the SAAU, for example, appoints the producer representatives to the marketing boards. But even on questions of broader interest, the government will turn to the SAAU for advice and comment: proposed industrial conciliation legislation (1953 and 1973), the repeal of the Masters and Servants Act (1974), and the Theron Commission Report on the "Coloured Population Group" (1976) all faced close SAAU scrutiny.[1]

In April and May of 1977, I conducted interviews with officers of the South African Agricultural Union (SAAU) and the provincial agricultural unions and with a small sample of white farmers. The interviews with organized agriculture normally involved a cluster of individuals who met for a half, sometimes an entire, day. The cluster might include, as it did in Natal, the president and director of the provincial union; as in the Transvaal, the secretary and assistant secretary of the provincial union, a member of the Dairy Board, and a representative of the Department of Agriculture; or, as in the Cape, the secretary of the provincial union, two

---

1. These consultations were reported in interviews with the officers of the Cape and Transvaal Agricultural Unions, as well as with the South African Agricultural Union.

wine farmers, and representatives from the Ko-operative Wijnbouwers Vereniging (Cooperative Winegrowers Association). The individual white farmers interviewed were carefully selected by the SAAU and were in no sense representative of the white farming community. It was valuable, nonetheless, to speak with white farm owners and occasionally black laborers in a setting that had nurtured labor-repressive agriculture.[2]

For documentary research, I concentrated on the published journals and annual reviews of the South African Agricultural Union and of the provincial agricultural unions.

> South African Agricultural Union: *Report of the Annual Congress* or *General Council* (1956–1975); *Organized Agriculture (Georganiseerde Landbou),* organ of the South African Agricultural Union and the Cooperative Movement (1962–70); *SALU Nuus,* newsletter of the South African Agricultural Union (1973–74)
>
> Natal Agricultural Union: *NAUNLU,* official organ of the Natal Agricultural Union (1951–73); *Annual Report* (1971/72)
>
> Free State Agricultural Union: *Agenda for the Annual Congress* (1966–70)
>
> Transvaal Agricultural Union: *Congress Report of the Transvaal Agricultural Union* (1968–73).

Alabama

The Alabama Farm Bureau Federation is the principal farm organization in the state, though based primarily in the former cotton-growing areas and the Black Belt—the center of black residence before World War II and of Alabama's "racial politics." Though there are competing organizations, such as the National Farmers' Organization, none has established a substantial influence on developing commercial agriculture. The Farm Bureau has been the principal farm lobby in the state legislature and probably the most effective organized interest supporting Black Belt ascendancy, racial segregation, and disenfranchisement of the black population. At the county level, the Farm Bureau, closely tied to the Agricultural Extension Service, had enrolled over 60,000 white members by 1950 and has grown considerably since (though drawing on other than farming communities).

---

2. The book does not normally provide footnote citations for factual material or quotes drawn from interviews, except where the text itself is ambiguous or silent on the source. In those exceptional cases, a citation is provided, indicating the type of interview and, in some cases, the specific organization represented.

During June 1975, I interviewed the president and assistant to the president of the Alabama Farm Bureau Federation and reviewed a number of Farm Bureau publications: the Annual Report and Presidential Address (1964–74). *Farm Bureau Policies* (1949–74), and the *Legislative Newsletter* (1970–74). I also reviewed the major Alabama newspapers for the post-World War II period, focusing upon Farm Bureau responses to the civil rights campaigns, court decisions, changes in legislative apportionment, and the emerging role of secondary manufacturing. As the Farm Bureau respondents had difficulty recalling events during the civil rights period and the Farm Bureau documentary materials only hinted at the debates and interests that underlay the organization's race and labor policies, I asked both businessmen and trade-union leaders to help fill out the picture of Farm Bureau activity, particularly in the state legislature. Unfortunately, my interviews did not reach down to the county Farm Bureaus, where problems of race and labor had been most acute. Time constraints and perhaps irrational concerns about personal safety prevented a more thorough investigation at that level.

BUSINESSMEN

South Africa

Between July 1973 and February 1974, I conducted open-ended, taped interviews with twenty-five business executives, principally managing directors of firms.[3] Each respondent represented a firm listed on both the South Africa Stock Exchange (to insure direct South African investment) and the *Financial Mail's* ranking of South Africa's one hundred largest employers or nine major mining houses. The firms were selected on a random basis from the ninety-three firms that met both selection criteria. Two firms were excluded from the sample population because of transportation problems and six (mainly in finance) because their employees were nearly all white-collar and white; four firms, including the important Frame Group, declined to participate in the survey. But, as can be seen from table 1, the participating firms were broadly representative of concerns in mining,

3. Trade-union and business interviews in Alabama and South Africa were recorded and transcribed; remaining interviews were handled with notetaking and detailed reports prepared after the completion of the interview. The principal consideration here was not the intrusive quality of recording equipment but the cost and time involved in gaining typewritten transcripts.

textiles, manufacturing, commerce, and construction. In the text itself, however, the specific firms and officers remain anonymous.[4]

Table 1. South African Firms

Firms	Industrial Groups
African Explosives and Chemical Industry	Chemicals
African Oxygen	Iron, Steel, and Engineering
Anglo-Alpha Cement	Construction
Anglo-American Corporation of South Africa	Mining
Anglo-Transvaal Consolidated Investment	Mining
Bruynzeel Plywoods	Construction
The Carpet Manufacturing Company	Textiles and Carpets
Dorman Long Corporation	Iron, Steel, and Engineering
Dunlop South Africa	Motor
Johannesburg Consolidated Investment Company	Mining
John Orr's and Company	Commerce
Kohler Brothers	Paper and Packaging
LTA	Construction
The Leyland Motor Corporation of South Africa	Motor
The Metal Box Company of South Africa	Paper and Packaging
O.K. Bazaars	Commerce
The Roberts Construction Company	Construction
Ropes and Mattings Holdings	Carpets and Textiles
Sentrachem	Chemicals
South African Iron and Steel Industrial Corp.	Iron, Steel, and Engineering
South African Pulp and Paper Industries	Paper and Packaging
Stewarts and Lloyds of South Africa	Iron, Steel, and Engineering
Toyota South Africa	Motor
Truworths	Commerce
Vereeniging Refractories	Iron, Steel, and Engineering

I relied upon business publications that met the following criteria: formal association with a business organization that represents a particular sector of South African industry, substantial concern with public policy rather than technical or trade issues, and regular publication of organization memoranda or accounts of representations to parliamentary commissions or cabinet ministers. I studied publications in four areas of industry.

Chamber of Mines: *Annual Report* (1890–1967); *Proceedings at the Annual General Meeting* (1935–47, 1960–73); various publications of the Gold Producers' Committee, supplemented by the *South Africa Mining and Engineering Journal* (1960).

4. To gain reasonable access and frankness, business respondents were given anonymity both for themselves and their firms. Trade-union respondents generally demanded only anonymity for themselves but not their unions. Because of the organizational position of the South African Agricultural Union, the Alabama Farm Bureau, and the Histadrut, organizational anonymity could not be provided, though I have tried not to refer to specific individuals or officers, except in the case of the Histadrut, where anonymity was not asked for and seemed unnecessary.

Federated Chamber of Industries: *FCI News* (1948); *The Manufacturer*, official journal of the S.A. Federated Chamber of Industries (1950–66); *FCI Viewpoint* (1967–71).

Association of Chambers of Commerce: *The Commercial Bulletin of South Africa* (1935), *Commercial Opinion* (1936–73), supplemented by *Blue Book of Southern African Business* (1960–63).

Afrikaanse Handelsinstituut: *Volkshandel* (1940–73).

Alabama

During the summer of 1975, I interviewed the presidents, Alabama directors, and, in two cases, senior public-relations officers of corporations conducting major operations in Alabama. The sixteen responding companies were selected on the basis of location and sector from a list prepared by the Associated Industries of Alabama of the thirty largest employers in Alabama (table 2). Among the responding companies was the International Paper Company, although the officer was uncommunicative and ended the interview prematurely; three companies—Scott Paper Company (Southern Operations), Republic Steel Corporation (Southern District), and Gulf State Paper Corporation—declined to be interviewed, in two cases because of current court proceedings. The final sample, however, included the major state utilities, the principal manufacturers in steel and rubber, and representative employers in textiles, metal fabricating, and retail trade.

I gathered additional background material by interviewing officers of the Associated Industries of Alabama and the Alabama Chamber of Commerce and a past officer of the Birmingham Chamber of Commerce from the civil rights period.

Table 2. Alabama Firms

Hayes International Corporation
American Cast Iron and Pipe Company
Stockham Valves and Fitting Company
Alabama Power Company
Sears, Roebuck and Company
Pizitz Department Stores
Winn-Dixie
International Paper Company
Alabama Dry Docks and Shipbuilding
Vanity Fair Mills
Southern Bell Telephone
United States Steel Corporation
United States Pipe and Foundry Company
Goodyear Tire Corporation
Monsanto Textile Company
Avondale Mills

Because none of the business associations regularly published their views on political and race questions, I spent a considerable amount of time reading extrabusiness sources: the extensive clippings files and documentary holdings of the Birmingham City Library, as well as selective materials available at the Mobile Public Library and the State Archive in Montgomery; reports on *Racial Policies of American Industry* prepared by the Wharton School of Finance and Commerce, University of Pennsylvania; civil proceedings taken against individual companies by the Equal Employment Opportunity Commission and the National Labor Relations Board; and hearings conducted by the United States Civil Rights Commission in Alabama.

Northern Ireland

During March and April of 1976, I conducted interviews with the managing directors of three of the largest firms in Northern Ireland. For security reasons, I cannot identify the firms or, for that matter, even the industrial sectors that they represent. The potential costs of disclosure are high, and few of the respondents were insensitive to them.[5] The firms, however, did meet the following criteria: each is the largest or sole employer in a major section of Northern Ireland industry; each is based in the Belfast area; each is Protestant owned and managed; and each employs a predominantly or exclusively Protestant labor force. Between them, these firms employed 20,000 workers in 1977 and have at other times employed more than 30,000. Three other firms meeting these criteria declined to be interviewed.

Because of the difficulties in interviewing officers of individual firms, I devoted most of my research time to the three major business organizations: the Engineering Employers' Northern Ireland Association, the Confederation of British Industry (CBI), and the Northern Ireland Chamber of Commerce and Industry (NICCI), particularly the latter. Of the three organizations, the Engineering Employers' Association was the least interested in broad questions of social policy and least communicative about its views. I conducted interviews with a present officer (by telephone) and a principal officer during the crucial 1969–71 period. The Northern Ireland Regional Committee of the Confederation of British Industry was formed in 1965 and represented firms employing, by various estimates, 60 to 70 percent of the workers in manufacturing. The CBI was represented on the Northern Ireland Economic Council and on the Working Party on Dis-

5. One respondent, for example, demanded assurance that I was not a "hit man" for some terrorist organization and insisted that we meet in a public place, like a hotel lobby, park, or restaurant.

crimination in the Private Sector. I interviewed its principal officer. The Northern Ireland Chamber of Commerce and Industry was probably the most visible, if not influential, of the business associations; its representatives served on a broad range of advisory committees and working parties and in the past actively lobbied ministers at Stormont. In 1965, when CBI was organizing a regional committee, the Belfast Chamber and the Northern Ireland Chamber consolidated and expanded their recruitment efforts in the manufacturing sector. The consolidated organization, the NICCI, took in 60 percent of the firms in manufacturing, including all the major Northern Ireland-based companies. I interviewed a present officer and three past presidents during the 1965–71 period.

The interviews were supplemented by a close reading of the Northern Ireland Chamber of Commerce and Industry's official journals: *Belfast Chamber of Commerce Journal* (1923–41), *Northern Ireland Progress* (1950–73), and *Business Letter* (1974–77).

WORKERS

South Africa

Between June 1973 and February 1974, I interviewed the officers of twenty-six major trade unions.[6] The unions selected did not strictly constitute a sample. They included the largest (white and mixed) trade unions in the Trade Union Council of South Africa (TUCSA), the South African Confederation of Labour and among the unaffiliated unions; they also included several smaller but strategically placed unions. White-collar unions (e.g., the S.A. Society of Bank Officials) were excluded from the sample. The twenty-six trade unions set out in table 3 encompass nearly every significant union in the construction, manufacturing, railroad, mining, and commercial fields.

In nearly every case, interviews were held with the secretary or general secretary of the union. In a few instances, however, where it seemed appropriate, the interviews involved the president of the union, the assistant general secretary, or a provincial secretary. To insure anonymity, I refer only to the trade-union "officer."

In order to build an historical record on the South African trade-union movement, I reviewed a number of individual union publications, which were only occasionally helpful, and the proceedings of annual meetings and

6. The interviews for trade-union as well as business leaders normally lasted about one and one half hours; the shortest, one hour, and the longest, almost four hours.

Table 3. South African Trade Unions

I. Artisan Unions

Artisan	*Artisan-Dominated*
S.A. Technical Officials (3,260)[a]	S.A. Footplate Staff Association (9,216)
National Association of Furniture and Allied Workers of S.A. (816)	Amalgamated Engineering Union (25,168)
Blanke Bouwerkersvakbond (2,396)	S.A. Electrical Workers' Union (16,000)
S.A. Diamond Workers' Union (773)	Johannesburg Municipal Transport Workers' Union (1,208)
Amalgamated Society of Woodworkers (4,866)	S.A. Boilermakers, Iron and Steel Workers and Welders' Society (15,712)
Underground Officials' Association (7,902)	S.A. Typographical Union (19,851)
Amalgamated Union of Building Trade Workers of S.A. (9,963)	Artisan Staff Association (20,192)
Motor Industry Employees' Union (19,096)	
S.A. Iron Moulders' Society (2,079)	

Apprenticeships:		
all positions	9	0
some positions	0	7
virtually none	0	0
Race Composition:		
white	4	2
white since 1956[b]	2	2
mixed[c]	3	3

II. Industrial Unions

Exclusive[d]	*Open*
Die Spoorbond (5,560)	Transvaal Leather and Allied Trades Industrial Union (2,621)
S.A. Postal Association (2,232)	Garment Workers' Union of S.A. (12,825)
Durban Municipal Employees' Society (3,030)	Garment Workers' Union of the Western Province (35,406)
Mine Workers' Union (17,624)	Garment Workers' Industrial Union (Natal) (25,268)
Yster-, Staal-, en Verwante Nywerhedeunie (34,457)	National Union of Distributive Workers (14,364)

Apprenticeships:		
all positions	0	0
some positions	3	0
virtually none	2	5
Race Composition:		
white	5	0
white since 1956	0	1
mixed	0	4

[a]Membership size

[b]Under the Industrial Conciliation Act of 1956, racially mixed (Coloured and white) unions were given the alternative of forming separate branches and maintaining a single white executive council or splitting into fully separate unions.

[c]Coloured and white membership but not including Africans.

[d]See Chapter 15 for a discussion of exclusive and open industrial unionism.

special conventions of the various labor federations, which were considerably more helpful. The latter reflected the temper of debate and also provided resolutions, correspondence with state officials, and descriptions of representations before various state agencies. The most useful among these publications are :

South African Trades and Labour Council: Minutes of Meeting of Trade Union Council and Cape Federation (1927); TUC Correspondence (1928); Minutes of All-In Trades Union Conference (1930); Minutes of Meeting of National Executive Committee of Trades and Labour Council (1930); Annual Report and Balance Sheet of the South African TUC (1928, 1931); Report of the Annual Conference, South African Trades and Labour Council (1933–52)

Trade Union Council of South Africa: Minutes of Special Conference of Trade Unions (1953); Minutes of Trade Union Unity Committee, Unity Conference (1954); Report of Proceedings, Annual Conference, South African Trade Union Council (1955–60); Report of Proceedings, Annual Conference, Trade Union Council of South Africa (1962–75)

Individual Union Publications: *Die Mynwerker,* publication of the Mine Workers' Union (1949–73); *Die S.A. Werker,* publication of the S.A. Yster-, Staal-, en Verwante Nywerhedeunie (1963–76); *The Woodworker,* publication of the Amalgamated Society of Woodworkers of South Africa (1973); *Metalworker,* publication of the Amalgamated Engineering Union (1973); *Power,* publication of the S.A. Electrical Workers' Association (1972–73)

Alabama

During May and June of 1975, I interviewed a variety of individuals involved in the trade-union movement in Alabama: labor leaders, like the president, former vice-president and legislative director of the state AFL-CIO and a former officer of the state CIO; informants, such as labor attorneys for the Steelworkers' and the Pulp, Sulphite and Paper Mill Workers' Unions, public-relations director for District 36 (Southern District) of the Steelworkers' Union, and director of the Labor Education and Research Program at the University of Alabama, Birmingham; and finally, and most important, a sample of officers from the larger industrial unions and the strategically placed artisan unions. The sample of seventeen business agents and presidents was drawn from a larger list of unions affiliated to the state Labor Council of the AFL-CIO, the Metal Trades Department, and the various local Building and Construction Trades

Councils, and a number of prominent independent unions, like the United Mine Workers' and the United Automobile Workers' Unions (table 4). The final sample included virtually every major union in iron and steel manufacturing, coal mining, secondary industry, and the building trades. It did not include any of the railway unions—their jurisdictions extended beyond Alabama and their offices were usually located elsewhere in the South—or any white-collar unions. Though two interviews could not be arranged because of scheduling conflicts, no trade-union leader declined to be interviewed.

Table 4. Alabama Trade Unions

Artisan Unions		*Industrial Unions*		
Typographical Union, Birmingham (356)[a]		United Steelworkers (26,000)		
Birmingham Building and Construction Trades (Carpenters and Joiners, 1,200)		United Automobile Workers (17,000)		
		United Mine Workers (not known)		
International Brotherhood of Electrical Workers (1,250)		Retail, Wholesale and Department Store Workers (6,400)		
Mobile Construction and Building Trades (12,000)		Communications Workers (3,000)		
		Paper, Pulp and Sulphite Workers (14,000)		
International Brotherhood of Boilermakers and Iron Shipbuilding (588)		Union of Marine and Shipbuilding Workers (3,500)		
		United Rubber Workers (2,800)		
		Amalgamated Clothing Workers (4,000)		
		International Ladies Garment Workers (6,000)		
		Electrical Workers, U-19 (3,400)		
		Laborers' Union, Birmingham (2,500)		
Apprenticeships:				
all	4		0	
some/most	1		5	
none	0		7	
Percentage Black:[b]				
under 10	5		3	
10–49	0		6	
over 49	0		3	
When Organized:				
before 1900	3		0	
1930–49	2		8	
after 1949	0		2	
don't know	0		2	

[a]Estimate of current membership
[b]Before 1964

I also reviewed a number of documentary sources: trade-union contracts; *Proceedings* of the Annual Convention of the Alabama Labor Council (1956–74); *Proceedings* of the Alabama State Industrial Union Council, CIO

(1941–57); *Legislative Report* of the Alabama Labor Council (1957–65); labor reporting in the *Birmingham News* (1946–75); Equal Employment Opportunity Commission (EEOC) reports for specific industries; and court proceedings involving current and past trade-union practices (e.g., *Local Union No. 12, United Rubber Workers* v. *National Labor Relations Board*).

Israel

The Histadrut (now the General Federation of Labor, previously Jewish Labor) is an overarching labor organization that has dominated the labor movement since its founding in 1920 and played a central role in the politics of the Jewish community both before and after partition in 1948. Initially, it incorporated the labor exchanges and trade-union activities of competing Jewish labor parties, but eventually it organized 85 percent of the Jewish working population and created an elaborate institutional framework of social welfare activity and worker-owned industrial enterprises. The labor leadership and parties that dominated the Histadrut also came to dominate the Jewish state: "The same political elements take the lead at both the national and the Histadrut levels," one former general secretary noted.[7]

During May and June of 1976, I interviewed a range of present and former leaders of the Histadrut; also officeholders in the state and governing Labor party who concentrated on problems of Arab labor. Among those interviewed were two former general secretaries of the Histadrut and the present general secretary (covering virtually the entire period since 1948), the founder and former director of the Arab Department of the Histadrut, the present director and assistant director of the Arab Department, the manager of the Galilee District of the Histadrut, the secretary of the Textile Workers' Union, the chairman of a workers council in a textile factory, the director of the Arab Department of the Labor party, and the deputy to the advisor on Arab affairs of the Prime Minister's Office.

The historical record for the Histadrut was attained primarily from secondary sources but also from a reading (and selective translation) of the *Proceedings of Histadrut Conventions* and *Reports of the Executive Council* through the tenth convention (1920 to 1966), review of *Labour in Palestine* and its successor *Israel Labour News* from 1946 to 1953, and use of the clippings files of the *Jerusalem Post* for the period 1958–74.

7. Aharon Becker, "Histadrut Faces the Future," pp. 12–13.

APPENDIX B

Statistical Tables

I. SOUTH AFRICA

A. Population

Year	Total	Whites	Coloureds	Asians	Africans
1904	5,174,827	1,117,234	444,991	112,311	3,490,291
1910	5,878,000	1,257,000	517,000	148,000	3,956,000
1915	6,436,000	1,380,000	541,000	159,000	4,356,000
1921	6,927,403	1,521,343	545,181	163,594	4,697,285
1925	7,664,000	1,650,000	608,000	181,000	5,225,000
1930	8,540,000	1,801,000	682,000	199,000	5,858,000
1936	9,587,863	2,003,334	769,241	219,691	6,595,597
1940	10,353,000	2,160,000	836,000	247,000	7,110,000
1946	11,415,925	2,372,044	928,062	285,260	7,830,559
1951	12,667,759	2,641,689	1,103,016	366,664	8,556,390
1955	13,669,000	2,856,000	1,242,000	410,000	9,161,000
1960[a]	17,122,000	3,069,000	1,500,000	476,000	12,077,000
1965	19,607,000	3,408,000	1,782,000	548,000	13,869,000
1970	22,469,000	3,835,000	2,074,000	642,000	15,918,000
1974	24,920,000	4,166,000	2,306,000	709,000	17,745,000

Sources: Union Statistics for Fifty Years, A8
Bulletin of Statistics (1974), vol. 8, no. 4; (1975), vol. 9, no. 4

Note: The tables and footnotes in this appendix were prepared by Kennieth Pittman.
[a]The substantial increase between 1955 and 1960 reflects in part a modification in the calculation of the African population. Three figures are available for the 1960 African population: 9,896,000 or 10,927,992 or 12,077,000.

B. Urban Population by Racial Group in Cities of More Than 5,000 Inhabitants
(By Percentage)

Year	Whites	Coloureds	Asians	Africans
1904	36.0	21.3	17.6	6.3
1911	35.6	23.2	29.4	8.7
1921	39.9	26.5	39.9	9.5
1936	49.5	32.3	50.7	13.8
1946	58.2	38.7	56.3	18.5
1951	61.9	44.5	60.7	22.1
1960	68.2	49.0	65.6	26.2

Sources: Bureau of Statistics, "Urban and Rural Population of South Africa 1904–1960," Report Number 02–02–01
Bureau of Statistics, *Population Census, 1970 Sample Tabulation,* Report Number 02–01–01 and 02

C.1. Agriculture: Employment

Year	Total	Whites[a]	Coloureds	Asians	Africans
1918	488,062	54,621	50,797	23,671	358,973
1925	689,165	160,685	76,792	16,503	435,185
1930	749,197	184,811	73,613	14,864	475,909
1937	469,410	205,261	31,930	12,265	608,412
1945	649,447	15,611		————633,836————	
1950	882,371	15,012		————867,359————	
1955	1,005,674	8,040	————129,837————		867,797
1960	913,345	13,329	125,507	6,802	767,707
1964	888,104	12,496	123,942	7,095	744,571

Sources: Union Statistics for Fifty Years, G3, I3
Statistical Yearbook (1966), H31
Agricultural Census No. 38 (1963–64), Report No. 06–01–03

Note: The data do not include "casual employees," a substantial proportion of the agricultural labor force—e.g., casual employees numbered 591,882 (498,898 African) in 1960. As only sketchy data on casual employees are available prior to 1958 and after 1963, the numbers are excluded. The figures refer to employees, including domestic servants, on white-, Coloured-, and Asian-owned farms.

[a]The data for 1925–1937 include farm owners together with their relations residing on the farm unit. If owners and relatives are excluded, "white employment" would drop to a fraction of the figures given—e.g., in 1925 there were 90,658 white farms; in 1930 there were 96,940; and in 1937 there were 104,544.

C.2. Agriculture: Production and Mechanization

Year	Volume of Agricultural Production $(1958/9-1960/1 = 100)$[a]	Number of Tractors
1911	28	
1915	30	
1918		231
1920	34	
1921		515
1925	39	
1926		1,302
1930	51	3,684
1935	47	
1937		6,019
1940	53	
1945	57	
1946		20,292
1950	67	48,422
1955	84	87,451
1960	99	120,920
1964		133,600
1965	116	
1970	144	
1971		157,100
1973		164,100
1975	169	

Sources: Union Statistics for Fifty Years, I22, I27
          Agrekon (1974), vol. 13, no. 1; (1975), vol. 14, no. 4
          Annual Report of the Secretary for Agricultural Economics and Marketing (1975–76)
          Agricultural Census No. 34 (1959–60), no. 4

[a]Data for 1911–1959 originally indexed for base year 1936/7–1938/39 were converted to index 1958/9–1960/1 as the base year.

D.1. Employment: Mining

Year	Total	Whites	Coloureds[a]	Asians	Africans
1910	291,377	31,810		4,073	255,494
1915	271,753	27,490		3,878	240,884
1920	306,554	37,939		3,129	266,092
1925	300,554	31,685		1,957	267,473
1930	349,031	35,674		1,234	213,861
1935[b]	400,274	42,315	1,542	854	355,703
1940	502,008	54,767	2,232	767	444,542
1945	462,392	52,581	1,592	580	410,132
1950	492,615	56,246	2,292	568	435,536
1955	526,919	66,580	2,804	414	460,398
1960	593,048	65,005	3,438	429	524,176
1965	607,119	63,866	4,523	440	538,290
1970	656,815	62,638	6,262	623	587,292
1974	664,600	62,678	7,300	526	594,096

Sources: Union Statistics for Fifty Years, G4–G5
Monthly Bulletin of Statistics (1962), vol. 41, no. 12; (1966), vol. 45, no. 12
Bulletin of Statistics (1971), vol. 5, no. 4; (1975), vol. 9, no. 4

[a]For 1910–30 Coloured workers are included with Africans.
[b]Data since 1930 include "quarrying" with mining; employment in quarrying is small by comparison, however, and has little impact on the data (e.g., 17,067 were employed in quarrying in 1960, of which 1,615 were whites).

D.2. Employment: Manufacturing

Year	Total	Whites	Coloureds	Asians	Africans
1916	101,178	39,624	15,271	11,318	35,065
1920	175,520	62,483		113,037	
1925	191,598	71,004		120,594	
1930	218,585	91,024	27,299	9,745	90,517
1935	234,295	95,592	25,840	10,048	102,815
1940	314,488	115,292	37,564	14,233	147,399
1945	431,402	133,518	55,329	18,014	224,541
1950	553,233	191,093	73,810	21,260	267,070
1955	632,773	176,963		113,660	342,150
1960	692,400	208,900		125,800	357,700
1965	929,500	233,900	150,100	50,900	494,600
1970	1,164,100	276,900	195,800	74,300	617,200
1975	1,327,500	295,500	223,300	82,500	726,200

Sources: Official Yearbook of the Union (1917), vol. 1 through (1936), vol. 17
Census of Industrial Establishments (1942–43); (1944–45)
Monthly Bulletin of Statistics (1957), vol. 36, no. 12 through (1966), vol. 45, no. 12
Bulletin of Statistics (1967), vol. 1, no. 3; (1974), vol. 8, no. 4
A Survey of Race Relations in South Africa (1975)

Note: Figures through 1930 include all manufacturing, public as well as private. As of 1950–51, census standards were revised in accordance with the United Nations International Standard Industrial Classification. As a result, the figures since 1950 are, on average, slightly lower than they would be according to the pre-1950 classification—e.g., Official Yearbook figures for total employment (old standard) for 1948–49 are 590,905; the figures of the Monthly Bulletin of Statistics (new standard) for the same period are 527,851. Note also that the data for 1916–45 appear to include working proprietors as well as paid employees.

D.3. Employment: Commerce (Wholesale and Retail)

Year	Total	Whites	Coloureds	Asians	Africans[a]
1921	84,569	62,382	8,554	13,633	
1936	132,671	101,614	13,858	17,199	
1946[b]	212,339	106,743	17,668	18,647	69,281
1951	290,093	143,890	24,241	22,807	99,155
1960	363,057	162,472	35,168	27,177	138,240
1970	451,600	192,900	47,800	24,600	186,300
1975	500,000	213,000	56,800	28,800	201,400

Sources: Union Statistics for Fifty Years, A34–A41
Statistical Yearbook (1966), H8–H9
Bulletin of Statistics (1974), vol. 8, no. 4
A Survey of Race Relations in South Africa (1975)

[a]Data for 1921 and 1936 exclude Africans.
[b]Data through 1946 appear to exclude working proprietors.

E. Contribution of Sectors to National Economy
(Percentage)

Year	Agriculture	Mining	Manufacturing	Commerce[a]	General Government	Other
1912	17.4	27.1	6.7	13.5		35.3
1920	20.9	21.3	10.7	16.8		30.3
1925	21.6	16.9	11.9	15.4		34.2
1930	13.9	17.3	15.4	14.5		38.9
1935	13.5	21.0	15.2	13.7		36.6
1940	11.8	22.8	17.5	14.3		33.6
1945	12.3	14.4	19.9	14.1		39.3
1950	17.8	13.3	18.3	14.7	7.7	28.2
1955	15.1	12.3	20.4	15.3	7.9	29.0
1960	12.1	13.8	20.7	14.1	8.5	30.8
1965	10.2	12.7	23.5	14.2	8.4	31.0
1970	8.3	10.3	24.2	15.1	9.6	32.5

Sources: Union Statistics for Fifty Years, S3
South African Reserve Bank Quarterly Bulletin (June 1971), Supplement; (March 1976)

Note: Data for 1912–45 are computed on the basis of national income; the base after 1945 is gross domestic product. For a discussion of the use of national income figures and their tendency to overstate the importance of manufacturing, see W. J. Bussehau, "The Expansion of Manufacturing Industry in the Union," The South African Journal of Economics, vol. 13, no. 3 (September 1945).

[a]The category is not strictly equivalent for the periods 1912–1945 and 1950–1974.

F. Trade-Union Membership

Year	Total	Whites	Coloureds and Asians	Africans[a]
1900	3,836			
1905	6,343			
1910	9,178			
1915	10,538			
1920	135,140			
1925	93,603			
1930	75,496			10,000
1935	121,348			
1940	235,051			28,672
1945	341,417			
1950	358,626	284,076	74,550	38,251
1955	395,132	304,107	91,025	
1961	404,889	310,427	94,462	59,952
1965	489,156	355,219	133,937	
1970	587,242	405,032	182,210	
1974	618,694	411,952	206,742	
1975	653,694	382,525	271,169	59,440

Sources: *Official Yearbook of the Union* (1923), vol. 6
Union Statistics for Fifty Years, G18
A Survey of Race Relations in South Africa (1961); (1966); (1971); (1974); (1975); (1976)
Muriel Horrell, *South African Trade Unionism*

[a]The figures from 1930 include the Non-European Trade Union Federation with its estimated 10,000 African members in 1928. The figures for 1940 are taken from Makabeni's Native Clothing Workers' Union (2,672 members) and Gordon's Joint Committee of African Trade Unions (26,000 members). The figures for 1961 and 1975 are taken from *A Survey of Race Relations in South Africa.*

II. ALABAMA

A. Population

Alabama

Year	Total	White	Black	Percent Black
1900	1,828,697	1,001,152	827,545	45.3
1910	2,138,093	1,228,832	909,261	42.5
1920	2,348,174	1,447,032	901,142	38.4
1930	2,646,248	1,700,775	945,473	35.7
1940	2,832,961	1,849,097	983,864	34.7
1950	3,061,743	2,079,591	982,152	32.1
1960	3,266,740	2,283,609	983,131	30.1
1970	3,444,165	2,533,831	910,334	26.4

Black Belt Counties[a]

Year	Total	White	Black	Percent Black
1900	379,220	87,184	292,036	77.0
1910	433,859	89,801	344,058	79.3
1920	397,807	101,714	296,093	74.4
1930	411,769	118,656	293,113	71.2
1940	436,234	137,859	298,375	68.4
1950	434,565	164,889	269,676	68.3
1960	444,197	196,329	247,868	55.8
1970	417,064	204,768	212,296	50.9

Sources: Economic Abstracts of Alabama—1966, 1975
          Twelfth Census of the United States-1900, vol.1
          Fourteenth Census of the United States-1920, vol. 3
          Sixteenth Census of the United States, vol. 2, part 1

[a]The Black Belt includes all counties with more than 70 percent black population in 1900.

B.1. Urban Population
(Residents in Incorporated Places of 2,500 or More Inhabitants)

Year	Percentage Urban	Year	Percentage Urban
1830	1.0	1910	17.3
1840	2.1	1920	21.7
1850	4.6	1930	28.1
1860	5.1	1940	30.2
1870	6.3	1950	40.1
1880	5.4	1960	51.7
1890	10.1	1970	58.4
1900	11.9		

Source: Donald B. Dodd and Wynelle S. Dodd, Historical Statistics of the South 1790-1970

B.2. Urban Population by Racial Group

Year	Percentage Urban White	Black
1900	11.8	5.8
1910	17.3	17.2
1920	21.5	21.9
1930	28.0	28.4
1940	29.2	32.1
1950	42.6	46.2
1960	54.1	56.5
1970	57.0	62.4

Source: Economic Abstract of Alabama—1966, 1975

C.1. Agriculture: Farms and Mechanization

Year	Number of Farms Alabama	Black Belt	Average Farm Size[a] Alabama	Black Belt	Number of Tractors Alabama	Black Belt
1850	41,964		289.2			
1860	55,128		346.5			
1870	67,382		222.0			
1880	135,864		138.8			
1890	157,772		125.8			
1900	223,220		92.7			
1910	262,901	64,947	78.9	62.2		
1920	256,099	54,223	76.4	68.8	811	
1925	237,631	45,644	70.4	67.7	2,465	343
1930	257,395	52,434	68.2	63.8	4,664	
1935	273,455	54,668	71.9	69.0		
1940	231,746	45,665	82.6	128.7	7,638	2,162
1945	223,369	37,356	85.4	157.4	16,616	2,153
1950	211,512	34,832	98.6	133.7	44,067	4,447
1954	176,949	29,536	117.7	165.6	62,526	6,404
1959	115,773	20,384	142.7	200.6	67,559	6,806
1964	92,530	15,525	164.5	251.5	71,925	8,135
1969	72,491	10,307	188.4	324.9	75,069	9,465
1974	56,678	6,677	209.1	458,0	68,521	8,612

Sources: Thirteenth Census of the United States, vol. 6, "Agriculture"
Fourteenth Census of the United States, vol. 6, "Agriculture," part 2
United States Census of Agriculture—1925
United States Census of Agriculture—1935, vols. 2, 3
United States Census of Agriculture—1945, vol. 1, part 21
United States Census of Agriculture—1954, vol. 1, part 21
United States Census of Agriculture—1959, vol. 1, part 32
1964 United States Census of Agriculture, vol. 1, part 32
1969 United States Census of Agriculture, vol. 1, part 32
1974 United States Census of Agriculture, vols. 1–2, part 32

[a]Measured in acres

C.2. Agriculture: Number of Tenants

Year	Alabama		Black Belt	
	White	Black	White	Black
1910	65,017	93,309	4,498	49,994
1920	70,395	77,874	3,586	39,362
1925	73,696	70,539	3,066	33,647
1930	88,545	77,875	42,601	
1935	100,705	75,542	5,207	38,813
1940	78,573	57,651	4,239	30,867
1945	60,867	48,823	2,418	23,211
1950	49,587	38,026	1,993	19,080
1954	32,814	27,739	1,721	14,703
1959	15,911	15,933	824	8,982
1964	9,368	10,043	585	6,105
1969	4,605	2,647	555	1,790
1974	3,443	581	447	361

Sources: Thirteenth Census of the United States, vol. 6, "Agriculture"
Fourteenth Census of the United States, vol. 6, "Agriculture," part 2
Sixteenth Census of the United States, Agriculture—Alabama, 1st Series
United States Census of Agriculture—1925
United States Census of Agriculture—1935, vols. 1–3
United States Census of Agriculture—1945, vol. 1, part 21
United States Census of Agriculture—1950, vol. 1, part 21
United States Census of Agriculture—1954, vol. 1, part 21
United States Census of Agriculture—1959, vol. 1, part 32
1964 United States Census of Agriculture, vol. 1, part 32
1974 United States Census of Agriculture, vols. 1–2

Note: Tenants are defined as those who rent all the land they operate or who work on shares. The census category includes cash tenants, share-cash tenants, crop-share tenants, livestock-share tenants, croppers, and unspecified tenants.

C.3. Agriculture: Cotton

Year	Alabama Acres	Bales	Black Belt Acres	Bales
1910	3,730,482	1,129,527	1,275,568	315,263
1920	2,628,154	714,163	641,528	99,973
1925	2,948,072	983,673	697,913	183,499
1930	3,566,498	1,312,963	752,011	
1935	2,130,062	934,396	435,234	144,885
1940	1,930,560	772,711	375,625	98,208
1945	1,373,194	966,158	269,365	151,346
1950	1,850,846	824,290	287,806	106,843
1954	1,153,514	707,152	197,468	103,164
1959	794,434	683,491	141,274	92,286
1964	804,094	853,522	138,072	128,883
1969	563,278	497,526	97,965	79,164
1974	539,888	481,198	98,084	84,262

Sources: *Thirteenth Census of the United States,* vol. 6, "Agriculture"
 United States Census of Agriculture—1925
 United States Census of Agriculture—1935, vols. 1–3
 United States Census of Agriculture—1945, vol. 1, part 21
 United States Census of Agriculture—1954, vol. 1, part 21
 United States Census of Agriculture—1959, vol. 1, part 32
 1964 United States Census of Agriculture, vol. 1, part 32
 1969 United States Census of Agriculture, vol. 1, part 32
 1974 United States Census of Agriculture, vol. 1, part 32

D. Employment: Annual Average of Employees in Nonagricultural Establishments (Thousands)

Year	Total	Mining and Quarrying	Manufacturing	Wholesale and Retail
1940	427.6	31.8	145.8	74.9
1945	579.1	28.7	223.4	87.0
1950	619.6	24.1	216.1	120.5
1955	702.9	15.0	236.3	138.3
1960	776.4	13.0	237.0	150.8
1965	886.5	8.9	277.0	166.9
1970	1,010.4	8.3	323.8	190.7
1974	1,164.1	9.2	351.1	226.9

Sources: *Alabama Employment Review, 1947–1964*
 Economic Abstracts of Alabama—1966, 1975

APPENDIX C

Interview Guidelines

I. BUSINESSMEN

A. South Africa

1. I need some basic information about the company.
   (a) How many employees come under your management?
   (b) What is the race composition of the work force?
   (c) Do you have an industrial council?
   (d) With which unions do you negotiate?
   (e) Is there a demarcation, in effect, above which nonwhites have not risen? Are there job categories that both whites and nonwhites fill?
   (f) Is your labour force mainly migratory or is it permanent?

2. Do you belong to any employers' organizations?
   (a) What role do they play in your labour negotiations?
   (b) How much do they influence your management practice?

3. What were your priorities in the last industrial council negotiations?
   (a) Were these different or similar to the priorities of other firms covered by the agreement?
   (b) To what extent do you have scope to structure labour-management relations independent of the agreement?
   (c) What were the priorities of the unions?

4. How were the wages of African employees determined?
   (a) Who first raised the question in negotiations?
   (b) What role did the trade unions play in this?
   (c) What role did the Department of Labour play?

5. Do all negotiated benefits extend to African workers?

6. Did you consult with African workers prior to negotiations?
   (a) Do you have works or liaison committees?

432

    (b) Do you view them as successful?

    (c) Are wages discussed?

    (d) Were you consulted by the government prior to the passage of the new works committee legislation?

7. When was the last union supported strike?

    (a) Have you had unofficial strikes?

    (b) What was at issue?

    (c) How was it resolved?

    (d) Were your operations affected by the Natal disturbances?

8. Would you favour a change in the labour laws that gave Africans the right to join registered trade unions?

    (a) How would you like to see them organized?

    (b) As separate or mixed unions?

9. What aspects of the social environment create the greatest difficulties for you in managing the company as you think it should be managed?

    (a) What would you like to see done to change this?

10. Do you have job reservation in the industry?

    (a) Did you oppose job reservation when it was first proposed?

11. Are you affected by influx control?

    (a) Would you like to see it abolished?

    (b) Would you like to see an end to migrant labour?

    (c) What kind of labour force would you prefer?

    (d) Are you affected by the Physical Planning Act?

    (e) Are you affected by border industry development?

12. Do you believe apartheid as a policy undermines or supports business interests?

13. Would you favour changes in the Apprenticeship Act or its administration that would allow Africans to be trained as apprentices?

14. Do you believe the gap between white and nonwhite wages is too large?

15. Do you ever use the poverty datum line in establishing wage levels for your firm?

16. Do you think there will ever be a time when whites will work under nonwhite supervisors?

17. Are there any changes in law or administration you would like to see come about?

    (a) Have you made representation to the government or a political party?

    (b) How receptive was the government to your overtures?

    (c) On what other kinds of issues have you made representation?

18. Do you believe farmers are getting special benefits at the expense of business?

19. How would you characterize your attitude toward the trade unions?

Alabama

1. I need some basic information about the company:

    (a) How many employees come under your management?

    (b) What is the racial composition of the work force? Can you estimate the composition in 1946 and 1960? Can these figures be broken down by skilled, semiskilled, and unskilled job categories?

    (c) Which unions are represented in your plants? What are the major ones? Which unions represent the bulk of black workers?

    (d) Do you consider your operations, in comparison with other industries in Alabama, capital or labor intensive? How has this changed since 1960?

    (e) Do you face labor shortages in any particular areas? What categories of jobs?

2. Do you belong to any employers' organizations?

    (a) How much do they influence your management practice?

    (b) Have they influenced your relations with labor organizations? Black employees? Government agencies?

3. Let us consider the 1950–60 period in industrial relations:

    (a) In negotiations with the unions, what kinds of priorities did management have? (e.g., hold down wages, changes in work practice)

    (b) What kinds of priorities did the unions have? (e.g., wages, job security, benefits, white employment)

    (c) How were the wages and working conditions of black employees determined? (e.g., negotiated by mixed union, white-dominated union, determined by management)

4. How had this changed by the late sixties?

    (a) What were management priorities?

    (b) What were union priorities?

    (c) How were black wages and working conditions determined?

    (d) What were the reasons for these changes?

5. Let us consider the wage pattern in the 1950–60 period:

    (a) Did blacks and whites in the same jobs receive the same wages?

    (b) Did whites tend to get premium rates or preference on overtime?

    (c) Did white employees have access to pension or benefit packages unavailable to blacks?

6. How had this changed by the late sixties? How do you account for these changes?

7. In the 1950–60 period, did the company face any strikes?

    (a) What unions or types of workers were involved?

    (b) What was at issue?

8. In the 1950–60 period, what aspects of the social environment created the greatest difficulties for you in managing the company as you think (thought) it should be managed? Had any of these difficulties been alleviated by the late sixties?

9. In the 1950–60 period, did the company have jobs that were considered "colored" and others considered "white"?

    (a) Had that changed by the late sixties?

    (b) What brought about the changes?

10. In the 1950–60 period, did the plant have segregated changing rooms, bathrooms, and eating areas?

    (a) When did that change?

    (b) Why did it change?

11. In the 1950–60 period, did white employees ever work under black supervisors?

    (a) Had that changed by the late sixties?

    (b) Why were these changes made?

12. Was the kind of racial discrimination and prejudice present in the fifties conducive or troublesome for business or did it make no real difference?

13. In the 1950–60 period, were there any changes in state law or administration that the company favored?

    (a) Did you make representation to the state legislature or governor?

    (b) How receptive were they to your overtures?

    (c) On what kinds of issues did you make representation in the late sixties?

14. Have you taken a position on
    (a) attempts to amend "right to work" laws?
    (b) minimum wage laws?
    (c) reapportionment issues?
    (d) educational appropriations and taxes?
    (e) state civil rights issues?

15. Were your operations in any way affected by the civil rights protests?
    (a) Did you make any response as a company?
    (b) Did you urge any business organizations to make any public response or representation?

16. Do you believe farmers are getting special benefits at the expense of business?

17. How would you characterize your attitude toward the trade unions?

II. WORKERS

A. South Africa

1. I need some basic information on the union:
    (a) When was the union founded?
    (b) What is the race composition of your union? The industry?
    (c) Which is the predominant language group?
    (d) Do you have a closed-shop agreement?
    (e) Do you belong to one of the labour federations? Which one?
    (f) Which workers fall within the jurisdiction of your union?

2. Has the membership increased in numbers in recent years? Do you devote funds to recruiting new members?

3. When was the last official (union-supported) strike?
    (a) What was at issue?
    (b) Have there been unofficial strikes? What was at issue?

4. What priorities did your union have in the last industrial council negotiations?
    (a) What were the priorities of management?
    (b) Was the issue of African labour an issue in the negotiations? Who raised the question?

     (c) Did the union consult with African workers prior to negotiations?

5. Would you favour a change in labour laws that gave Africans the right to join registered trade unions?

6. What aspect of the current social situation poses the greatest threat to the position of the white workers?
     (a) What is the best way a trade union can protect its position?
     (b) Do you believe there is any conflict between economic growth and a protected position for the white worker?

7. Do you think your union would be organized differently if the Industrial Conciliation Act were amended to include Africans?

8. Do you believe apartheid as a policy undermines or supports trade-union interests? In what ways?

9. Would you prefer to see:
     (a) more rapid implementation of separate development?
     (b) a more flexible approach by the government?
     (c) the dismantling of separate development?
     (d) the policy just as it is?

10. Could you elaborate your views on:
     (a) job reservation?
     (b) development of border and homeland industries?
     (c) the urban African?

11. Would you favour compulsory education for all groups in South Africa?
     (a) If yes, even if it meant higher taxes?
     (b) Would your membership?

12. Would you favour changes in the Apprenticeship Act or its administration that provided more training for Africans?

13. Do you believe the gap between white and nonwhite wages is too large?
     (a) Would you be willing to forego sizable salary increases in order that the gap be reduced?

14. Do you think all African workers should be guaranteed an income at least equal to the poverty datum line?

15. Do you think there will ever be a time when whites will work under nonwhite supervisors?

16. Are there any changes in labour law or other laws that your union would like to see brought about?

    (a) Have you ever informed a party or public official of your views on these matters?

    (b) How receptive was the government to your overtures?

17. Do you believe farmers are getting special benefits at the expense of workers?

18. What do you believe the union's attitude should be toward management?

B. Alabama

1. I need some basic information about the (union).
   (a) When did the (union) first begin organizing workers in Alabama?
   (b) Which became the principal locals? At which companies?
   (c) At (1), (2) and (3) local, how did the union gain recognition?
   (d) Did you represent specific occupations or crafts? Or did you seek to represent all positions in the plant? Which occupations?
   (e) Do you belong to any union councils or federations? Did you ever belong to the state Labor Council? Why did you not affiliate? Why did you withdraw?
   (f) How many members are there in the (union)? Has that increased, decreased or stayed the same over the past fifteen years?

2. When these principal locals were first organized, what was the union's position on black workers? (e.g., separate locals, auxiliaries, exclusion, incorporation)
   (a) What was the racial composition of the union?
   (b) When was the racial pattern changed?
   (c) What brought about the change?
   (d) Did you ever adopt the UMW formula for choosing leaders? (i.e., black vice-president)

3. (if incorporated) Why did you choose to organize on an integrated basis?

4. Let us consider the 1950–60 period of industrial relations.
   (a) In negotiations with management, what kinds of priorities did the union have? (e.g., wages, job security, benefits, white employment)
   (b) What were the priorities of management? (e.g., hold down wages, changes in work practice)

(c) How were the wages and working conditions of black employees determined? (e.g., negotiated by mixed union, white dominated union, determined by management)

5. How had this changed by the late sixties?
   (a) What were union priorities?
   (b) What were management priorities?
   (c) How were black wages and working conditions determined?

6. Let us consider the wage pattern in the 1950–60 period.
   (a) Did blacks and whites in the same jobs receive the same wages?
   (b) Did whites tend to get premium rates or preference on overtime?
   (c) Did white employees have access to pension or benefit packages unavailable to blacks?
   (d) Were there separate seniority lists for black and white employees?

7. How had this changed by the late sixties? How do you account for these changes?

8. In the 1950–60 period, did the union call any major strikes?
   (a) What locals or types of workers were involved?
   (b) What was at issue?
   (c) Was race ever an issue?

9. What about the 1960–70 period?
   (a) What locals or types of workers were involved?
   (b) What was at issue?
   (c) Was race ever an issue?

10. In the 1950–60 period, what aspect of the social-economic situation in Alabama posed the greatest threat to the position of your members?
    (a) What is the best way the trade union could protect the members' position?
    (b) What aspects threatened the workers' position?
    (c) How could his position best be protected?

11. In the 1950–60 period, did the plants have jobs that were considered "colored" and others considered "white?"
    (a) Had that changed by the late sixties?
    (b) What brought about the changes?
    (c) Did the union challenge this job pattern? Did it resist change?
    (d) What about management?

12. In the 1950–60 period, did the plants have segregated changing rooms, bathrooms, and eating areas?
    (a) When did that change?
    (b) Why were these changes made?
    (c) Did the union or members or management resist or encourage this change?

13. In the 1950–60 period, did white employees ever work under black supervisors?
    (a) Had that changed by the late sixties?
    (b) Why were these changes made?
    (c) Did the union or the members or management resist or encourage this change?

14. Did the kind of racial practices and attitudes present in the fifties undermine or support your union's position?

15. Would you favor changes in apprenticeships (or seniority) that provided more opportunities for black workers?

16. In the 1950–60 period, were there any changes in state law or administration that the union favored?
    (a) Did you make representation to the state legislature or governor?
    (b) How receptive were they to your overtures?
    (c) What kinds of issues did you make representation on in the late sixties?

17. Have you taken positions on:
    (a) attempts to amend right to work laws
    (b) state minimum-wage legislation
    (c) reapportionment issues
    (d) education appropriations
    (e) state civil rights issues
    (f) poverty programs?

18. How was the (union) affected by the civil rights protests?
    (a) How did your members respond?
    (b) Did you make any response as a union?
    (c) Did you urge any labor councils to respond?

19. Do you believe farmers are getting special benefits at the expense of workers?

20. What do you believe the union's attitude should be toward management?

21. Do you believe management has ever taken advantage of racial differences among the (sector) workers? How?

22. In the 1950–60 period, with which groups did labor form a coalition? On what kinds of issues?
    (a) Associated Industries of Alabama
    (b) Chambers of Commerce
    (c) Alabama Farm Bureau
    (d) Small farmers
    (e) Civil rights groups

23. How had this changed in the 1960–70 period?
    (a) Associated Industries of Alabama
    (b) Chambers of Commerce
    (c) Alabama Farm Bureau
    (d) Small farmers
    (e) Civil rights groups

APPENDIX D

Another Account of Capitalist Development in Two Racially Divided Societies

(Statement by Ambassador Andrew Young, United States Permanent Representative to the United Nations, to South African businessmen, Johannesburg, South Africa, 21 May 1977)

UNITED STATES MISSION TO THE UNITED NATIONS

799 UNITED NATIONS PLAZA
NEW YORK, N.Y. 10017

PRESS RELEASE

FOR IMMEDIATE RELEASE   Press Release USUN-30(77)
                                        May 27, 1977

I come tonight, I think, neither as an ambassador nor as a politician, but I see the situation here as a situation in which in spite of all that is wrong, in spite of the enormous difficulties, in spite of, in fact, the sin and the injustice that engulfs us, that there is a tremendous need for hope and that there is a longing to find a way out of the situation in which we find ourselves. I think there are some aspects of the situation in which I grew up, an intensely racial situation, in southern Louisiana, in the United States, that may have some relevance to your situation, but I leave that for you to decide. But as we now look at the United States of America as the champion of human rights around the world, it was not so long ago that it was not so, and that we too have a heritage of shame which in many respects surpasses yours. . . . And out of my experiences I've come to think of the business community as in many respects being the key. . . .

What I contend is that there can be a conscious contribution to development made by the technology and the market system which is developed in the West. But that can only be done as we take a good hard look at that system and see what it is in fact that makes it work. . . .

There's a funny thing about capitalism, and I almost hate to call it that. Because it's not what the sociologists write about it, or what they used to write about as capitalism in the 19th century. Something happens to capitalism when the poor rise up. The system that we enjoy in the United States is a system born of struggle. . . .

Twelve years ago it was very difficult and almost impossible for black people in the South to even vote. In 1976 it was black voters essentially that elected Jimmy Carter President of the United States. It was as late as 1969 that I was in jail in Atlanta, Georgia. And in 1972 I became the Congressman from the same district. A district which incidentally was 62 percent white. How we achieved that kind of miraculous change is beyond me. But at no point in 1965 when we were marching from Selma to Montgomery and being tear gassed and brutalized and killed by our police force did I ever anticipate that I would ever be elected to the Congress of the United States, much less be Ambassador to the United Nations.

And yet, it all happened. And because so much happened to us so fast, and so good, I guess I tend to be idealistic to the point of being naive. I don't care what is, I don't care what has been, all I'm concerned about in life is what can be. And I see in the economic power the economic potential of this nation something that can be, and the government doesn't have a thing to do with it. There's nothing they can do to help it, and there's nothing they can do to stop it. It's almost irrelevant.

For when in Atlanta, Georgia, five banks decided that it was bad for business to have racial turmoil, racial turmoil ceased. Because those five banks controlled the loans that went to all of the businesses in that community. And when they decided that racism was not good for business, and the word went down from five major banks the newspapers picked it up, the small businesses picked it up, taxi-drivers picked it up, workers picked it up. They decided that prejudice cost too much. And they put up four million dollars to develop a public relations campaign for our city, a city too busy to hate. And since that day in early 1970, they've been a city busy making money. They are too busy to hate, they don't have time. Everybody's enjoying the prosperity of the market system.

But it wasn't always that easy. In Birmingham, Alabama, there was an intransigent government. A very violent situation in which in a six-month time there were 50 bombings of black homes and churches and businesses. Nobody was arrested, nobody condemned. And the situation was so totally out of hand that only a massive non-violent protest by the black community made the business community aware of its responsibilities. For an important part of that responsibility was the black community deciding that things were so bad that they would not cooperate with the economic system anymore. So for almost six months they didn't buy anything but food and medicine.

During that period we also had thousands of people in jail. And the government, even under a very liberal President, John Kennedy, said to us there was nothing that he could do. The Supreme Court held our cases from 1963 and didn't decide on them until 1967, so they were really of no help. And then they decided to put us back in jail for seven days just for kicks. It was all over by then. . . . But the Congress of the United States refused to respond, except to call us communists. The major newspapers attacked us for stirring up trouble. . . .

But in the midst of that situation, one of the things that happened was that Martin Luther King and I had lunch one day with two presidents of corporations that were the major employers in Birmingham, Alabama, and I don't even remember what we talked about, but we discussed the situation in detail very quietly and answered their questions. Following that meeting the managers of those plants were changed, policies were changed, within a week's time we had a committee of 100 businessmen in that city. Those 100 businessmen negotiated the end of apartheid in Birmingham, Alabama, in spite of the fact that on the books of law it was still illegal to desegregate anything. But in their own business interests and in the interest of the future of that community, a committee of 100 began to lead that city, not only from racial hatred but into a kind of prosperity that would have been impossible otherwise.

And there seems to be something about the free market system that means that you don't have to take from the rich to give to the poor. That when you take in more consumers into the system you expand the markets, you expand profits, and you create more jobs. That expansion of market potential created the kind of growth in the United States of America that transformed our Southland from an impoverished region to a region that literally dominates both the politics and the economy of our nation right now. Now I know South Africa is different: none of that will work here, but I just pass it on because Mr. Oppenheimer invited me. Since this is a better dinner than I usually get, I've got to do something to earn my supper. But already the Cape Town Chamber of Commerce called on its members for a no-discrimination pledge, already committees of American businessmen and bankers are meeting regularly in small private groups to discuss the implications of their involvement here in this nation. And I would contend that the market potential of blacks in South Africa is far greater than the market potential of blacks ever was in the United States of America. For you're not talking just about the 16 million black citizens here, you're talking essentially about the southern half of the continent that is a potential market for a system which could relate to it as brothers. . . .

I would think that there is an opportunity for change. And that change can come through the marketplace. And it can be non-violent, productive, and humane. But it can't be that way by accident. There has got to be some deliberate intent to respond to the challenge that's faced by history, that's brought on by history to us in this nation. And I would think that that challenge is to draw a majority of your own citizens into the market system that you enjoy and advocate. That's kind of what happened to us. When blacks became a part of the free market system in the South, not only did that system explode, but blacks had very much a stake in it. And when you've got a stake in a society you don't vote to change it, outlaw it, or overthrow it. And yet in giving blacks a stake in that society the tragic irony in some ways is that nothing was taken from the whites but the income gap between whites and blacks actually expanded. But blacks were so much better off than they ever thought that they would be or could be. They were so involved and there did seem to be an openness within that system to advance economically and then politically. . . .

So much has happened in my lifetime that I never thought possible, that I just don't believe that there's anything that is impossible. And I don't believe it's impossible for 22 million citizens to share in the wealth and richness of this land. I don't believe it's impossible for this industrial empire to one day feed and clothe all of southern Africa. . . .

God bless you.

BIBLIOGRAPHY

GENERAL WORKS

Alavi, Hamza. "The State in Post-Colonial Societies: Pakistan and Bangladesh." *New Left Review* 74 (1972).

Alexis, Marcus. "A Theory of Labor Market Discrimination with Interdependent Utilities." *American Economic Review* 63, no. 2 (May 1973).

Allport, Gordon W. *The Nature of Prejudice.* Garden City, N.Y.: Doubleday Anchor Books, 1958.

Apter, David E. *Choice and the Politics of Allocation.* New Haven: Yale University Press, 1971.

————. *Political Change: Collected Essays.* London: Frank Cass, 1973.

————. *The Politics of Modernization.* Chicago: The University Press, 1967.

Arrighi, Giovanni. "Labour Supplies in Historical Perspective: A Study of the Proletarianization of the African Peasantry in Rhodesia." *The Journal of Development Studies* 6, no. 3 (April 1970).

————. "International Corporations, Labor Aristocracies, and Economic Development in Tropical Africa," in Giovanni Arrighi and John S. Saul, *Essays on the Political Economy of Africa.* New York: Monthly Review Press, 1973.

————, and John S. Saul. *Essays on the Political Economy of Africa.* New York: Monthly Review Press, 1973.

Arrow, Kenneth J. "The Theory of Discrimination," in Orley Ashenfelter and Albert Rees, eds., *Discrimination in Labor Markets.* Princeton, N.J.: Princeton University Press, 1973.

Ashenfelter, Orley. "Discrimination and Trade Unions," in Orley Ashenfelter and Albert Rees, eds., *Discrimination in Labor Markets.* Princeton, N.J.: Princeton University Press, 1973.

————, and Albert Rees, eds., *Discrimination in Labor Markets.* Princeton, N.J.: Princeton University Press, 1973.

Ashton, T.S. *The Industrial Revolution, 1760–1830.* London: Oxford University Press, 1964.

Banaji, Jarius. "Summary of Selected Parts of Kautsky's *The Agrarian Question.*" *Economy and Society* 5, no. 1 (February 1976).

Banton, Michael. *Race Relations.* New York: Basic Books, 1967.

Baran, Paul A. *The Longer View: Essays Toward a Critique of Political Economy.* New York: Monthly Review Press, 1969.

————. "On the Political Economy of Backwardness," in Charles V. Wilber, ed., *The Political Economy of Development and Underdevelopment.* New York: Random House, 1973.

—————. *The Political Economy of Growth*. New York: Monthly Review Press, 1968.

Baxter, Paul, and Basil Sansom, eds. *Race and Social Difference*. Baltimore: Penguin Books, 1972.

Becker, Gary S. *The Economics of Discrimination*. Chicago: The University Press, 1971.

Beckford, George L. *Persistent Poverty: Underdevelopment in Plantation Economies of the Third World*. New York: Oxford University Press, 1972.

Beer, Samuel H. *British Politics in the Collectivist Age*. New York: Alfred A. Knopf, 1967.

Bell, Duran, Jr. "The Economic Basis of Employer Discrimination," in George M. Von Furstenberg, Ann R. Horowitz, and Beatrice Harrison, eds., *Patterns of Racial Discrimination*. Lexington, Mass.: D. C. Heath, 1974.

Bell, Wendell, and Walter E. Freeman, eds., *Ethnicity and Nation-Building: Comparative, International, and Historical Perspectives*. Beverly Hills, Calif.: Sage Publications, 1973.

Bender, Gerald J. *Angola Under the Portuguese: The Myth and the Reality*. Berkeley: University of California Press, 1978.

Berger, Suzanne. *Peasants Against Politics*. Cambridge, Mass.: Harvard University Press, 1972.

Bernstein, Irving. *The Lean Years*. Boston: Houghton Mifflin Co., 1962.

—————. *Turbulent Years*. Boston: Houghton Mifflin Co., 1971.

Black, C. E. *The Dynamics of Modernization*. New York: Harper and Row, 1966.

Blank, Stephen. *Industry and Government in Britain*. Lexington, Mass.: Lexington Books, 1973.

Blauner, Robert. *Racial Oppression in America*. New York: Harper and Row, 1972.

Bloch, Marc. *Feudal Society*. Chicago: The University Press, 1961.

—————. *French Rural History*. Berkeley: University of California Press, 1970.

Blumer, Herbert. "Industrialization and Race Relations," in Guy Hunter, ed., *Industrialization and Race Relations*. London: Oxford University Press, 1965.

Bonilla, Frank, and Robert Girling, eds. *Structures of Dependency*. Published by the authors, 1973.

Briggs, Asa. "Chartism's Geographic and Economic Divisions," in May Lynn McDougall, ed., *The Working Class in Modern Europe*. Lexington, Mass.: D. C. Heath, 1975.

Brink, William, and Louis Harris. *Black and White*. New York: Simon and Schuster, 1967.

Brody, David. *Steelworkers in America*. New York: Harper Torchbooks, 1969.

Brooks, Thomas R. *Toil and Trouble*. New York: Delta, 1964.

Cardoso, Fernando Henrique. "Imperialism and Dependency in Latin America," in Frank Bonilla and Robert Girling, eds., *Structures of Dependency*. Published by the authors, 1973.

Cardwell, Lucy A., and Mark R. Rosenzweig. "Monopsonistic Discrimination and Sex Differences in Wages." Center Discussion Paper No. 222, Economic Growth Center, Yale University, January 1975.

Castells, Manuel. "Immigrant Workers and Class Struggles in Advanced Capitalism: the Western European Experience." *Politics and Society* 5, no. 1 (1975).

Caudill, Harry M. *Night Comes to the Cumberlands.* Boston: Little, Brown and Co., 1963.

Cole, G. D. H. *A Short History of the British Working-Class Movement, 1889–1947.* London: George Allen & Unwin, 1948.

Cotler, Julio. "The Mechanics of Internal Domination and Social Change in Peru," in Irving Louis Horowitz, ed., *Masses in Latin America.* New York: Oxford University Press, 1970.

Cox, Oliver Cromwell. *Caste, Class, and Race: A Study in Social Dynamics.* New York: Monthly Review Press, 1959.

————. *Race Relations: Elements and Social Dynamics.* Detroit: Wayne State University Press, 1976.

Davis, David Brion. *The Problem of Slavery in Western Culture.* Ithaca, N.Y.: Cornell University Press, 1969.

Davis, Stanley M. "The Politics of Organizational Underdevelopment: Chile," in Stanley M. Davis and Louis Wolf Goodman, eds., *Workers and Managers in Latin America.* Lexington, Mass.: D. C. Heath, 1972.

Davis, Stanley M., and Louis Wolf Goodman, eds. *Workers and Managers in Latin America.* Lexington, Mass.: D. C. Heath, 1972.

Degler, Carl N. *Neither Black Nor White: Slavery and Race Relations in Brazil and the United States.* New York: Macmillan Publishing Co., 1971.

Deutsch, Karl W. *Nationalism and Social Communication.* Cambridge, Mass.: M.I.T. Press, 1966.

Diegues, Manuel, Jr. "Land Tenure and Use in the Brazilian Plantation System," in *Plantation Systems of the New World.* Washington: Pan American Union, 1959.

Dobb, Maurice. *Studies in the Development of Capitalism.* New York: International Publishers, 1963.

DuBois, W. E. Burghardt. *The Souls of Black Folk.* Greenwich, Conn.: Fawcett Publications, 1961.

Dunlop, John T. "The Development of Labor Organization: A Theoretical Framework," in Richard Lester and Joseph Shister, eds., *Insights in Labor Issues.* New York: Macmillan Company, 1948.

————. "Structural Changes in the American Labor Movement and Industrial Relations System," in Walter Galenson and Seymour Martin Lipset, eds., *Labor and Trade Unionism: An Interdisciplinary Reader.* New York: John Wiley and Sons, 1960.

Ehrman, Henry W. *Organized Business in France.* Princeton, N.J.: Princeton University Press, 1957.

Engels, Frederick. *The Condition of the Working-Class in England.* Moscow: Progress Publishers, 1973.

————. *The Origin of the Family, Private Property and the State.* New York: International Publishers, 1972.

————. *The Peasant War in Germany.* Moscow: Progressive Publishers, 1956.

Enloe, Cynthia. *Ethnic Conflict and Political Development*. Boston: Little, Brown and Company, 1973.

Estall, R. C., and R. Ogilvie Buchanan. *Industrial Activity and Economic Geography*. London: Hutchinson University Library, 1966.

Eulau, Heinz. *Micro-Macro Political Analysis*. Chicago: Aldine Publishing Company, 1969.

Fernbach, David. "Introduction," in *Karl Marx: The First International and After*. New York: Vintage Books, 1974.

Foltz, William J. "Ethnicity, Status, and Conflict," in Wendell Bell and Walter E. Freeman, eds., *Ethnicity and Nation-Building: Comparative, International, and Historical Perspectives*. Beverly Hills, Calif.: Sage Publications, 1973.

Frank, André Gunder. *Capitalism and Underdevelopment in Latin America*. New York: Monthly Review Press, 1967.

Franklin, John Hope, ed. *Color and Race*. Boston: Beacon Press, 1968.

Frazier, E. Franklin. *Black Bourgeoisie*. New York: Collier Books, 1962.

Freeman, Richard B. "Alternative Theories of Labor Market Discrimination: Individual and Collective Behavior," in George M. Von Furstenberg, Ann R. Horowitz, and Beatrice Harrison, eds., *Patterns of Racial Discrimination*. Lexington, Mass.: D. C. Heath, 1974.

Furnivall, J. S. *Colonial Policy and Practice*. New York: New York University Press, 1956.

Galenson, Walter. *Comparative Labor Movements*. New York: Prentice-Hall, Inc., 1952.

——————, ed. *Labor in Developing Economies*. Berkeley: University of California Press, 1962.

Galenson, Walter, and Seymour Martin Lipset, eds. *Labor and Trade Unionism: An Interdisciplinary Reader*. New York: John Wiley and Sons, 1960.

Galarza, Ernesto. *Merchants of Labor: The Mexican Bracero Story*. Santa Barbara, Calif.: McNally and Loftin, 1964.

Geertz, Clifford. "The Integrative Revolution: Primordial Sentiments and Civil Politics in the States," in *Old Societies and New States*. New York: Free Press, 1963.

——————, ed. *Old Societies and New States*. New York: Free Press, 1963.

Genovese, Eugene D. *In Red and Black: Marxian Explorations in Southern and Afro-American History*. New York: Vintage Books, 1972.

Gerth, H. H., and C. Wright Mills, eds. *From Max Weber: Essays in Sociology*. New York: Oxford University Press, 1958.

Giddens, Anthony. *The Class Structure of the Advanced Societies*. London: Hutchinson University Library, 1973.

——————. *New Rules of Sociological Method: A Positive Critique of Interpretative Sociologies*. New York: Basic Books, 1976.

Gitlow, Abraham L. *Labor and Industrial Society*. Homewood, Ill.: Richard D. Irwin, Inc., 1963.

Glazer, Nathan, and Daniel P. Moynihan, eds. *Ethnicity*. Cambridge, Mass.: Harvard University Press, 1975.

Goody, Jack. *Technology, Tradition, and the State in Africa.* London: Oxford University Press, 1971.

Gordon, David M., ed. *Problems in Political Economy.* Lexington, Mass.: D. C. Heath, 1971.

_____. *Theories of Poverty and Underemployment.* Lexington, Mass.: Lexington Books, 1972.

Gordon, Milton M. *Assimilation in American Life.* New York: Oxford University Press, 1964.

Gramsci, Antonio. "The Intellectuals," in Quintin Hoare and Geoffrey Nowell Smith, eds., *Selections from the Prison Notebooks.* New York: International Publishers, 1971.

_____. "The Modern Prince," in Quintin Hoare and Geoffrey Nowell Smith, eds., *Selections from the Prison Notebooks.* New York: International Publishers, 1971.

_____. "Notes on Italian History," in Quintin Hoare and Geoffrey Nowell Smith, eds., *Selections from the Prison Notebooks.* New York: International Publishers, 1971.

_____. "State and Civil Society," in Quintin Hoare and Geoffrey Nowell Smith, eds., *Selections from the Prison Notebooks.* New York: International Publishers, 1971.

Greaves, Ida C. "Plantation in World Economy," in *Plantation Systems of the New World.* Washington: Pan American Union, 1959.

Greenberg, Stanley B. *Politics and Poverty: Modernization and Response in Five Poor Neighborhoods.* New York: John Wiley and Sons, 1974.

Greenstone, J. David. *Labor in American Politics.* New York: Vintage Books, 1970.

Gregor, A. James. *Contemporary Radical Ideologies.* New York: Random House, 1968.

Handlin, Oscar. *Boston's Immigrants.* New York: Atheneum, 1974.

Harbison, Frederick H., Robert K. Burns, and Robert Dubin. "Toward a Theory of Labor-Management Relations," in Richard A. Lester and Joseph Shister, eds., *Insights in Labor Issues.* New York: Macmillan Company, 1948.

Harris, Marvin. *Patterns of Race in the Americas.* New York: Walker and Company, 1964.

Hartz, Louis, ed. *The Founding of New Societies.* New York: Harcourt, Brace and World, 1964.

Hechter, Michael. *Internal Colonialism: The Celtic Fringe in British National Development 1536-1966.* Berkeley: University of California Press, 1975.

Herbert, Sydney. *The Fall of Feudalism in France.* New York: Barnes and Noble, 1969.

Hobsbawm, E. J. *The Age of Revolution 1789-1848.* New York: Mentor Book, 1962.

_____. "A Case of Neo-Feudalism: La Convención, Peru." *Journal of Latin American Studies* 1, no. 1 (May 1969).

_____. *Industry and Empire.* Baltimore: Penguin Books, 1969.

_____. *Labouring Men.* New York: Basic Books, Inc., 1964.

_____. *Primitive Rebels.* New York: W. W. Norton and Company, 1965.

Holt, Robert T., and John E. Turner, eds. *The Methodology of Comparative Research*. New York: The Free Press, 1969.

Horowitz, Daniel L. *The Italian Labor Movement*. Cambridge, Mass.: Harvard University Press, 1963.

Horowitz, Donald L. "Cultural Movements and Ethnic Change." *Annals* 433 (September 1977).

—————. "Ethnic Identity," in Nathan Glazer and Daniel P. Moynihan, eds., *Ethnicity*. Cambridge, Mass.: Harvard University Press, 1975.

Horowitz, Irving Louis, ed. *Masses in Latin America*. New York: Oxford University Press, 1970.

Hoxie, Robert Franklin. *Trade Unionism in the United States*. New York: D. Appleton and Co., 1923.

Hunter, Guy. "Conclusion," in Guy Hunter, ed., *Industrialization and Race Relations*. London: Oxford University Press, 1965.

—————, ed. *Industrialization and Race Relations*. London: Oxford University Press, 1965.

Huntington, Samuel P. "The Change to Change." *Comparative Politics* 3, no. 3 (April 1971).

—————. *Political Order in Changing Societies*. New Haven: Yale University Press, 1968.

Isaacs, Harold R. "Basic Group Identity: The Idols of the Tribe," in Nathan Glazer and Daniel P. Moynihan, eds., *Ethnicity*. Cambridge, Mass.: Harvard University Press, 1975.

Jacobson, Julius, ed. *The Negro and the American Labor Movement*. Garden City, N.Y.: Anchor Books, 1968.

Kahl, Joseph A. *Modernization, Exploitation and Dependency in Latin America*. New Brunswick, N.J.: Transaction Books, 1976.

Kerr, Clark. "The Balkanization of Labor Markets," in Lloyd G. Reynolds, Stanley M. Master, and Collette Moser, eds., *Readings in Labor Economics and Labor Relations*. Englewood Cliffs, N.J.: Prentice-Hall, 1974.

Kindleberger, Charles P. *Economic Development*. 2nd Ed. New York: McGraw-Hill Book Company, 1965.

Knowles, Louis L., and Kenneth Prewitt. *Institutional Racism in America*. Englewood Cliffs, N.J.: Prentice-Hall, 1969.

Kuper, Leo. "Plural Societies: Perspectives and Problems," in Leo Kuper and M. G. Smith, eds., *Pluralism in Africa*. Berkeley: University of California Press, 1971.

—————. "Political Change in White Settler Societies: The Possibilities of Peaceful Democratization," in Leo Kuper and M. G. Smith, eds., *Pluralism in Africa*. Berkeley: University of California Press, 1971.

Kuper, Leo, and M. G. Smith, eds. *Pluralism in Africa*. Berkeley: University of California Press, 1971.

Laclau, Ernesto. "Feudalism and Capitalism in Latin America." *New Left Review*, no. 67 (May–June 1971).

Landes, David S. *The Unbound Prometheus*. Cambridge: The University Press, 1969.

LaPalombara, Joseph. *Interest Groups in Italian Politics*. Princeton, N.J.: Princeton University Press, 1964.

————. "Parsimony and Empiricism in Comparative Politics: An Anti-Scholastic View," in Robert T. Holt and John E. Turner, eds., *The Methodology of Comparative Research*. New York: The Free Press, 1969.

Latham, Earl. *The Group Basis of Politics*. Ithaca, N.Y.: Cornell University Press, 1952.

Lawrence, Paul R., and Jay W. Lorsh. *Organization and Environment*. Cambridge, Mass.: Harvard University Press, 1967.

Lefebvre, Henri. *The Sociology of Marx*. New York: Vintage Books, 1969.

Lenin, V. I. "Critical Remarks on the National Question," in *National Liberation, Socialism, and Imperialism*. New York: International Publishers, 1968.

————. *Imperialism*. New York: International Publishers, 1969.

————. *National Liberation, Socialism, and Imperialism*. New York: International Publishers, 1968.

————. "The Question of Nationalities or 'Autonomisation,' " in *National Liberation, Socialism and Imperialism*. New York: International Publishers, 1968.

————. "The Right of Nations to Self-Determination," in *National Liberation, Socialism, and Imperialism*. New York: International Publishers, 1968.

————. *The State and Revolution*, in *Selected Works*. Vol. 2. Moscow: Progress Publishers, 1975.

————. *What Is to Be Done?* in Dan N. Jacobs, ed., *The New Communist Manifesto*. New York: Harper Torchbooks, 1965.

Lerner, Daniel. *The Passing of Traditional Society*. New York: The Free Press, 1964.

Lester, Richard A., and Joseph Shister, eds. *Insights in Labor Issues*. New York: Macmillan Company, 1948.

Leys, Colin. *Underdevelopment in Kenya*. London: Heinemann, 1975.

Lipset, Seymour Martin. *Political Man*. New York: Doubleday and Company, 1960.

Lorwin, Val R. "France," in Walter Galenson, ed., *Comparative Labor Movements*. New York: Prentice-Hall, 1952.

————. *The French Labor Movement*. Cambridge, Mass.: Harvard University Press, 1954.

McConnell, Grant. *The Decline of Agrarian Democracy*. Berkeley: University of California Press, 1953.

————. *Private Power and American Democracy*. New York: Vintage Books, 1975.

McCormick, B. J., and Owen E. Smith, eds. *The Labour Market*. Baltimore: Penguin Books, 1968.

McDougall, May Lynn, ed. *The Working Class in Modern Europe*. Lexington, Mass.: D. C. Heath and Company, 1975.

Mandle, Jay R. "The Plantation Economy: An Essay in Definition." *Science and Society* 36, no. 1 (Spring 1972).

————. *The Plantation Economy: Population and Economic Change in Guyana 1838–1960*. Philadelphia: Temple University Press, 1973.

Marx, Karl. *Capital*. Vol. 1. New York: International Publishers, 1967.

—————. *The Eighteenth Brumaire of Louis Bonaparte*. New York: International Publishers, 1963.

—————. *Grundrisse*. New York: Vintage Books, 1973.

—————. "Letters on Ireland," in David Fernbach, ed., *Karl Marx: The First International and After*. New York: Vintage Books, 1974.

Marx, Karl, and Frederick Engels. "The Manifesto of the Communist League," in Dan Jacobs, ed., *The New Communist Manifesto*. New York: Harper Torchbooks, 1965.

Merton, Robert. *Social Theory and Social Structure*. New York: The Free Press, 1968.

Mills, C. Wright. *The Sociological Imagination*. London: Oxford University Press, 1967.

Mintz, Sidney W. "The Plantation as a Socio-Cultural Type," in *Plantation Systems of the New World*. Washington: Pan American Union, 1959.

Moore, Barrington, Jr. *Political Power and Social Theory*. New York: Harper Torchbooks, 1965.

—————. *Social Origins of Dictatorship and Democracy*. Boston: Beacon Press, 1967.

Morazé, Charles. *The Triumph of the Middle Class*. Garden City, N.Y.: Anchor Books, 1968.

Morse, Richard M. "The Heritage of Latin America," in Louis Hartz, ed., *The Founding of New Societies*. New York: Harcourt, Brace and World, 1964.

Myrdal, Gunnar. *An American Dilemma: The Negro Problem and Modern Democracy*. Vols. 1–2. New York: Harper Torchbooks, 1969.

O'Connor, James. *The Fiscal Crisis of the State*. New York: St. Martin's Press, 1973.

Ollman, Bertell. "Prolegomenon to a Debate of Marx's 'Method.' " *Politics and Society* 3, no. 4 (Summer 1973).

Olson, Mancur, Jr. *The Logic of Collective Action*. New York: Schocken Books, 1968.

Paige, Jeffrey M. *Agrarian Revolution*. New York: The Free Press, 1975.

Pennock, J. R. " 'Responsible Government,' Separated Powers, and Special Interests: Agricultural Subsidies in Britain and America." *American Political Science Review* 56, no. 3 (September 1962).

Perlman, Selig. *A Theory of the Labor Movement*. New York: Macmillan, 1928.

Perlo, Victor. *Economics of Racism U.S.A.* New York: International Publishers, 1975.

Petras, James. *Politics and Social Forces in Chilean Development*. Berkeley: University of California Press, 1969.

Polanyi, Karl. *The Great Transformation*. Boston: Beacon Press, 1957.

Poulantzas, Nicos. *Classes in Contemporary Capitalism*. London: New Left Books, 1975.

Preobrazhensky, Evgenii. "Peasants and the Political Economy of the Early Stages of Industrialization," in Teodor Shanin, ed., *Peasants and Peasant Societies*. Baltimore: Penguin Books, 1971.

Rees, Albert. *The Economics of Work and Pay*. New York: Harper and Row, 1973.

Reich, Michael. "The Economics of Racism," in David M. Gordon, ed., *Problems in Political Economy*. Lexington, Mass.: D. C. Heath, 1971.

Reich, Michael, David M. Gordon, and Richard C. Edwards. "A Theory of Labor Market Segmentation." *American Economic Review* 63, no. 2 (May 1973).

Rex, John. *Race Relations in Sociological Theory*. London: Weidenfeld and Nicolson, 1970.

Reynolds, Lloyd G., Stanley M. Master, and Collette Moser, eds. *Readings in Labor Economics and Labor Relations*. Englewood Cliffs, N.J.: Prentice-Hall, 1974.

Rose, Peter I., ed. *Slavery and Its Aftermath*. New York: Atherton Press, 1970.

Rudé, George. *The Crowd in History*. New York: John Wiley and Sons, 1964.

Samoff, Joel. "Class, Class Conflict, and the State: Notes on the Political Economy of Africa." Paper presented at the Annual Meeting of the African Studies Association, Houston, Texas, November 1977.

Sartre, Jean-Paul. *Search for a Method*. New York: Vintage Books, 1968.

Saul, John S., and Giovanni Arrighi. *Essays on the Political Economy of Africa*. New York: Monthly Review Press, 1973.

Saul, John S., and Roger Woods. "African Peasantries," in Teodor Shanin, ed., *Peasants and Peasant Societies*. Baltimore: Penguin Books, 1971.

Schermerhorn, R. A. *Comparative Ethnic Relations: A Framework for Theory and Research*. New York: Random House, 1970.

Schumpeter, Joseph A. *Capitalism, Socialism and Democracy*. New York: Harper and Row, 1962.

Scott, James C. *The Moral Economy of the Peasantry*. New Haven: Yale University Press, 1976.

Self, Peter, and Herbert J. Storing. *The State and the Farmer*. London: George Allen and Unwin, 1962.

Shanin, Teodor, ed. *Peasant Societies*. Baltimore: Penguin Education, 1971.

Shils, Edward. "Color, the Universal Intellectual Community, and the Afro-Asian Intellectual," in John Hope Franklin, ed., *Color and Race*. Boston: Beacon Press, 1968.

Shonfield, Andrew. *Modern Capitalism*. London: Oxford University Press, 1965.

Smith, M. G. "Institutional and Political Conditions of Pluralism," in Leo Kuper and M. G. Smith, eds., *Pluralism in Africa*. Berkeley: University of California Press, 1971.

————. "The Plural Framework of Jamaican Society," in Paul Baxter and Basil Sansom, eds., *Race and Social Difference*. Baltimore: Penguin Books, 1972.

Spero, Sterling D., and Abram L. Harris. *The Black Worker*. New York: Atheneum, 1972.

Stavenhagen, Rodolfo. "Classes, Colonialism and Acculturation," in Irving Louis Horowitz, ed., *Masses in Latin America*. New York: Oxford University Press, 1970.

————. *Social Classes in Agrarian Societies*. Garden City, N.Y.: Anchor Books, 1975.

Stepan, Alfred C. *State and Society. Peru in Comparative Perspective*. Princeton, N.J.: Princeton University Press, 1978.

Stiglitz, Joseph E. "Theories of Discrimination and Economic Policy," in George M. Von Furstenberg, Ann R. Horowitz, and Bennett Harrison, eds., *Patterns of Racial Discrimination*. Lexington, Mass.: D. C. Heath, 1974.

Sweezy, Paul M., and Maurice Dobb. "Communications—The Transition From Feudalism to Capitalism." *Science and Society* 14, no. 2 (Spring 1950).

Taft, Philip, and Phillip Ross. "American Labor Violence: Its Causes, Character, and Outcome," in Hugh Davis Graham and Ted Robert Gurr, eds., *Violence in America*. New York: Signet Books, 1969.

Takahahi, H. K. "The Transition From Feudalism to Capitalism: A Contribution to the Sweezy-Dobb Controversy." *Science and Society* 16, no. 4 (Fall 1952).

Tannenbaum, Frank. *A Philosophy of Labor*. New York: Alfred A. Knopf, 1962.

Thompson, E. P. *The Making of the English Working Class*. New York: Vintage Books, 1963.

Thompson, James D. *Organizations in Action*. New York: McGraw-Hill Book Company, 1967.

Tilly, Charles, ed. *The Formation of Nation States in Western Europe*. Princeton, N.J.: Princeton University Press, 1975.

————. "Reflections on the History of European State-Making," in *The Formation of Nation States in Western Europe*. Princeton, N.J.: Princeton University Press, 1975.

————. *The Vendée*. Cambridge, Mass.: Harvard University Press, 1964.

Toynbee, Arnold. *The Industrial Revolution*. Boston: Beacon Press, 1956.

Tucker, Robert C. *Stalin As Revolutionary 1879–1929: A Study in History and Personality*. New York: W. W. Norton, 1974.

Turner, H. A. *Trade Union Growth: Structure and Policy*. Toronto: University of Toronto Press, 1962.

————. "Trade Union Organization," in B. J. McCormick and E. Owen Smith, eds., *The Labour Market*. Baltimore: Penguin Books, 1968.

Turner, John E., and Robert T. Holt, eds. *The Methodology of Comparative Research*. New York: The Free Press, 1969.

Van den Berghe, Pierre L. *Race and Racism*. New York: John Wiley and Sons, 1967.

Von Furstenberg, George M., Ann R. Horowitz, and Bennett Harrison, eds. *Patterns of Racial Discrimination*. Lexington, Mass.: Lexington Books, 1974.

Wallerstein, Immanuel. *The Modern World-System*. New York: Academic Press, 1974.

Webb, Sidney and Beatrice. *The History of Trade Unionism*. London: Longmans, Green and Co., 1935.

————. *Industrial Democracy*. London: Longmans, Green and Co., 1902.

Weber, Max. *General Economic History*. New York: Greenberg, Publisher, 1927.

Wilber, Charles K., ed. *The Political Economy of Development and Underdevelopment*. New York: Random House, 1973.

Wilson, James Q. *Political Organizations*. New York: Basic Books, 1973.

Wilson, William J. *Power, Racism, and Privilege*. New York: Macmillan Company, 1973.

Wolf, Eric R. "Aspects of Group Relations in a Complex Society: Mexico," in Teodor Shanin, ed., *Peasant Societies*. Baltimore: Penguin Books, 1971.

_____. *Peasant Wars of the Twentieth Century.* New York: Harper Torchbooks, 1973.

_____. "Specific Aspects of Plantation Systems in the New World: Community Sub-Cultures and Social Classes," in *Plantation Systems of the New World.* Washington: Pan American Union, 1959.

Wolff, Richard D. *The Economics of Colonialism.* New Haven: Yale University Press, 1974.

Young, Crawford. *The Politics of Cultural Pluralism.* Madison: The University of Wisconsin Press, 1976.

Zeigler, Harmon. *Interest Groups in American Society.* Englewood Cliffs, N.J.: Prentice-Hall, 1964.

Zwerman, William L. *New Perspectives on Organization Theory.* Westport, Conn.: Greenwood Publishing Corporation, 1970.

SOUTH AFRICA (AND SOUTHERN AFRICA)

Adam, Heribert. *Modernizing Racial Domination.* Berkeley: University of California Press, 1971.

_____. "The South African Power-Elite: A Survey of Ideological Commitment," in *South Africa: Sociological Perspectives.* London: Oxford University Press, 1971.

Africa, Reggie. "Mechanisation in South African Agriculture 1936–1974." SALDRU Farm Labour Conference, Paper No. 35, September 1976.

Alexander, Ray, and H. J. Simons. *Job Reservation and the Trade Unions.* Woodstock, Cape: Enterprise, 1959.

Altman, J. R. "Leadership Problems of Registered Trade Unions in South Africa." *South African Labour Bulletin* 3, no. 2 (September 1976).

Antrobus, G. G. "Farm Labour in the Eastern Cape, 1950–1973." SALDRU Farm Labour Conference, September 1976.

Archer, Sean. "Inter-racial Income Distribution in South Africa." Unpublished paper, 1971.

Biesheuvel, S. "The Black-White Wage Gap." South African Institute of Race Relations, Johannesburg, November 1972.

Bozzoli, Belinda. "The Origins, Development and Ideology of Local Manufacturing in South Africa." *Journal of Southern African Studies* 1, no. 2 (April 1975).

Bransky, Dennis. "The Causes of the Boer War: Towards a Synthesis." Workshop on the Social and Economic History of Southern Africa, Oxford University, Institute of Commonwealth Studies, September 1974.

Bundy, Colin. "The Abolishion of the Masters and Servants Act." *South African Labour Bulletin* 2, no. 1 (May–June 1975).

_____. "The Emergence and Decline of a South African Peasantry." *African Affairs* 71, no. 285 (October 1972).

Bunting, Brian. *The Rise of the South African Reich.* Middlesex: Penguin Books, 1969.

Burawoy, Michael. "Another Look at the Mineworker." *African Social Research* 14 (December 1972).

Cape of Good Hope. *Report of the Select Committee on the Labour Question*, C2–1892.

––––––––. *Report of the Select Committee, Supply of the Labour Market*, A.26–1879.

Cape Province Agricultural Union. "The Responsibilities of the Farmer as Employer." Mimeo. Paarl, Cape, 5 December 1974.

Chamber of Mines (Witwatersrand Chamber of Mines, Transvaal Chamber of Mines, Transvaal and Orange Free State Chamber of Mines). *Annual Report*. 1890–1967.

––––––––. "The Mining Industry," *Evidence and Report of the Industrial Commission of Enquiry*.

––––––––. *The Native Workers on the Witwatersrand Gold Mines*, 1947.

––––––––. *Proceedings at the Annual General Meeting*. Johannesburg, 1935–47, 1960–73.

––––––––. *Tribal Natives and Trade Unionism*. Johannesburg, 1946.

Chamber of Mines (Witwatersrand Chamber of Mines, Transvaal Chamber of Mines, Transvaal and Orange Free State Chamber of Mines), Gold Producers' Committee. (Statement of Evidence). *Commission for the Socio-Economic Development of the Native Areas Within the Union of South Africa*, 1955.

––––––––. (Statement of Evidence). *Economic and Wage Commission*. No. 2 and 3. Johannesburg, 1925.

––––––––. (Statement of Evidence). *Low Grade Ore Commission 1930–32*. No. 7.

––––––––. (Statement of Evidence). *Native Laws Commission of Enquiry*. No. 2. Johannesburg, 1947.

––––––––. *Party Programmes and the Mines: A Business Statement*. Johannesburg, 1924.

––––––––. (Statement of Evidence). *Select Committee on the Industrial Conciliation and Wage Bills*. Johannesburg, 1937.

Commercial Opinion. Association of Chambers of Commerce of South Africa, 1936–73.

Davies, Robert. "The White Working Class in South Africa." *New Left Review*, no. 82 (November–December 1973).

––––––––. "Mining Capital, The State and Unskilled White Workers in South Africa, 1901–1913." *Journal of Southern African Studies* 3, no. 1 (October 1976).

Davies, Robert, David Kaplan, Mike Morris, and Dan O'Meara. "Class Struggle and the Periodisation of the State in South Africa." *Review of African Political Economy*, no. 7 (September–December 1976).

De Kiewiet, C. W. *A History of South Africa: Social and Economic*. London: Oxford University Press, 1957.

Dekker, L. C. G. Douwes. "Are Works Committees Trade Unions?" Johannesburg: South African Institute of Race Relations, 1973.

––––––––, David Hemson, J. S. Kane-Berman, J. Lever, and L. Schlemmer. "Case Studies in African Labor Action in South and South West Africa." Mimeo, 1973.

De Villiers, René. "Afrikaner Nationalism," in Monica Wilson and Leonard Thompson, eds., *The Oxford History of South Africa*. Vol 2. New York: Oxford University Press, 1971.

Doxey, G. V. *The Industrial Colour Bar in South Africa*. Cape Town: Oxford University Press, 1961.

Desmond, Cosmas. *The Discarded People*. Baltimore: Penguin Books, 1971.

DuToit, André. *Afrikaner Political Thought, 1780–1850*. Forthcoming.

Elphick, Richard. *Kraal and Castle: Khoikhoi and the Founding of White South Africa*. New Haven: Yale University Press, 1977.

Etheredge, D. A. "Wages, Productivity and Opportunity." South African Institute of Race Relations and South African Institute of Personnel Management, Conference on Closing the Wage Gap. Johannesburg, January 1973.

F.C.I. News. Federated Chamber of Industries, 1948.

F.C.I. Viewpoint. Federated Chamber of Industries, 1967–71.

Federated Chamber of Industries. "Report No. 3 of the Ad Hoc Labour Legislation Committee: Native Trade Unions." Ballinger Papers. University of the Witwatersrand, 1946.

Feit, Edward. *Workers Without Weapons*. Hamden, Conn.: Archon Books, 1975.

Finlay, William. "South Africa: Capitalist Agriculture and the State." B. Soc. Sc. thesis, University of Cape Town, November 1976.

Fortes, Meyer. "The Plural Society in Africa," in Adrian Leftwich, ed., *South Africa: Economic Growth and Political Change*. London: Allison and Busby, 1974.

Fransman, Martin. "The Role of the Non-Capitalist Mode in the Periphery of Southern Africa." Workshop on the Social and Economic History of Southern Africa, Oxford University, Institute of Commonwealth Studies, September 1974.

Giliomee, Hermann. "The Economic Advance of Afrikanerdom." Unpublished paper.

Giliomee, Hermann, and Richard Elphick. "The Shaping of South African Society, 1652–1820." Paper Presented to the Yale South African Research Program, 2 October 1977.

————, eds. *The Shaping of South African Society, 1652–1820*. Cape Town: Longman's, 1979.

Gitsham, Ernest, and James F. Trembath. *Labour Organisation in South Africa*. Durban: E. P. Commercial Printing Co., 1926.

Gregory, Theodore. *Ernest Oppenheimer and the Economic Development of South Africa*. Cape Town: Oxford University Press, 1962.

Grosskopf, J. F. W. *Rural Impoverishment and Rural Exodus*, in *Report of the Carnegie Commission: The Poor White Problem in South Africa*. Stellenbosch, 1932.

Harris, Peter. "Industrial Workers in Rhodesia, 1946–1972: Working Class Elites or Lumpenproletariat?" *Journal of Southern African Studies* 1, no. 2 (April 1975).

Hemson, David. "Black Strikes, Prices and Trade Union Organisation 1939–73." Mimeo, 21 May 1973.

Hendrie, Delia, and Dudley Horner. "The People and Workers of the Cape Peninsula: A Sketch." *South African Labour Bulletin* 3, no. 2 (September 1976).

Hepple, Alex. *Trade Unions in Travail.* Johannesburg: Unity Publications, 1954.

Herd, Norman. *1922: The Revolt on the Rand.* Johannesburg: Blue Crane Books, 1966.

Horner, J. A. "Black Pay and Productivity in South Africa." Johannesburg: South African Institute of Race Relations, September 1972.

Horrell, Muriel. *The African Homelands of South Africa.* Johannesburg: South African Institute of Race Relations, 1973.

————. *Legislation and Race Relations.* Johannesburg: South African Institute of Race Relations, 1971.

————. *South African Trade Unionism.* Johannesburg: South African Institute of Race Relations, 1961.

————. *South Africa's Workers.* Johannesburg: South African Institute of Race Relations, 1969.

————. *A Survey of Race Relations in South Africa 1967.* Johannesburg: South African Institute of Race Relations, 1968.

————. *A Survey of Race Relations in South Africa 1968.* Johannesburg: South African Institute of Race Relations, 1969.

Horrell, Muriel, and Tony Hodgson. *A Survey of Race Relations 1975.* Johannesburg: South African Institute of Race Relations, 1976.

Horrell, Muriel, and Dudley Horner. *A Survey of Race Relations, 1973.* Johannesburg: South African Institute of Race Relations, 1974.

Horrell, Muriel, Dudley Horner, and Jane Hudson. *A Survey of Race Relations, 1974.* Johannesburg: South African Institute of Race Relations, 1975.

Horrell, Muriel, Dudley Horner, John Kane-Berman, and Robin Margo. *A Survey of Race Relations in South Africa 1972.* Johannesburg: South African Institute of Race Relations, 1973.

Horwitz, Ralph. *The Political Economy of South Africa.* London: Weidenfeld and Nicolson, 1967.

Houghton, D. Hobart. "Economic Development, 1865–1965," in Monica Wilson and Leonard Thompson, eds., *The Oxford History of South Africa.* Vol 2. New York: Oxford University Press, 1971.

————. *The South African Economy.* Cape Town: Oxford University Press, 1964.

Hughes, K. R. "Challenges from the Past: Reflections on Liberalism and Radicalism in the Writing of Southern African History." *Social Dynamics* 3, no. 1 (1977).

Humphriss, Dercyk, and David G. Thomas. *Benoni: Son of My Sorrow.* Town Council of Benoni, 1968.

Johannesburg Chamber of Commerce. "Memorandum Submitted to the Commission of Enquiry into Laws Affecting Natives in or near Urban Areas." Ballinger Papers. University of the Witwatersrand, 22 February 1947.

Johnstone, Frederick A. "Class Conflict and Colour Bars in the South African Gold Mining Industry, 1910–1926." *The Societies of Southern Africa in the 19th and 20th Centuries.* Vol. 1. London: University of London, Institute of Commonwealth Studies, 1971.

————. "Class and Race Relations in the South African Gold Mining Industry, 1910–26." Ph.D. dissertation. University of Oxford, March 1972.

Rheinallt Jones, Edith B. "Farm Labour in the Transvaal." *Race Relations* 12, no. 1 (1945).

Kallaway, Peter, "Preliminary Notes Towards a Study of Labour on the Diamond Fields of Griqualand West." Workshop on the Social and Economic History of Southern Africa, Oxford University, Institute of Commonwealth Studies, September 1974.

Kaplan, David, "Capitalist Development in South Africa: Class Conflict and the State." Workshop on the Social and Economic History of Southern Africa, Oxford University Institute of Commonwealth Studies, September 1974.

Katzen, M. F. "White Settlers and the Origins of a New Society, 1652–1778," in Monica Wilson and Leonard Thompson, eds., *The Oxford History of South Africa*. Vol. 1. New York: Oxford University Press, 1969.

Leftwich, Adrian, ed. *South Africa: Economic Growth and Political Change*. London: Allison and Busby, 1974.

Legassick, Martin. "Development and Underdevelopment in South Africa." Seminar paper. Institute of Commonwealth Studies, February 1971.

————. "Legislation, Ideology and Economy in Post-1948 South Africa." *Journal of Southern African Studies* 1, no. 1 (October 1974).

————. "South Africa: Capital Accumulation and Violence." *Economy and Society* 3, no. 3 (August 1974).

Leistner, G. M. E. "Non-Whites in the South African Economy," in N. J. Rhoodie, ed., *South African Dialogue*. Johannesburg: McGraw-Hill Book Company, 1972.

Lerumo, A. *Fifty Fighting Years: The South African Communist Party 1921–1971*. London: Inkululeko Publications, 1971.

Lever, Jeffrey. "White Organised Labour and the Development of Non-White South Africans," in Wolfgang H. Thomas, ed., *Labour Perspectives on South Africa*. Cape Town: David Philip, 1974.

Lewsen, Phyllis, ed. *Selections from the Correspondence of John X. Merriman 1905–24*. Cape Town: The Van Riebeeck Society, 1969.

Lipton, Merle. "White Farming: A Case History of Change in South Africa." Johannesburg: South African Institute of Race Relations, 1975.

Luthuli, Albert. *Let My People Go*. New York: Meridian Books, 1962.

MacCrone, I. D. *Race Attitudes in South Africa*. London: Oxford University Press, 1937.

Management Responsibility and African Employment in South Africa. Johannesburg: Ravan Press, 1973.

The Manufacturer. Federated Chamber of Industries, 1950–66.

Market Research Africa. Prepared for Professor E. Feit and the Anglo-American Corporation of South Africa. *A Summary of a Study of Artisan Attitudes in South Africa*. Johannesburg.

Marquard, Leo. "The Native Farm Labour Committee Report." *Race Relations* 7, no. 2 (1940).

Macobey, John, "Afrikaner Women of the Garment Union during the 'Thirties and 'Forties." *South African Labour Bulletin* 2, no. 1 (May–June 1975).

Mokgatle, Naboth. *The Autobiography of an Unknown South African*. Berkeley: University of California Press, 1975.

Monthly Bulletin. Natal Employers' Association, 1974.
Monthly Bulletin. Steel and Engineering Industries Federation of South Africa, 1973.
Morris, M. L. "Capitalism and Apartheid: A Critique of Some Current Conceptions of Cheap Labour Power." Workshop on the Social and Economic History of Southern Africa, Oxford University, Institute of Commonwealth Studies, September 1974.
_____. "The Development of Capitalism in South African Agriculture: Class Struggle in the Countryside." *Economy and Society* 5, no. 3 (August 1976).
Morris, Mike, and David Kaplan, "Labour Policy in a State Corporation: A Case Study of the South African Iron and Steel Corporation, Article Two," *South African Labour Bulletin* 2, no. 8 (April 1976).
Die Mynwerker. Mine Workers' Union, 1949–73.
Natal Agricultural Union (Council). *Annual Report 1971/2.*
NAUNLU. Natal Agricultural Union, 1951–73.
Nedbank Group. *South Africa: An Appraisal.* Johannesburg, 1977.
O'Dowd, Michael. "South Africa in the Light of the Stages of Economic Growth," in Adrian Leftwich, ed., *South Africa: Economic Growth and Political Change.* London: Allison and Busby, 1974.
O'Meara, Dan. "Analyzing Afrikaner Nationalism: The 'Christian-National' Assault on White Trade Unionism in South Africa, 1934–1948." *African Affairs* 77, no. 306 (January 1978).
_____. "The 1946 African Mine Workers' Strike in the Political Economy of South Africa." *Journal of Commonwealth and Comparative Politics* 13, no. 2 (July 1975).
Organised Agriculture. South African Agricultural Union, 1962–70.
Raiford, William N. "International Credit and South Africa," in *U.S. Corporate Interests in Africa: Report to the Committee on Foreign Relations, U.S. Senate.* Washington, D.C.: Government Printing Office, January 1978.
Report of the Carnegie Commission: The Poor White Problem in South Africa. Stellenbosch, 1932.
Report of the Economics Commission of the Study Project on Christianity in Apartheid Society. *Power, Privilege and Poverty.* Johannesburg, 1972.
Republic of South Africa. "Agreement for the National Industrial Council for Iron, Steel, Engineering and Metallurgical Industry." *Government Gazette.* No. 3721, 1 December 1972.
_____. *Second Report of the Commission of Enquiry into Agriculture.* R.P. 84–1970.
_____. *South Africa: Official Yearbook of the Republic of South Africa.* Pretoria, 1977.
_____. *Statistical Yearbook.* Pretoria, 1966.
_____. *Third Final Report of the Commission of Enquiry into Agriculture.* R.P. 19–1972.
Republic of South Africa, Department of Agricultural Economics and Marketing. *Annual Report of the Secretary for Agricultural Economics and Marketing.* Pretoria, 1975–76.

Republic of South Africa, Department of Industries. "White Paper on the Report by the Inter-Departmental Committee on the Decentralisation of Industries."

Republic of South Africa, Department of Labour and of Mines. *Report of the Commission of Inquiry into Labour Legislation.* Part 1. R.P. 47–1979.

Republic of South Africa, Department of Statistics. *Bulletin of Statistics* (quarterly). Pretoria, 1967–75.

Rex, John. "The Plural Society: The South African Case," in Adrian Leftwich, ed., *South Africa: Economic Growth and Political Change.* London: Allison and Busby, 1974.

Rhoodie, N. J., ed. *South African Dialogue.* Johannesburg: McGraw-Hill Book Company, 1972.

Riekert, P. J. "Increasing Productivity as a Condition of Economic Growth in South Africa." Seventh Academic Congress, AIESEC, University of Pretoria, 5–6 July 1973.

Roberts, Margaret. *Labour in the Farm Economy.* Johannesburg: South African Institute of Race Relations, 1958.

Robertson, H. M. "150 Years of Economic Contact Between Black and White." *The South African Journal of Economics* 3, no. 1 (March 1935).

Routh, Guy. "Industrial Relations and Race Relations." Johannesburg: South African Institute of Race Relations.

Roux, Edward. *Time Longer Than Rope.* Madison: The University of Wisconsin Press, 1964.

Rutherford, T. C. "African Workers and the South African Typographical Union," in Wolfgang H. Thomas, ed., *Labour Perspectives on South Africa.* Cape Town: David Philip, 1974.

Sachs, Solly. *The Choice Before South Africa.* New York: Philosophical Library, 1952.

Savage, Michael. "The Challenge of Change and Some Arithmetic of Apartheid." Johannesburg: South African Institute of Race Relations, 1977.

Scheepers, Anna. "The Garment Workers Face the Challenge," in Wolfgang H. Thomas, ed., *Labour Perspectives on South Africa.* Cape Town: David Philip, 1974.

Schlemmer, Lawrence. "Employment Opportunity and Race in South Africa." Johannesburg: South African Institute of Race Relations, R.R. 42–1973.

Seidman, Ann and Neva. *South African and U.S. Multi-national Corporations.* Westport, Conn.: Lawrence Hill and Co., 1977.

Simons, H. J. and R. E. *Class and Colour in South Africa, 1850–1950.* Baltimore: Penguin Books, 1969.

Simson, Howard. "The Myth of the White Working Class in South Africa." *African Review* (Dar Es Salaam) 4, no. 2 (1974).

South Africa Reserve Bank. *South Africa Reserve Bank Quarterly Bulletin.* Pretoria, 1971–76.

South African Agricultural Union. "Bantu Wage Policy." Mimeo, 1974.

————. "Memorandum for Submission to the Commission of Enquiry into Agriculture." May 1967.

————. *Report of the Annual Congress for Submission to the General Council,* 1971/72–1973/74.

————. *Report of the General Council for Submission to the Annual Congress,* 1956/57–1974/75.

South African Institute of Race Relations. "Employment Earnings in Some Economic Sectors." R.R. 81/73, RW 28/5/73, January 1973.

————. *Farm Labour in the Orange Free State.* Johannesburg, April 1939.

South African Labour and Development Research Unit, "Farm Labour in South Africa: A Review Article." *Social Dynamics* 2, no. 2 (December 1976).

South African Republic. "The Mining Industry," in the *Industrial Commission of Enquiry. Evidence and Report.* Johannesburg: Witwatersrand Chamber of Mines, 1897.

South African Trades and Labour Council. *Annual Report and Balance Sheet,* 1928, 1931.

————. *Report of the Annual Conference,* 1933–52.

Stadler, A. W. "Agricultural Policy and Agrarian Politics." SALDRU Farm Labour Conference, Cape Town, September 1976.

————. "The Party System in South Africa, 1910–1948." Ph.D. dissertation, University of the Witwatersrand, Johannesburg, 1970.

Stone, John. *Colonist or Uitlander?* Oxford: Clarendon Press, 1973.

S.A. (Suid Afrika) Werker. Yster-, Staal-, en Verwante Nywerhedeunie, 1963–76.

Thomas, Wolfgang H., ed. *Labour Perspectives on South Africa.* Cape Town: David Philip, 1974.

Thompson, Leonard, ed. *African Societies in Southern Africa.* London: Heinemann, 1969.

————. "Co-operation and Conflict: The High Veld," in Monica Wilson and Leonard Thompson, eds., *The Oxford History of South Africa.* Vol. 1. Oxford: Oxford University Press, 1969.

Thorne, L. D. "Lessons to Learn." Mimeo, Natal Agricultural Union, 27 February 1973.

Tinley, J. T. *The Native Labor Problem in South Africa.* Chapel Hill: University of North Carolina Press, 1942.

Trade Union Council of South Africa (also South African Trade Union Council). *Minutes of the Trade Union Unity Committee, Unity Conference.* Cape Town, 1954.

————. *Report of Proceedings.* Annual and Special Conferences, 1955–75.

Transvaal. *Report of the Mining Industry Commission 1907–08.* 579–3/2/08–2000.

————. *Report of the Transvaal Indigency Commission 1906–08.* T.G. 13–1908.

————. *Report of the Transvaal Labour Commission: Report and Evidence.* Cd. 1894, Cd. 1896, 1904.

Trapido, Stanley. "South Africa in a Comparative Study of Industrialization." *Journal of Developmental Studies* 7, no. 3 (April 1971).

Trollope, Anthony. *South Africa.* Cape Town: A. A. Balkema, 1973. (Reprint of a 1878 edition.)

Union of South Africa. *Report of the Commission of Inquiry into European Occupancy of the Rural Areas,* G.P.–S.7029095–1959.

_____. *Report of the Commission for the Socio-Economic Development of the Native Areas Within the Union of South Africà.* U.G. 61–1955.

_____. *Report of the Department of Labour.* U.G. No. 36, 1940.

_____. *Report of the Economic and Wage Commission 1925.* U.G. 14–1926.

_____. *Report of the Industrial Legislation Commission.* U.G. 37–1935.

_____. *Report of the Industrial Legislation Commission of Enquiry.* U.G. 62–1951.

_____. *Report of the Low Grade Mines Commission.* U.G. 34–1920.

_____. *Report of the Mine Natives' Wages Commission.* U.G. 21–1944.

_____. *Report of the Mining Industry Board.* U.G. 39–1922.

_____. *Report of the Mining Regulations Commission.* U.G. 36–1925.

_____. *Report of the Native Economic Commission 1930–32.* U.G. 22–1932.

_____. *Report of the Native Farm Labour Committee, 1937–39.* G.P.–S 3396–1939–102.

_____. *Report of the Natives Land Commission. Minutes.* U.G. 25–1916.

_____. *Report of the Select Committee on the Industrial Conciliation Bill.* S.C. 5–1923.

_____. *Report of the Select Committee on the Wage Bill.* S.C. 14–1925.

_____. *Report of the Witwatersrand Mine Natives' Wages Commission.* U.G. No. 21–1944.

Union of South Africa. Bureau of Census and Statistics. *Monthly Bulletin of Statistics.* Pretoria, 1957–66. (Becomes the *Bulletin of Statistics* in 1967.)

_____. *Union Statistics for Fifty Years, 1910–1960.* Pretoria, 1960.

Union of South Africa. Bureau of Statistics. *Agricultural Census No. 34, Report on Agricultural and Pastoral Production 1959–60, South Africa and Southwest Africa.* No. 4. Pretoria.

_____. *Agricultural Census No. 38.* Pretoria, 1959–60.

Union of South Africa. Department of Labour. *Work Reservation.* Pretoria, 31 December 1960.

Union of South Africa. Office of Census and Statistics. *Census of Industrial Establishments.* Pretoria, 1942–45.

_____. *Official Yearbook of the Union.* Pretoria, 1917–36.

Urban Foundation. *Proceedings of the Businessmen's Conference on the Quality of Life of Urban Communities.* Johannesburg, November 1976.

Van den Berghe, Pierre. *South Africa. A Study in Conflict.* Berkeley: University of California Press, 1970.

Van der Horst, Sheila T. *Native Labour in South Africa.* London: Oxford University Press, 1942.

Van der Merwe, H. W., M. J. Ashley, N. C. J. Charton, and B. J. Huber. *White South African Elites.* Cape Town: Juta and Company, 1974.

Van Onselen, Charles. *Chibaro: African Mine Labour in Southern Rhodesia, 1900–1933.* London: Pluto Press, 1976.

Verwoerd, H. F. "Die Bestryding Van Armoede en die Herorganisaie van Welvaartswerk." *Report of the National Conference on the Poor White Problem.* Kimberley, 1934.

Volkshandel. Afrikaanse Handelsinstituut, 1940–73.

Walker, Ivan L., and Ben Weinbren. *2000 Casualties*. Johannesburg: S.A Trade Union Council, 1961.

Welsh, David. "The Growth of Towns," in Monica Wilson and Leonard Thompson, eds., *The Oxford History of South Africa*. Vol. 2. New York: Oxford University Press, 1971.

————. "The Political Economy of Afrikaner Nationalism," in Adrian Leftwich, ed., *South Africa: Economic Growth and Political Change*. London: Allison and Busby, 1974.

————. *The Roots of Segregation*. Cape Town: Oxford University Press, 1971.

Wilson, Francis. "Farming, 1866–1966," in Monica Wilson and Leonard Thompson, eds. *The Oxford History of South Africa*. Vol. 2. New York: Oxford University Press, 1971.

————. *Labour in the South African Gold Mines 1911–1969*. Cambridge: The University Press, 1972.

————. *Migrant Labour in South Africa*. Johannesburg: South African Council of Churches and SPRO-CAS, 1972.

Wilson, Monica. "Cooperation and Conflict: The Eastern Cape Frontier," in Monica Wilson and Leonard Thompson, eds., *The Oxford History of South Africa*. Vol 1. Oxford: Oxford University Press, 1969.

————. "The Growth of Peasant Communities," in Monica Wilson and Leonard Thompson, eds., *The Oxford History of South Africa*. Vol. 2. Oxford: Oxford University Press, 1971.

Wilson, Monica and Leonard Thompson, eds. *The Oxford History of South Africa*. Vols. 1 and 2. New York: Oxford University Press, 1969, 1971.

Wolpe, Harold. "Capitalism and Cheap Labour-Power in South Africa: From Segregation to Apartheid." *Economy and Society* 1, no. 4 (November 1972).

————. "The Theory of Internal Colonialism—The South African Case." Mimeo. Institute of Commonwealth Studies, University of London, 31 January 1973.

Yudelman, David. "From Laissez Faire to Interventionist State: Subjugation and Co-optation of Organised Labour on the South African Gold Mines, 1902–1939." Ph.D. dissertation, Yale University, 1977.

————. "Industrialization, Race Relations and Change in South Africa." *African Affairs* 74, no. 294 (January 1975).

ALABAMA (AND THE SOUTH)

Adamson, W. M. *Industrial Activity in Alabama, 1913–1932*. Bureau of Business Research, University of Alabama.

Alabama Business Research Council. *Transition in Alabama*. University, Ala.: University of Alabama Press, 1962.

Alabama Department of Industrial Relations. *Alabama Employment Review: 1947–1964*. May 1965.

Alabama Farm Bureau Federation. "President's Report to Annual Meeting," 1964–74.

──────. *Farm Bureau Policies,* 1949–74.

Alabama Labor Council, American Federation of Labor and Congress of Industrial Organizations. *Legislative Report and Voting Records,* 1957–65.

──────. *Convention and Special Convention of the Alabama Labor Council, AFL-CIO,* 1956–1974.

Alabama Labor Council, Railroad Brotherhoods of Alabama, and the United Mine Workers of America. *Joint Legislative Report, Regular Legislative Session 1957.*

Alabama Power Company, Commercial Department. *The Textile Industry in Alabama.* Birmingham, approximate date of publication 1925.

Alabama State Advisory Committee to the U.S. Commission on Civil Rights. "The Agricultural Stabilization and Conservation Service in the Alabama Black Belt." April 1968.

──────. "ASCS Operations in Twenty-Six Alabama Counties." May 1967.

──────. "Dothan Open Meeting." 29 July 1966.

Alabama State Industrial Union Council (CIO). *Proceedings of Constitutional Convention,* 1942, 1954.

Armes, Ethel. *The Story of Coal and Iron in Alabama.* Chamber of Commerce, Birmingham, Alabama, 1910.

Bailey v. Alabama 211 U.S. 452 (1911).

Barnum, Darold T. *The Negro in the Bituminous Coal Mining Industry.* The Wharton School of Finance and Commerce, University of Pennsylvania, 1970.

Bond, Horace Mann. *Negro Education in Alabama: A Study in Cotton and Steel.* Washington, D.C.: The Associated Publishers, Inc., 1939.

Campbell, Christina. *The Farm Bureau: A Study of the Making of National Farm Policy 1933–40.* Urbana: University of Illinois Press, 1962.

Cantor, Milton, ed. *Black Labor in America.* Westport, Conn.: Negro University Press, 1969.

Cash, W. J. *The Mind of the South.* New York: Vintage Books, 1941.

Chapman, H. H. *The Iron and Steel Industries of the South.* University, Ala.: University of Alabama Press, 1953.

Clark, Thomas D. *The South Since Reconstruction.* Indianapolis, Ind.: Bobbs-Merrill Company, 1973.

Danhof, Clarence H. "Thought on the South's Economic Problems," in Melvin Greenhut and W. Jaye Whitman, eds., *Essays in Southern Economic Development.* Chapel Hill: University of North Carolina Press, 1964.

Daniel, Pete. *The Shadow of Slavery: Peonage in the South 1901–1969.* Urbana: University of Illinois Press, 1972.

Davis, Allison, Burleigh B. Gardner, and Mary R. Gardner. *Deep South.* Chicago: Phoenix Books, 1965.

DeCanio, Stephen J. *Agriculture in the Postbellum South: The Economics of Production and Supply.* Cambridge, Mass.: The MIT Press, 1974.

Dewey, Donald, "Negro Employment in Southern Industry." *The Journal of Political Economy* 60, no. 4.

Dodd, Donald B., and Wynelle S. Dodd. *Historical Statistics of the South 1790–1970.* University, Ala.: University of Alabama Press, 1973.

DuBois, W. E. Burghardt. *Black Reconstruction in America 1860–1880.* New York: Atheneum, 1969.

Edwards, Thomas J. "The Tenant System and Some Changes Since Emancipation." Reprinted in August Meier and Elliott Rudwick, eds., *The Making of Black America.* New York: Atheneum, 1971.

Elmore, Nancy Ruth. "The Birmingham Coal Strike of 1908." M.A. thesis, University of Alabama, 1966.

Fulmer, John Leonard. *Agricultural Progress in the Cotton Belt Since 1920.* Chapel Hill: The University of North Carolina Press, 1950.

Furse, Sally. "History of the International Union of Mine, Mill and Smelter Workers in the Jefferson County Area." Unpublished paper, University of Alabama in Birmingham, 1974.

Garrow, David J. *Protest at Selma: Martin Luther King, Jr., and the Voting Rights Act of 1965.* New Haven: Yale University Press, 1978.

Genovese, Eugene D. *The Political Economy of Slavery: Studies in the Economy and Society of the Slave South.* New York: Vintage Books, 1967.

————. *Roll, Jordan, Roll: The World the Slaves Made.* New York: Pantheon Books, 1974.

————. *The World the Slaveholders Made.* New York: Vintage Books, 1971.

Going, Allen Johnston. *Bourbon Democracy in Alabama 1874–1890.* University, Ala.: University of Alabama Press, 1951.

Greenhut, Melvin L., and W. Tate Whitman, eds. *Essays in Southern Economic Development.* Chapel Hill: University of North Carolina Press, 1964.

Griffith, Lucille. *Alabama: A Documentary History to 1900.* University, Ala.: The University of Alabama Press, 1972.

Gutman, Herbert G. "The Negro and the United Mine Workers of America," in Julius Jacobson, ed., *The Negro and the American Labor Movement.* New York: Anchor Books, 1968.

Hackney, Sheldon. *Populism To Progressivism in Alabama.* Princeton, N.J.: Princeton University Press, 1969.

Hansen, Fay. "Political Conflict and Consensus in a Local Union." Unpublished paper, June 1973.

Harris, Carl V. *Political Power in Birmingham, 1871–1921.* Knoxville: The University of Tennessee Press, 1977.

Harrison, Mary Phyllis. "A Change in the Government of the City of Birmingham: 1962–63." M.A. thesis, University of Montevallo, Montevallo, Alabama, 1974.

Havard, William C. "The South, A Shifting Perspective," in William C. Havard, ed., *The Changing Politics of the South.* Baton Rouge: Louisiana State University Press, 1972.

Havens, Murray Clark. *City Versus Farm? Urban-Rural Conflict in the Alabama Legislature.* University, Ala.: University of Alabama, Bureau of Public Administration, 1959.

Head, Holman. "The Development of the Labor Movement in Alabama Prior to 1900." M.B.A. thesis, University of Alabama, 1955.

Hoffman, Alice, and Jack Spiese. "An Interview With Ruben Farr." Oral History Project, Pennsylvania State University, 1968.

Howard, John C. *The Negro in the Lumber Industry.* Wharton School of Finance and Commerce, University of Pennsylvania, 1970.

Johnson, Charles S. "Growing up in the Black Belt: Ten Profiles," in Peter I. Rose, ed., *Slavery and its Aftermath.* New York: Atherton Press, 1970.

Johnson, Charles S., Edwin R. Embree, and W. W. Alexander. *The Collapse of Cotton Tenancy: Summary of Field Studies and Statistical Surveys 1933–1935.* Chapel Hill: The University of North Carolina Press, 1935.

Key, V. O. *Southern Politics.* New York: Vintage Books, 1949.

Kile, Orville Merton. *The Farm Bureau Movement.* New York: Macmillan Company, 1921.

————. *The Farm Bureau Through Three Decades.* Baltimore: Waverly Press, 1948.

King, Martin Luther, Jr. *Why We Can't Wait.* New York: Signet Book, 1964.

Kousser, J. Morgan. *The Shaping of Southern Politics.* New Haven: Yale University Press, 1974.

Kundahl, George Gustavus, Jr. "Organized Labor in Alabama State Politics." Ph.D. dissertation, University of Alabama, 1967.

Local Union No. 12, United Rubber, Cork, and Linoleum and Plastic Workers of America, AFL-CIO v. National Labor Relations Board 368 F. 2d 12 (1966).

Maddox, James G. *The Advancing South: Manpower Prospects and Problems.* New York: The Twentieth Century Fund, 1967.

Marshall, F. Ray. *Labor in the South.* Cambridge, Mass.: Harvard University Press, 1967.

————. *The Negro Worker.* New York: Random House, 1967.

Marshall, Ray, and Lamond Godwin. *Co-Operatives and Rural Poverty in the South.* Baltimore: Johns Hopkins Press, 1971.

Mitchell, Broadus, and George Sinclair Mitchell. *The Industrial Revolution in the South.* Baltimore: The Johns Hopkins Press, 1930.

Moore, Albert Burton. *History of Alabama.* Tuscaloosa, Ala.: Alabama Book Store, 1934.

Nicholls, William H. "Southern Tradition and Regional Economic Progress." *The Southern Economic Journal* 26, no. 3 (January 1960).

————. *Southern Tradition and Regional Progress.* Chapel Hill: The University of North Carolina Press, 1960.

Northrup, Herbert R. *The Negro in the Paper Industry.* Wharton School of Finance and Commerce, University of Pennsylvania, 1969.

————. "The Negro in the Rubber Tire Industry," in *Negro Employment in Basic Industry: A Study of Racial Policies in Six Industries.* Wharton School of Finance and Commerce, University of Pennsylvania, 1970.

————. "The Negro and the United Mine Workers of America." *Southern Economic Journal* 9 (1942–43).

————. *Organized Labor and the Negro.* New York: Harper and Brothers, 1944.

Peirce, Neal R. *The Deep South States of America.* New York: W. W. Norton and Company, 1974.

Pettway v. American Cast Iron Pipe Company 494 F.2d 211 (1974).

Phillips, Charles L. "A History of the United Rubber Workers in Gadsden, Alabama, 1936–1943." M.A. thesis, University of Alabama in Birmingham, 1974.

Phillips, Ulrich B. *Life and Labor in the Old South.* Boston: Little, Brown and Company, 1963.

Raines, Howell. *My Soul Is Rested: Movement Days in the Deep South Remembered.* New York: G. P. Putnam and Sons, 1977.

Ransom, Roger L., and Richard Sutch. "Debt Peonage in the Cotton South After the Civil War." *Journal of Economic History* 32, no. 3 (September 1972).

————. "The Ex-Slave in the Post-Bellum South: A Study of the Economic Impact of Racism in a Market Environment." *Journal of Economic History* 33, no. 1 (March 1973).

Raper, Arthur F. *Preface to Peasantry.* New York: Atheneum, 1969. (Originally published in 1936.)

Ratchford, B. U. "Patterns of Economic Development." *The Southern Economic Journal* 20, no.3 (January 1954).

Risher, Howard W., Jr. *The Negro in the Railroad Industry.* Wharton School of Finance and Commerce, University of Pennsylvania, 1971.

Rogers, William Warren. *The One-Gallused Rebellion: Agrarianism in Alabama, 1865–1896.* Baton Rouge: Louisiana State University Press, 1970.

Rosengarten, Theodore. *All God's Dangers: The Life of Nate Shaw.* New York: Alfred A. Knopf, 1974.

Rowan, Richard L. *The Negro in the Steel Industry.* The Wharton School of Finance and Commerce, University of Pennsylvania, 1968.

————. *The Negro in the Textile Industry.* The Wharton School of Finance and Commerce, University of Pennsylvania, 1970.

Rubin, Lester. *The Negro in the Shipbuilding Industry.* The Wharton School of Finance and Commerce, University of Pennsylvania, 1970.

Rudwick, Elliott M. *Race Riot at East St. Louis, July 2, 1917.* Carbondale: Southern Illinois University Press, 1964.

Stevenson v. International Paper Company, Mobile, Ala. 352 F. Supp. 230 (1972).

Straw, Richard A. "The Collapse of Bi-racial Unionism: The Alabama Coal Strike of 1908." *Alabama Historical Quarterly* (Summer 1975).

Strong, Donald S. "Alabama, Transition and Alienation," in William C. Havard, ed., *The Changing Politics of the South.* Baton Rouge: Louisiana State University Press, 1972.

Tindall, George B. *The Emergence of the New South 1913–1945.* Baton Rouge: Louisiana State University Press, 1967.

Twelve Southerners. *I'll Take My Stand: The South and the Agrarian Tradition.* New York: Harper and Brothers, 1930.

United States Department of Commerce, United States Bureau of the Census. *United States Census of Agriculture.* Washington, D.C.: U.S. Government Printing Office, 1925, 1935, 1945, 1950, 1954, 1959, 1964, 1969, 1974.

United States Department of Commerce and Labor, United States Bureau of the Census. *12th–16th Census of the United States.* Washington, D.C.: U.S. Government Printing Office, 1900, 1910, 1920, 1930, 1940.

United States Department of Labor. *Labor in the South*. Bulletin No. 898. Washington, D.C.: U.S. Government Printing Office, 1947.

United States Steel Corporation, Tennessee Coal and Iron Division. *Biography of a Business*. 1960.

United States v. United States Steel Corporation 371 F. Supp. 1045 (1973).

United States v. Hayes International Corporation 415 F.2d 1038 (1969).

University of Alabama, Center for Business and Economic Research. *Economic Abstracts of Alabama*. Graduate School of Business, University of Alabama, 1963, 1966, 1975.

Washington, Booker T. *The Future of the American Negro*. Boston: George H. Ellis, 1899.

————. "The Negro and the Labor Unions." *Atlantic Monthly*, June 1913.

Watkins, Elijah, et al. v. Scott Paper Company 6 EPD (1973).

Wharton, Vernon Lane. *The Negro in Mississippi 1865–1890*. New York: Harper and Row, 1965.

Wiener, Jonathan. "Planter Persistence and Social Change: Alabama, 1850–1870." *Journal of Interdisciplinary History* 7, no. 2 (Autumn 1976).

————. "Planter-Merchant Conflict in Reconstruction Alabama." *Past and Present*, no. 68 (August 1975).

Woodman, Harold D. "Sequel to Slavery: The New History Views the Postbellum South." *The Journal of Southern History* 43, no. 4 (November 1977).

Woodward, C. Vann. *Origins of the New South, 1877–1913*. Baton Rouge: Louisiana State University Press, 1951.

————. *Tom Watson: Agrarian Rebel*. New York: Rinehart and Winston, 1938.

Worthman, Paul B. "Black Workers and Labor Unions in Birmingham, Alabama, 1897–1904," in Milton Cantor, ed., *Black Labor in America*. Westport, Conn.: Negro University Press, 1969.

Zeichner, Oscar. "The Legal Status of the Agricultural Laborer in the South." *Political Science Quarterly* 55, no. 3 (September 1940).

————. "The Transition from Slave to Free Agricultural Labor in the Southern States." *Agricultural History* 3, no. 1 (January 1939).

NORTHERN IRELAND

Aunger, Edmund A. "Religion and Occupational Class in Northern Ireland." *Economic and Social Studies* 7, no. 7 (1975).

Barritt, Dennis P., and Arthur Booth. *Orange and Green*. Northern Ireland Friends Peace Board, 1972.

Barritt, Dennis P., and Charles F. Carter. *The Northern Ireland Problem*. London: Oxford University Press, 1962.

Belfast Chamber of Commerce. "Petition of the Belfast Chamber of Commerce, 12 November 1783," in the Northern Ireland Chamber of Commerce and Industry, *Year Book, 1977*.

Belfast Chamber of Commerce Journal. Belfast and Northern Ireland Chamber of Commerce and Industry, 1923–41.

Bell, Geoffrey. *The Protestants of Ulster*. London: Pluto Press, 1976.

Boal, F. W. "Territoriality and Class: A Study of Two Residential Areas in Belfast." *Irish Geography* 6, no. 3 (1971).

──────. "Territoriality on the Shankill-Falls Divide, Belfast." *Irish Geography* 6, no. 1 (1969).

──────, and R. H. Buchanan. "The 1969 Northern Ireland Election." *Irish Geography* 6, no. 1 (1969).

Boserup, Anders. *Who Is the Principal Enemy? Contradictions and Struggles in Northern Ireland*. London: National Labour Press, 1972.

Boyle, J. W. "Belfast and the Origins of Northern Ireland," in J. C. Beckett and R. E. Glasscock, eds., *Belfast: The Origin and Growth of an Industrial City*. London: British Broadcasting Corporation, 1967.

Budge, Ian, and Cornelius O'Leary. *Belfast: Approach to Crisis*. London: Macmillan, 1973.

Business Letter. Belfast and Northern Ireland Chamber of Commerce and Industry, 1974-77.

Busteed, M. A. *Northern Ireland*. London: Oxford University Press, 1974.

The Campaign for Social Justice in Northern Ireland. *Northern Ireland: The Plain Truth*. 2nd ed. Castlefields, Dungannon, 15 June 1969.

Crawford, W. H. "Ulster Landowners and the Linen Industry," in J. T. Ward and R. G. Wilson, eds., *Land and Industry: The Landed Estates and the Industrial Revolution*. Newton Abbot: David and Charles, 1971.

Fisk, Robert. *The Point of No Return*. London: Times Books, 1975.

Gardner, Louis. *Resurgence of the Majority*. Ulster Vanguard Publications, February 1971.

Gray, Tony. *Psalms and Slaughter*. London: Heinemann Publishers, 1972.

Greaves, C. Desmond. *The Life and Times of James Connolly*. London: Lawrence and Wishart, 1976.

Green, E. R. R. "Business Organization and the Business Class," in T. W. Moody and J. C. Beckett, eds., *Ulster Since 1880: A Social Survey*. London: British Broadcasting Corporation, 1957.

Hunter, R. J. "Plantations in Ulster, c. 1600-41." Education Facsimile No. 171. Public Record Office of Northern Ireland, 1975.

Jones, Emrys. "Belfast," in T. W. Moody and J. C. Beckett, eds., *Ulster Since 1800: A Social Survey*. London: British Broadcasting Corporation, 1957.

──────. *A Social Geography of Belfast*. London: Oxford University Press, 1960.

Kee, Robert. *Ourselves Alone*. London: Quartet Books, 1976.

Lijphart, Arend. "Review Article: The Northern Ireland Problem; Cases, Theories and Solutions." *British Journal of Political Science* 5, pt. 1 (January 1975).

Marx, Karl. "Letters on Ireland, 1867-1870," in David Fernbach, ed., *Karl Marx: The First International and After*. New York: Vintage Books, 1974.

McCann, Eamonn. *War and an Irish Town*. Middlesex, England: Penguin Books, 1974.

Moody, T. W., and J. C. Beckett. *Ulster Since 1800: A Social Survey*. London: British Broadcasting Corporation, 1957.

Northern Ireland. *Disturbances in Northern Ireland: Report of the Commission Appointed by the Governor of Northern Ireland.* Belfast, Cmd. 532, 1969.

—————. *Religious Tables, Northern Ireland.* Northern Ireland General Register Office. Belfast: Her Majesty's Stationery Office, 1975.

—————. *Report of the Joint Working Party on the Economy of Northern Ireland.* Belfast, Cmd. 446, October 1962.

—————. *Report and Recommendation of the Working Party on Discrimination in the Private Sector of Employment.* Ministry of Health and Social Services. Belfast: Her Majesty's Stationery Office, 1973.

—————. *Social and Economic Trends in Northern Ireland.* Belfast: Her Majesty's Stationery Office, 1976.

Northern Ireland Community Relations Commission. *First Annual Report 1971; Second Annual Report,* 1 January 1971 to 30 April 1972.

Northern Ireland Progress. Belfast and Northern Ireland Chamber of Commerce and Industry, 1950–73.

De Paor, Liam. *Divided Ulster.* New York: Penguin Books, 1971.

Rose, Richard. *Governing Without Consensus.* Boston: Beacon Press, 1972.

United Kingdom. *Fair Employment (Northern Ireland) Act 1976.* Chapter 25. London: Her Majesty's Stationery Office, 1976.

Wallace, Martin. *Drums and Guns: Revolution in Ulster.* London: Geoffrey Chapman, 1970.

Ward, J. T., and R. G. Wilson, eds. *Land and Industry: The Landed Estate and the Industrial Revolution.* Newton Abbot: David and Charles, 1971.

ISRAEL

Allon, Moshe. "The Histadrut in the State of Israel," in *Society.* Jerusalem: Keter Publishing House, 1974.

The Arab Higher Committee. *The Palestine Arab Case.* April 1947.

Arlosoroff, Chaim. "The Economic Background of the Arab Problem," in Enzo Sereni and R. E. Ashery, eds., *Jews and Arabs in Palestine.* New York: Hechalutz Press, 1936.

—————. "Land, Immigration and the Shaw Report," in the Executive Committee of the General Federation of Jewish Labour in Palestine, *Documents and Essays on Jewish Labour Policy in Palestine.* Tel Aviv, 1930.

Aruri, Naseer, ed. *The Palestinian Resistance to Israeli Occupation.* Wilmette, Ill.: The Medina University Press International, 1970.

Avineri, Shlomo. "Israel: Two Nations," in Michael Curtis and Mordecai Chertoff, eds., *Israel: Social Structure and Change.* New Brunswick, N.J.: Transaction Books, 1973.

Bastumi, Rustum. "The Arab Israelis," in Michael Curtis and Mordecai Chertoff, eds., *Israel: Social Structure and Change.* New Brunswick, N.J.: Transaction Books, 1973.

Becker, Aharon. "Histadrut Faces the Future." General Federation of Labor. Tel Aviv.

Ben-Porath, Yoram. *The Arab Labor Force in Israel.* Jerusalem: The Maurice Falk Institute for Economic Research in Israel, 1966.

Borochov, Ber. *Nationalism and Class Struggle.* New York: Poale Zion-Zeire of America and the Young Poale Zion Alliance of America, 1937.

Brawer, A. J., et al. "Jewish Communities ('Edot')," in *Society.* Jerusalem: Keter Publishing House, 1974.

Carmi, Shulamit, and Henry Rosenfeld. "The Origins of the Process of Proletarianization and Urbanization of Arab Peasants in Palestine." *Annals of New York Academy of Sciences* 220 (1974).

Carpi, Daniel, and Gedalia Yogev, eds. *Zionism.* Tel Aviv: Massada Publishing Company, 1975.

Cohen, Abner. *Arab Border Villages in Israel.* Manchester University Press, 1965.

Curtis, Michael, and Mordecai Chertoff, eds. *Israel: Social Structure and Change.* New Brunswick, N.J.: Transaction Books, 1973.

Eisenstadt, S. N. *Israel Society.* London: Weidenfeld and Nicolson, 1967.

Elizur, Yuval, and Eliahu Salpeter. *Who Rules Israel?* New York: Harper and Row, 1917.

Flapan, Simha. "National Inequality in Israel." *New Outlook* (November–December 1964).

General Federation of Jewish Labor (Histadrut). *Conventions of the Histadrut.* Second to Tenth, 1923–66.

————. *Report on Histadrut Activities in Palestine.* Tel Aviv, 1947.

————. *Survey of Histadrut Activities.*

General Federation of Jewish Labor (Histadrut), Executive Committee. "Letter of the Central Committee of the Palestine Jewish Labour Party on Jewish and Arab Labour to Sir John Hope-Simpson, H.M. Special Commissioner, July, 1930," in *Documents and Essays on Jewish Labour Policy in Palestine.* Tel Aviv, 1930.

————. *Documents and Essays on Jewish Labour Policy in Palestine.* Tel Aviv, 1930.

————. "Memorandum Submitted to the Palestine Commission of Inquiry, December, 1929," in *Documents and Essays on Jewish Labour Policy in Palestine.* Tel Aviv, 1930.

————. *A Report Prepared by the Executive Committee for the Convention.* Third and Fourth Conventions, 1927, 1933.

General Federation of Jewish Labour in Palestine and the Zionist Socialist Labour Party. "Joint Reply to Questionnaire on Subject Peoples, Migration and Socialism." Submitted to the British Commonwealth Conference, 1928, in the Executive Committee of the General Federation, in *Documents and Essays on Jewish Labour Policy in Palestine.* Tel Aviv, 1930.

Giladi, Dan. "The Economic Crises During the Fourth Aliya (1926-27)," in Daniel Carpi and Gedalia Yogev, eds., *Zionism.* Tel Aviv: Massada Publishing Co., 1975.

Gordon, A. D. "Our Task Ahead," in Arthur Hertzberg, ed., *The Zionist Idea.* Garden City, N.Y.: Doubleday and Company and Herzl Press, 1959.

————. "People and Labor," in Arthur Hertzberg, ed., *The Zionist Idea.* Garden City, N.Y.: Doubleday and Company and Herzl Press, 1959.

Gorni, Yosef. "Changes in the Social and Political Structure of the Second Aliya Between 1904 and 1940," in Daniel Carpi and Gedalia Yogev, eds., *Zionism*. Tel Aviv: Massada Publishing Co., 1975.

Ben-Gurion, David. *Jewish Labour*. London: Hechalutz Organization of England, 1935.

_____. *The Peel Report and the Jewish State*. London: Palestine Labour Studies Group, 1938.

Halevi, Nadav, and Ruth Klinov-Malul. *The Economic Development of Israel*. New York: Frederick A. Praeger, 1968.

Harrari, Yechiel, ed. *The Arab in Israel, Statistics and Facts*. Givat Haviva: Center for Arab and Afro-Asian Studies, 1970.

Hertzberg, Arthur, ed. *The Zionist Idea*. Garden City, N.Y.: Doubleday and Company and Herzl Press, 1959.

Hobman, J. B., ed. *Palestine's Economic Future*. London: Lund Humphries and Co., 1947.

Horowitz, David. "Arab Economy in Palestine," in J. B. Hobman, ed., *Palestine's Economic Future*. London: Lund Humphries and Co., 1947.

_____. *The Economics of Israel*. Oxford: Pergamon Press, 1967.

Hurwitz, David. "The Agrarian Problem of the Fellahin," in Enzo Sereni and R. E. Ashery, eds., *Jews and Arabs in Palestine*. New York: Hechalutz Press, 1936.

Israel, Central Bureau of Statistics. *Statistical Abstract of Israel 1976*. No. 27. Jerusalem, 1976.

Israel Labour News. General Federation of Jewish Labour, 1948–53.

Jewish Socialist Labour Confederation Poale-Zion. *The Jewish Labour Movement in Palestine*. Submitted to the Labour and Socialist International Congress, Brussels, August 1928. Berlin: Verbandsburo Poale-Zion, 1928.

Kalvarisky, H. M. "Jewish-Arab Relations Before the Great War." *Jewish-Arab Affairs*. Jerusalem: 'Brit-Shalom' Society, June 1931.

Katznelson, Berl. "Reaction v. Progress in Palestine." Palestine Labour Studies Group, 1937.

_____. "The Political Future of Palestine," in Enzo Sereni and R. E. Ashery, eds., *Jews and Arabs in Palestine*. New York: Hechalutz Press, 1936.

Kayyali, Abdul-Wahab. "Zionism and Imperialism: The Historical Origins." *Journal of Palestine Studies* 6, no. 3 (Spring 1977).

Khalidi, Endriss P. "Palestinian Arab Villages in Israel." *Arab World* (May–June 1972).

Kurland, Samuel. *Co-operative Palestine*. New York: National Committee for Labor Palestine, 1947.

Labour in Palestine. General Federation of Jewish Labour, 1946–47.

Lador-Lederer, Dr. Joseph J. "In the State of Israel," in *Society*. Jerusalem: Keter Publishing House, 1974.

Landau, Jacob M. "The Arabs and the Histadrut." Department of Labour Studies, Tel Aviv University and the Department of Higher Education, Histadrut, Tel Aviv, 1976.

_____. *The Arabs in Israel*. London: Oxford University Press, 1969.

Laqueur, Walter. *A History of Zionism*. New York: Schocken Books, 1976.

Lipset, Seymour Martin. "The Israeli Dilemma," in Michael Curtis and Mordecai Chertoff, eds., *Israel: Social Structure and Change.* New Brunswick, N.J.: Transaction Books, 1973.

Lucatz, Noah. "Histadrut as a Nationalist and Socialist Movement, 1882–1948." Ph.D. dissertation, Washington University, 1961.

Malkosh, Noah. *Histadrut in Israel.* Tel Aviv: Histadrut.

Medding, Peter Y. *Mapai in Israel: Political Organization and Government in a New Society.* Cambridge: At the University Press, 1972.

Muenzer, G. *Jewish Labour Economy in Palestine.* London: Victor Gollancz Ltd., 1945.

Nakhleh, Khalil. "Anthropological and Sociological Studies on the Arabs in Israel: A Critique." *Journal of Palestine Studies* 6, no. 4 (Summer 1977).

Palestine. *Report of the Commission on the Palestine Disturbances of August, 1929* (Shaw). London, 1930.

Pali, Santiago Quintana. "The Arabs in Israel: A Class Formation Analysis." Unpublished essay, Yale University, January 1978.

Peres, Yochanan. "Modernization and Nationalism in the Identity of the Israeli Arab." *The Middle East Journal* (1970).

Peretz, Don. *Israel and the Palestine Arabs.* Washington, D.C.: Middle East Institute, 1958.

Preuss, Walter. *The Labour Movement in Israel.* Jerusalem: Rubin Mass, 1965.

Public Hearings Before the Anglo-American Committee of Inquiry on Jewish Problems in Palestine and Europe. Jerusalem, 25 March 1946.

Revusky, Abraham. *The Histadrut: A Labor Commonwealth in the Making.* New York: League for Labor Palestine, 1938.

Ro'i Yaacov. "Relations Between Rehourt and its Arab Neighbors, 1890–1914," in Daniel Carpi and Gedalia Yogev, eds., *Zionism.* Tel Aviv: Massada Publishing Co., 1975.

Rosenfeld, Henry. "The Arab Village Proletariat." *New Outlook: Middle East Quarterly* 5, no. 3 (March–April 1962).

Seminar of Arab Jurists on Palestine. *The Palestine Question.* Beirut: The Institute for Palestine Studies, 1968.

Sereni, Enzo, and R. E. Ashery, eds. *Jews and Arabs in Palestine.* New York: Hechalutz Press, 1936.

Shapira, Anita. "The Struggles for the Employment of Jewish Labour." Ph.D. dissertation, Tel-Aviv University, 1974.

Shapiro, Anita. "The Ideology and Practice of the Joint Jewish-Arab Labour Union in Palestine 1920–1939." Mimeo.

Sharon, Nahum. "The Histadrut in 1966." *New Outlook* (February 1966).

Shubat, Ibrahim. "The Twenty-Five Years Seen Through Arab Eyes." *New Middle East* (May 1973).

Sobel, Irwin. "Israel," in Walter Galenson, ed., *Labor in Developing Economies.* Berkeley: University of California Press, 1962.

Stock, Ernest. *From Conflict to Understanding.* New York: Institute of Human Relations Press, American Jewish Committee, 1968.

Sussman, Svi. "The Policy of the Histadrut with Regard to Wage Differentials." Ph.D. dissertation, Hebrew University, Jerusalem, April 1969.

Weingrod, Alex. *Israel, Group Relations in a New Society.* New York: Frederick A. Praeger, 1965.

Zureik, Elia. "Toward a Sociology of the Palestinians." *Journal of Palestine Studies* 6, no. 4 (Summer 1977).

Zureik, Elia T. "Transformation of Class Structure Among the Arabs in Israel: From Peasantry to Proletariat." *Journal of Palestine Studies* 6, no. 1 (Autumn 1976).

INDEX

Abernathy, the Reverend Ralph, 236
Absentees' Property Law (*1950*), 48
Accommodative school, 129–31
African: distinguished from black, 36*n*25
African Mine Workers' Union (AMWU), 157, 170
African National Congress, 173
Africans: limitations of rights in South Africa, 37; as proportion of South Africa's population, 49. *See also* Cheap labor; Labor; Peasants and peasantry; Strikes; Unions
Afrikaanse Handelsinstituut. *See* Handelsinstituut, Afrikaanse
Agricultural Adjustment Administration (AAA), 111, 114, 122
Agricultural Extension Service, 120
Agricultural Stabilization and Conservation Service (ASCS), 123
Agriculture, capitalist: transition to, in Germany, 57, 58; definition of, 58, 71; Kautsky on transition to, 60; and racism, 387
—South Africa: transition to, 70–72, 79–86; World War II and crisis in, 85; and governments, 89; importance of, 89; development of, 94; Africanization of, 95; and decline of labor control in, 102
—Alabama: declining importance of, 218, 219; convict labor in, 221–22
Agriculture, subsistence. *See* Peasantry
Agudat Israel workers, 367
Ahdut Haavoda (Working Class Union), 361, 371, 372. *See also* Poale Zion
Alabama Bankers Association, 241
Alabama Chamber of Commerce, 233, 234
Alabama Farm Bureau, 119–25, 404; and businessmen, 233, 234
Alabama Labor Council, 233, 355
Alabama Slave Code (*1852*), 115
Alavi, Hamza, 388
Aldrich, Truman, 333
Aliya: First (*1882–1904*), 47, 359–60; Second (*1904–14*), 47, 360, 364; Fourth (*1924–31*), 363
Amalgamated Association of Iron, Steel and Tin Workers, 334

Amalgamated Association of Steel Workers, 226
Amalgamated Engineering Union, 302, 304, 305
Amerindians, 33, 39
Anarcho-syndicalism, 278
Anglo-American Corporation, 149, 169, 174–75
Anglo-Irish Treaty of *1821*, 44
Anglovaal, 206
Angola, 33, 65, 66
Apartheid, 391, 393, 394, 402, 406; origins of, 72; farmers support of, 105; labor repression and, 152; FCI on, 177; Confederation of Labour on, 301; artisan unions and, 301, 309–10; unions' attitude to, 324–26; waning support for, 327
Apprenticeship Act (*1922*), 292, 303, 305, 318
Apter, David, 8, 12
Arab Carpenters' Union, 369
Arab Railwaymen's Union, 370
Arabs: become laborers, 47; denied citizenship, 48; limited participation in Histadrut, 376. *See also* Discrimination; Fellahin; Labor, Arab; Unions, Israel
Aristocracy of labor, 20, 274, 276–77
Arlosoroff, Chaim, 357, 359*n*14
Armes, Ethel, 212
Arrighi, Giovanni and John Saul, 20
Arrow, Kenneth, 142, 143, 144
Artisan Staff Association, 301, 302*n*62, 304*n*67
Artisans. *See* Unions, artisan
Associated Industries of Alabama, 233, 234, 237, 241
Associated Trade Unions of South Africa, 292
Association of Chambers of Commerce (ASSOCOM), 90, 172, 176, 190, 192–93, 194, 204; labor control and, 179; opposed to job reservation, 185; African trade unionism and, 197, 198; and Sharpeville, 202, 203; and the racial order, 206
"Atlanta Compromise," 7
Aunger, Edmund, 256